EARTHBOY
JACOBUS™

OTHER BOOKS
BY DOUG TENNAPEL

GEAR

CREATURE TECH

TOMMYSAURUS REX

EARTHBOY
JACOBUS™

BY
DOUG TENNAPEL

Doug TenNapel – Artist/Writer
Kenny Hitt – Cover Artist
Jennifer Barker – Scanner/Text
Font – Nate Piekos
Thomas Krajewski - Proofreader
Deven Polley – Production Assistant
Matt Dougherty – Production Assistant
Angie TenNapel – Office Queen

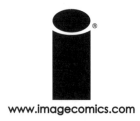

www.imagecomics.com

Erik Larsen - Publisher
Todd McFarlane - President
Marc Silvestri - CEO
Jim Valentino - Vice-President

Eric Stephenson - Executive Director
Brett Evans - Production Manager
Missie Miranda - Controller
Jim Demonakos - PR & Marketing Coordinator
Allen Hui - Production Artist
Joe Keatinge - Traffic Manager
Mia MacHatton - Administrative Assistant
Jonathan Chan - Production Assistant

Earthboy Jacobus, 2005. Published by Image Comics, Inc., Office of publication: 1942 University Avenue, Suite 305, Berkeley, California 947

PRINTED IN CANADA

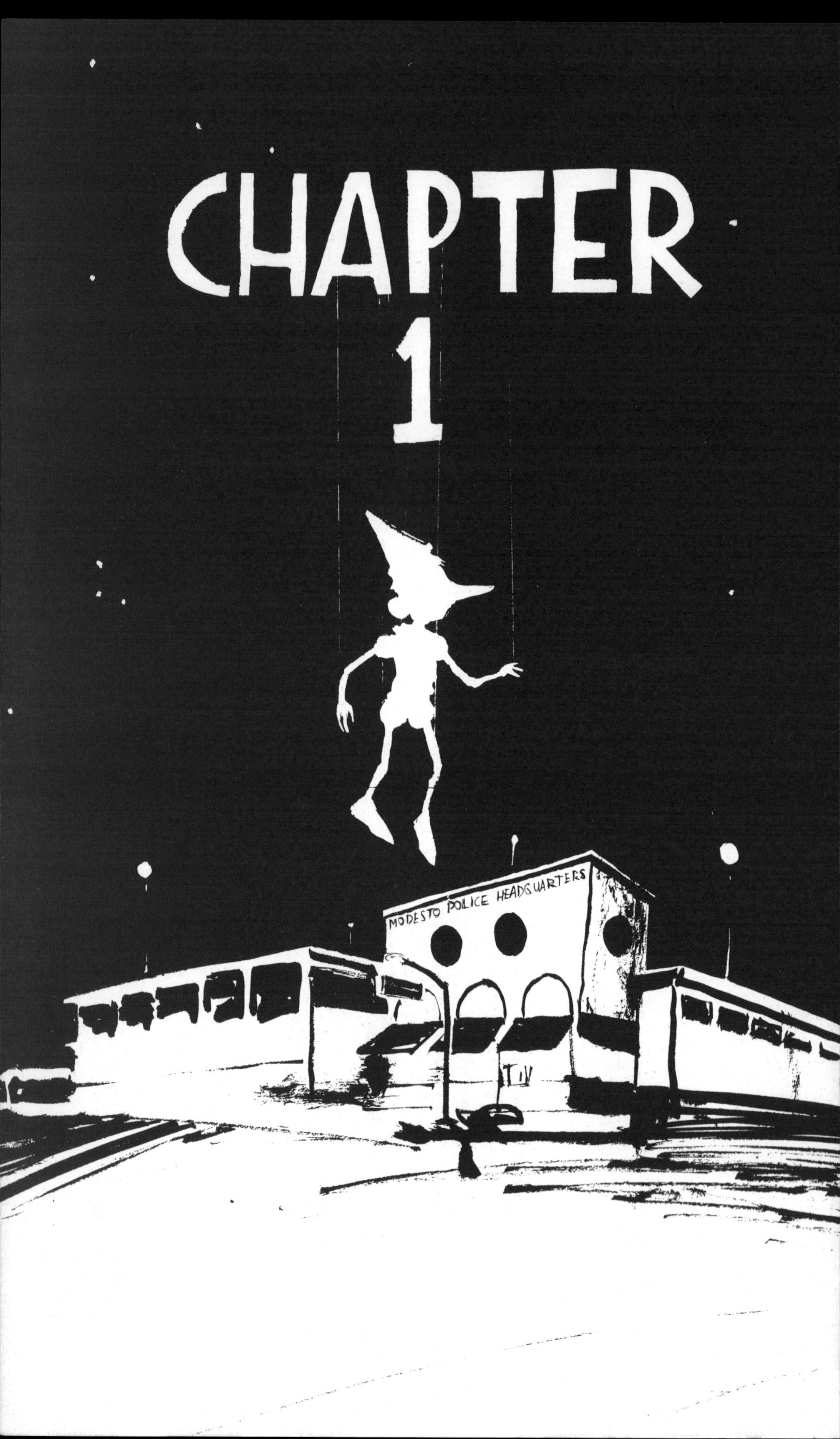
CHAPTER
1
MODESTO POLICE HEADQUARTERS

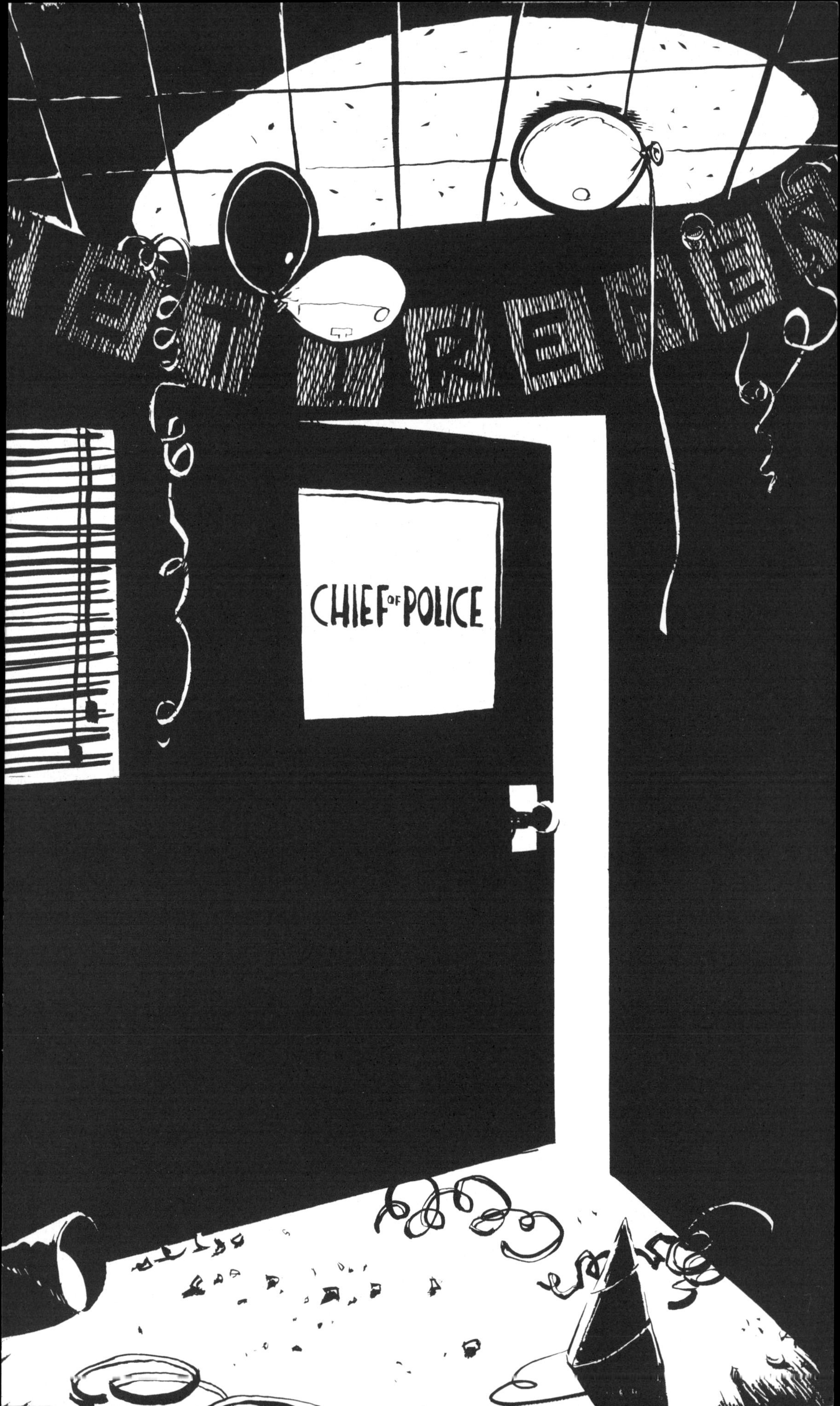
CHIEF OF POLICE

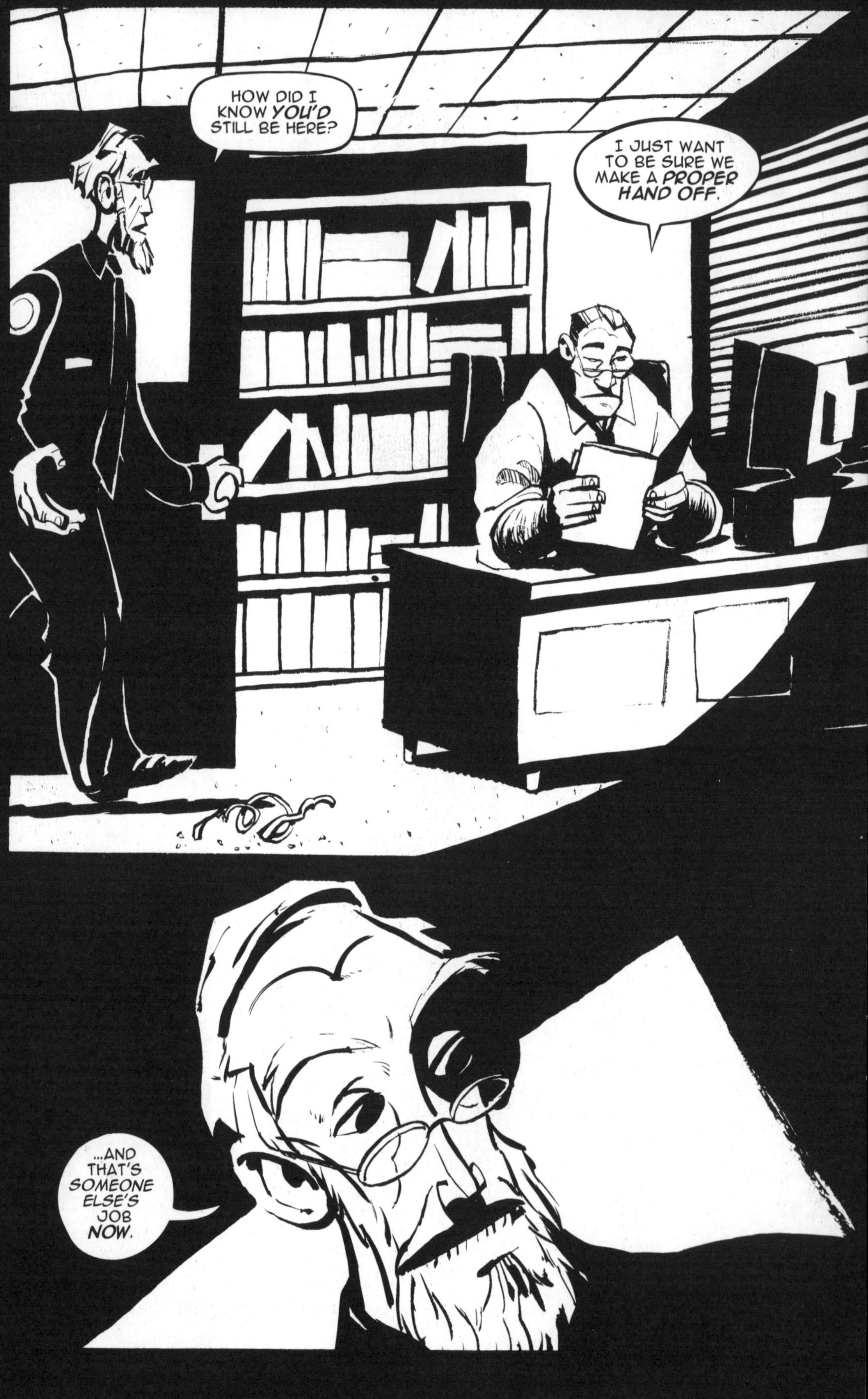
HOW DID I KNOW YOU'D STILL BE HERE?
I JUST WANT TO BE SURE WE MAKE A PROPER HAND OFF.
...AND THAT'S SOMEONE ELSE'S JOB NOW.

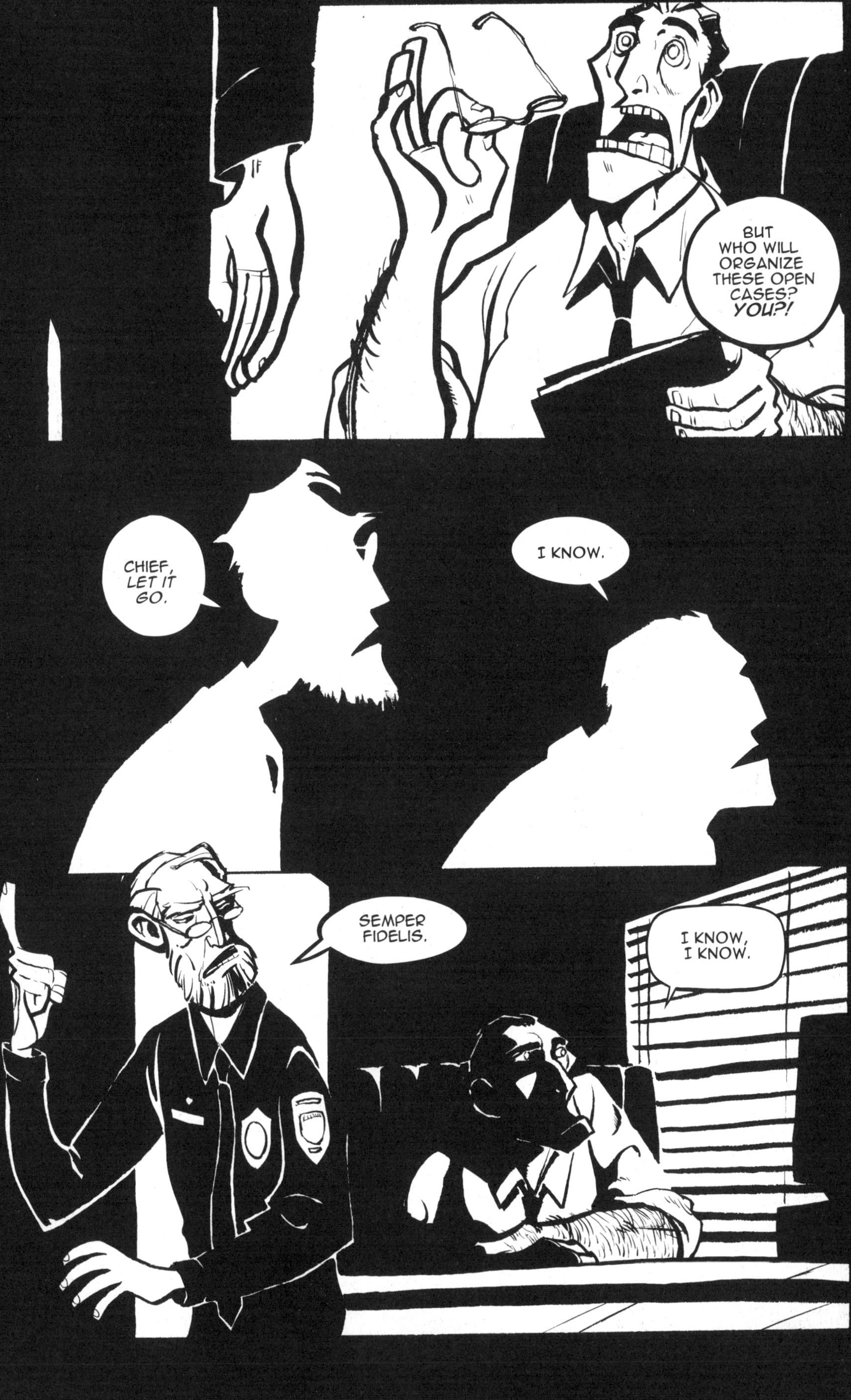
BUT WHO WILL ORGANIZE THESE OPEN CASES? YOU?!
CHIEF, LET IT GO.
I KNOW.
SEMPER FIDELIS.
I KNOW, I KNOW.

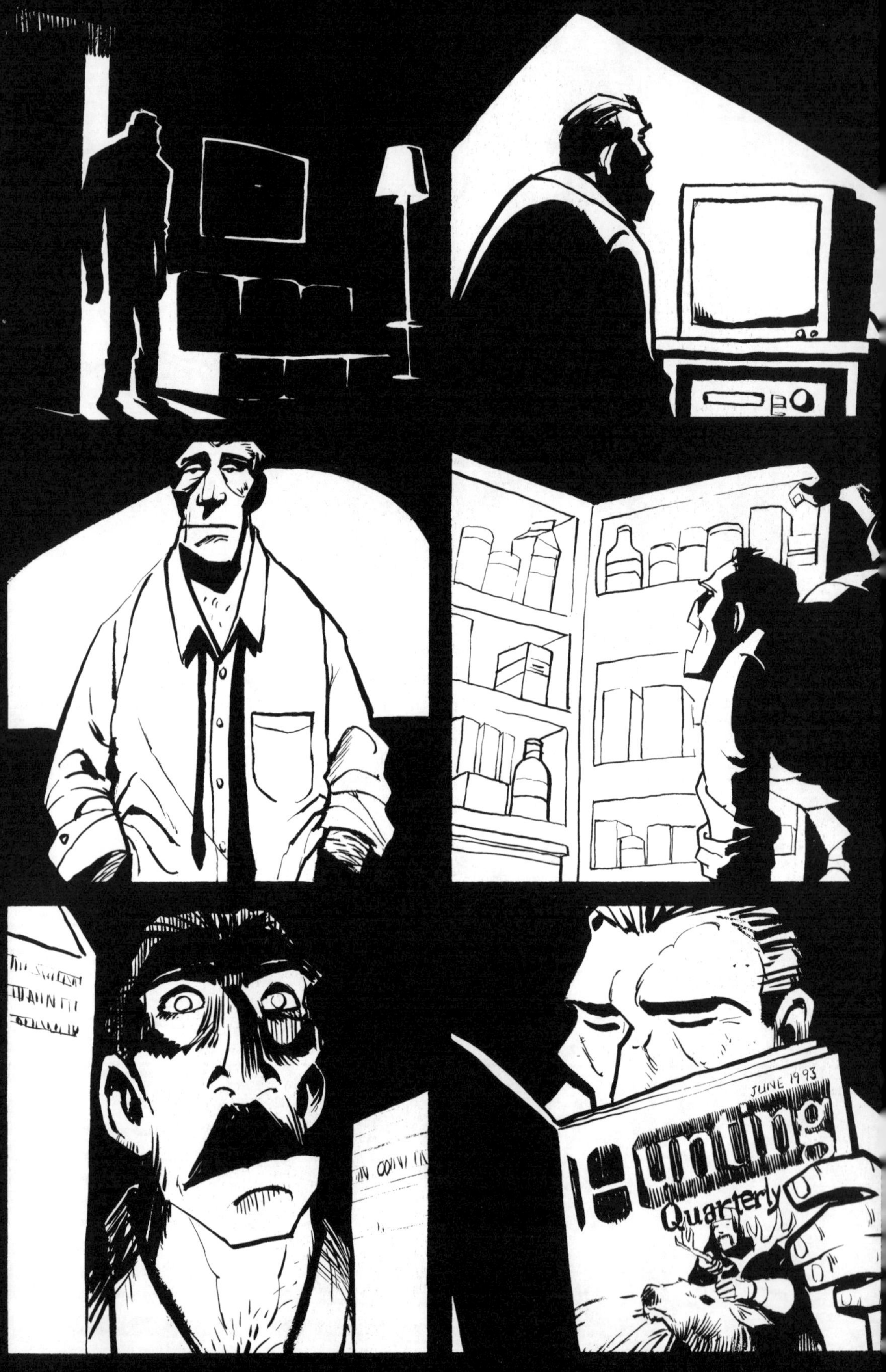
JUNE 1993
Hunting
Quarterly

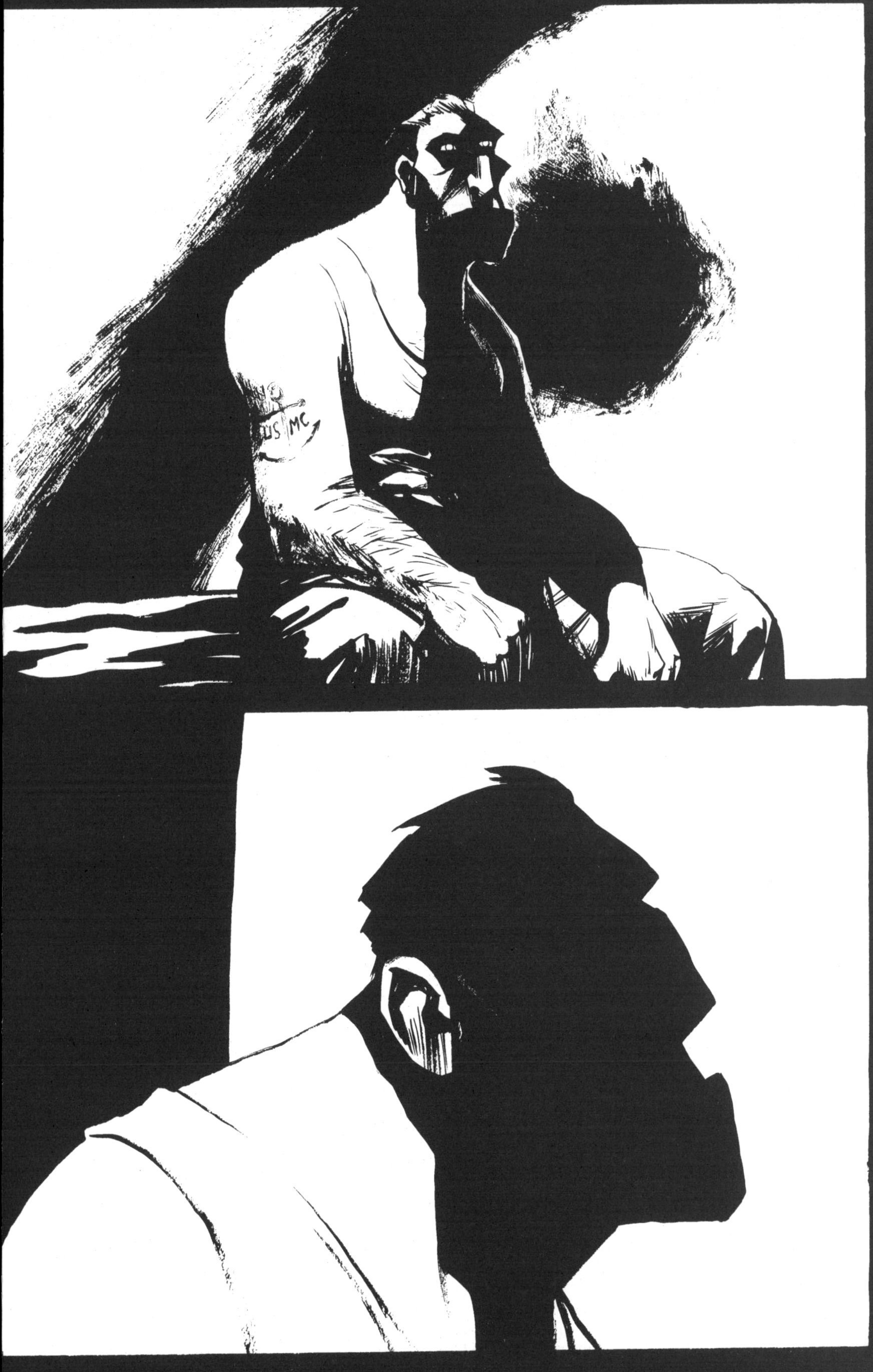
US MC

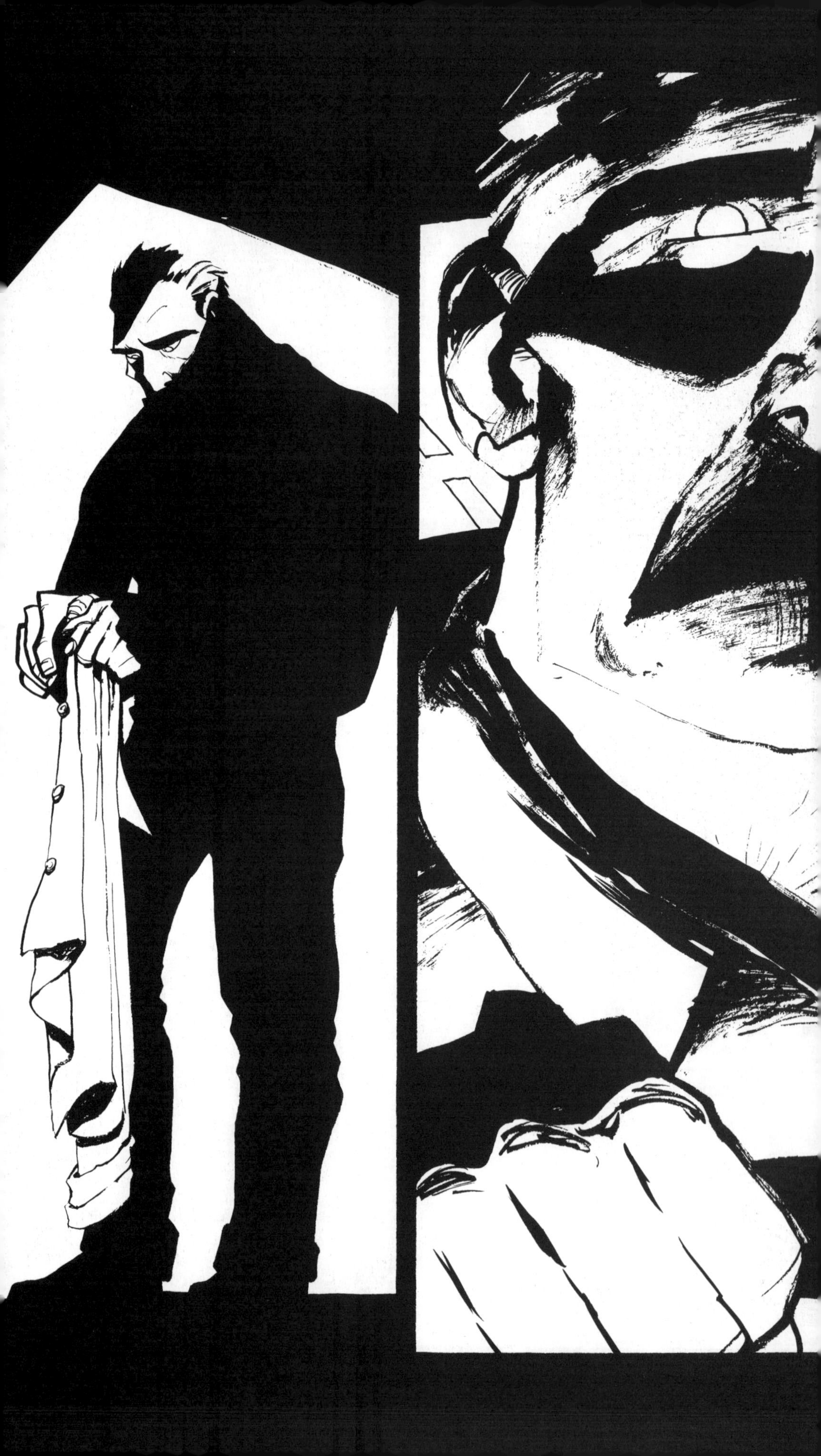

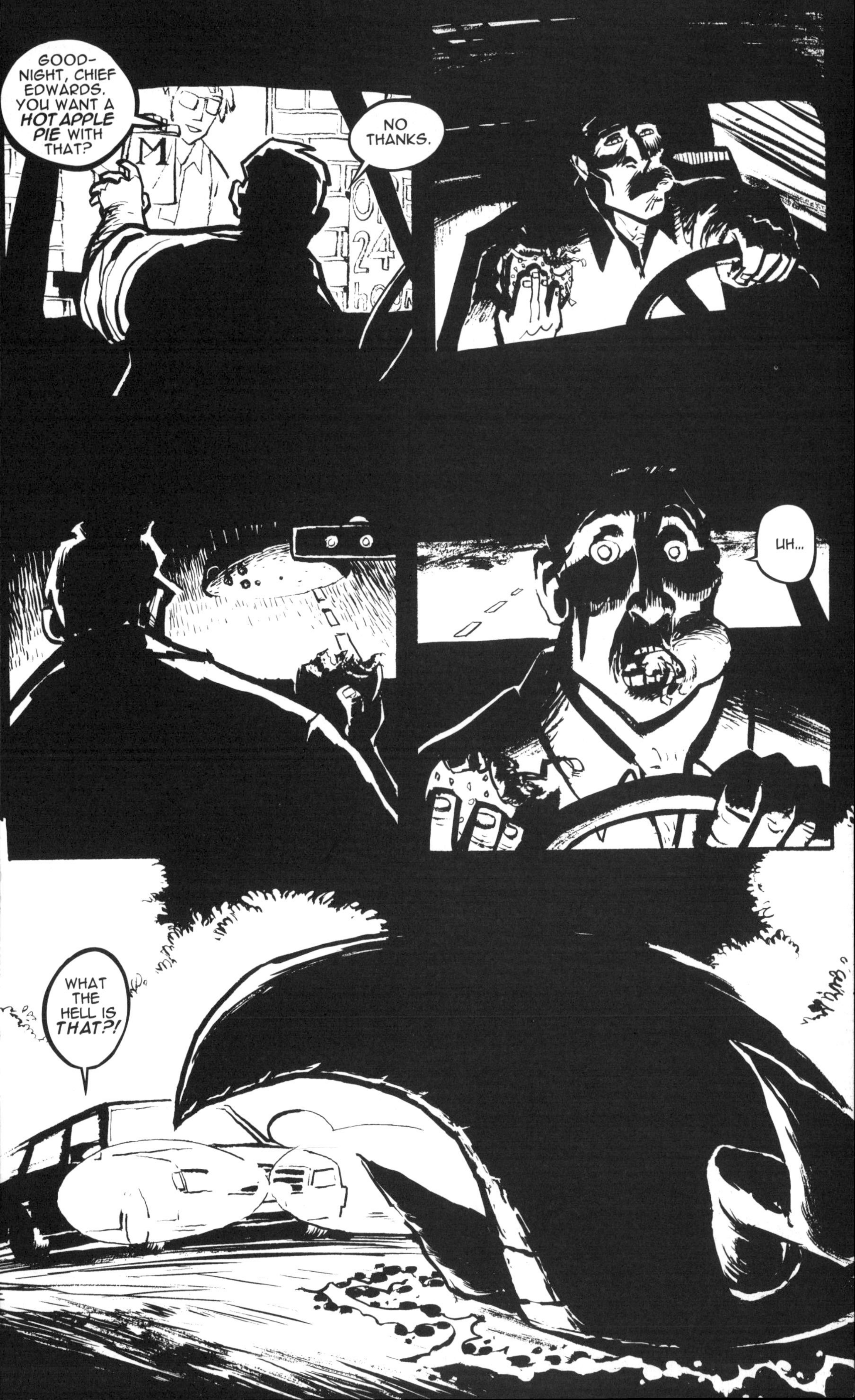
GOOD-NIGHT, CHIEF EDWARDS. YOU WANT A HOT APPLE PIE WITH THAT?
NO THANKS.
UH...
WHAT THE HELL IS THAT?!

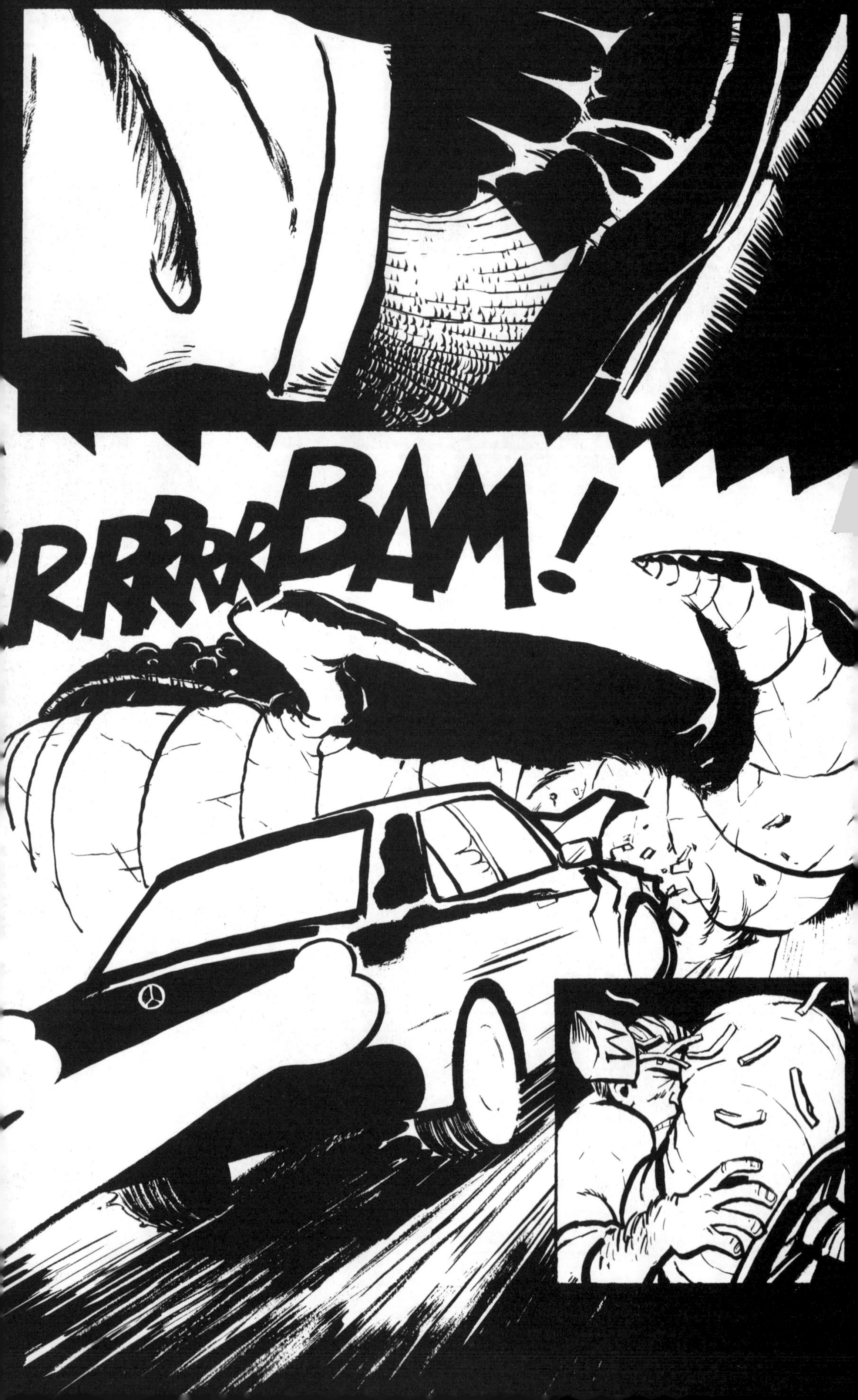
RRRRRRBAM!

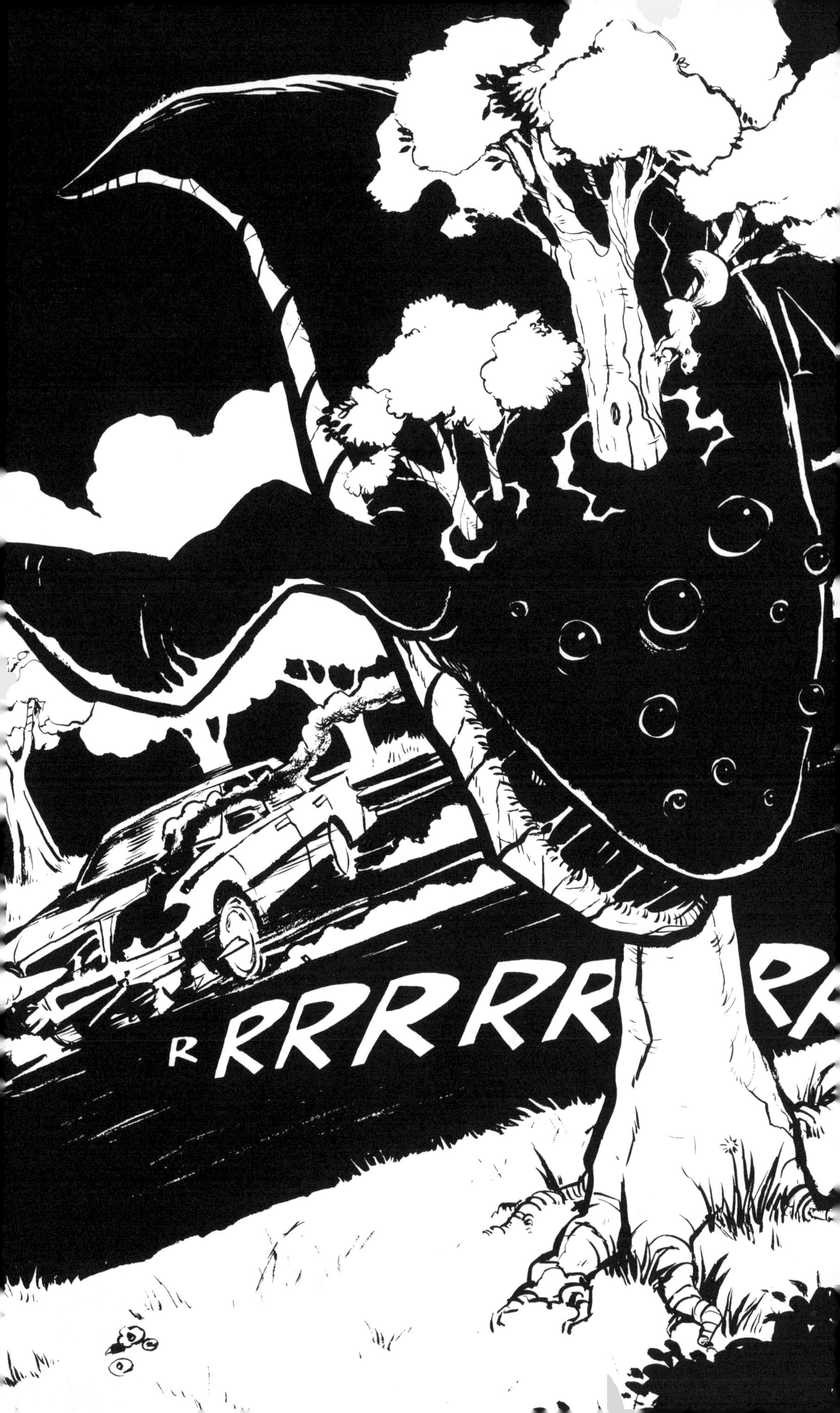
rRRRRR

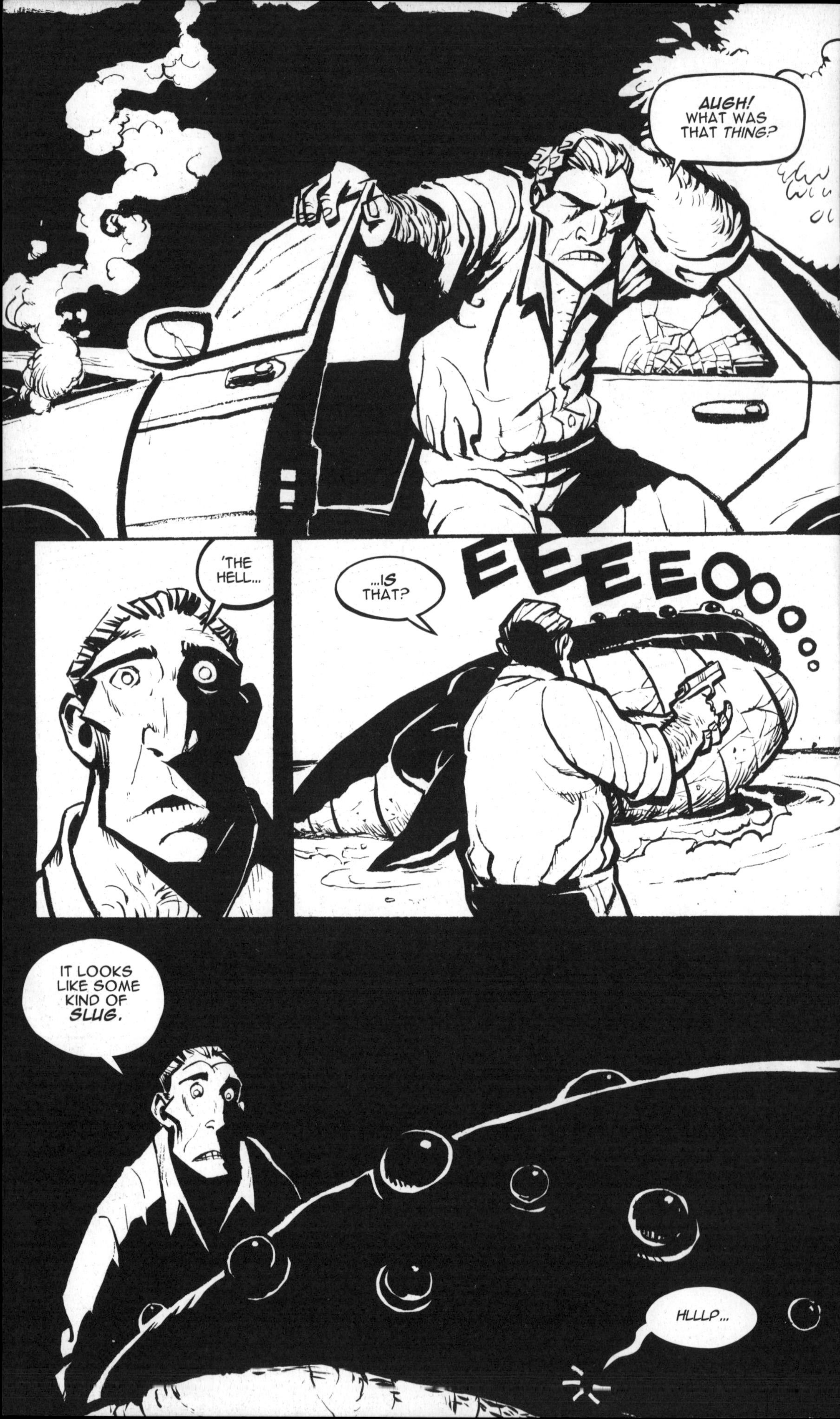
AUGH! WHAT WAS THAT THING?
'THE HELL...
...IS THAT?
EEEEOOOooo
IT LOOKS LIKE SOME KIND OF SLUG.
HLLLP...

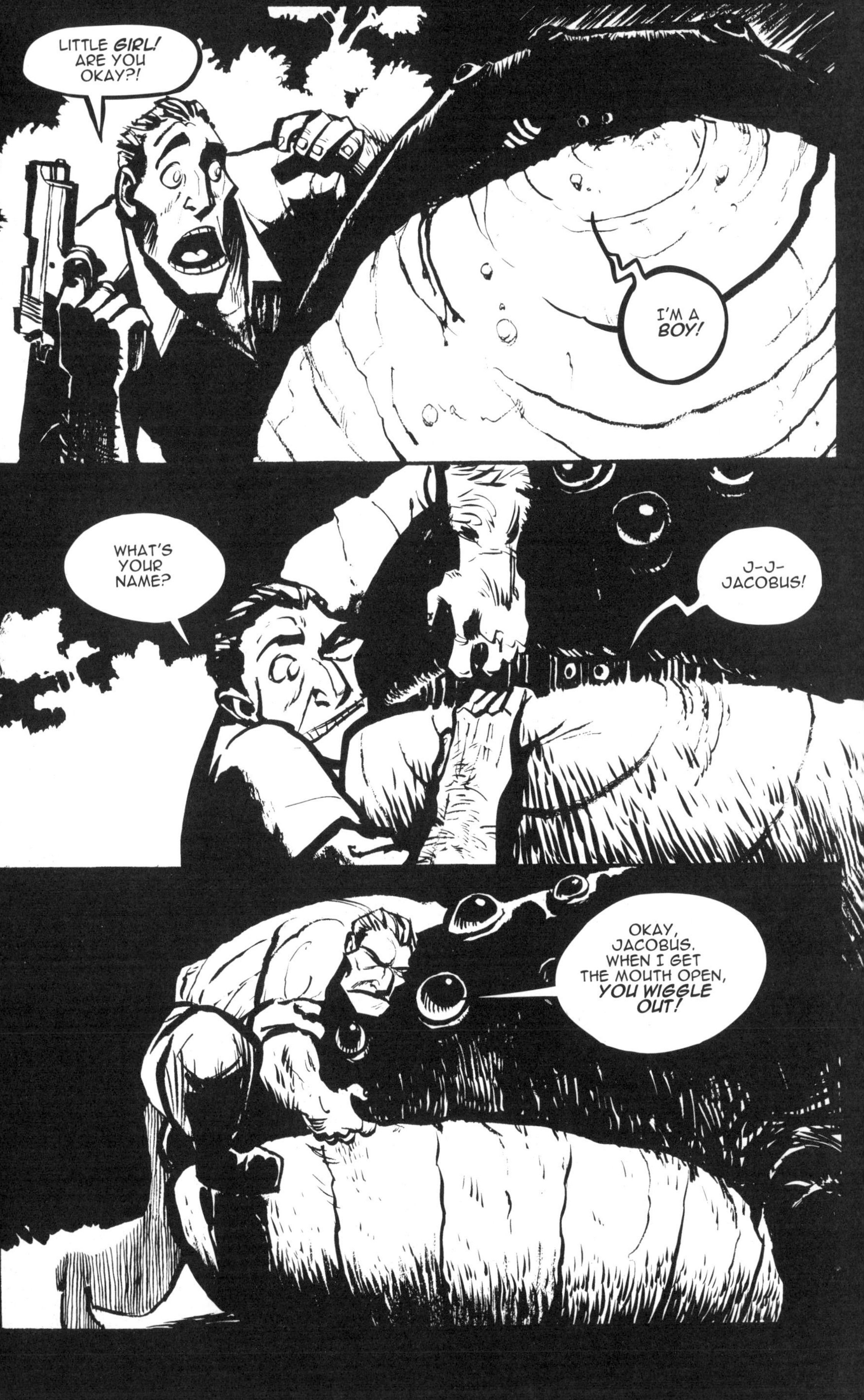
LITTLE GIRL! ARE YOU OKAY?!
I'M A BOY!
WHAT'S YOUR NAME?
J-J-JACOBUS!
OKAY, JACOBUS. WHEN I GET THE MOUTH OPEN, YOU WIGGLE OUT!

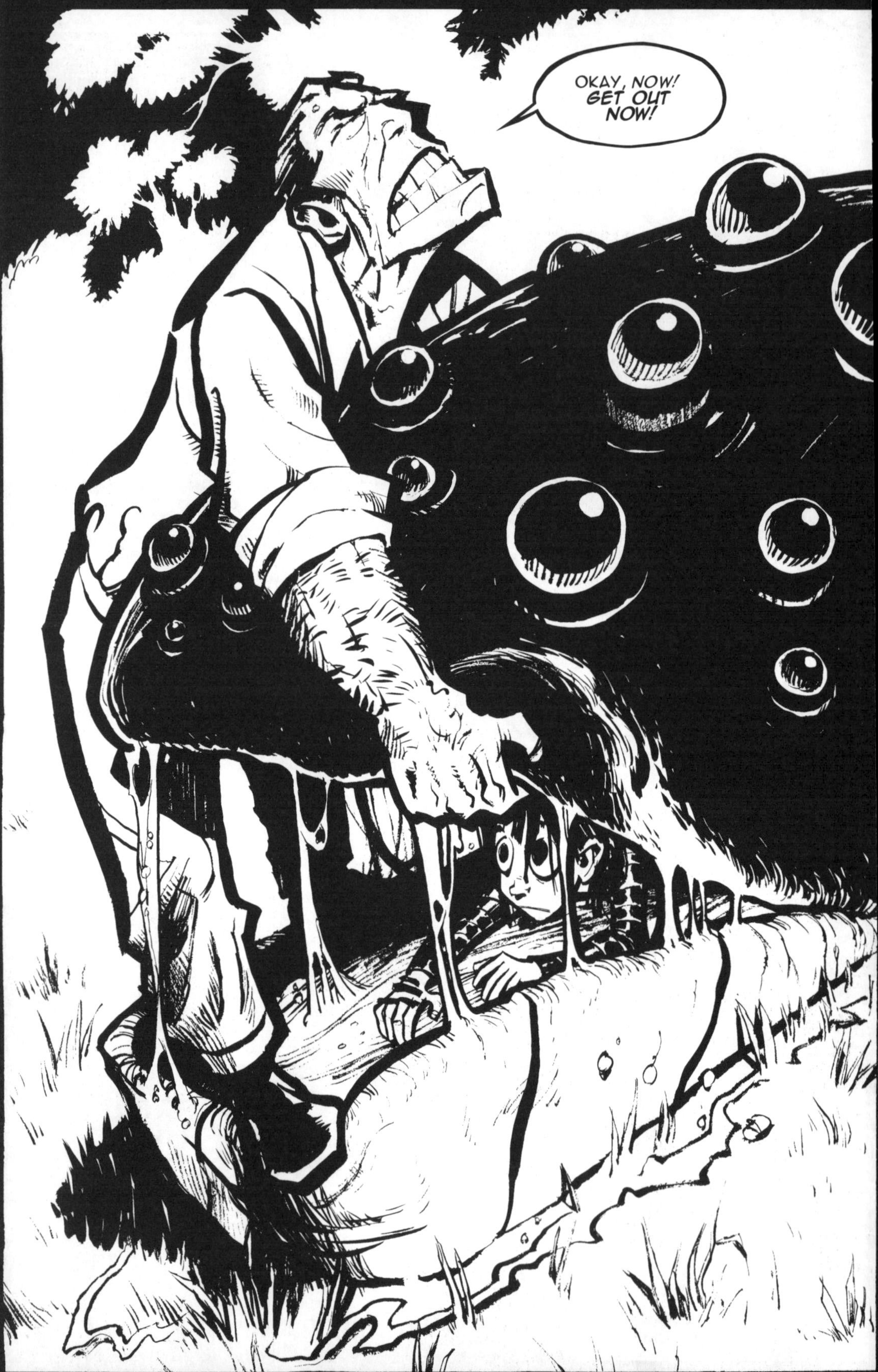
OKAY, NOW! GET OUT NOW!

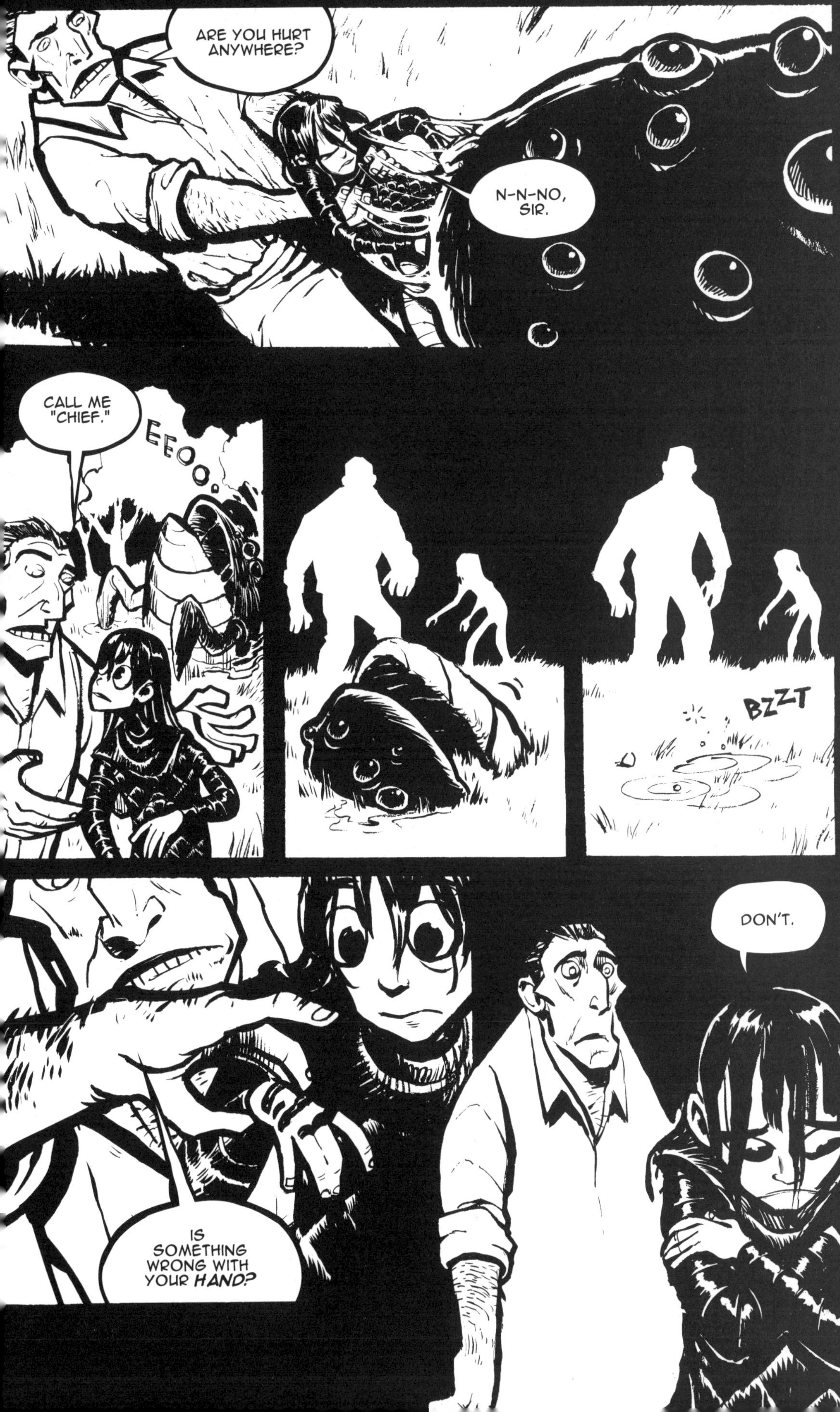
ARE YOU HURT ANYWHERE?
N-N-NO, SIR.
CALL ME "CHIEF."
EEOO..
BZZT
IS SOMETHING WRONG WITH YOUR HAND?
DON'T.

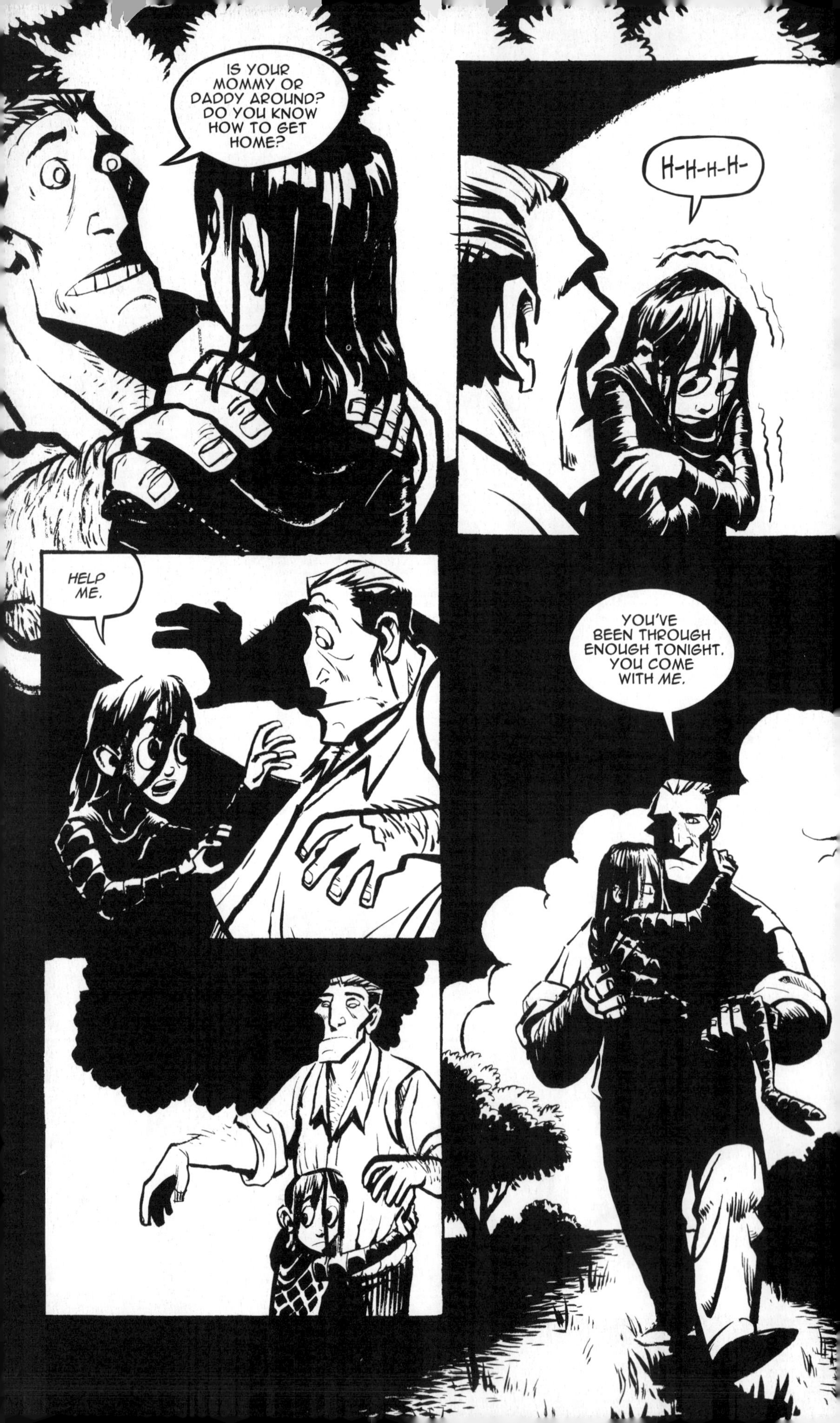
IS YOUR MOMMY OR DADDY AROUND? DO YOU KNOW HOW TO GET HOME?
H-H-H-H-
HELP ME.
YOU'VE BEEN THROUGH ENOUGH TONIGHT. YOU COME WITH ME.

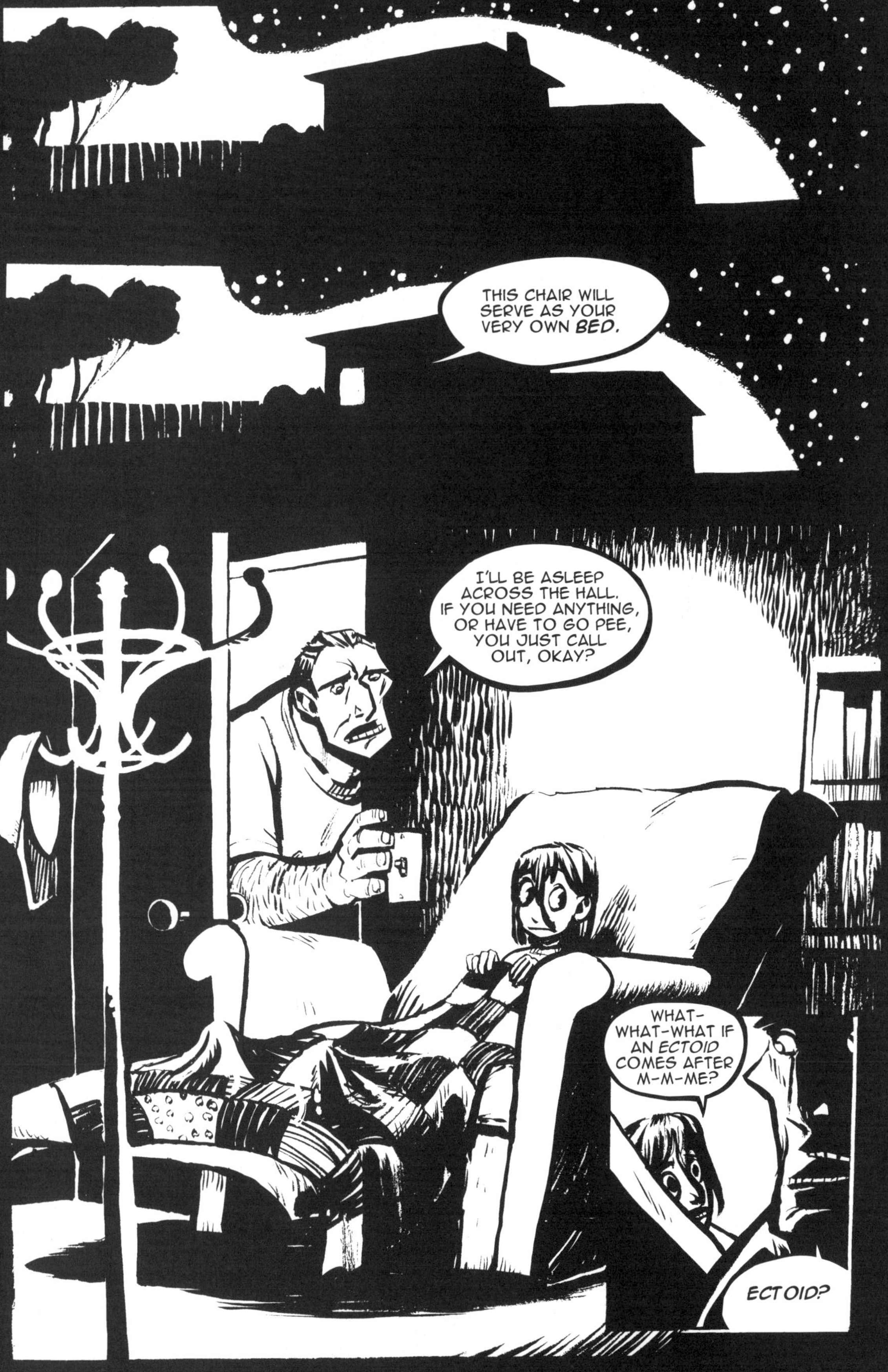

THIS CHAIR WILL SERVE AS YOUR VERY OWN BED.
I'LL BE ASLEEP ACROSS THE HALL. IF YOU NEED ANYTHING, OR HAVE TO GO PEE, YOU JUST CALL OUT, OKAY?
WHAT-WHAT-WHAT IF AN ECTOID COMES AFTER M-M-ME?
ECTOID?

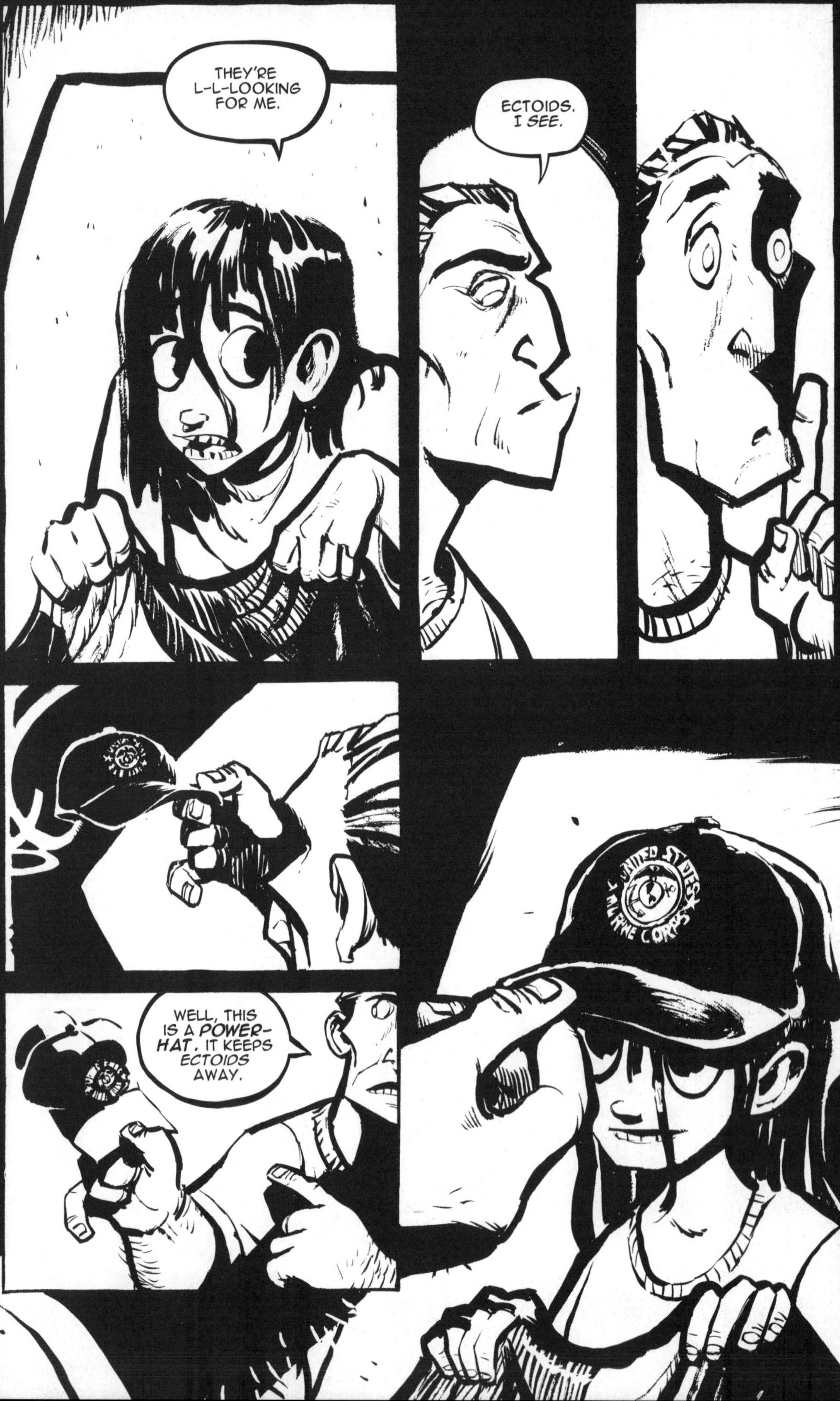
THEY'RE L-L-LOOKING FOR ME.
ECTOIDS. I SEE.
WELL, THIS IS A POWER-HAT. IT KEEPS ECTOIDS AWAY.
UNITED STATES MARINE CORPS

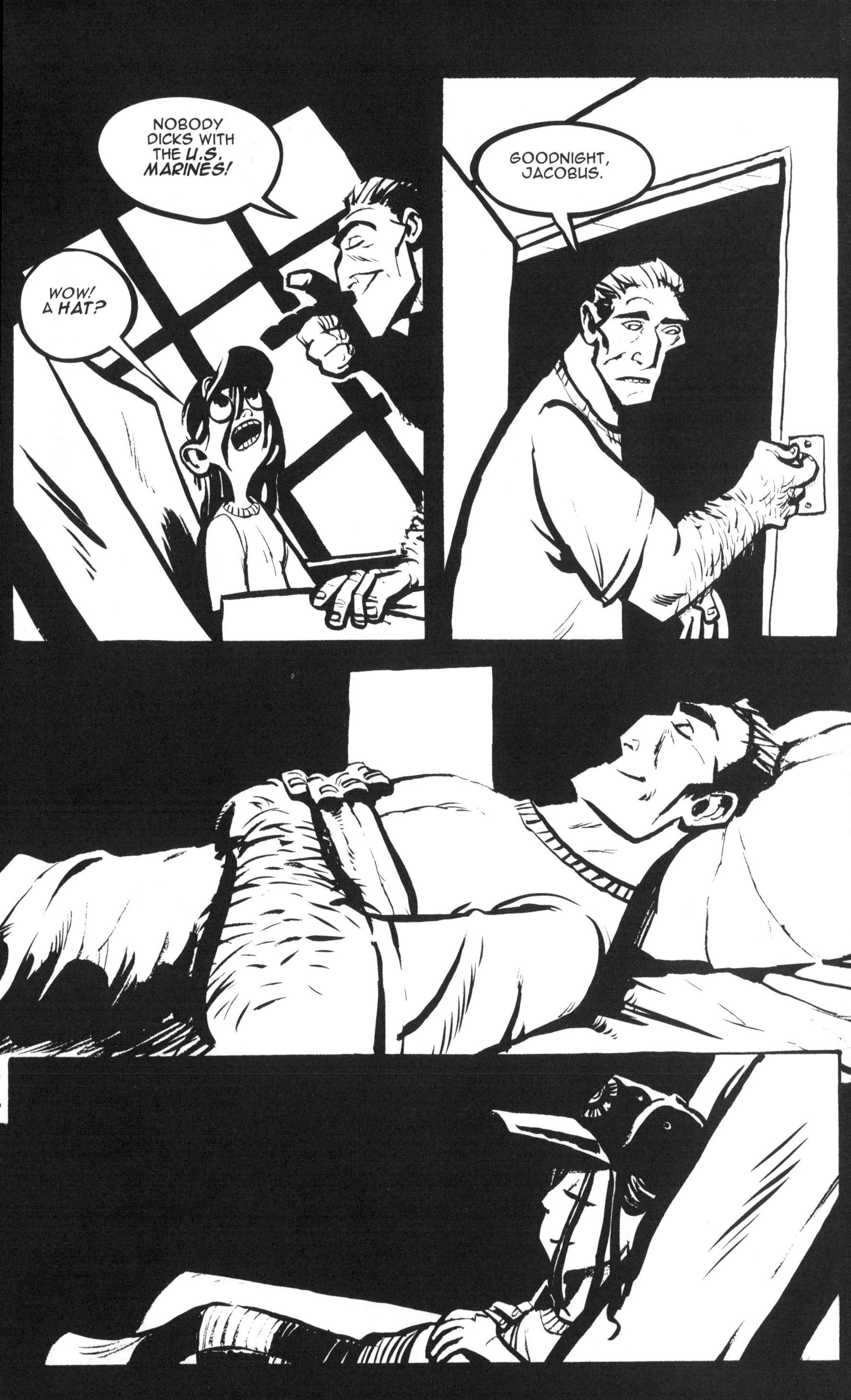
NOBODY DICKS WITH THE U.S. MARINES!
WOW! A HAT?
GOODNIGHT, JACOBUS.

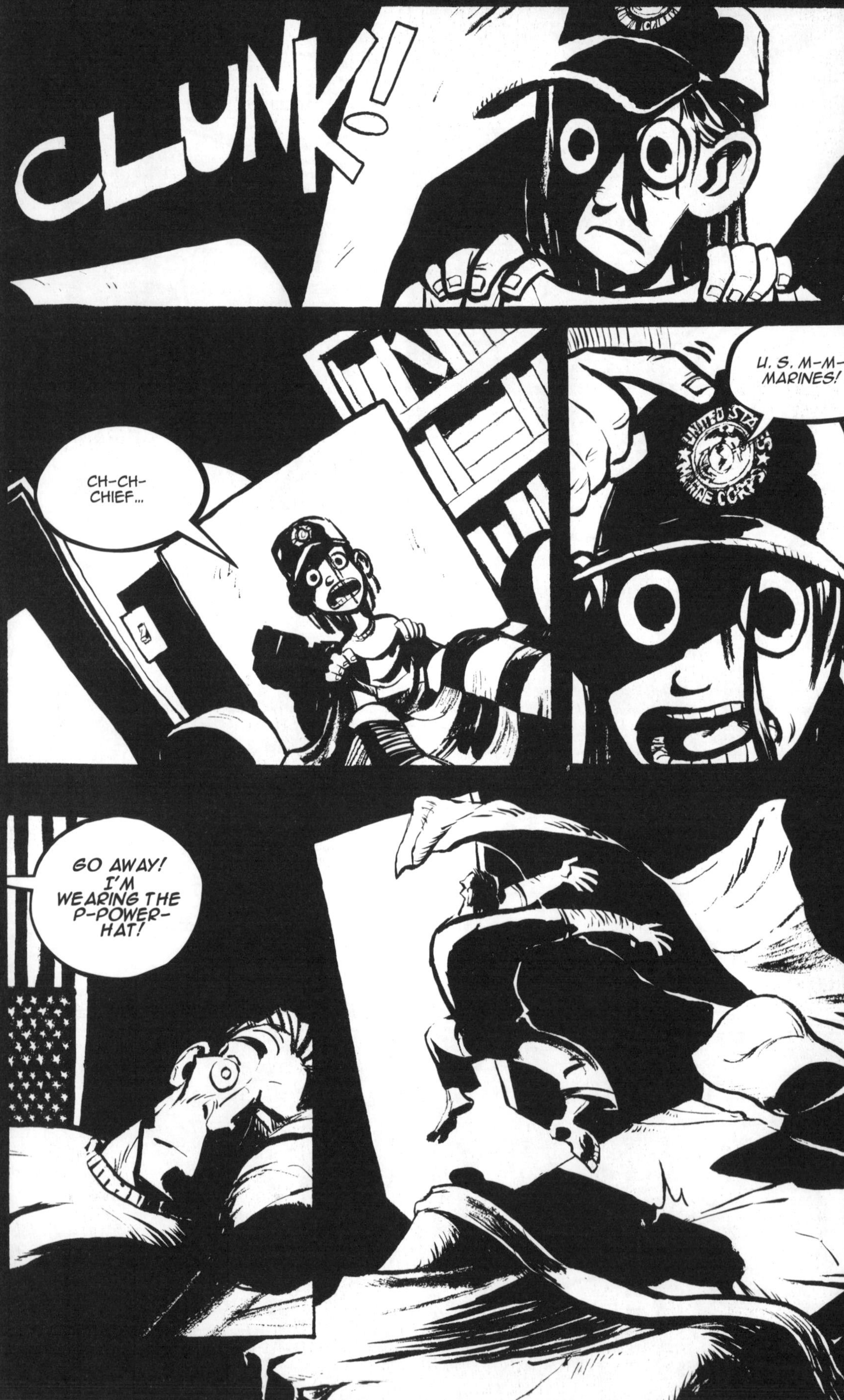
CLUNK!
CH-CH-CHIEF...
U. S. M-M-MARINES!
UNITED STATES MARINE CORPS
GO AWAY! I'M WEARING THE P-POWER-HAT!

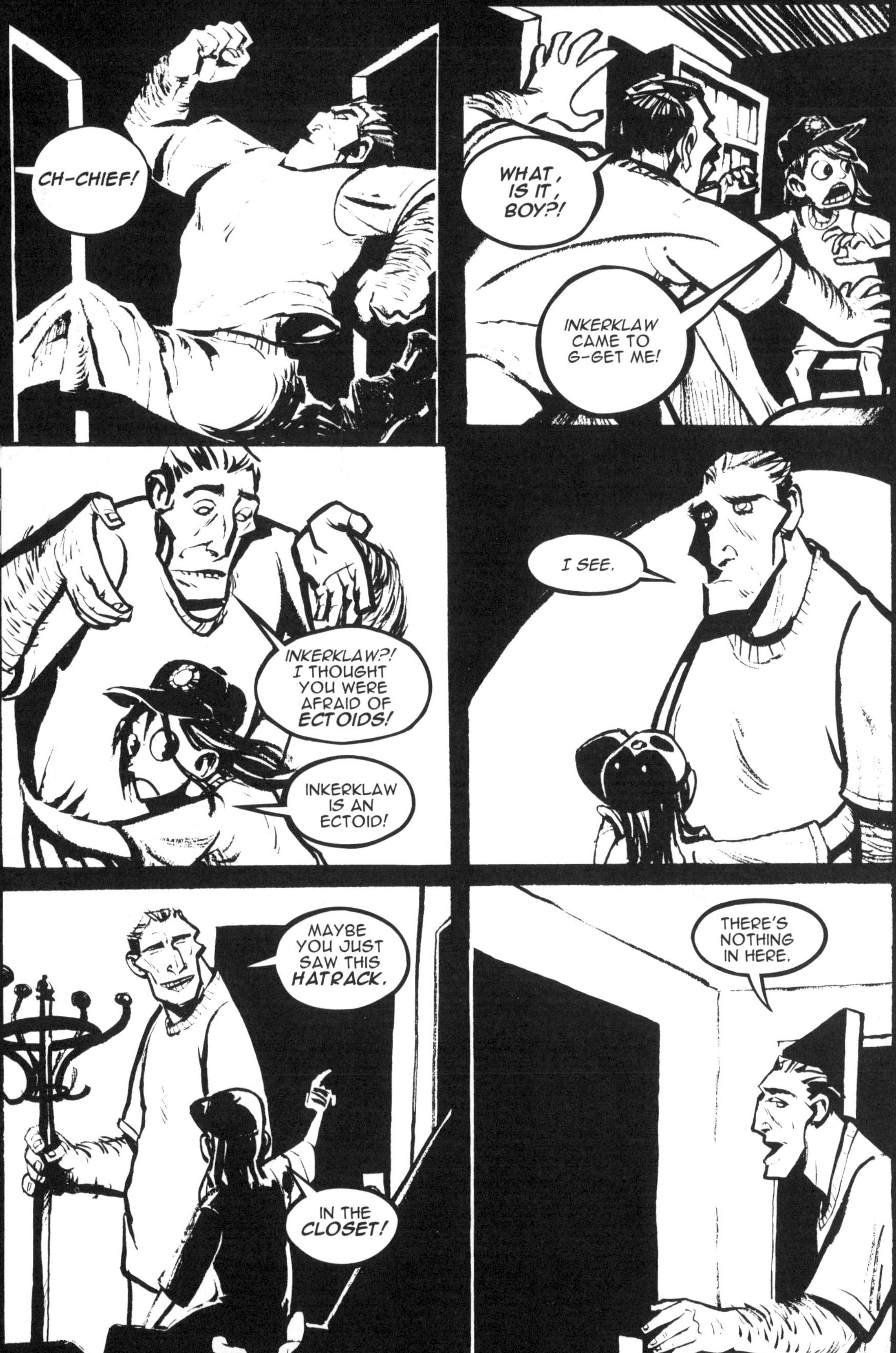
CH-CHIEF!
WHAT, IS IT, BOY?!
INKERKLAW CAME TO G-GET ME!
INKERKLAW?! I THOUGHT YOU WERE AFRAID OF ECTOIDS!
INKERKLAW IS AN ECTOID!
I SEE.
MAYBE YOU JUST SAW THIS HATRACK.
IN THE CLOSET!
THERE'S NOTHING IN HERE.

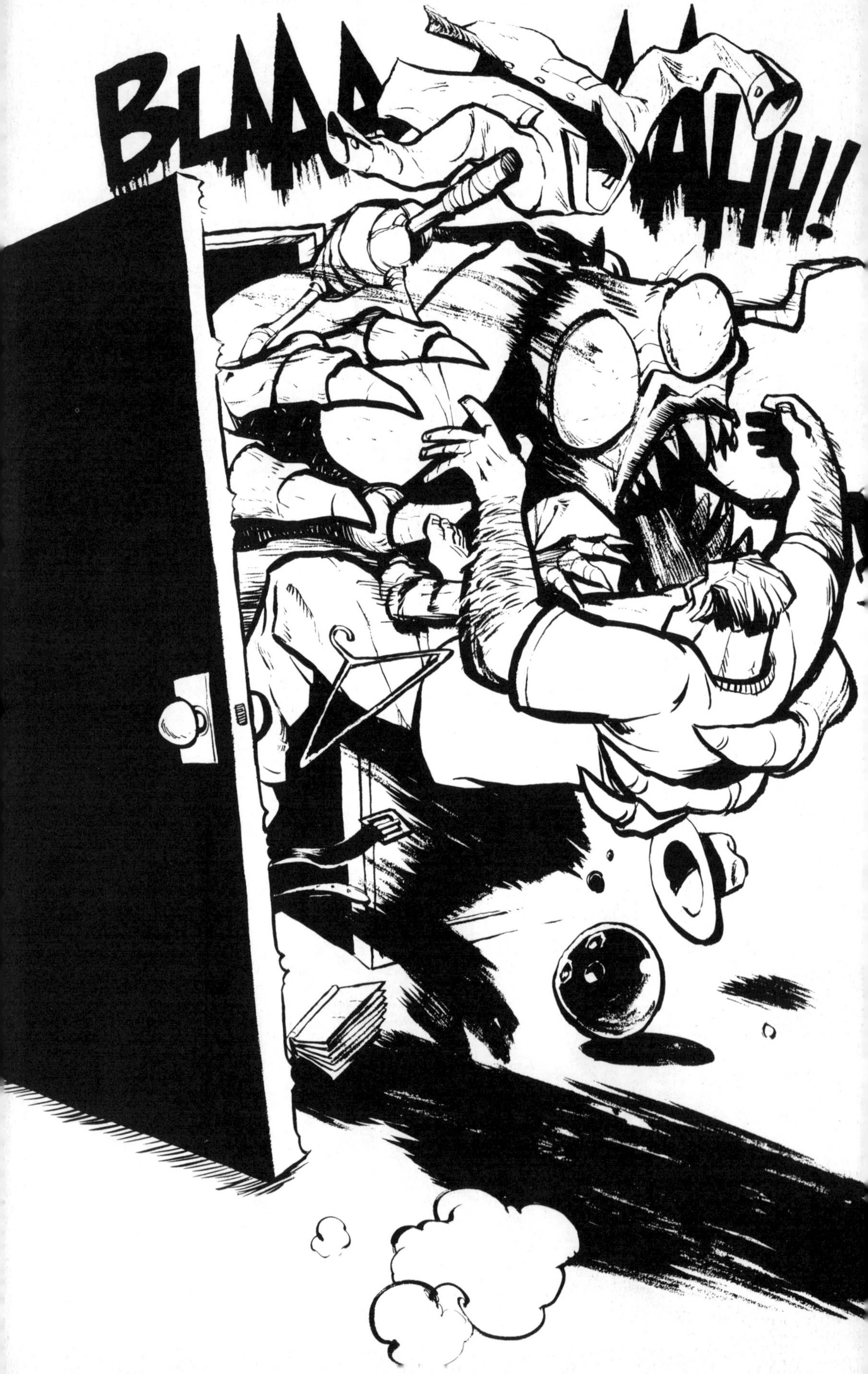
BLAA AHH!

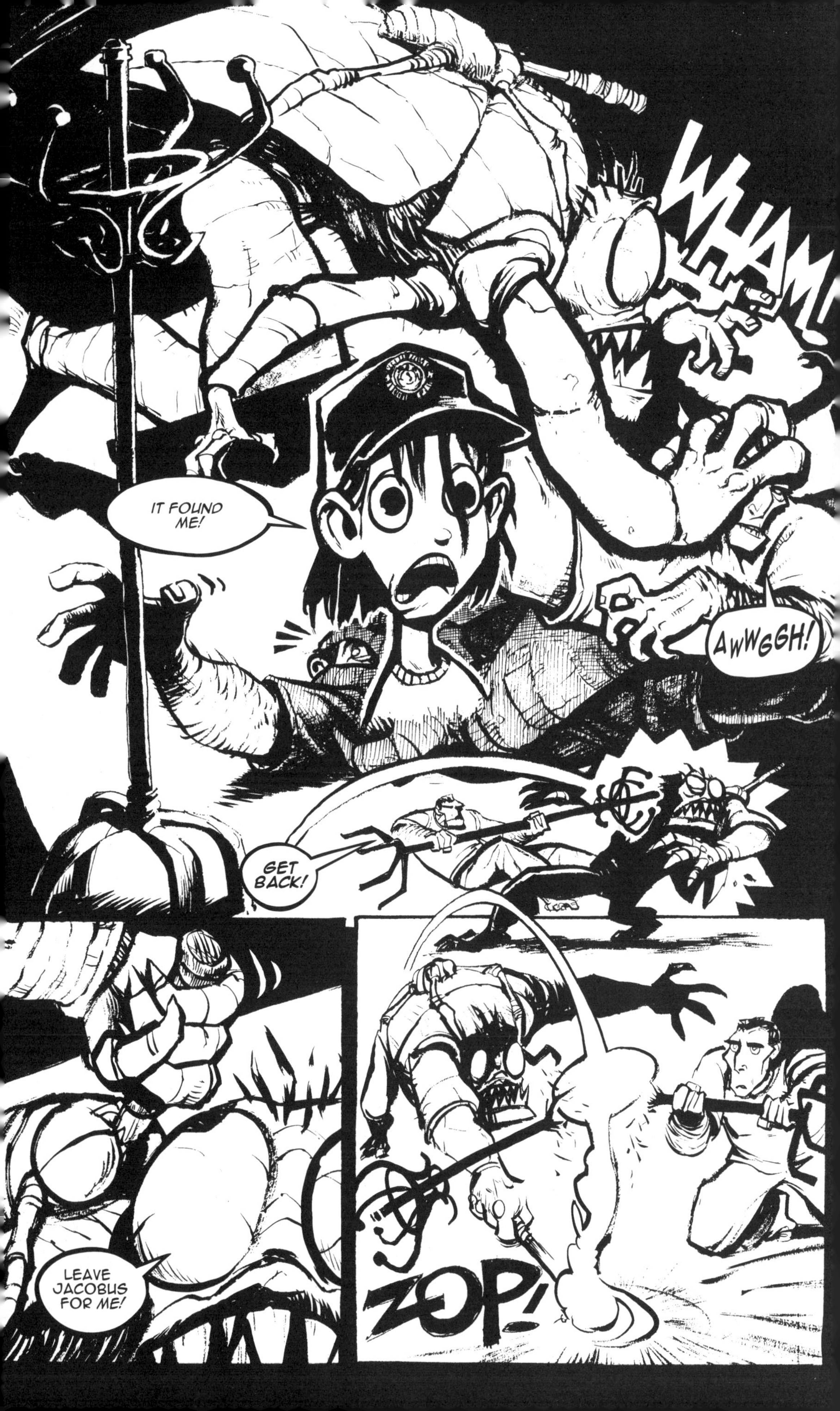
WHAM!
IT FOUND ME!
AWWGGH!
GET BACK!
LEAVE JACOBUS FOR ME!
ZOP!

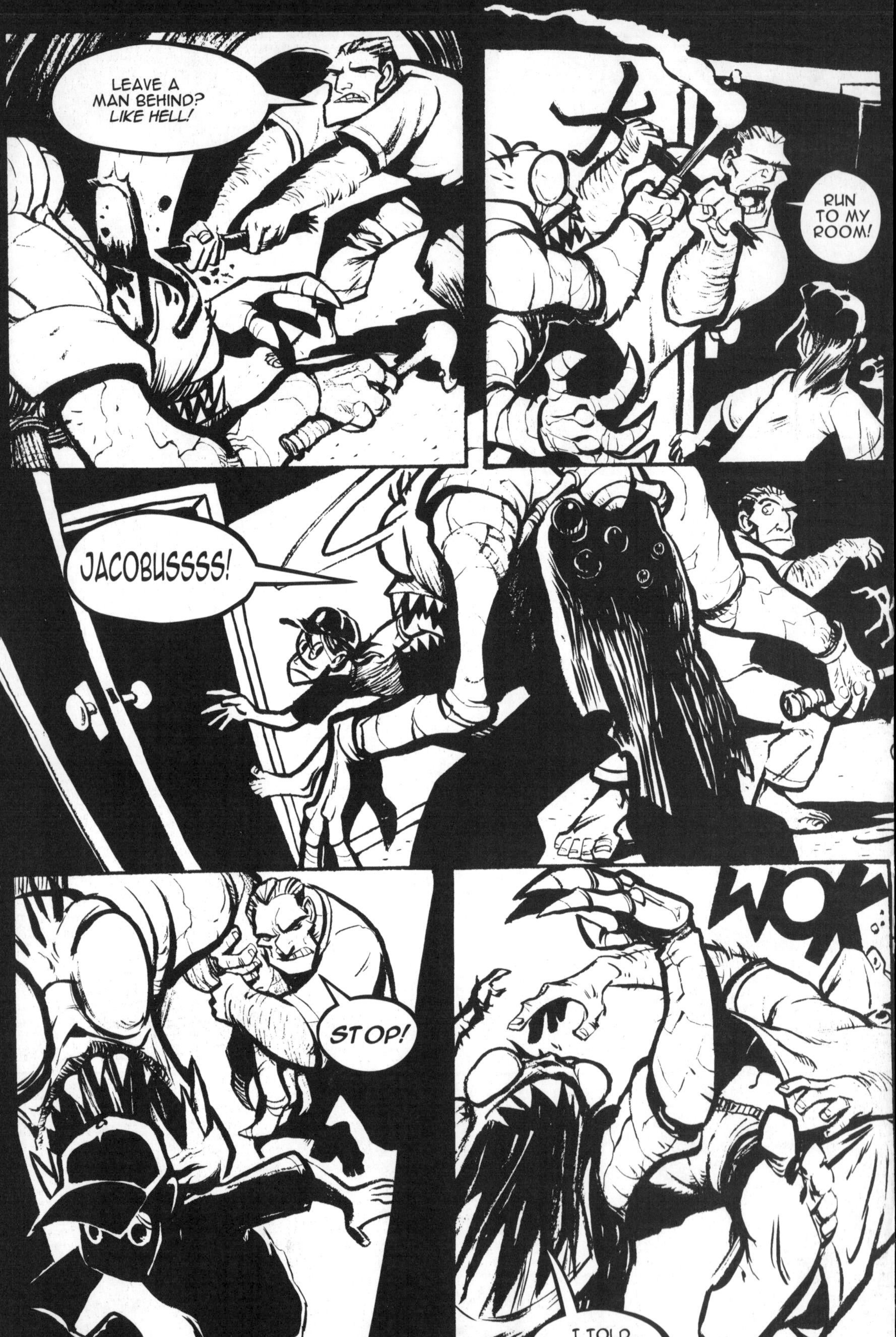
LEAVE A MAN BEHIND? LIKE HELL!
RUN TO MY ROOM!
JACOBUSSSS!
STOP!
WOK
I TOLD YOU TO LEAVE US!

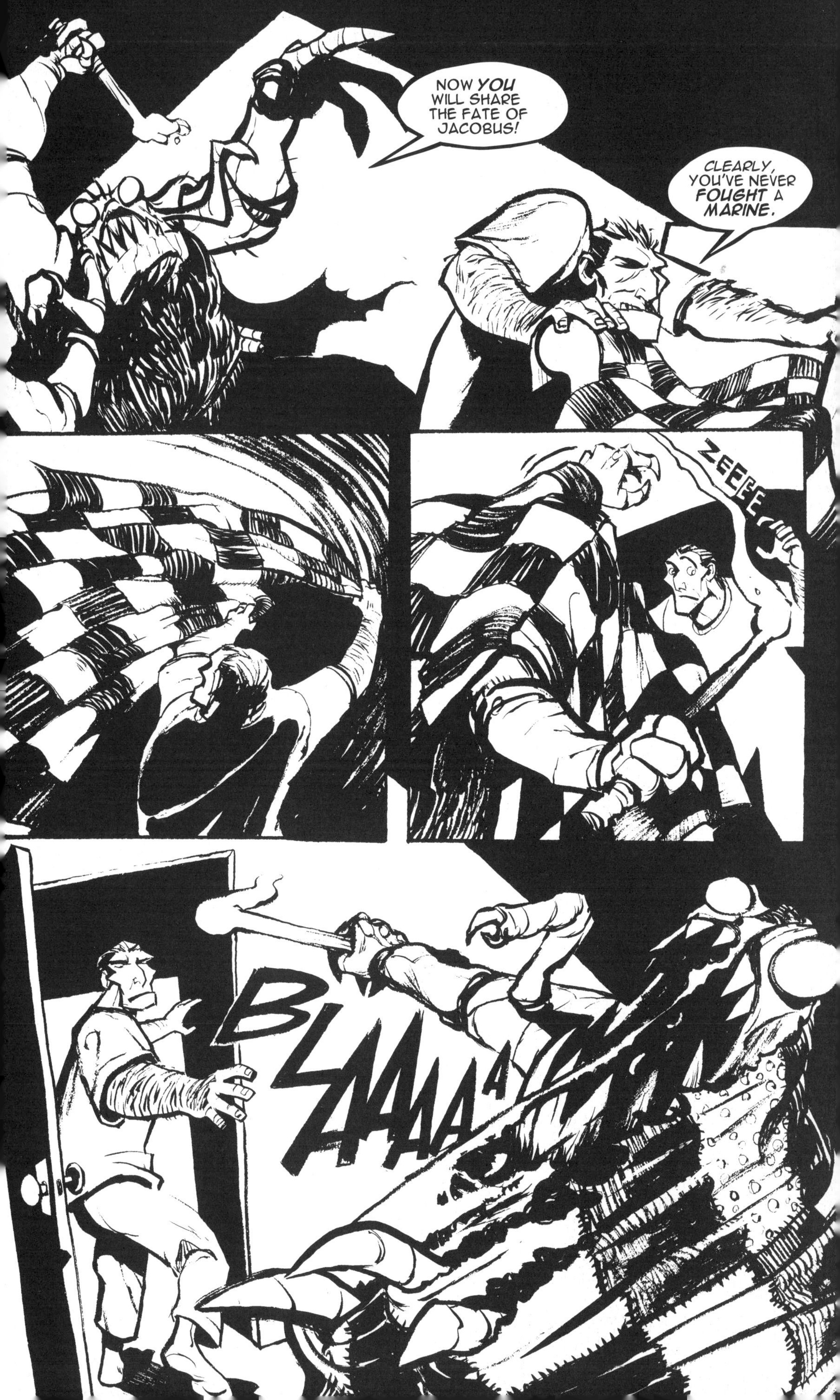
NOW YOU WILL SHARE THE FATE OF JACOBUS!
CLEARLY, YOU'VE NEVER FOUGHT A MARINE.
ZEEEE
BLAAAAAA

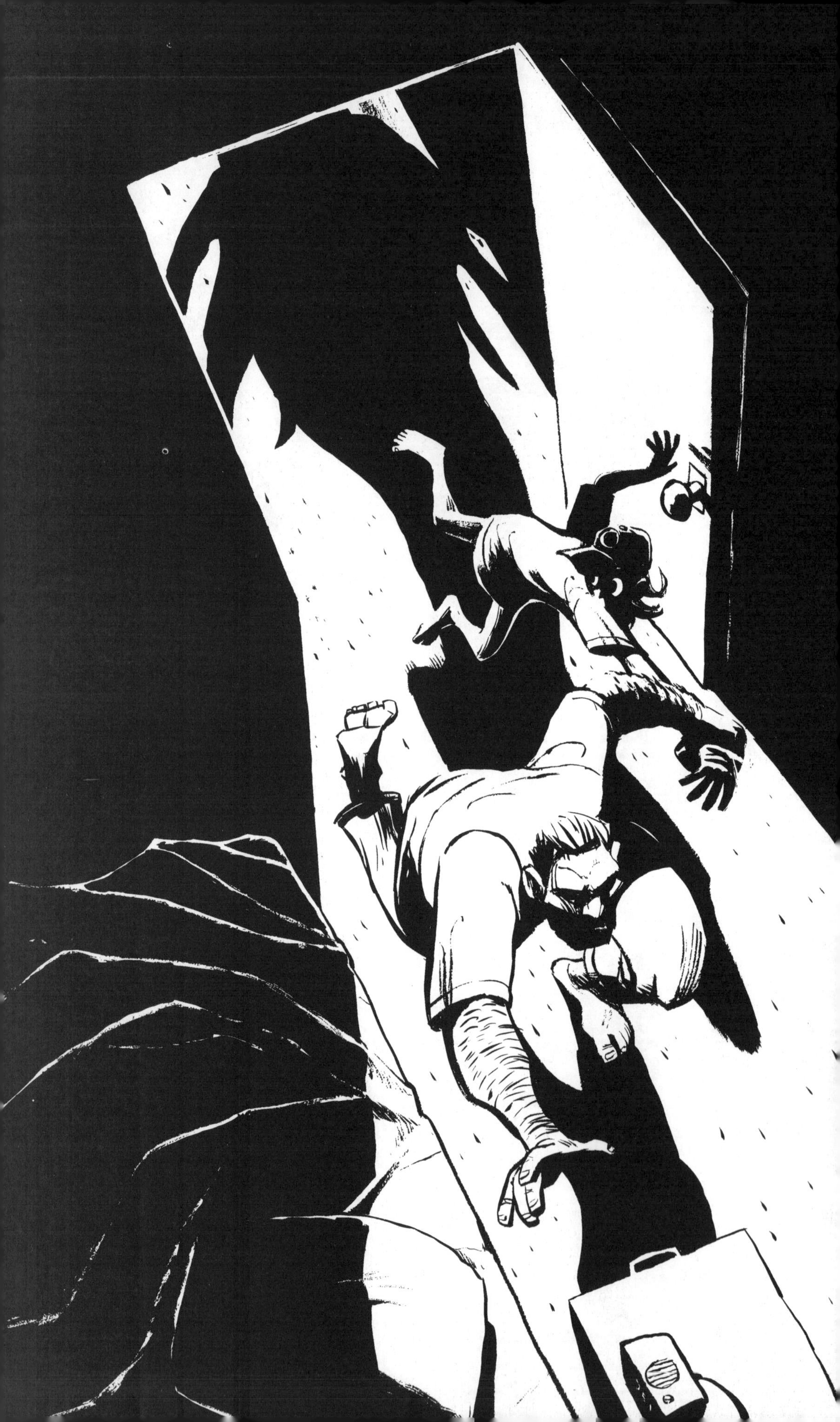

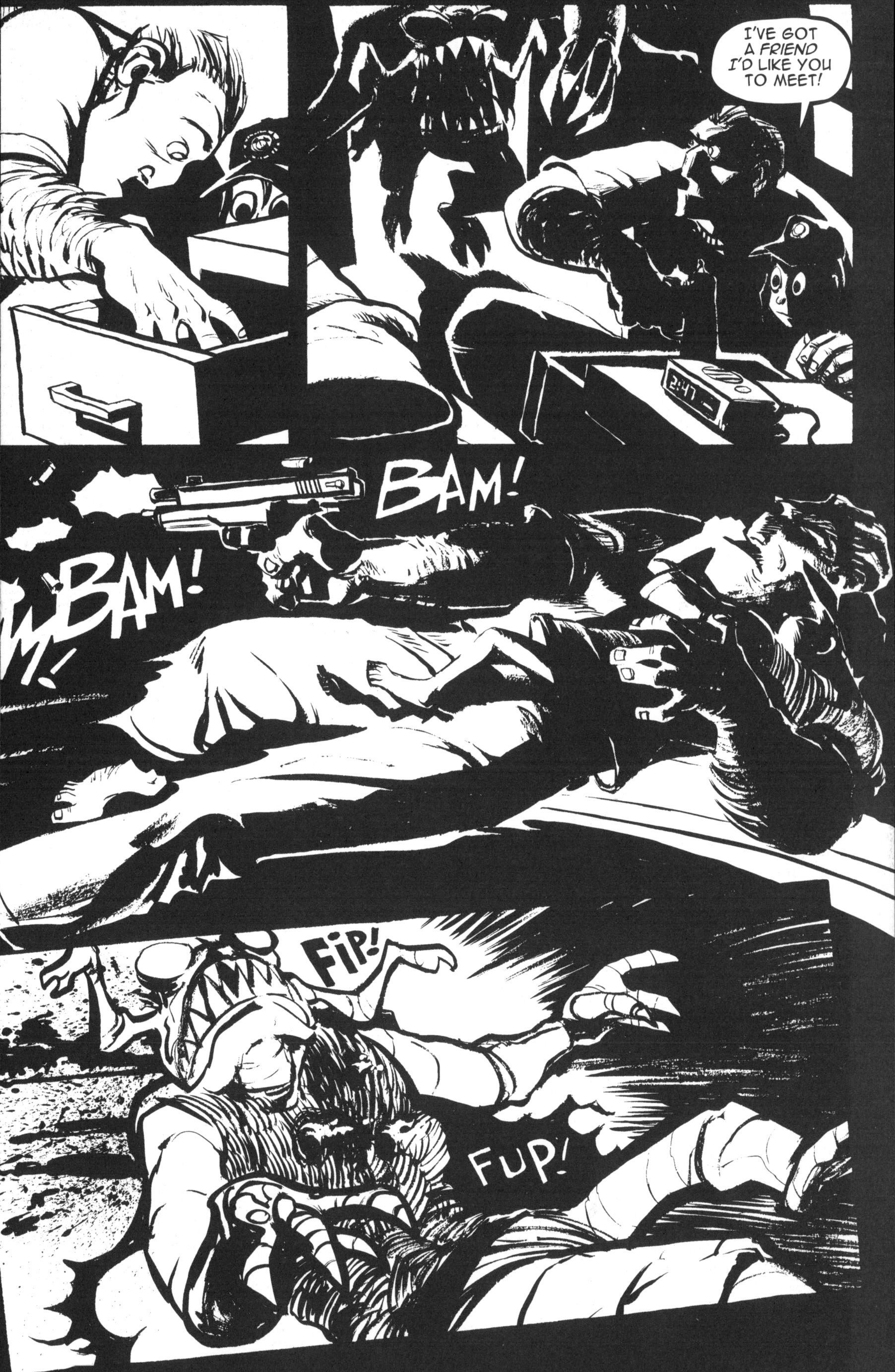
I'VE GOT A FRIEND I'D LIKE YOU TO MEET!
BAM!
BAM!
FIP!
FUP!

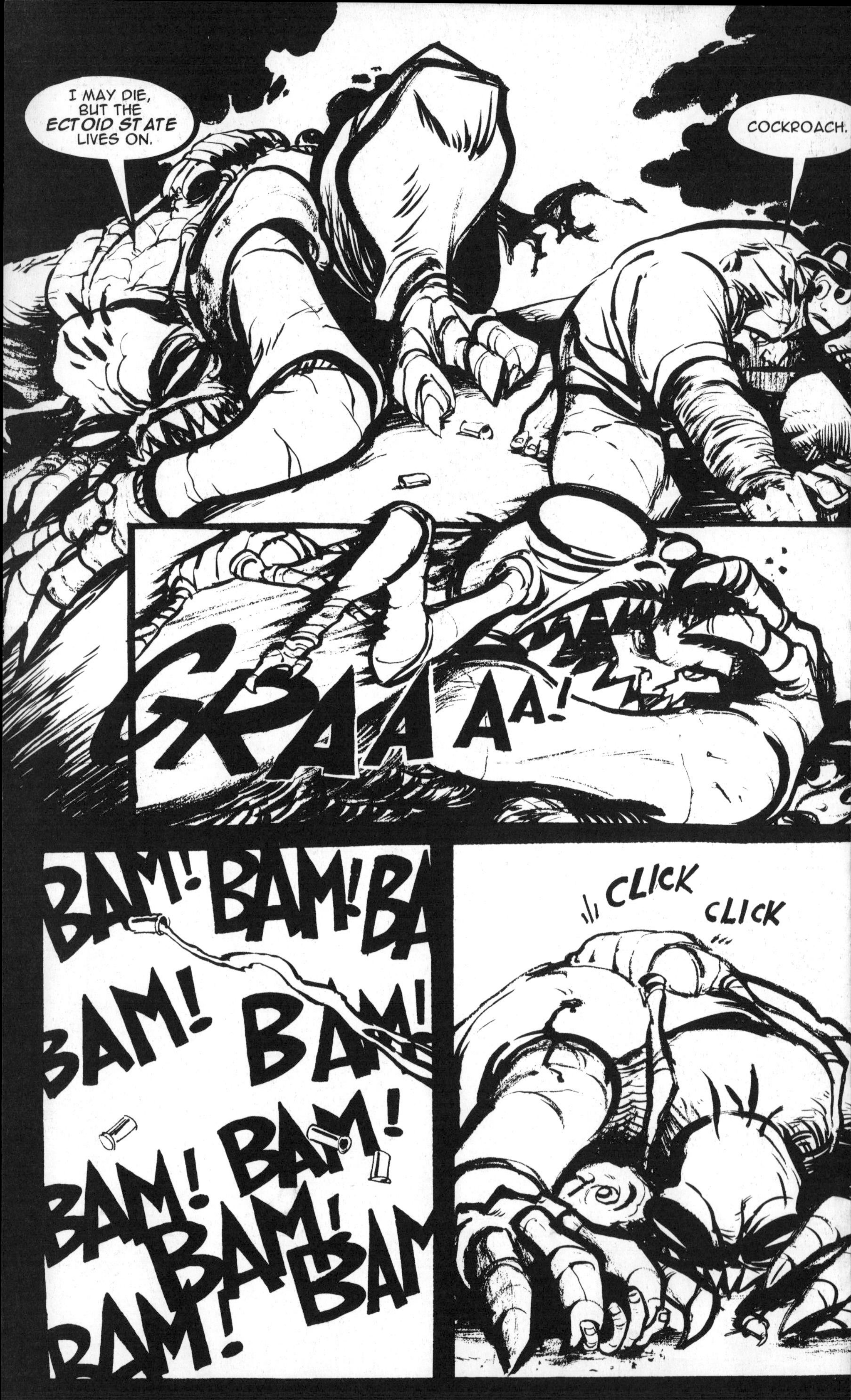
I MAY DIE, BUT THE ECTOID STATE LIVES ON.
COCKROACH.
GRAAAAA!
BAM! BAM! BA
BAM! BAM!
BAM! BAM! BAM!
BAM! BAM! BAM
BAM!
CLICK
CLICK

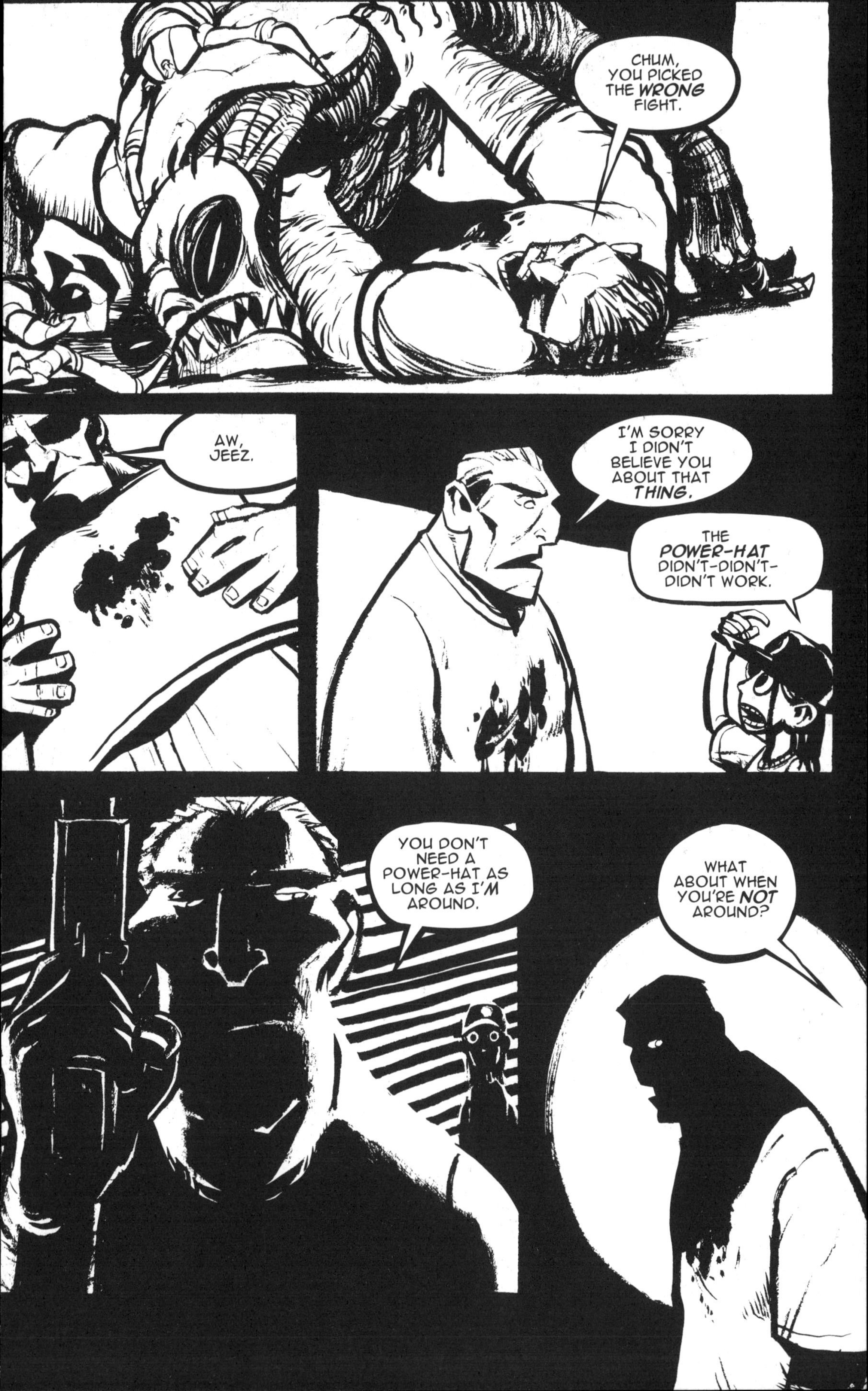
CHUM, YOU PICKED THE WRONG FIGHT.
AW, JEEZ.
I'M SORRY I DIDN'T BELIEVE YOU ABOUT THAT THING.
THE POWER-HAT DIDN'T-DIDN'T-DIDN'T WORK.
YOU DON'T NEED A POWER-HAT AS LONG AS I'M AROUND.
WHAT ABOUT WHEN YOU'RE NOT AROUND?

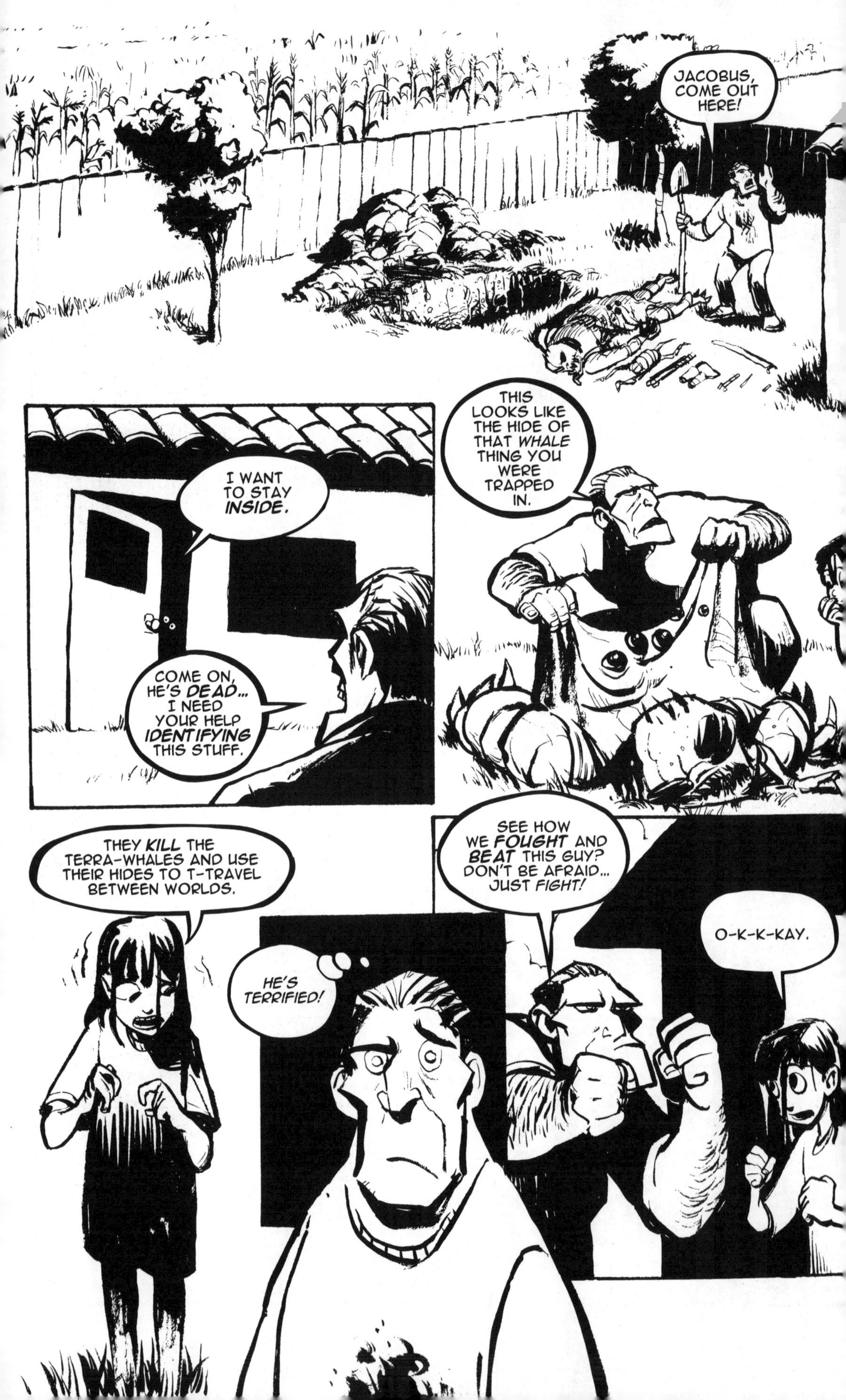
JACOBUS, COME OUT HERE!
I WANT TO STAY INSIDE.
COME ON, HE'S DEAD... I NEED YOUR HELP IDENTIFYING THIS STUFF.
THIS LOOKS LIKE THE HIDE OF THAT WHALE THING YOU WERE TRAPPED IN.
THEY KILL THE TERRA-WHALES AND USE THEIR HIDES TO T-TRAVEL BETWEEN WORLDS.
HE'S TERRIFIED!
SEE HOW WE FOUGHT AND BEAT THIS GUY? DON'T BE AFRAID... JUST FIGHT!
O-K-K-KAY.

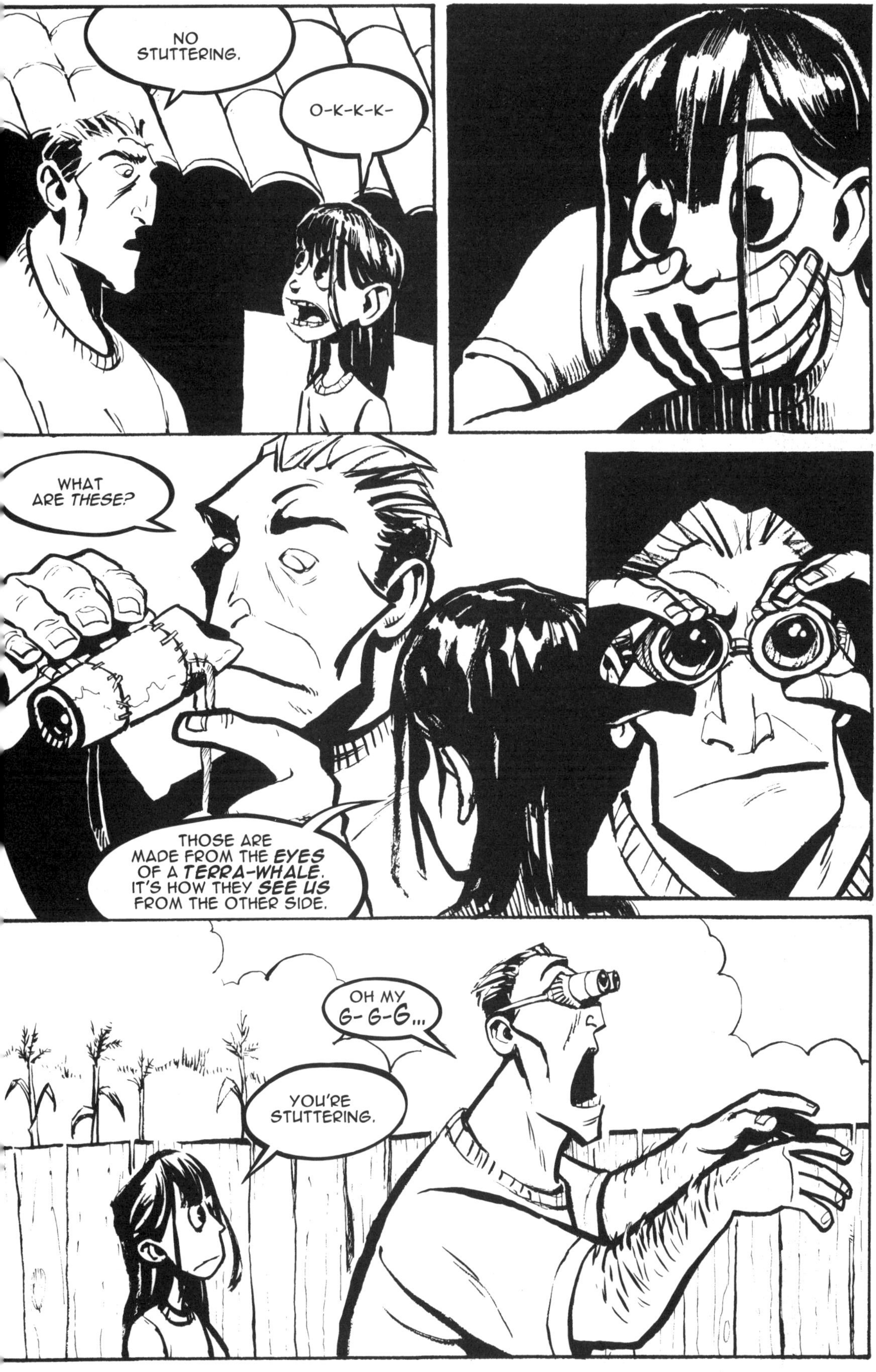
NO STUTTERING.
O-K-K-K-
WHAT ARE *THESE?*
THOSE ARE MADE FROM THE *EYES* OF A *TERRA-WHALE*. IT'S HOW THEY *SEE US* FROM THE OTHER SIDE.
OH MY G-G-G...
YOU'RE STUTTERING.

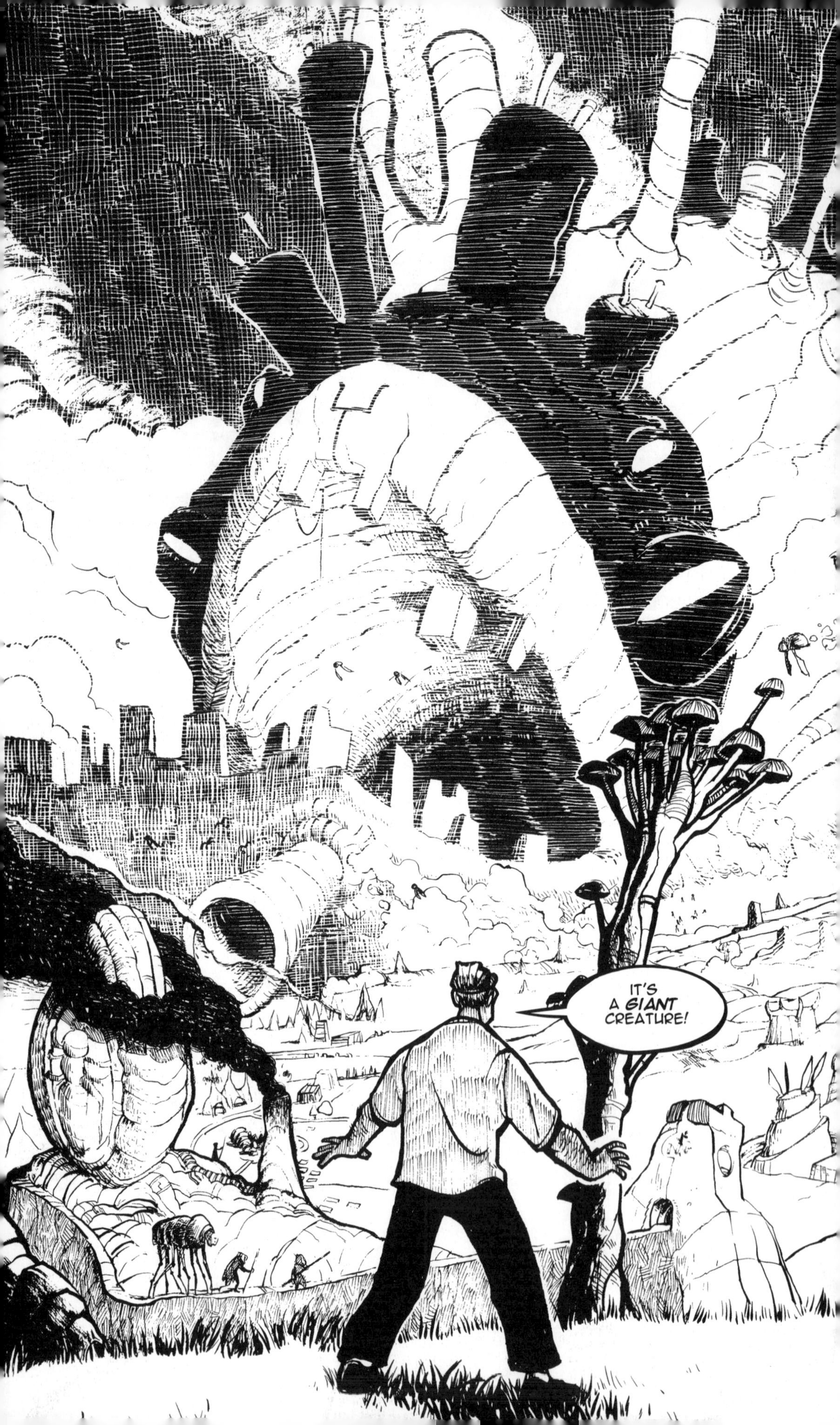
IT'S A GIANT CREATURE!

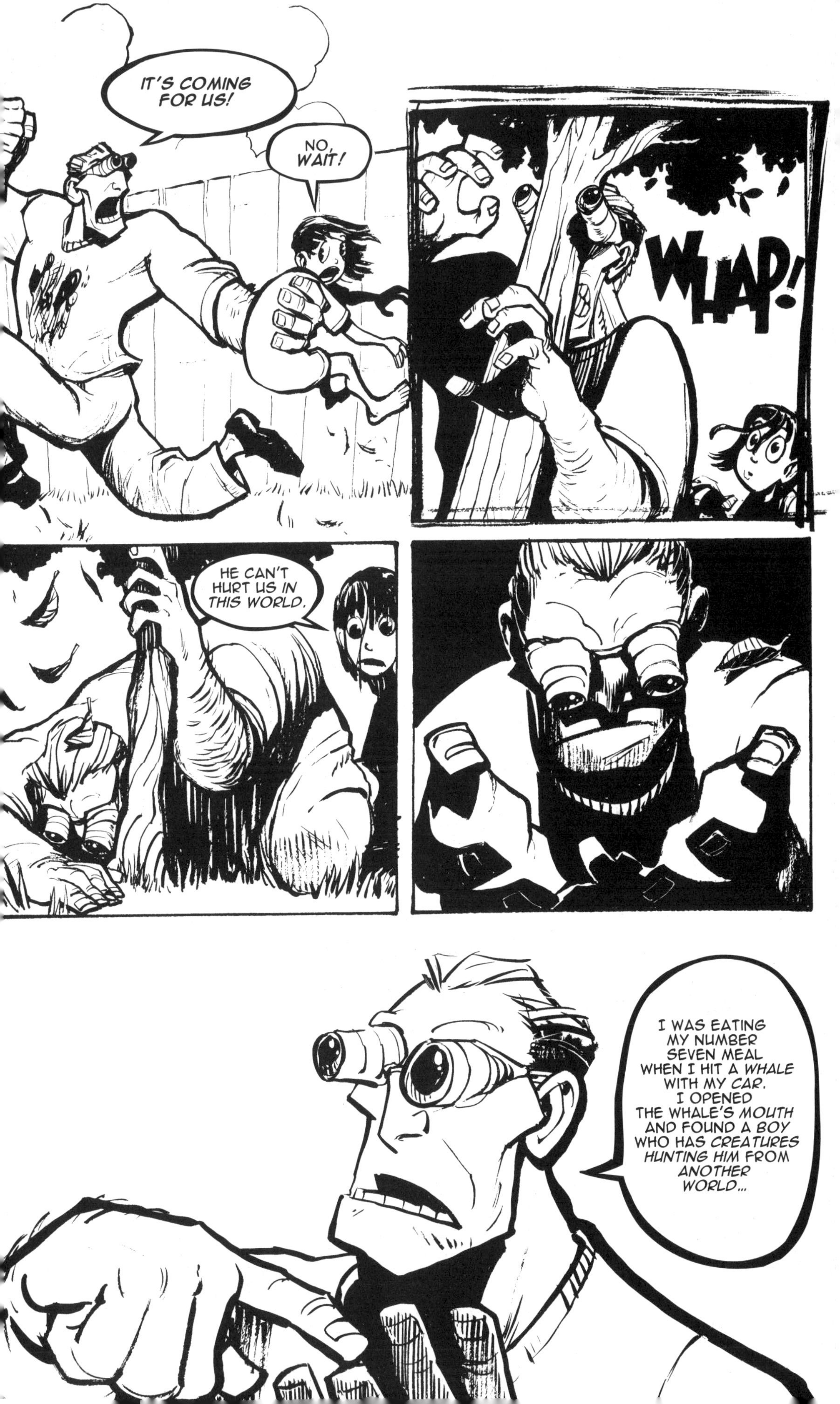
IT'S COMING FOR US!
NO, WAIT!
WHAP!
HE CAN'T HURT US IN THIS WORLD.
I WAS EATING MY NUMBER SEVEN MEAL WHEN I HIT A WHALE WITH MY CAR. I OPENED THE WHALE'S MOUTH AND FOUND A BOY WHO HAS CREATURES HUNTING HIM FROM ANOTHER WORLD...

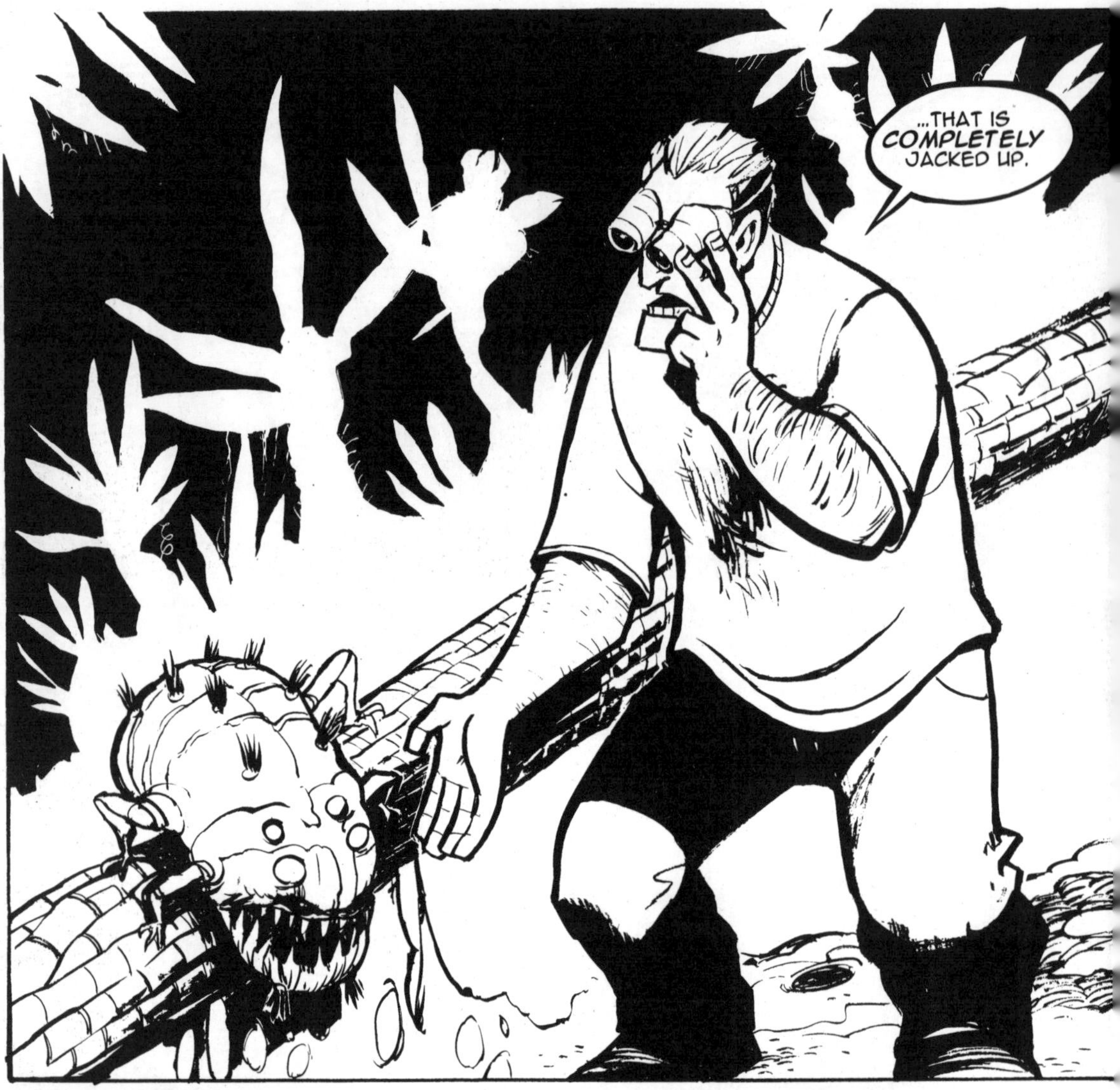
...THAT IS COMPLETELY JACKED UP.

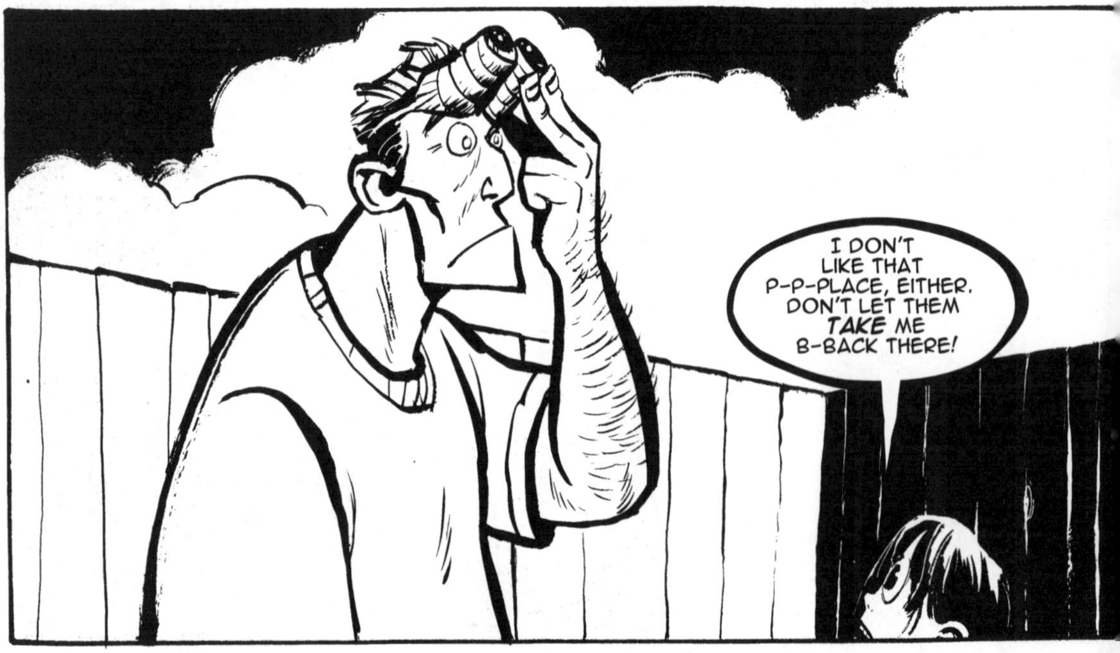
I DON'T LIKE THAT P-P-PLACE, EITHER. DON'T LET THEM TAKE ME B-BACK THERE!

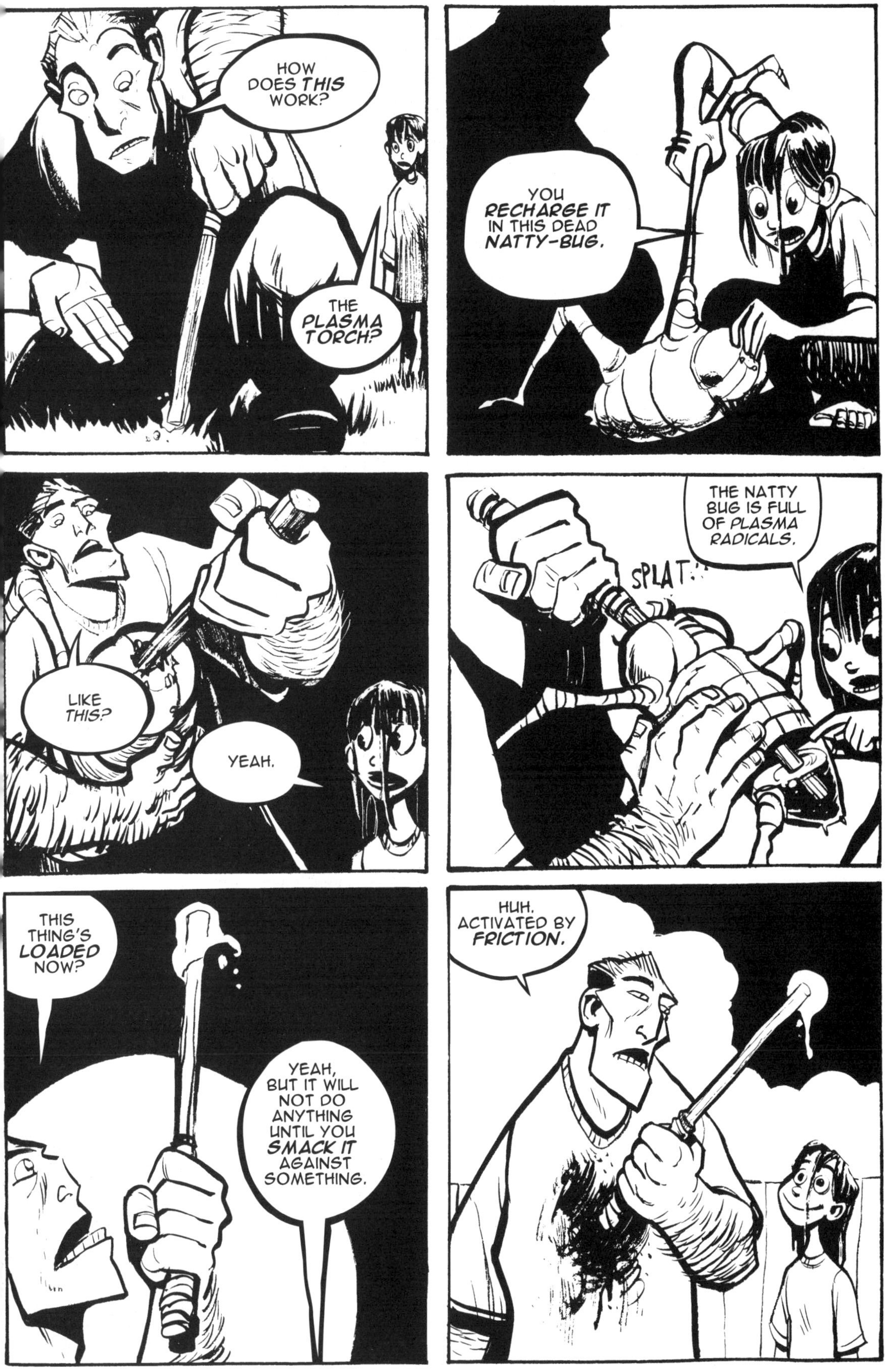
HOW DOES THIS WORK?
THE PLASMA TORCH?
YOU RECHARGE IT IN THIS DEAD NATTY-BUG.
LIKE THIS?
YEAH.
THE NATTY BUG IS FULL OF PLASMA RADICALS.
SPLAT!
THIS THING'S LOADED NOW?
YEAH, BUT IT WILL NOT DO ANYTHING UNTIL YOU SMACK IT AGAINST SOMETHING.
HUH. ACTIVATED BY FRICTION.

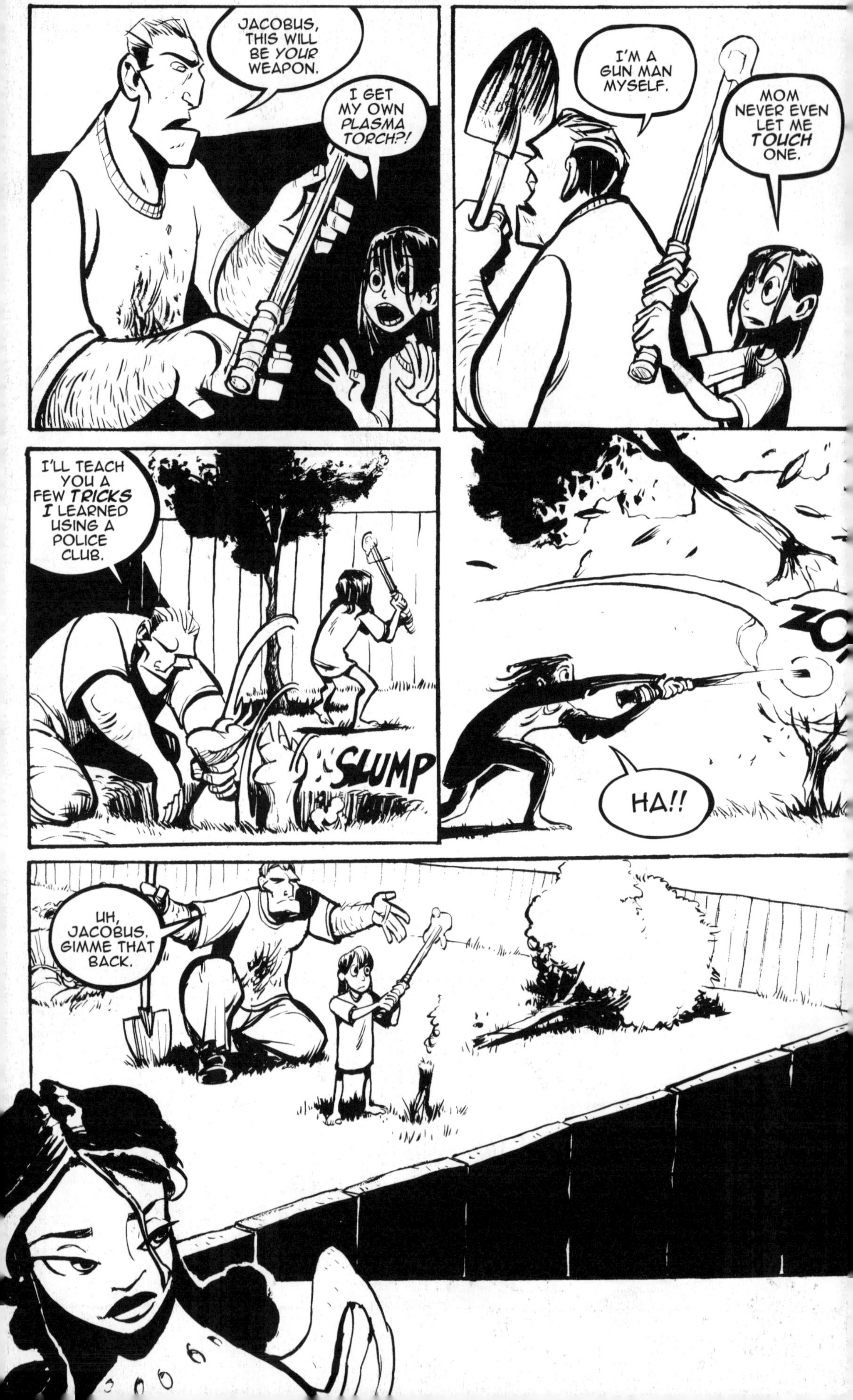
JACOBUS, THIS WILL BE YOUR WEAPON.
I GET MY OWN PLASMA TORCH?!
I'M A GUN MAN MYSELF.
MOM NEVER EVEN LET ME TOUCH ONE.
I'LL TEACH YOU A FEW TRICKS I LEARNED USING A POLICE CLUB.
SLUMP
HA!!
UH, JACOBUS. GIMME THAT BACK.

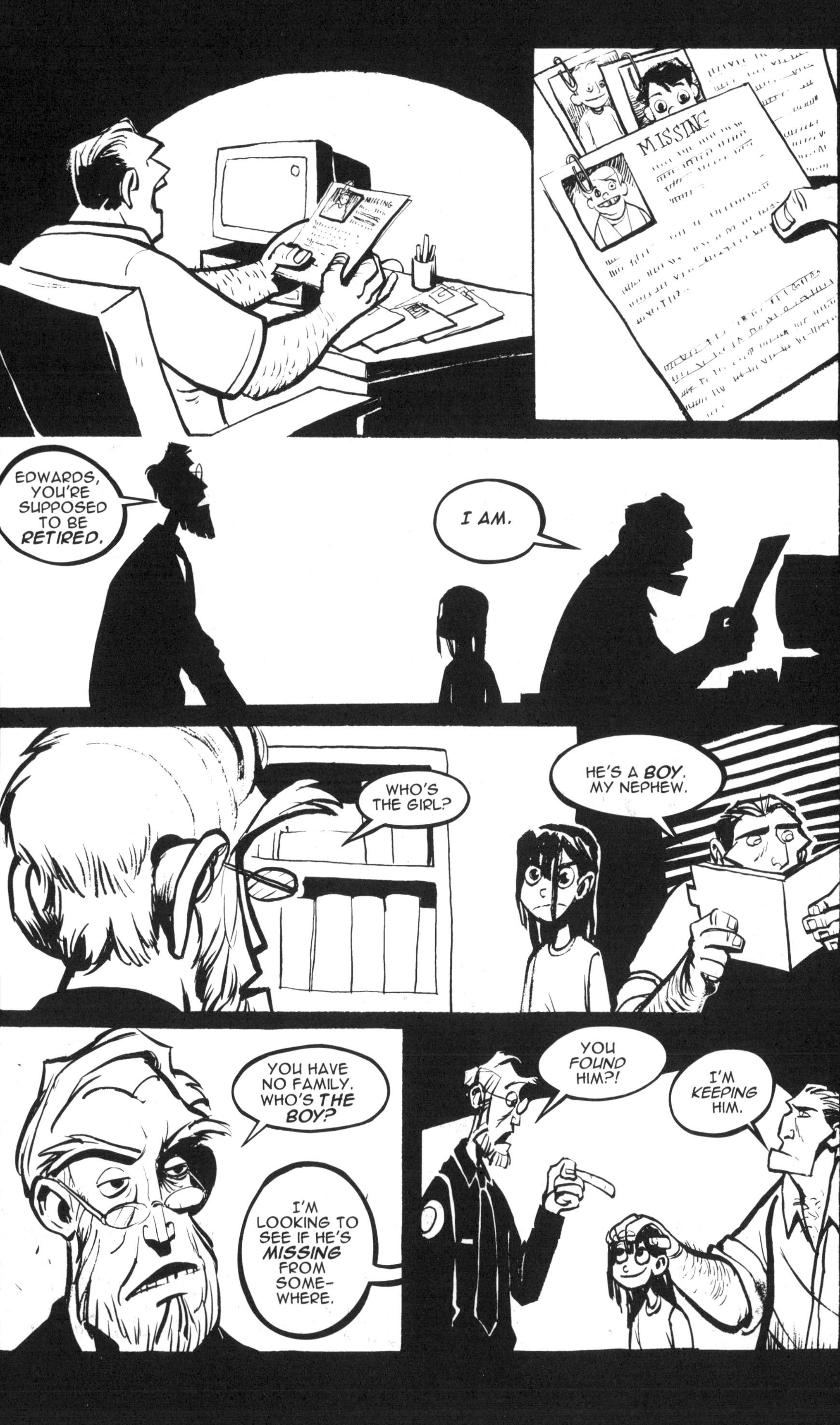
MISSING
EDWARDS, YOU'RE SUPPOSED TO BE RETIRED.
I AM.
WHO'S THE GIRL?
HE'S A BOY. MY NEPHEW.
YOU HAVE NO FAMILY. WHO'S THE BOY?
I'M LOOKING TO SEE IF HE'S MISSING FROM SOME-WHERE.
YOU FOUND HIM?!
I'M KEEPING HIM.

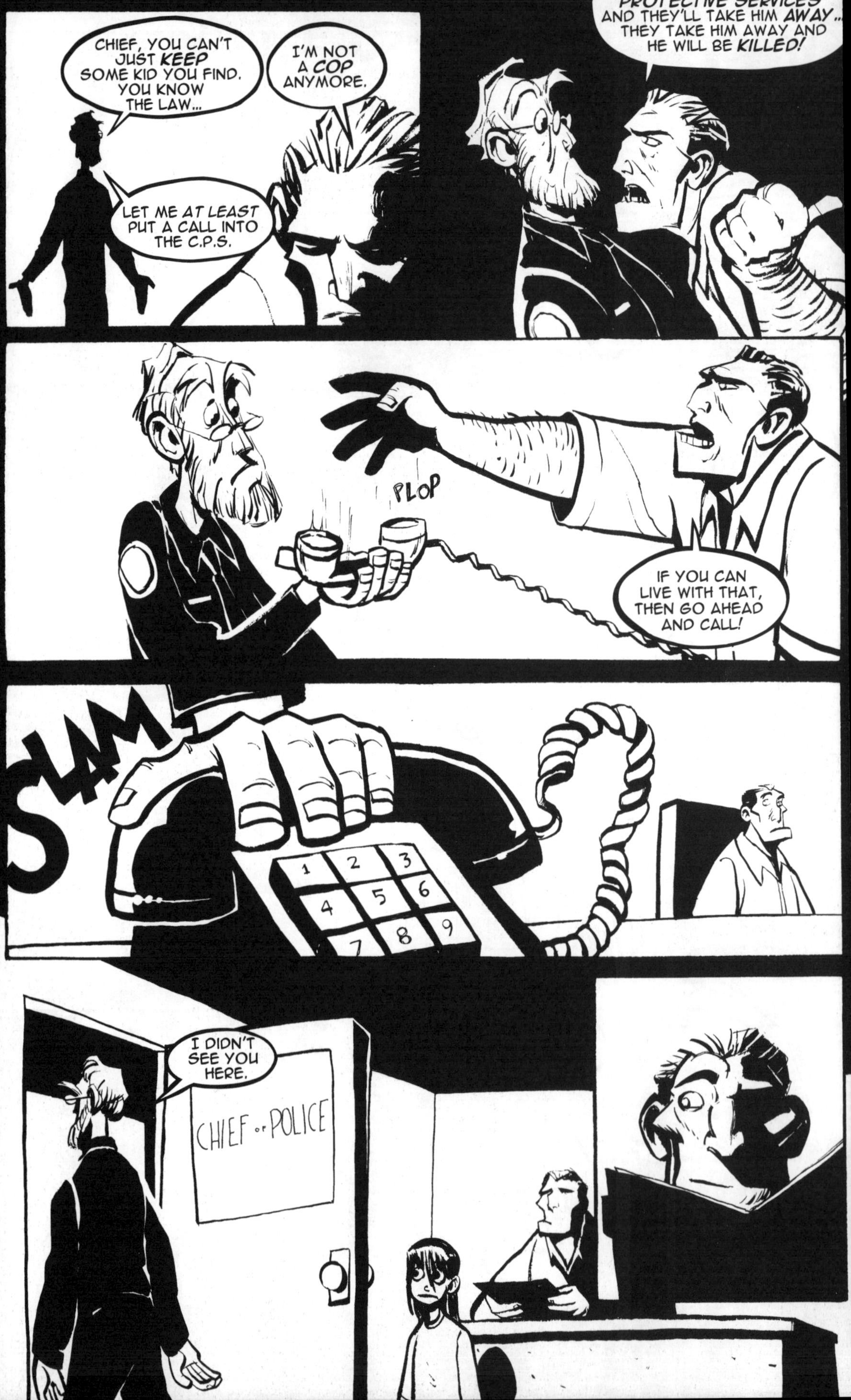

CHIEF, YOU CAN'T JUST KEEP SOME KID YOU FIND. YOU KNOW THE LAW...
I'M NOT A COP ANYMORE.
LET ME AT LEAST PUT A CALL INTO THE C.P.S.
YOU CALL CHILD PROTECTIVE SERVICES AND THEY'LL TAKE HIM AWAY... THEY TAKE HIM AWAY AND HE WILL BE KILLED!
PLOP
IF YOU CAN LIVE WITH THAT, THEN GO AHEAD AND CALL!
SLAM
1 2 3
4 5 6
7 8 9
I DIDN'T SEE YOU HERE.
CHIEF OF POLICE

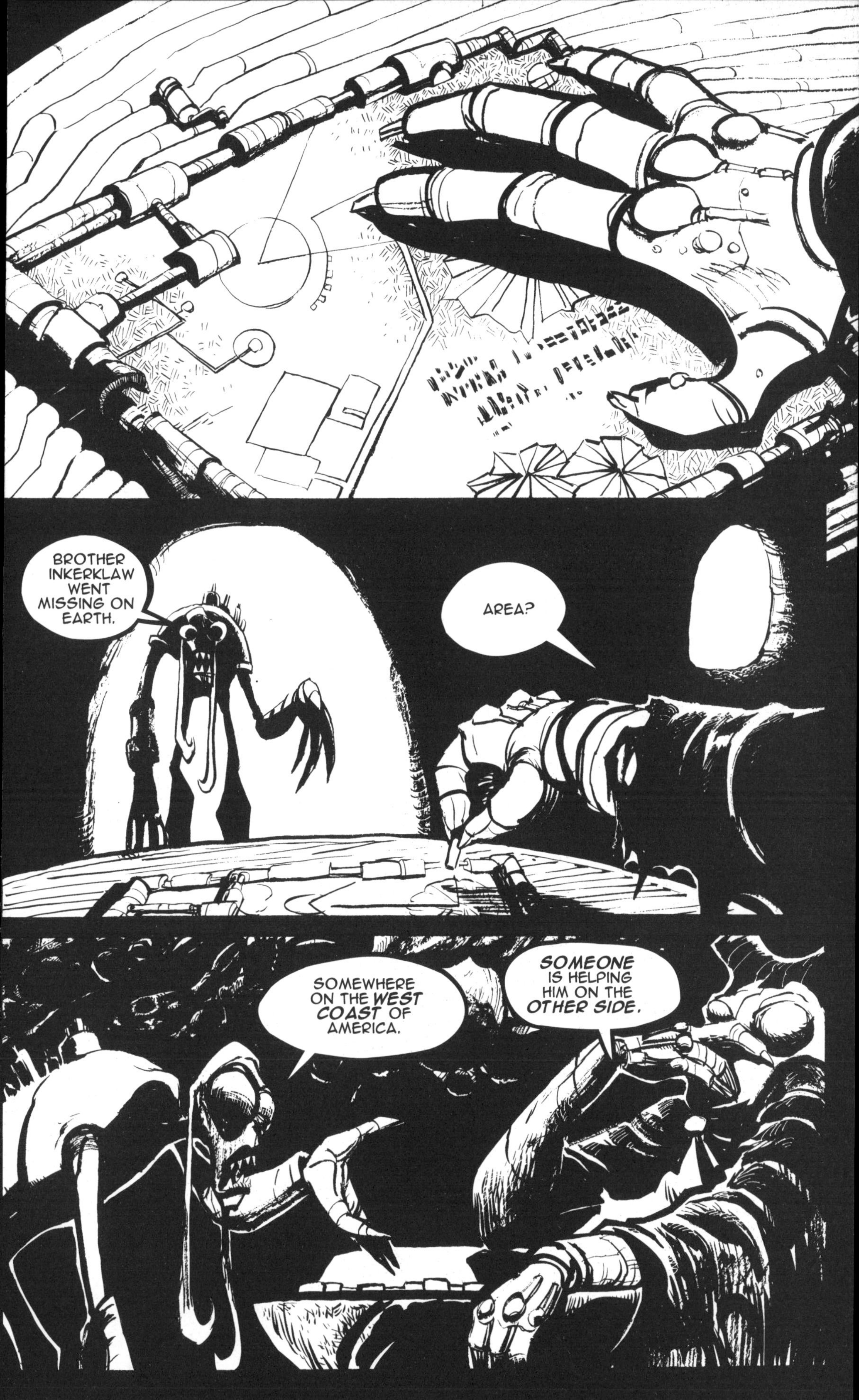
BROTHER INKERKLAW WENT MISSING ON EARTH.
AREA?
SOMEWHERE ON THE WEST COAST OF AMERICA.
SOMEONE IS HELPING HIM ON THE OTHER SIDE.

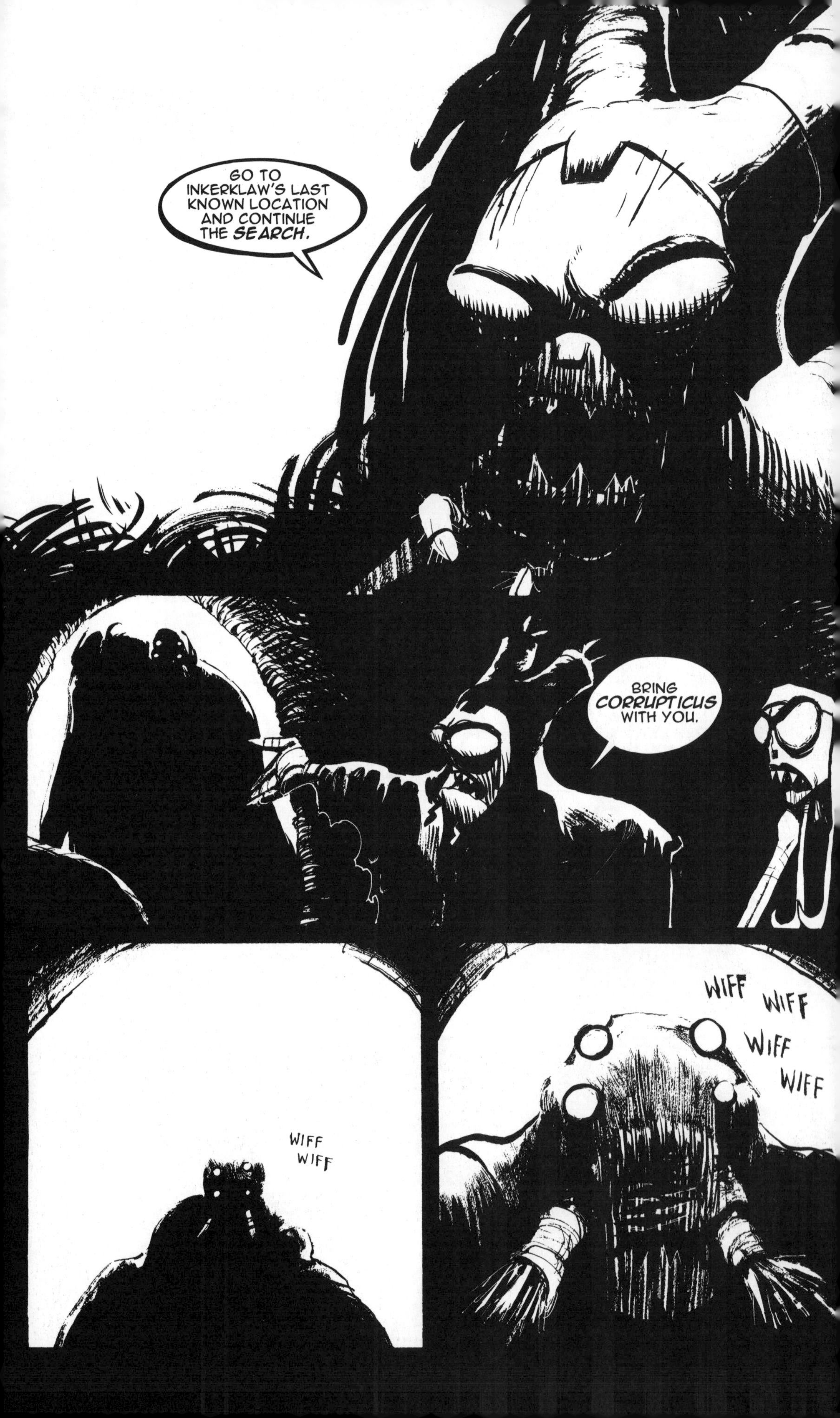
GO TO INKERKLAW'S LAST KNOWN LOCATION AND CONTINUE THE *SEARCH*.
BRING **CORRUPTICUS** WITH YOU.
WIFF WIFF
WIFF WIFF WIFF WIFF

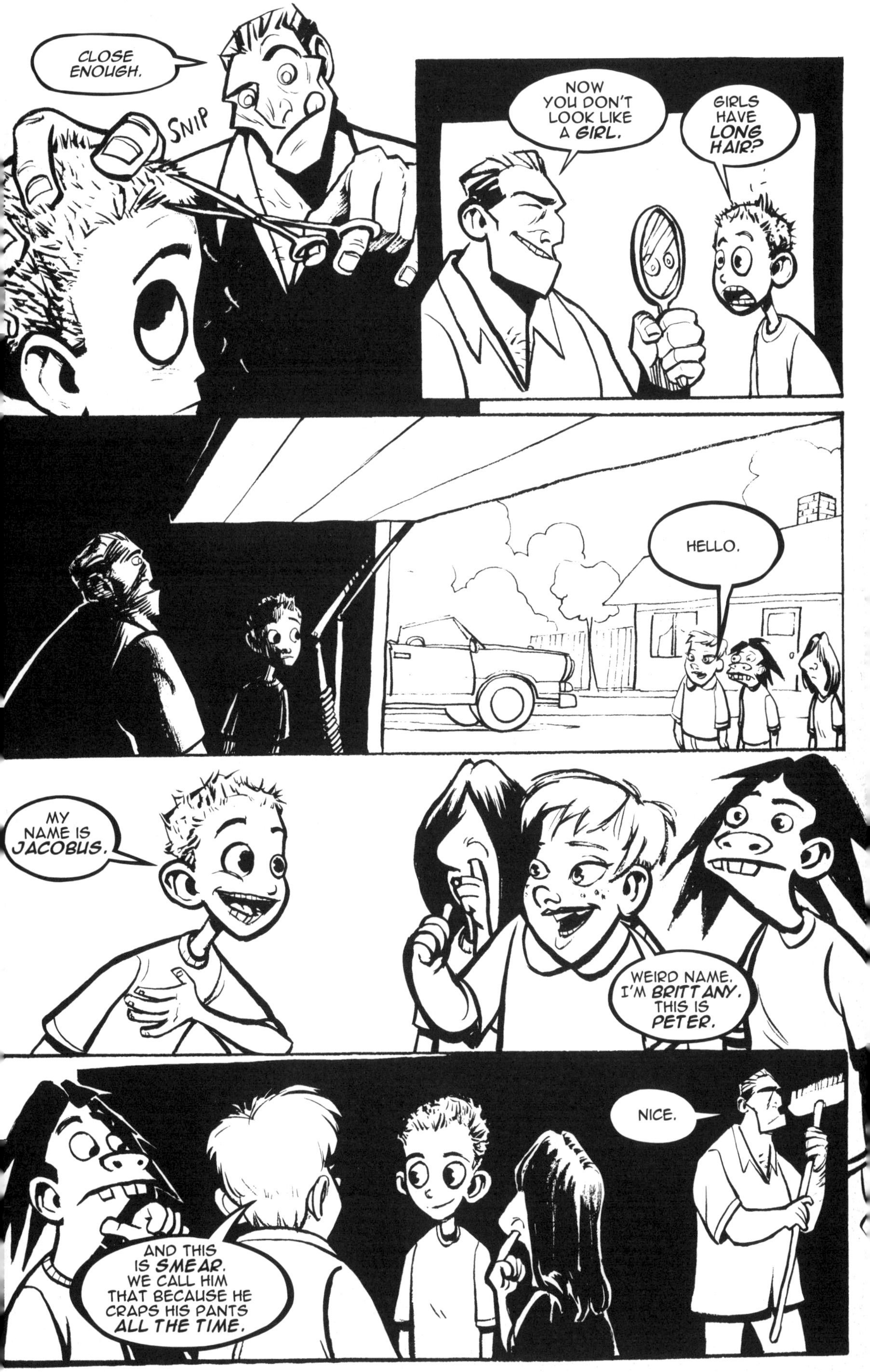
CLOSE ENOUGH.
SNIP
NOW YOU DON'T LOOK LIKE A GIRL.
GIRLS HAVE LONG HAIR?
HELLO.
MY NAME IS JACOBUS.
WEIRD NAME. I'M BRITTANY. THIS IS PETER.
AND THIS IS SMEAR. WE CALL HIM THAT BECAUSE HE CRAPS HIS PANTS ALL THE TIME.
NICE.

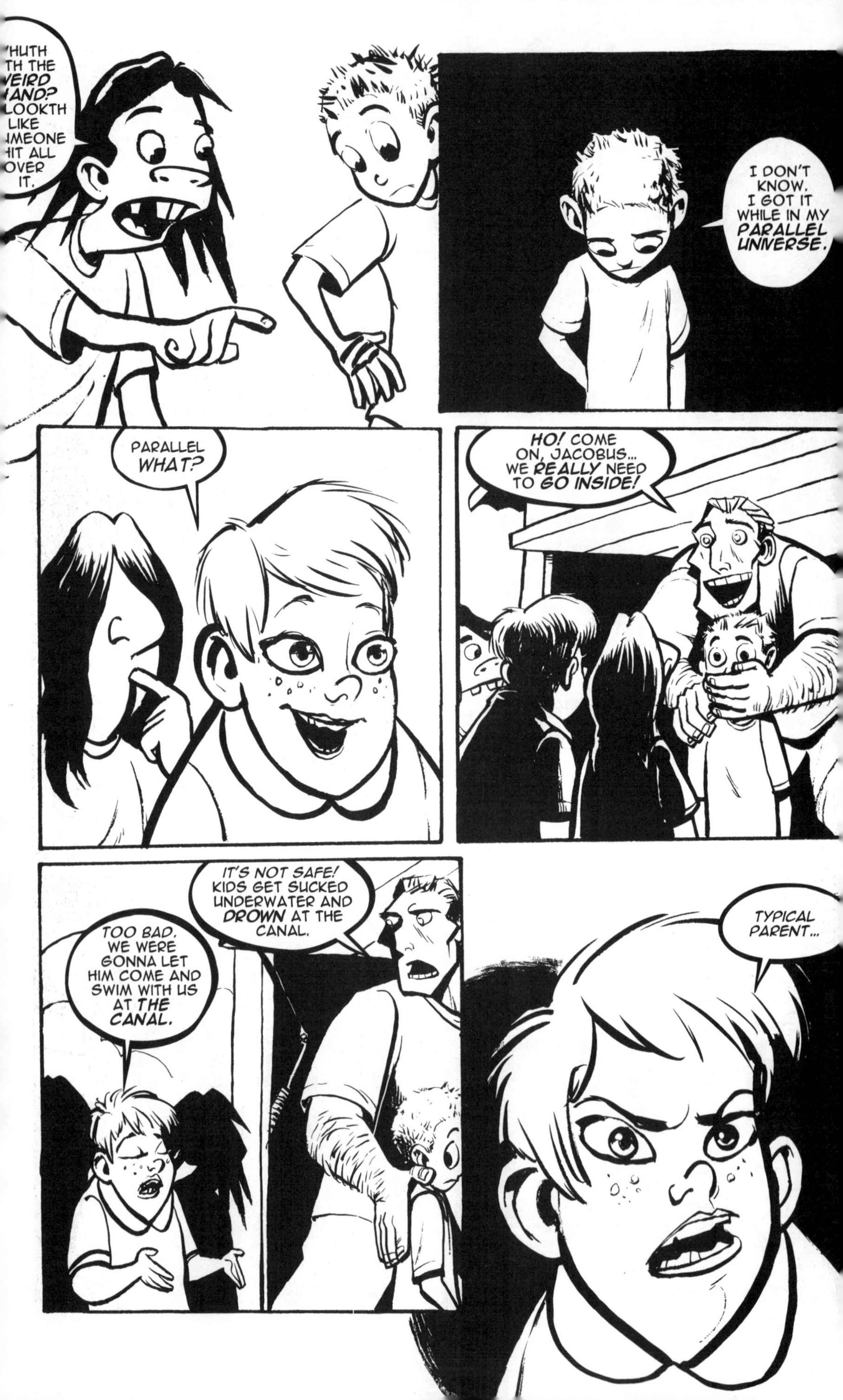

'HUTH
'TH THE
VEIRD
'AND?
LOOKTH
LIKE
'MEONE
'HIT ALL
OVER
IT.
I DON'T KNOW. I GOT IT WHILE IN MY PARALLEL UNIVERSE.
PARALLEL WHAT?
HO! COME ON, JACOBUS... WE REALLY NEED TO GO INSIDE!
TOO BAD. WE WERE GONNA LET HIM COME AND SWIM WITH US AT THE CANAL.
IT'S NOT SAFE! KIDS GET SUCKED UNDERWATER AND DROWN AT THE CANAL.
TYPICAL PARENT...

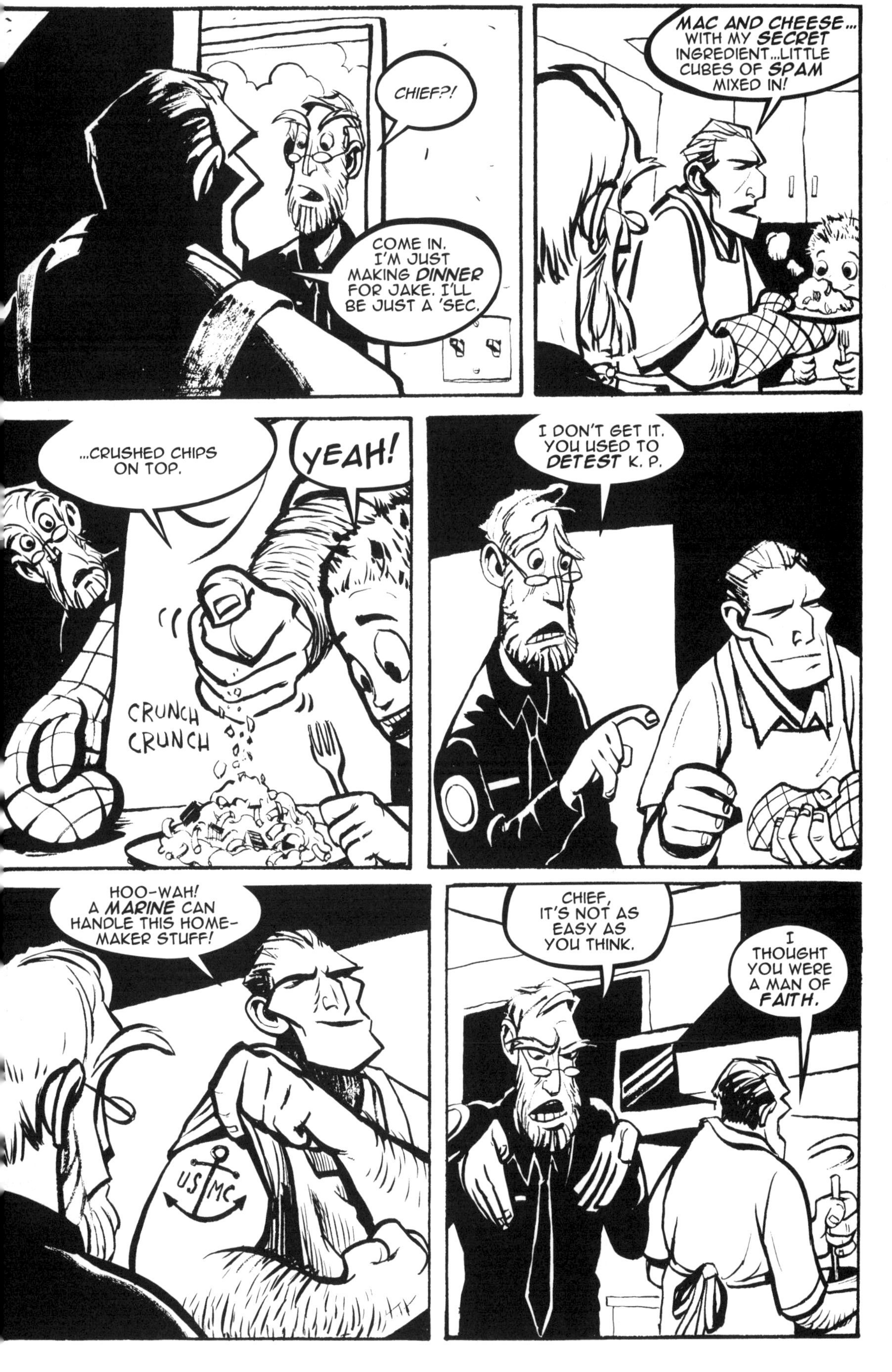
CHIEF?!
COME IN. I'M JUST MAKING DINNER FOR JAKE. I'LL BE JUST A 'SEC.
MAC AND CHEESE... WITH MY SECRET INGREDIENT...LITTLE CUBES OF SPAM MIXED IN!
...CRUSHED CHIPS ON TOP.
YEAH!
CRUNCH CRUNCH
I DON'T GET IT. YOU USED TO DETEST K. P.
HOO-WAH! A MARINE CAN HANDLE THIS HOME-MAKER STUFF!
US MC
CHIEF, IT'S NOT AS EASY AS YOU THINK.
I THOUGHT YOU WERE A MAN OF FAITH.

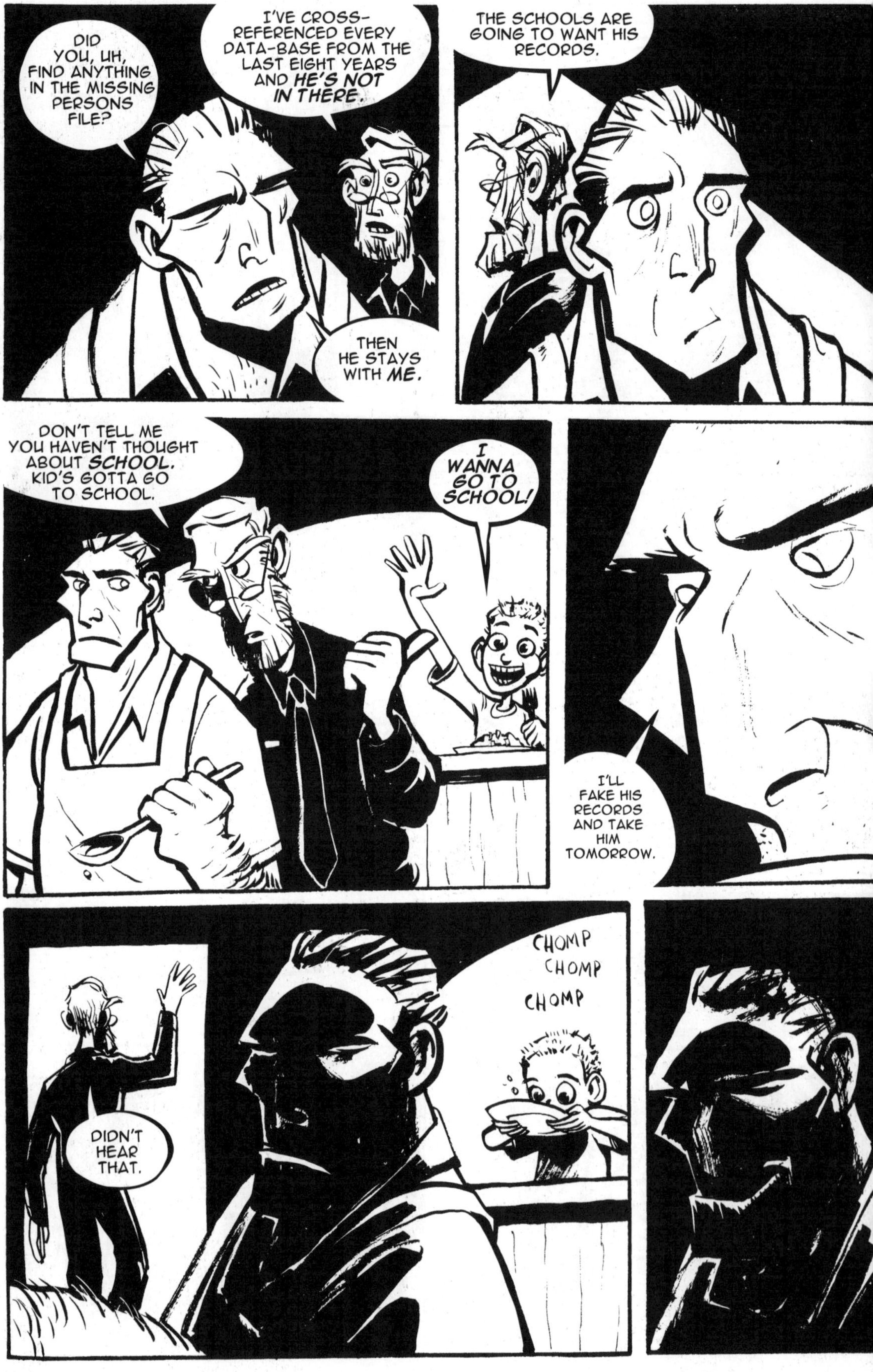
DID YOU, UH, FIND ANYTHING IN THE MISSING PERSONS FILE?
I'VE CROSS-REFERENCED EVERY DATA-BASE FROM THE LAST EIGHT YEARS AND *HE'S NOT IN THERE*.
THEN HE STAYS WITH *ME*.
THE SCHOOLS ARE GOING TO WANT HIS RECORDS.
DON'T TELL ME YOU HAVEN'T THOUGHT ABOUT *SCHOOL*. KID'S GOTTA GO TO SCHOOL.
I WANNA GO TO SCHOOL!
I'LL FAKE HIS RECORDS AND TAKE HIM TOMORROW.
DIDN'T HEAR THAT.
CHOMP
CHOMP
CHOMP

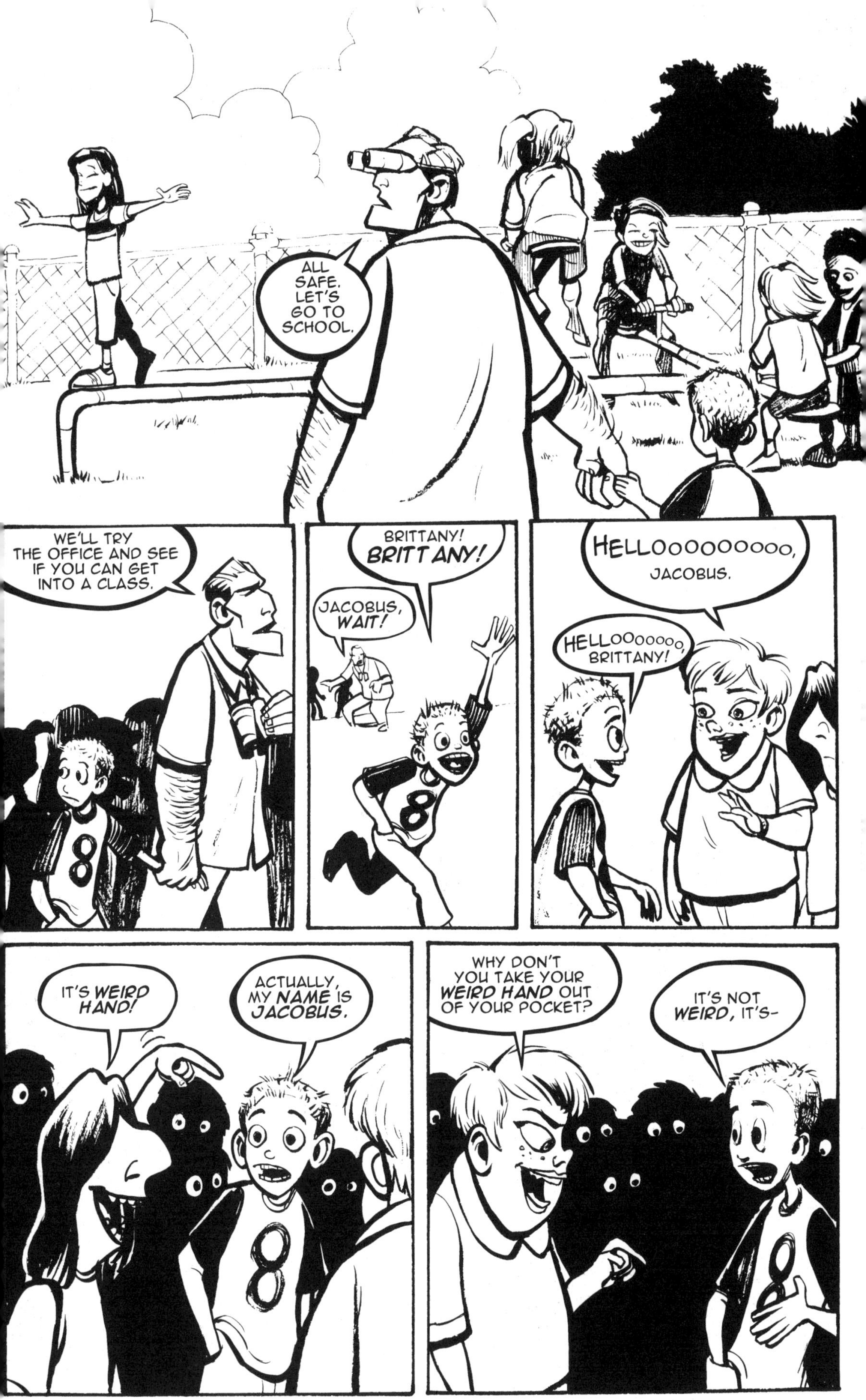

ALL SAFE. LET'S GO TO SCHOOL.
WE'LL TRY THE OFFICE AND SEE IF YOU CAN GET INTO A CLASS.
BRITTANY! BRITTANY!
JACOBUS, WAIT!
HELLOoooooooo, JACOBUS.
HELLOoooooo, BRITTANY!
IT'S WEIRD HAND!
ACTUALLY, MY NAME IS JACOBUS.
WHY DON'T YOU TAKE YOUR WEIRD HAND OUT OF YOUR POCKET?
IT'S NOT WEIRD, IT'S-

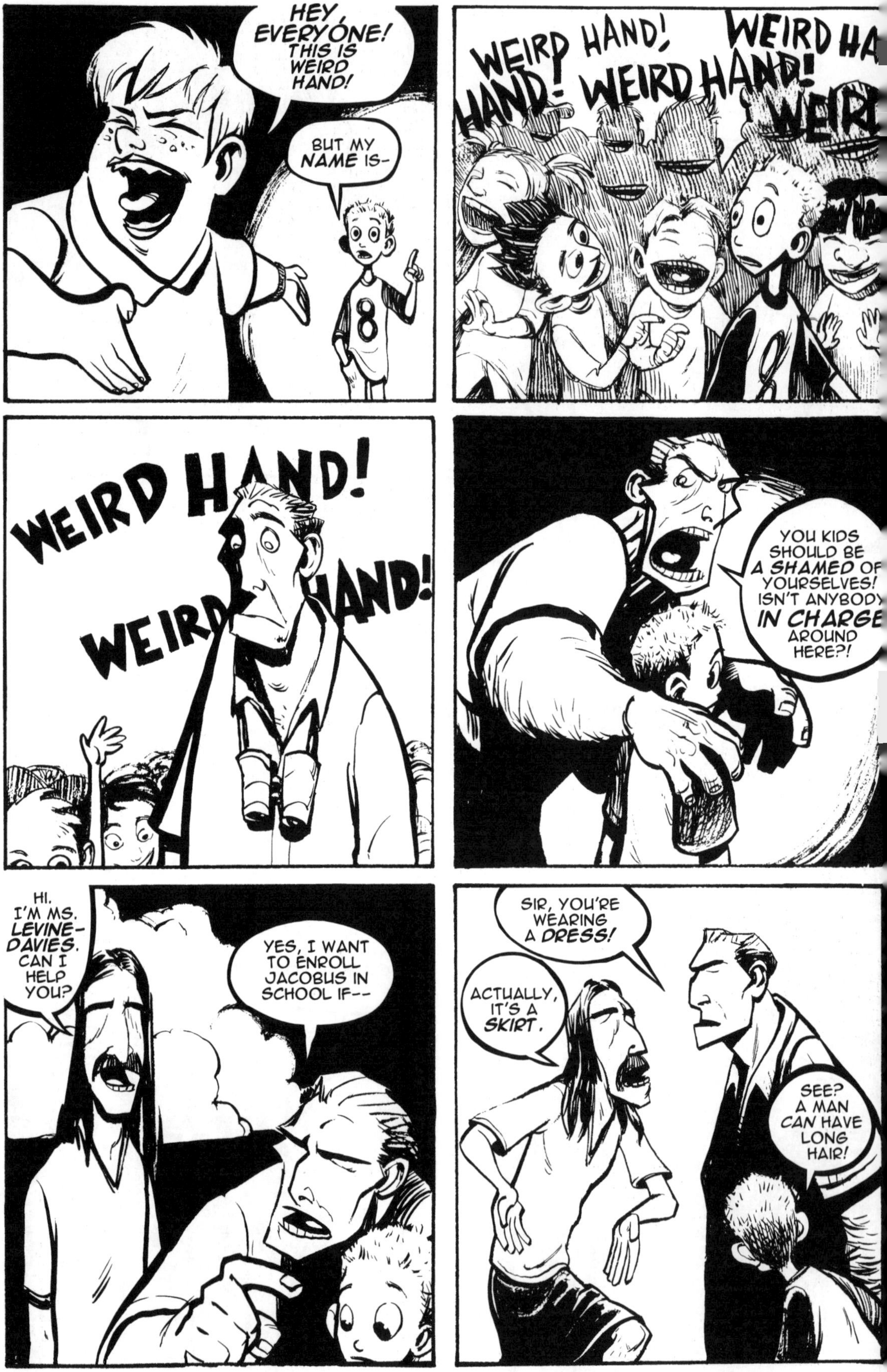
HEY, EVERYONE! THIS IS WEIRD HAND!
BUT MY NAME IS-
WEIRD HAND! WEIRD HA
HAND! WEIRD HAND!
WEIRD HAND!
WEIRD HAND!
YOU KIDS SHOULD BE A SHAMED OF YOURSELVES! ISN'T ANYBODY IN CHARGE AROUND HERE?!
HI. I'M MS. LEVINE-DAVIES. CAN I HELP YOU?
YES, I WANT TO ENROLL JACOBUS IN SCHOOL IF--
SIR, YOU'RE WEARING A DRESS!
ACTUALLY, IT'S A SKIRT.
SEE? A MAN CAN HAVE LONG HAIR!

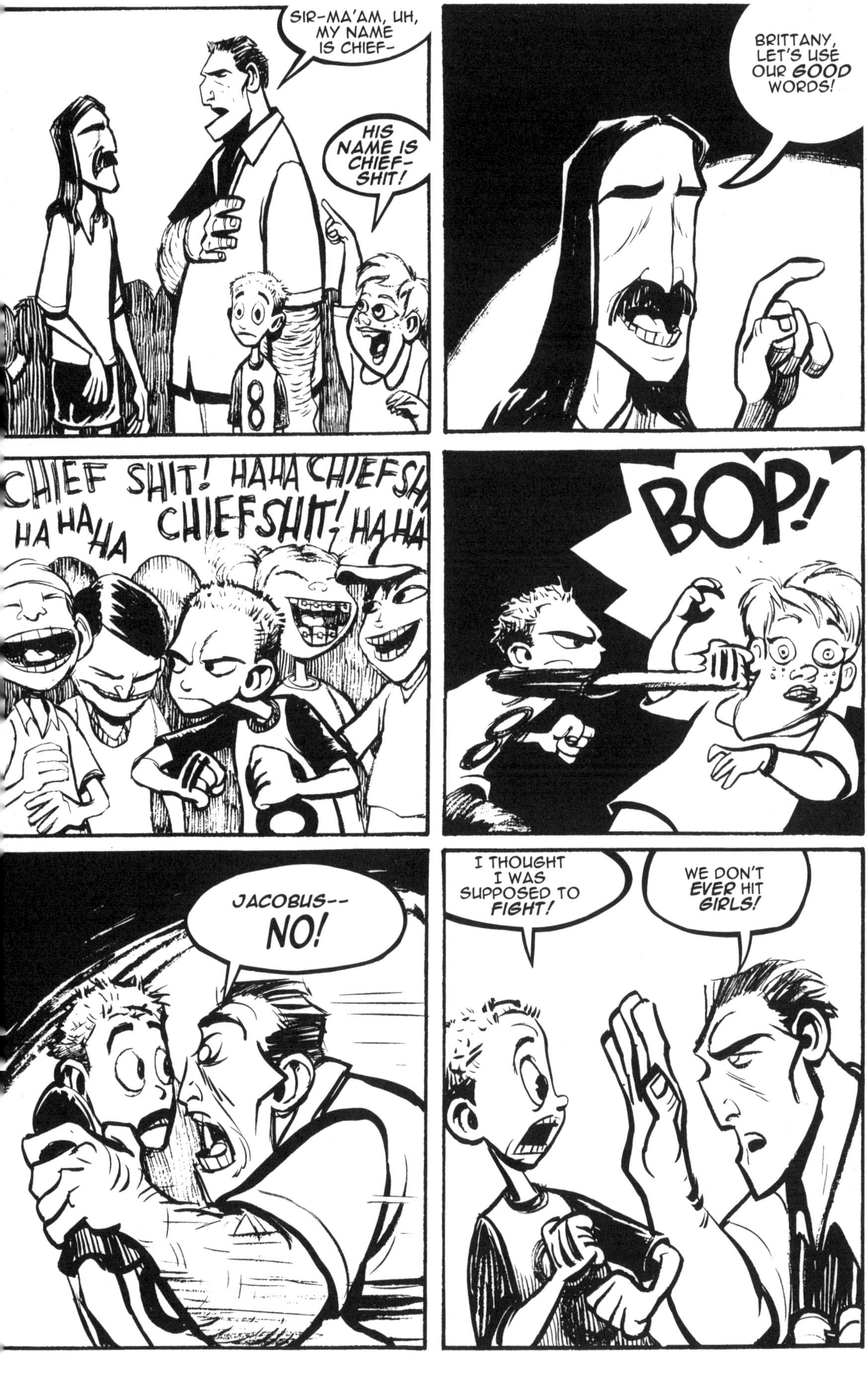
SIR-MA'AM, UH, MY NAME IS CHIEF-
HIS NAME IS CHIEF-SHIT!
BRITTANY, LET'S USE OUR GOOD WORDS!
CHIEF SHIT! HAHA CHIEFSH
HA HA HA
CHIEFSHIT! HA HA
BOP!
JACOBUS-- NO!
I THOUGHT I WAS SUPPOSED TO FIGHT!
WE DON'T EVER HIT GIRLS!

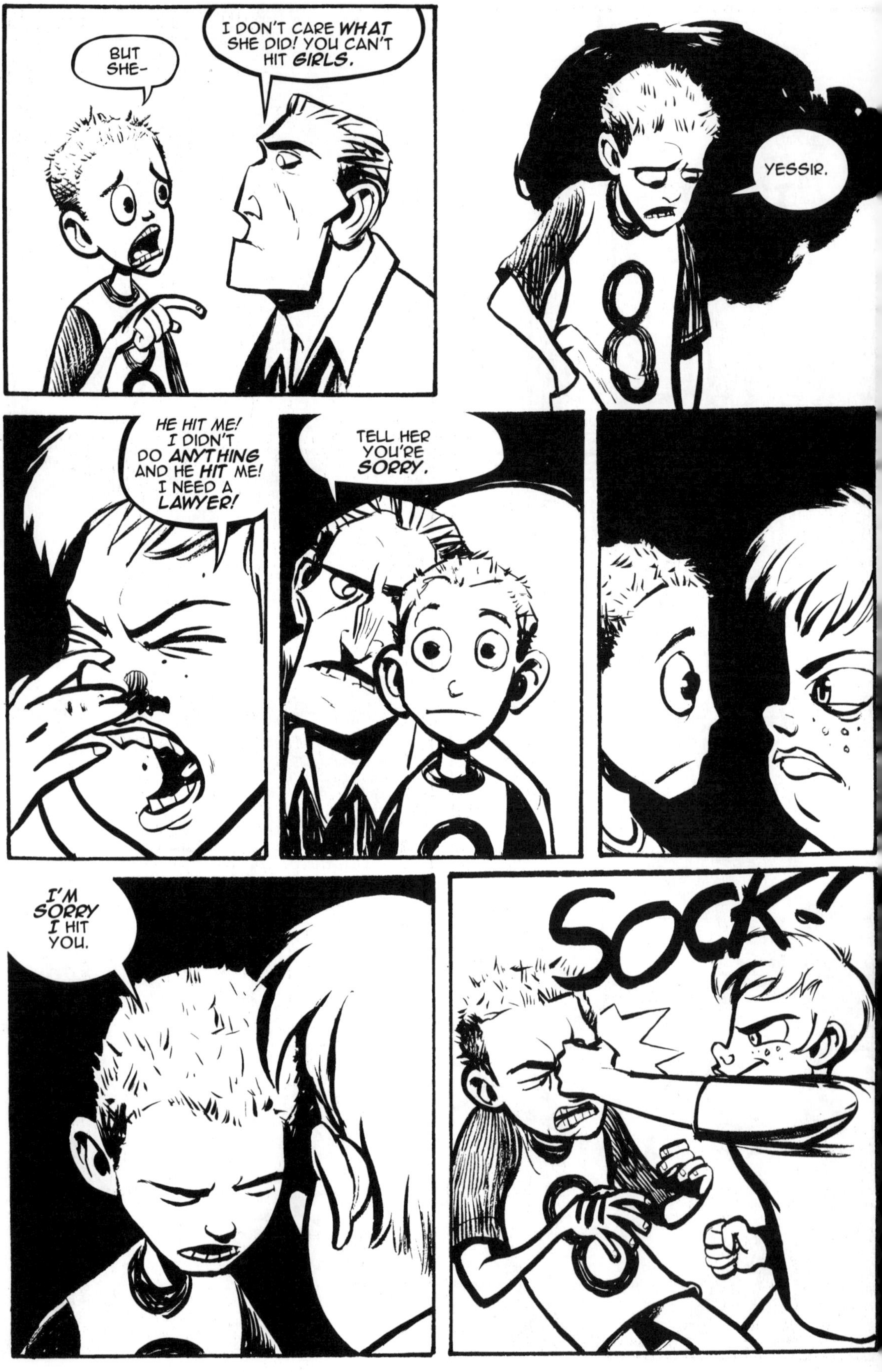
BUT SHE-
I DON'T CARE WHAT SHE DID! YOU CAN'T HIT GIRLS.
YESSIR.
HE HIT ME! I DIDN'T DO ANYTHING AND HE HIT ME! I NEED A LAWYER!
TELL HER YOU'RE SORRY.
I'M SORRY I HIT YOU.
SOCK!

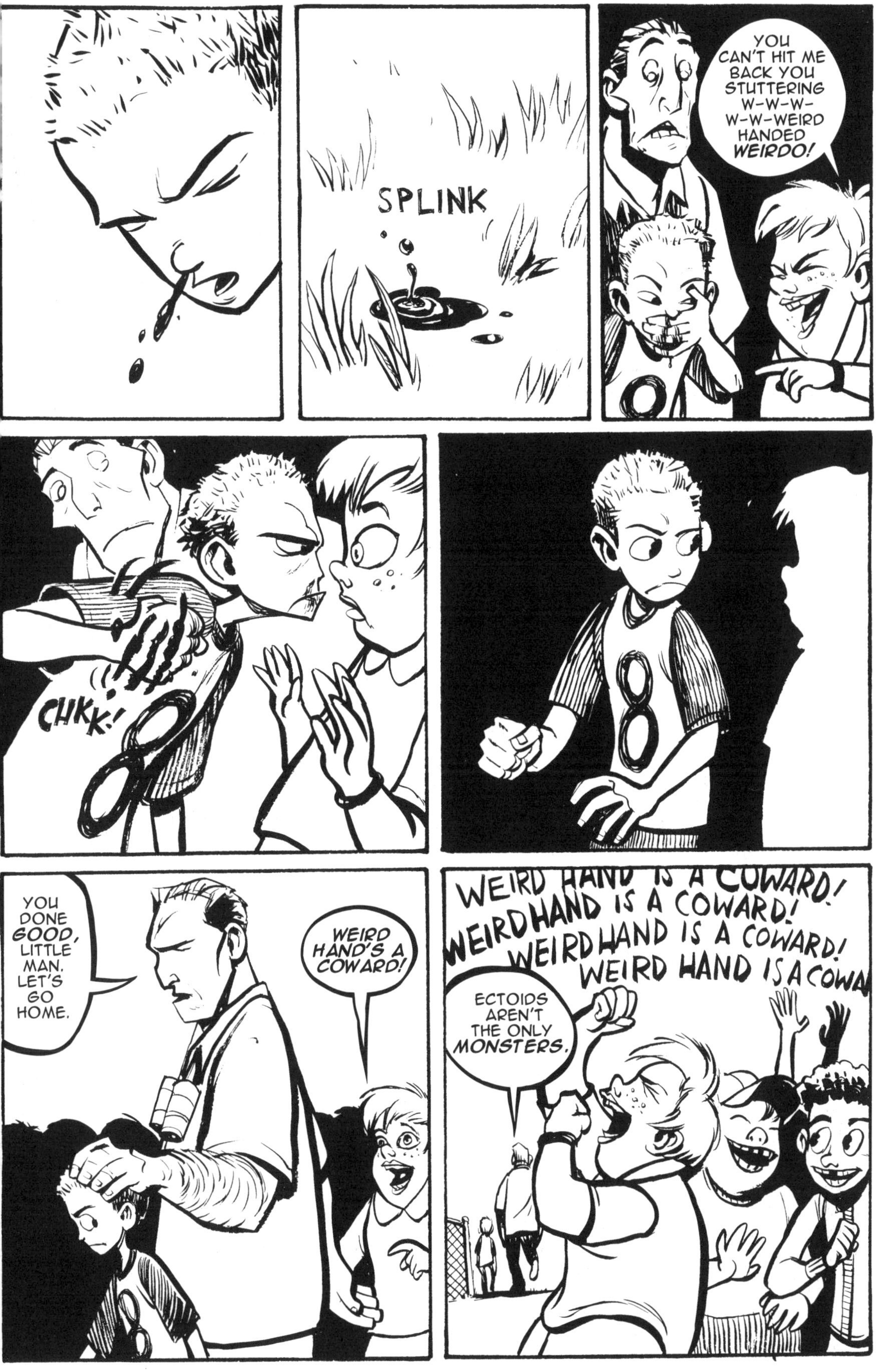

SPLINK
YOU CAN'T HIT ME BACK YOU STUTTERING W-W-W-W-W-WEIRD HANDED WEIRDO!
CHKK!
YOU DONE GOOD, LITTLE MAN. LET'S GO HOME.
WEIRD HAND'S A COWARD!
WEIRD HAND IS A COWARD!
WEIRD HAND IS A COWARD!
WEIRD HAND IS A COWARD!
WEIRD HAND IS A COWA
ECTOIDS AREN'T THE ONLY MONSTERS.

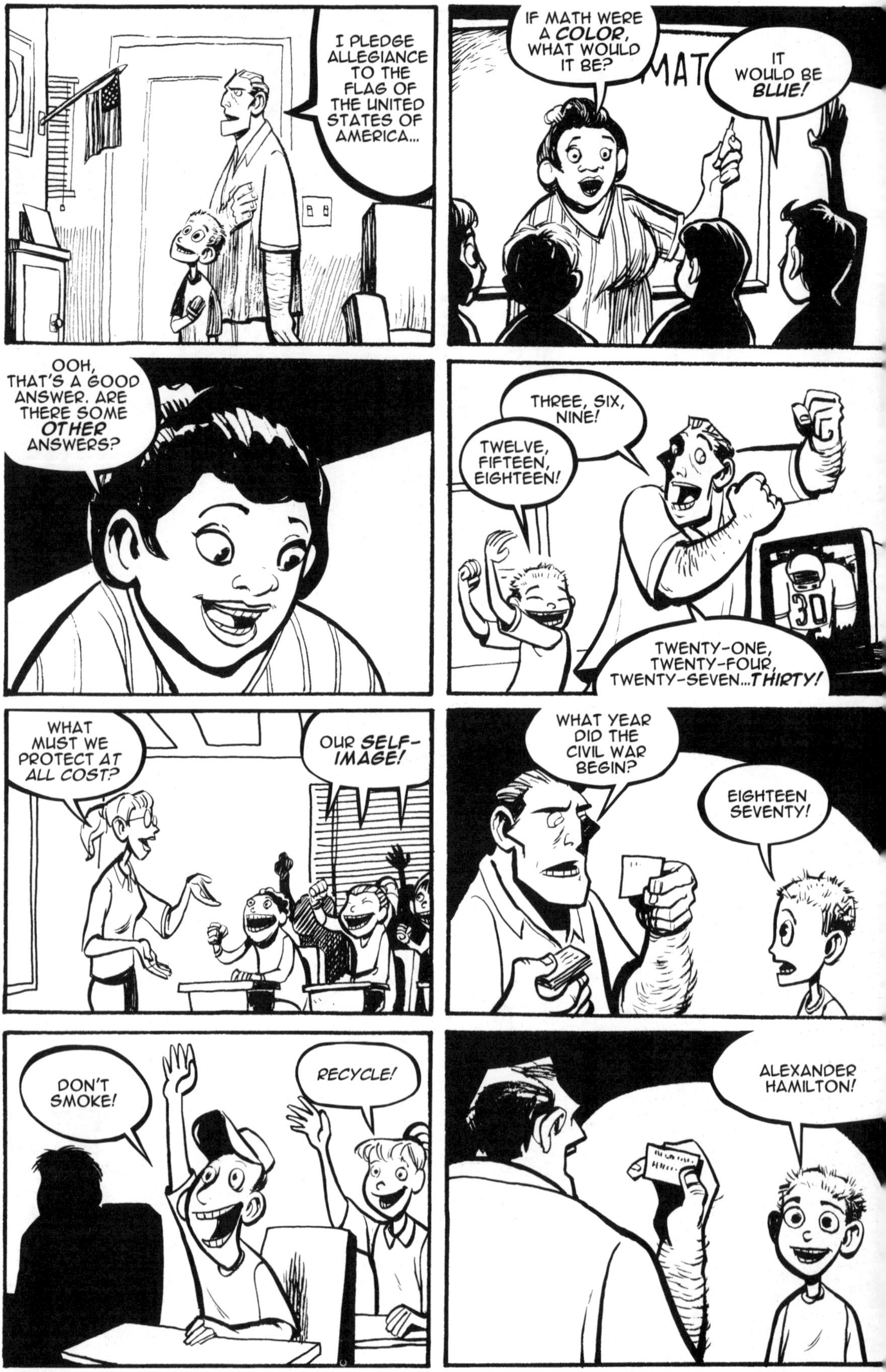
I PLEDGE ALLEGIANCE TO THE FLAG OF THE UNITED STATES OF AMERICA...
IF MATH WERE A *COLOR*, WHAT WOULD IT BE?
IT WOULD BE *BLUE!*
OOH, THAT'S A GOOD ANSWER. ARE THERE SOME *OTHER* ANSWERS?
THREE, SIX, NINE!
TWELVE, FIFTEEN, EIGHTEEN!
TWENTY-ONE, TWENTY-FOUR, TWENTY-SEVEN...*THIRTY!*
WHAT MUST WE PROTECT AT *ALL COST?*
OUR *SELF-IMAGE!*
WHAT YEAR DID THE CIVIL WAR BEGIN?
EIGHTEEN SEVENTY!
DON'T SMOKE!
RECYCLE!
ALEXANDER HAMILTON!

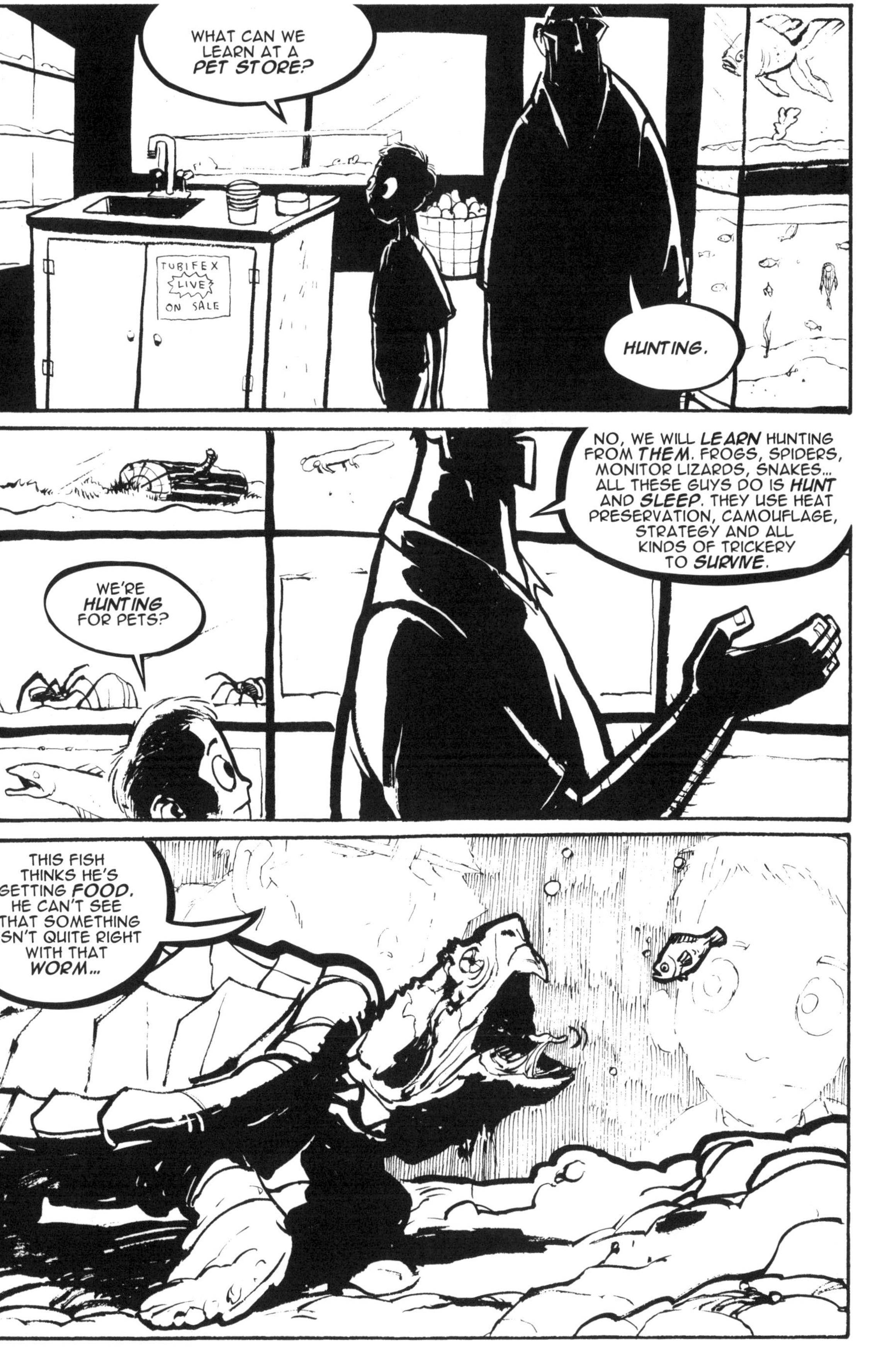
WHAT CAN WE LEARN AT A PET STORE?
TUBIFEX LIVE ON SALE
HUNTING.
WE'RE HUNTING FOR PETS?
NO, WE WILL LEARN HUNTING FROM THEM. FROGS, SPIDERS, MONITOR LIZARDS, SNAKES... ALL THESE GUYS DO IS HUNT AND SLEEP. THEY USE HEAT PRESERVATION, CAMOUFLAGE, STRATEGY AND ALL KINDS OF TRICKERY TO SURVIVE.
THIS FISH THINKS HE'S GETTING FOOD. HE CAN'T SEE THAT SOMETHING ISN'T QUITE RIGHT WITH THAT WORM...

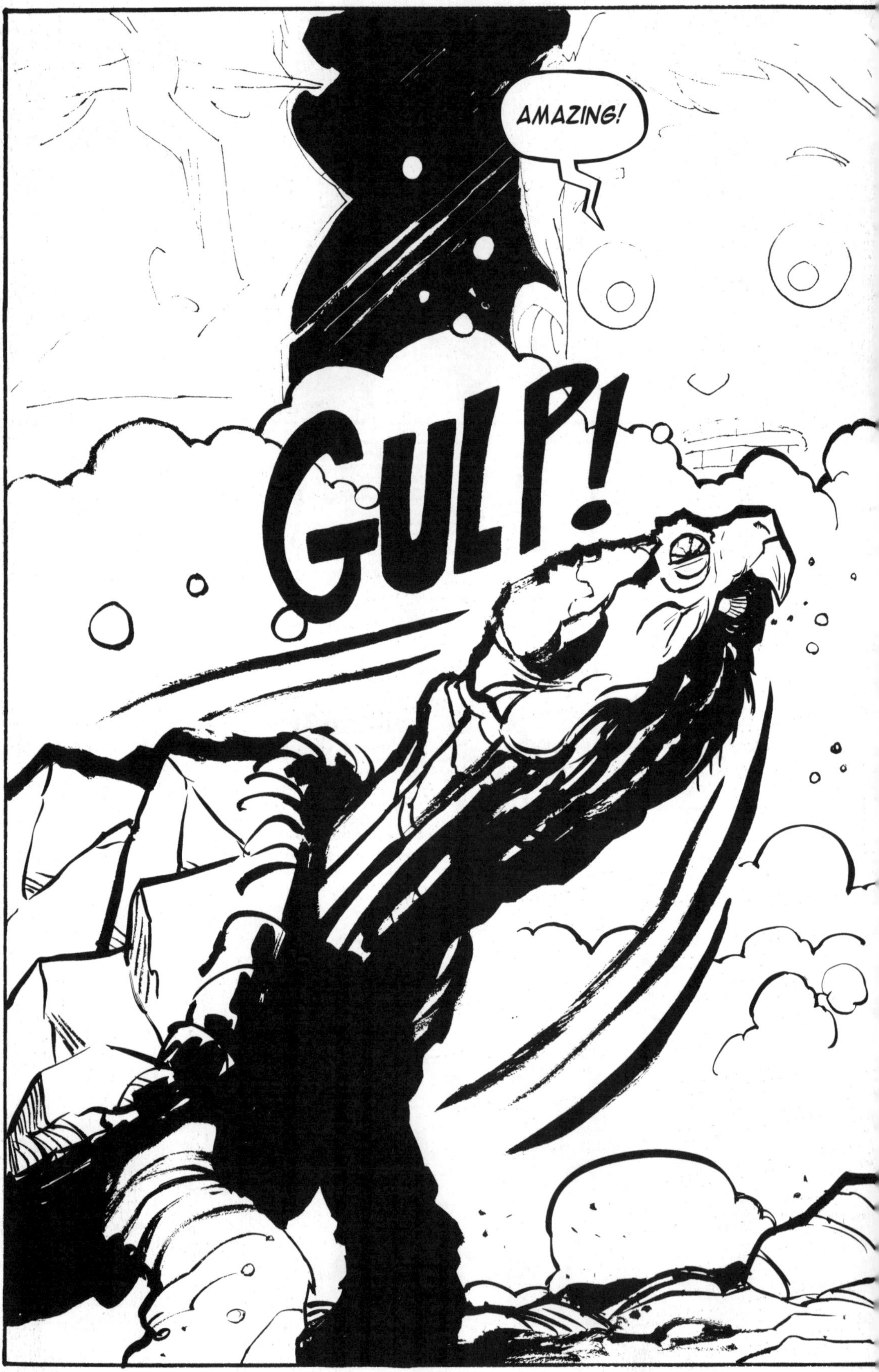
AMAZING!
GULP!

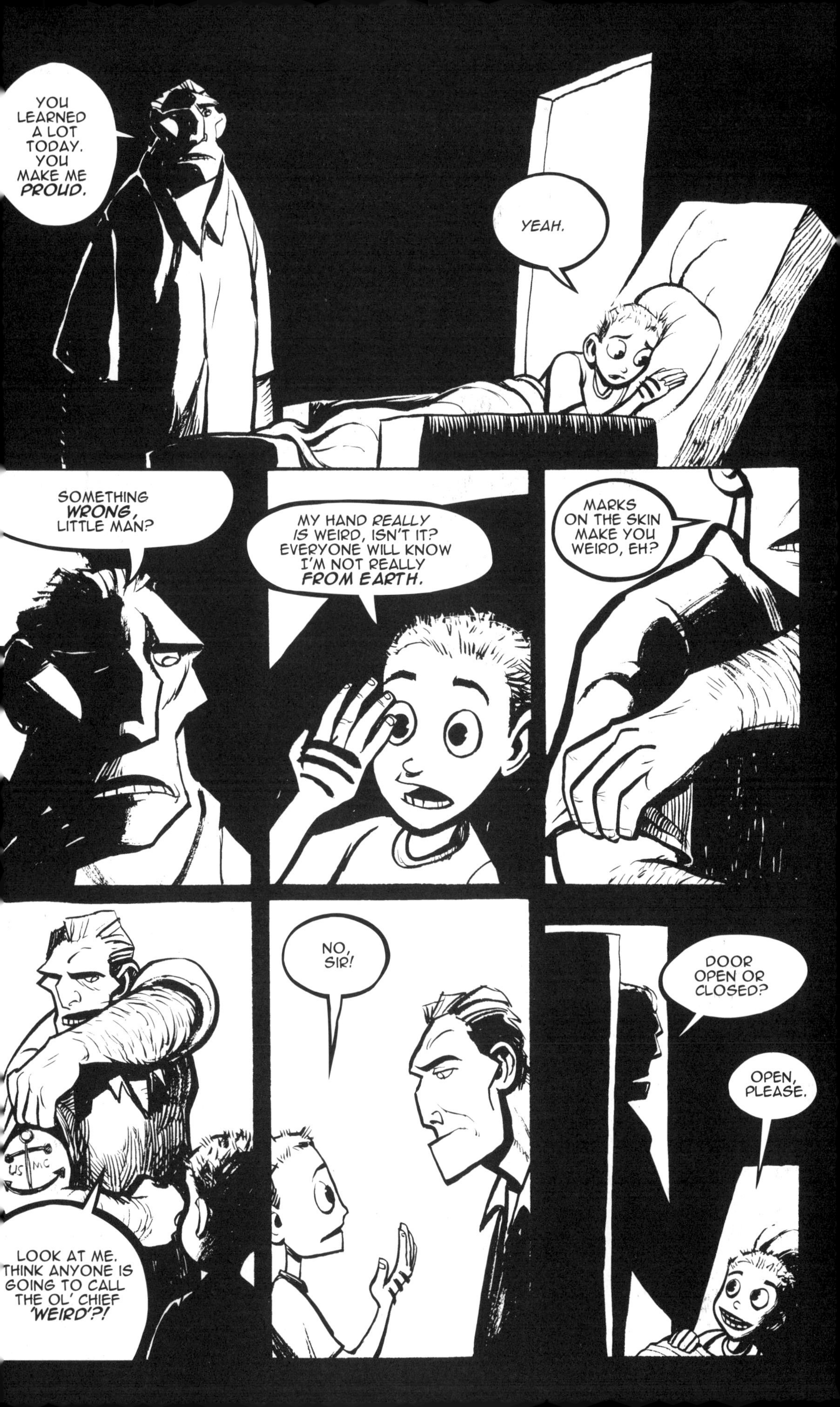
YOU LEARNED A LOT TODAY. YOU MAKE ME PROUD.
YEAH.
SOMETHING WRONG, LITTLE MAN?
MY HAND REALLY IS WEIRD, ISN'T IT? EVERYONE WILL KNOW I'M NOT REALLY FROM EARTH.
MARKS ON THE SKIN MAKE YOU WEIRD, EH?
LOOK AT ME. THINK ANYONE IS GOING TO CALL THE OL' CHIEF 'WEIRD'?!
US MC
NO, SIR!
DOOR OPEN OR CLOSED?
OPEN, PLEASE.

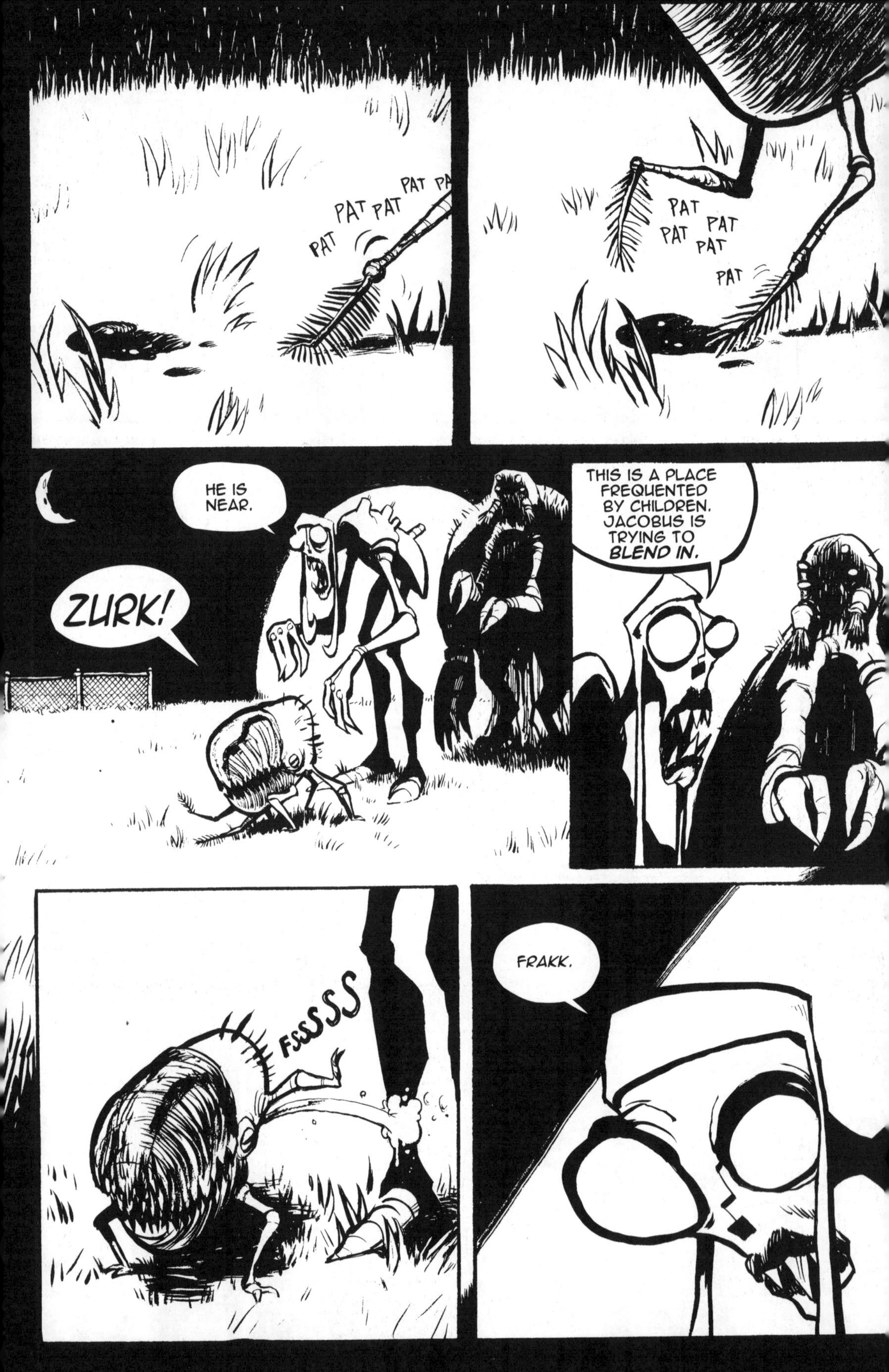
PAT PAT PAT PAT PA
PAT PAT PAT PAT PAT
PAT
HE IS NEAR.
ZURK!
THIS IS A PLACE FREQUENTED BY CHILDREN. JACOBUS IS TRYING TO *BLEND IN.*
FsSSSS
FRAKK.

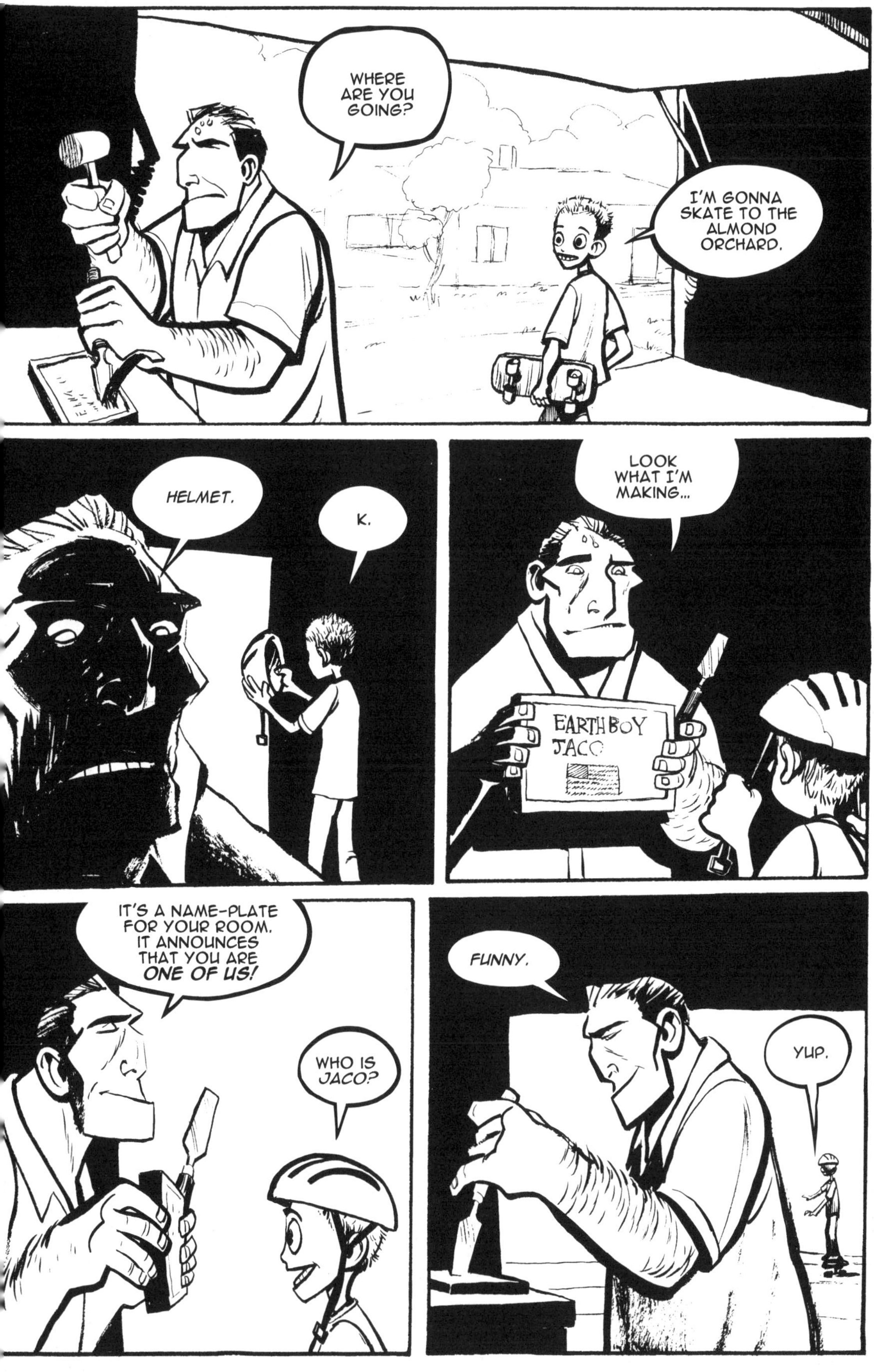
WHERE ARE YOU GOING?
I'M GONNA SKATE TO THE ALMOND ORCHARD.
HELMET.
K.
LOOK WHAT I'M MAKING...
EARTH BOY JACO
IT'S A NAME-PLATE FOR YOUR ROOM. IT ANNOUNCES THAT YOU ARE ONE OF US!
WHO IS JACO?
FUNNY.
YUP.

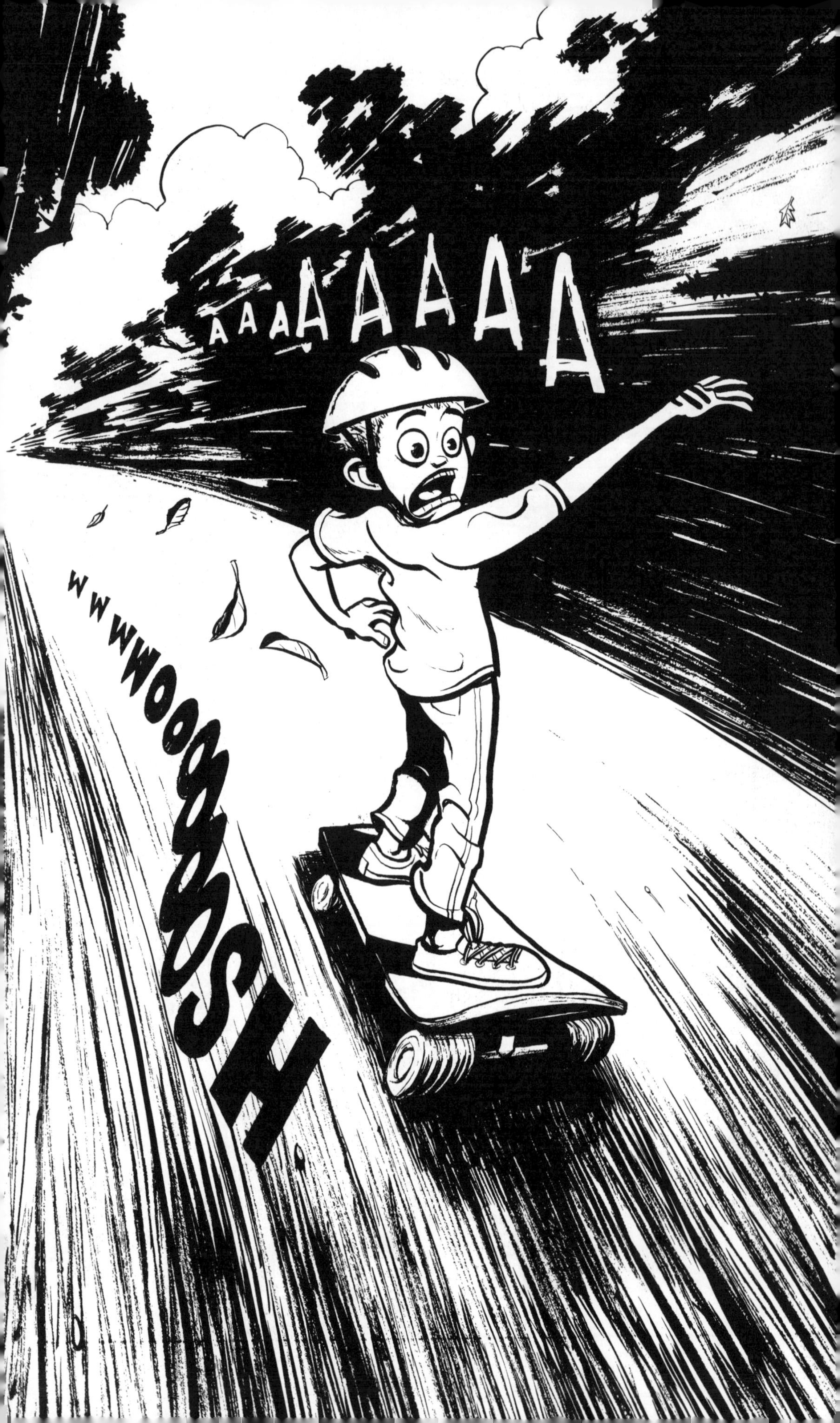
AAAAAAAA
WWWWOOOOOOOOSH

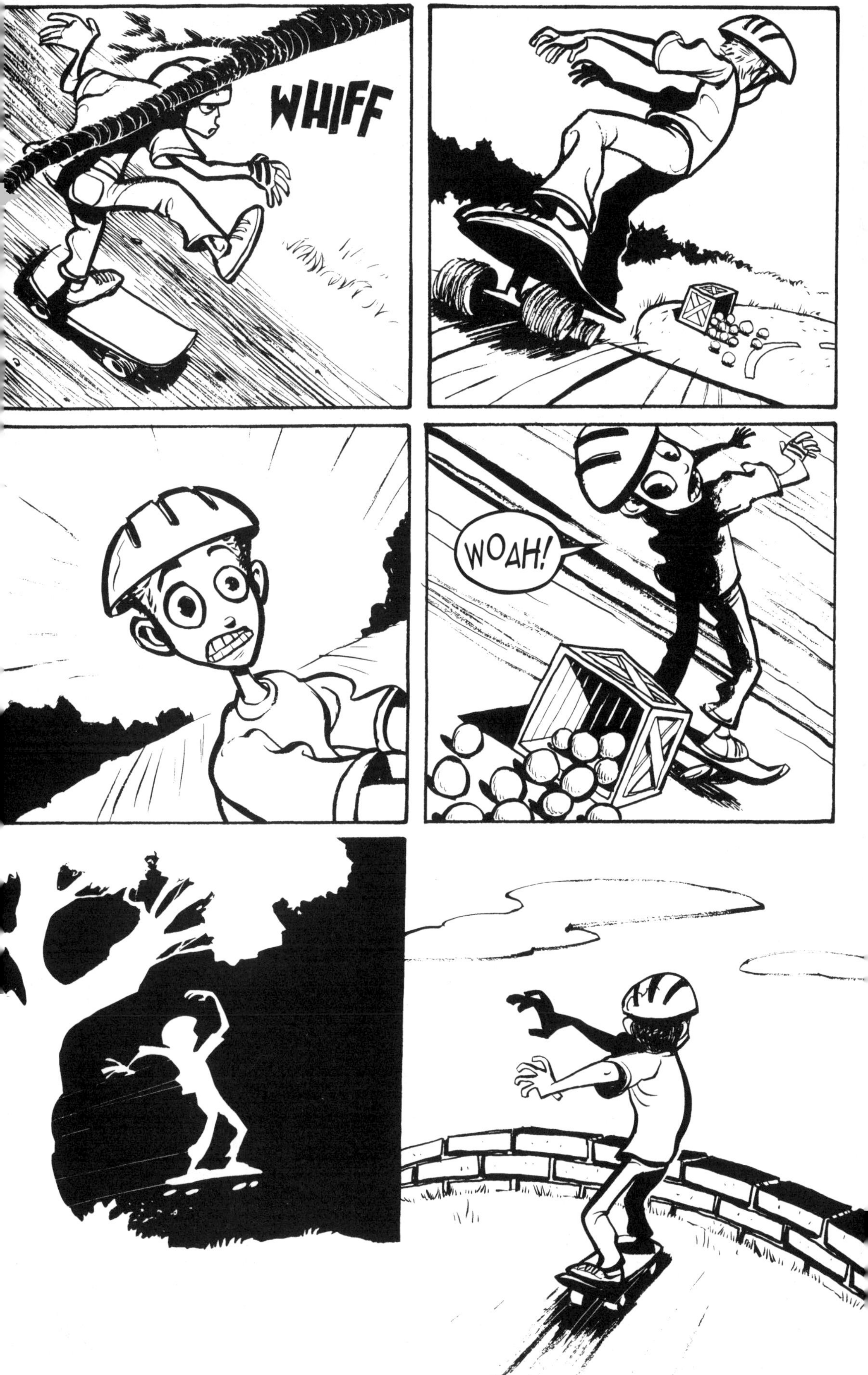
WHIFF
WOAH!

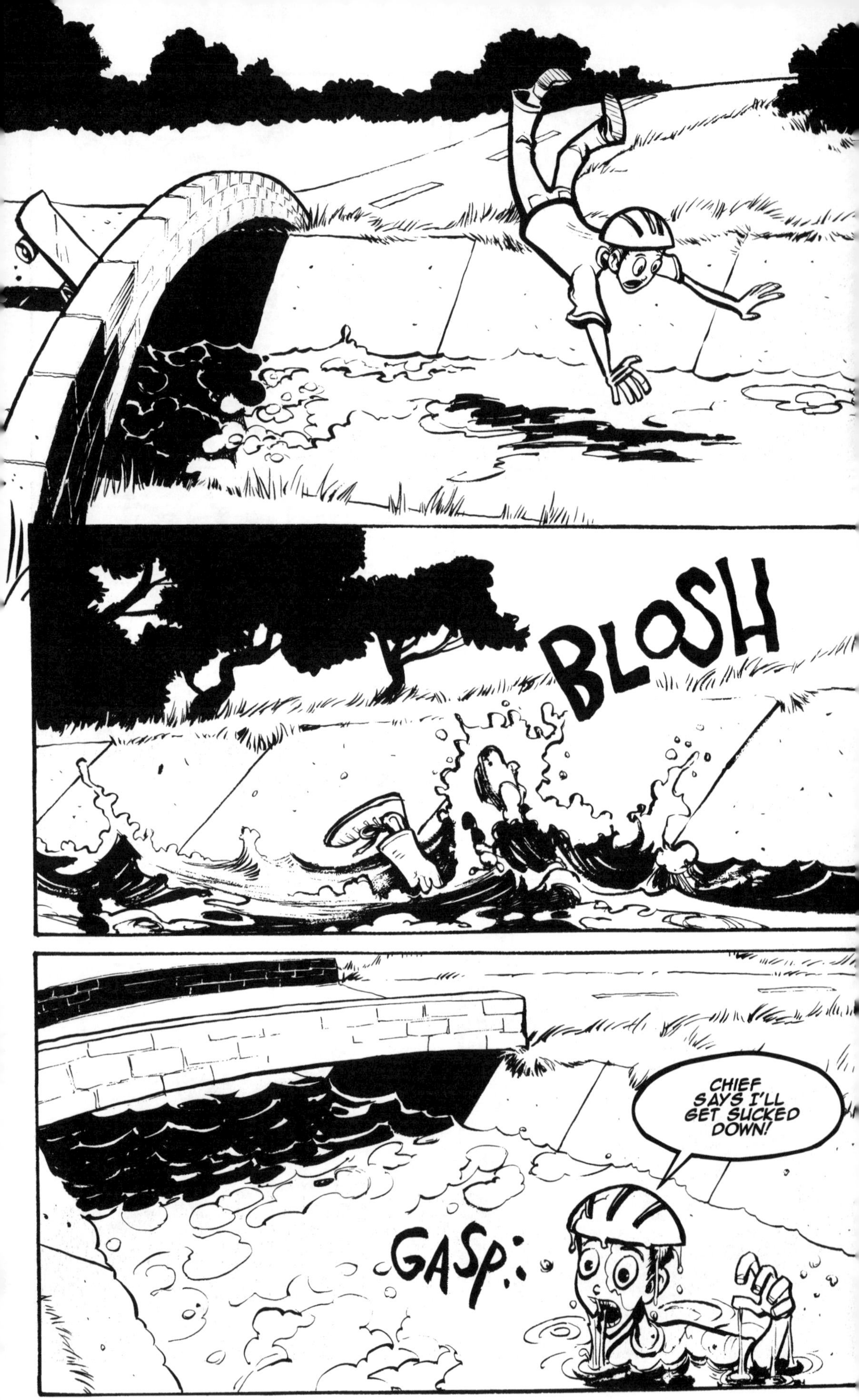
BLOSH
CHIEF SAYS I'LL GET SUCKED DOWN!
GASP

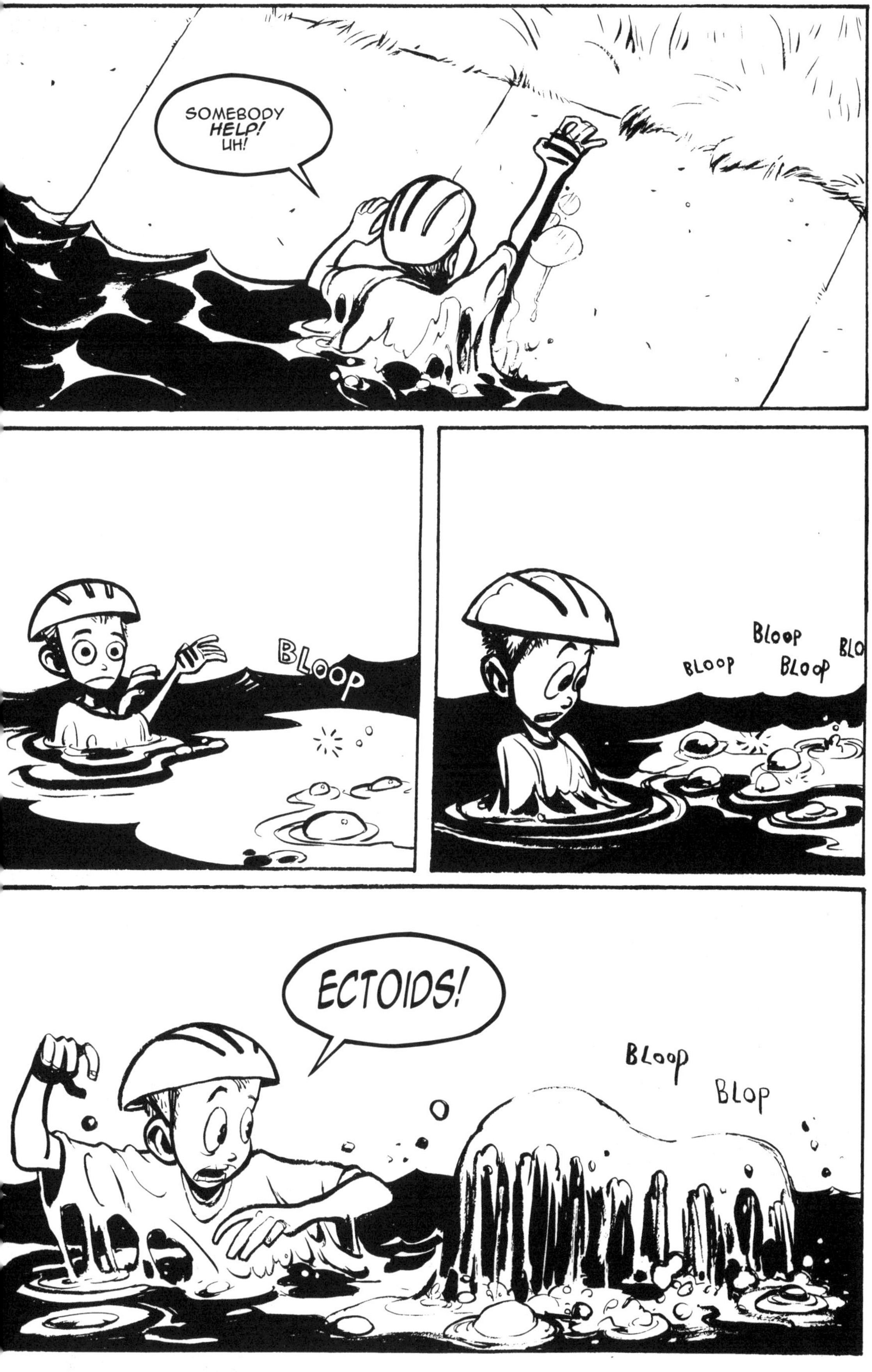
SOMEBODY HELP! UH!
BLOOP
BLOOP
BLOOP
BLOOP
BLO
ECTOIDS!
BLOOP
BLOP

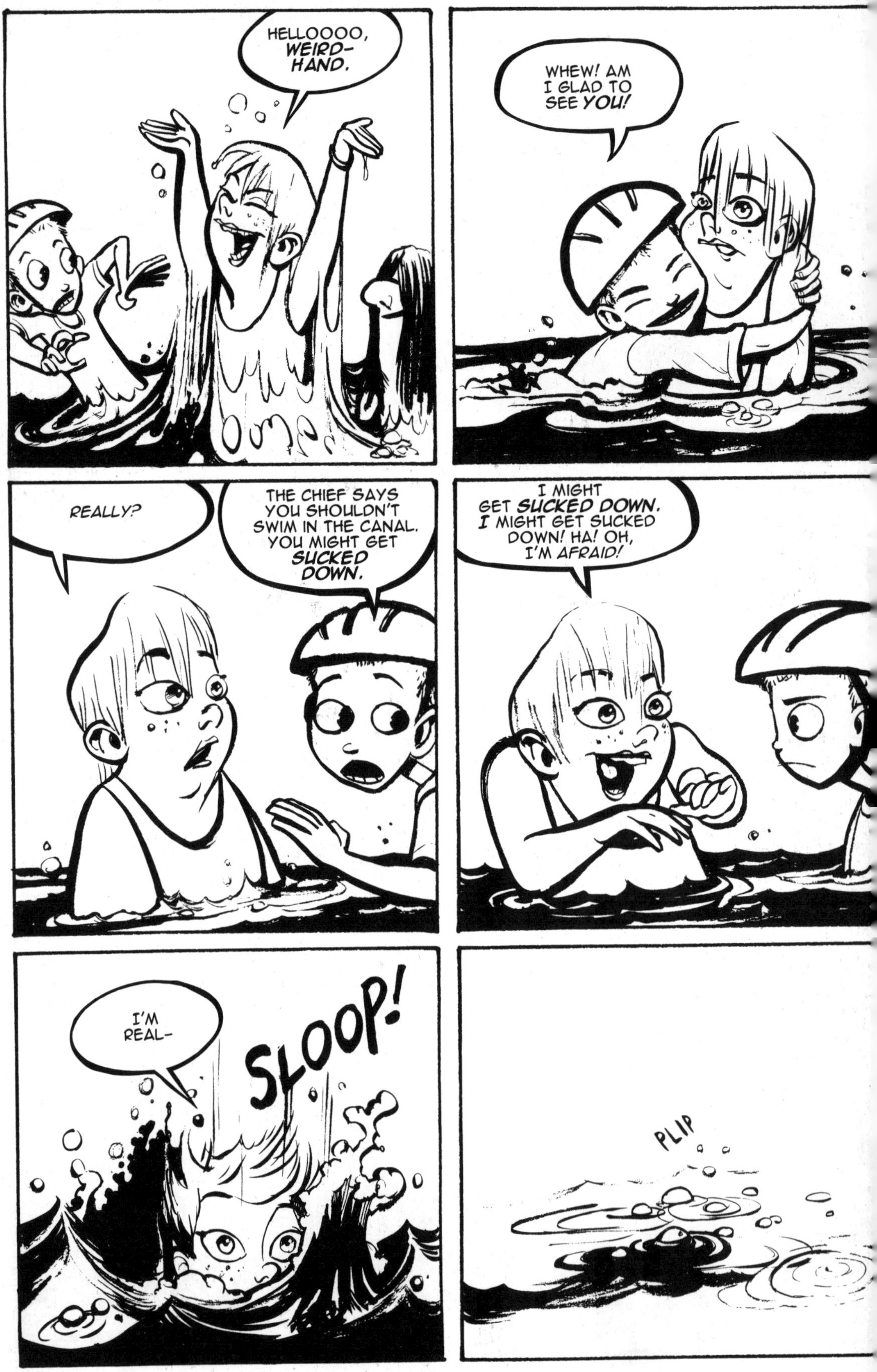
HELLOOOO, WEIRD-HAND.
WHEW! AM I GLAD TO SEE YOU!
REALLY?
THE CHIEF SAYS YOU SHOULDN'T SWIM IN THE CANAL. YOU MIGHT GET SUCKED DOWN.
I MIGHT GET SUCKED DOWN. I MIGHT GET SUCKED DOWN! HA! OH, I'M AFRAID!
I'M REAL-
SLOOP!
PLIP

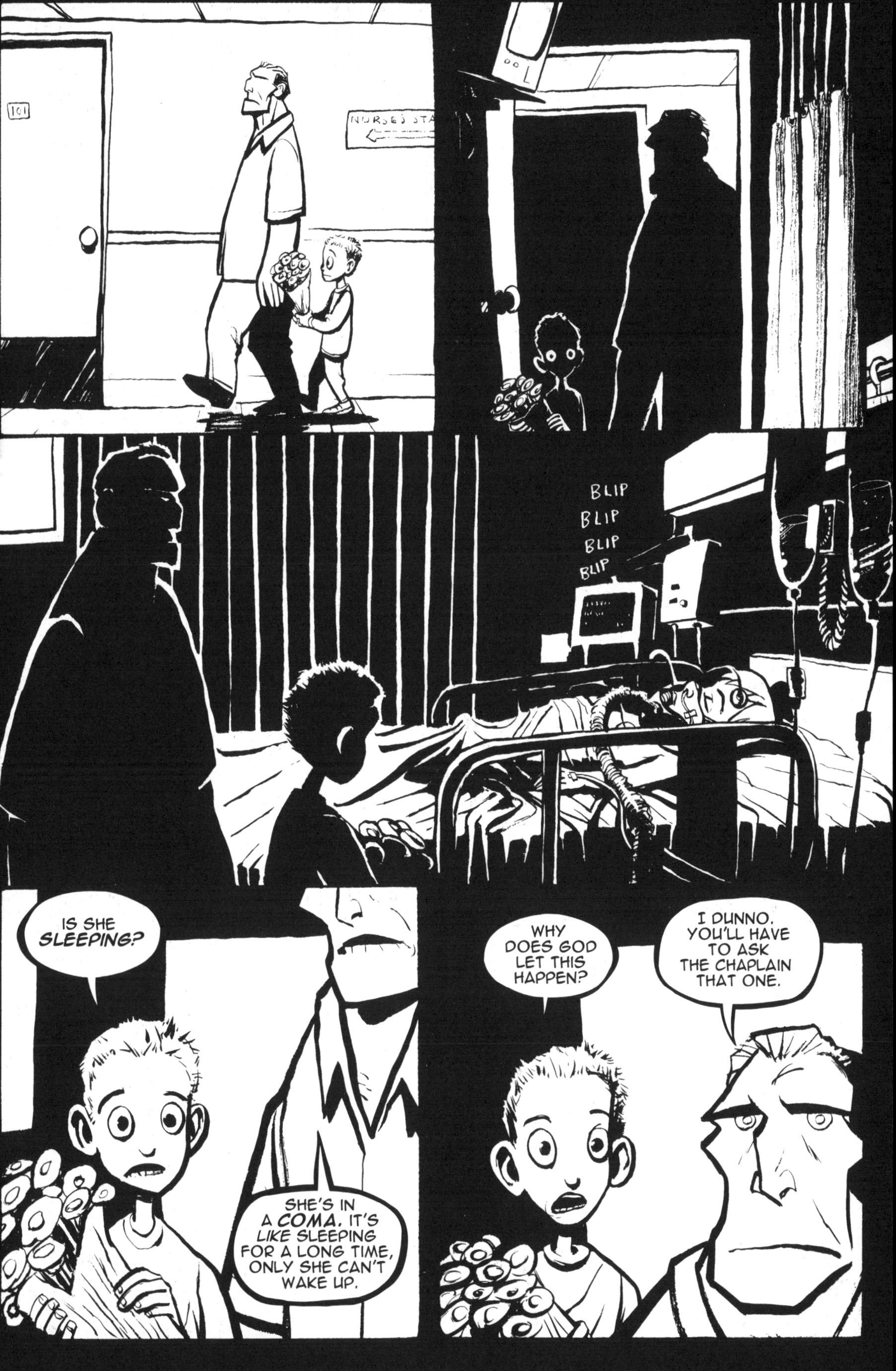
101
NURSES STA
BLIP
BLIP
BLIP
BLIP
IS SHE SLEEPING?
SHE'S IN A COMA. IT'S LIKE SLEEPING FOR A LONG TIME, ONLY SHE CAN'T WAKE UP.
WHY DOES GOD LET THIS HAPPEN?
I DUNNO. YOU'LL HAVE TO ASK THE CHAPLAIN THAT ONE.

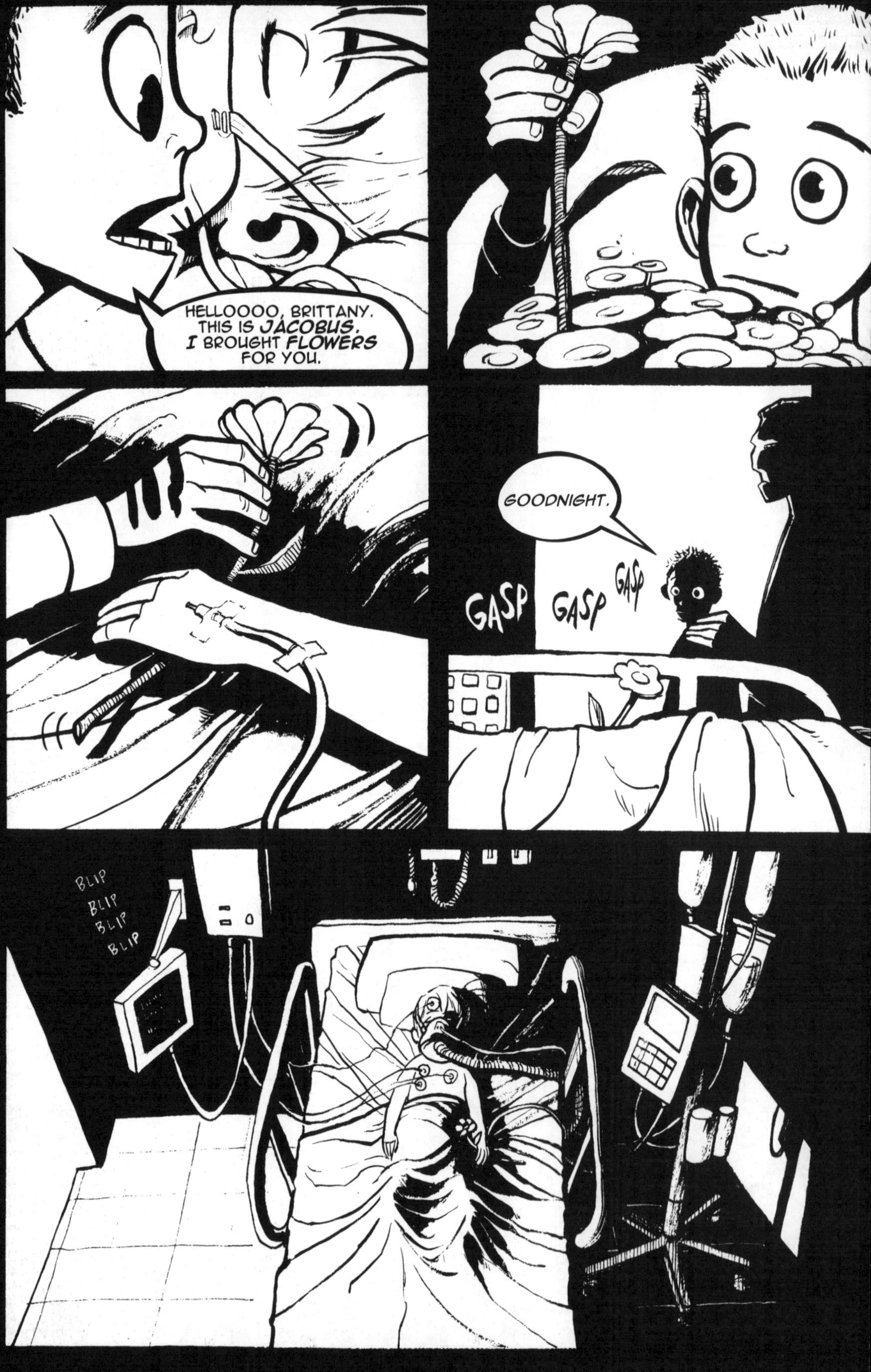
HELLOOOO, BRITTANY. THIS IS JÁCOBUS. I BROUGHT FLOWERS FOR YOU.
GOODNIGHT.
GASP GASP GASP
BLIP BLIP BLIP BLIP

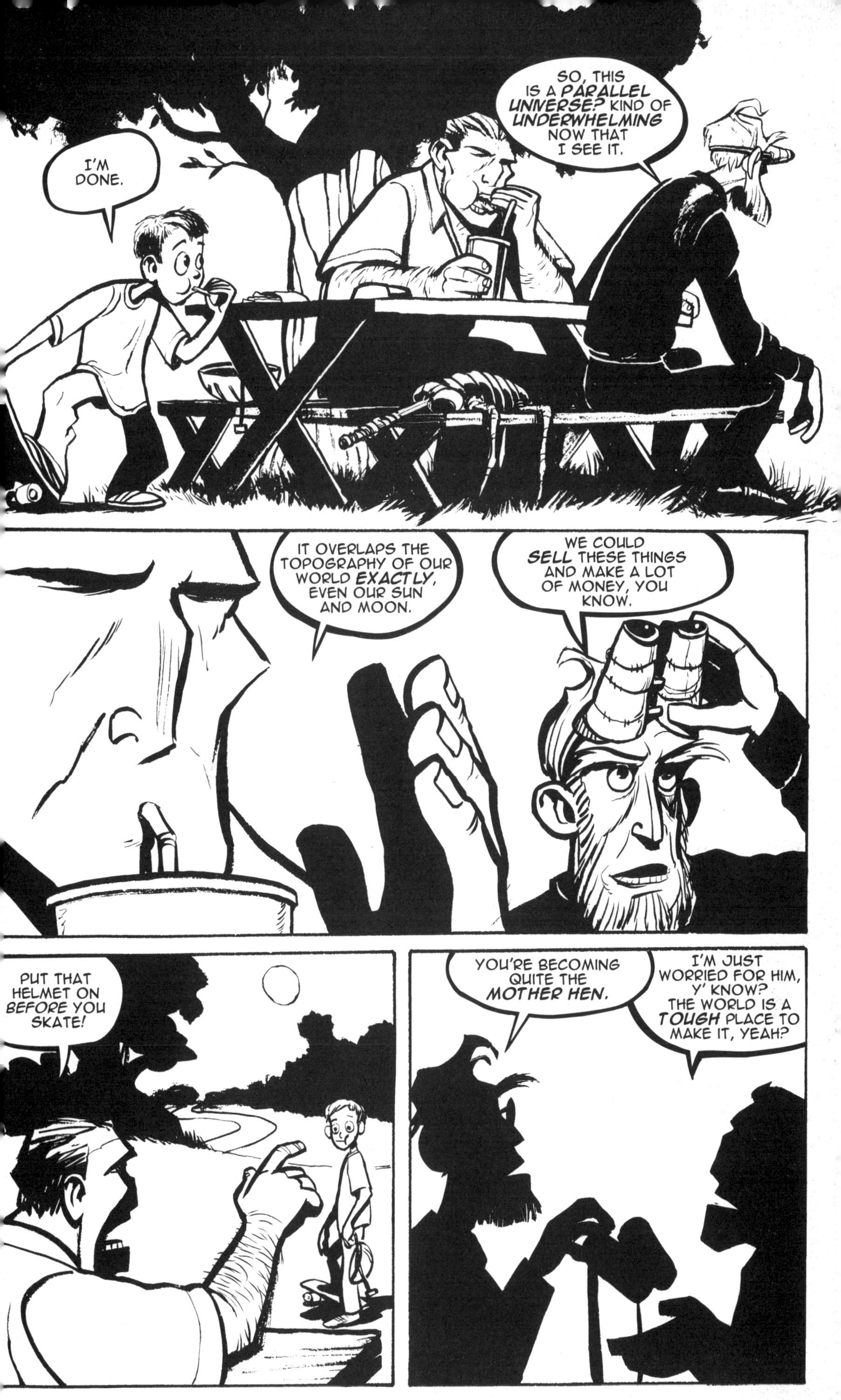
I'M DONE.
SO, THIS IS A PARALLEL UNIVERSE? KIND OF UNDERWHELMING NOW THAT I SEE IT.
IT OVERLAPS THE TOPOGRAPHY OF OUR WORLD EXACTLY, EVEN OUR SUN AND MOON.
WE COULD SELL THESE THINGS AND MAKE A LOT OF MONEY, YOU KNOW.
PUT THAT HELMET ON BEFORE YOU SKATE!
YOU'RE BECOMING QUITE THE MOTHER HEN.
I'M JUST WORRIED FOR HIM, Y' KNOW? THE WORLD IS A TOUGH PLACE TO MAKE IT, YEAH?

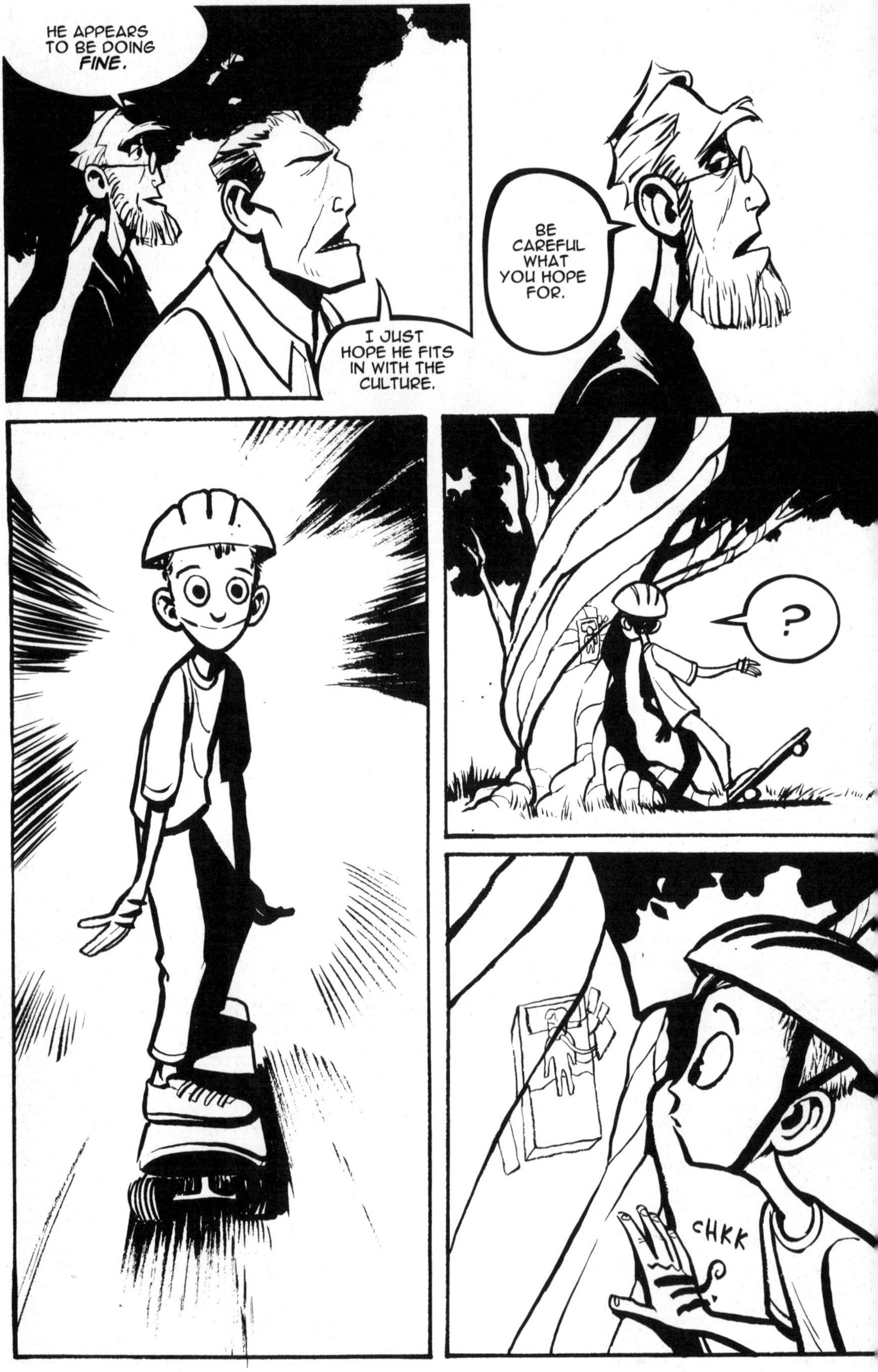
HE APPEARS TO BE DOING *FINE.*
I JUST HOPE HE FITS IN WITH THE CULTURE.
BE CAREFUL WHAT YOU HOPE FOR.
?
CHKK

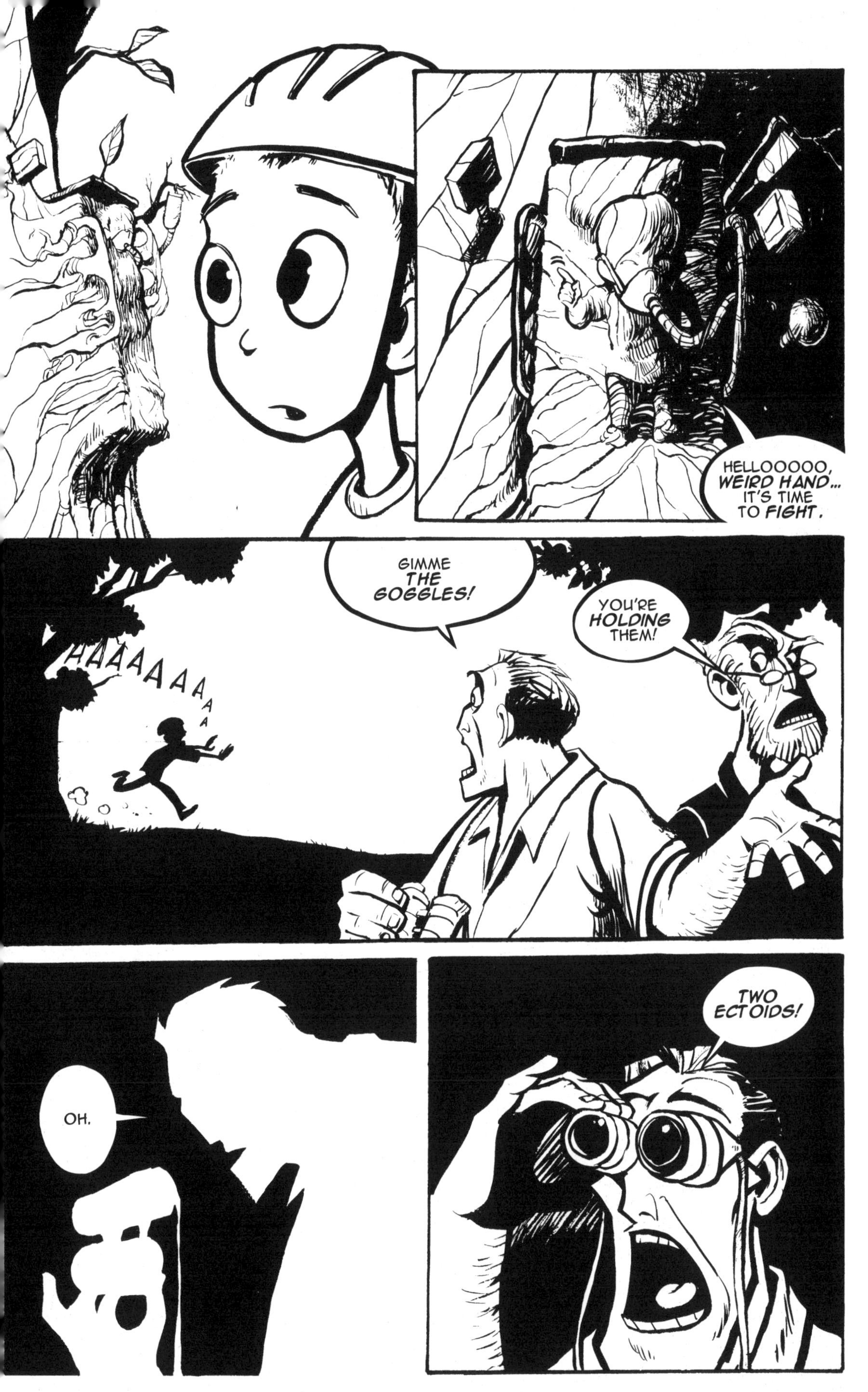
HELLOOOOO, WEIRD HAND... IT'S TIME TO FIGHT.
GIMME THE GOGGLES!
YOU'RE HOLDING THEM!
AAAAAAAAAA
OH.
TWO ECTOIDS!

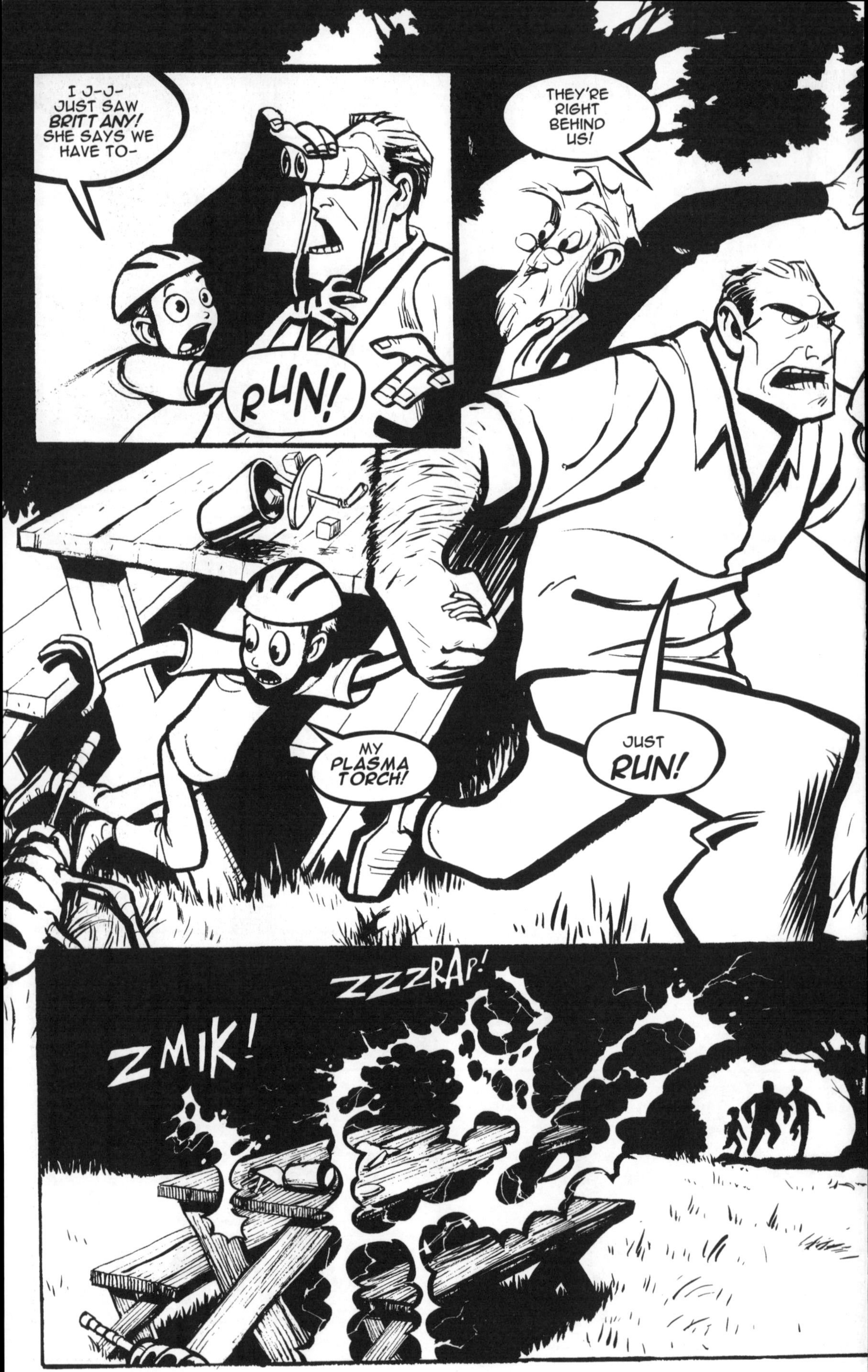
I J-J- JUST SAW BRITTANY! SHE SAYS WE HAVE TO-
RUN!
THEY'RE RIGHT BEHIND US!
MY PLASMA TORCH!
JUST RUN!
ZZZRAP!
ZMIK!

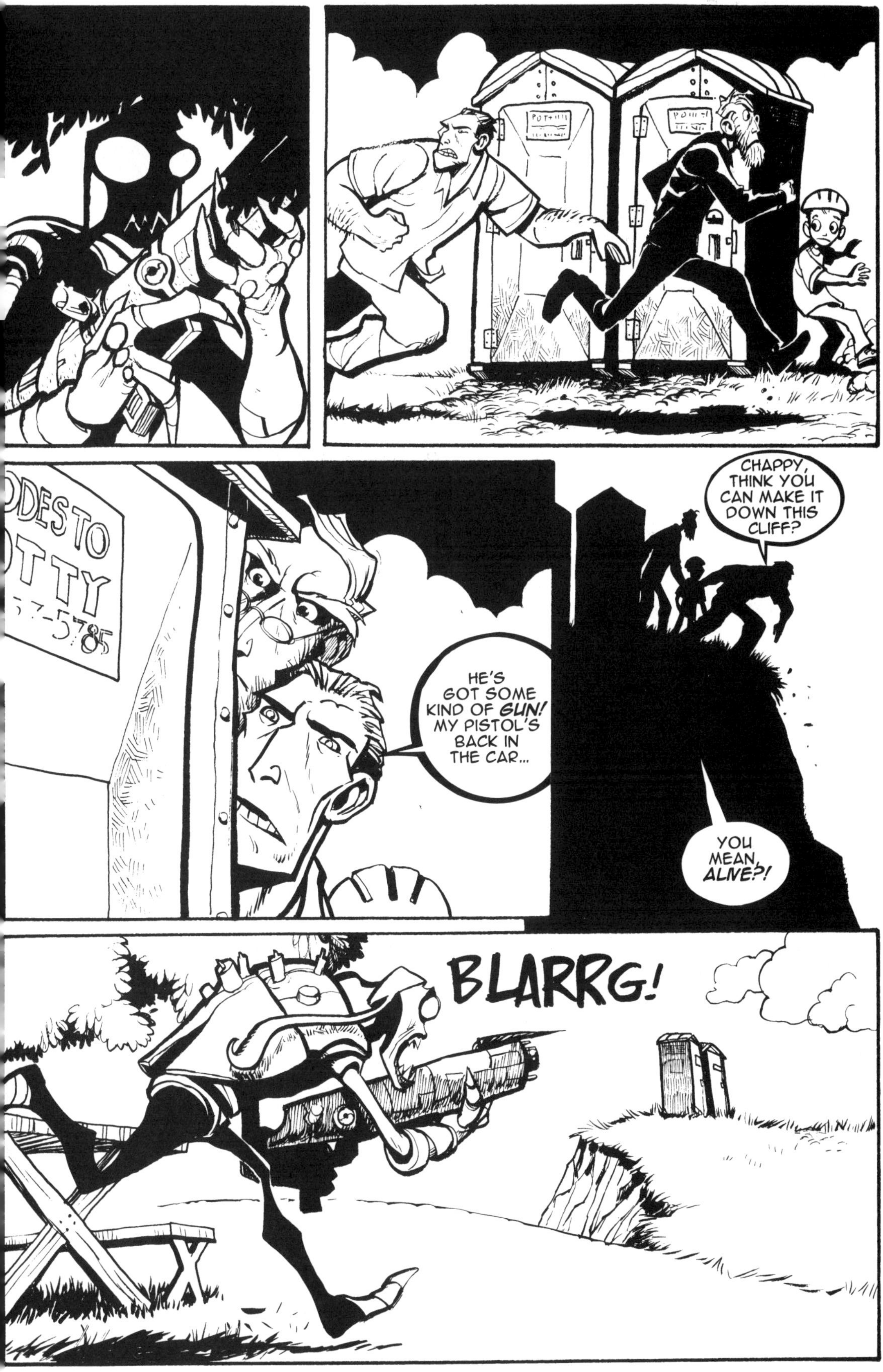

HE'S GOT SOME KIND OF GUN! MY PISTOL'S BACK IN THE CAR...
CHAPPY, THINK YOU CAN MAKE IT DOWN THIS CLIFF?
YOU MEAN, ALIVE?!
BLARRG!

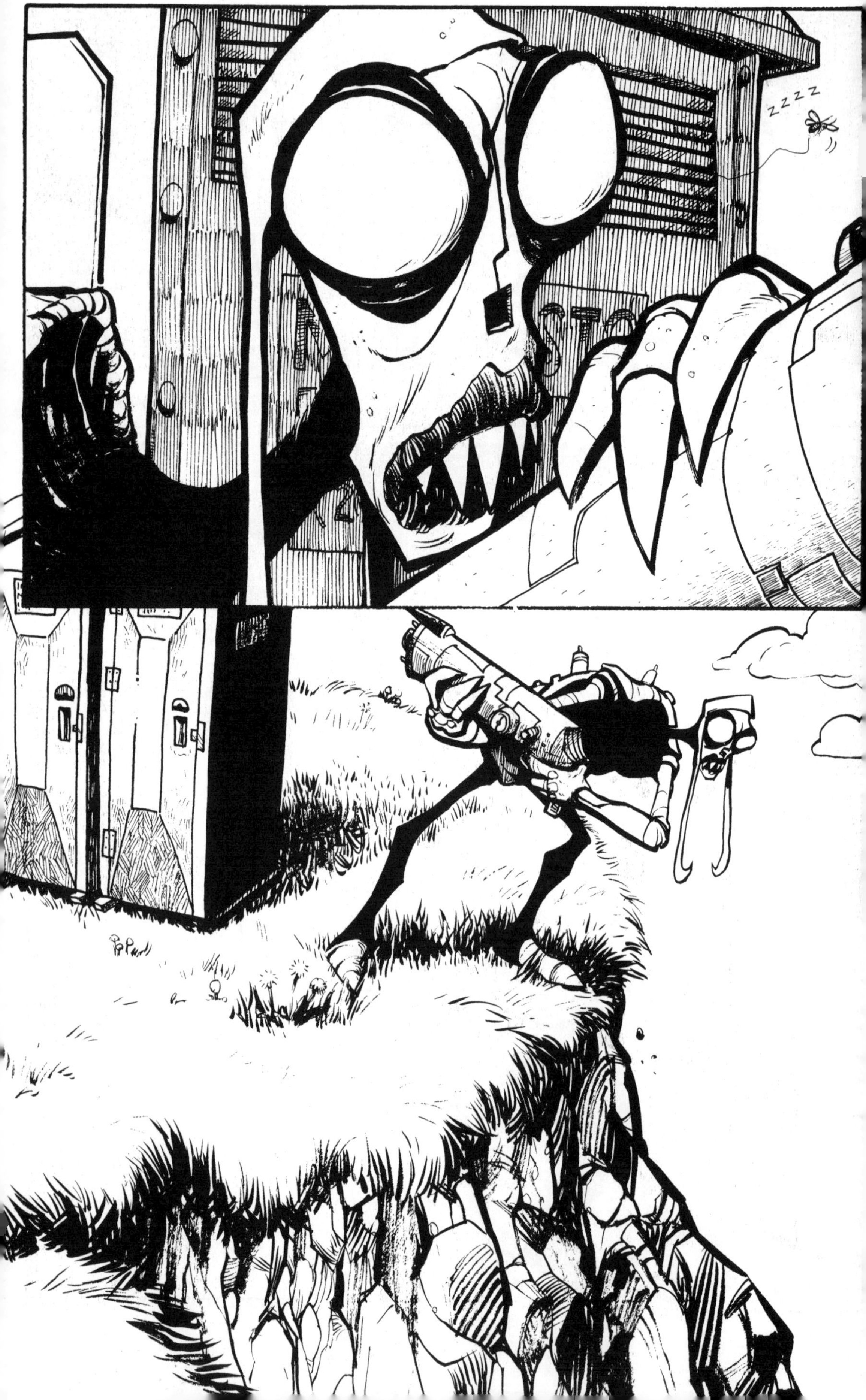
ZZZZ

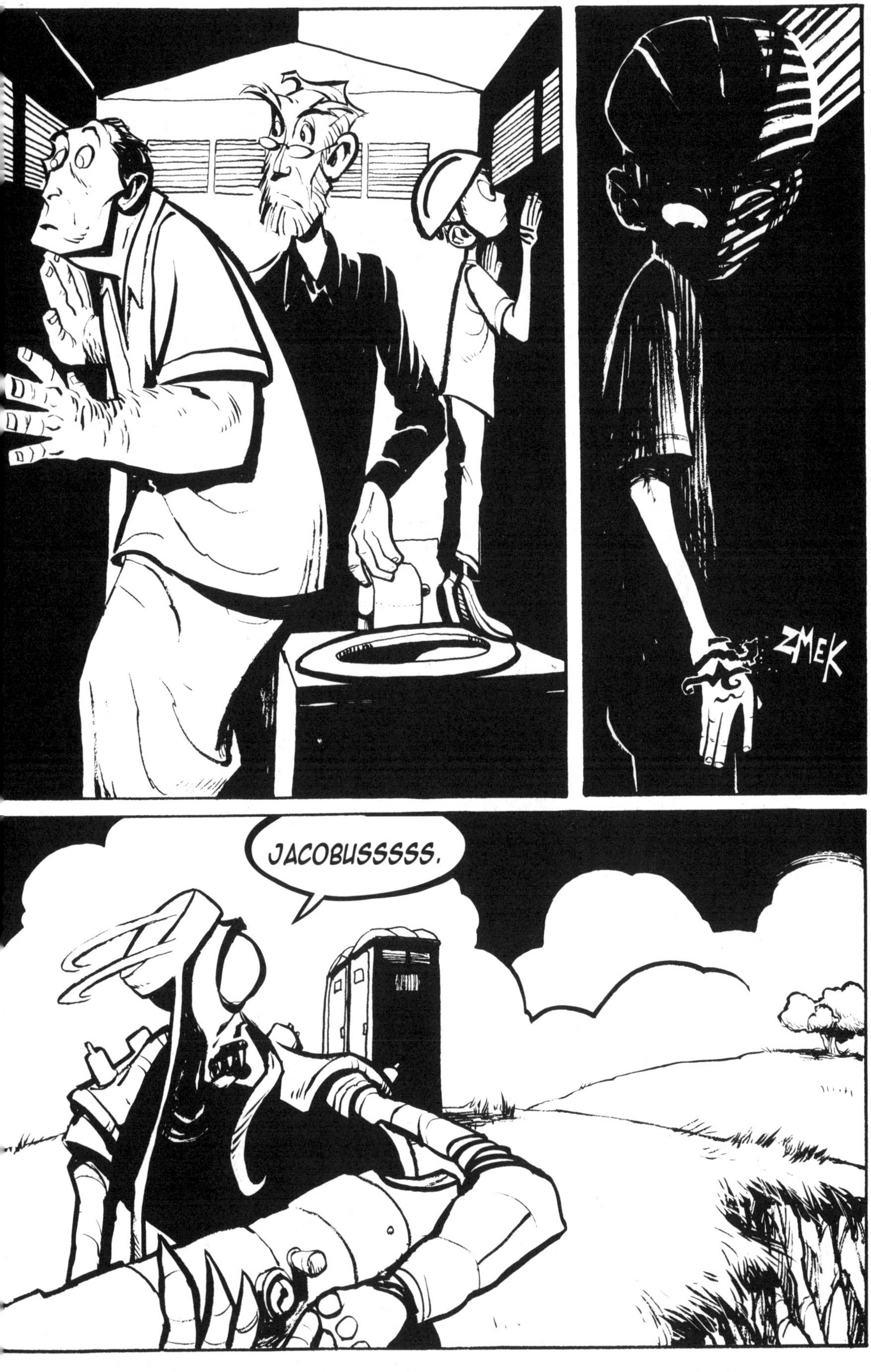
ZMEK
JACOBUSSSSS.

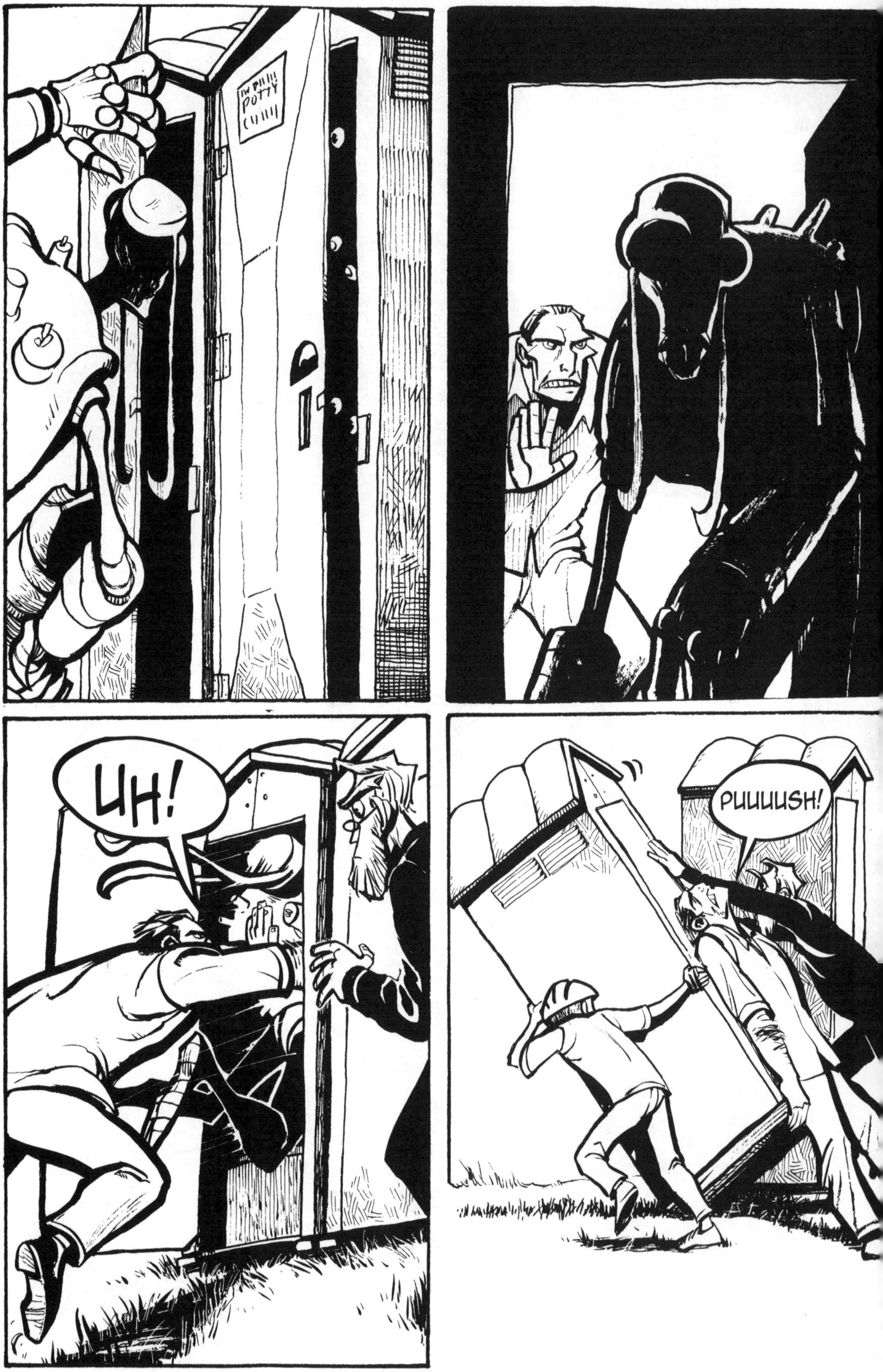
POTTY
UH!
PUUUUSH!

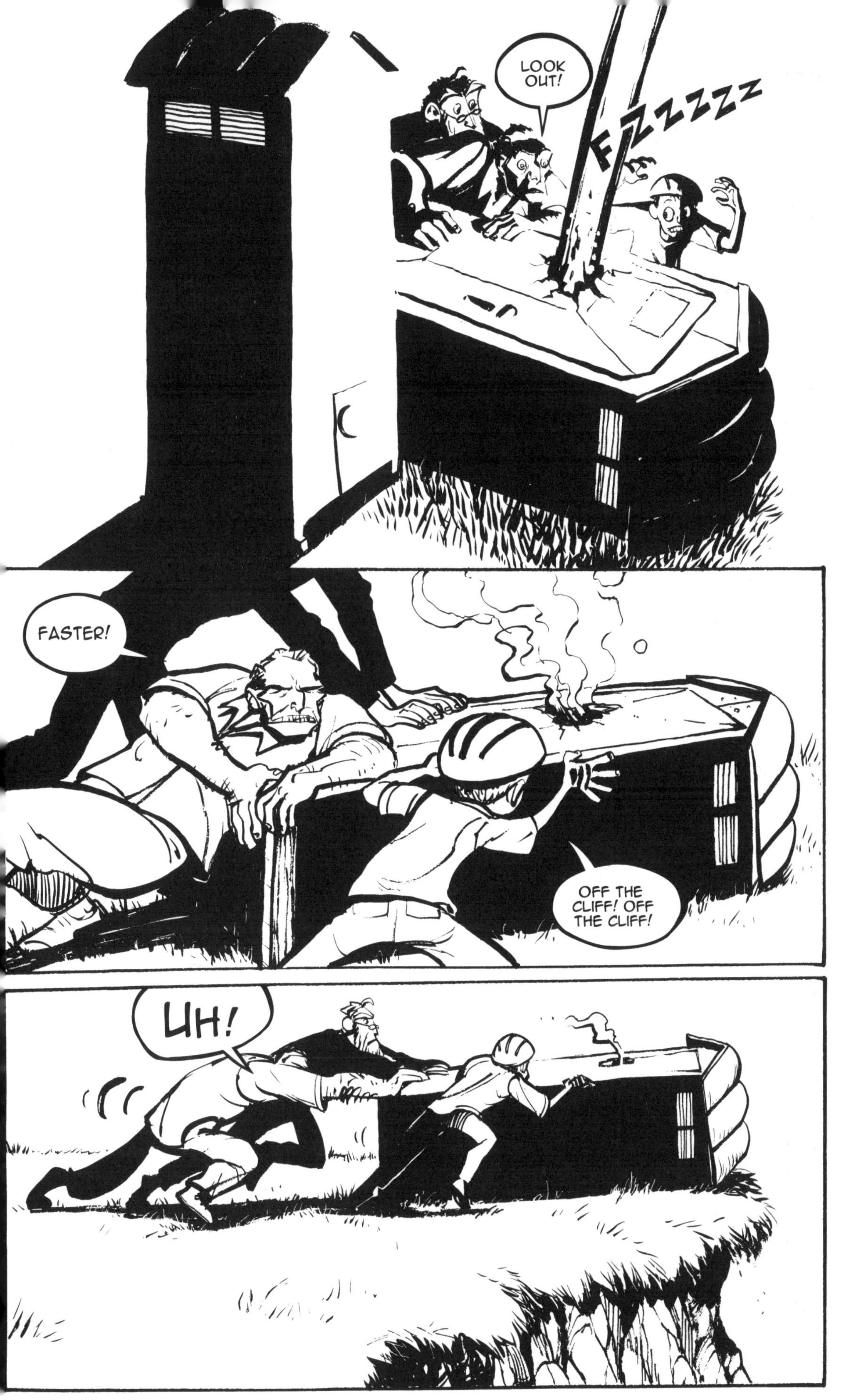

LOOK OUT!
FZZZZZZ
FASTER!
OFF THE CLIFF! OFF THE CLIFF!
UH!

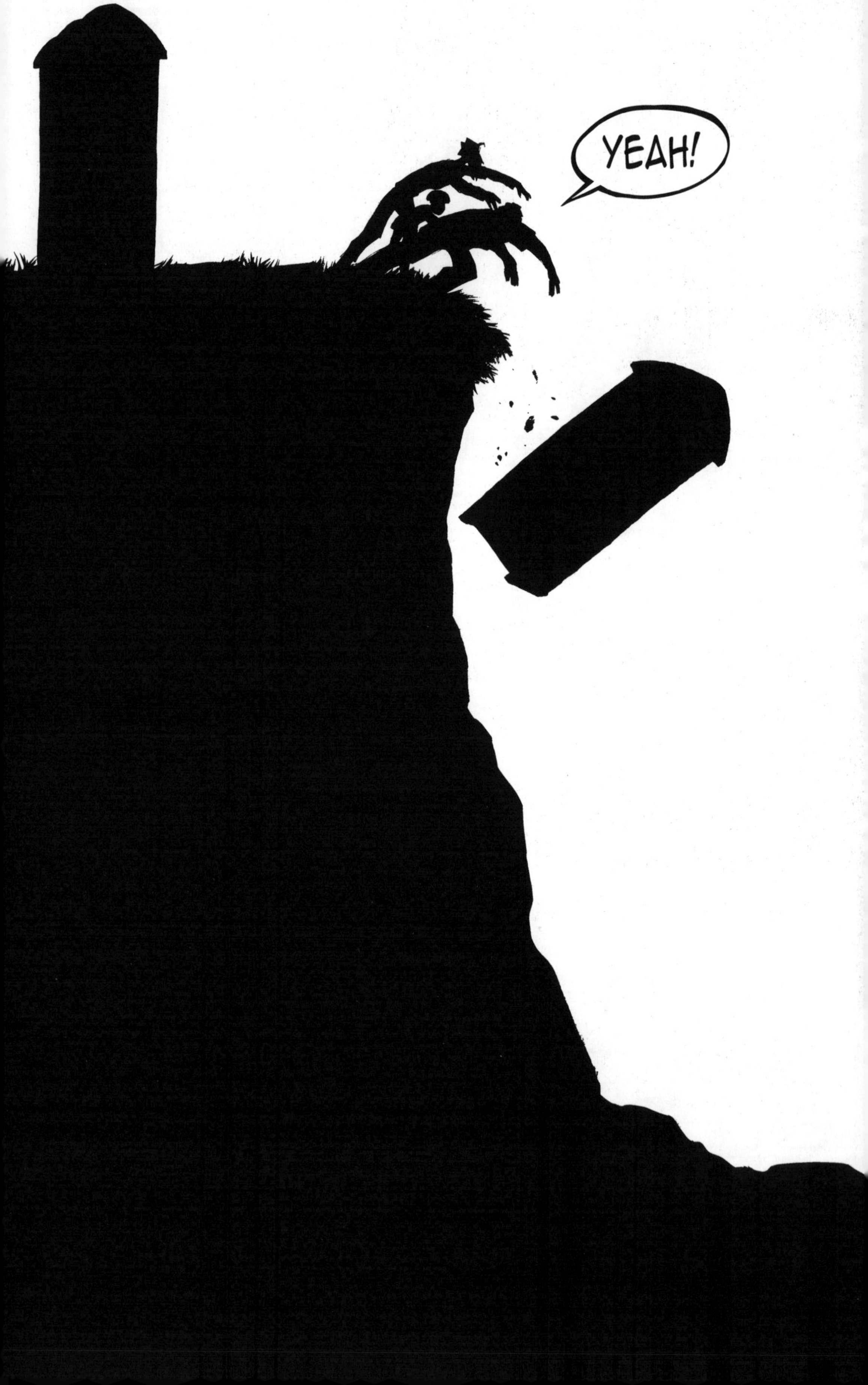
YEAH!

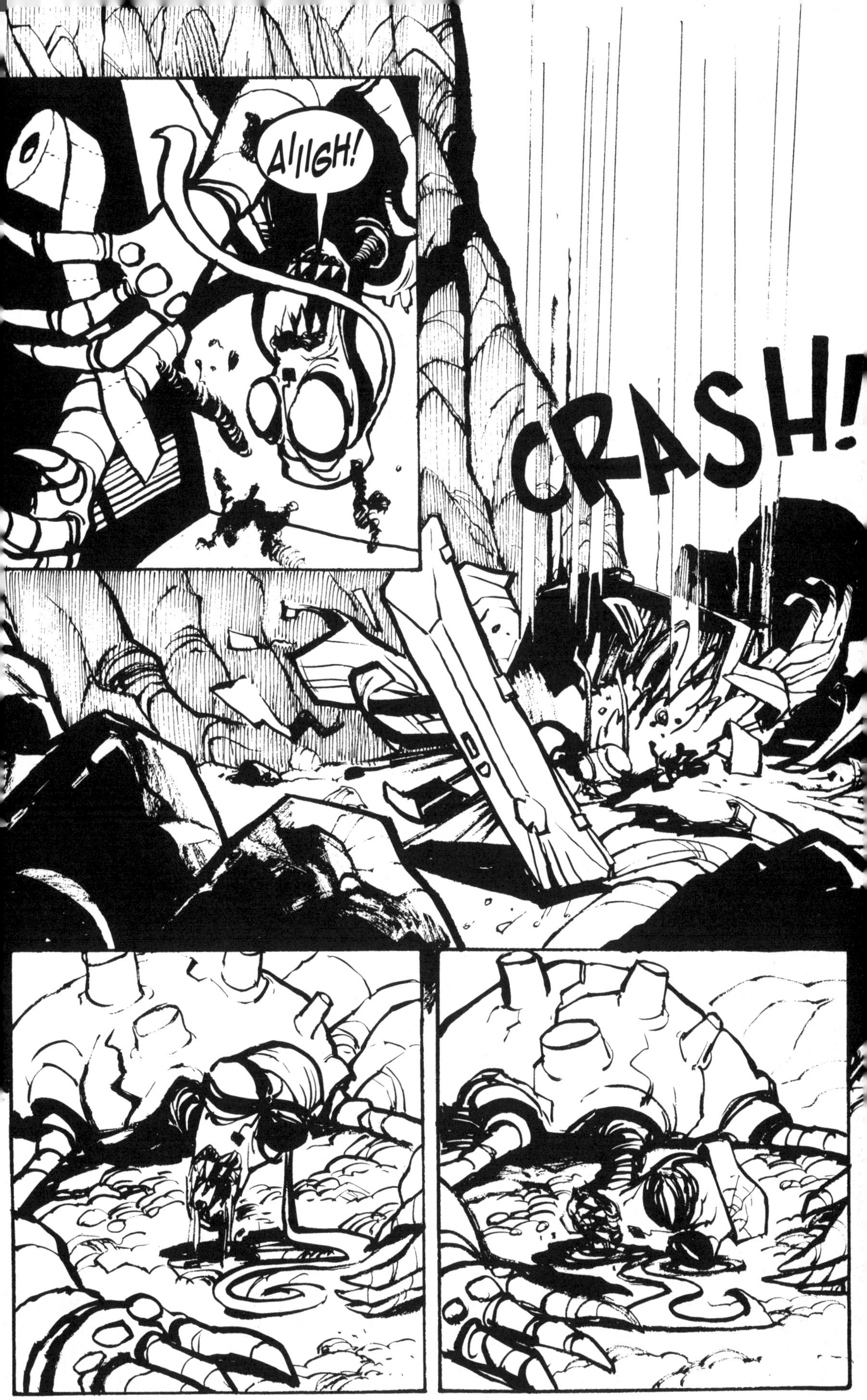
AIIIGH!
CRASH!!

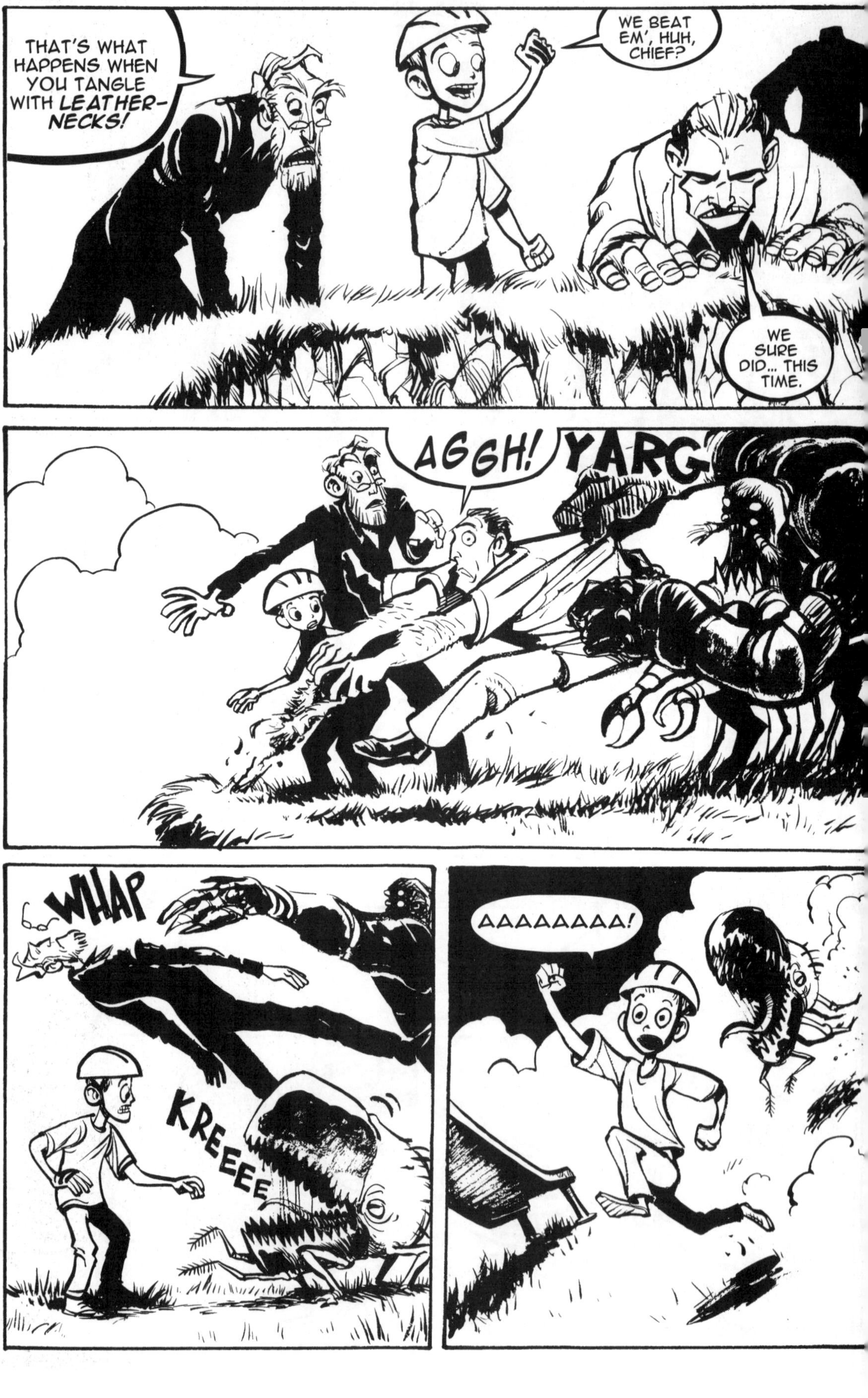
THAT'S WHAT HAPPENS WHEN YOU TANGLE WITH LEATHER-NECKS!
WE BEAT EM', HUH, CHIEF?
WE SURE DID... THIS TIME.
AGGH!
YARG
WHAP
KREEEEE
AAAAAAAA!

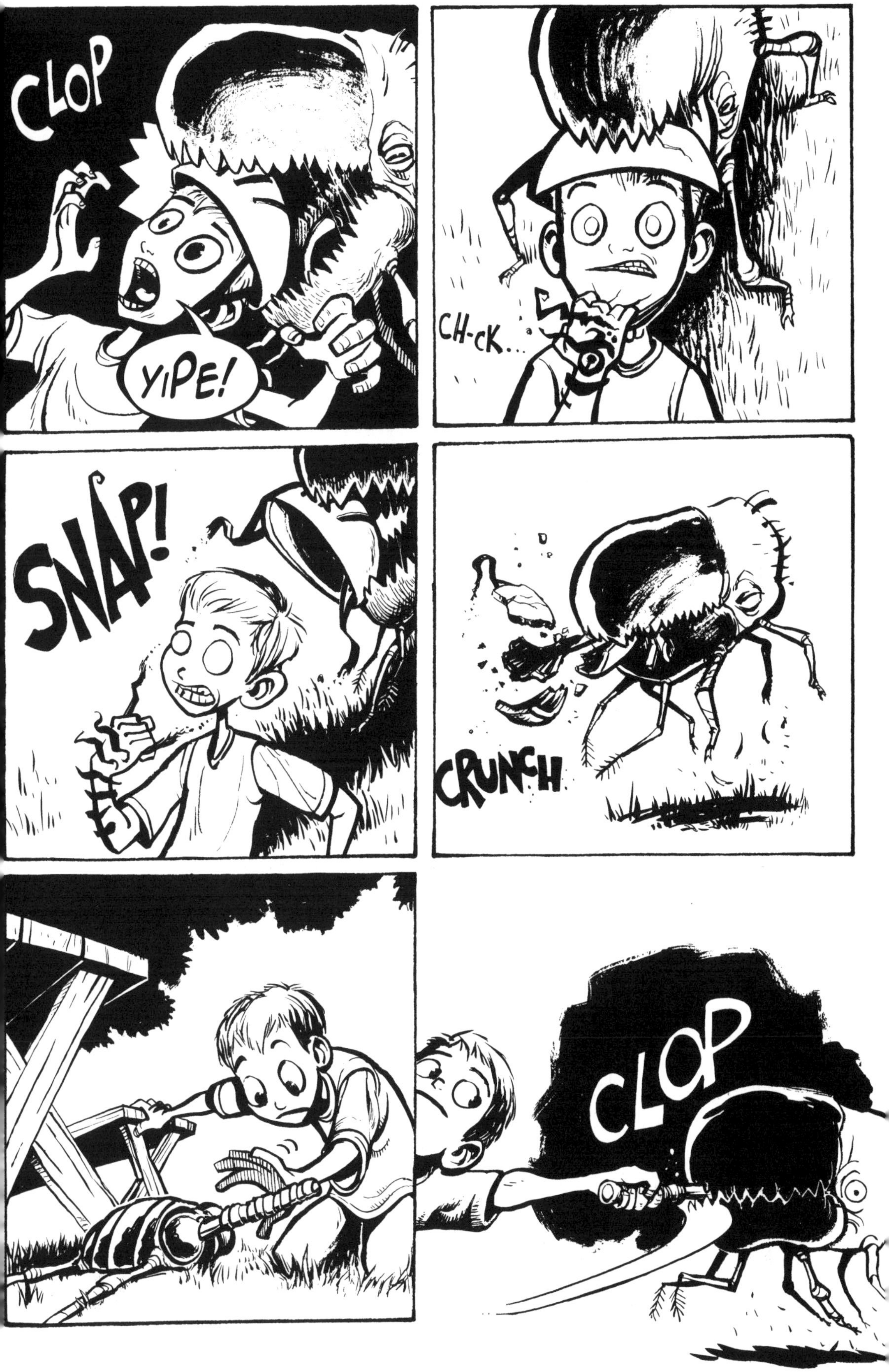
CLOP
YIPE!
CH-CK...
SNAP!
CRUNCH
CLOP

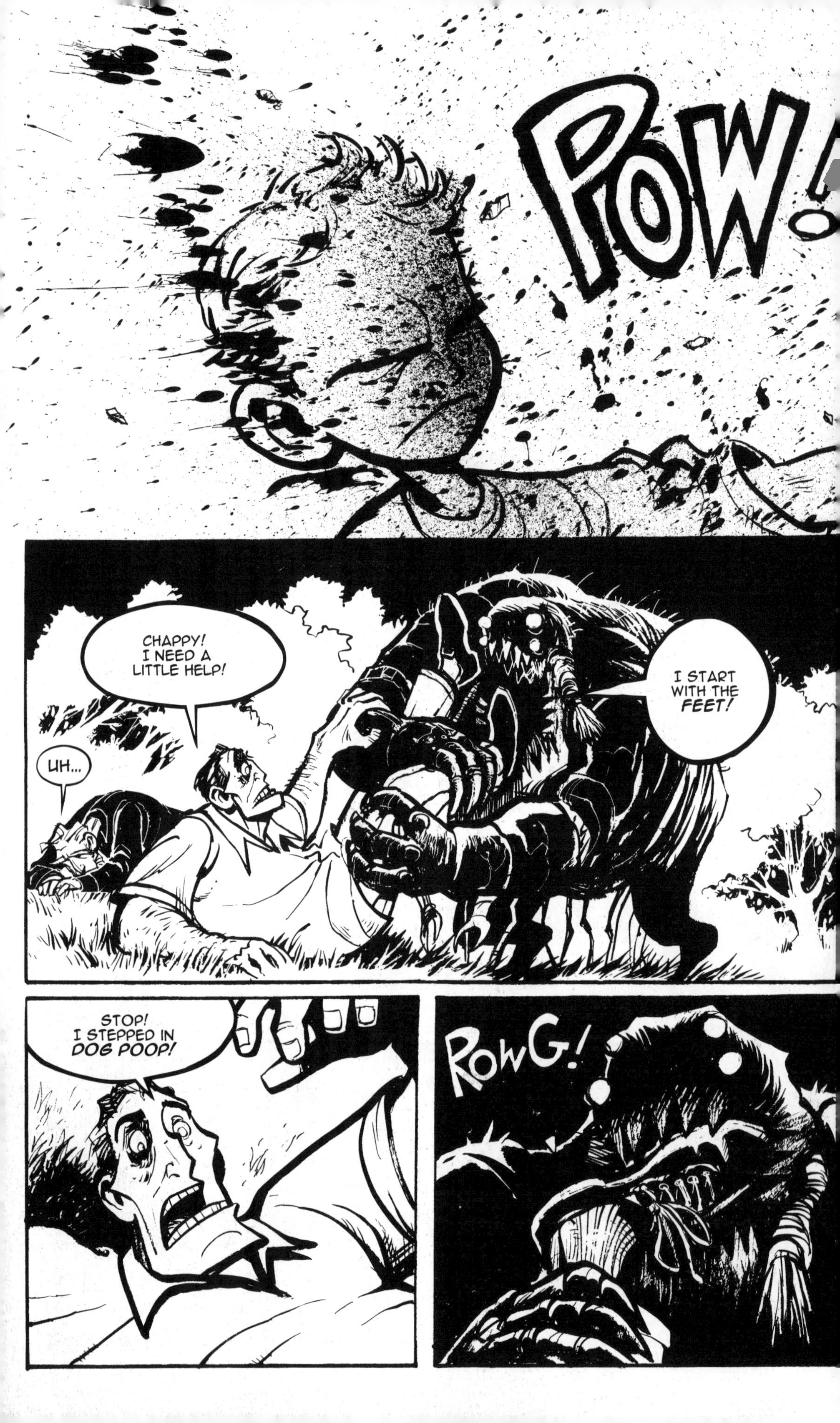
POW!
CHAPPY! I NEED A LITTLE HELP!
UH...
I START WITH THE FEET!
STOP! I STEPPED IN DOG POOP!
ROWG!

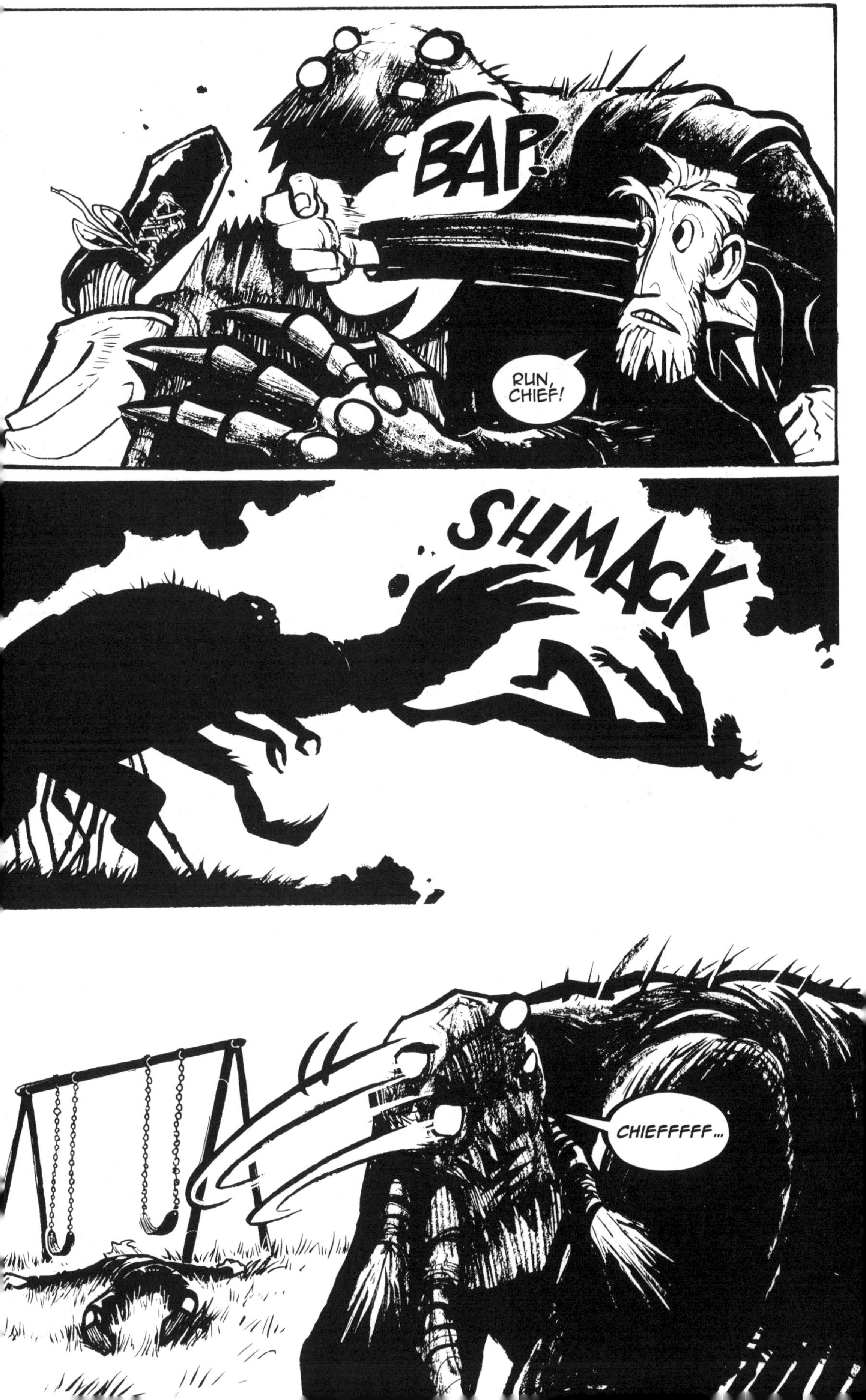
BAP!
RUN, CHIEF!
SHMACK
CHIEFFFFF...

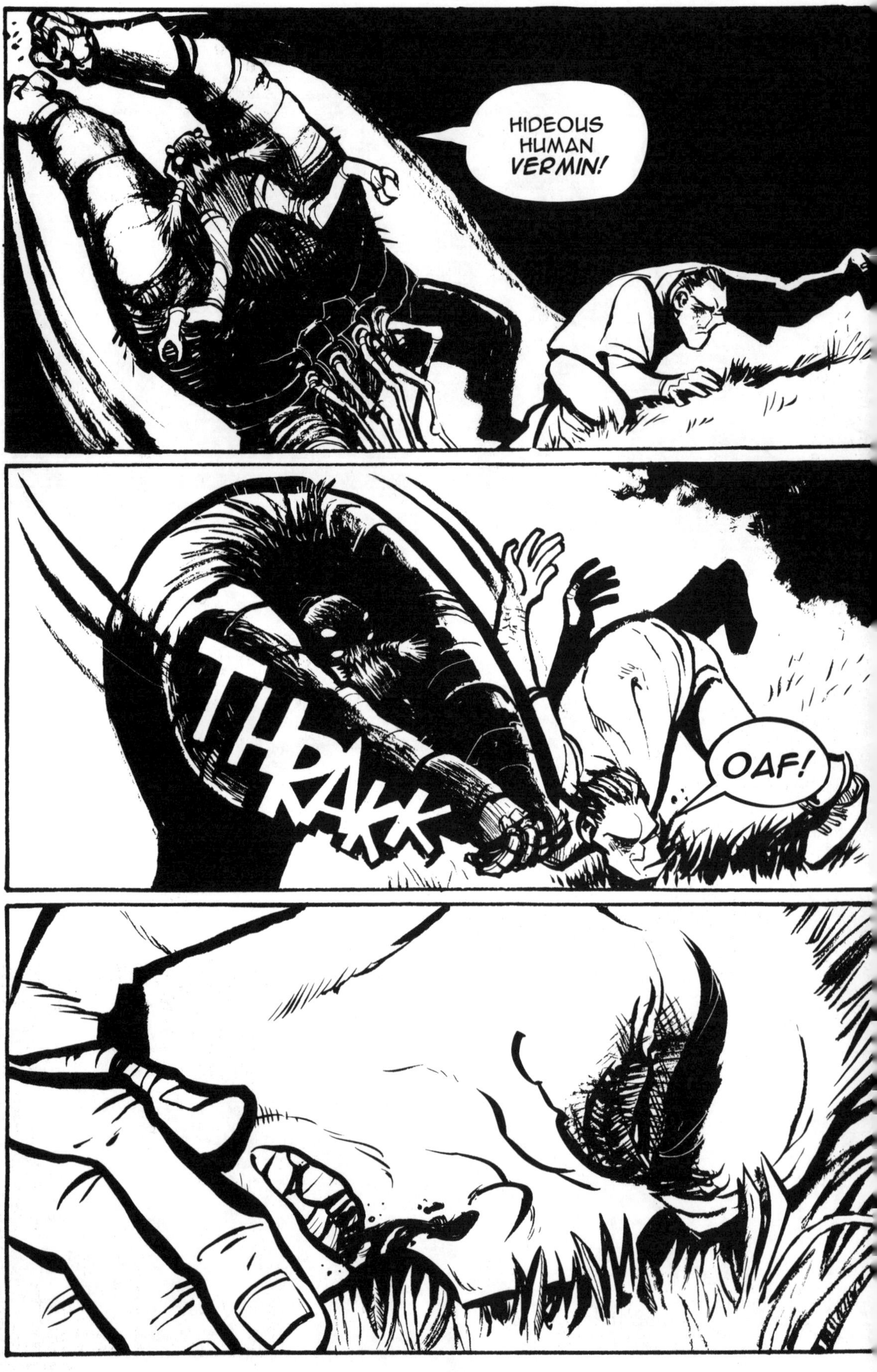
HIDEOUS HUMAN VERMIN!
THRAKK
OAF!

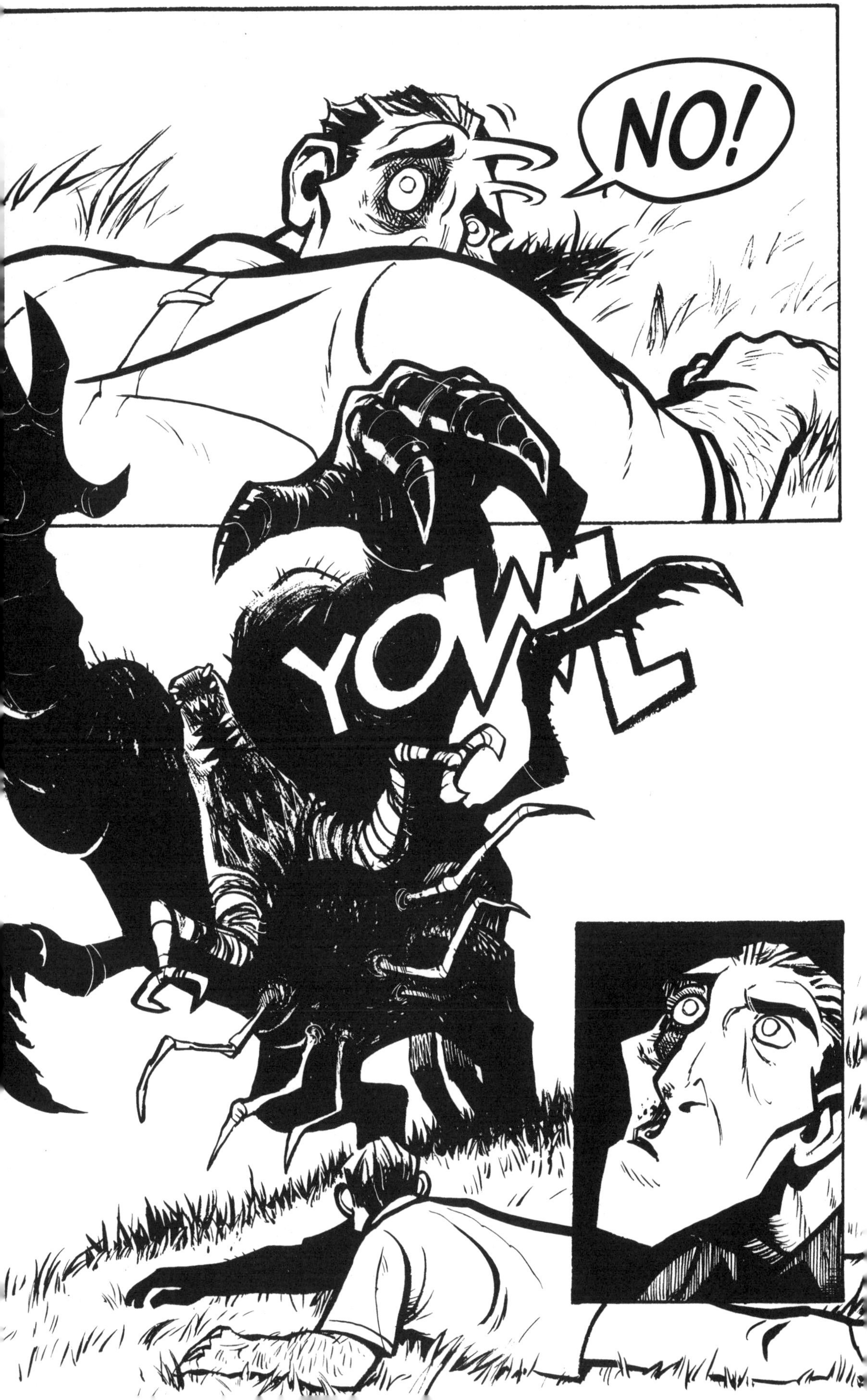
NO!
YOWL

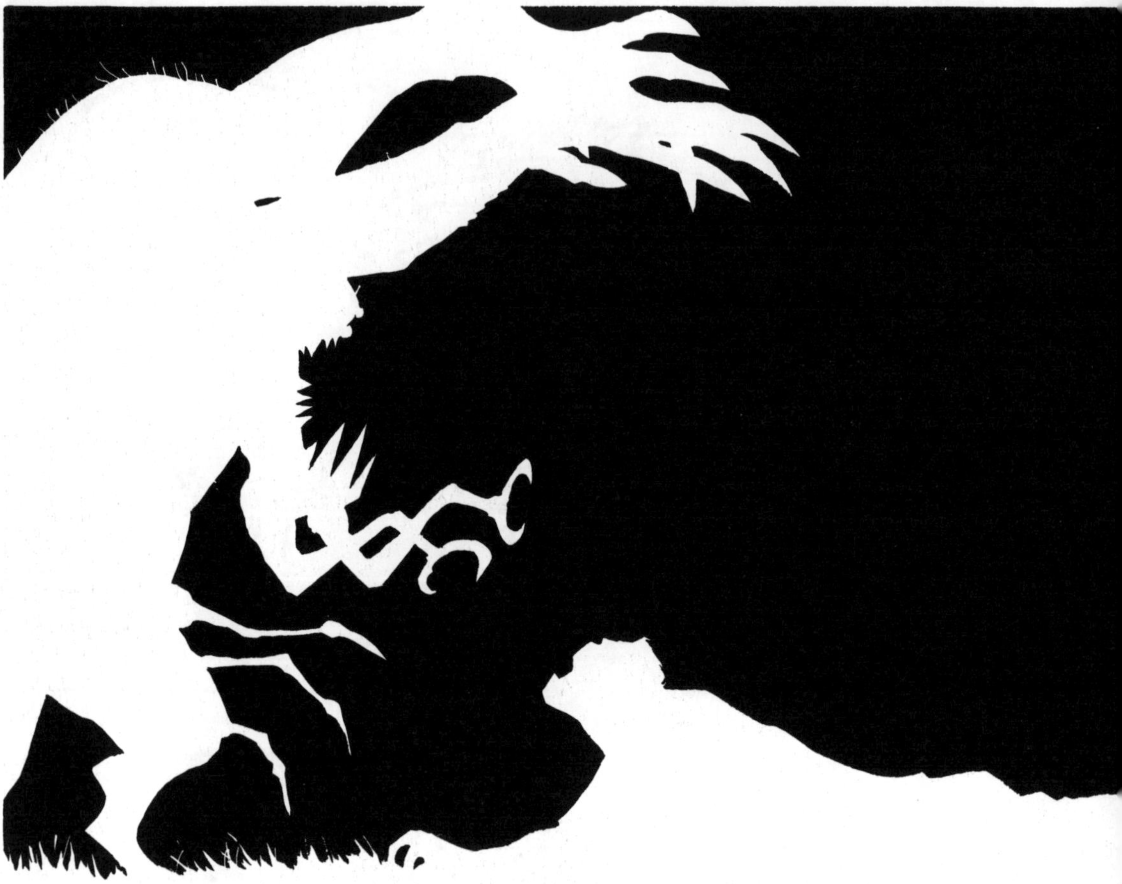

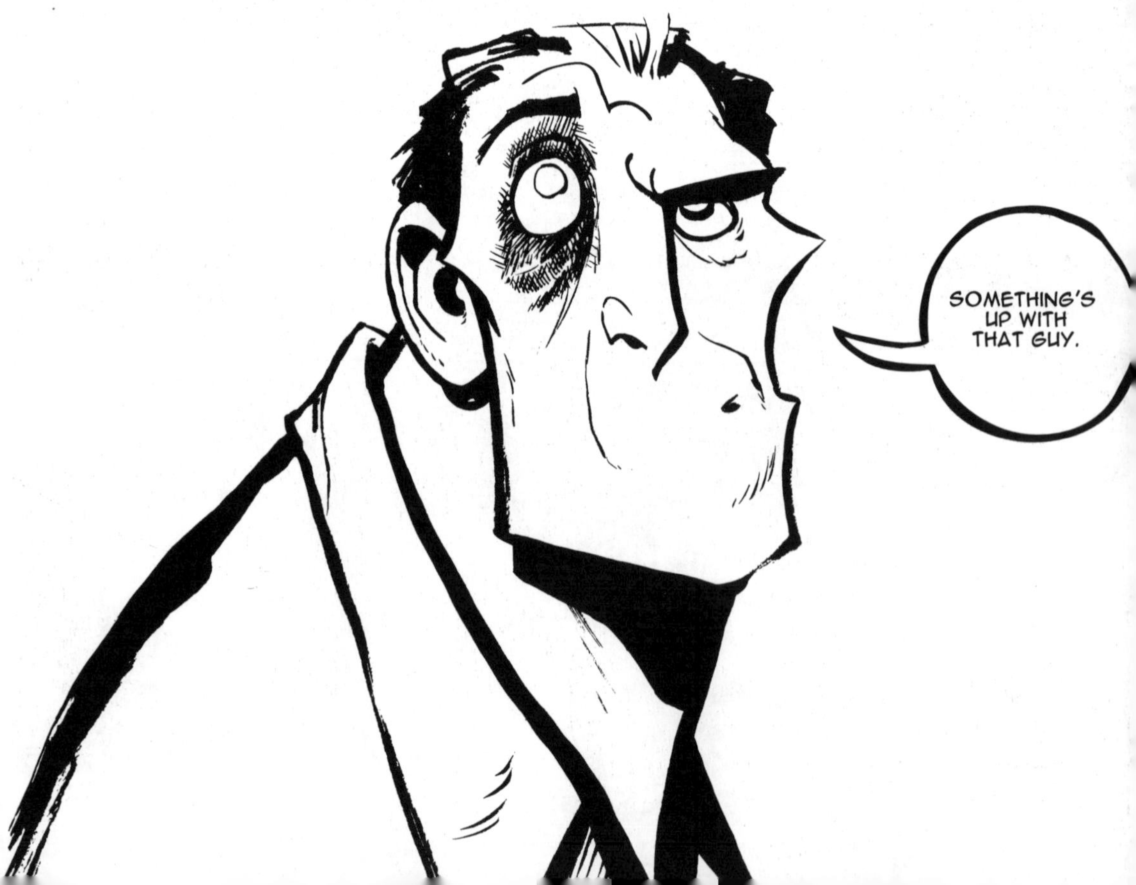

SOMETHING'S UP WITH THAT GUY.

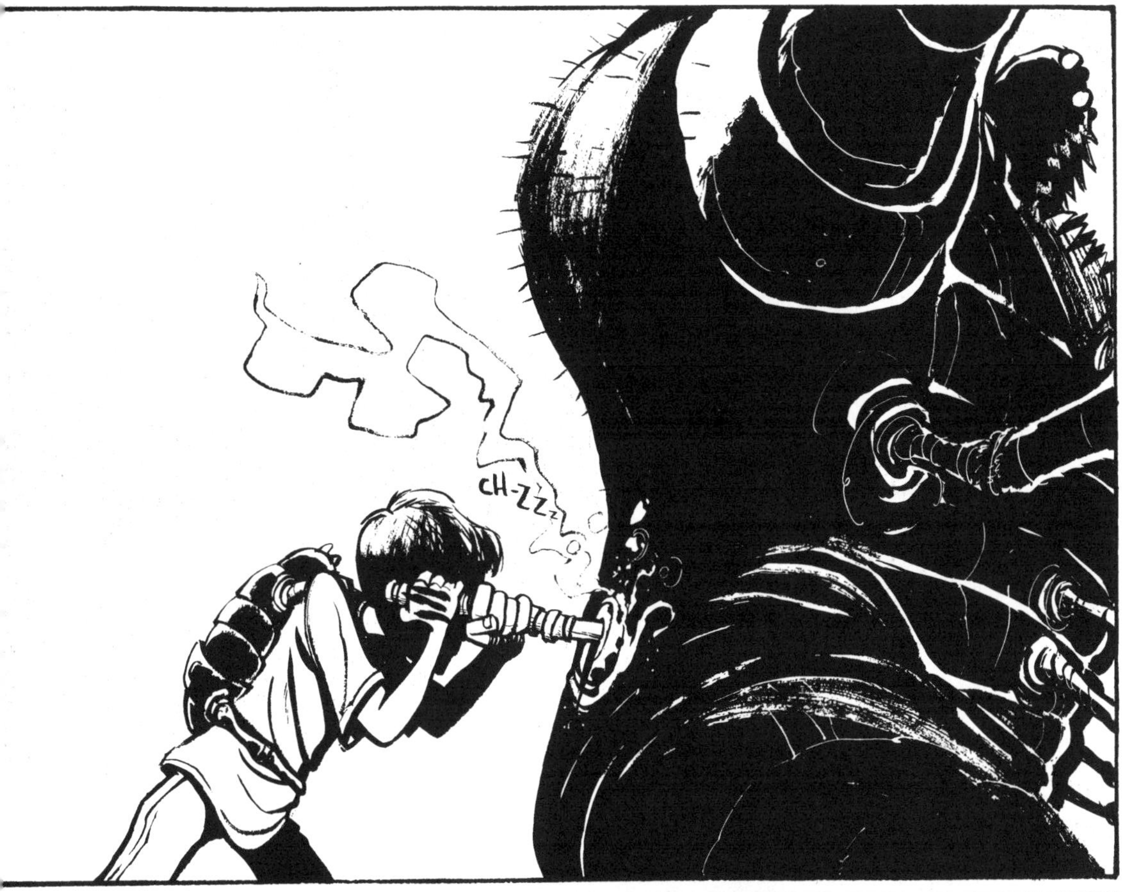
CH-ZZZZ

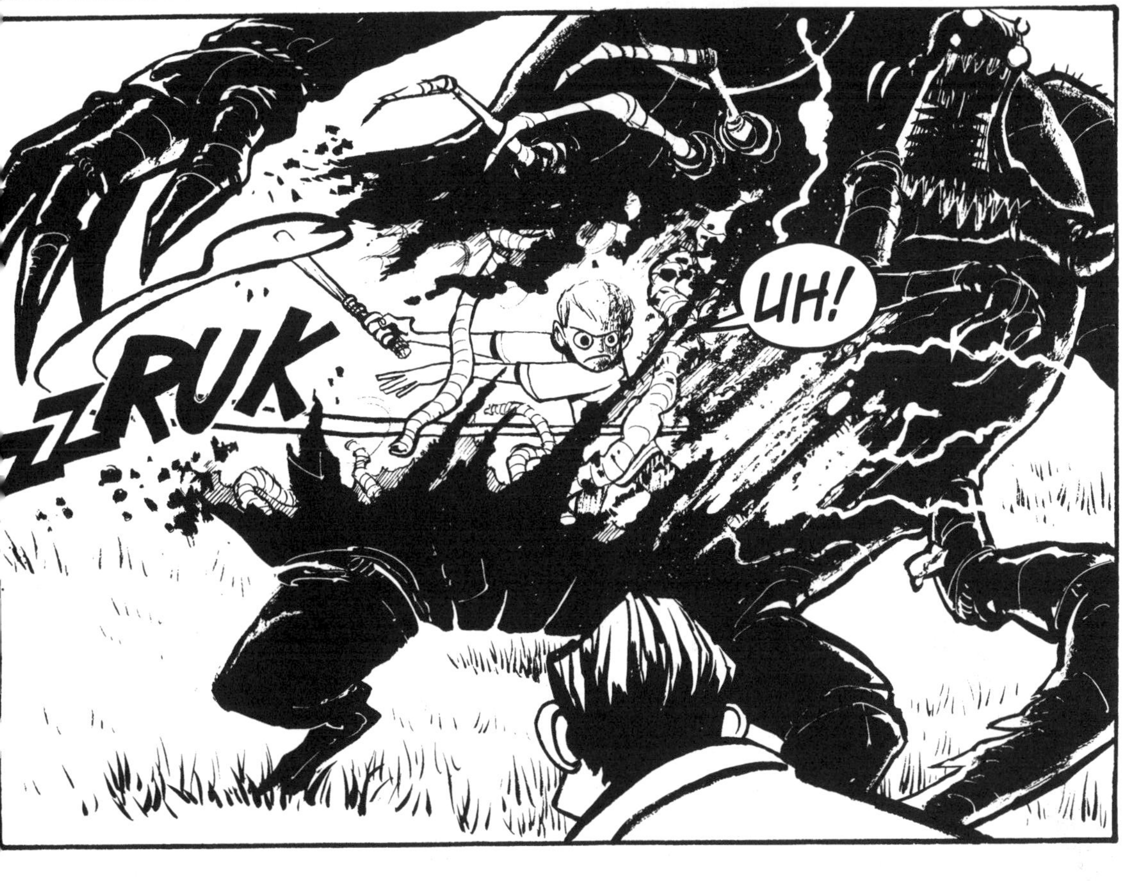
ZZRUK
UH!

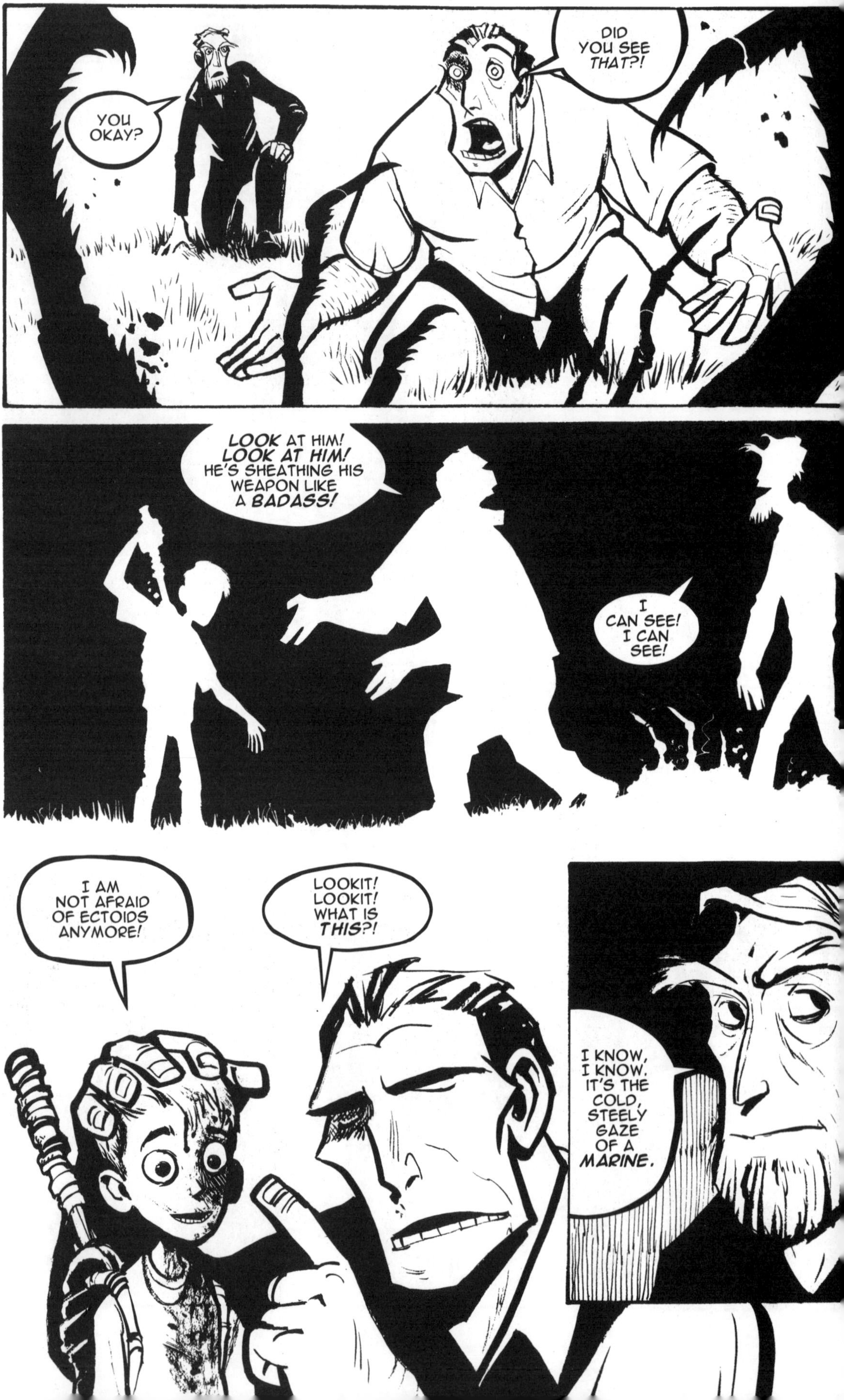
DID YOU SEE THAT?!
YOU OKAY?
LOOK AT HIM! LOOK AT HIM! HE'S SHEATHING HIS WEAPON LIKE A BADASS!
I CAN SEE! I CAN SEE!
I AM NOT AFRAID OF ECTOIDS ANYMORE!
LOOKIT! LOOKIT! WHAT IS THIS?!
I KNOW, I KNOW. IT'S THE COLD, STEELY GAZE OF A MARINE.

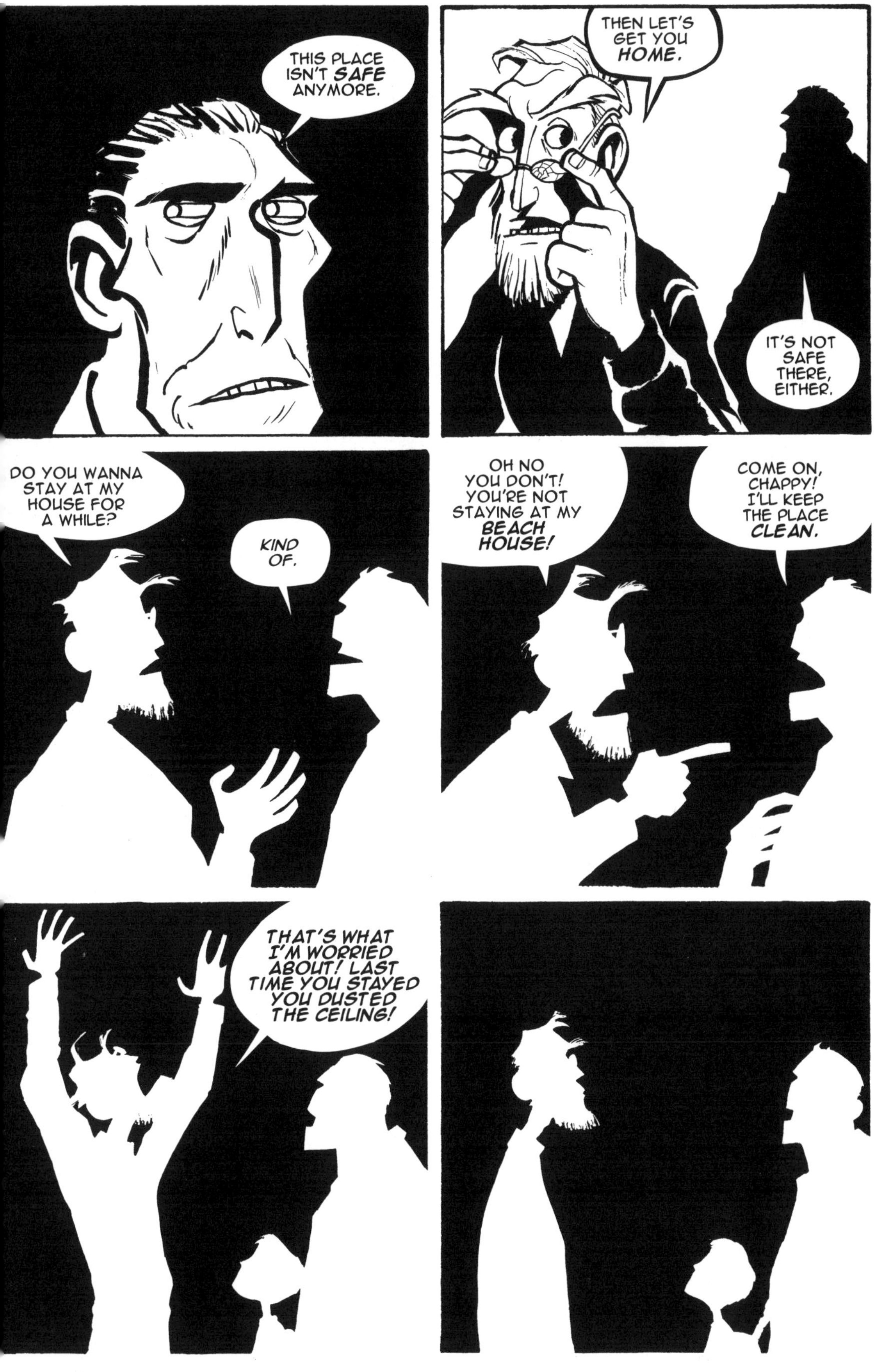
THIS PLACE ISN'T SAFE ANYMORE.
THEN LET'S GET YOU HOME.
IT'S NOT SAFE THERE, EITHER.
DO YOU WANNA STAY AT MY HOUSE FOR A WHILE?
KIND OF.
OH NO YOU DON'T! YOU'RE NOT STAYING AT MY BEACH HOUSE!
COME ON, CHAPPY! I'LL KEEP THE PLACE CLEAN.
THAT'S WHAT I'M WORRIED ABOUT! LAST TIME YOU STAYED YOU DUSTED THE CEILING!

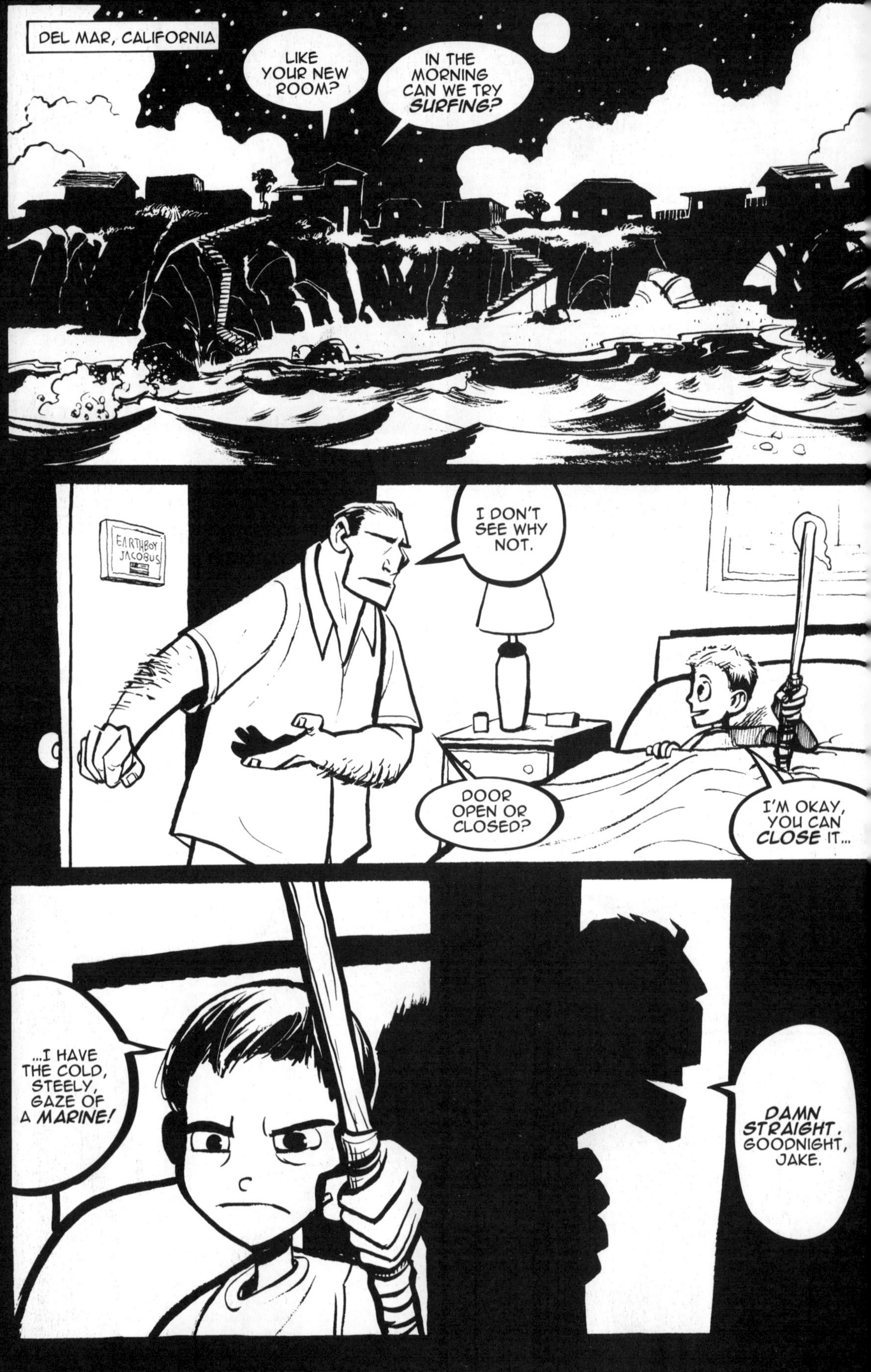
DEL MAR, CALIFORNIA
LIKE YOUR NEW ROOM?
IN THE MORNING CAN WE TRY *SURFING?*
EARTHBOY JACOBUS
I DON'T SEE WHY NOT.
DOOR OPEN OR CLOSED?
I'M OKAY, YOU CAN *CLOSE* IT...
...I HAVE THE COLD, STEELY, GAZE OF A *MARINE!*
DAMN STRAIGHT. GOODNIGHT, JAKE.

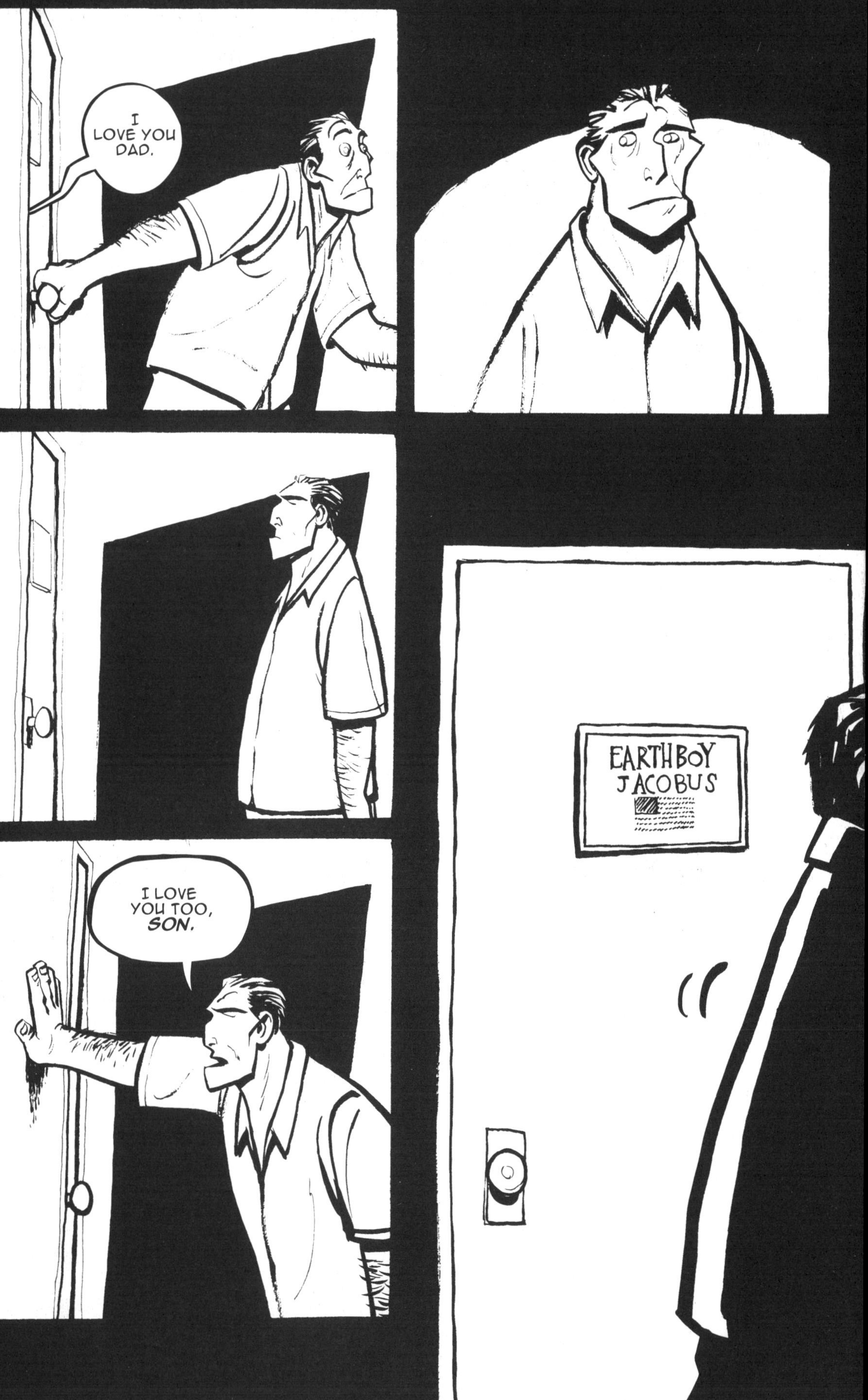
I LOVE YOU DAD.
I LOVE YOU TOO, SON.
EARTHBOY JACOBUS

CHAPTER
2

Jonah 2:5

The waters compassed
me about, *even* to the
soul: the depth closed
me round about, the
weeds were wrapped
about my head.

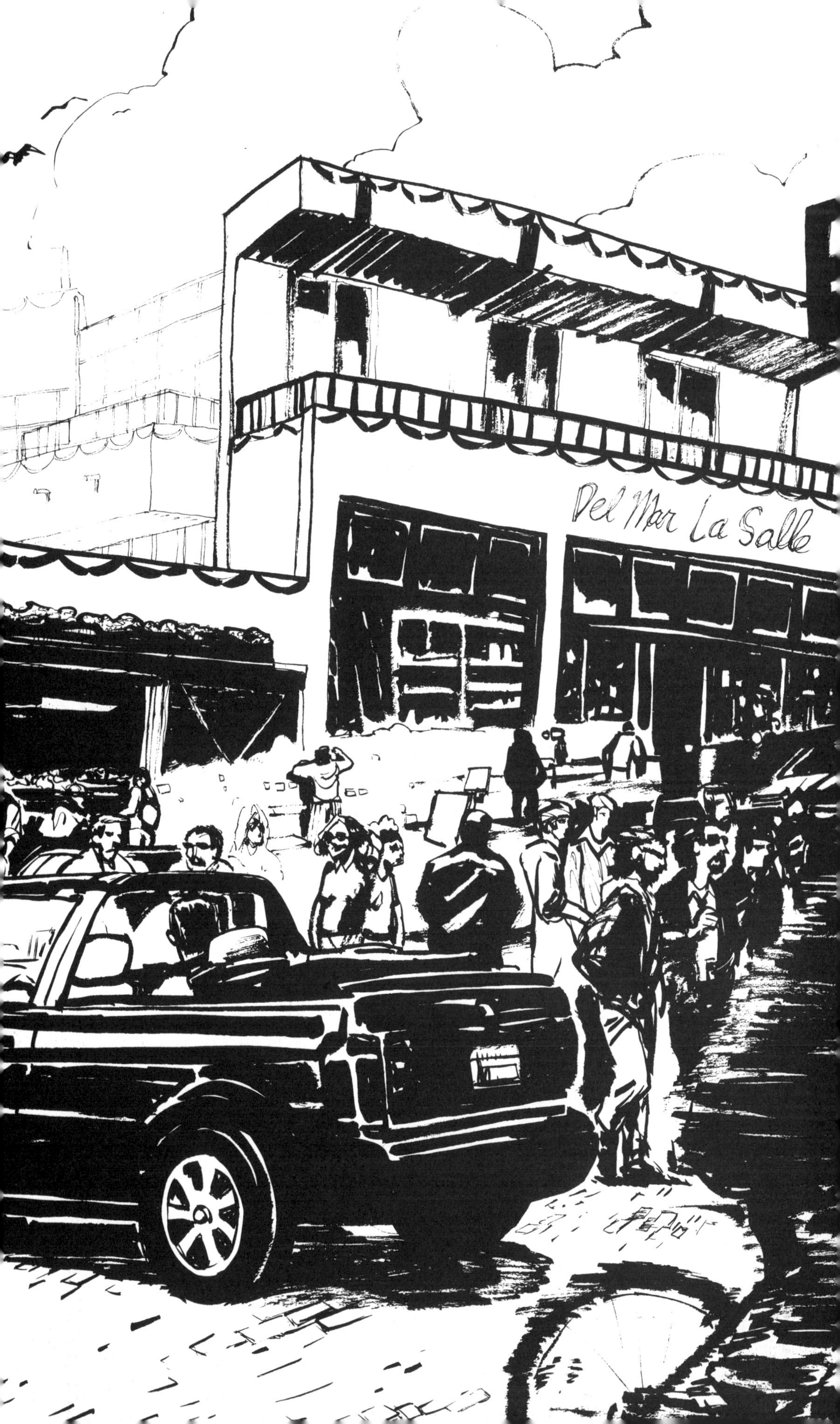
Del Mar La Salle

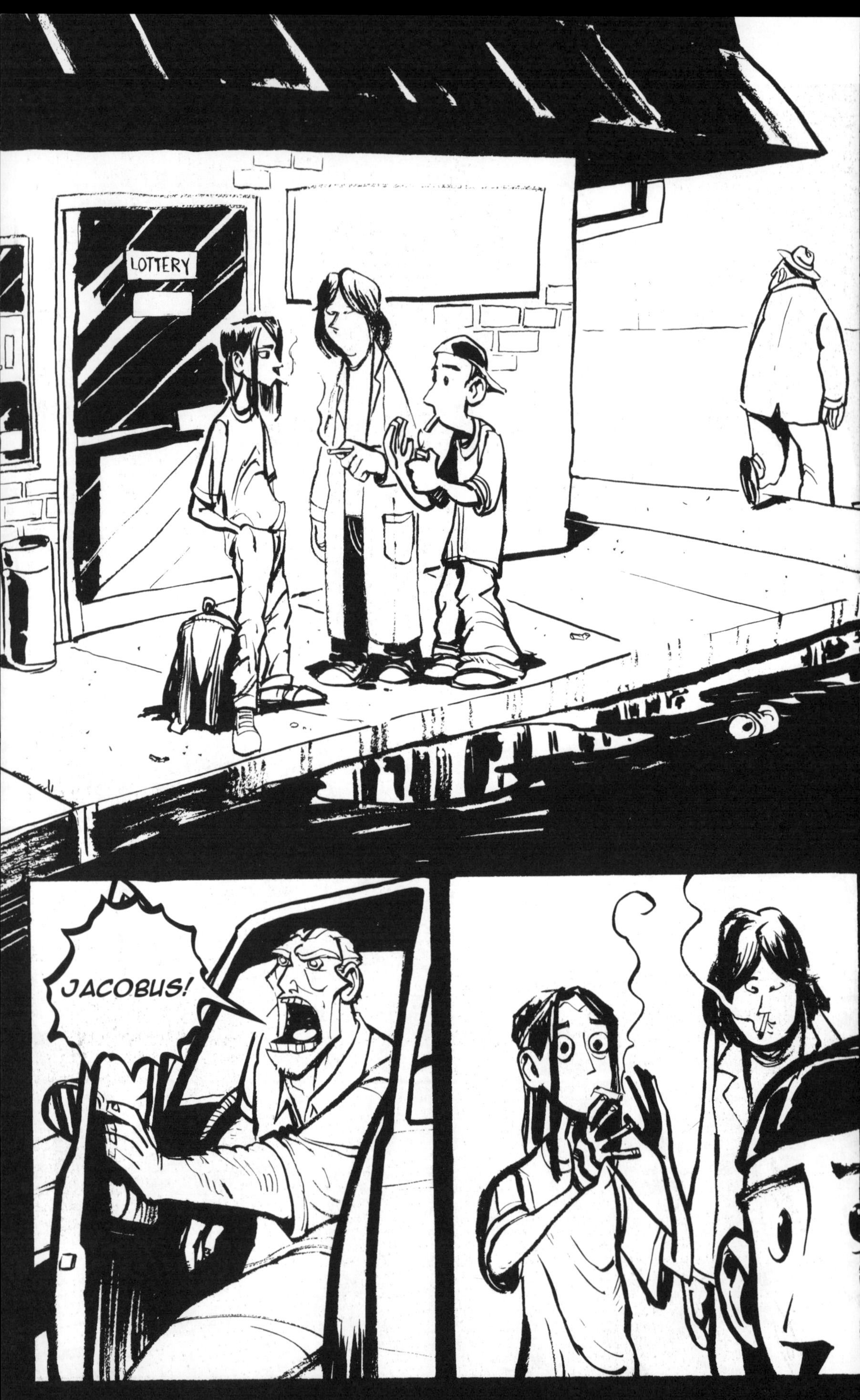
LOTTERY
JACOBUS!

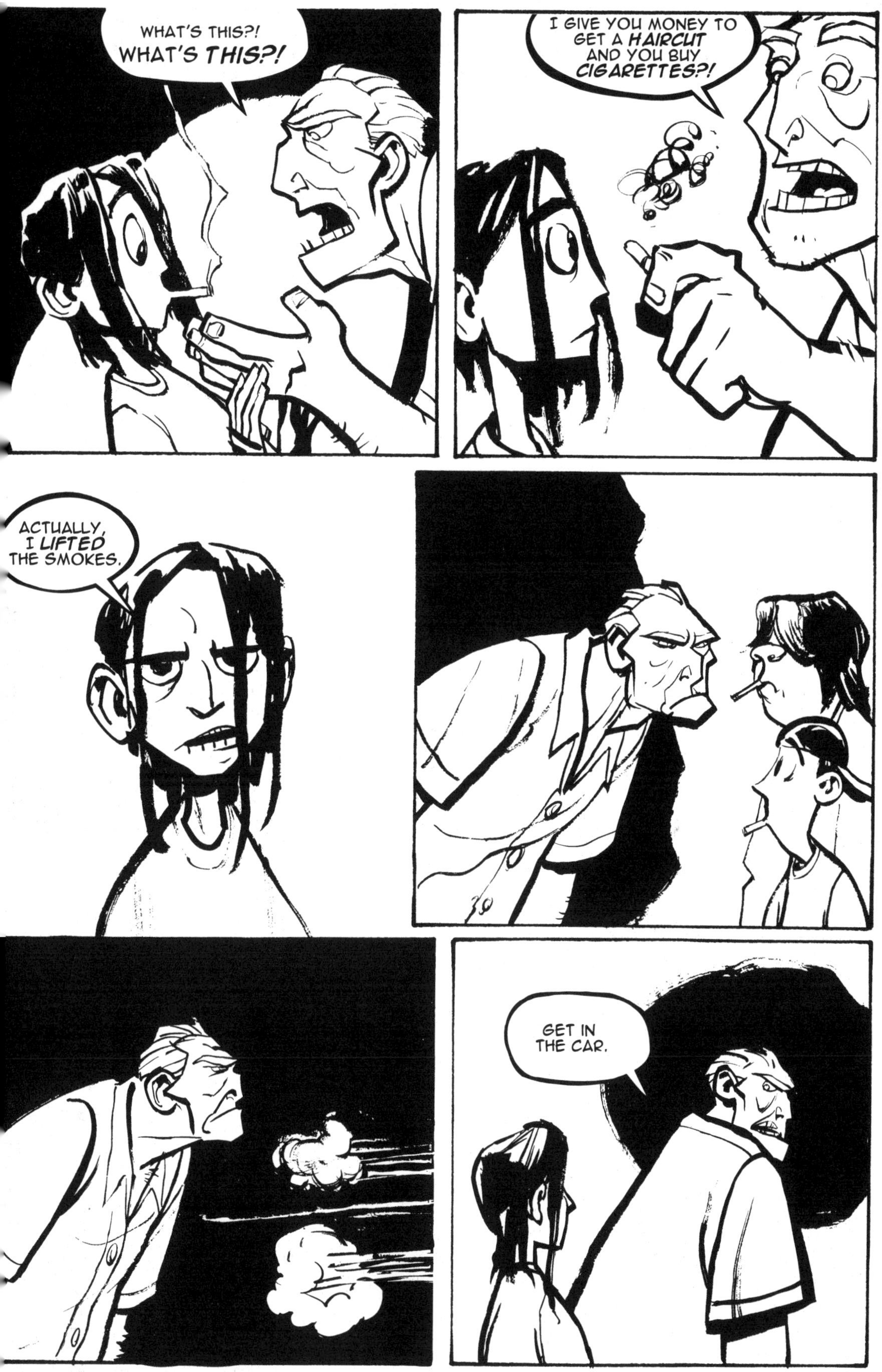
WHAT'S THIS?!
WHAT'S THIS?!
I GIVE YOU MONEY TO GET A HAIRCUT AND YOU BUY CIGARETTES?!
ACTUALLY, I LIFTED THE SMOKES.
GET IN THE CAR.

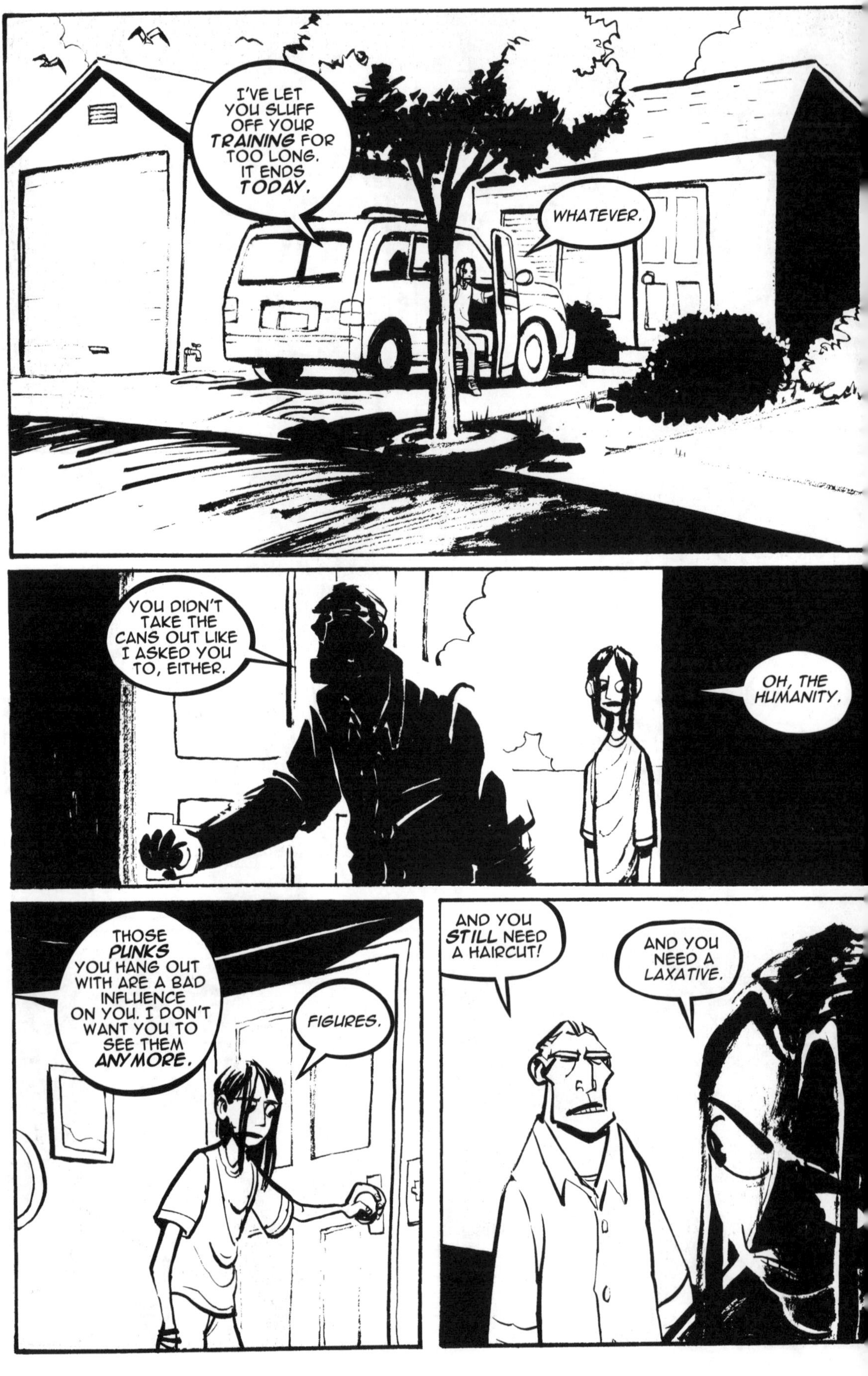
I'VE LET YOU SLUFF OFF YOUR TRAINING FOR TOO LONG. IT ENDS TODAY.
WHATEVER.
YOU DIDN'T TAKE THE CANS OUT LIKE I ASKED YOU TO, EITHER.
OH, THE HUMANITY.
THOSE PUNKS YOU HANG OUT WITH ARE A BAD INFLUENCE ON YOU. I DON'T WANT YOU TO SEE THEM ANYMORE.
FIGURES.
AND YOU STILL NEED A HAIRCUT!
AND YOU NEED A LAXATIVE.

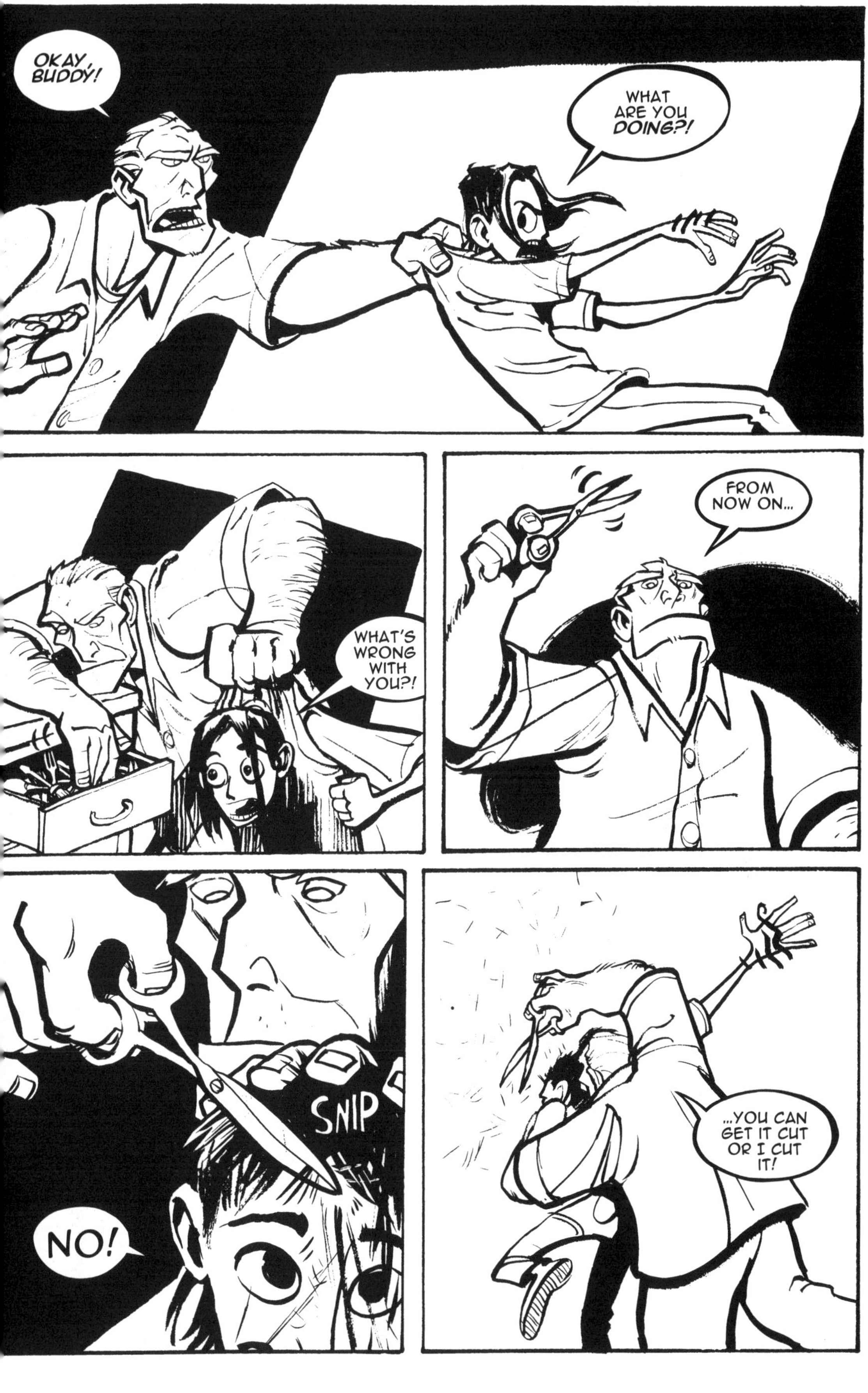
OKAY, BUDDY!
WHAT ARE YOU DOING?!
WHAT'S WRONG WITH YOU?!
FROM NOW ON...
SNIP
NO!
...YOU CAN GET IT CUT OR I CUT IT!

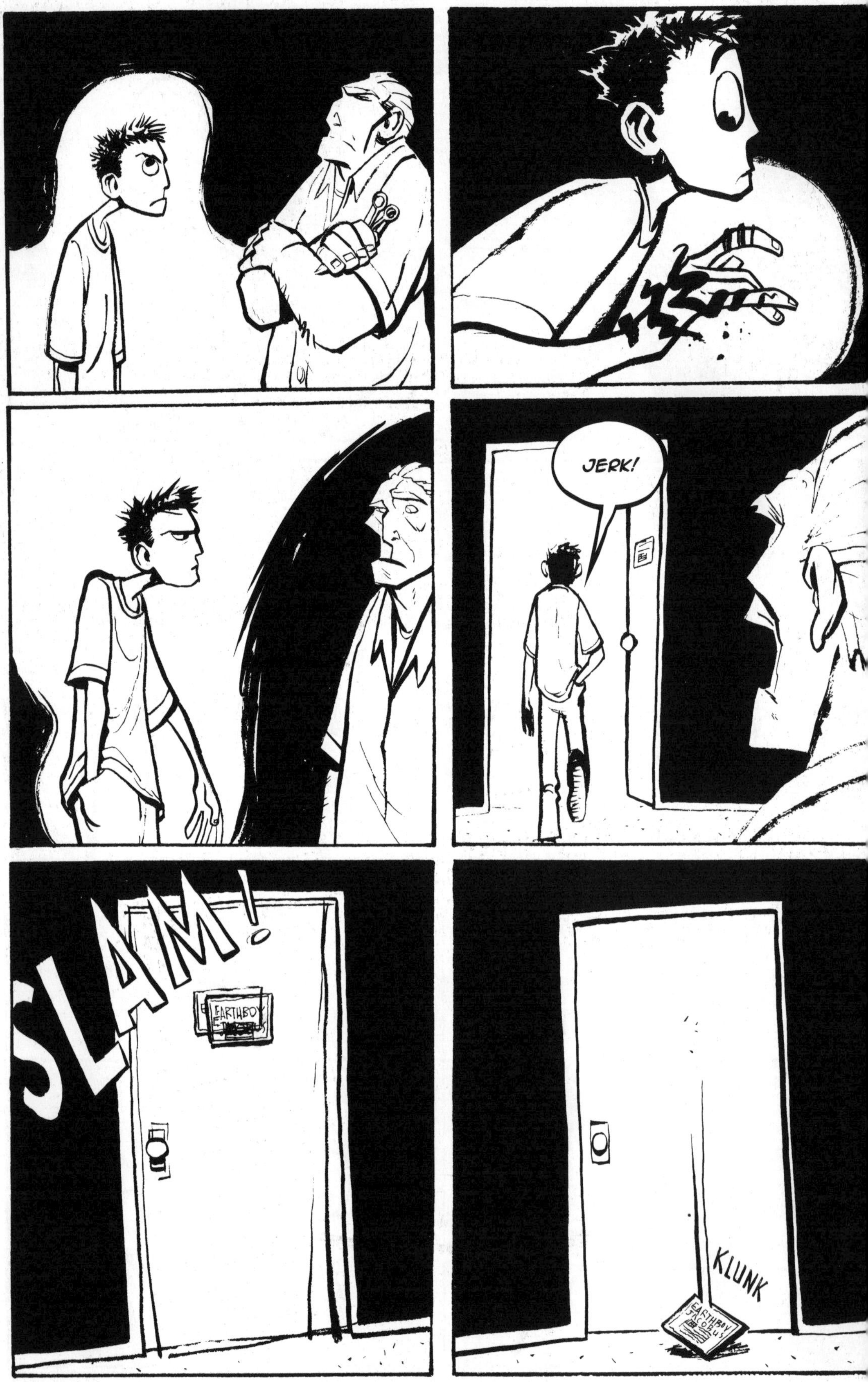
JERK!
SLAM!
EARTHBOY
KLUNK
EARTHBOY JACOBUS

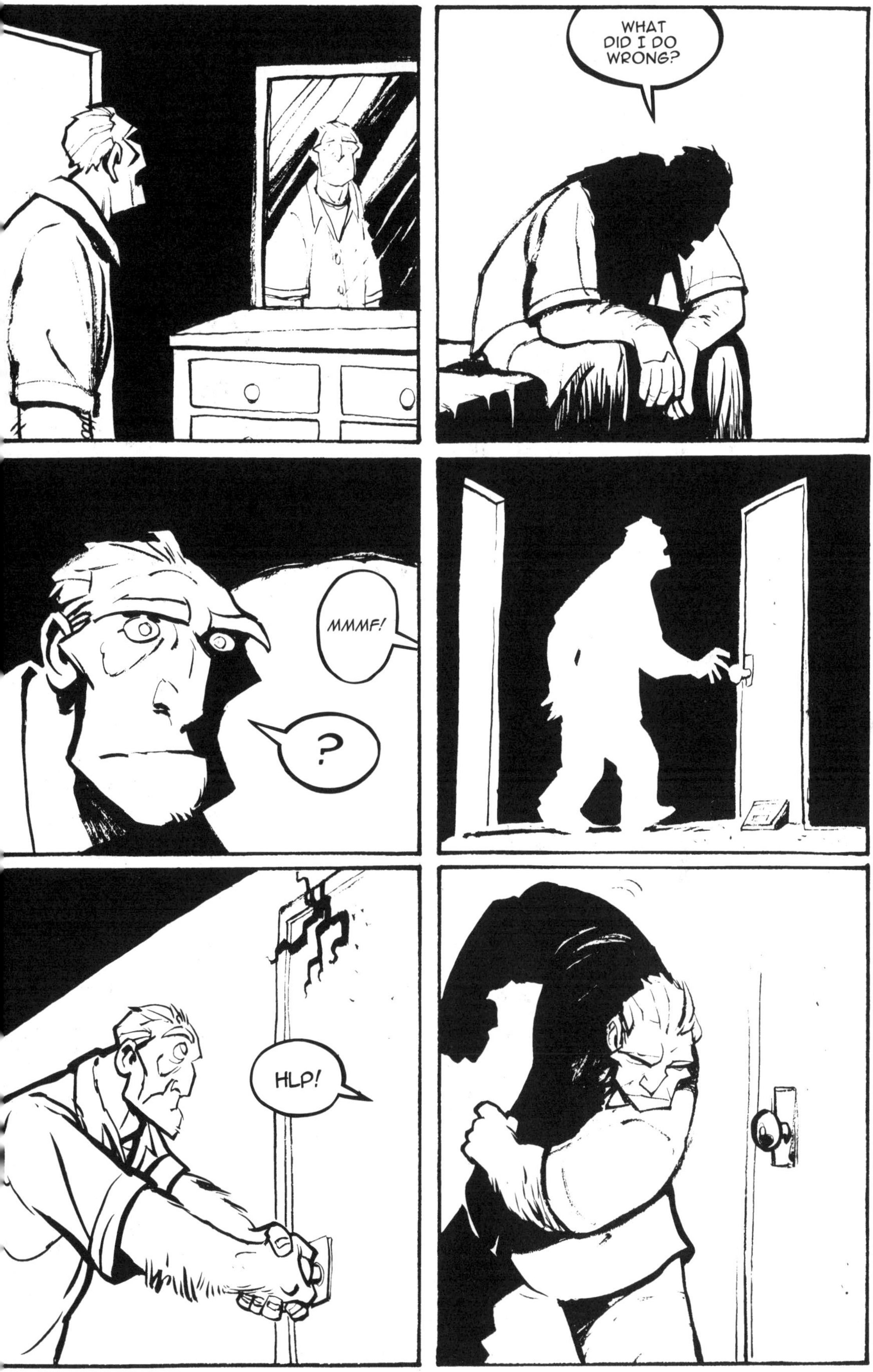
WHAT DID I DO WRONG?
MMMF!
?
HLP!

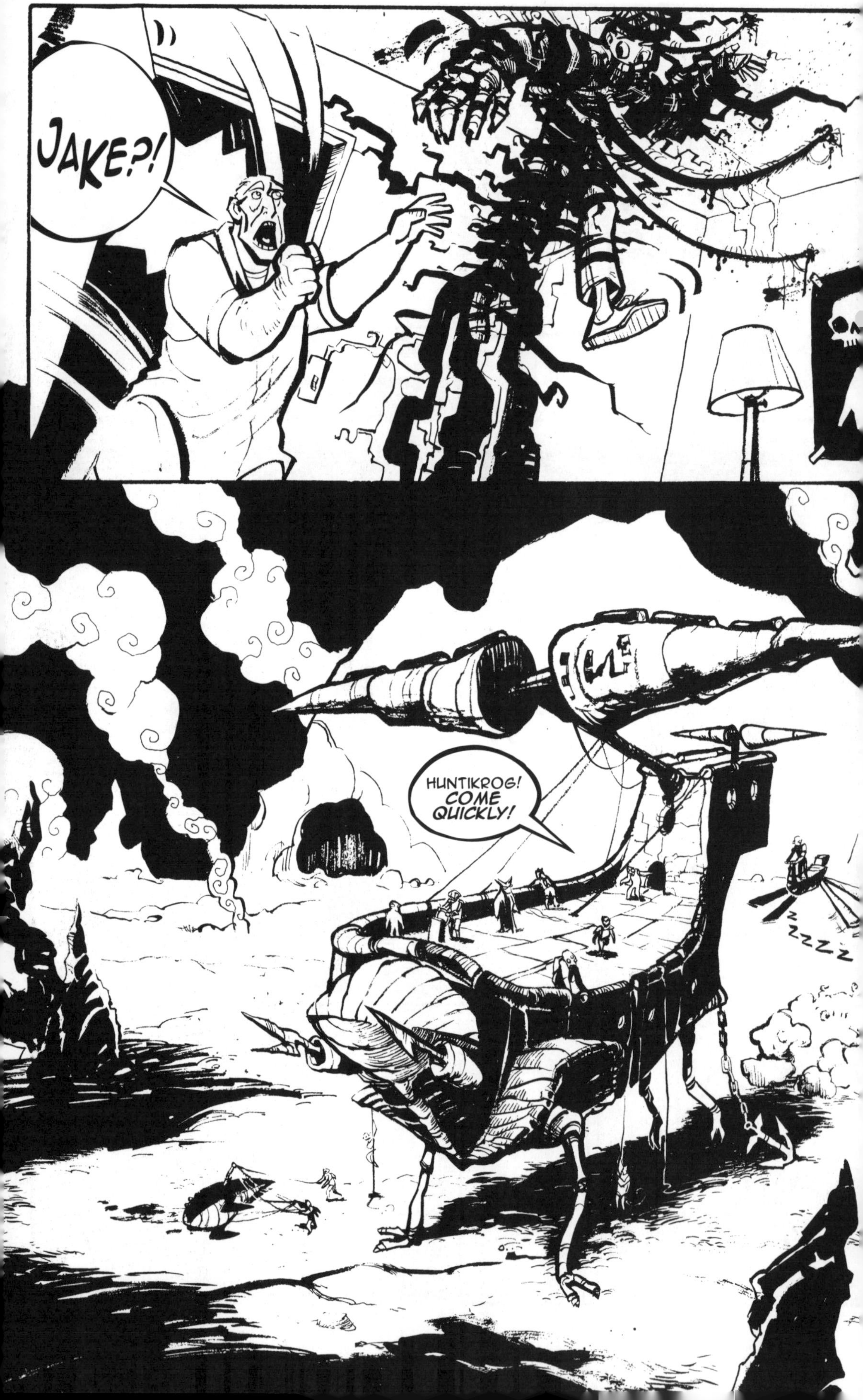
JAKE?!
HUNTIKROG! COME QUICKLY!
ZZZZZ

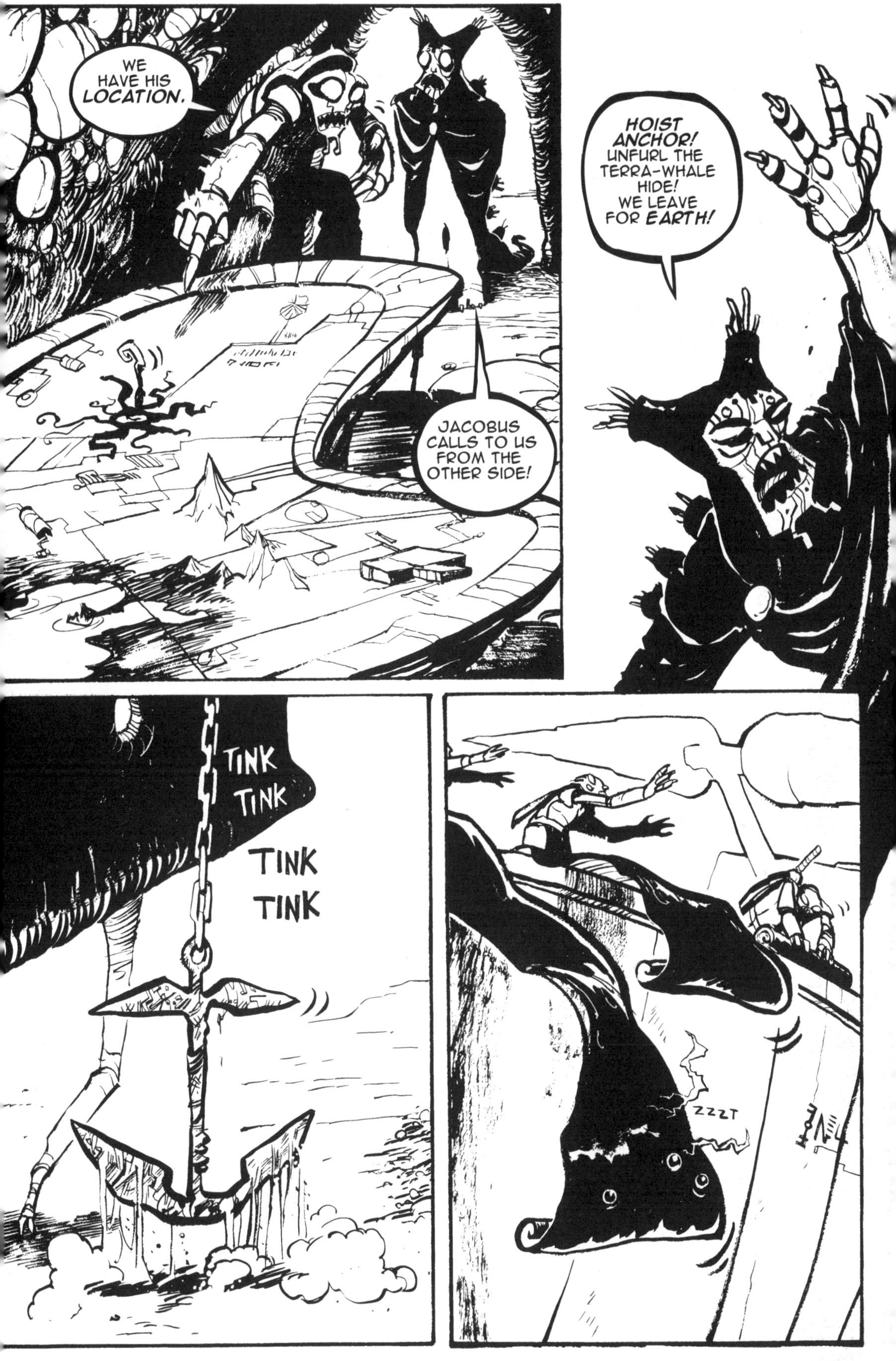
WE HAVE HIS LOCATION.
JACOBUS CALLS TO US FROM THE OTHER SIDE!
HOIST ANCHOR! UNFURL THE TERRA-WHALE HIDE! WE LEAVE FOR EARTH!
TINK TINK
TINK TINK
ZZZT

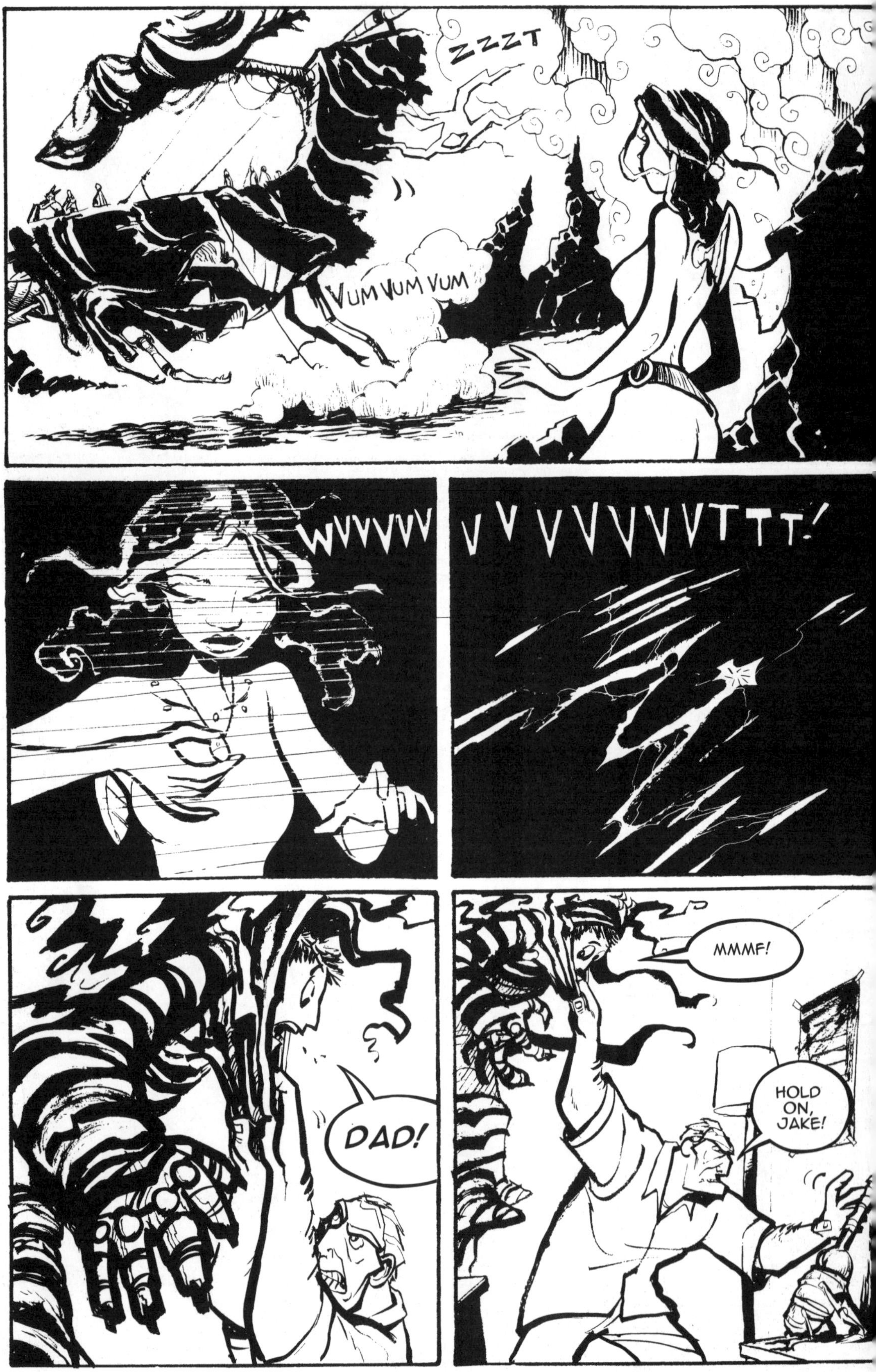
ZZZT
VUM VUM VUM
WVVVVV
V V VVVVVVTTT!
DAD!
MMMF!
HOLD ON, JAKE!

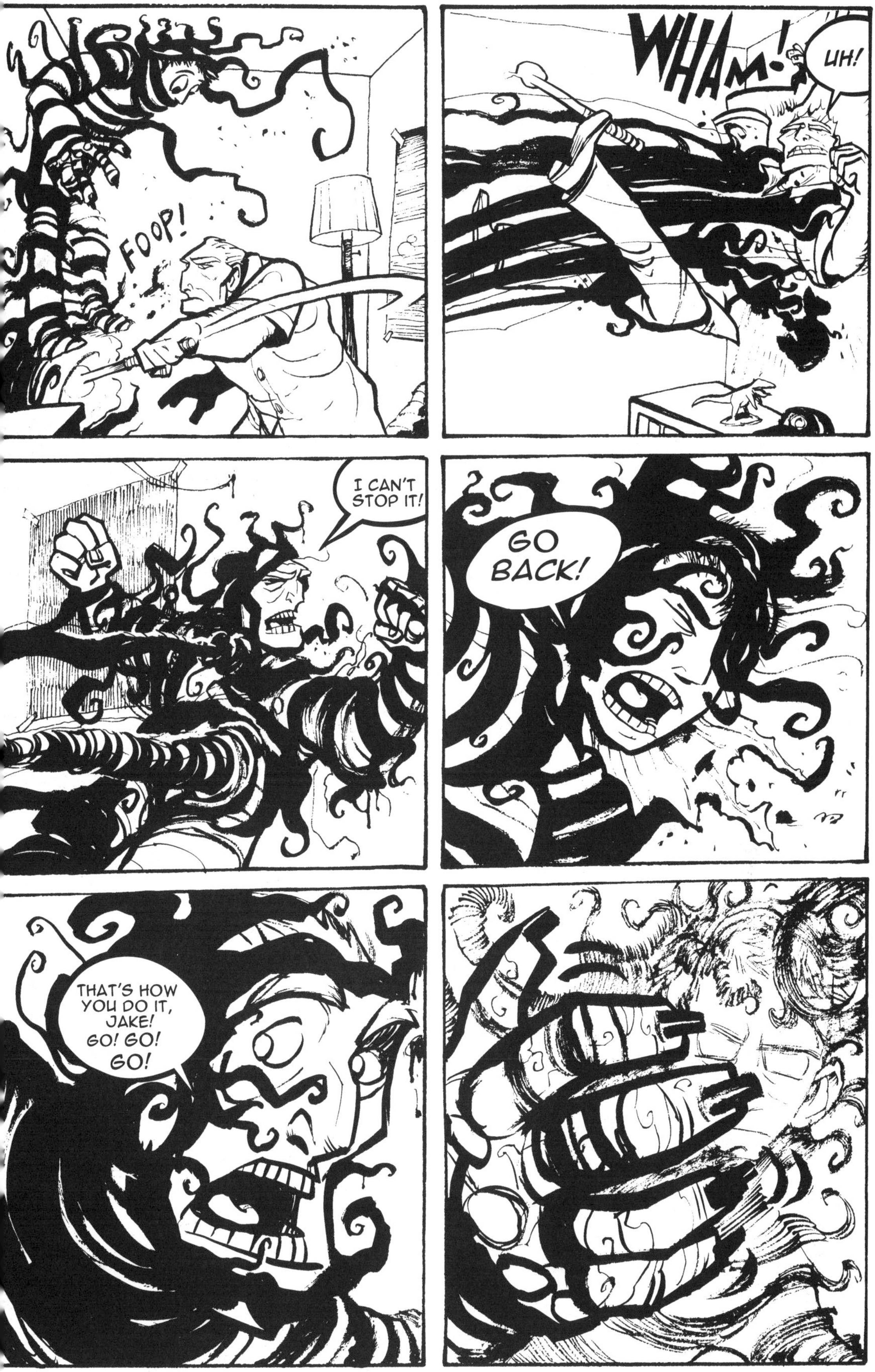
FOOP!
WHAM!
UH!
I CAN'T STOP IT!
GO BACK!
THAT'S HOW YOU DO IT, JAKE! GO! GO! GO!

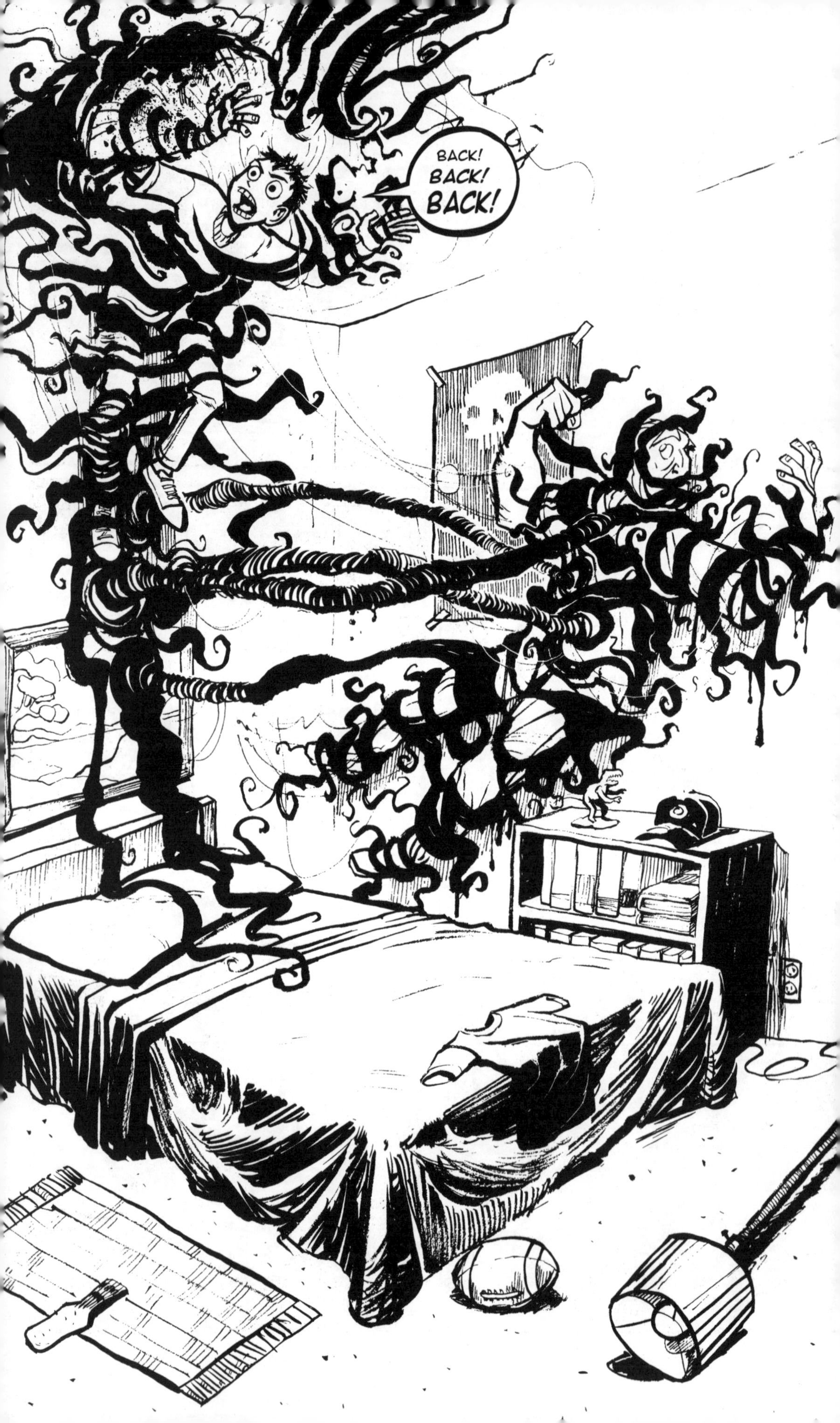
BACK! BACK! BACK!

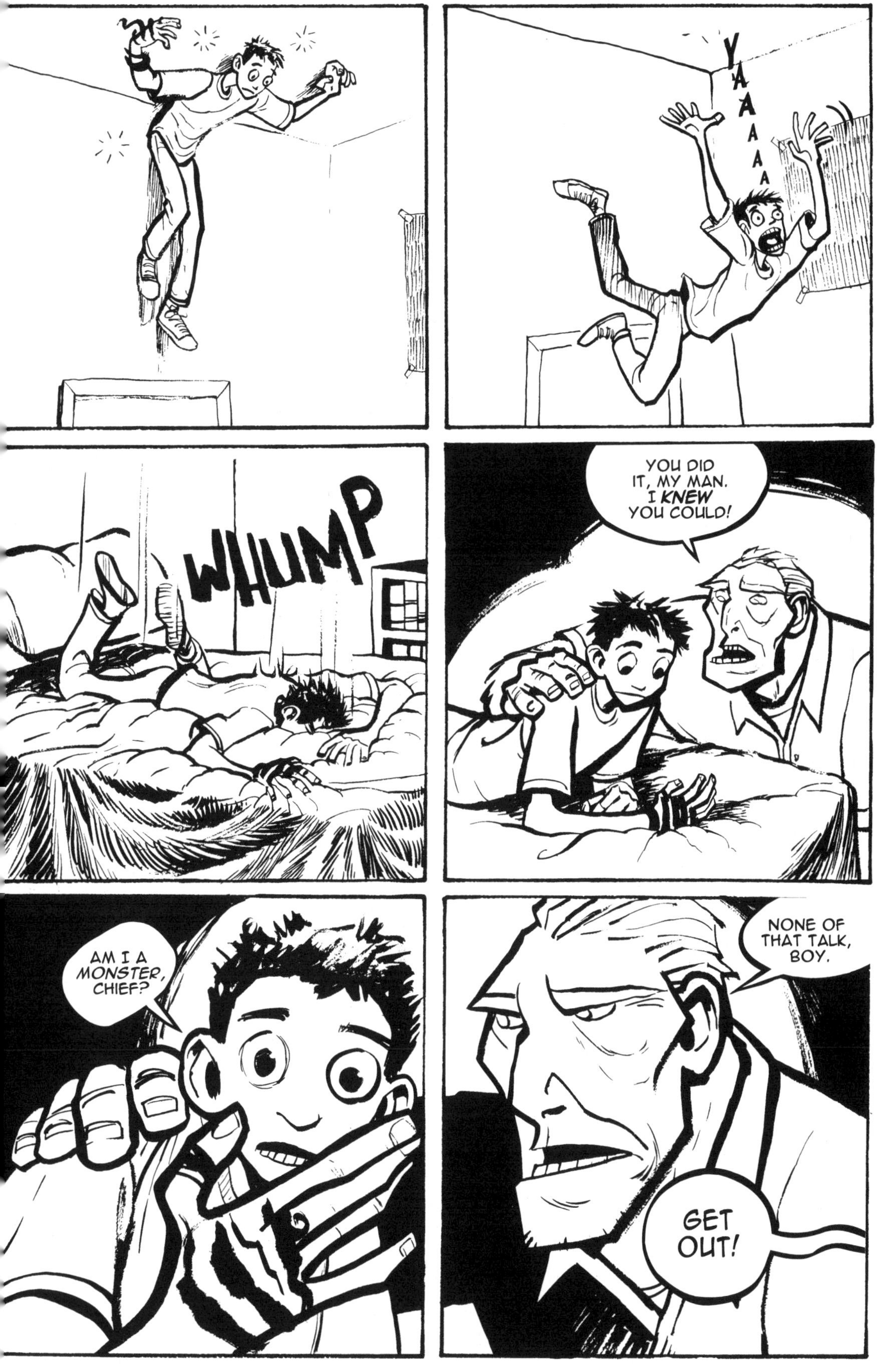
YAAAAAA
WHUMP
YOU DID IT, MY MAN. I *KNEW* YOU COULD!
AM I A MONSTER, CHIEF?
NONE OF THAT TALK, BOY.
GET OUT!

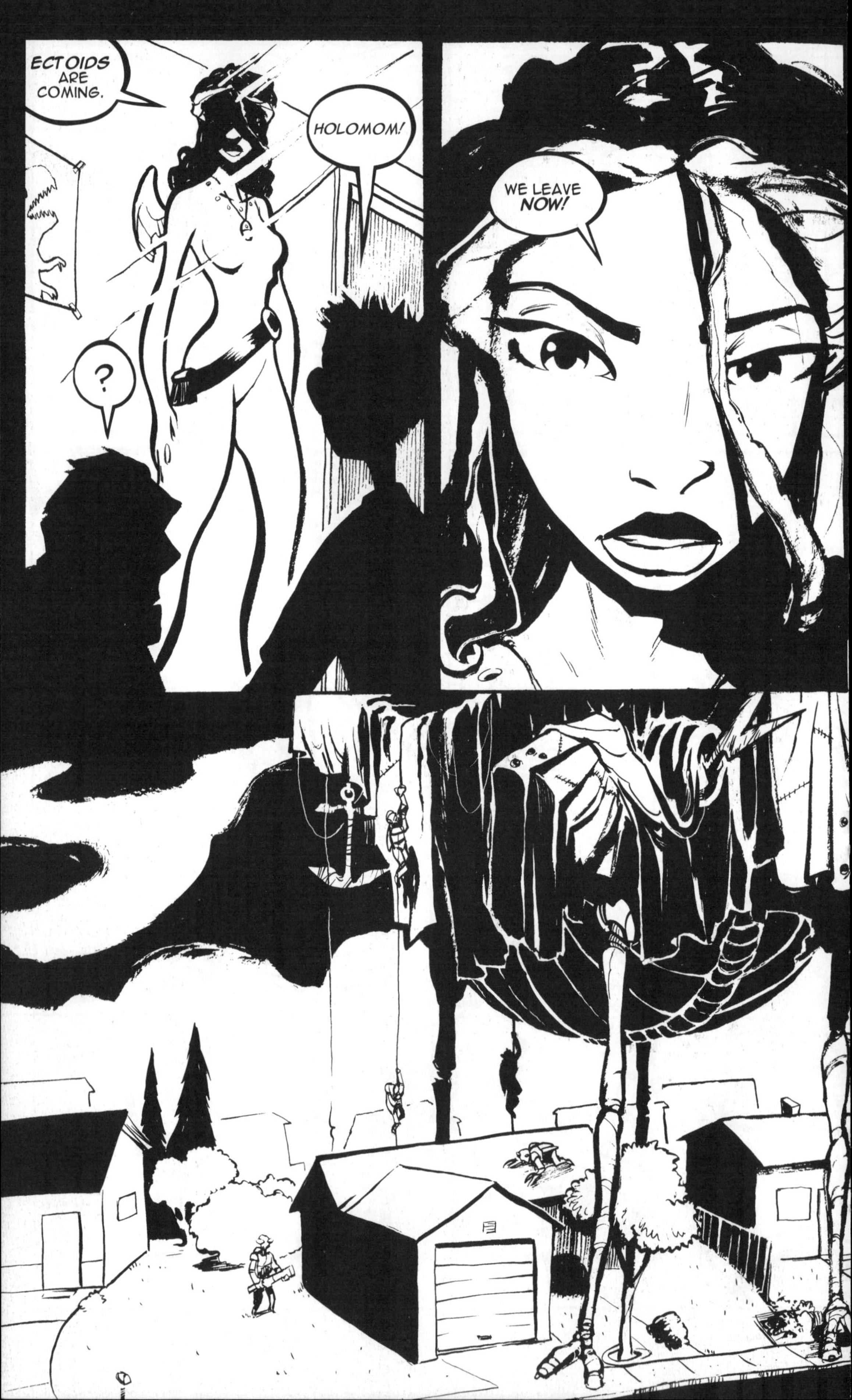
ECTOIDS ARE COMING.
HOLOMOM!
?
WE LEAVE NOW!

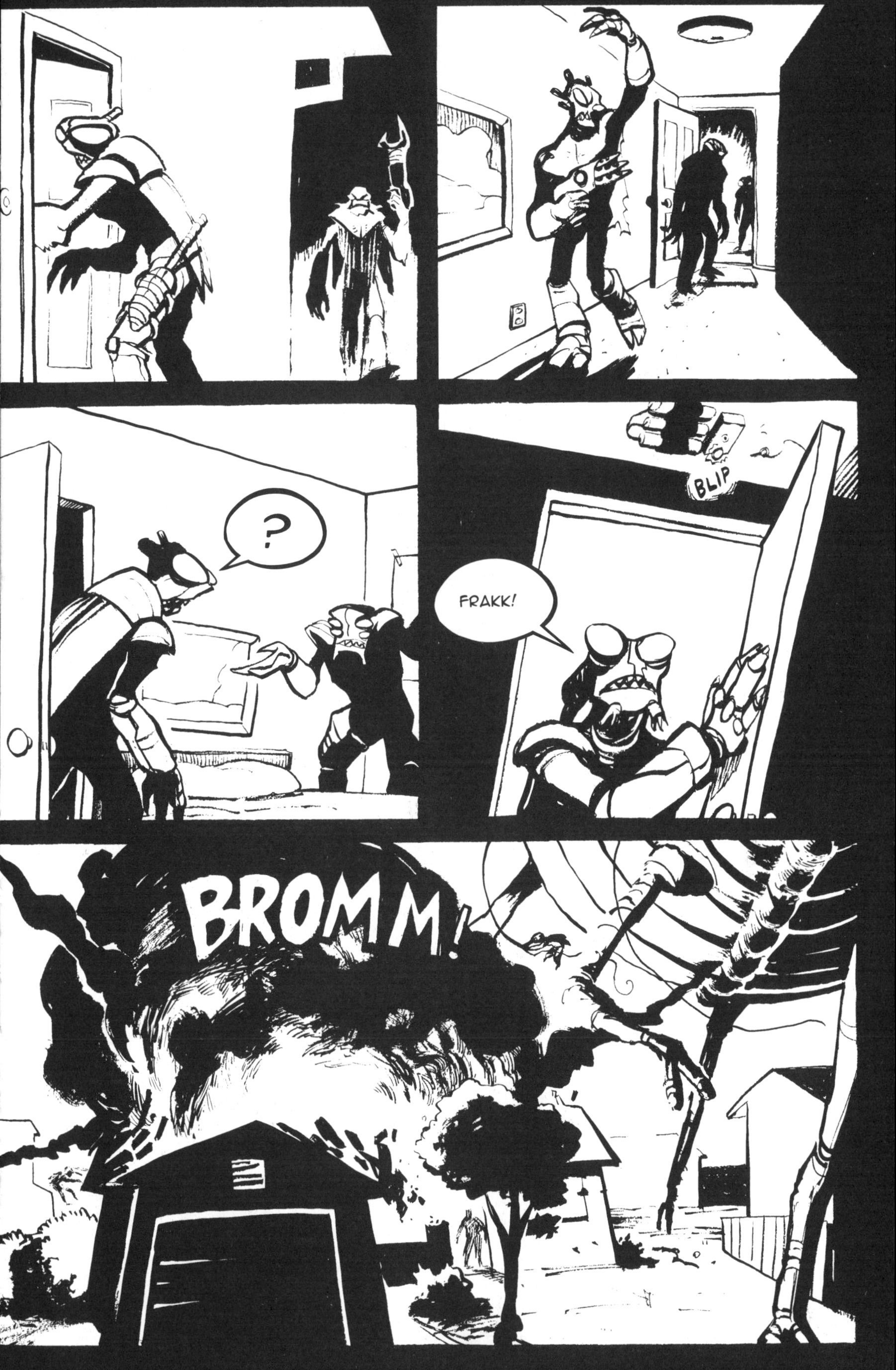
?
FRAKK!
BLIP
BROMM!

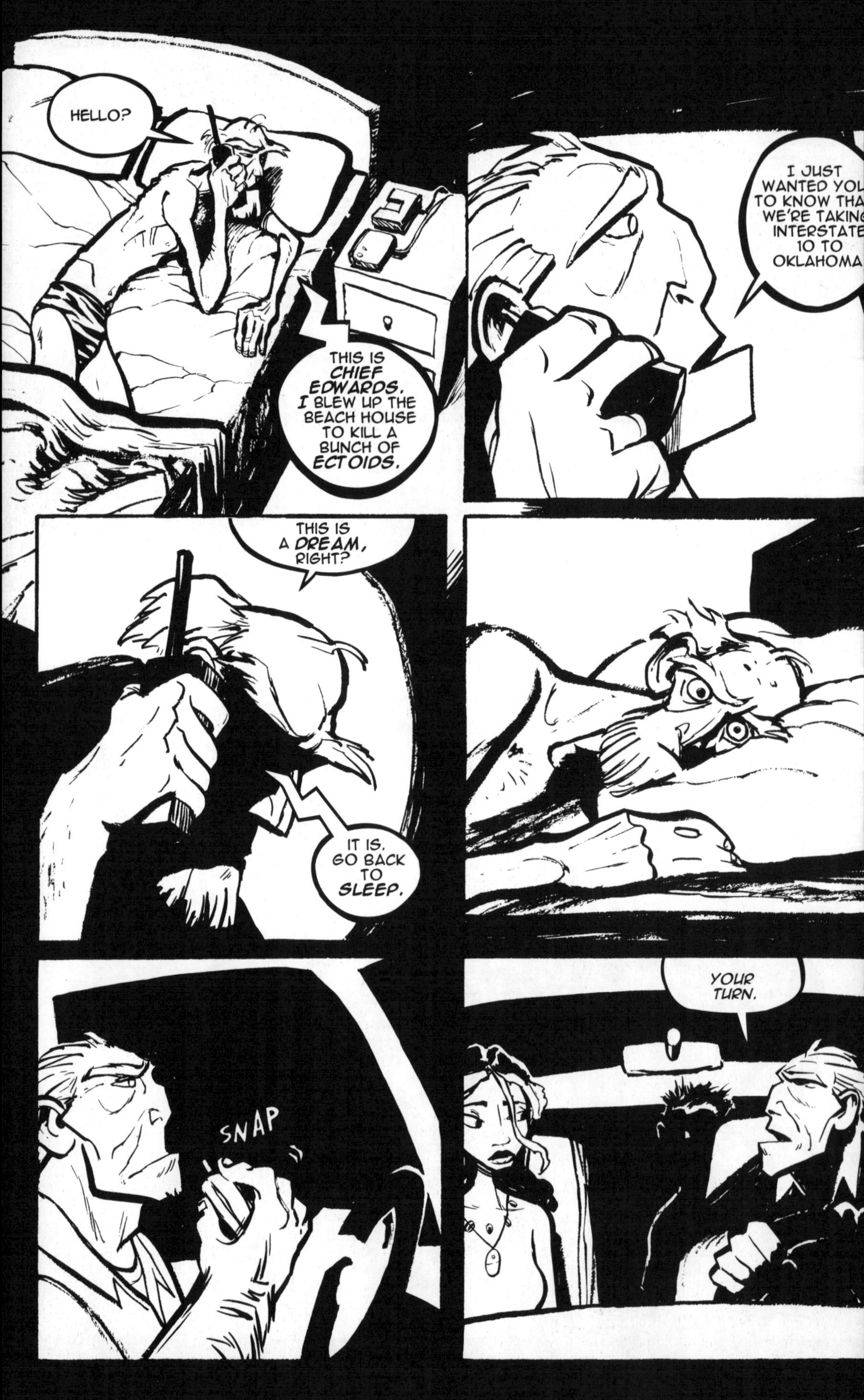
HELLO?
THIS IS CHIEF EDWARDS. I BLEW UP THE BEACH HOUSE TO KILL A BUNCH OF ECTOIDS.
I JUST WANTED YOU TO KNOW THAT WE'RE TAKING INTERSTATE 10 TO OKLAHOMA.
THIS IS A DREAM, RIGHT?
IT IS. GO BACK TO SLEEP.
SNAP
YOUR TURN.

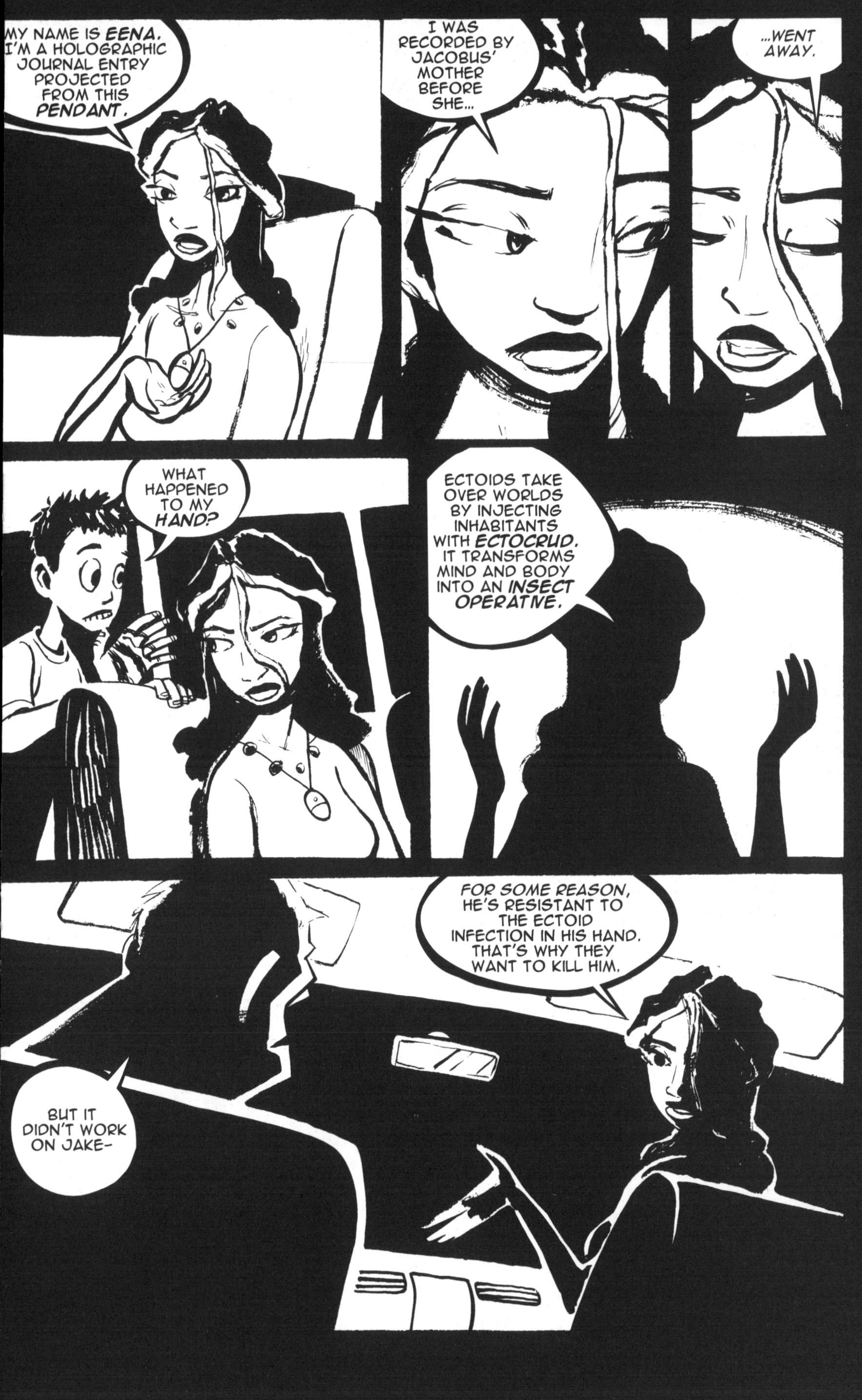
MY NAME IS EENA. I'M A HOLOGRAPHIC JOURNAL ENTRY PROJECTED FROM THIS PENDANT.
I WAS RECORDED BY JACOBUS' MOTHER BEFORE SHE...
...WENT AWAY.
WHAT HAPPENED TO MY HAND?
ECTOIDS TAKE OVER WORLDS BY INJECTING INHABITANTS WITH ECTOCRUD. IT TRANSFORMS MIND AND BODY INTO AN INSECT OPERATIVE.
BUT IT DIDN'T WORK ON JAKE-
FOR SOME REASON, HE'S RESISTANT TO THE ECTOID INFECTION IN HIS HAND. THAT'S WHY THEY WANT TO KILL HIM.

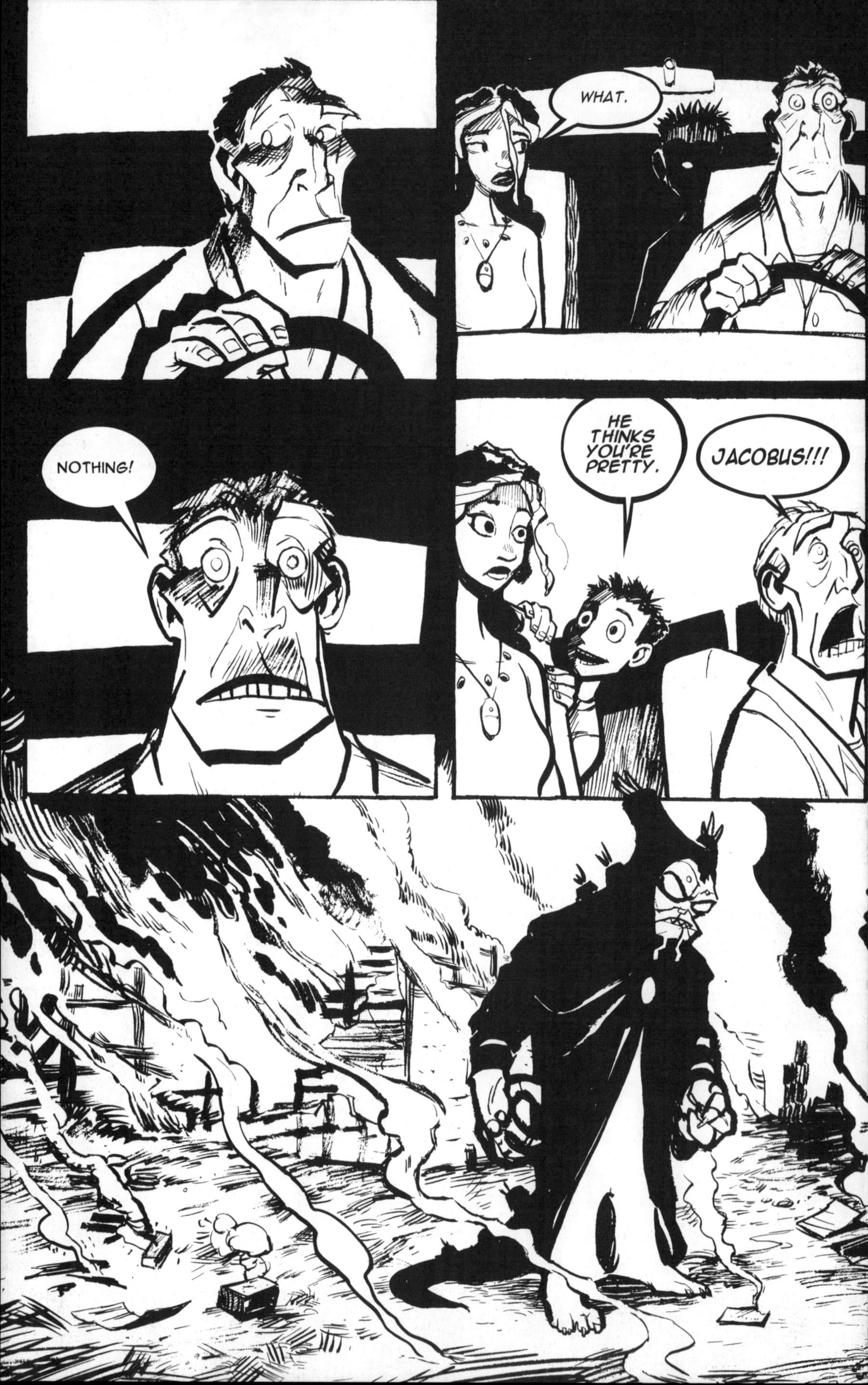
WHAT.
NOTHING!
HE THINKS YOU'RE PRETTY.
JACOBUS!!!

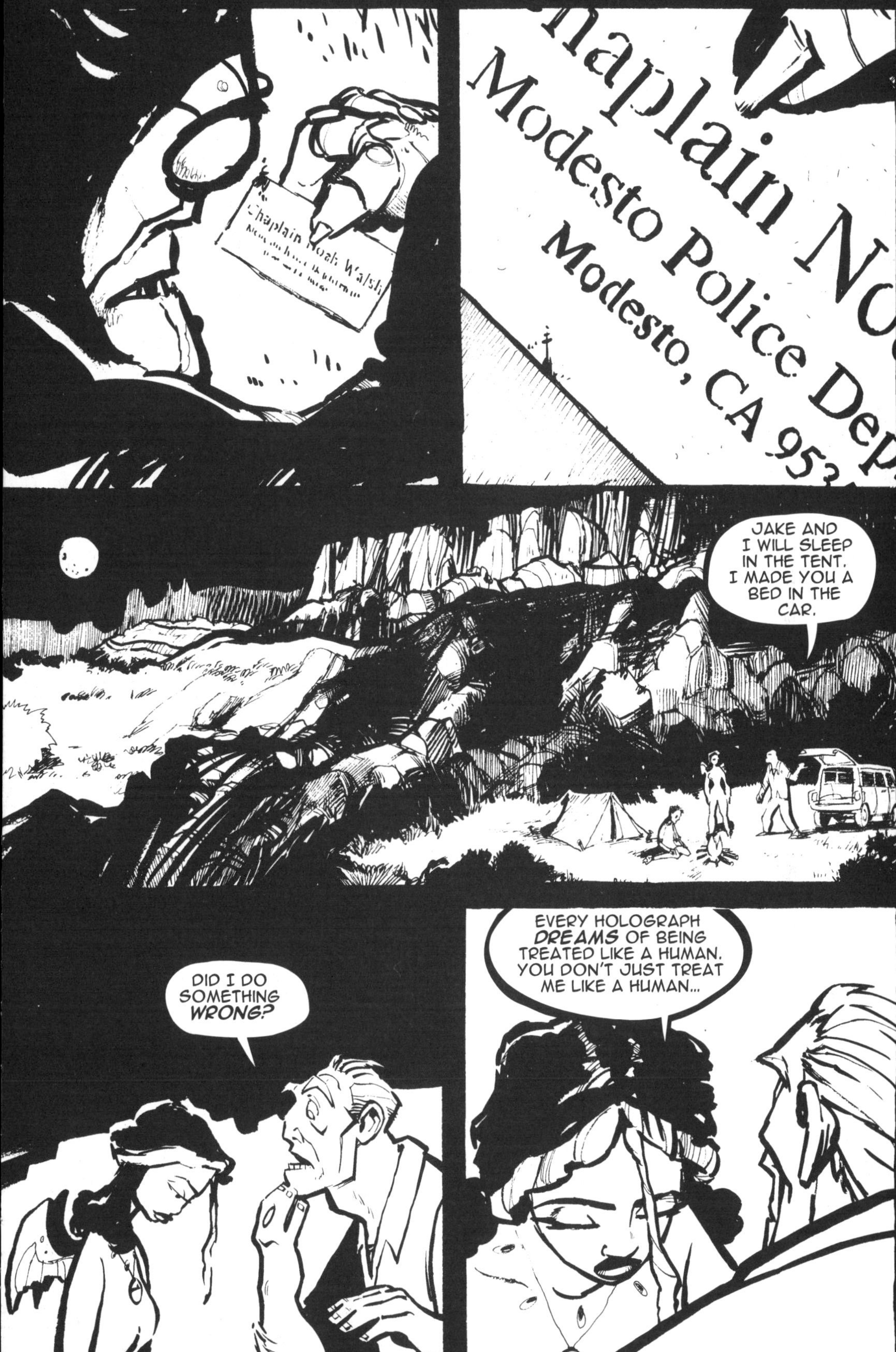

Chaplain Noah Walsh
Modesto Police Dep
Modesto, CA 953
JAKE AND I WILL SLEEP IN THE TENT. I MADE YOU A BED IN THE CAR.
DID I DO SOMETHING WRONG?
EVERY HOLOGRAPH DREAMS OF BEING TREATED LIKE A HUMAN. YOU DON'T JUST TREAT ME LIKE A HUMAN...

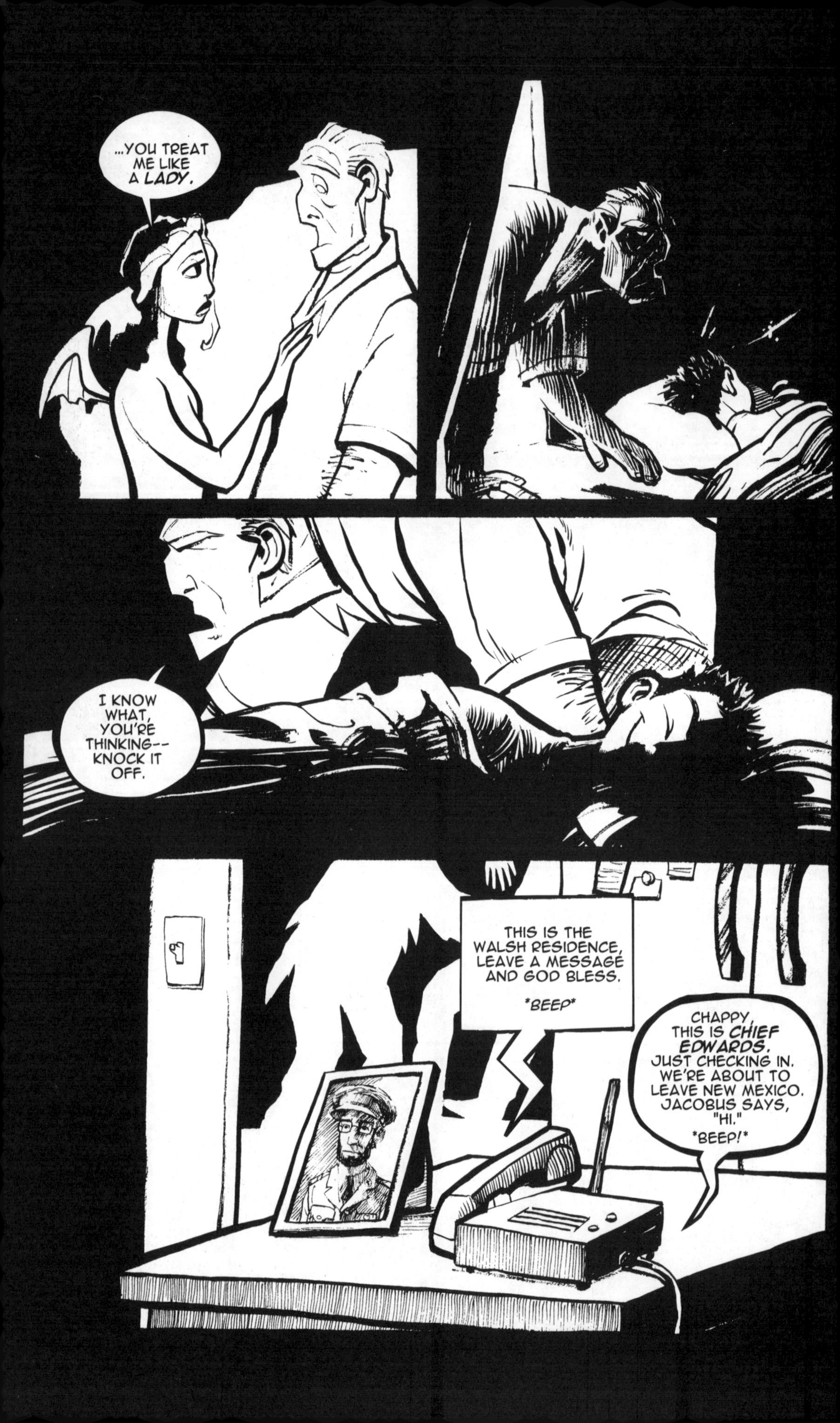
...YOU TREAT ME LIKE A LADY.
I KNOW WHAT, YOU'RE THINKING-- KNOCK IT OFF.
THIS IS THE WALSH RESIDENCE, LEAVE A MESSAGE AND GOD BLESS.
BEEP
CHAPPY, THIS IS CHIEF EDWARDS. JUST CHECKING IN. WE'RE ABOUT TO LEAVE NEW MEXICO. JACOBUS SAYS, "HI."
BEEP!

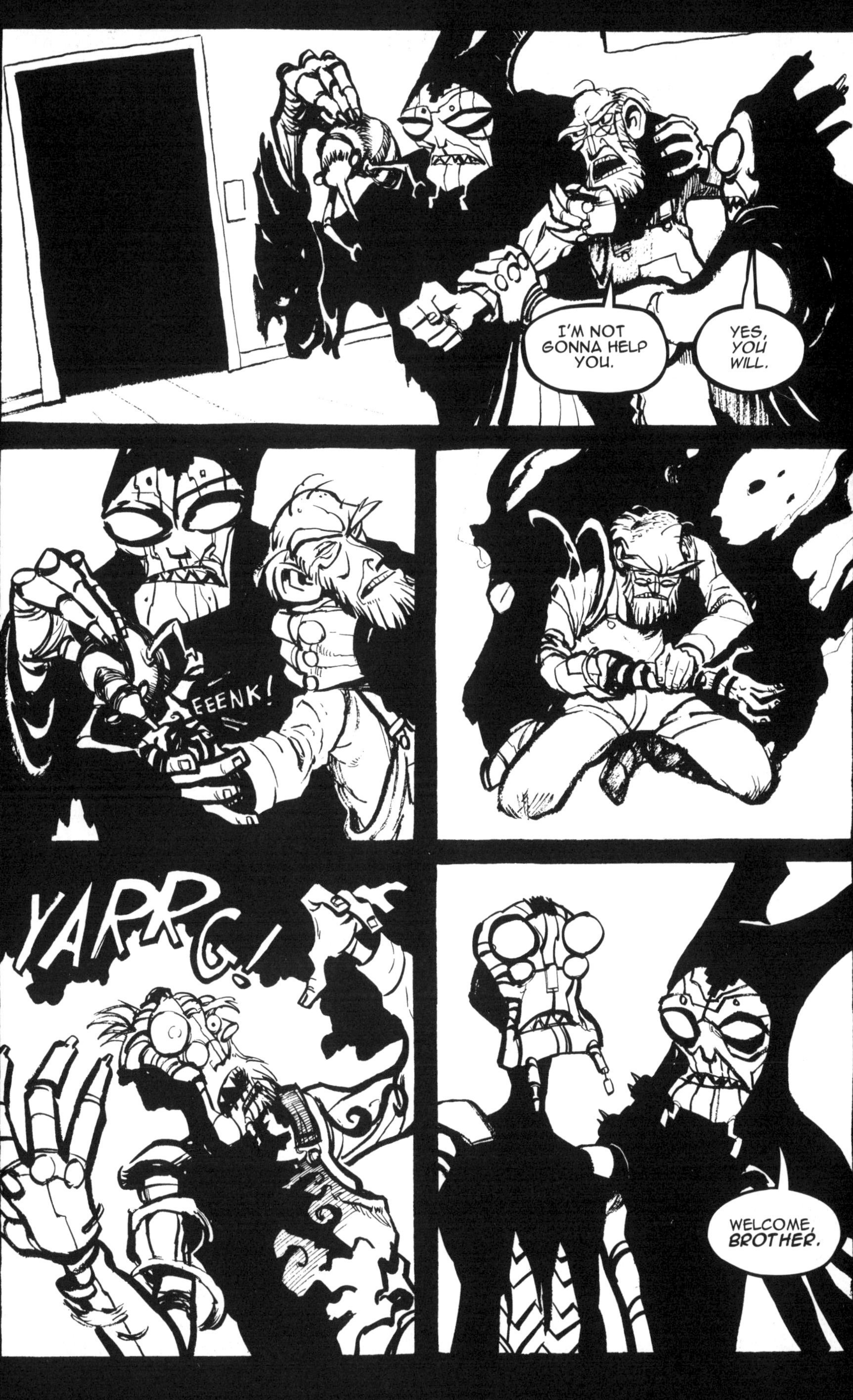
I'M NOT GONNA HELP YOU.
YES, YOU WILL.
EEENK!
YARRG!
WELCOME, BROTHER.

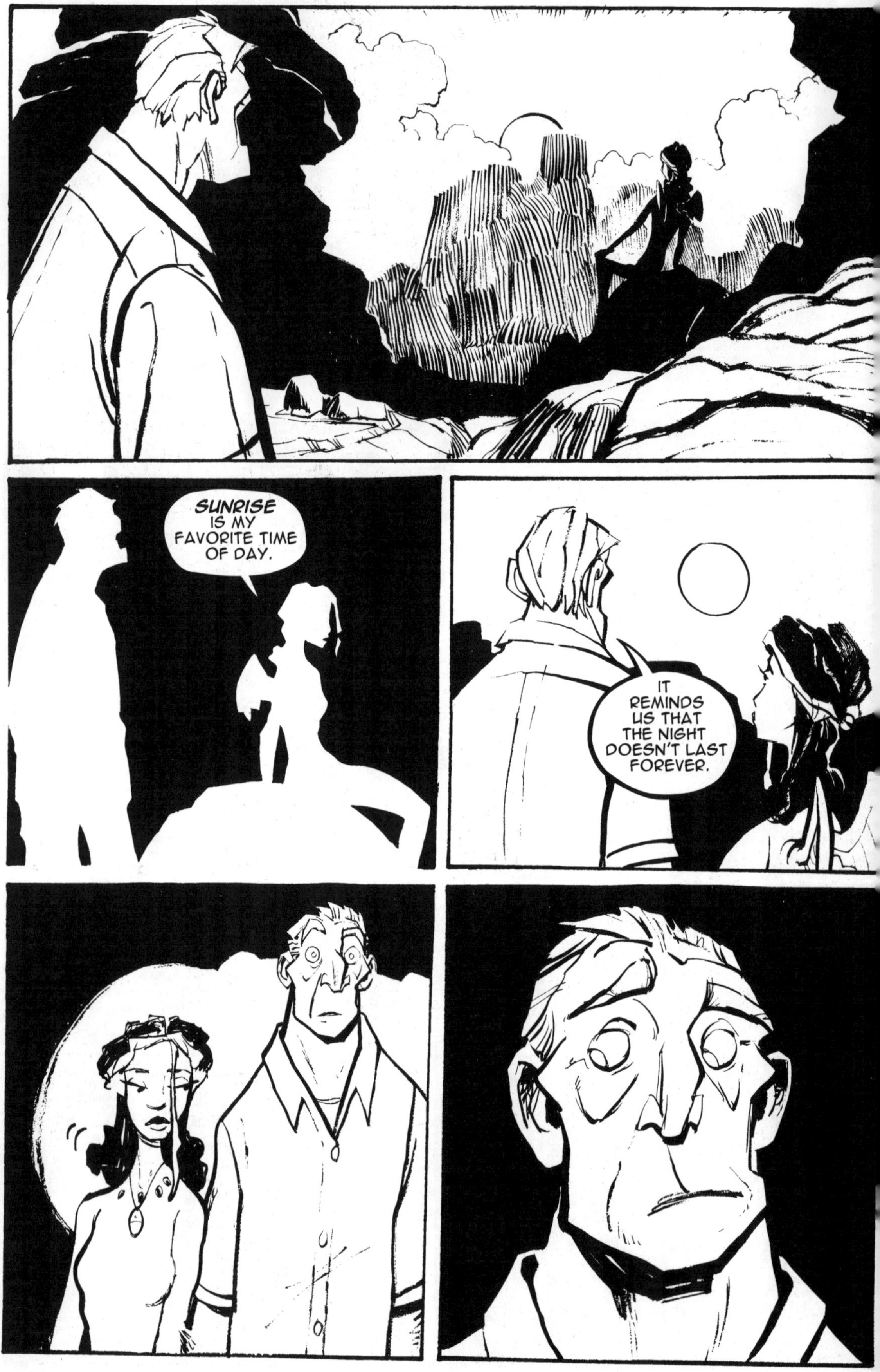
SUNRISE IS MY FAVORITE TIME OF DAY.
IT REMINDS US THAT THE NIGHT DOESN'T LAST FOREVER.

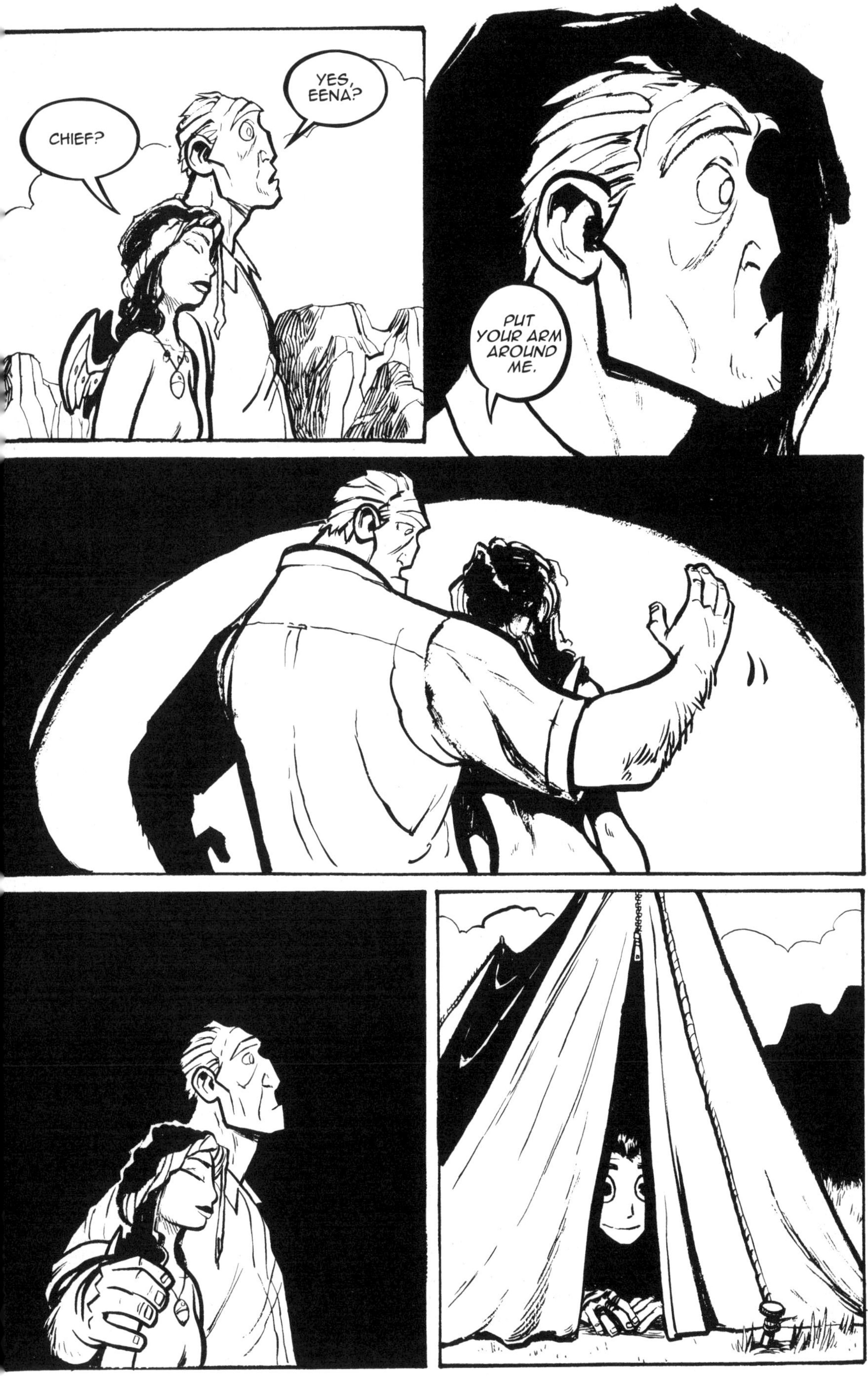
CHIEF?
YES, EENA?
PUT YOUR ARM AROUND ME.

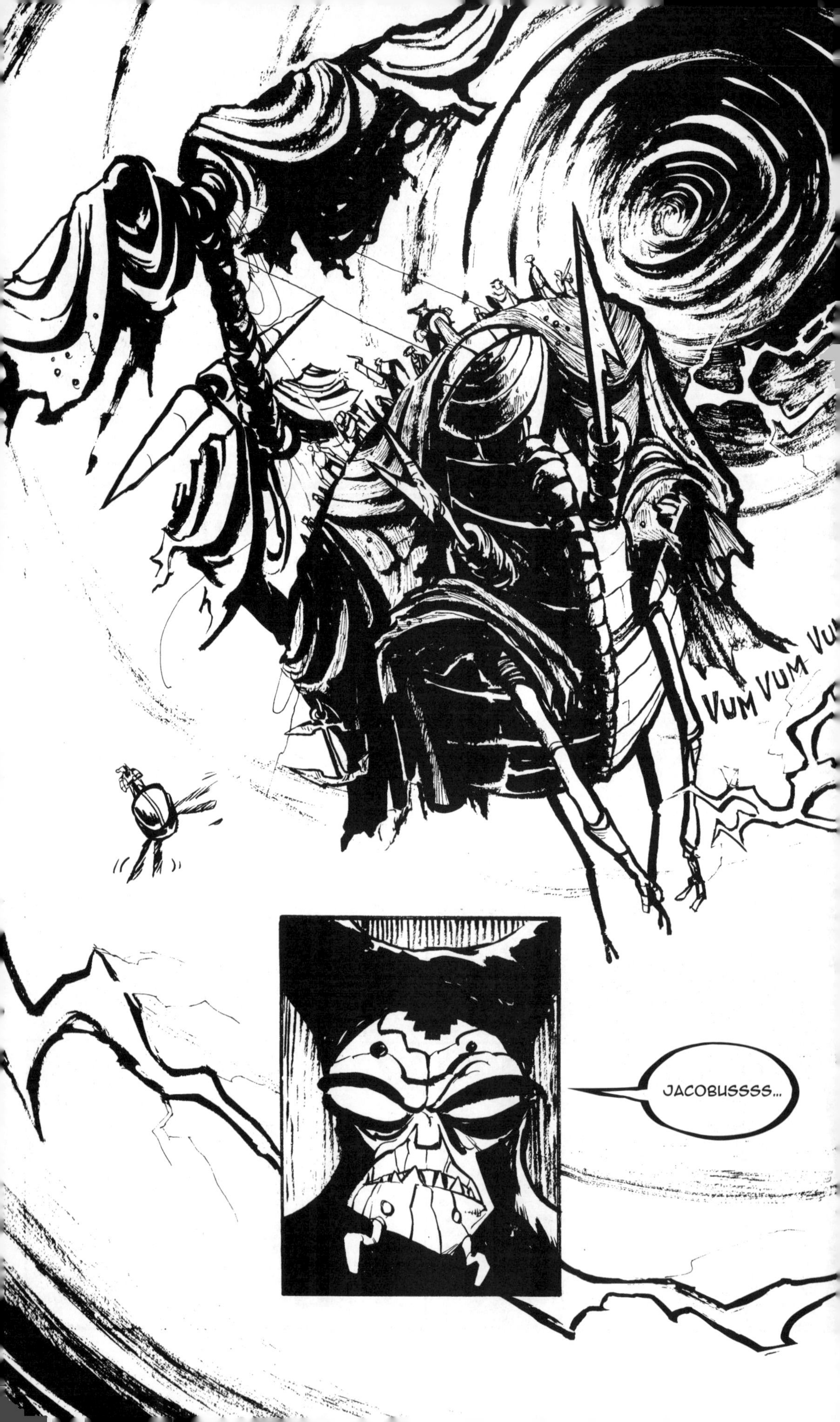
VUM VUM VU
JACOBUSSSS...

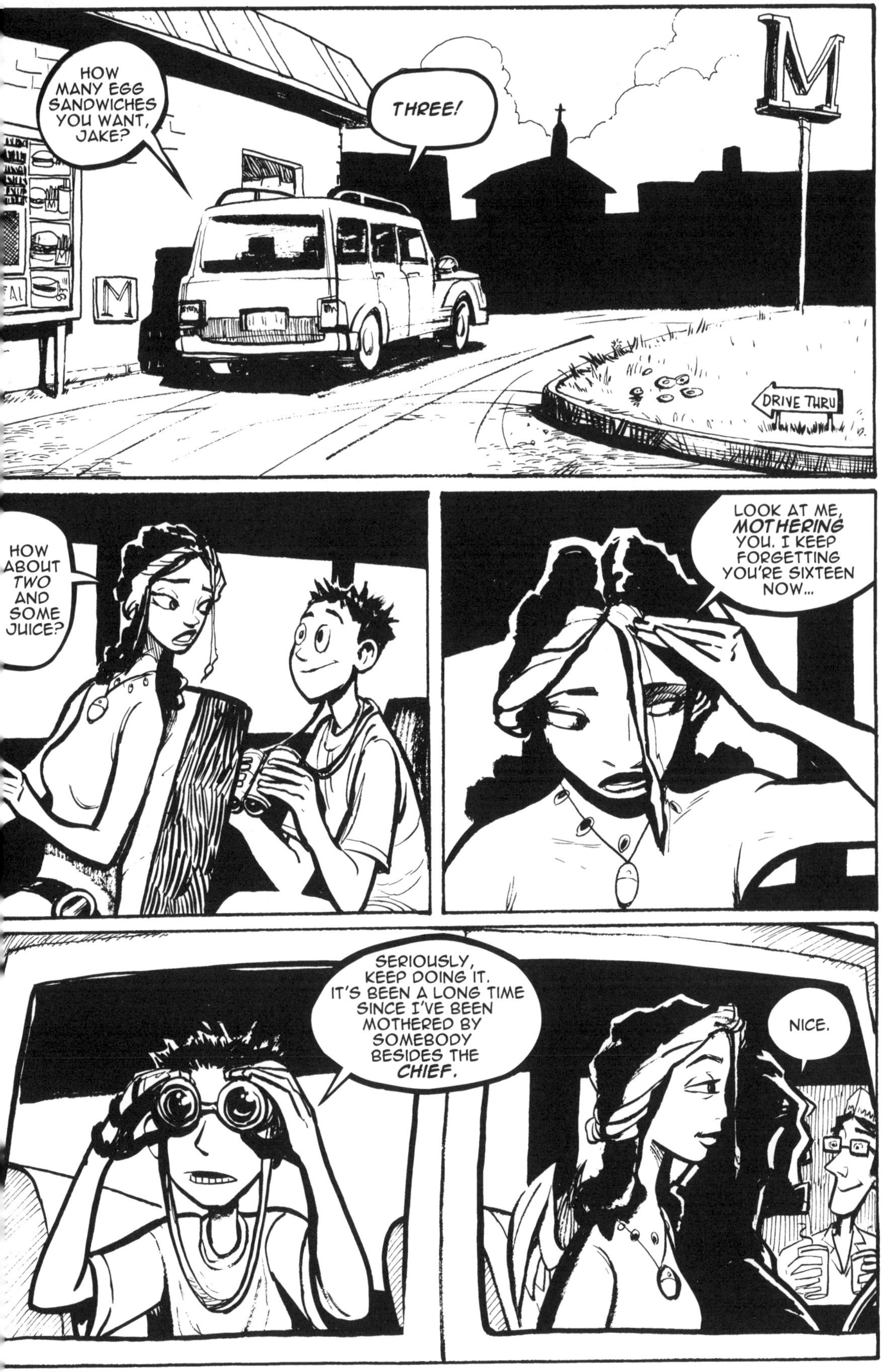
HOW MANY EGG SANDWICHES YOU WANT, JAKE?
THREE!
M
DRIVE THRU
HOW ABOUT TWO AND SOME JUICE?
LOOK AT ME, MOTHERING YOU. I KEEP FORGETTING YOU'RE SIXTEEN NOW...
SERIOUSLY, KEEP DOING IT. IT'S BEEN A LONG TIME SINCE I'VE BEEN MOTHERED BY SOMEBODY BESIDES THE CHIEF.
NICE.

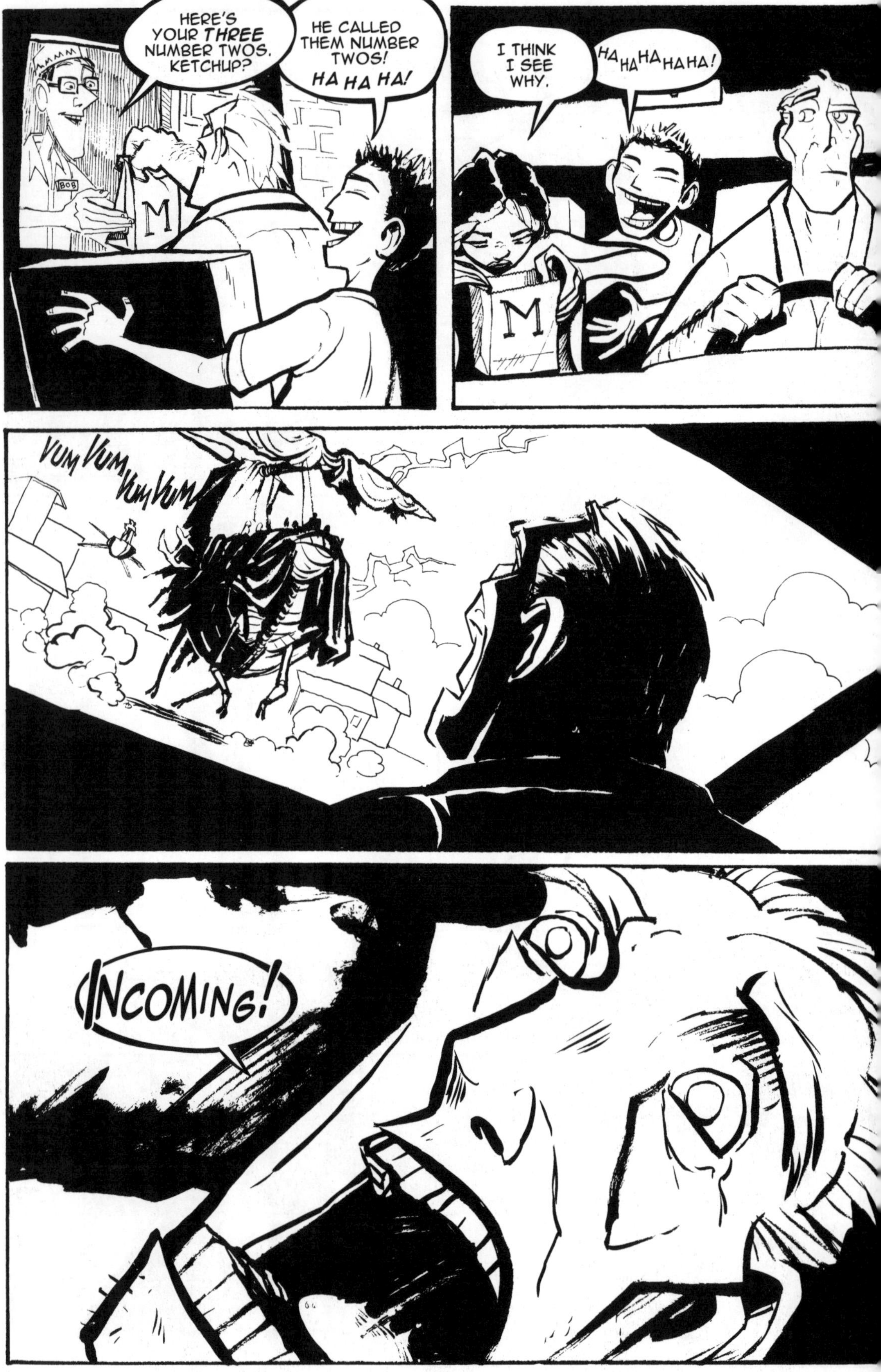
HERE'S YOUR THREE NUMBER TWOS. KETCHUP?
HE CALLED THEM NUMBER TWOS! HA HA HA!
BOB
I THINK I SEE WHY.
HA HA HA HA HA!
VUM VUM VUM VUM
INCOMING!

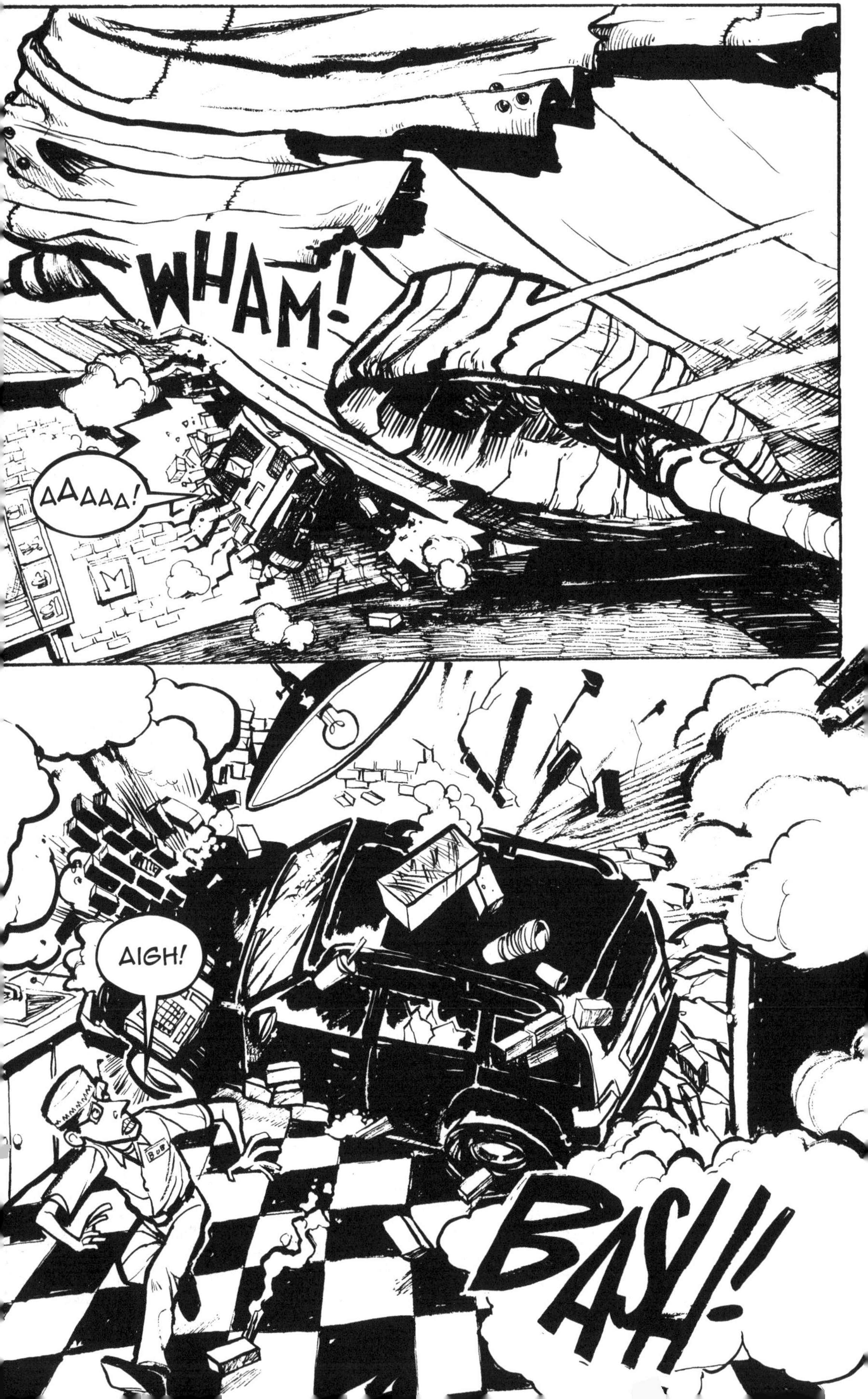
WHAM!
AAAAA!
AIGH!
BASH!

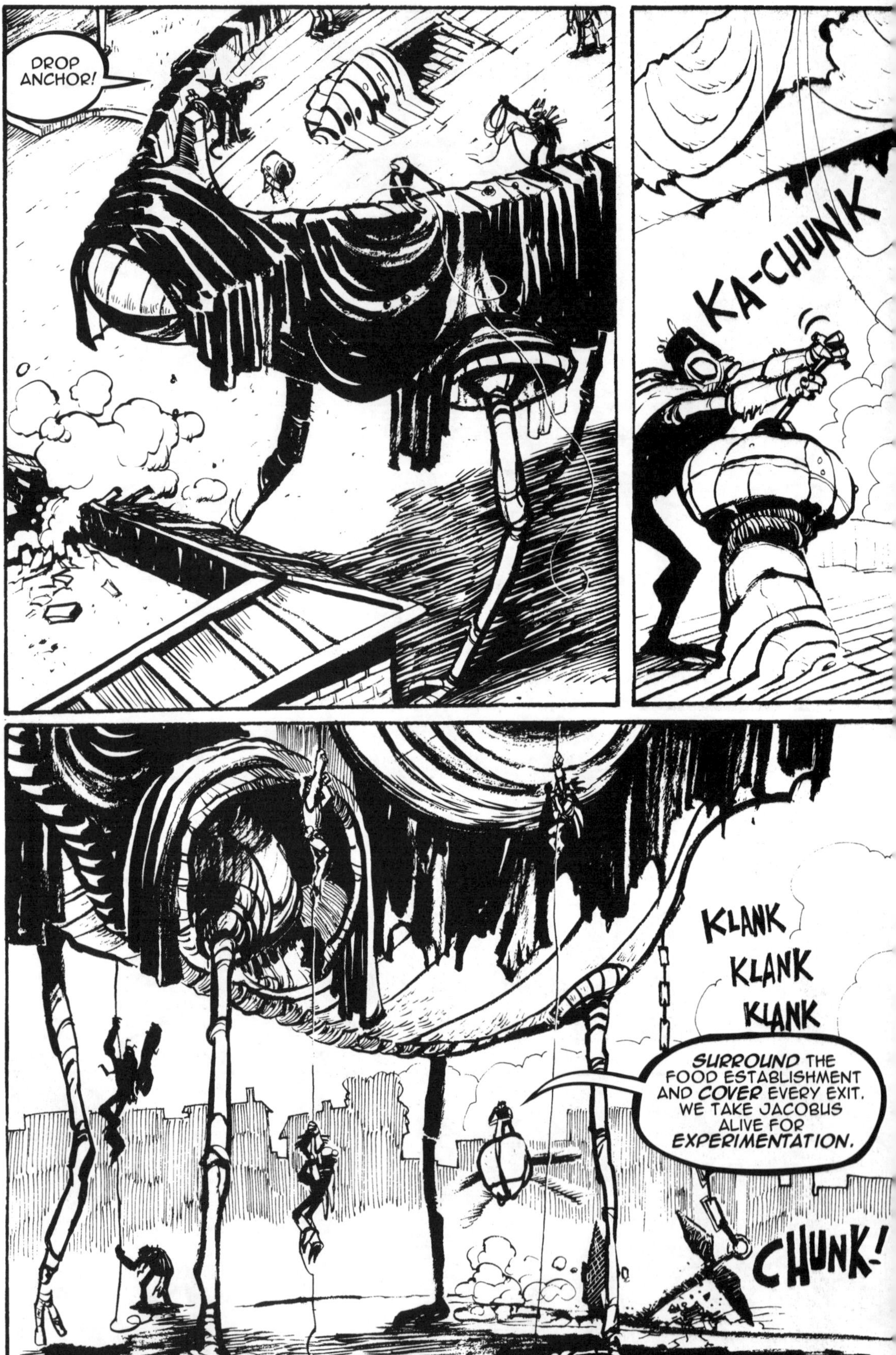
DROP ANCHOR!
KA-CHUNK
KLANK
KLANK
KLANK
SURROUND THE FOOD ESTABLISHMENT AND COVER EVERY EXIT. WE TAKE JACOBUS ALIVE FOR EXPERIMENTATION.
CHUNK!

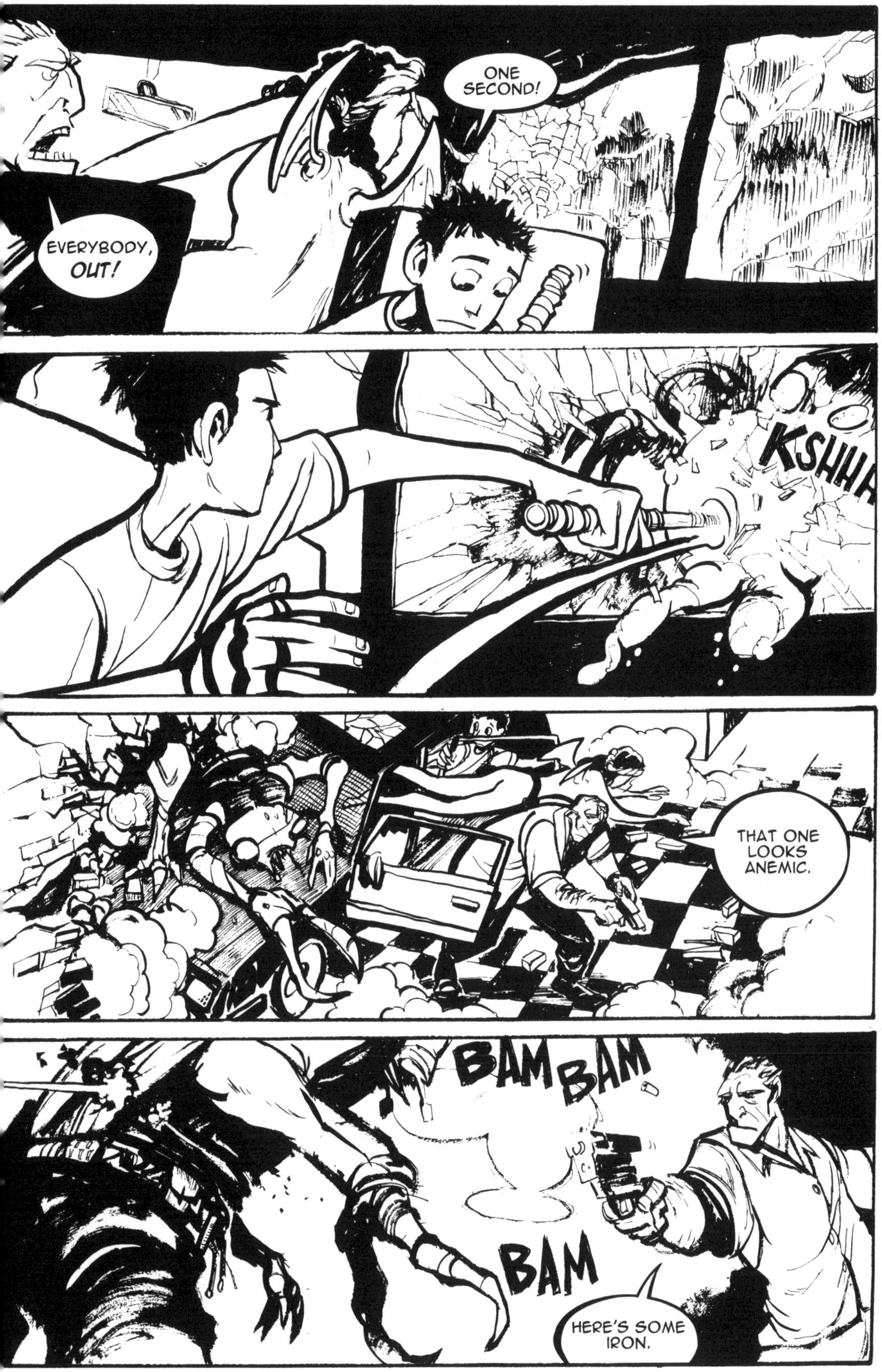
ONE SECOND!
EVERYBODY, OUT!
KSHHA
THAT ONE LOOKS ANEMIC.
BAM BAM
BAM
HERE'S SOME IRON.

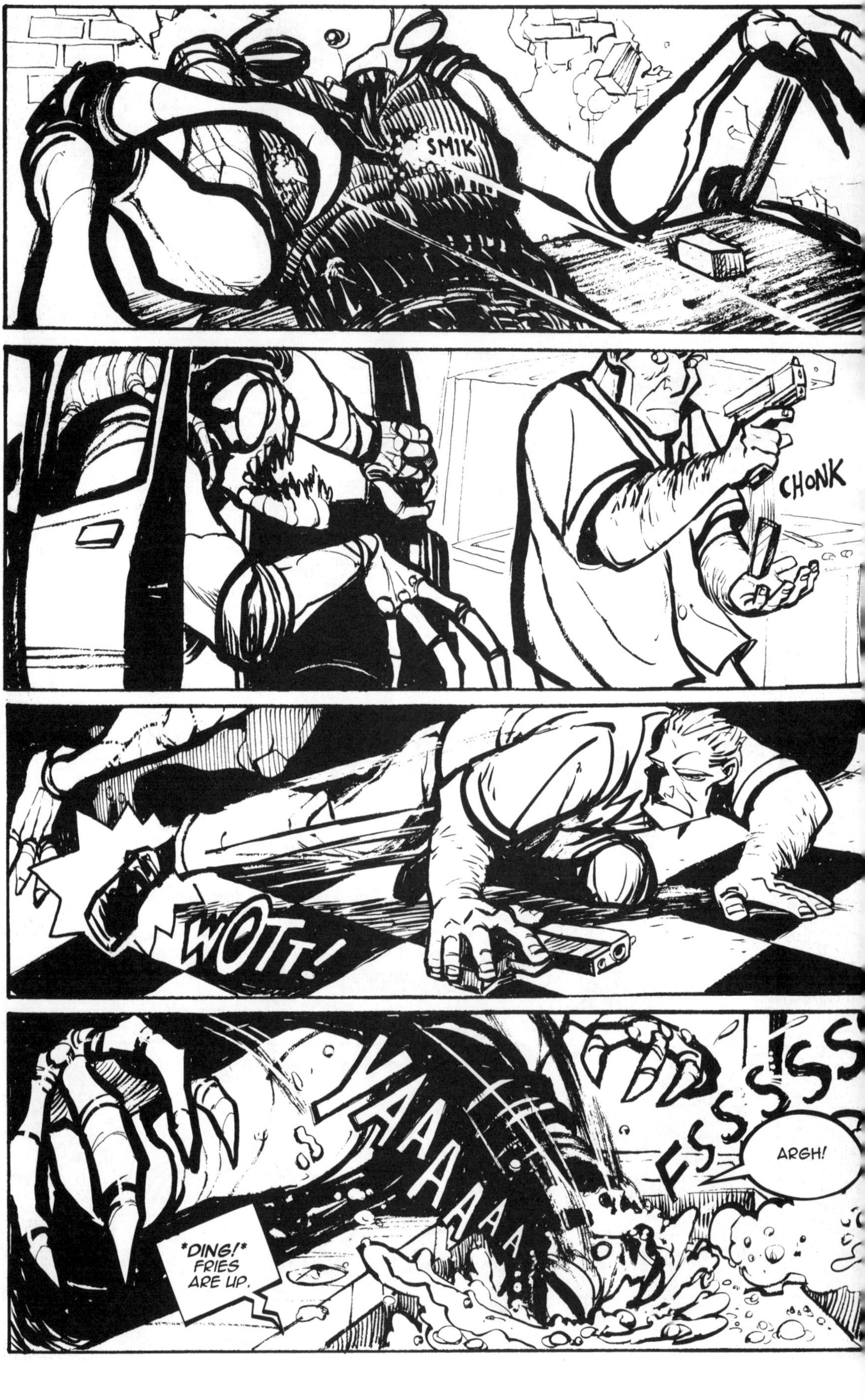
SMIK
CHONK
WOTT!
YAAAAAAA...
FSSSSSSS
ARGH!
DING! FRIES ARE UP.

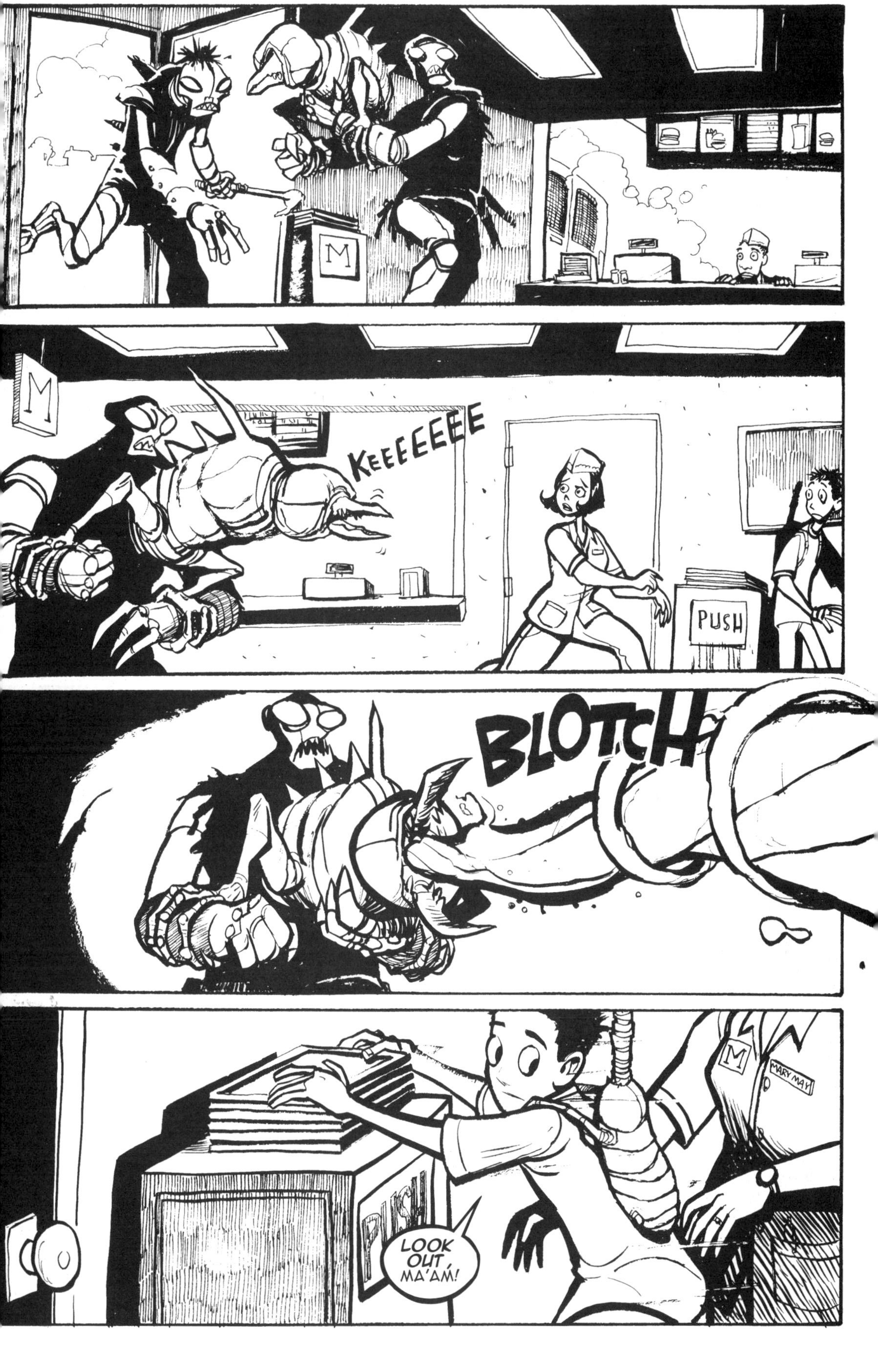

M
M
KEEEEEEE
PUSH
BLOTCH
M
MARY MAY
PUSH
LOOK OUT, MA'AM!

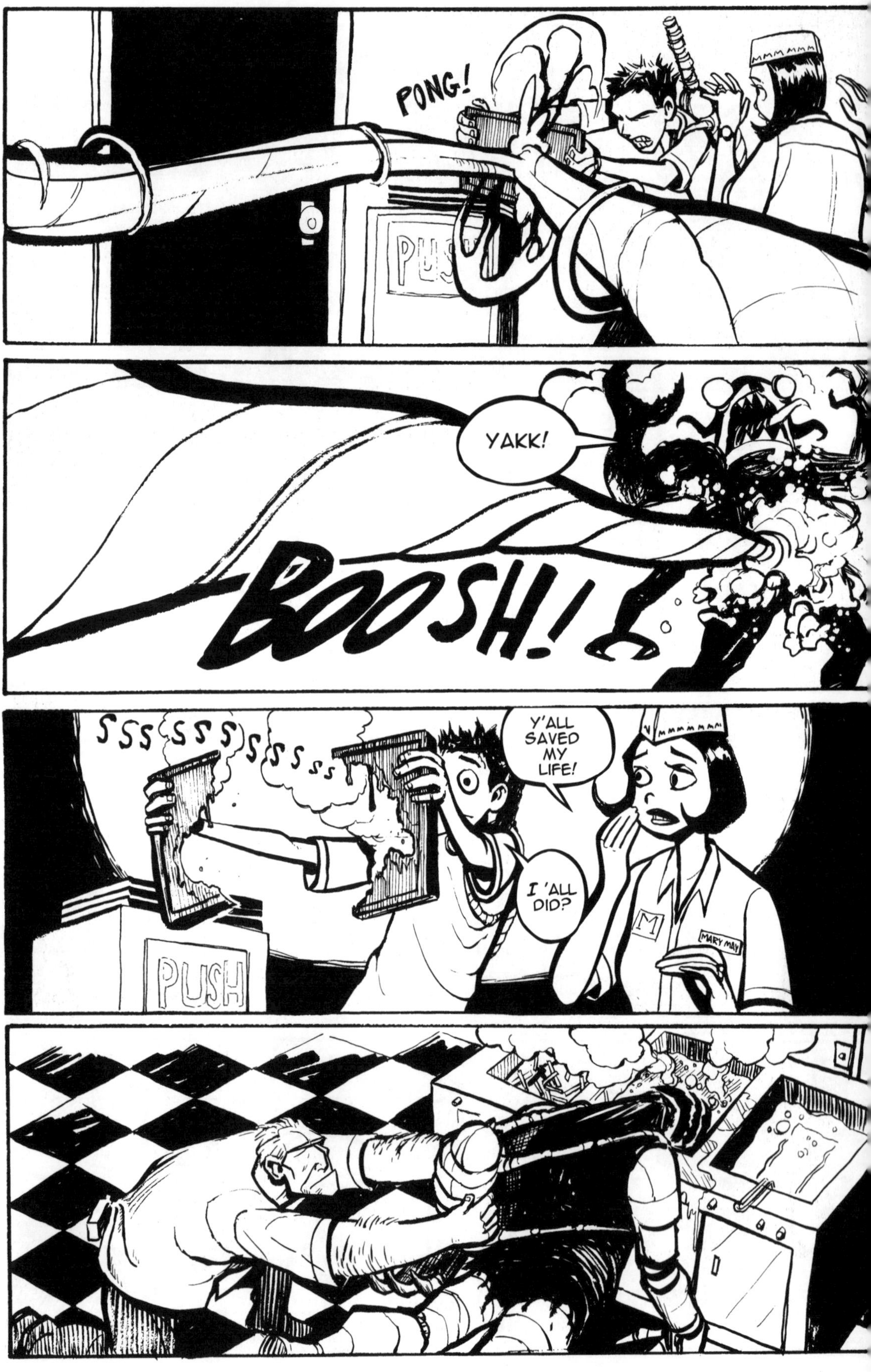
PONG!
PUSH
YAKK!
BOOSH!!
SSSSSSSSSSSsss
Y'ALL SAVED MY LIFE!
I 'ALL DID?
M
MARY MAY
PUSH

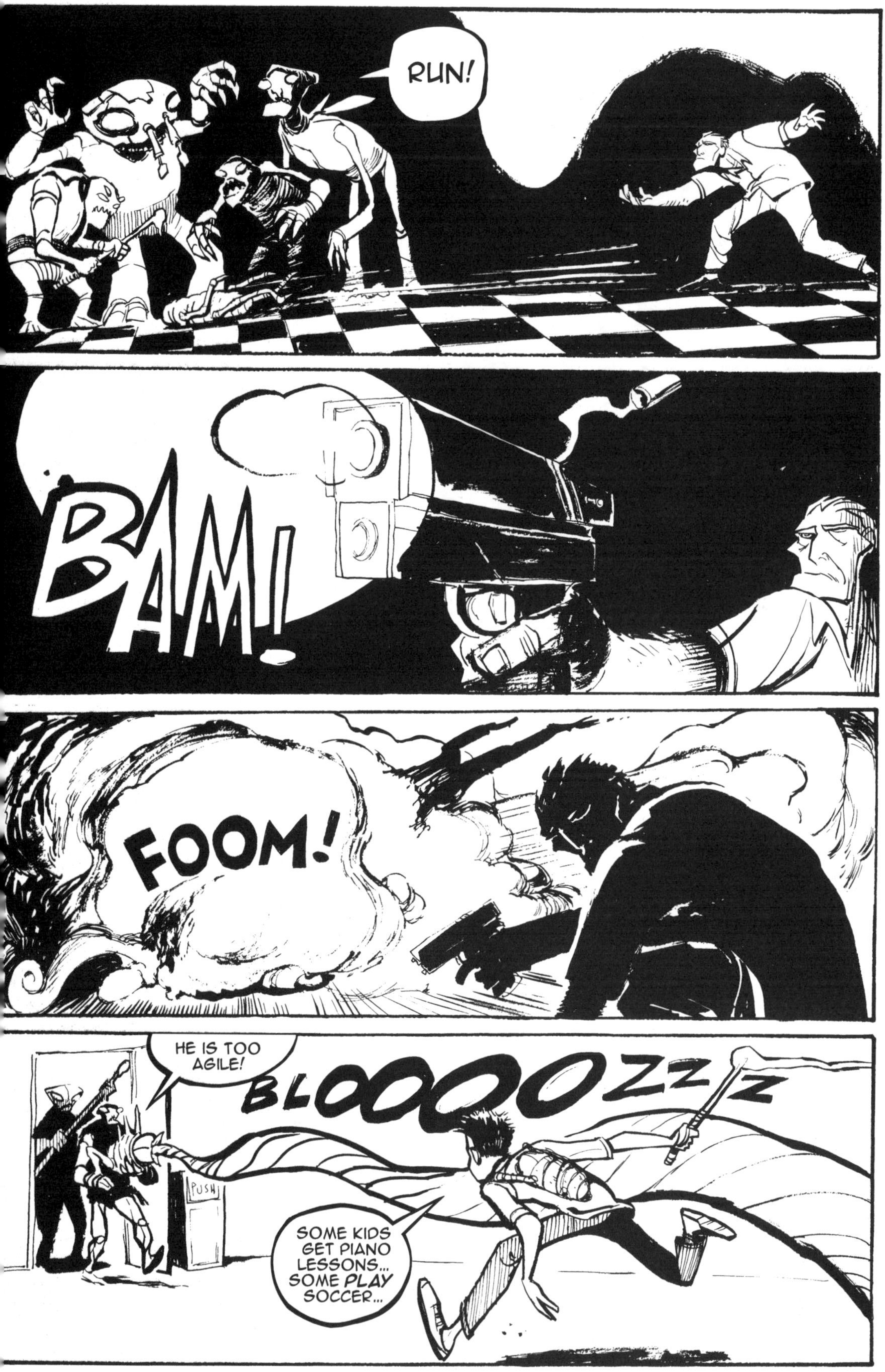
RUN!
BAM!
FOOM!
HE IS TOO AGILE!
BLOOOOOZZZ
SOME KIDS GET PIANO LESSONS... SOME PLAY SOCCER...

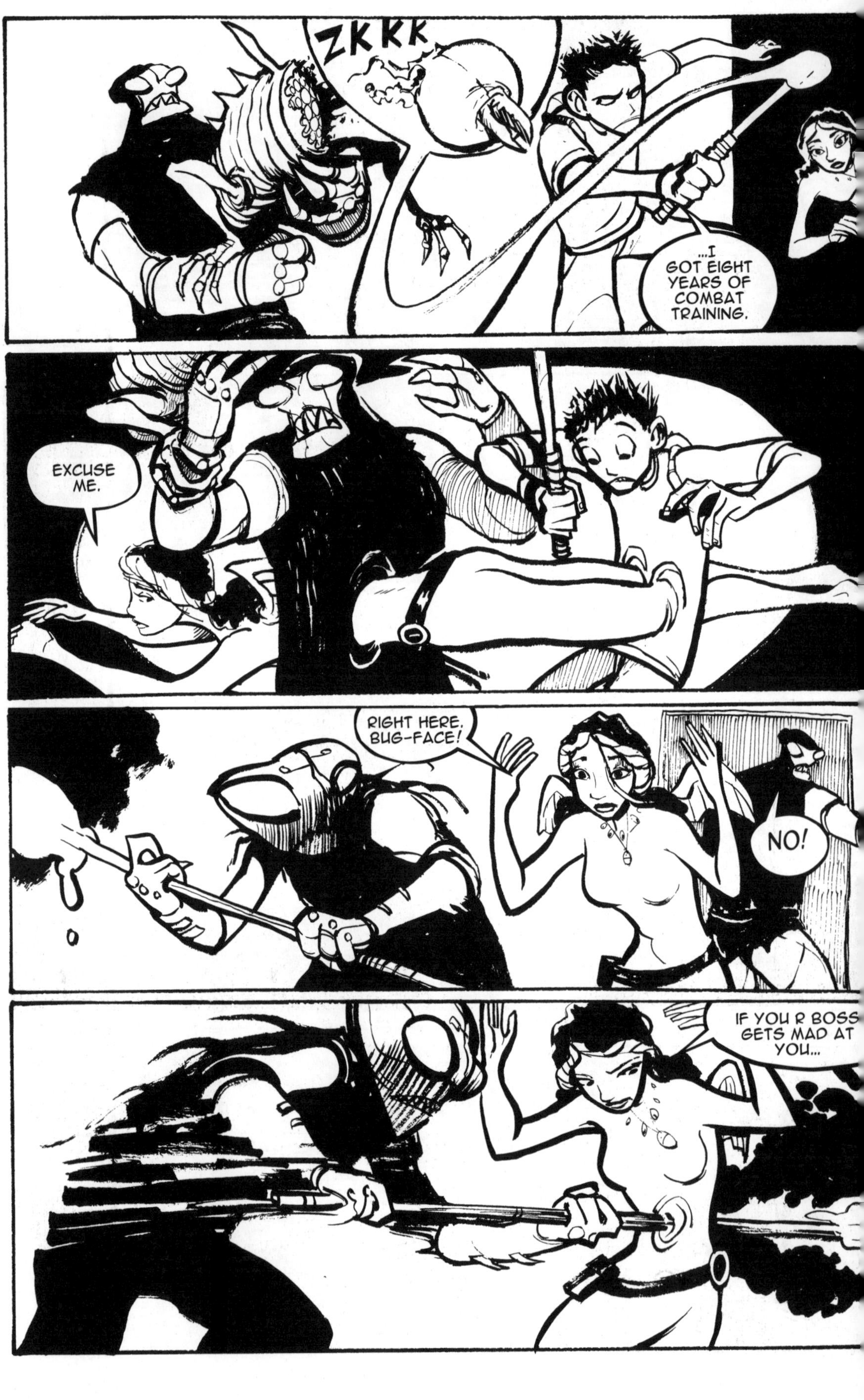
ZKKK
...I GOT EIGHT YEARS OF COMBAT TRAINING.
EXCUSE ME.
RIGHT HERE. BUG-FACE!
NO!
IF YOUR BOSS GETS MAD AT YOU...

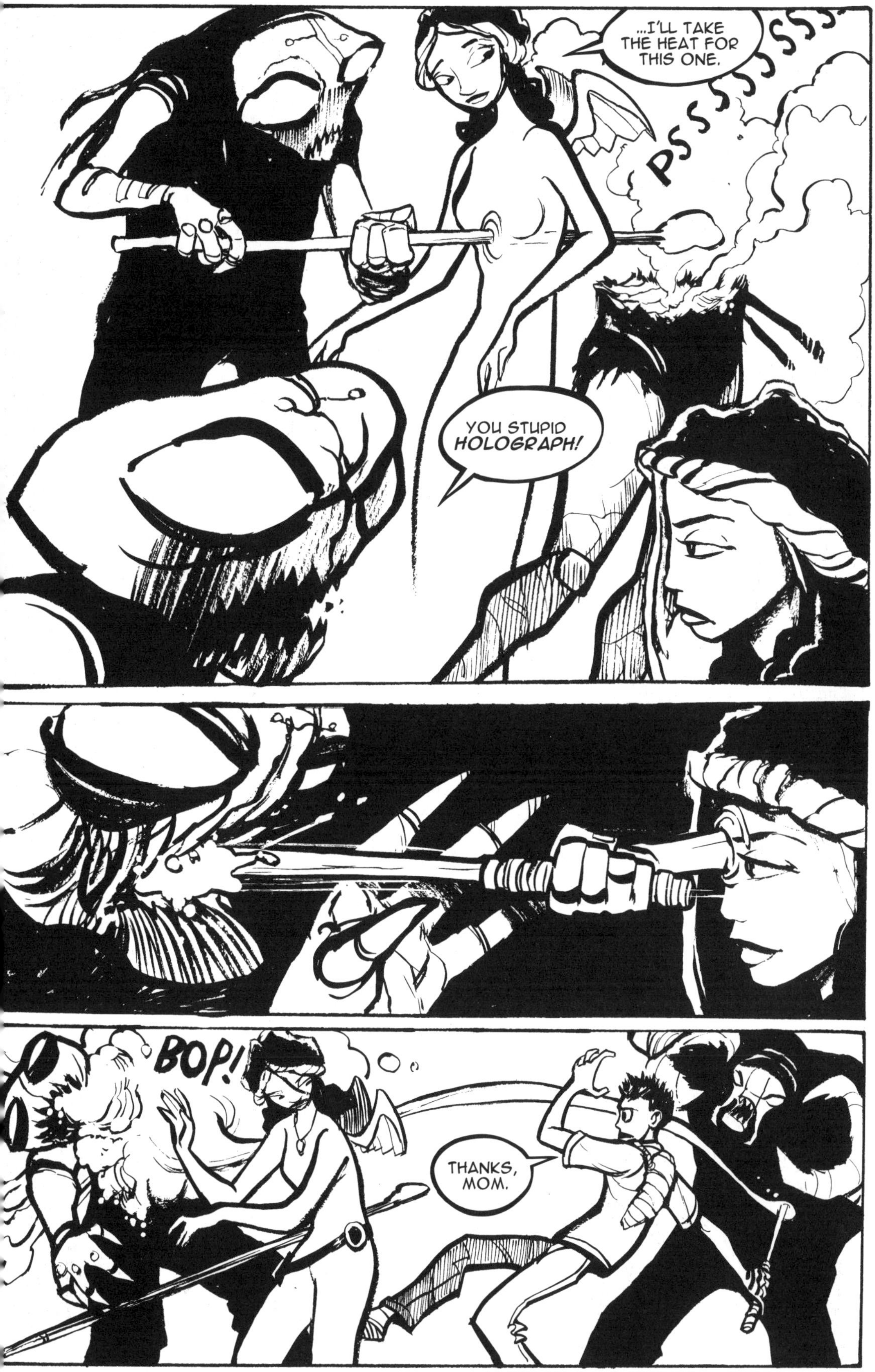
...I'LL TAKE THE HEAT FOR THIS ONE.
PSSSSSSSS
YOU STUPID HOLOGRAPH!
BOP!
THANKS, MOM.

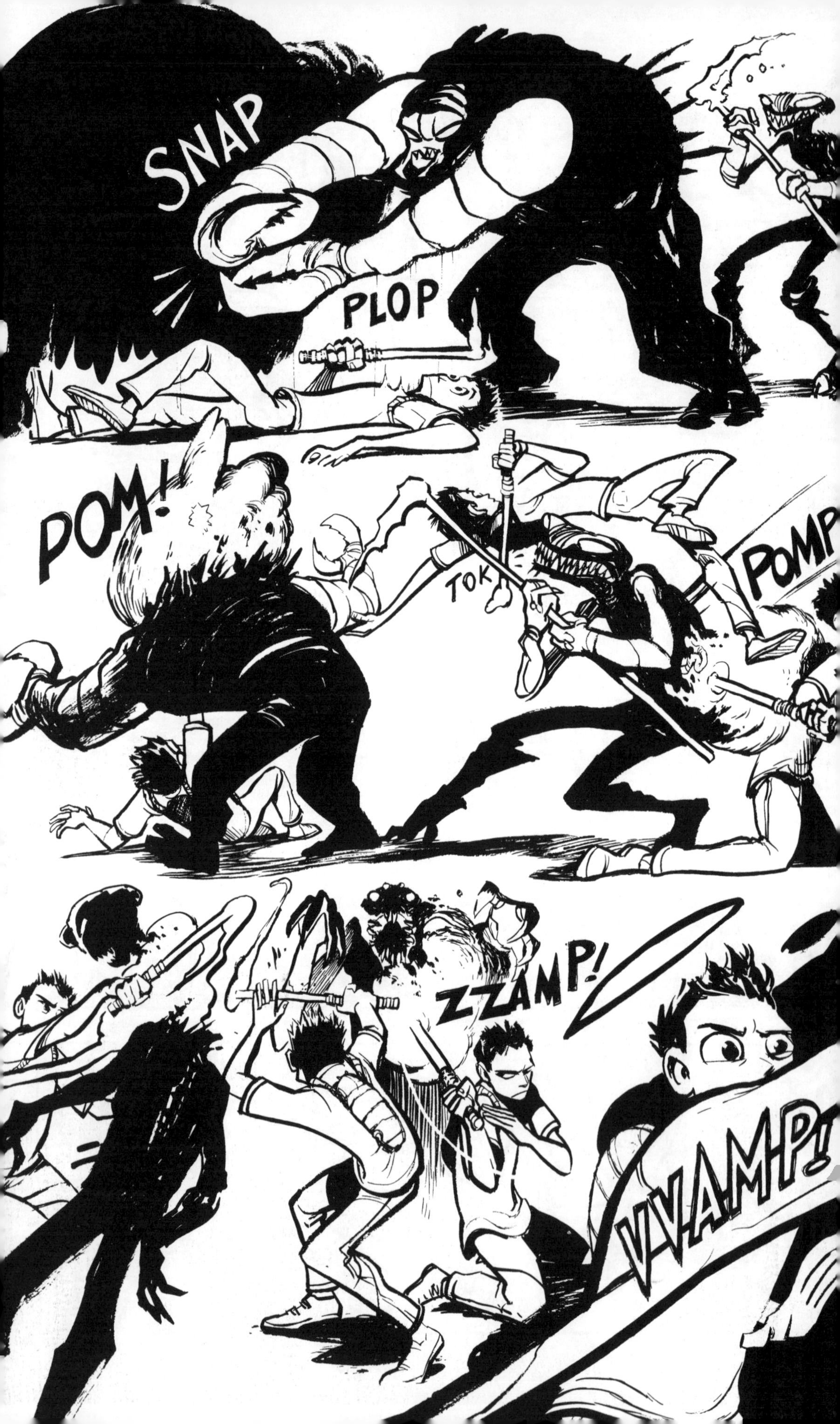
SNAP
PLOP
POM!
TOK
POMP
ZZAMP!
VVAMP!

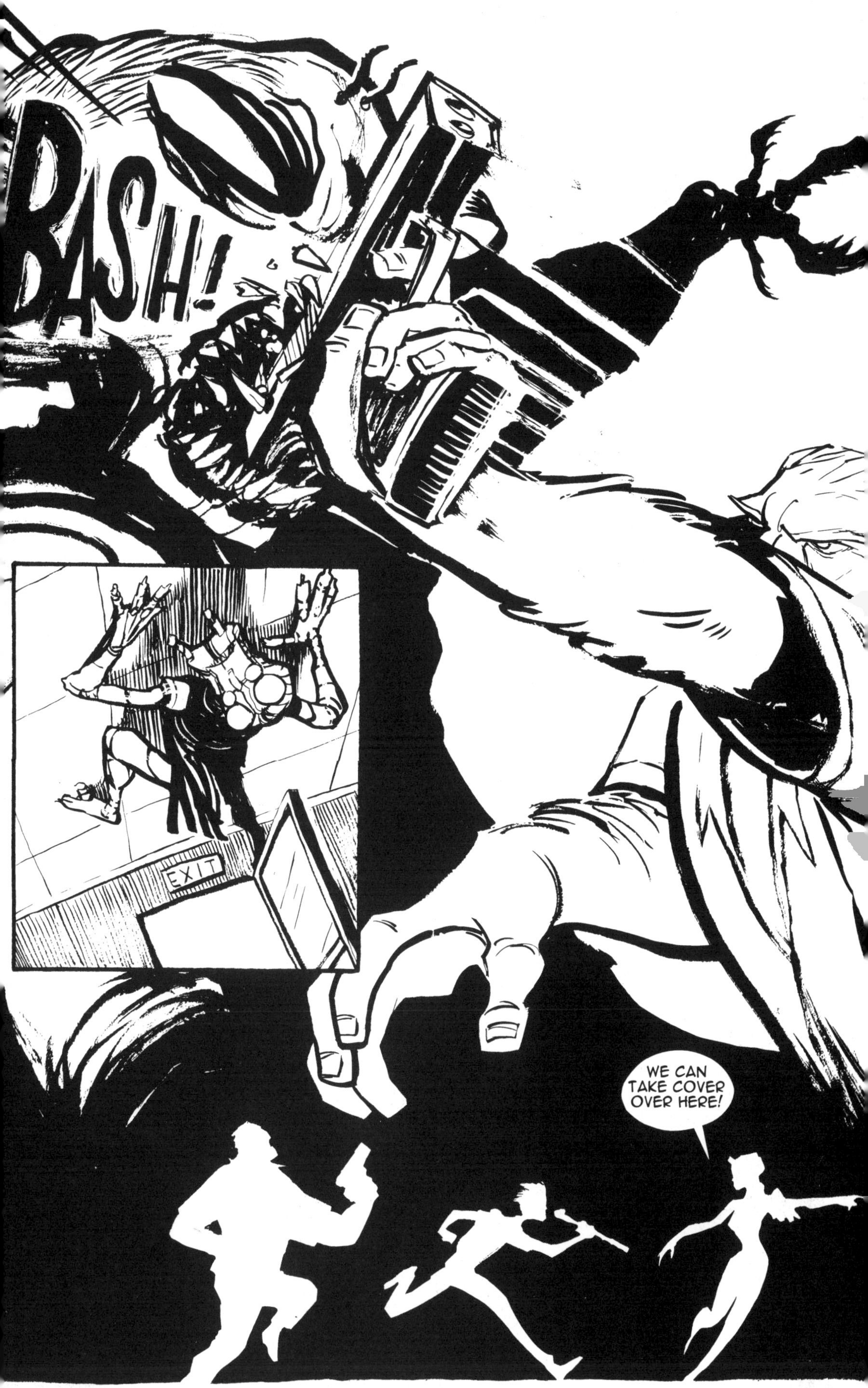
BASH!
EXIT
WE CAN TAKE COVER OVER HERE!

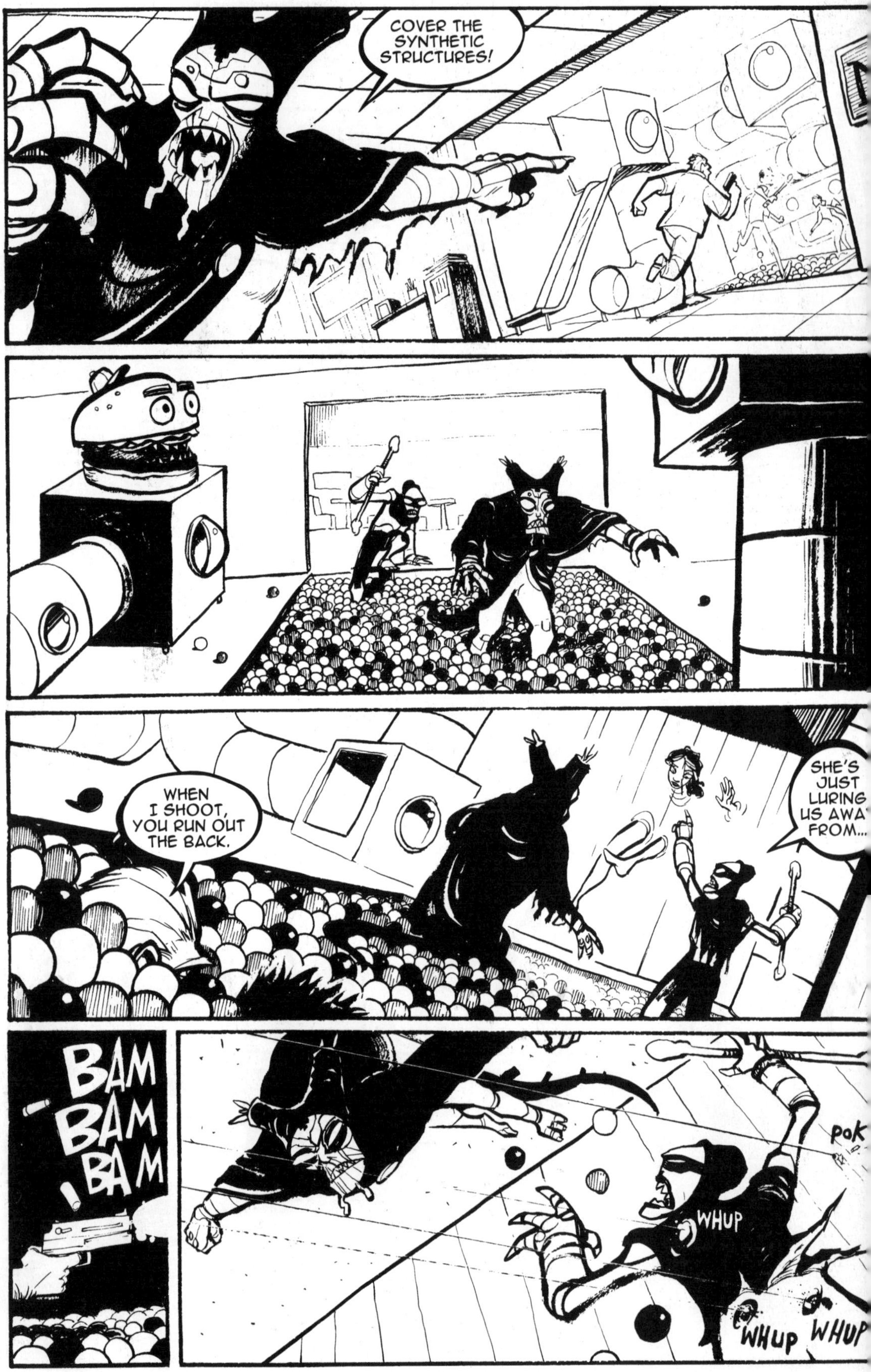
COVER THE SYNTHETIC STRUCTURES!
WHEN I SHOOT, YOU RUN OUT THE BACK.
SHE'S JUST LURING US AWA FROM...
BAM BAM BAM
POK
WHUP
WHUP WHUP

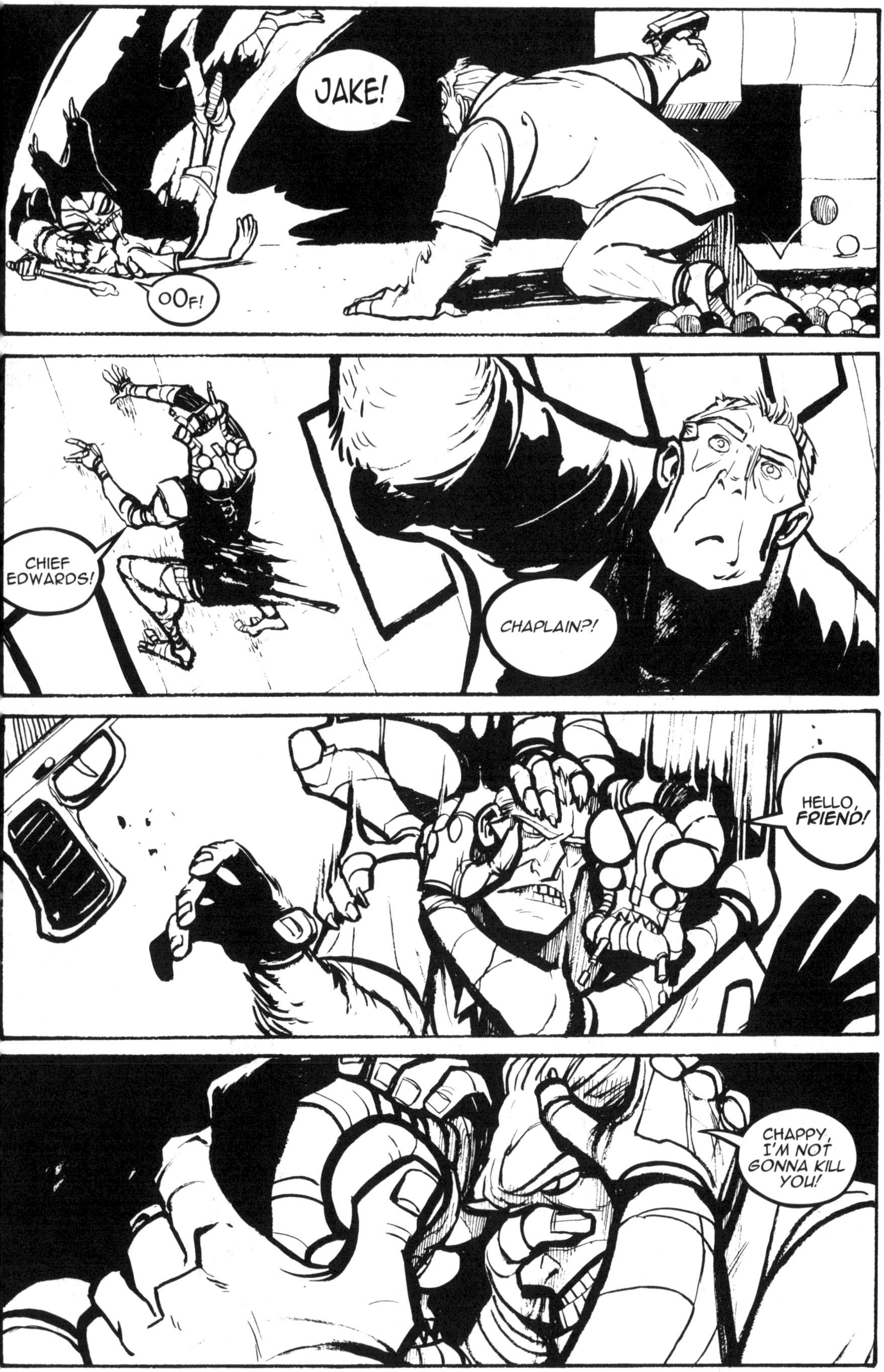
JAKE!
OOF!
CHIEF EDWARDS!
CHAPLAIN?!
HELLO, FRIEND!
CHAPPY, I'M NOT GONNA KILL YOU!

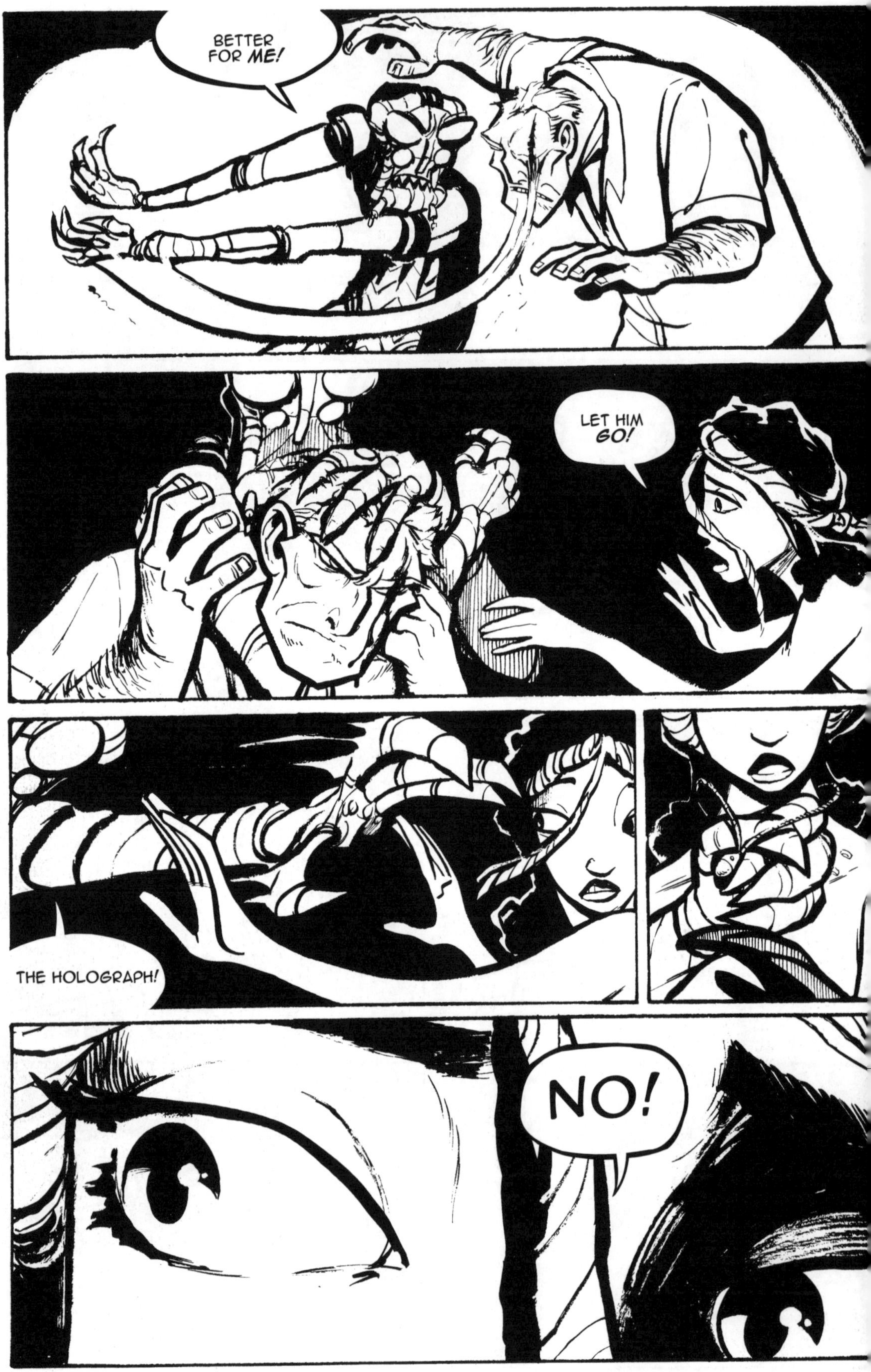
BETTER FOR ME!
LET HIM GO!
THE HOLOGRAPH!
NO!

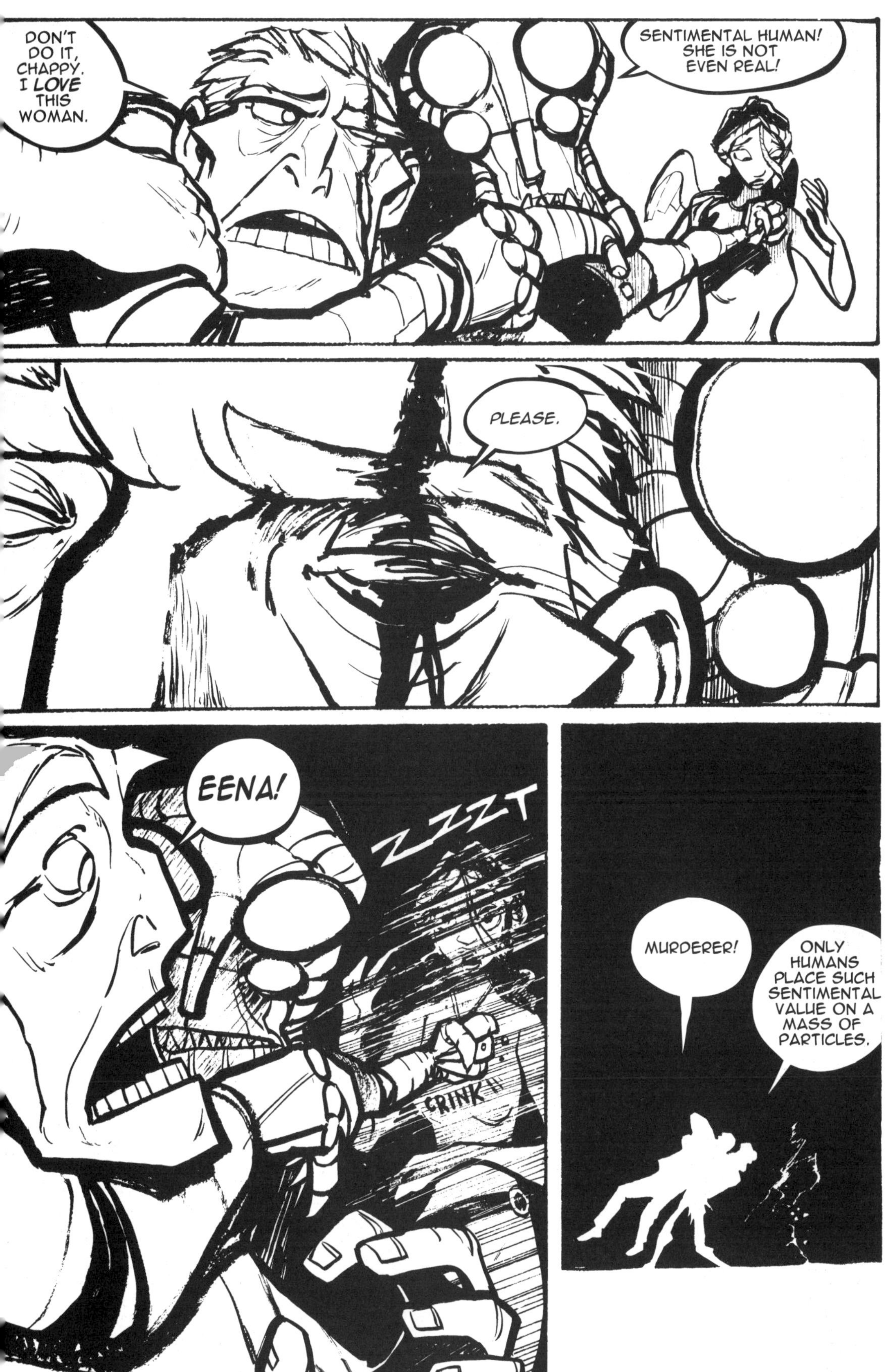
DON'T DO IT, CHAPPY. I LOVE THIS WOMAN.
SENTIMENTAL HUMAN! SHE IS NOT EVEN REAL!
PLEASE.
EENA!
ZZZT
CRINK
MURDERER!
ONLY HUMANS PLACE SUCH SENTIMENTAL VALUE ON A MASS OF PARTICLES.

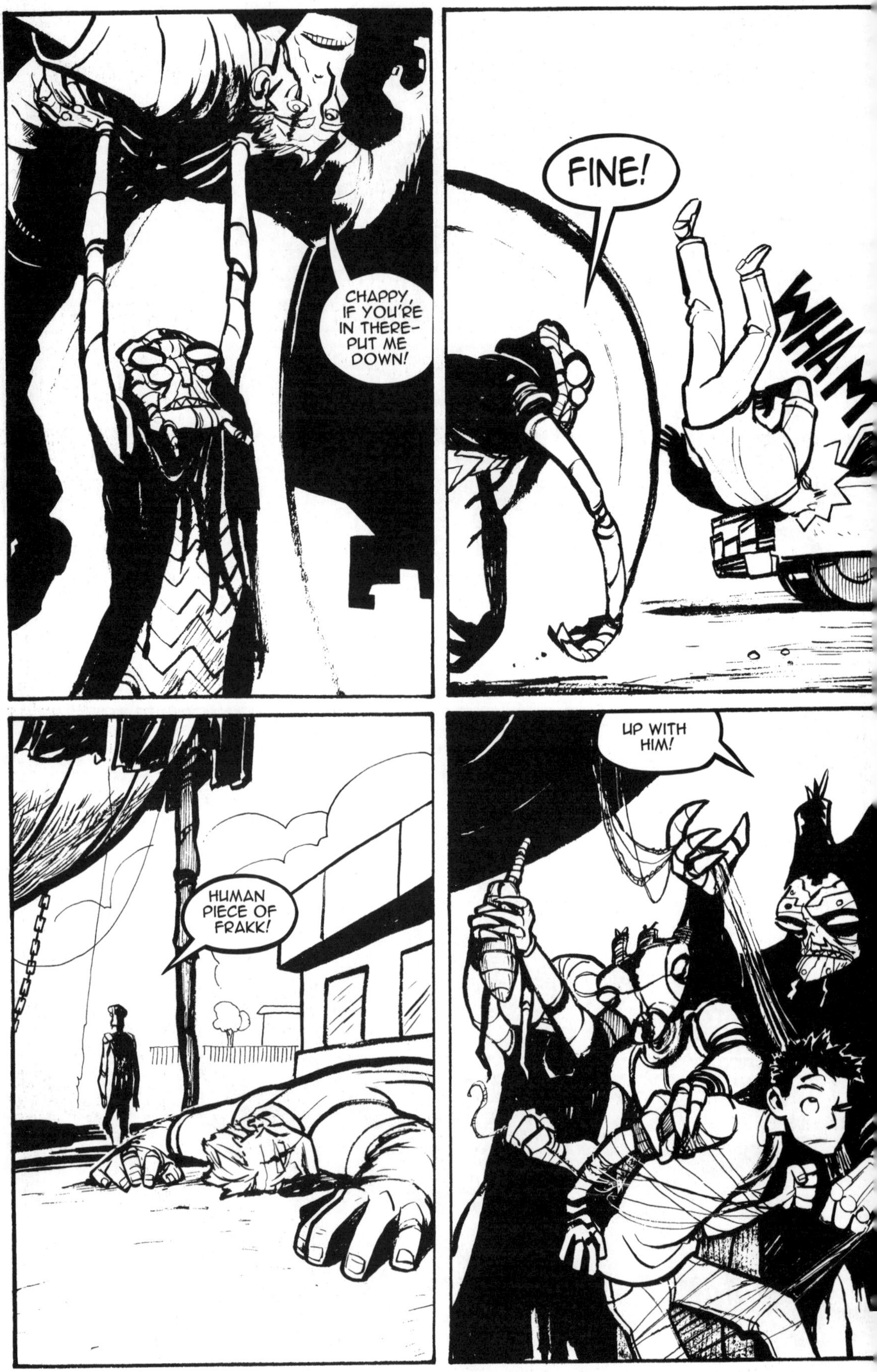
CHAPPY, IF YOU'RE IN THERE-PUT ME DOWN!
FINE!
WHAM
HUMAN PIECE OF FRAKK!
UP WITH HIM!

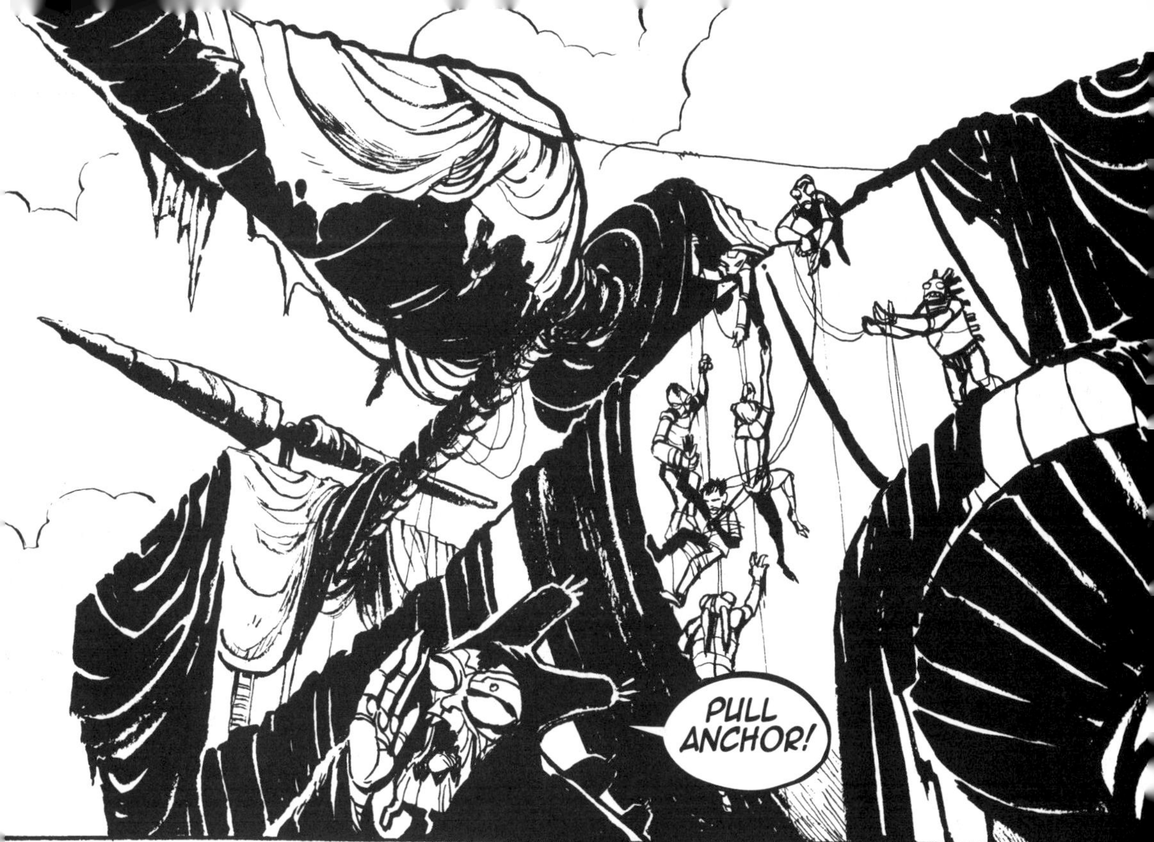
PULL ANCHOR!

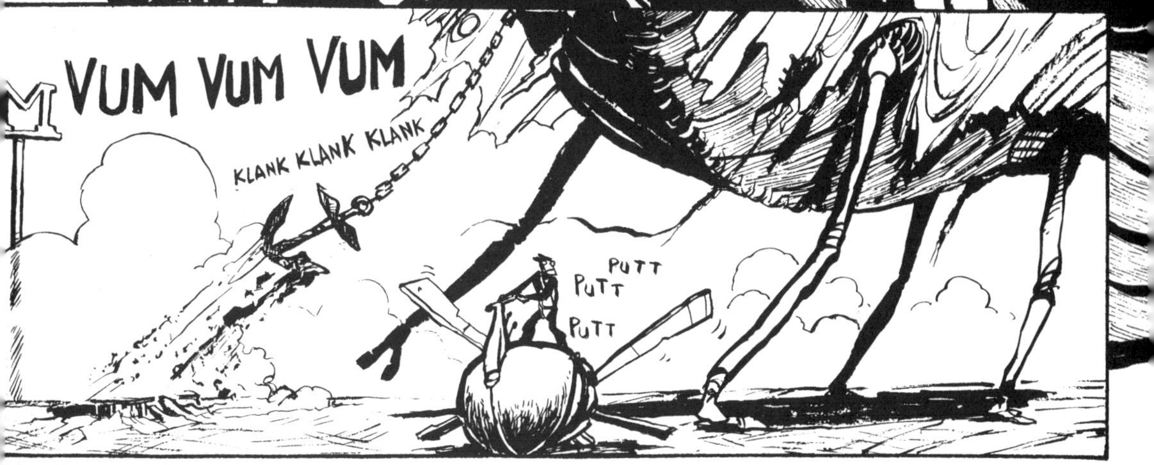
VUM VUM VUM
KLANK KLANK KLANK
PUTT PUTT PUTT PUTT

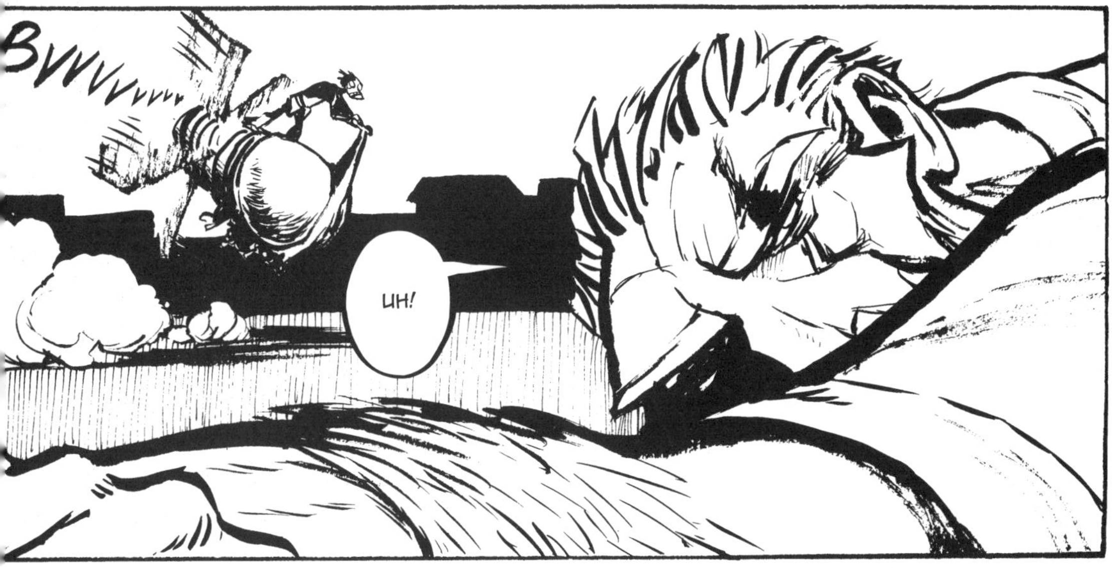
BVVVVVVVVV
UH!

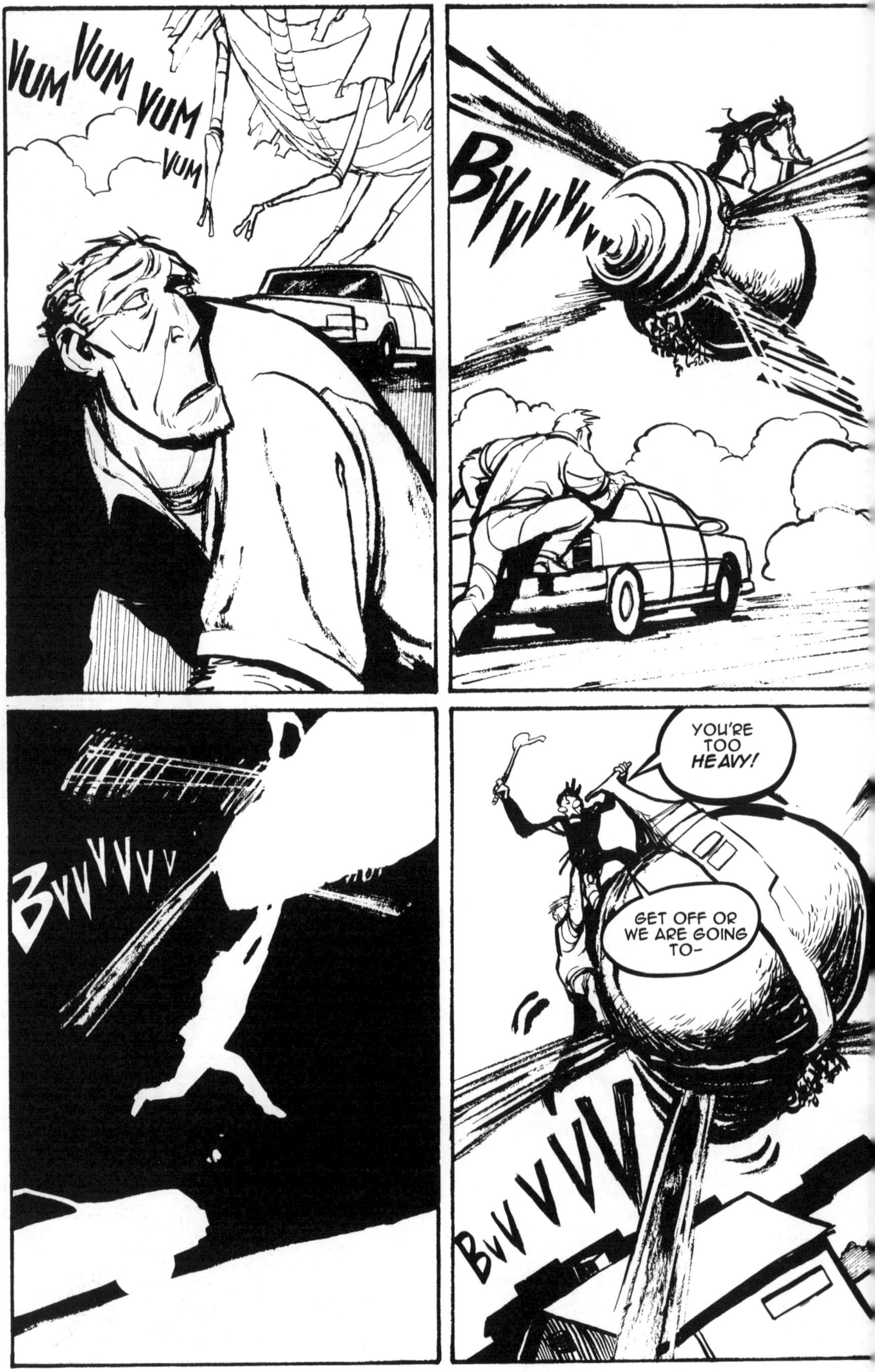
VUM VUM VUM VUM
BVVVVVV
BVVVVVV
YOU'RE TOO HEAVY!
GET OFF OR WE ARE GOING TO-
BVVVVV

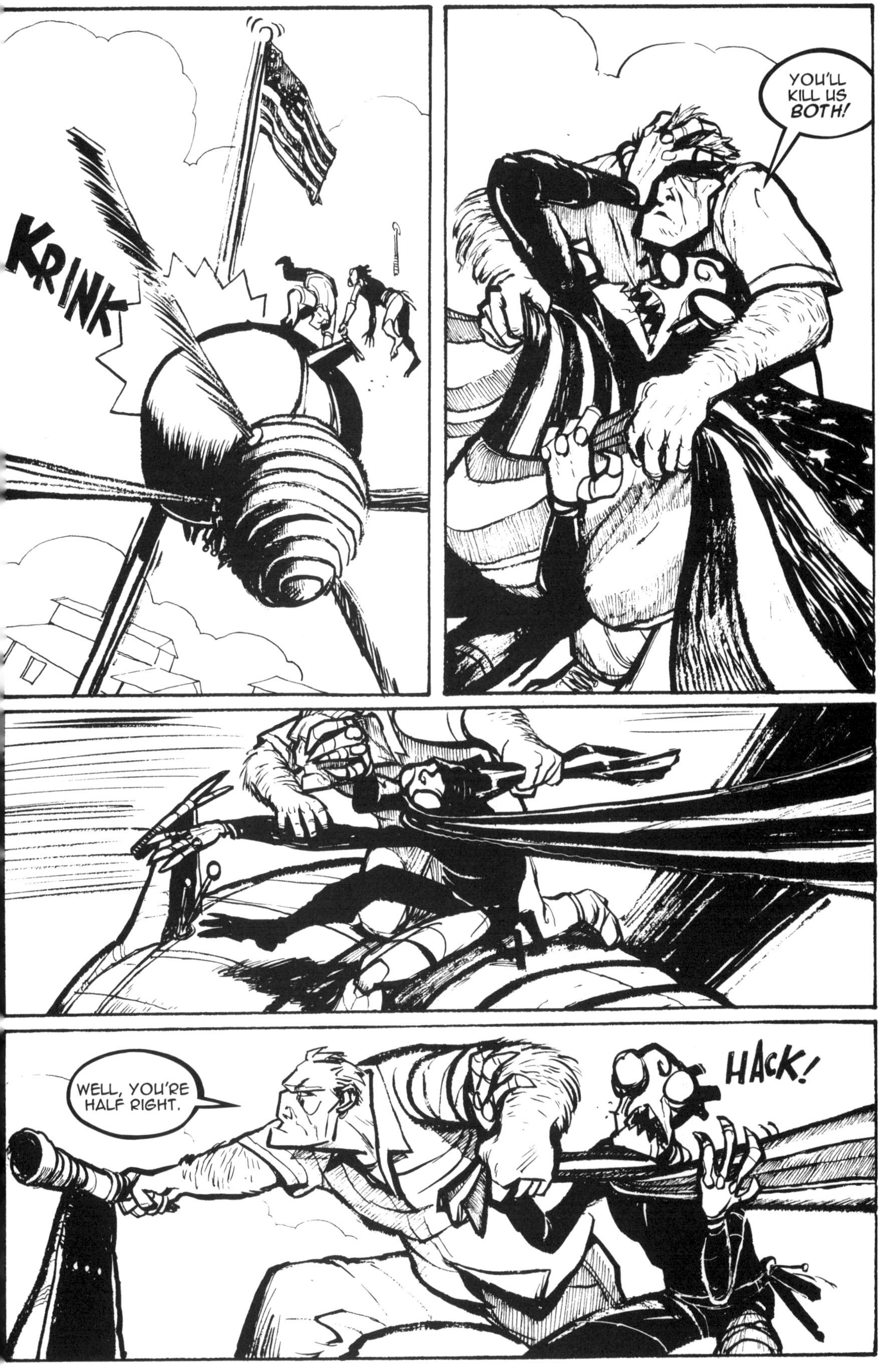
KRINK
YOU'LL KILL US BOTH!
WELL, YOU'RE HALF RIGHT.
HACK!

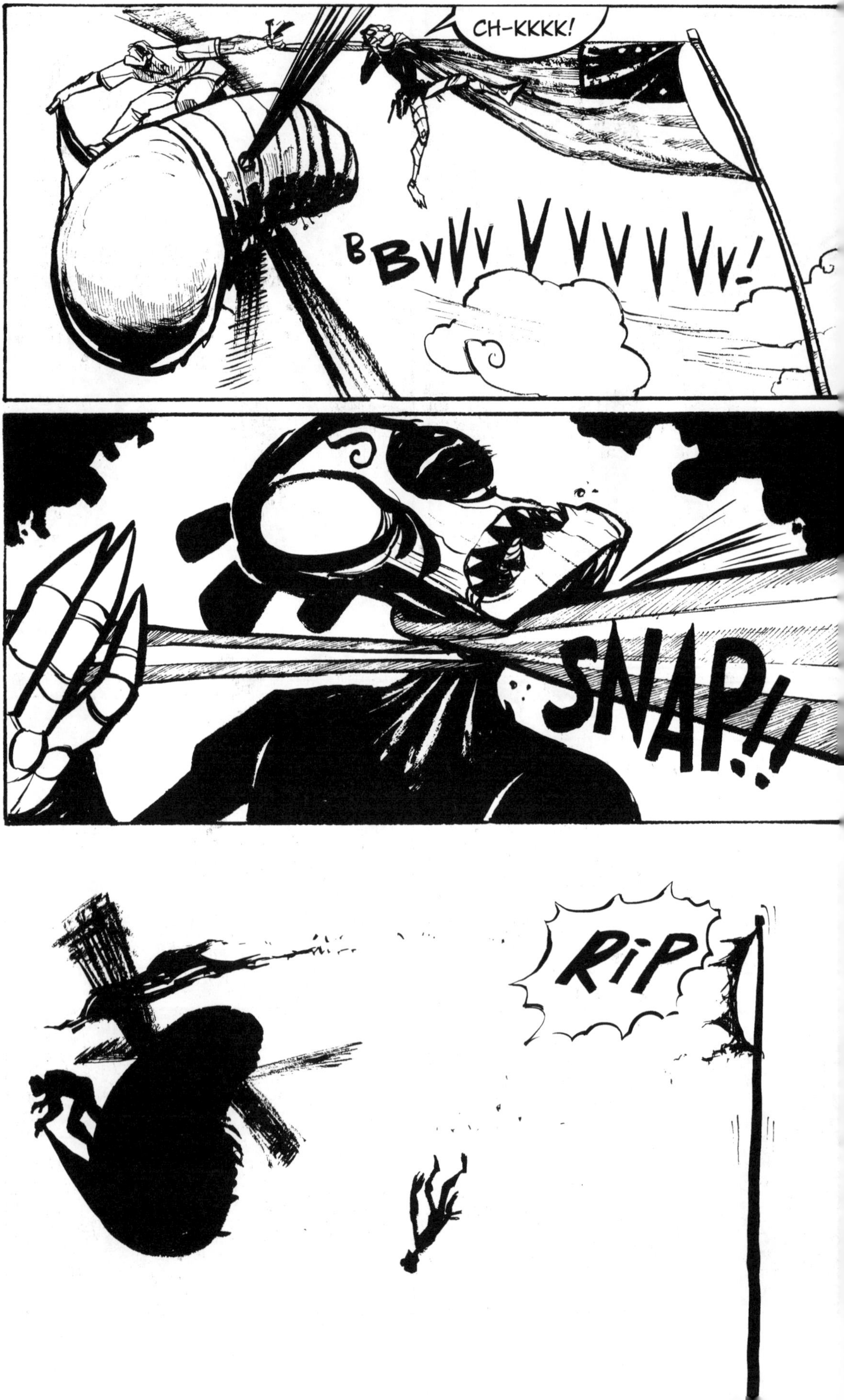
CH-KKKK!
BBVVVV VVVVVVV!
SNAP!!
RIP

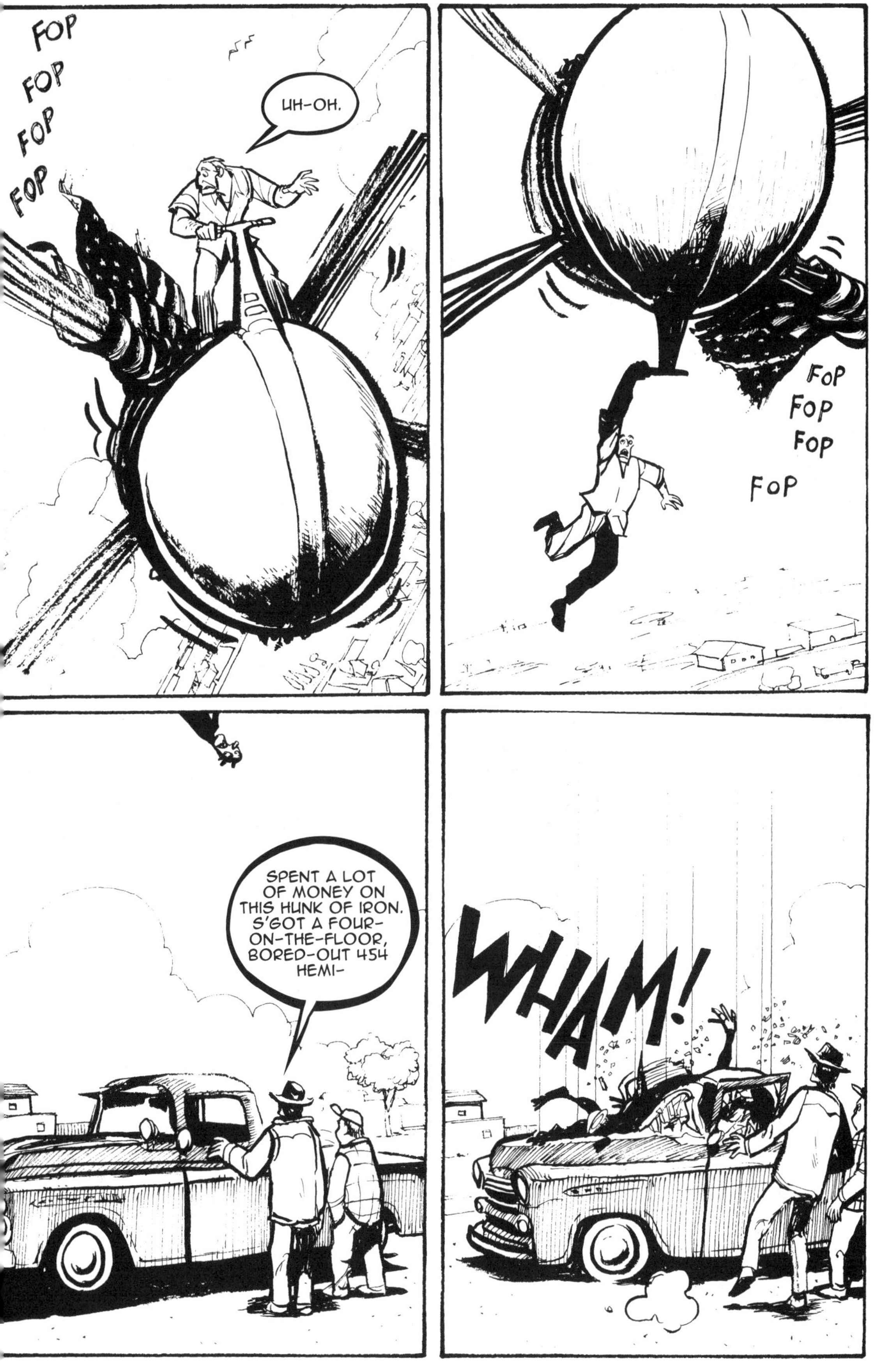
FOP
FOP
FOP
FOP
UH-OH.
FOP
FOP
FOP
FOP
SPENT A LOT OF MONEY ON THIS HUNK OF IRON. S'GOT A FOUR-ON-THE-FLOOR, BORED-OUT 454 HEMI-
WHAM!

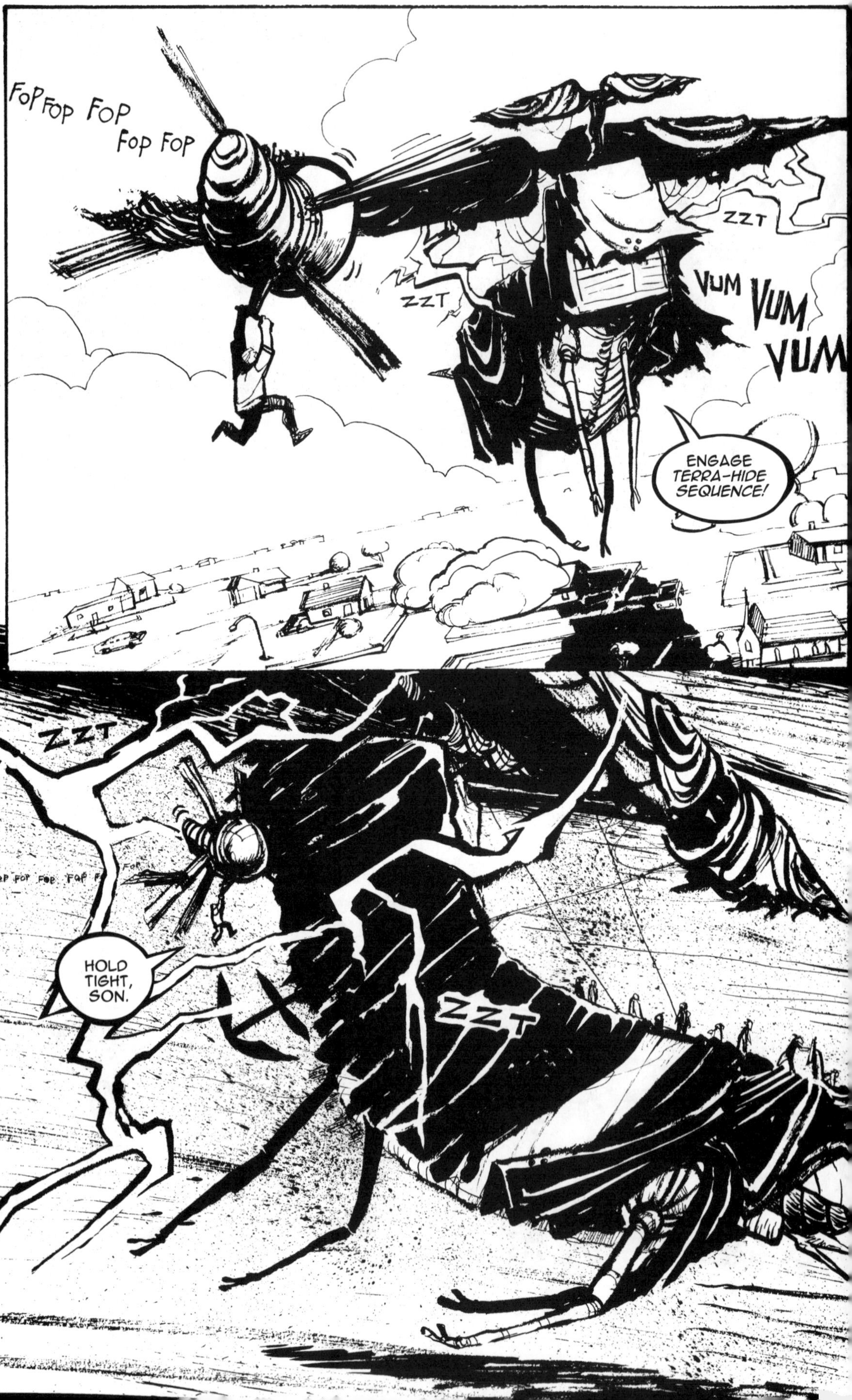
FOP FOP FOP
FOP FOP
ZZT
ZZT
VUM VUM VUM
ENGAGE TERRA-HIDE SEQUENCE!
ZZT
HOLD TIGHT, SON.
ZZT

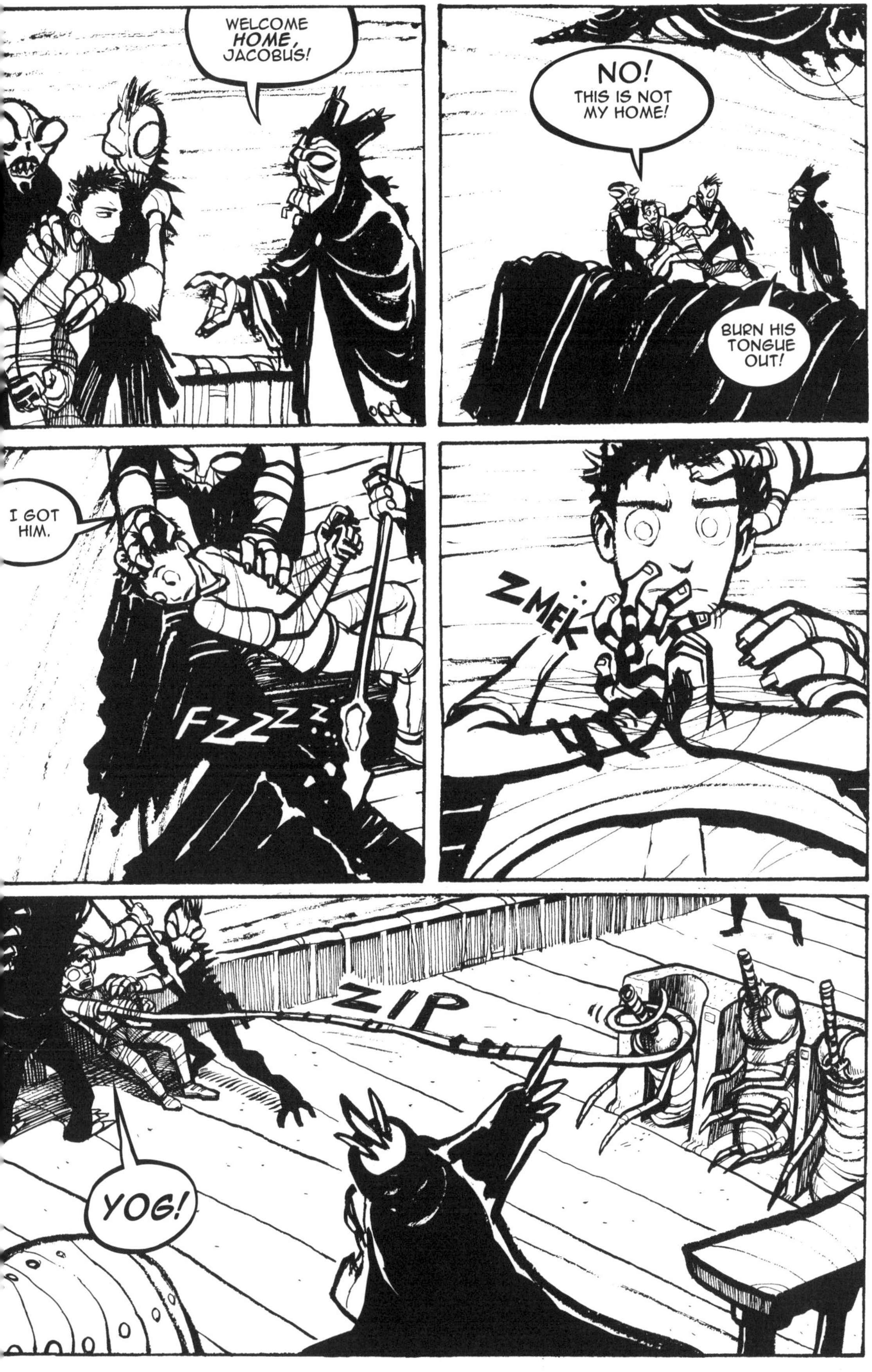
WELCOME *HOME*, JACOBUS!
NO! THIS IS NOT MY HOME!
BURN HIS TONGUE OUT!
I GOT HIM.
FZZZZZ
ZMEK
ZIP
YOG!

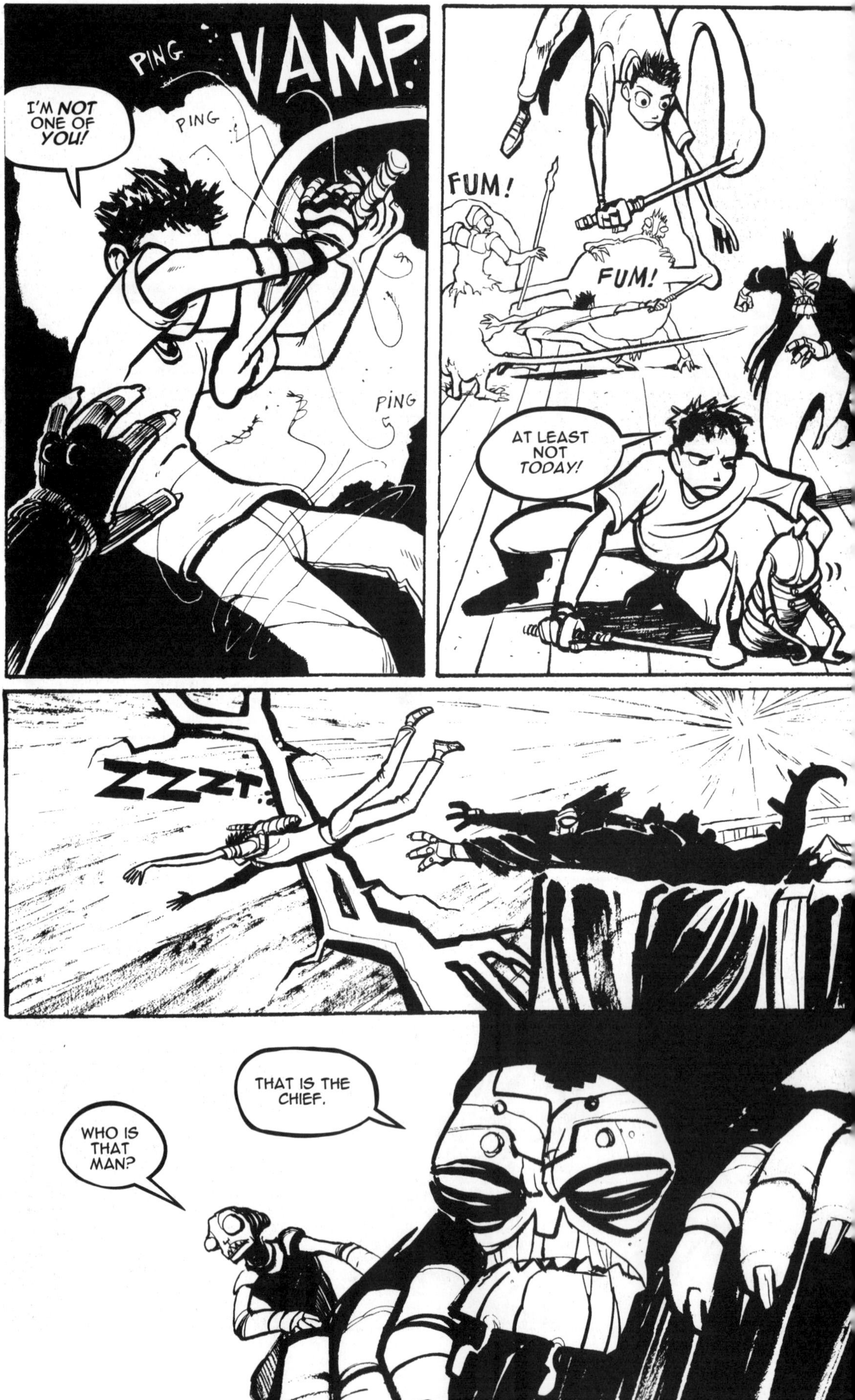

PING
VAMP
I'M NOT ONE OF YOU!
PING
PING
FUM!
FUM!
AT LEAST NOT TODAY!
ZZZT
THAT IS THE CHIEF.
WHO IS THAT MAN?

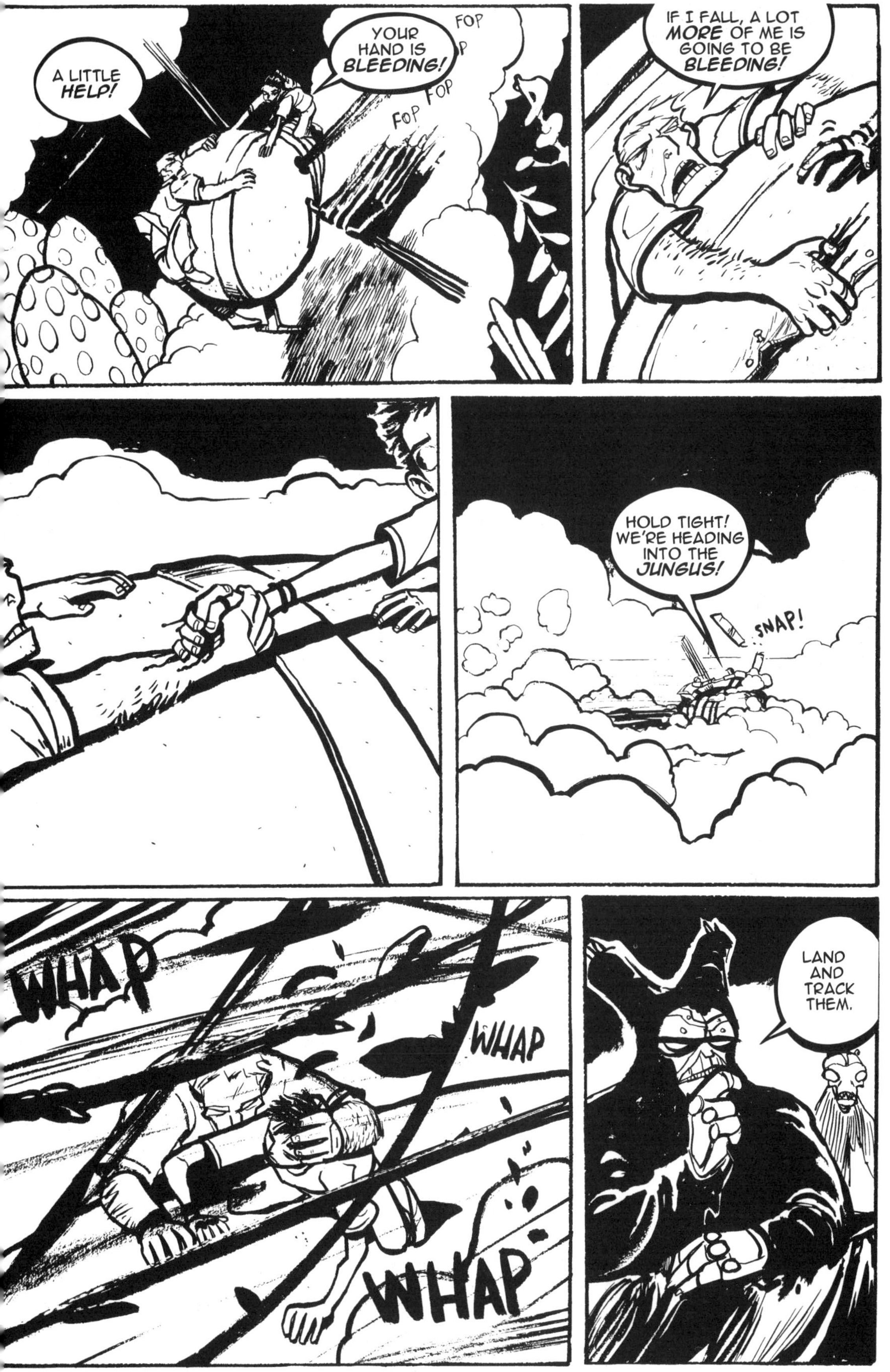
A LITTLE HELP!
YOUR HAND IS BLEEDING!
FOP
P
FOP FOP
IF I FALL, A LOT MORE OF ME IS GOING TO BE BLEEDING!
HOLD TIGHT! WE'RE HEADING INTO THE JUNGUS!
SNAP!
WHAP
WHAP
WHAP
LAND AND TRACK THEM.

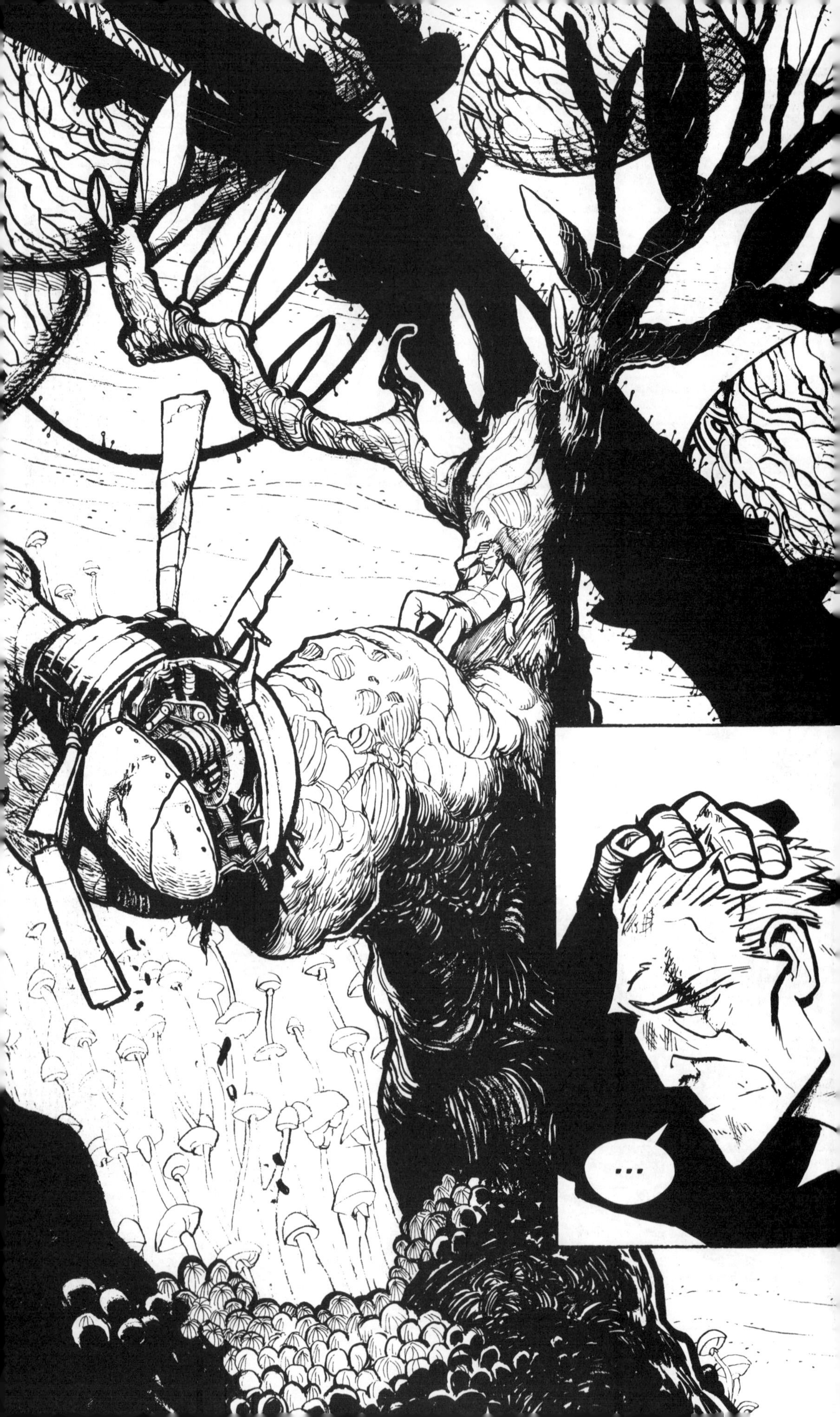
...

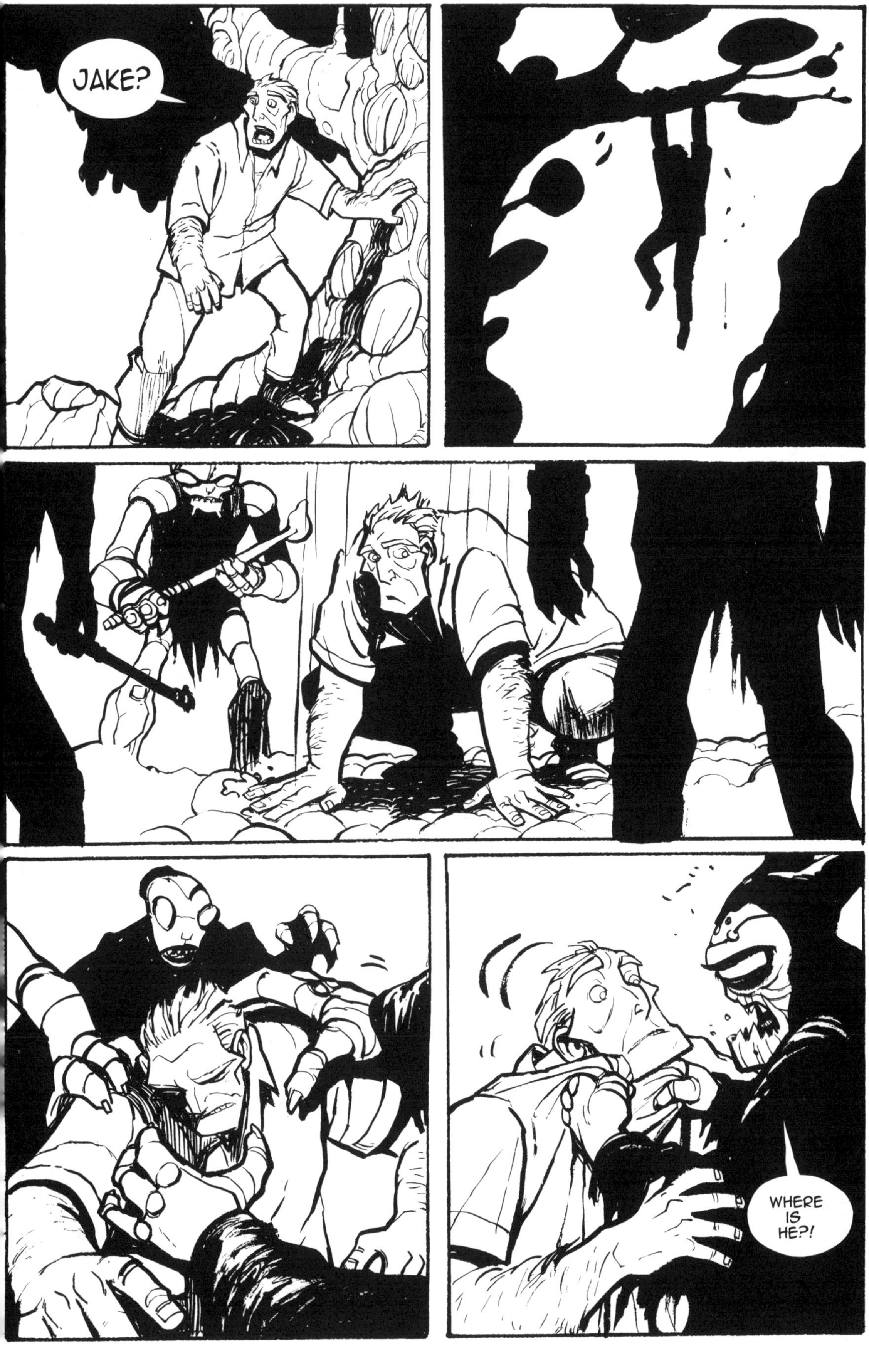
JAKE?
WHERE IS HE?!

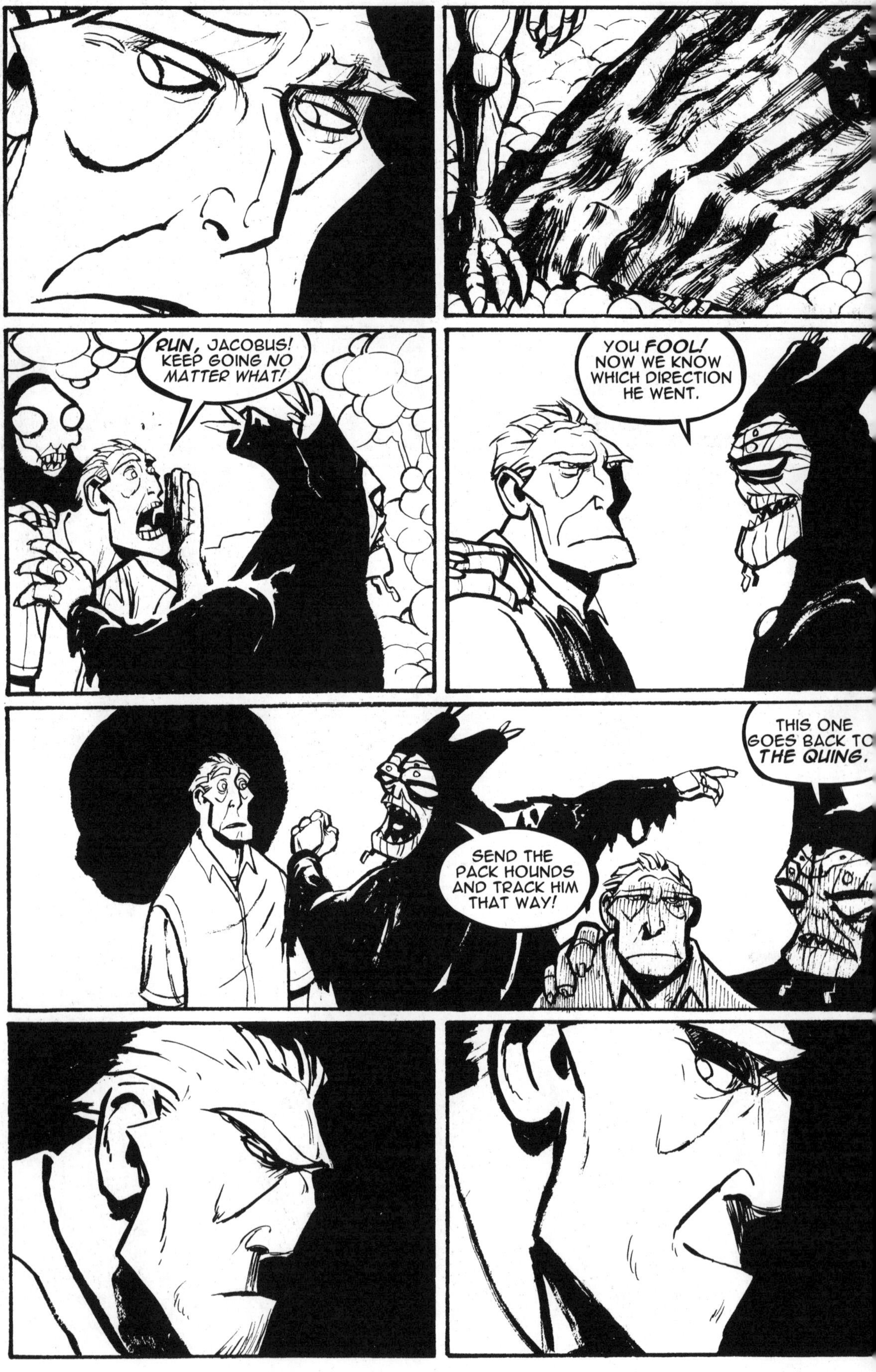
RUN, JACOBUS! KEEP GOING NO MATTER WHAT!
YOU FOOL! NOW WE KNOW WHICH DIRECTION HE WENT.
THIS ONE GOES BACK TO THE QUING.
SEND THE PACK HOUNDS AND TRACK HIM THAT WAY!

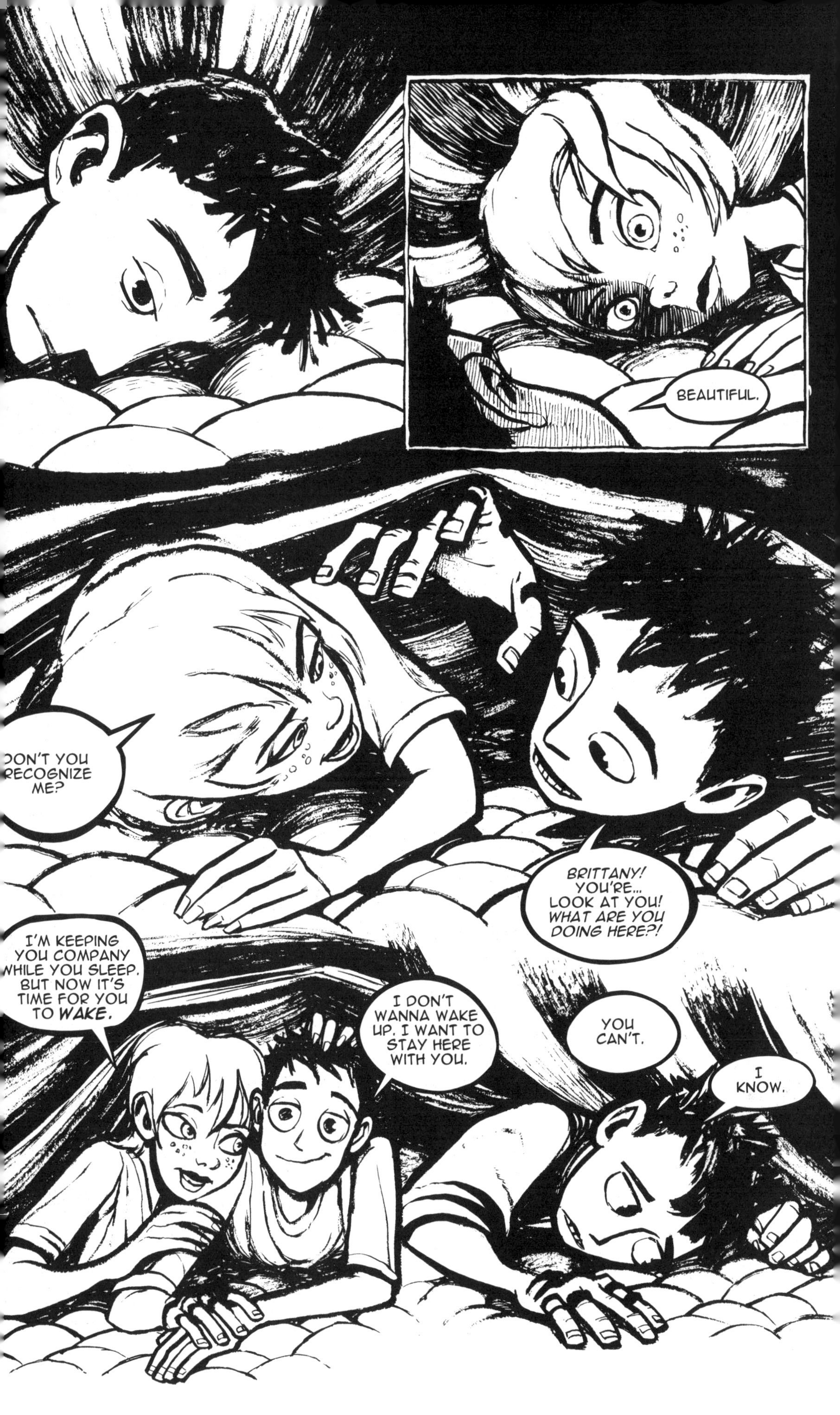
BEAUTIFUL.
DON'T YOU RECOGNIZE ME?
BRITTANY! YOU'RE... LOOK AT YOU! WHAT ARE YOU DOING HERE?!
I'M KEEPING YOU COMPANY WHILE YOU SLEEP. BUT NOW IT'S TIME FOR YOU TO WAKE.
I DON'T WANNA WAKE UP. I WANT TO STAY HERE WITH YOU.
YOU CAN'T.
I KNOW.

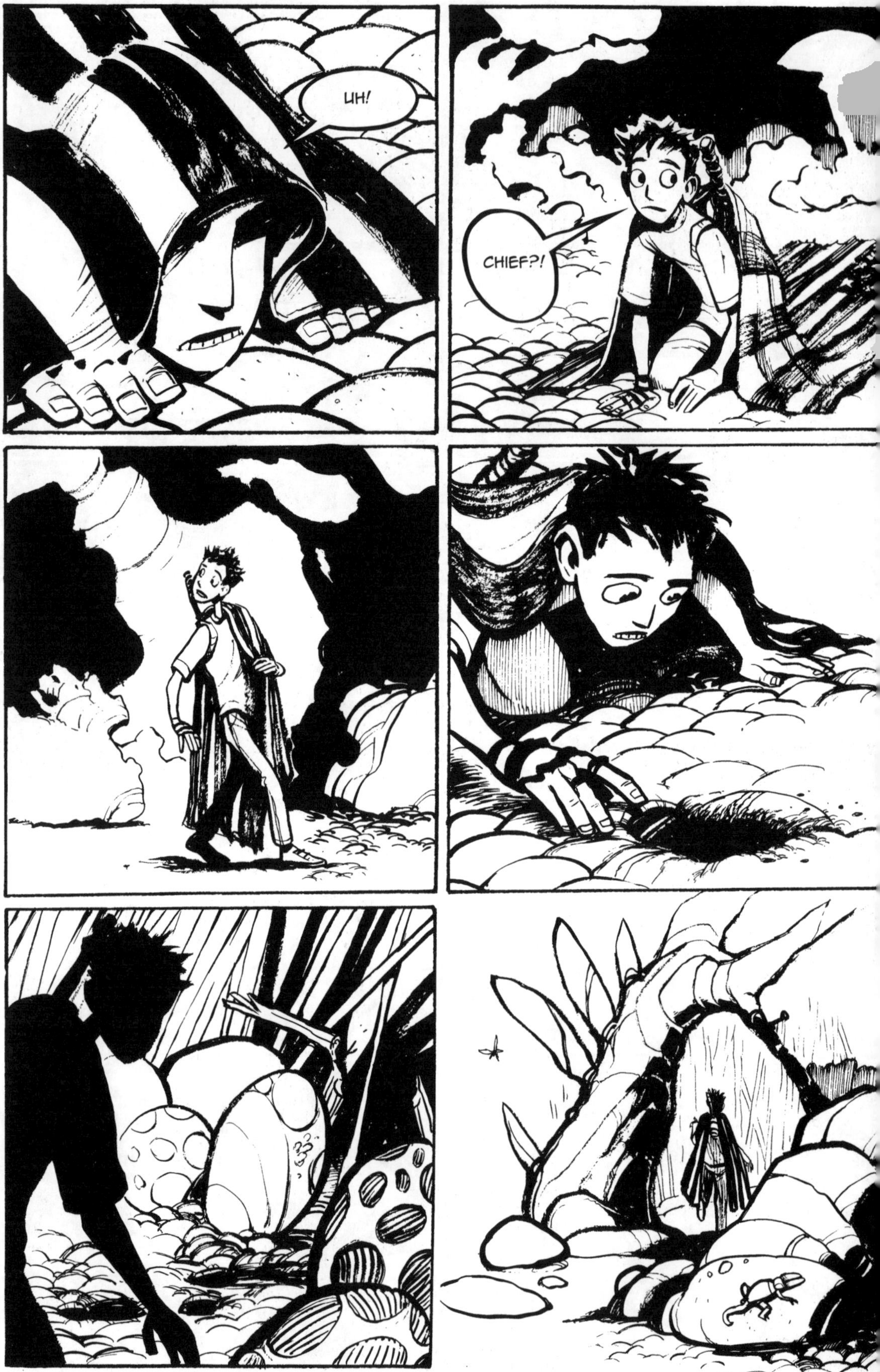
UH!
CHIEF?!

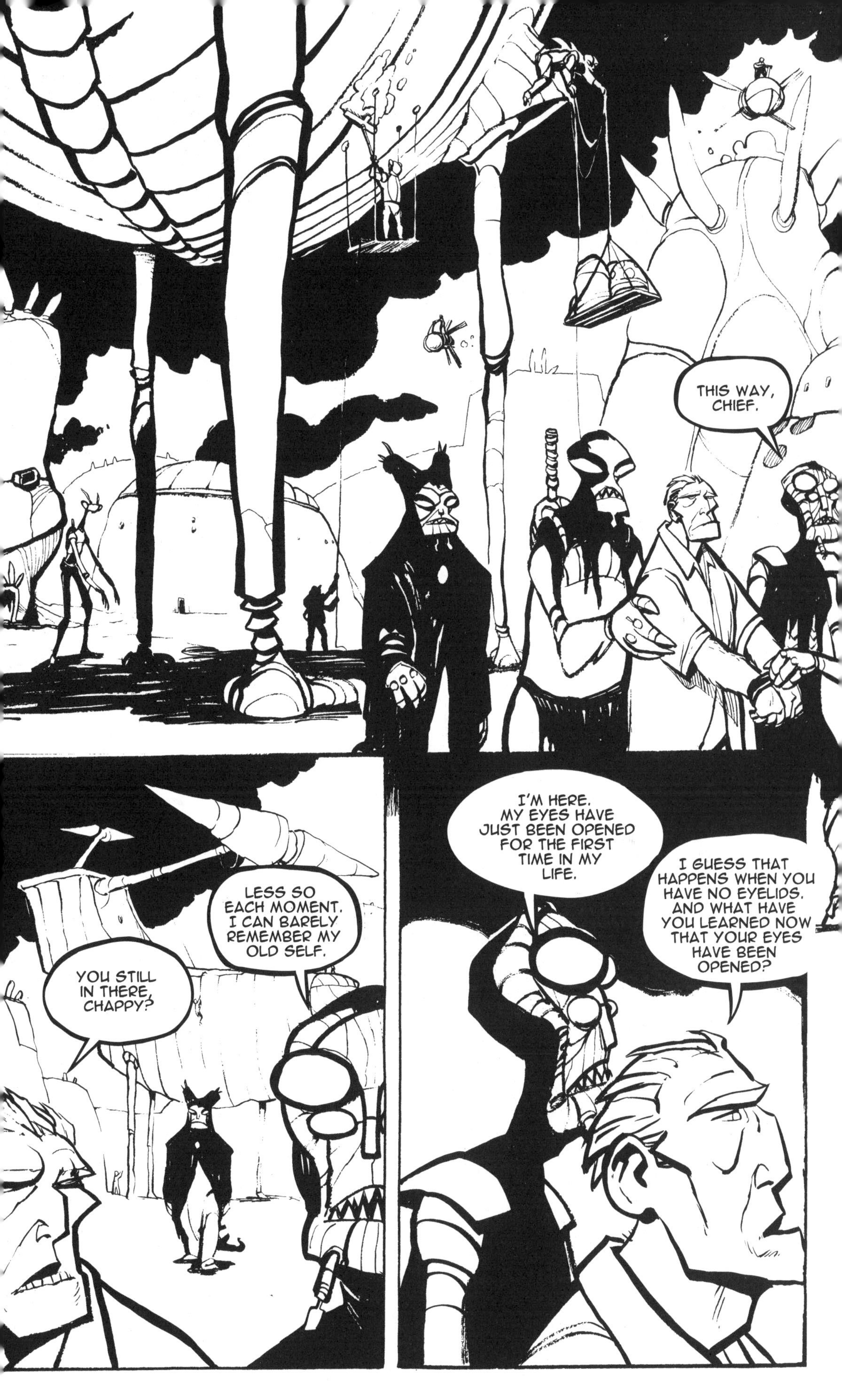
THIS WAY, CHIEF.
YOU STILL IN THERE, CHAPPY?
LESS SO EACH MOMENT. I CAN BARELY REMEMBER MY OLD SELF.
I'M HERE. MY EYES HAVE JUST BEEN OPENED FOR THE FIRST TIME IN MY LIFE.
I GUESS THAT HAPPENS WHEN YOU HAVE NO EYELIDS. AND WHAT HAVE YOU LEARNED NOW THAT YOUR EYES HAVE BEEN OPENED?

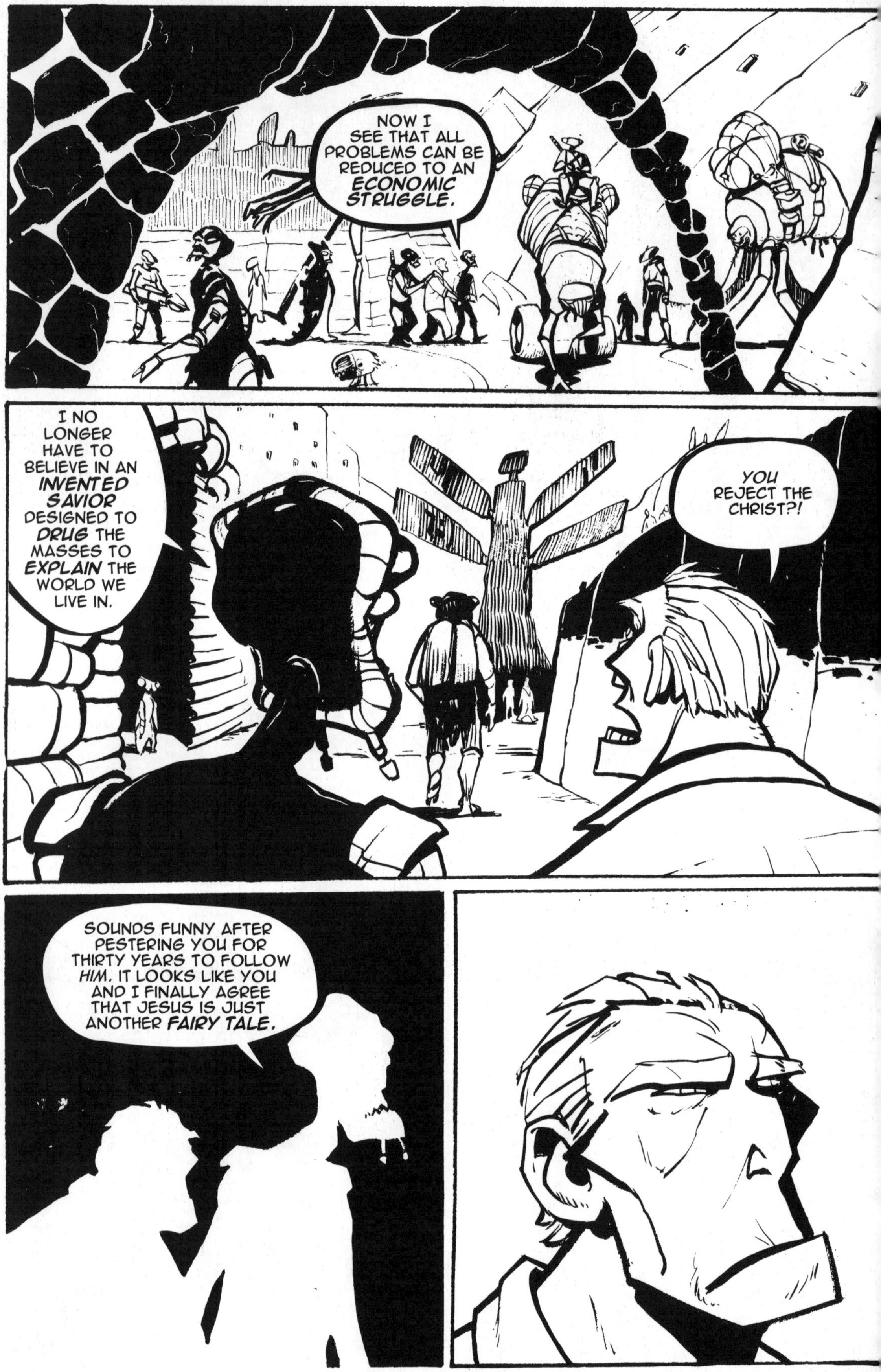
NOW I SEE THAT ALL PROBLEMS CAN BE REDUCED TO AN ECONOMIC STRUGGLE.
I NO LONGER HAVE TO BELIEVE IN AN INVENTED SAVIOR DESIGNED TO DRUG THE MASSES TO EXPLAIN THE WORLD WE LIVE IN.
YOU REJECT THE CHRIST?!
SOUNDS FUNNY AFTER PESTERING YOU FOR THIRTY YEARS TO FOLLOW HIM. IT LOOKS LIKE YOU AND I FINALLY AGREE THAT JESUS IS JUST ANOTHER FAIRY TALE.

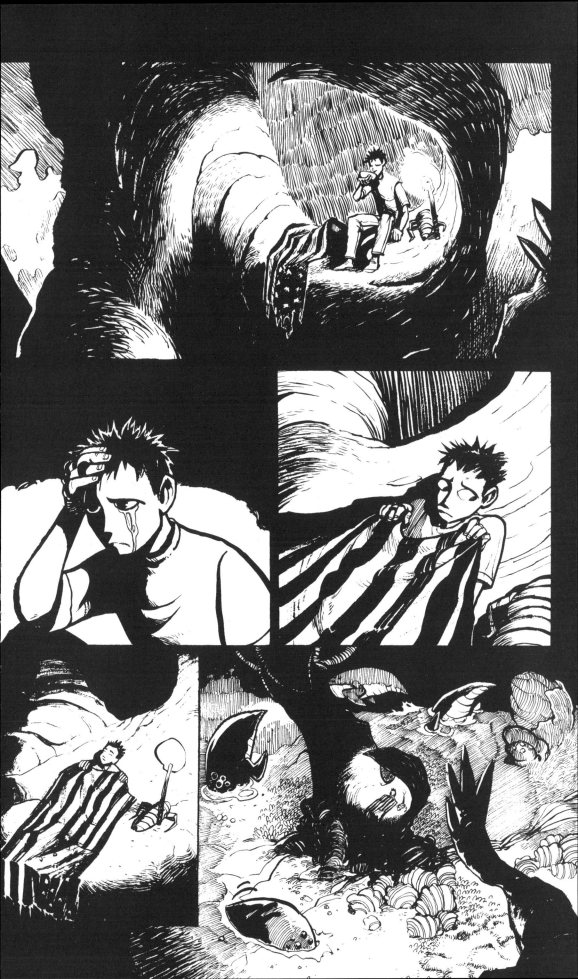

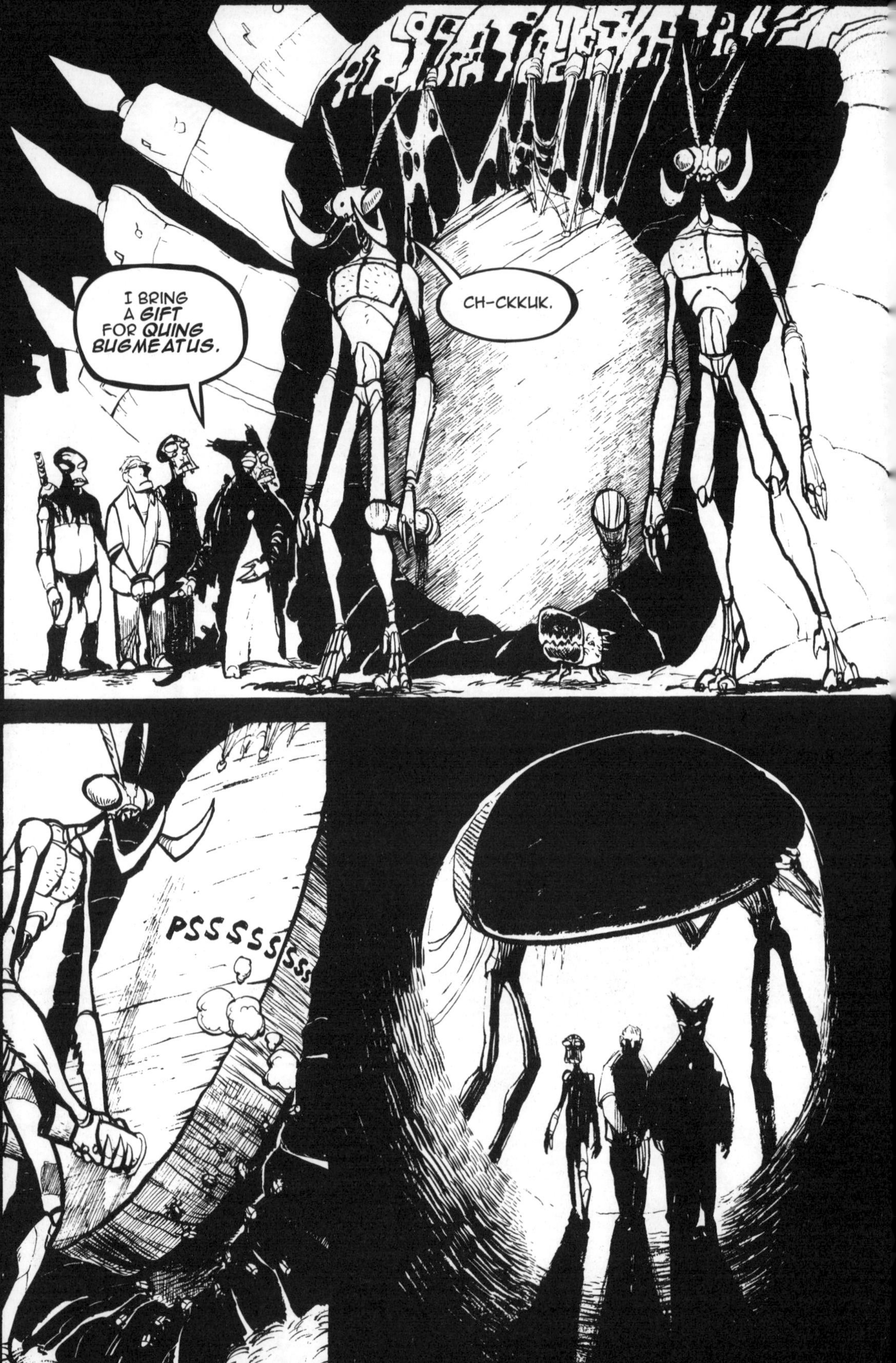
I BRING A GIFT FOR QUING BUGMEATUS.
CH-CKKUK.
PSSSSSSSSS

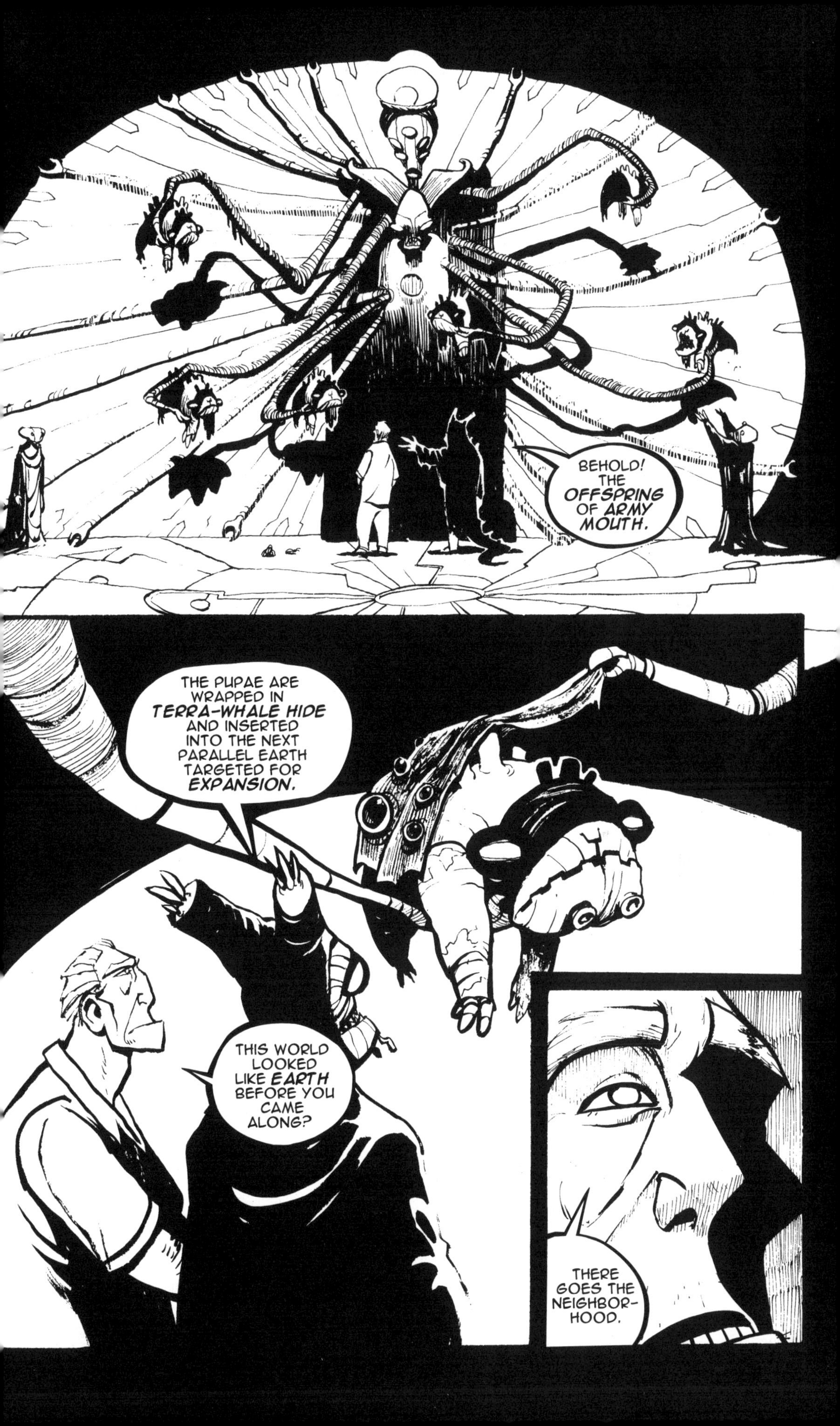
BEHOLD! THE OFFSPRING OF ARMY MOUTH.
THE PUPAE ARE WRAPPED IN TERRA-WHALE HIDE AND INSERTED INTO THE NEXT PARALLEL EARTH TARGETED FOR EXPANSION.
THIS WORLD LOOKED LIKE EARTH BEFORE YOU CAME ALONG?
THERE GOES THE NEIGHBOR-HOOD.

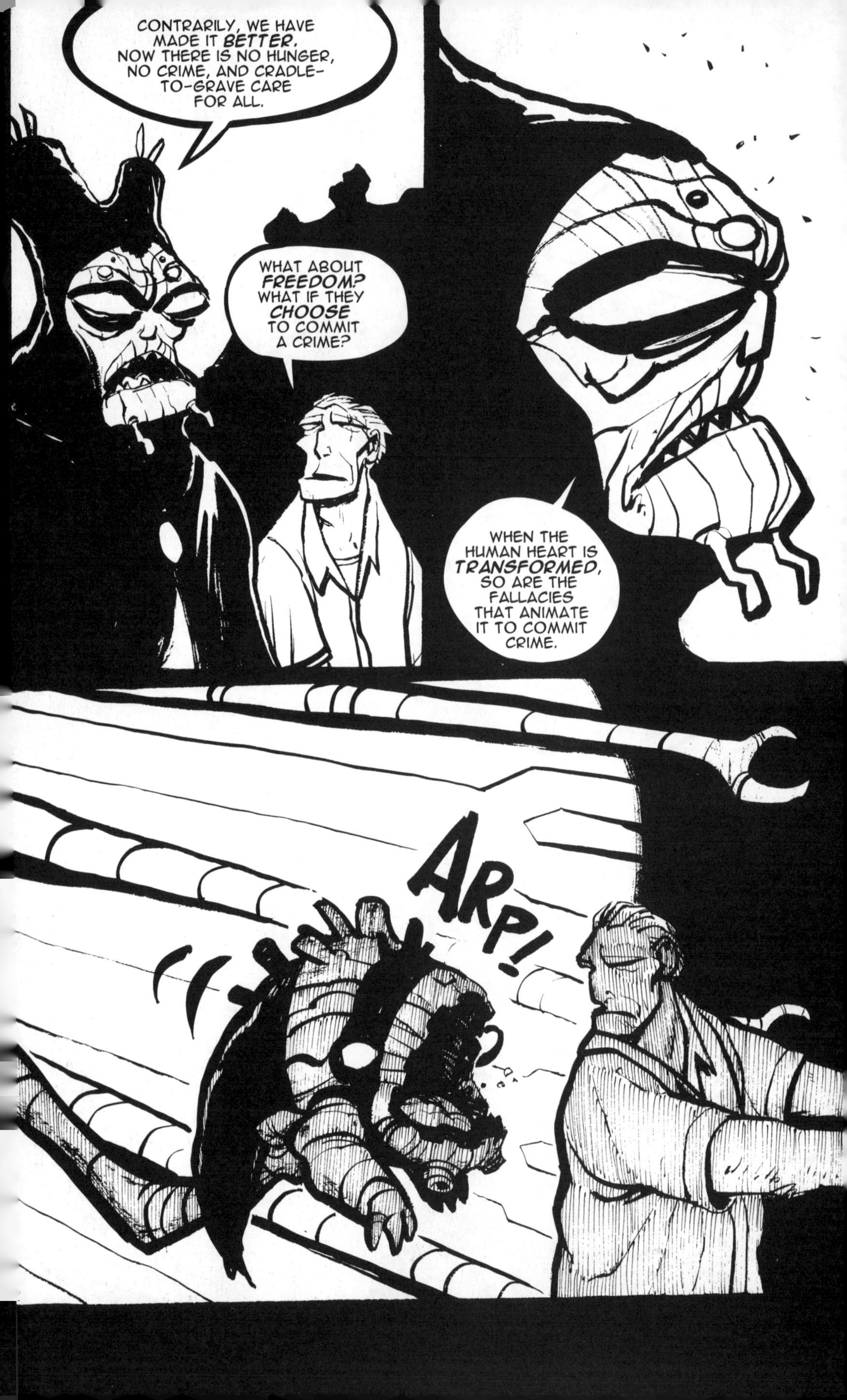
CONTRARILY, WE HAVE MADE IT BETTER. NOW THERE IS NO HUNGER, NO CRIME, AND CRADLE-TO-GRAVE CARE FOR ALL.
WHAT ABOUT FREEDOM? WHAT IF THEY CHOOSE TO COMMIT A CRIME?
WHEN THE HUMAN HEART IS TRANSFORMED, SO ARE THE FALLACIES THAT ANIMATE IT TO COMMIT CRIME.
ARP!

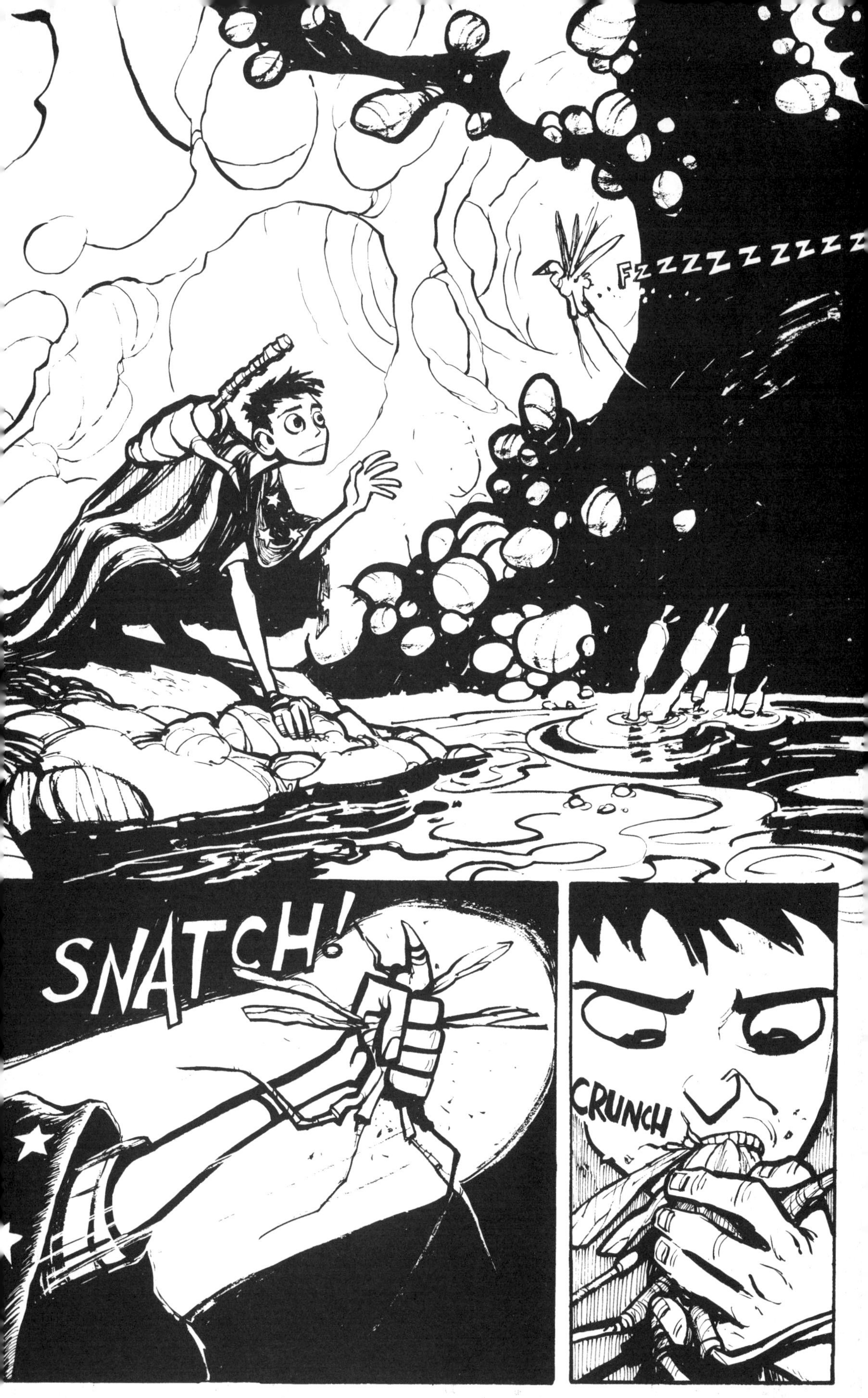

FZZZZZZZZZZ
SNATCH!
CRUNCH

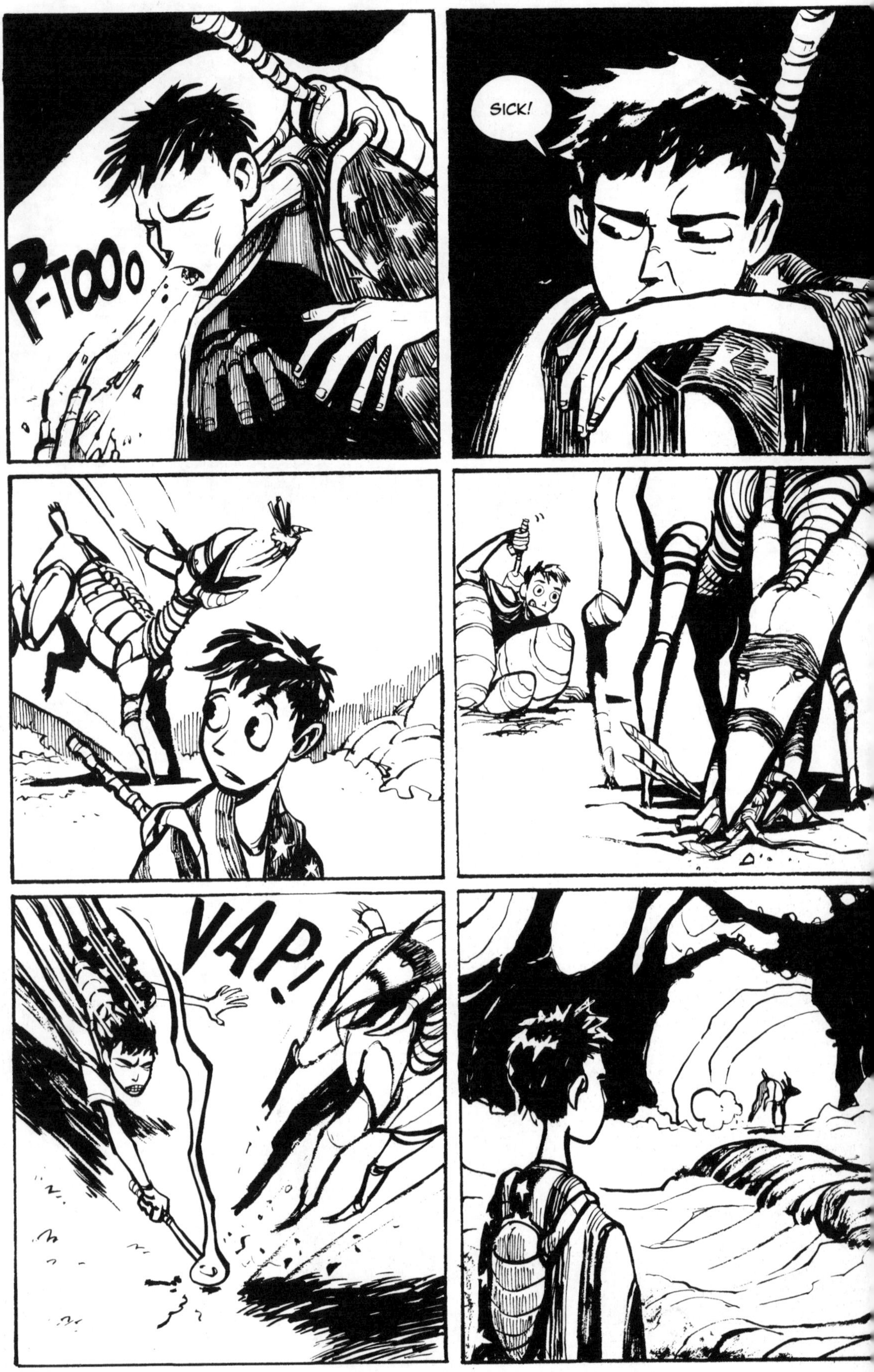
P-TOOO
SICK!
VAP!

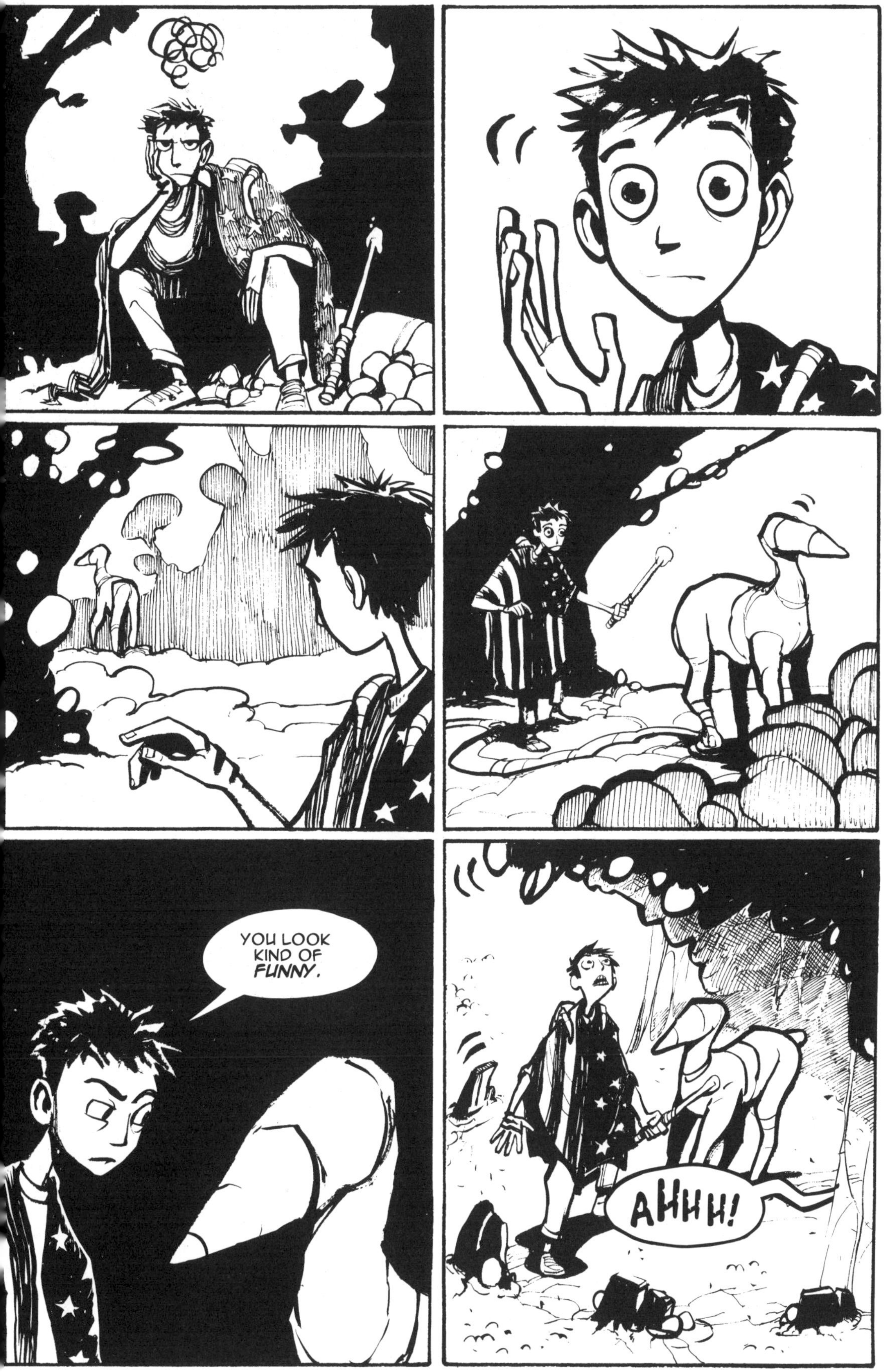
YOU LOOK KIND OF FUNNY.
AHHH!

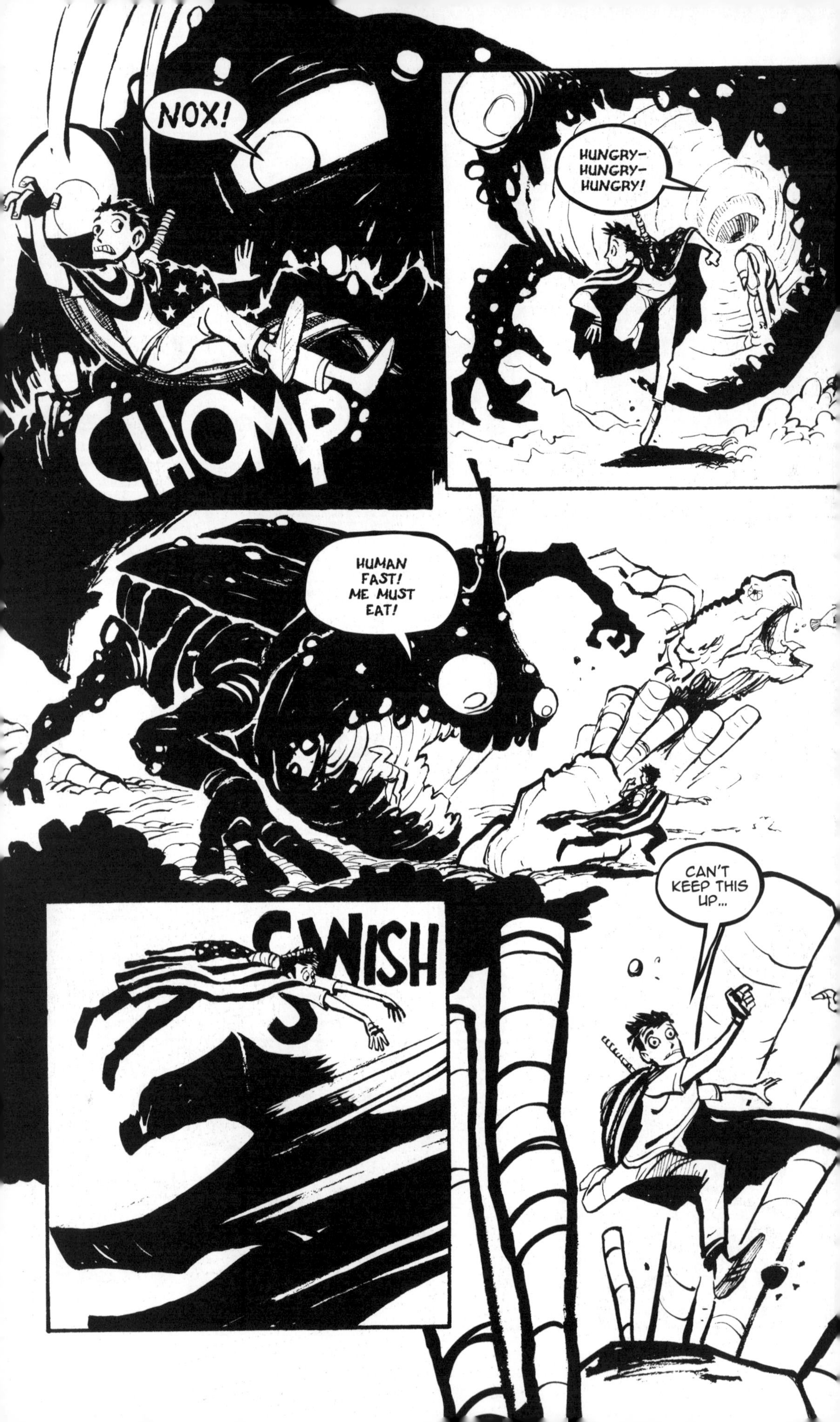
NOX!
CHOMP
HUNGRY-
HUNGRY-
HUNGRY!
HUMAN FAST! ME MUST EAT!
SWISH
CAN'T KEEP THIS UP...

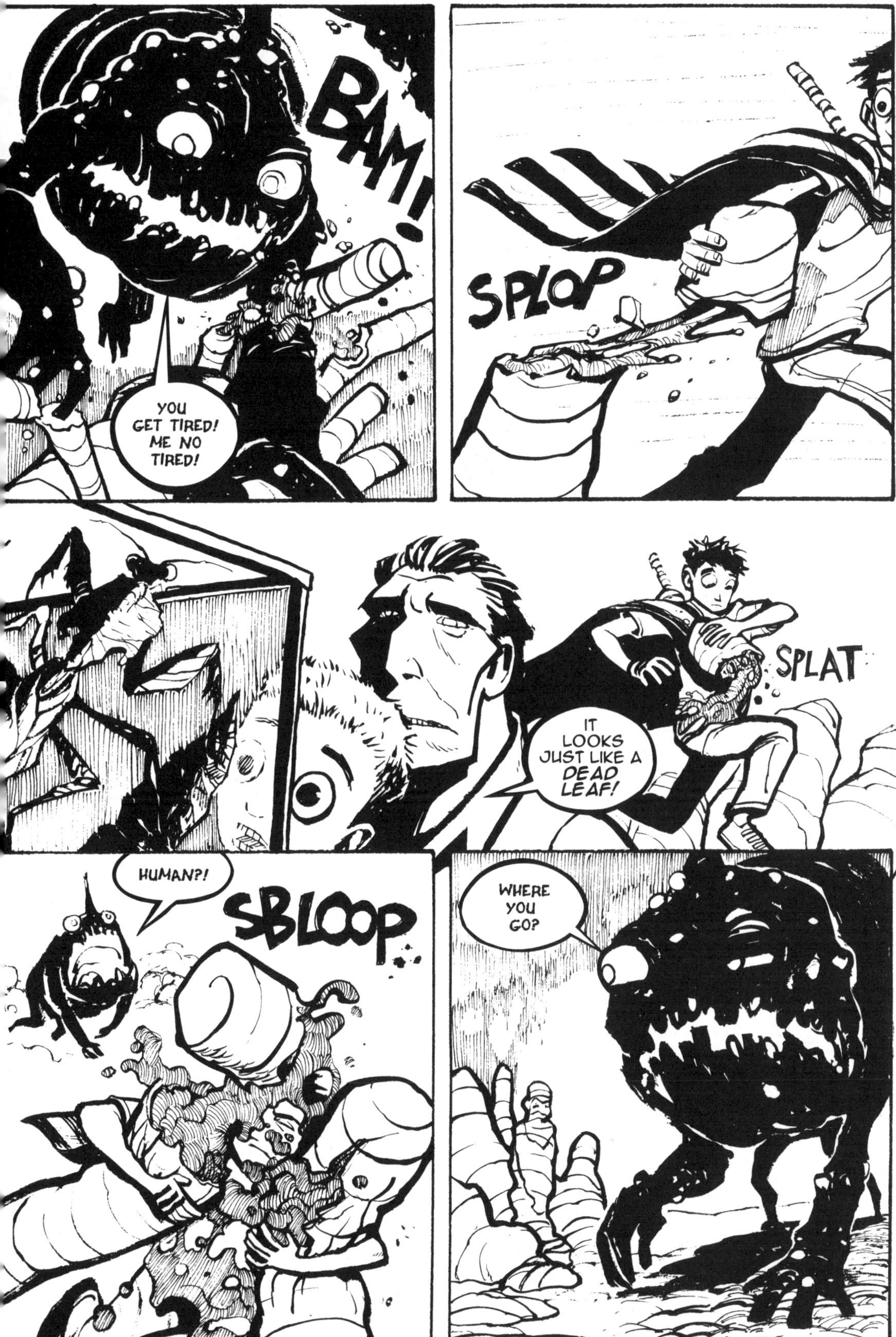
BAM!!
YOU GET TIRED! ME NO TIRED!
SPLOP
IT LOOKS JUST LIKE A DEAD LEAF!
SPLAT
HUMAN?!
SBLOOP
WHERE YOU GO?

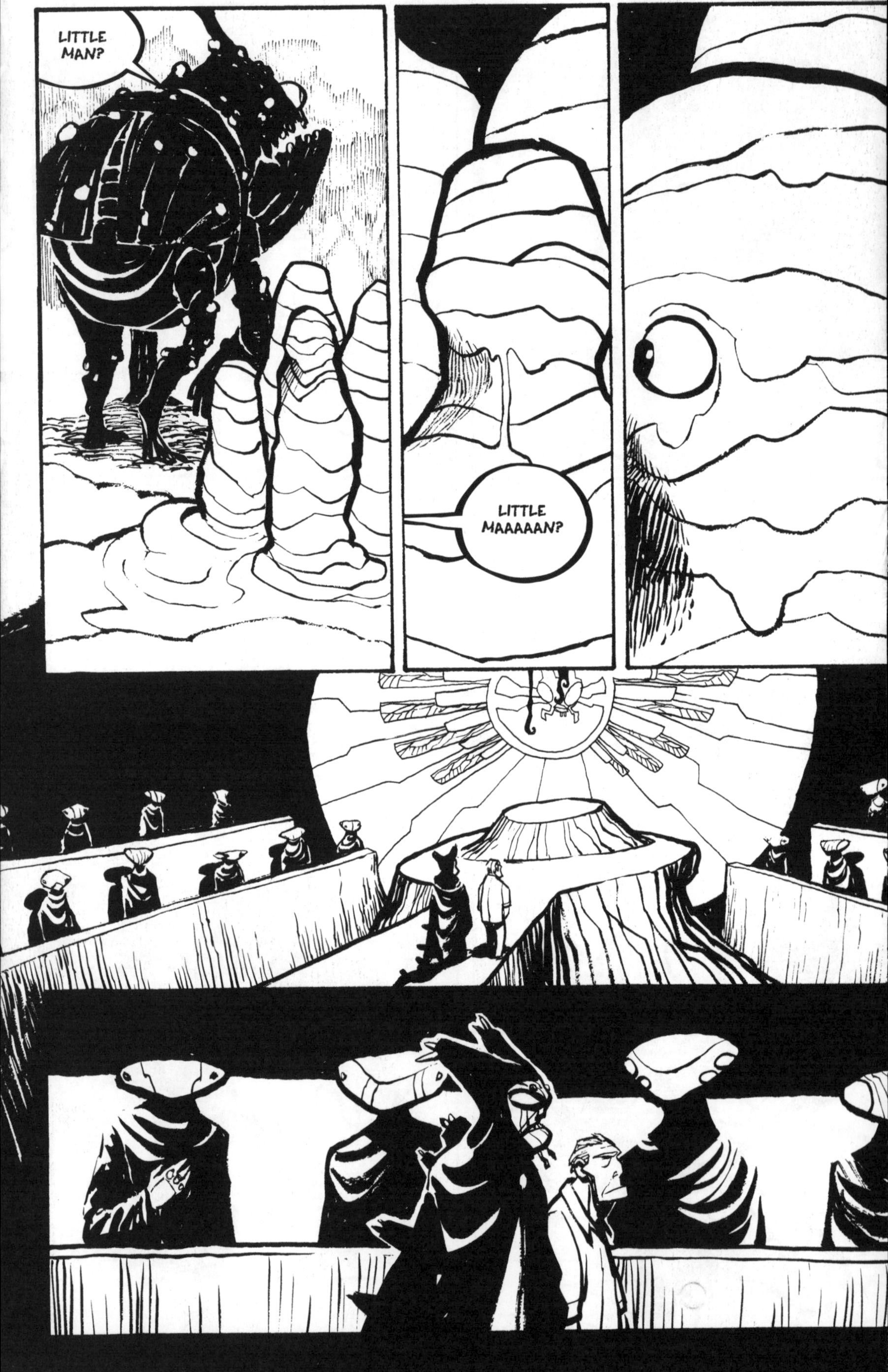
LITTLE MAN?
LITTLE MAAAAAN?

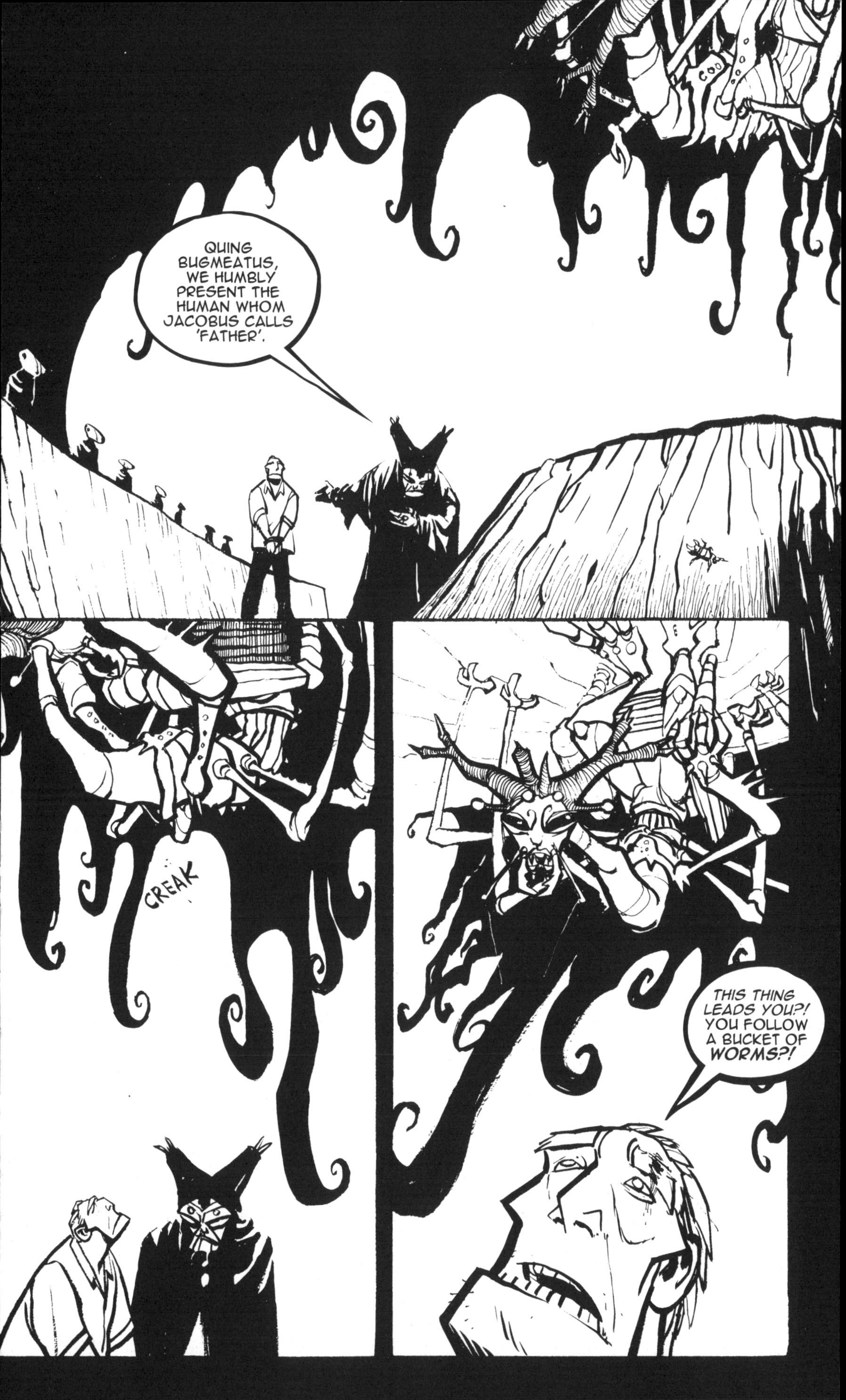
QUING BUGMEATUS, WE HUMBLY PRESENT THE HUMAN WHOM JACOBUS CALLS 'FATHER'.
CREAK
THIS THING LEADS YOU?! YOU FOLLOW A BUCKET OF WORMS?!

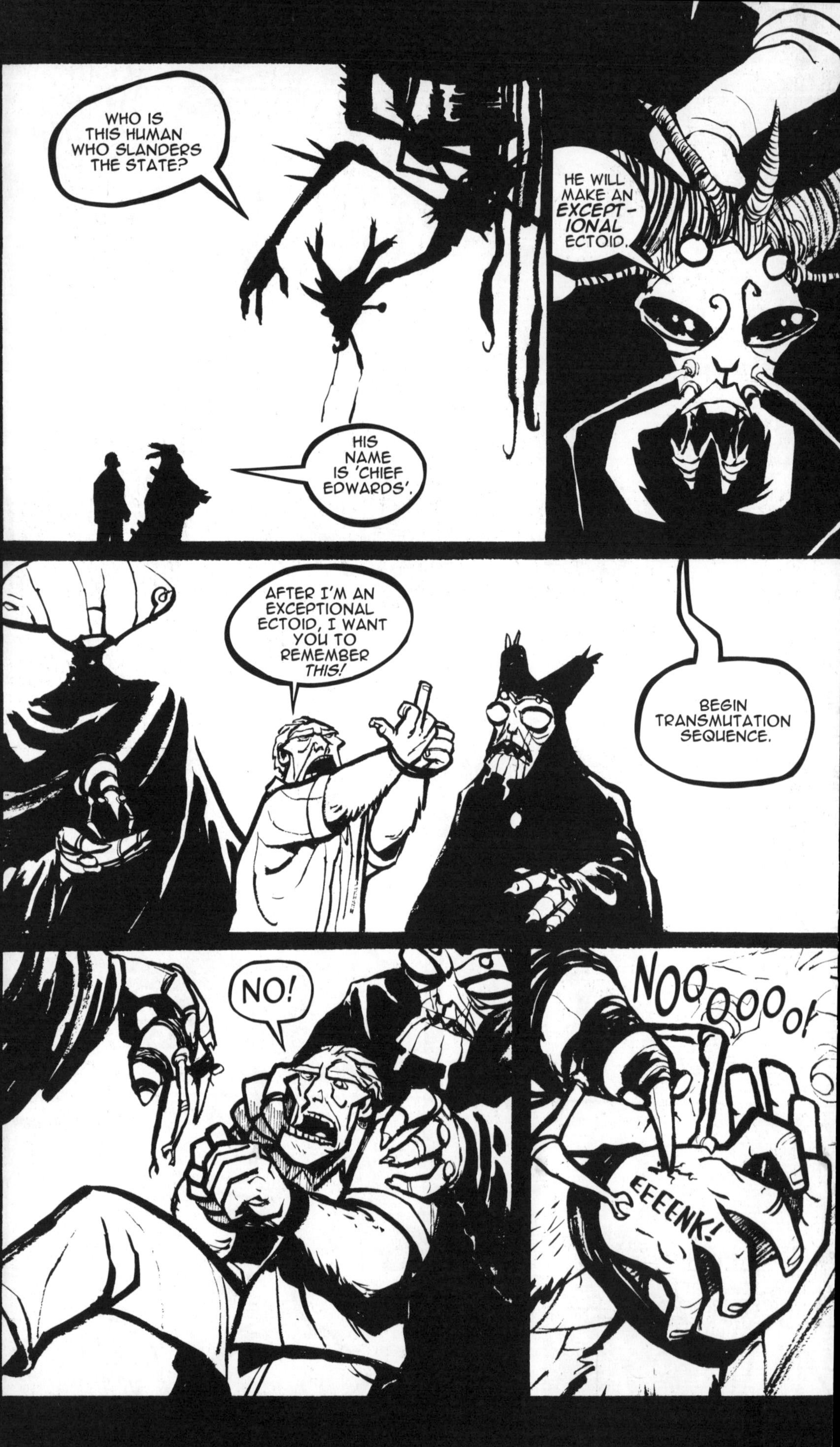
WHO IS THIS HUMAN WHO SLANDERS THE STATE?
HIS NAME IS 'CHIEF EDWARDS'.
HE WILL MAKE AN EXCEPT-IONAL ECTOID.
AFTER I'M AN EXCEPTIONAL ECTOID, I WANT YOU TO REMEMBER THIS!
BEGIN TRANSMUTATION SEQUENCE.
NO!
NOOOOOOO!
EEEENK!

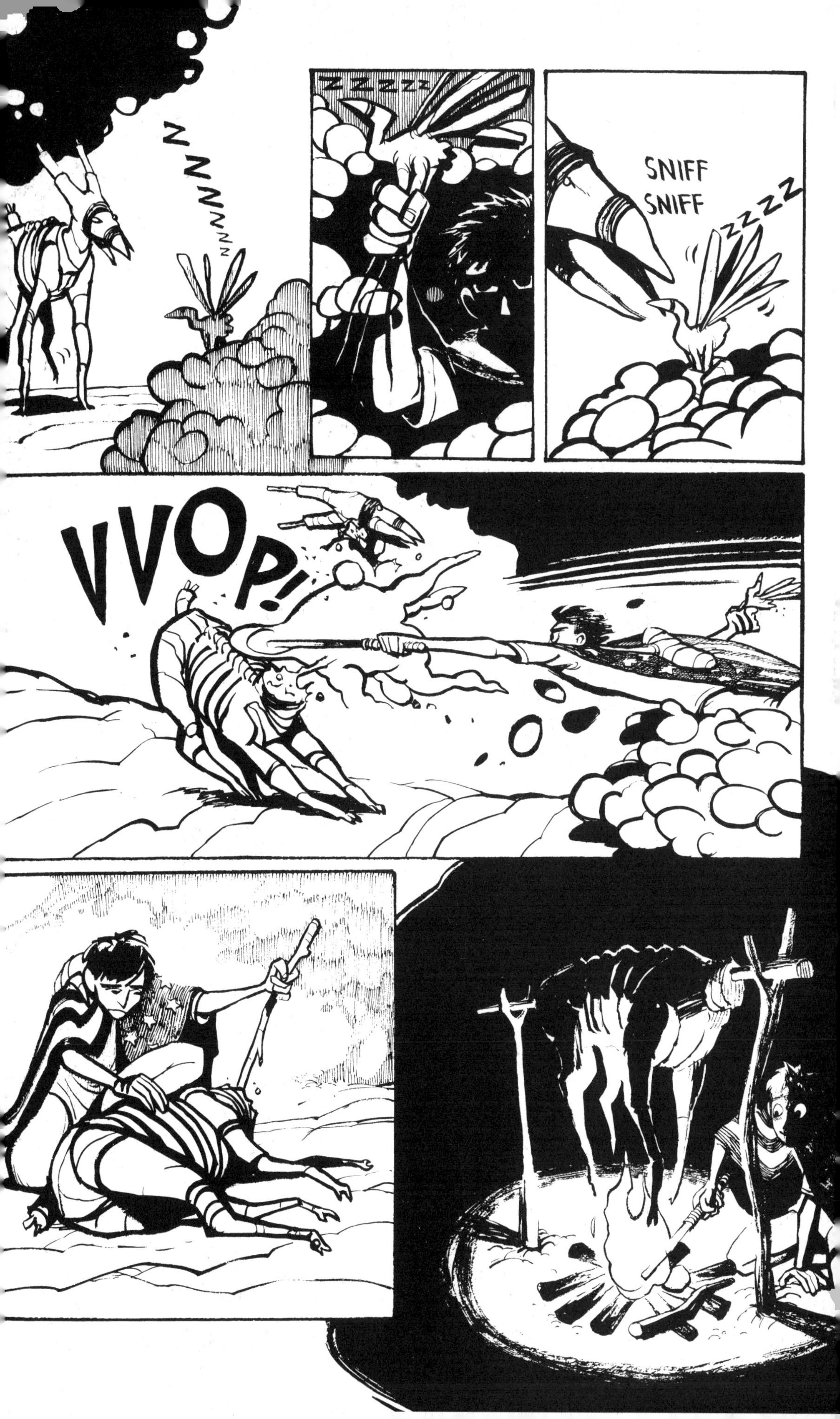
ZZZZZZZ
ZZZZZ
SNIFF
SNIFF
ZZZZ
VVOP!

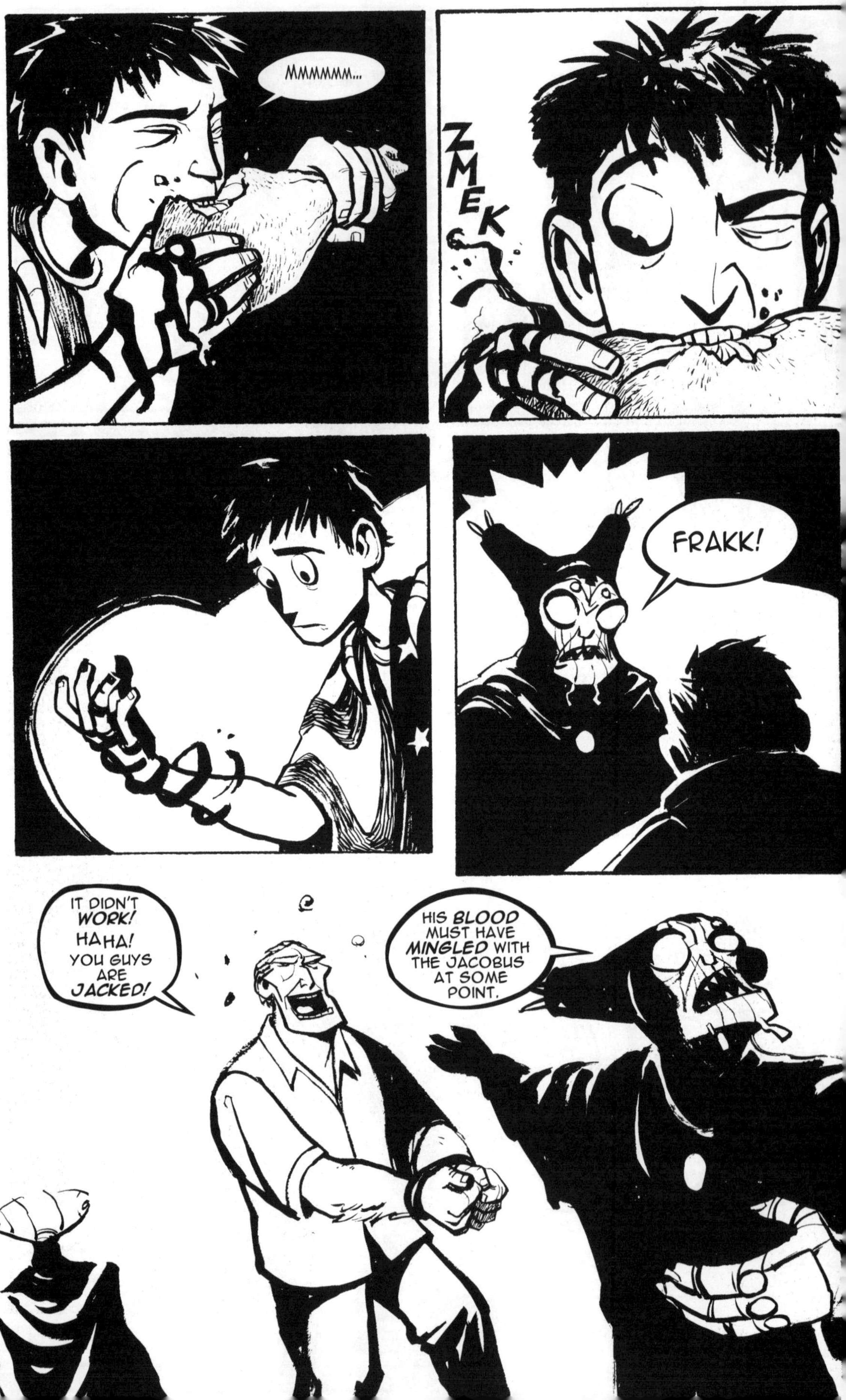
MMMMMM...
ZMEK
FRAKK!
IT DIDN'T WORK! HAHA! YOU GUYS ARE JACKED!
HIS BLOOD MUST HAVE MINGLED WITH THE JACOBUS AT SOME POINT.

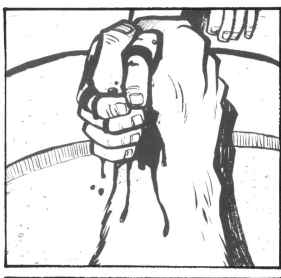

YOU'RE SCARED!

FEED HIM TO ARMY MOUTH!

YOU'RE ALL SCARED!

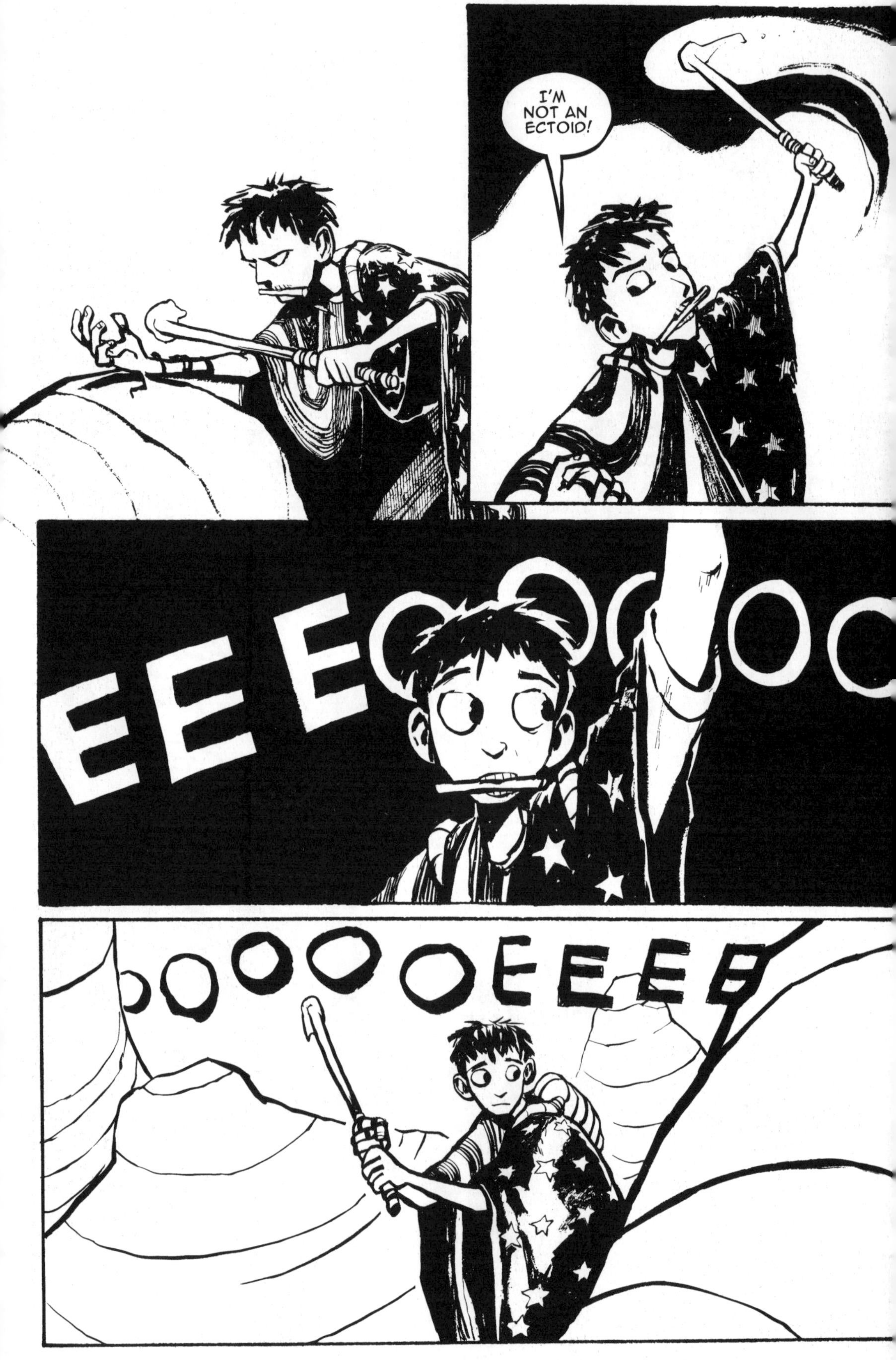
I'M NOT AN ECTOID!
EEEOOOO
OOOOOEEEE

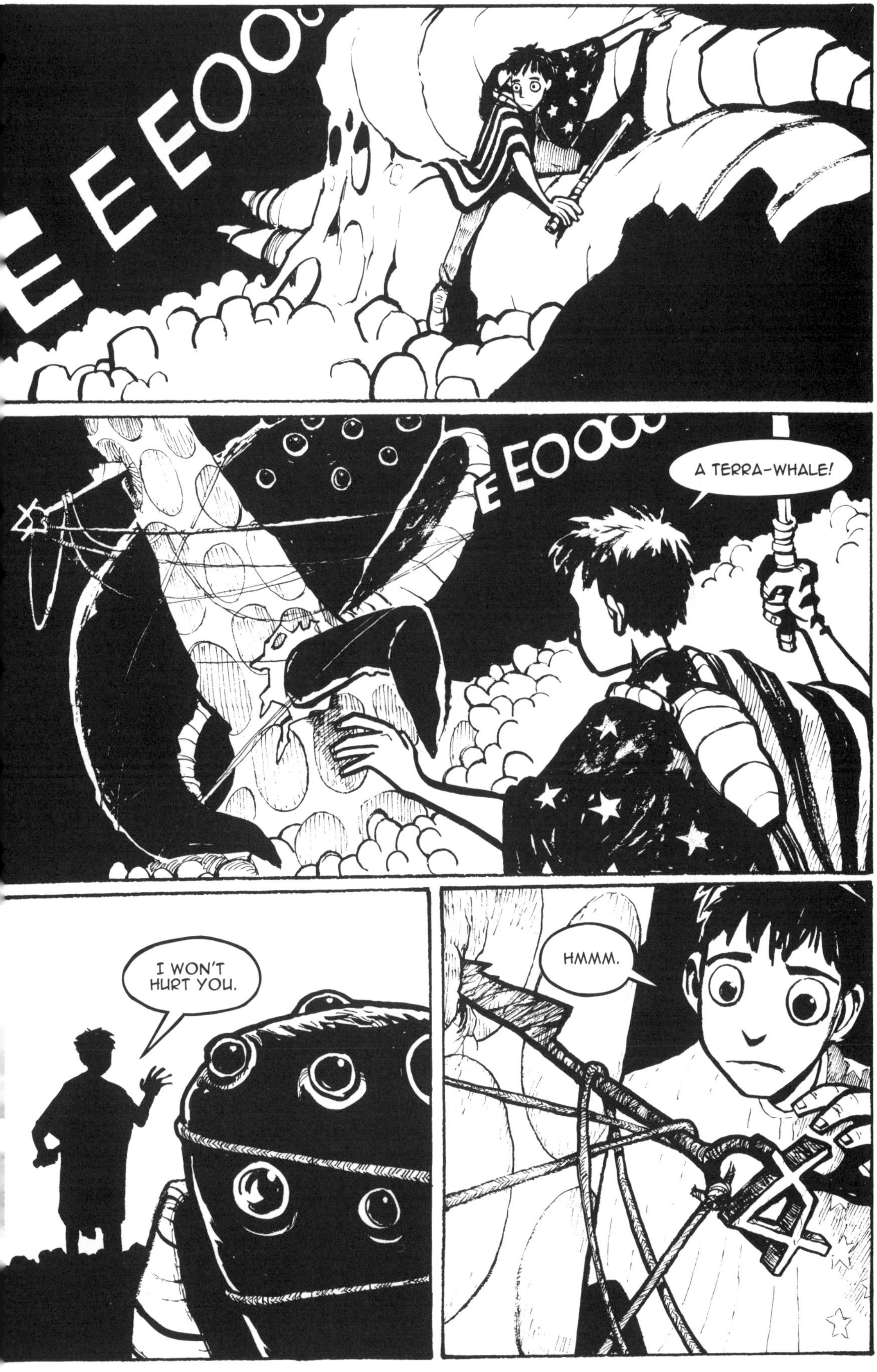
EEEOO
EEOO
A TERRA-WHALE!
I WON'T HURT YOU.
HMMM.

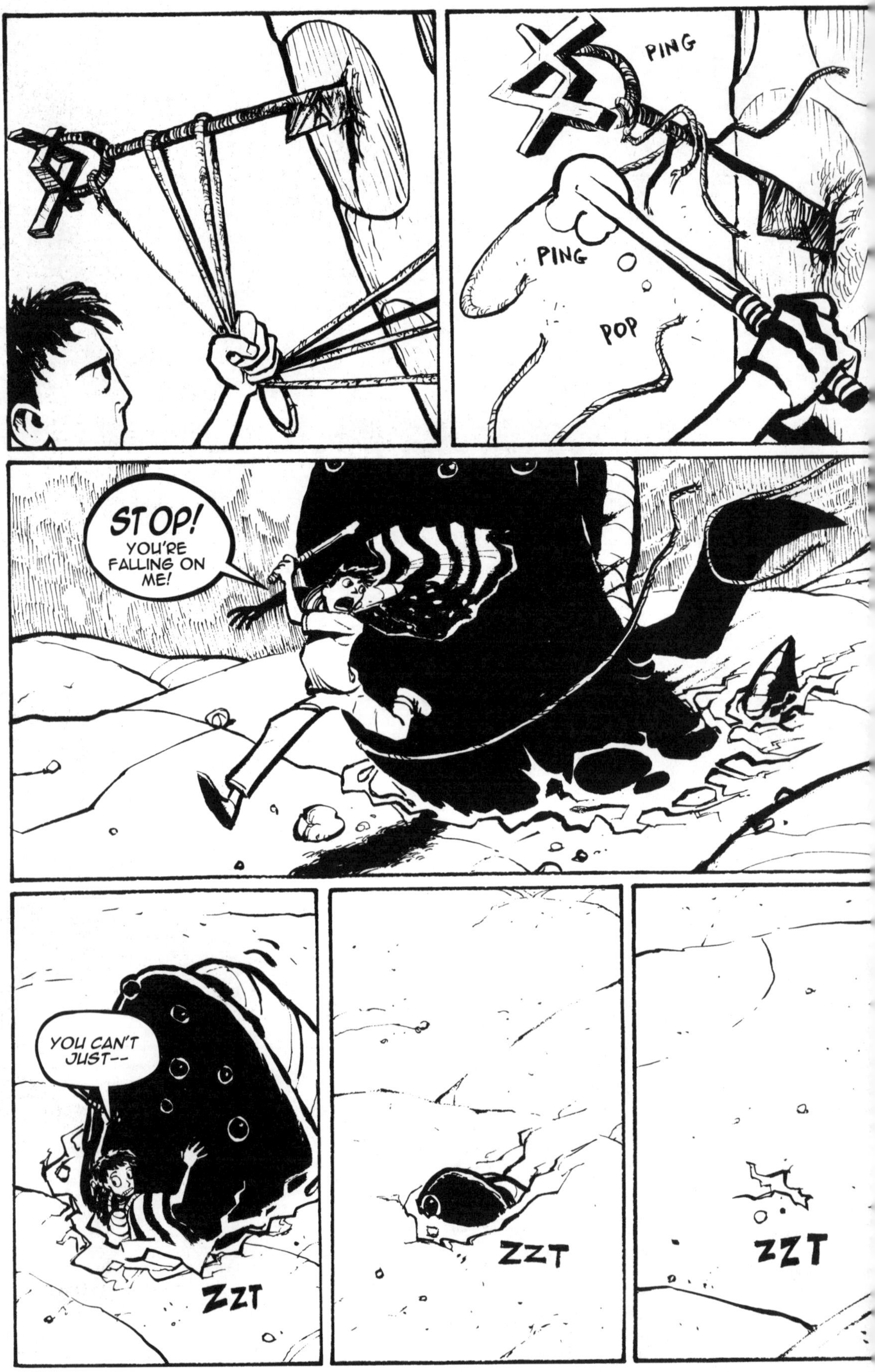
PING
PING
POP
STOP! YOU'RE FALLING ON ME!
YOU CAN'T JUST--
ZZT
ZZT
ZZT

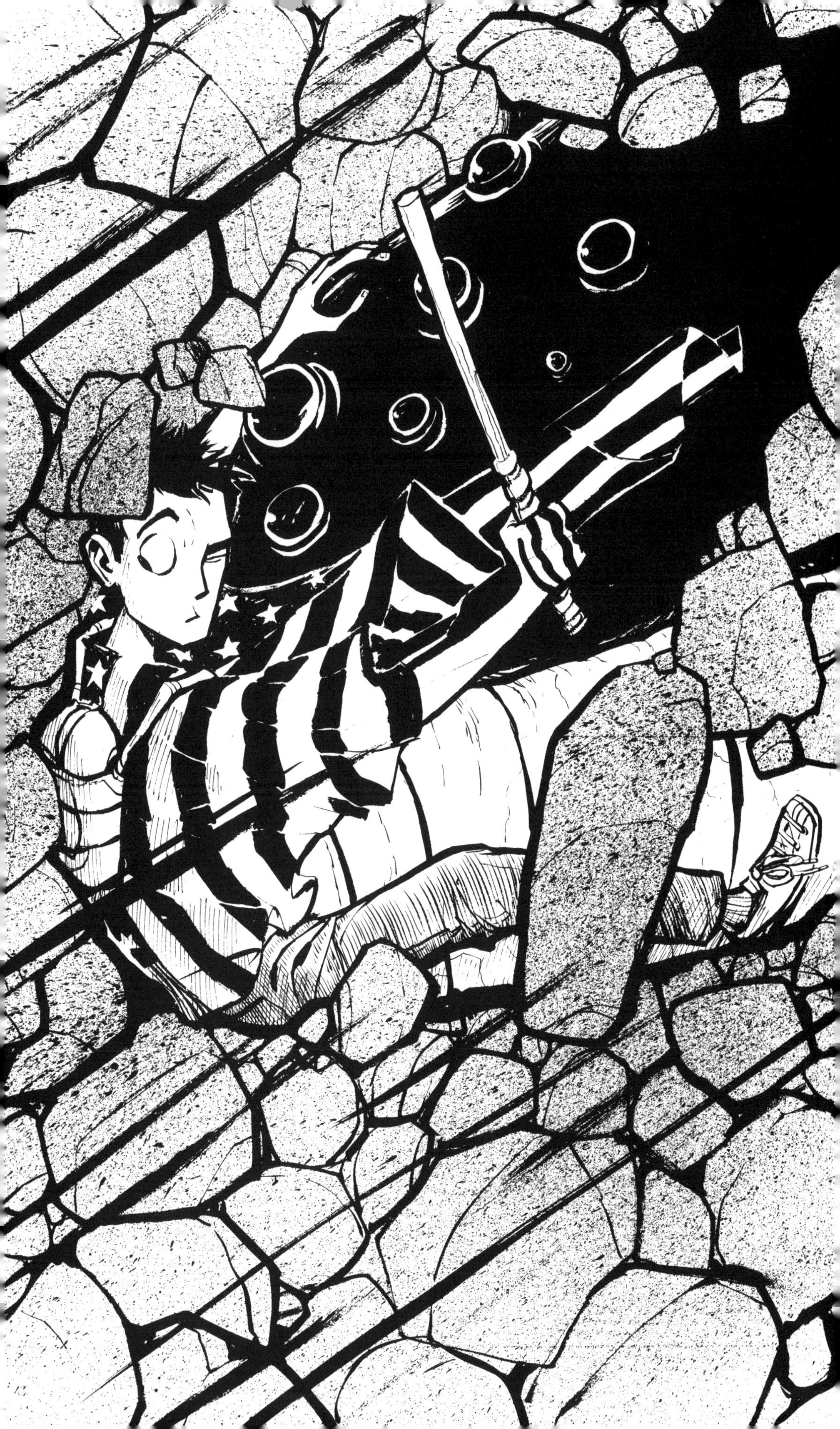

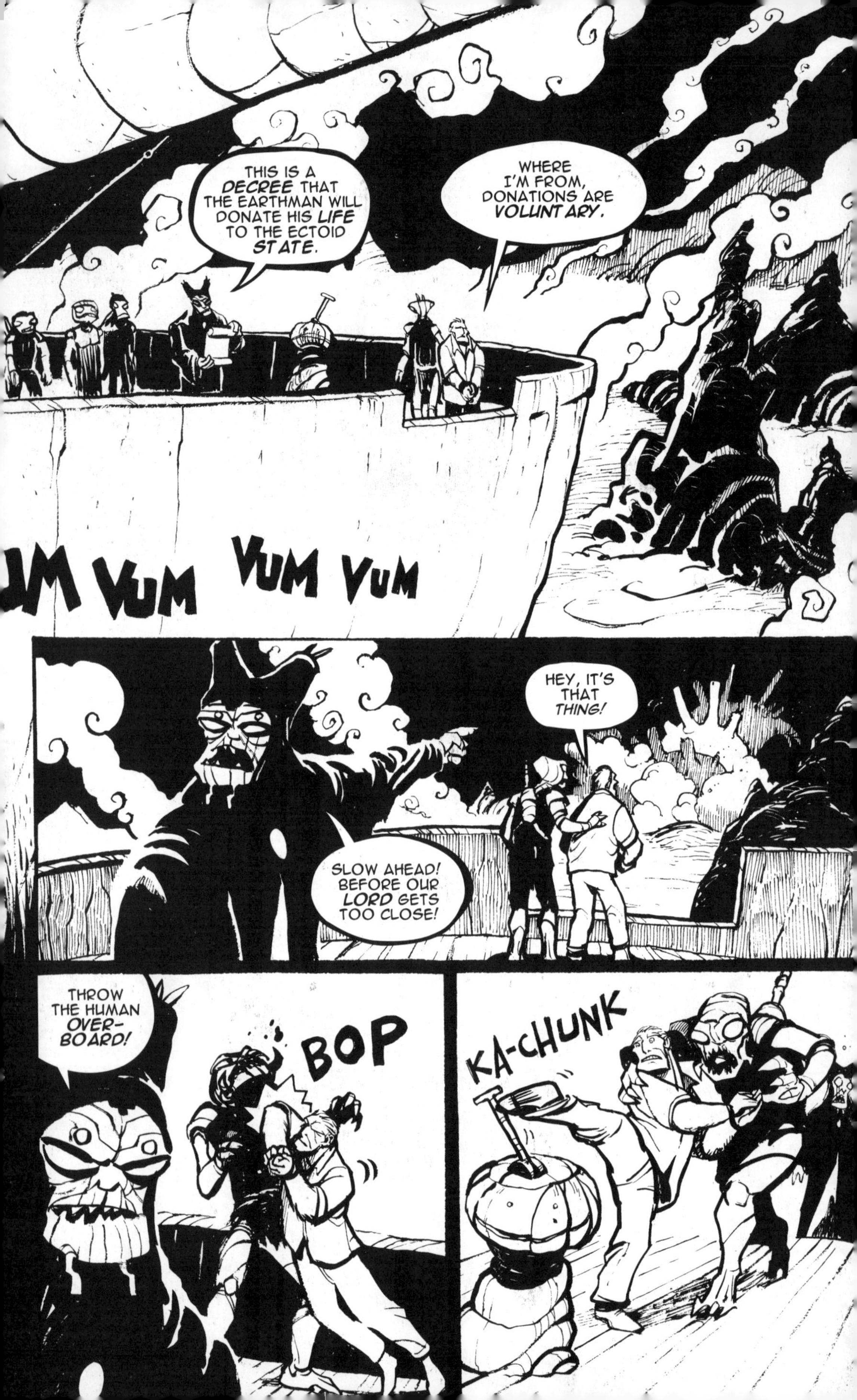
THIS IS A DECREE THAT THE EARTHMAN WILL DONATE HIS LIFE TO THE ECTOID STATE.
WHERE I'M FROM, DONATIONS ARE VOLUNTARY.
UM VUM VUM VUM
HEY, IT'S THAT THING!
SLOW AHEAD! BEFORE OUR LORD GETS TOO CLOSE!
THROW THE HUMAN OVER-BOARD!
BOP
KA-CHUNK

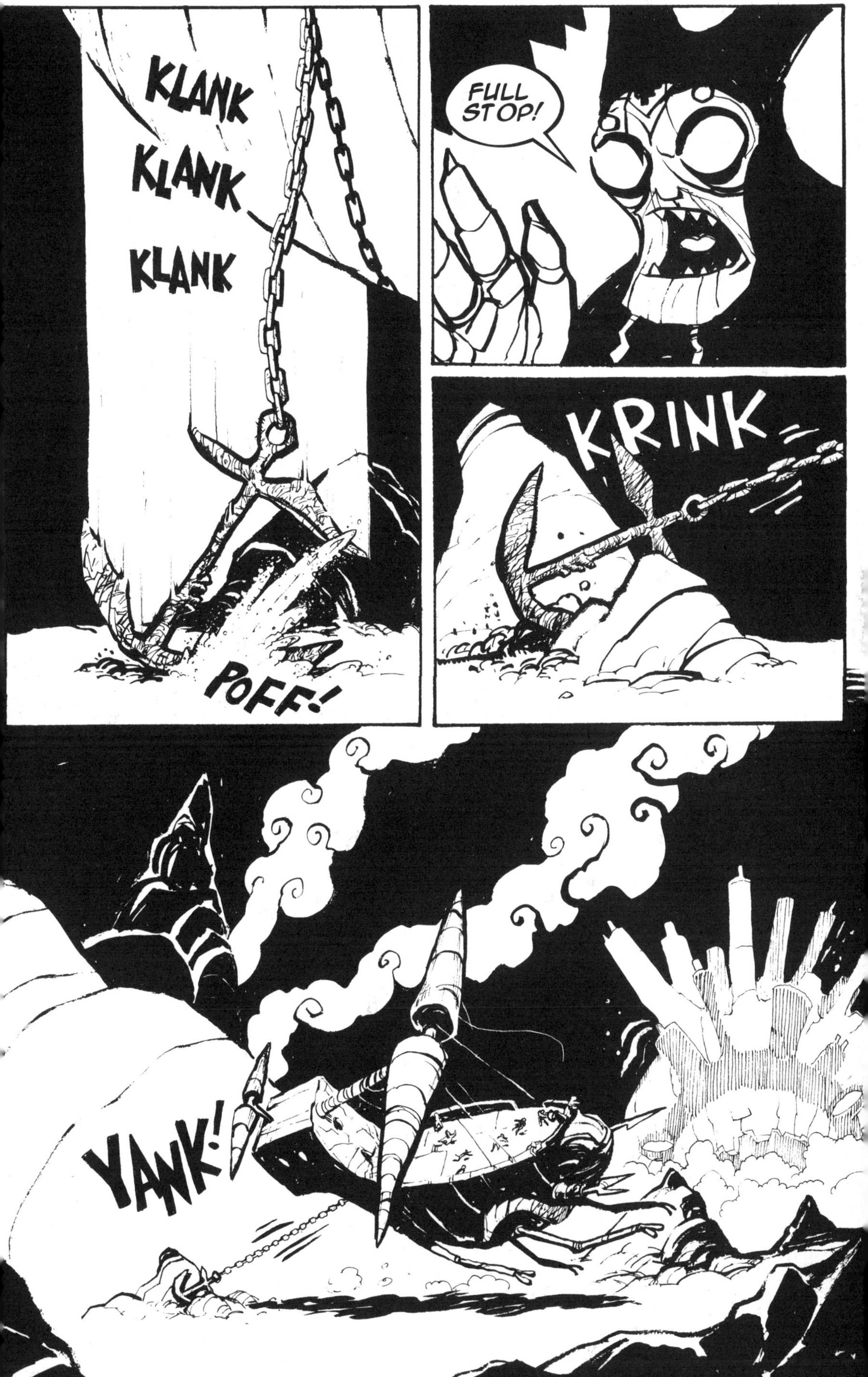
KLANK
KLANK
KLANK
POFF!
FULL STOP!
KRINK
YANK!

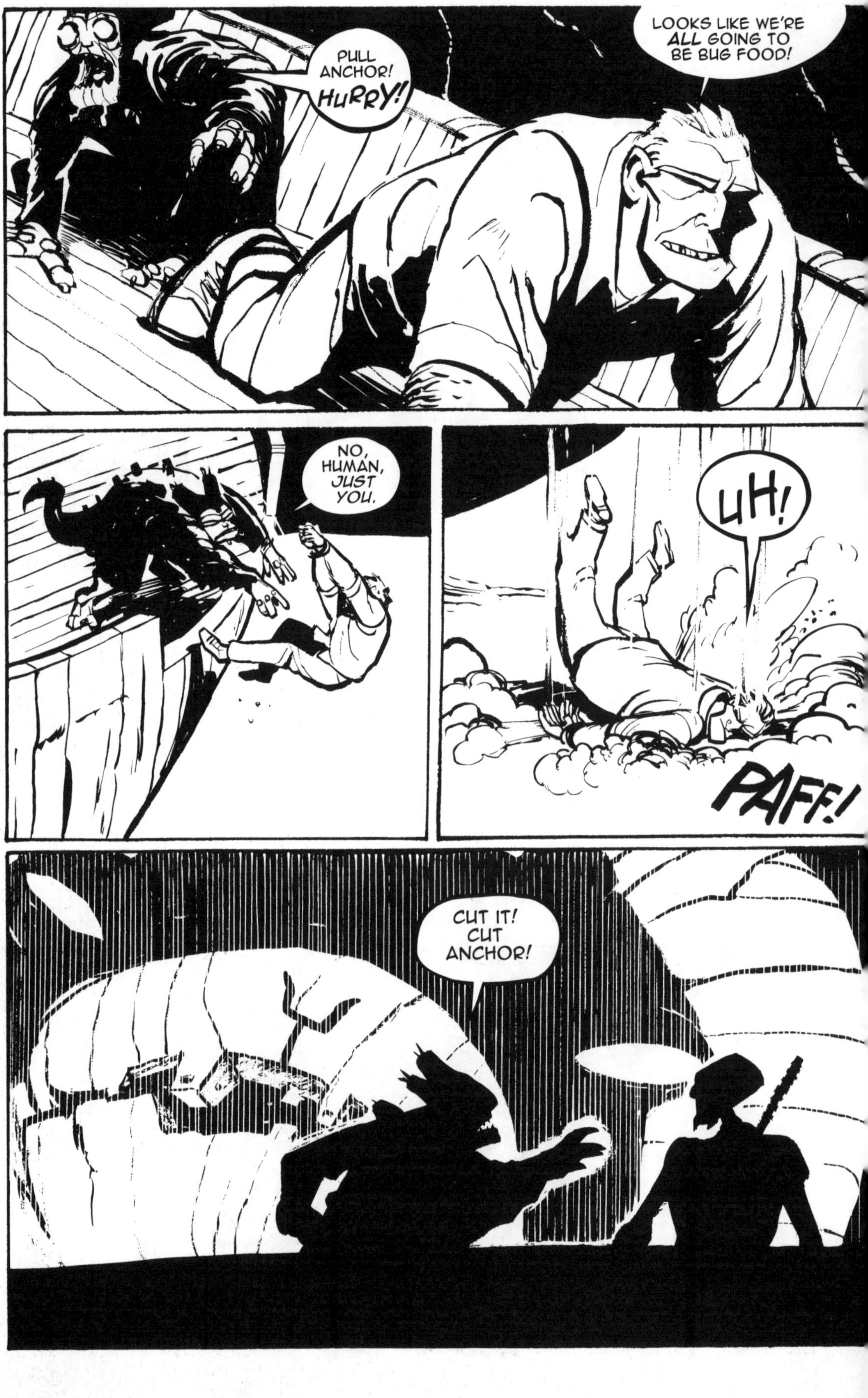
PULL ANCHOR! HURRY!
LOOKS LIKE WE'RE ALL GOING TO BE BUG FOOD!
NO, HUMAN, JUST YOU.
UH!
PAFF!
CUT IT! CUT ANCHOR!

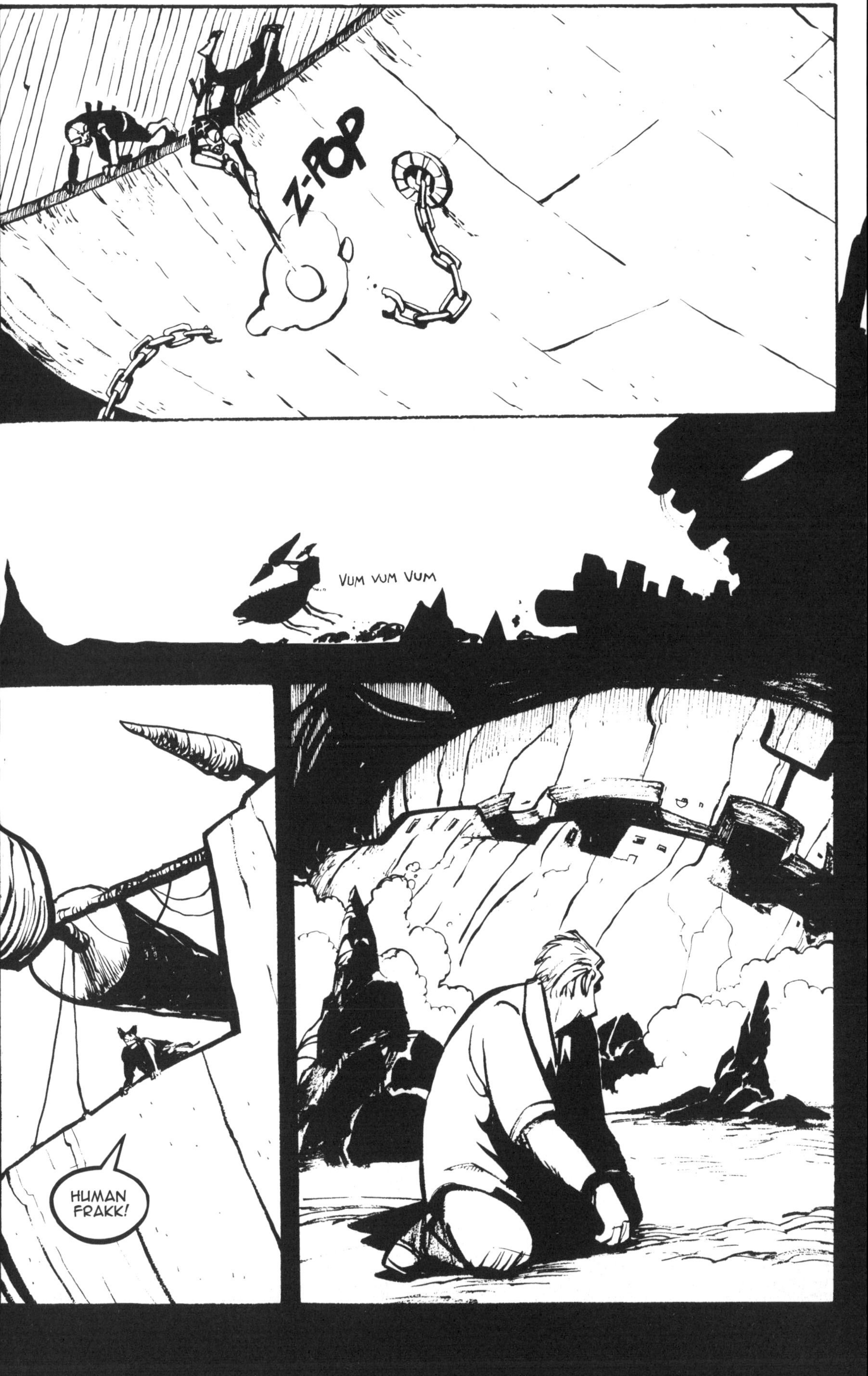
Z-POP
VUM VUM VUM
HUMAN FRAKK!

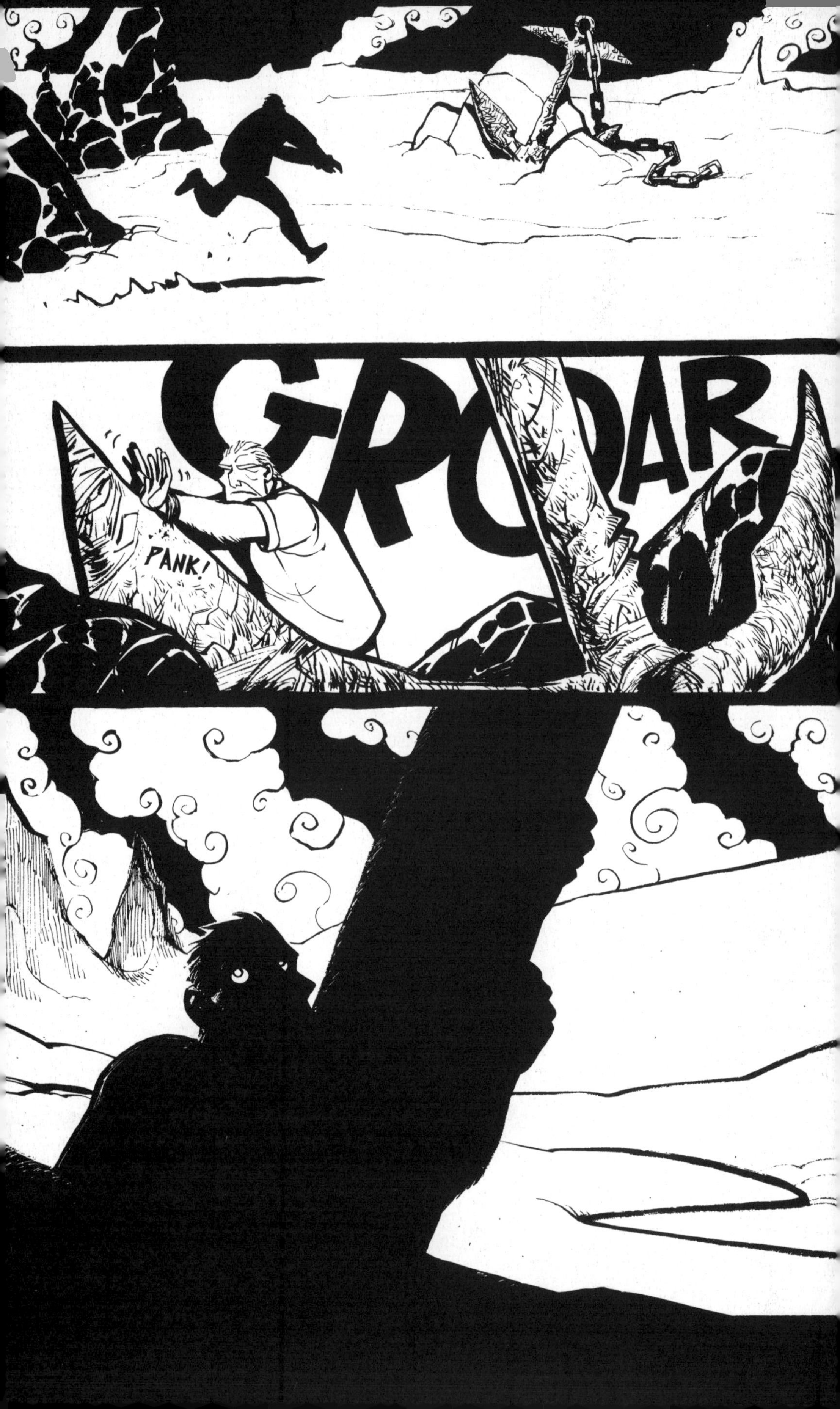
GROAR
PANK!

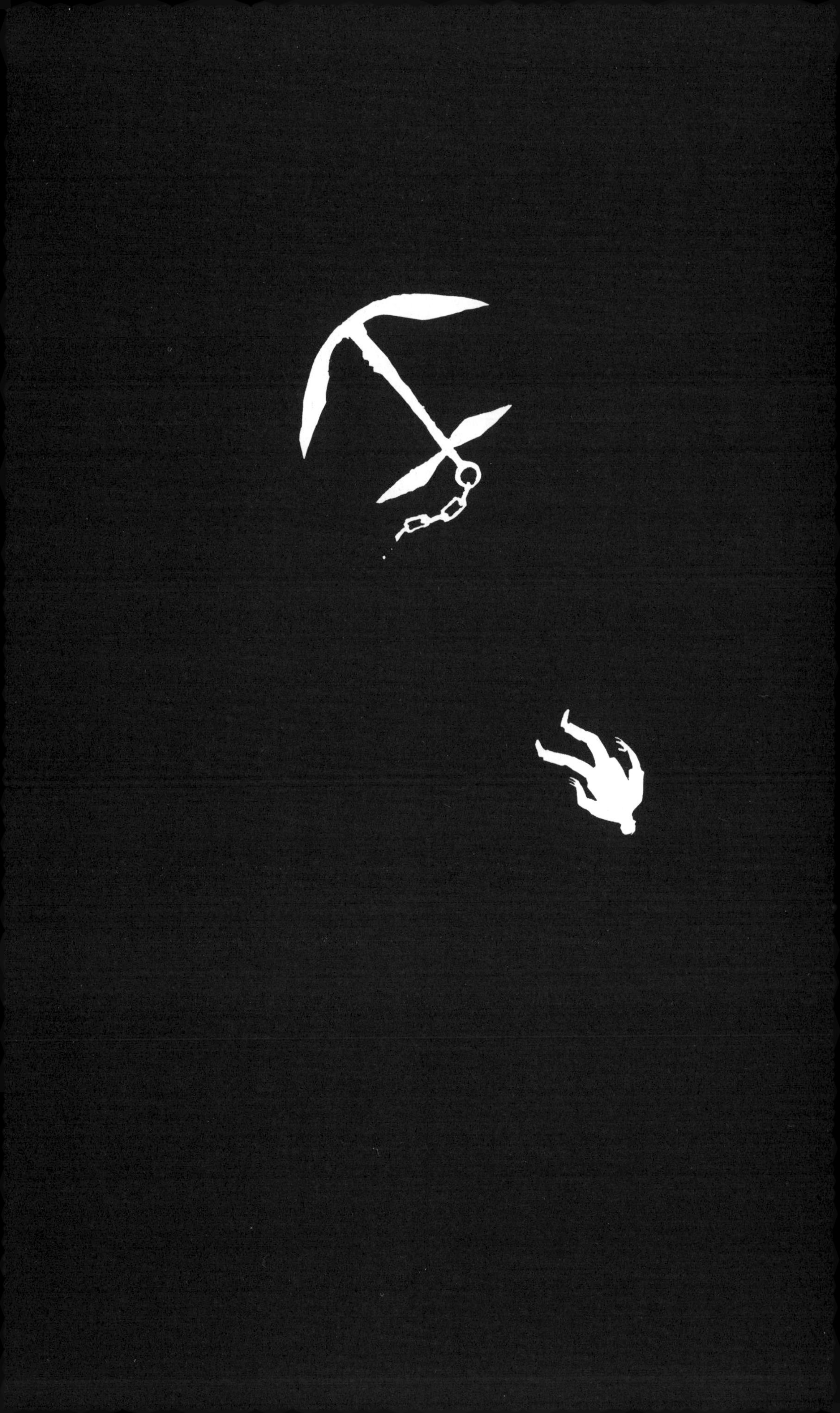

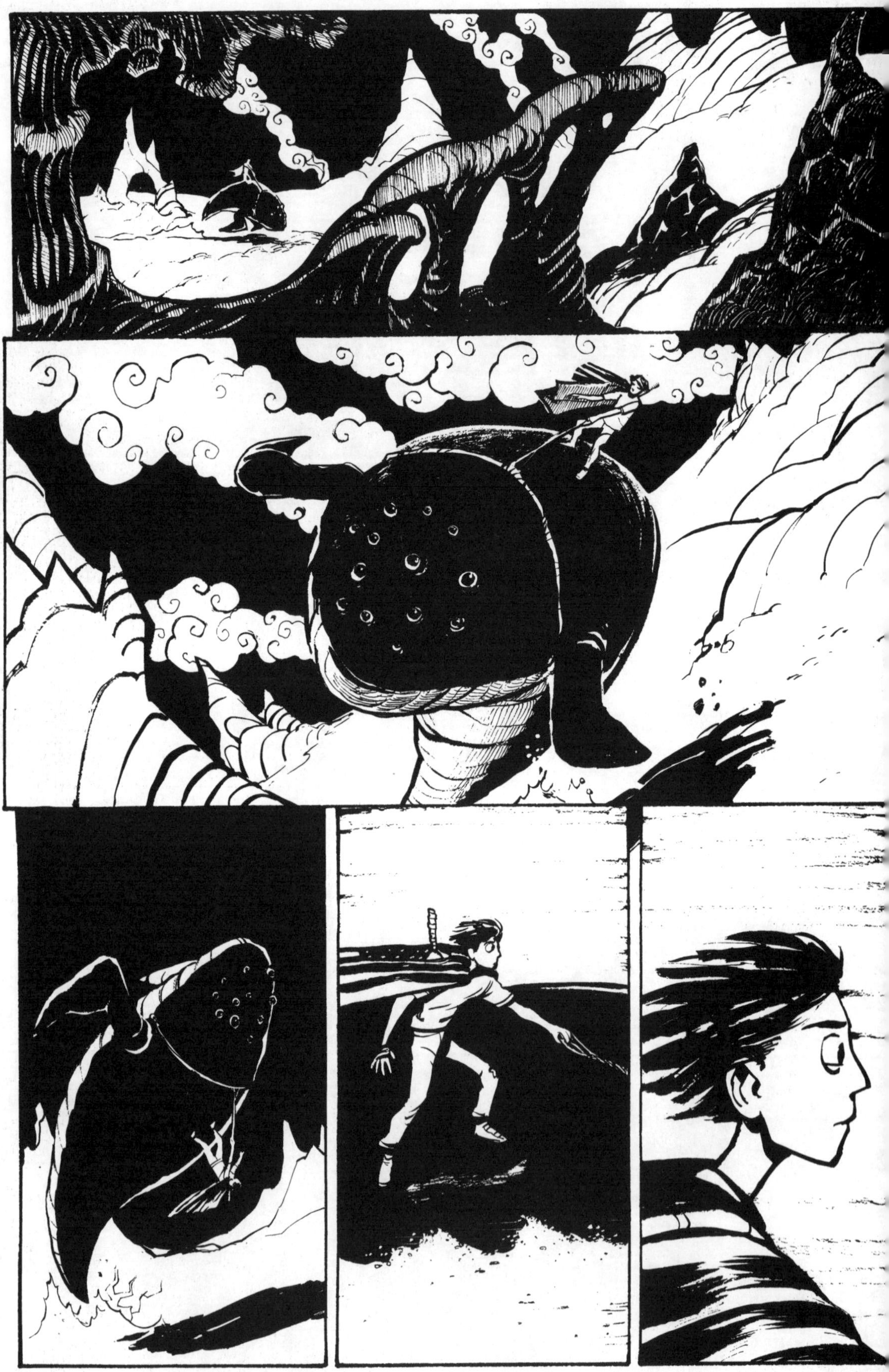

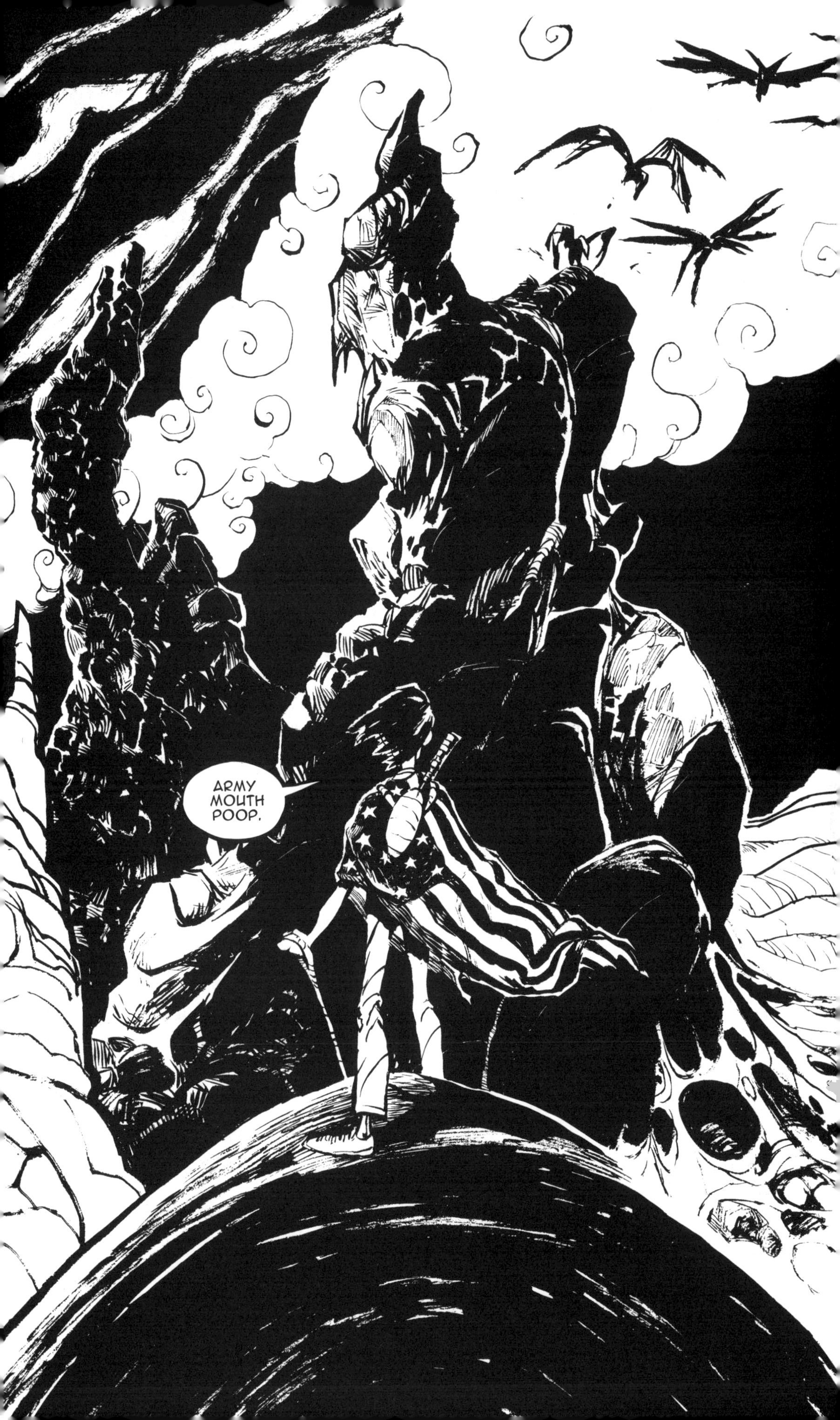
ARMY MOUTH POOP.

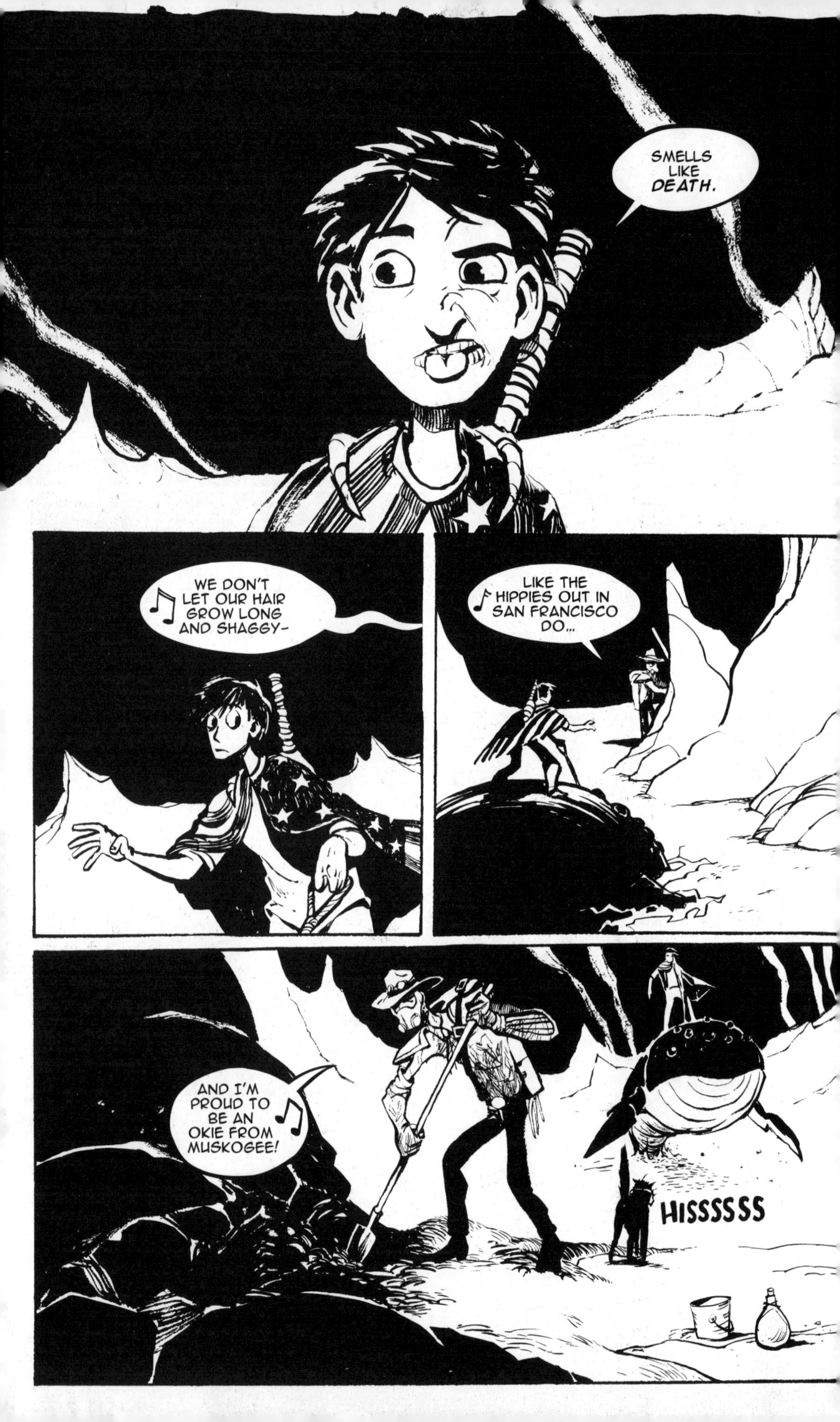
SMELLS LIKE DEATH.
WE DON'T LET OUR HAIR GROW LONG AND SHAGGY-
LIKE THE HIPPIES OUT IN SAN FRANCISCO DO...
AND I'M PROUD TO BE AN OKIE FROM MUSKOGEE!
HISSSSSS

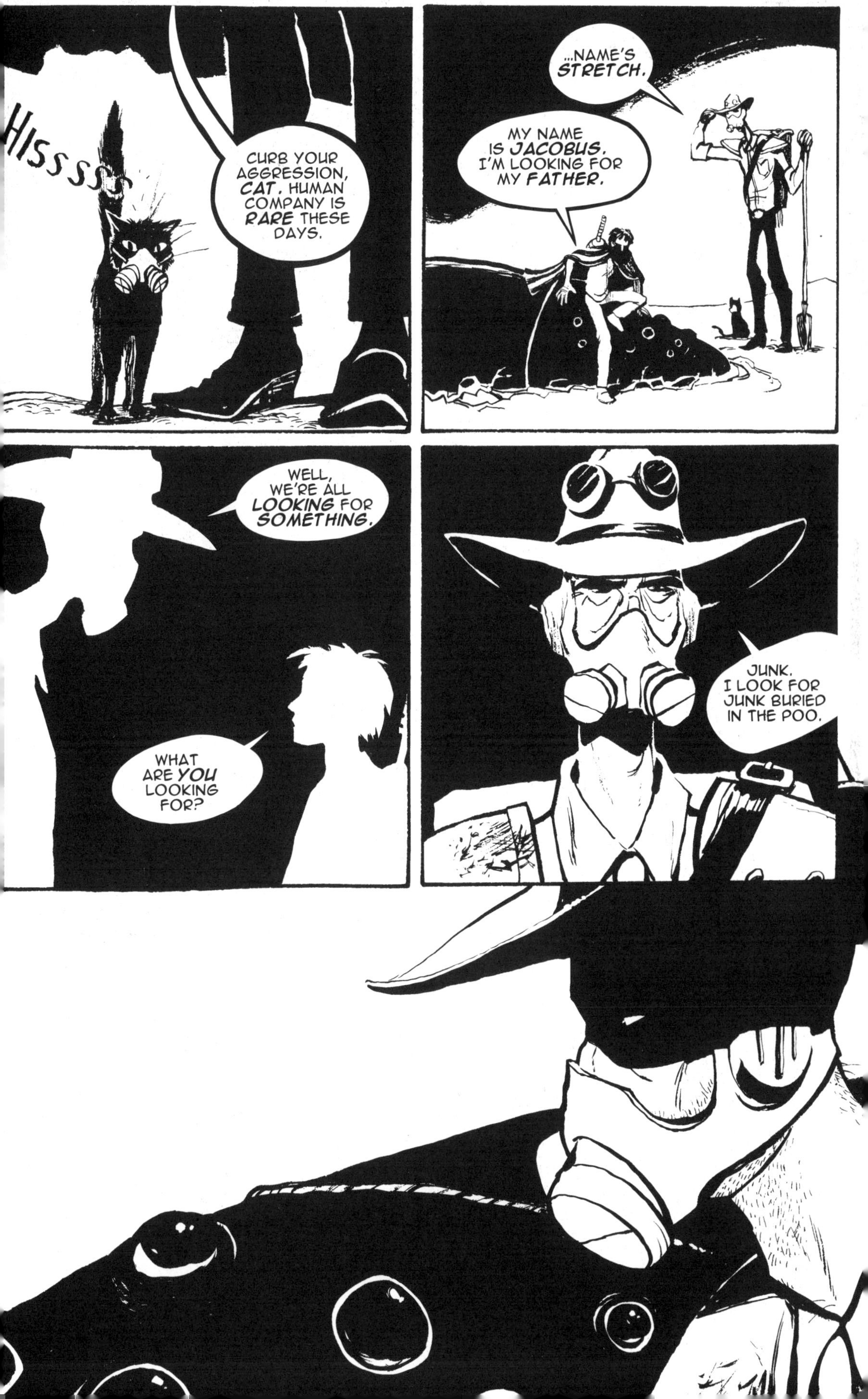
HISSSSS
CURB YOUR AGGRESSION, CAT. HUMAN COMPANY IS RARE THESE DAYS.
...NAME'S STRETCH.
MY NAME IS JACOBUS. I'M LOOKING FOR MY FATHER.
WELL, WE'RE ALL LOOKING FOR SOMETHING.
WHAT ARE YOU LOOKING FOR?
JUNK. I LOOK FOR JUNK BURIED IN THE POO.

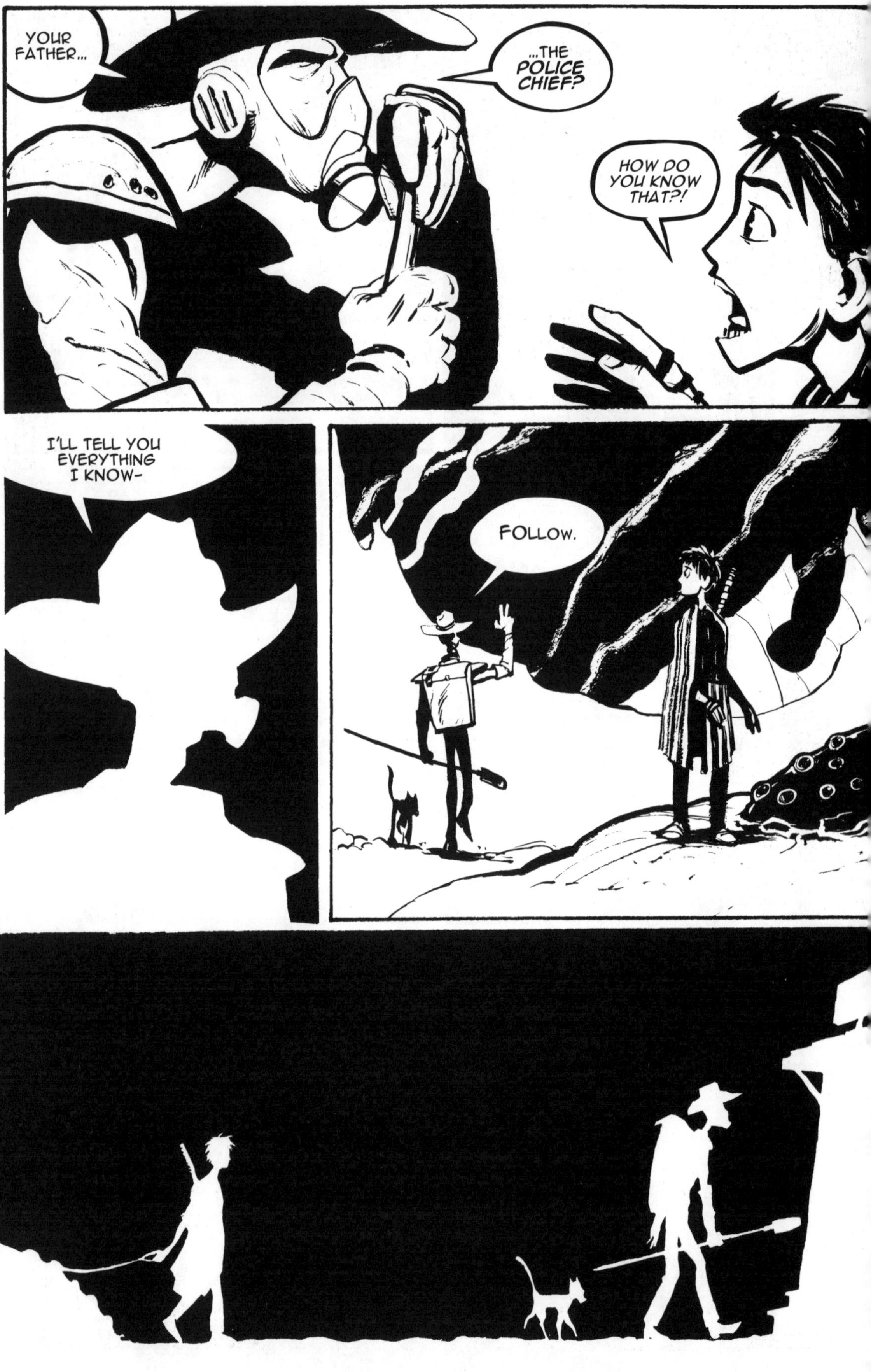
YOUR FATHER...
...THE POLICE CHIEF?
HOW DO YOU KNOW THAT?!
I'LL TELL YOU EVERYTHING I KNOW-
FOLLOW.

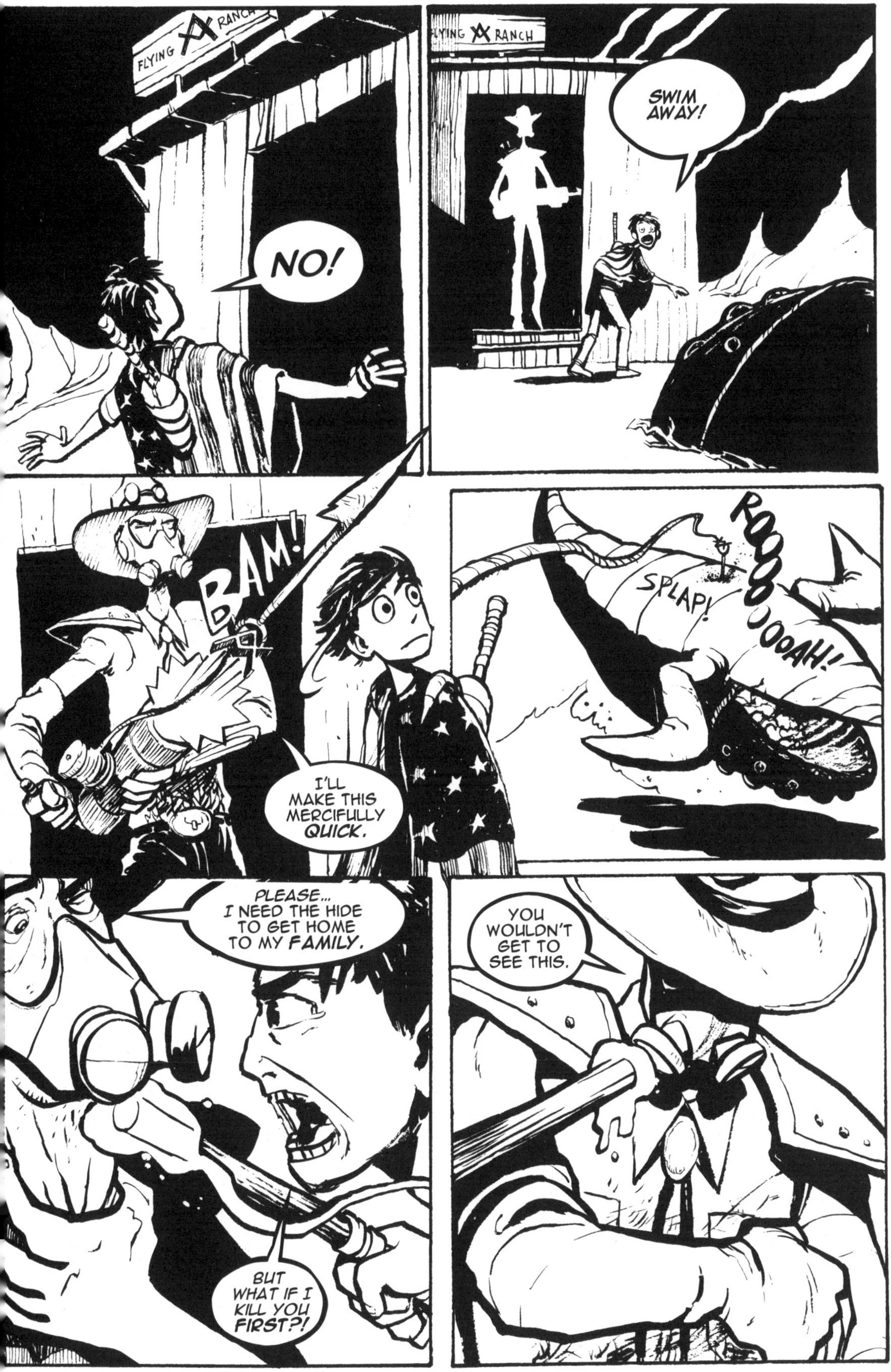
FLYING RANCH
NO!
FLYING RANCH
SWIM AWAY!
BAM!
I'LL MAKE THIS MERCIFULLY QUICK.
ROOOOOOOAH!
SPLAP!
PLEASE... I NEED THE HIDE TO GET HOME TO MY FAMILY.
BUT WHAT IF I KILL YOU FIRST?!
YOU WOULDN'T GET TO SEE THIS.

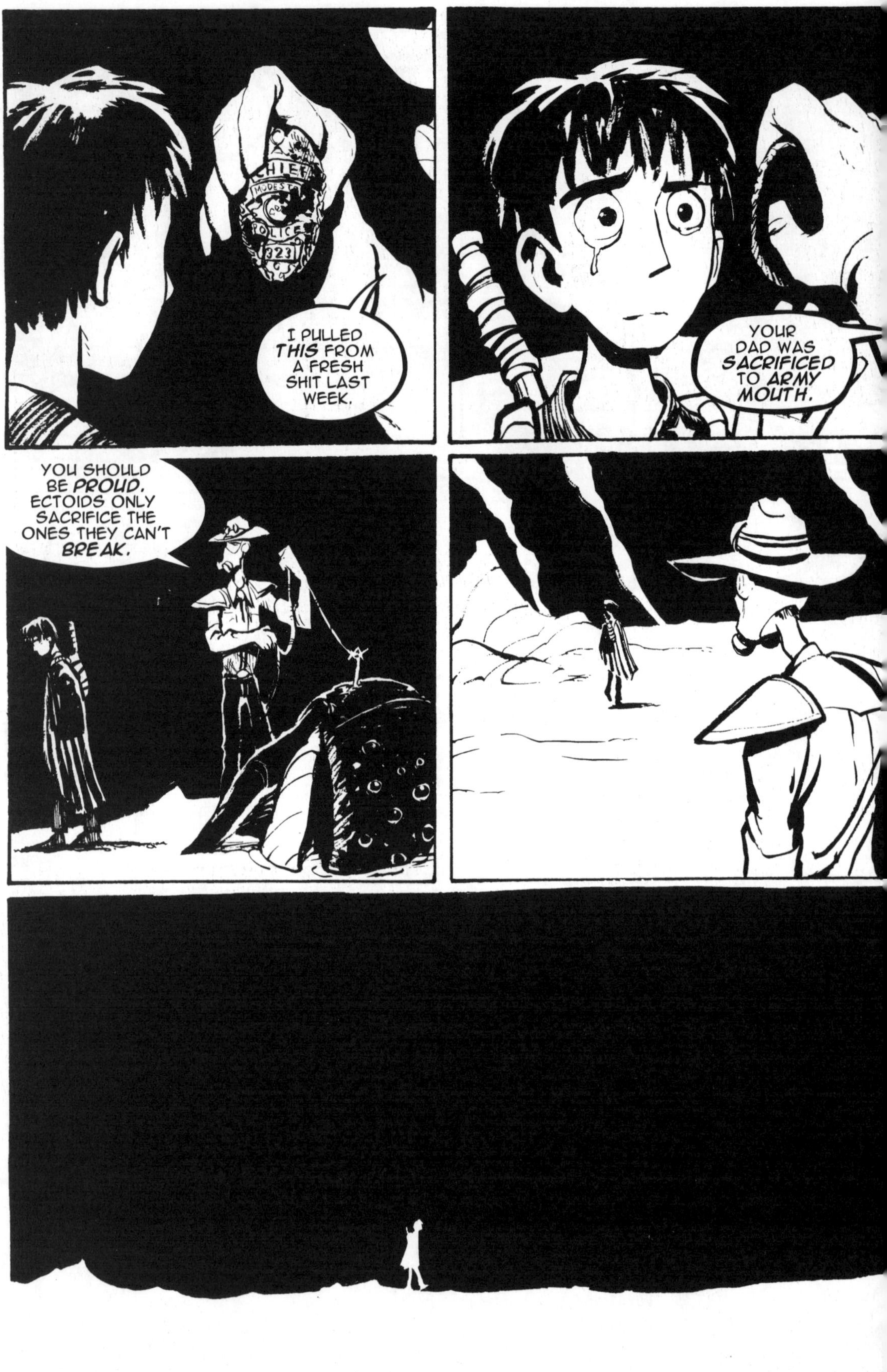
I PULLED THIS FROM A FRESH SHIT LAST WEEK.
YOUR DAD WAS SACRIFICED TO ARMY MOUTH.
YOU SHOULD BE PROUD. ECTOIDS ONLY SACRIFICE THE ONES THEY CAN'T BREAK.

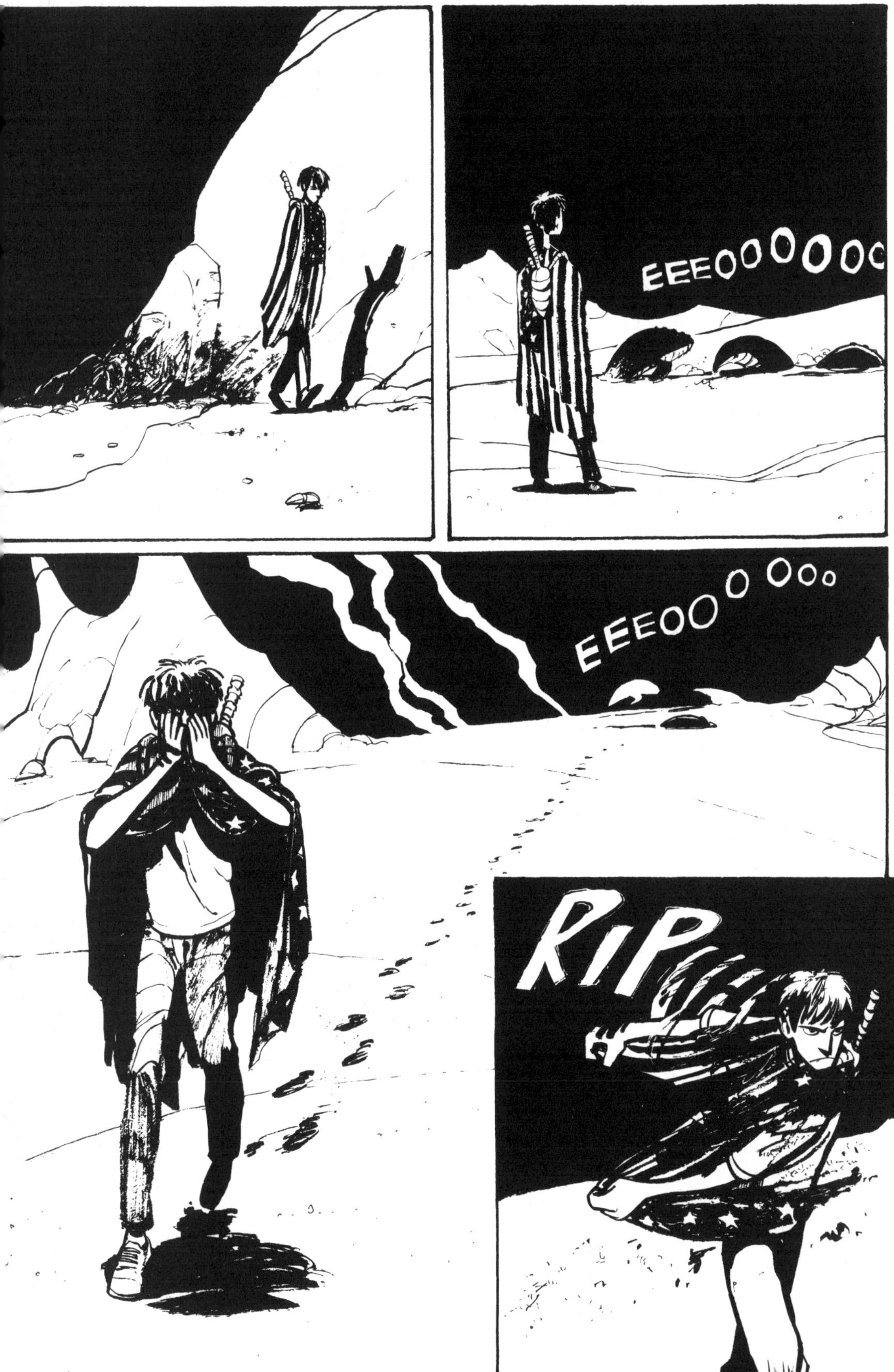
EEEOOOOOO
EEEOOOOOO
RIP

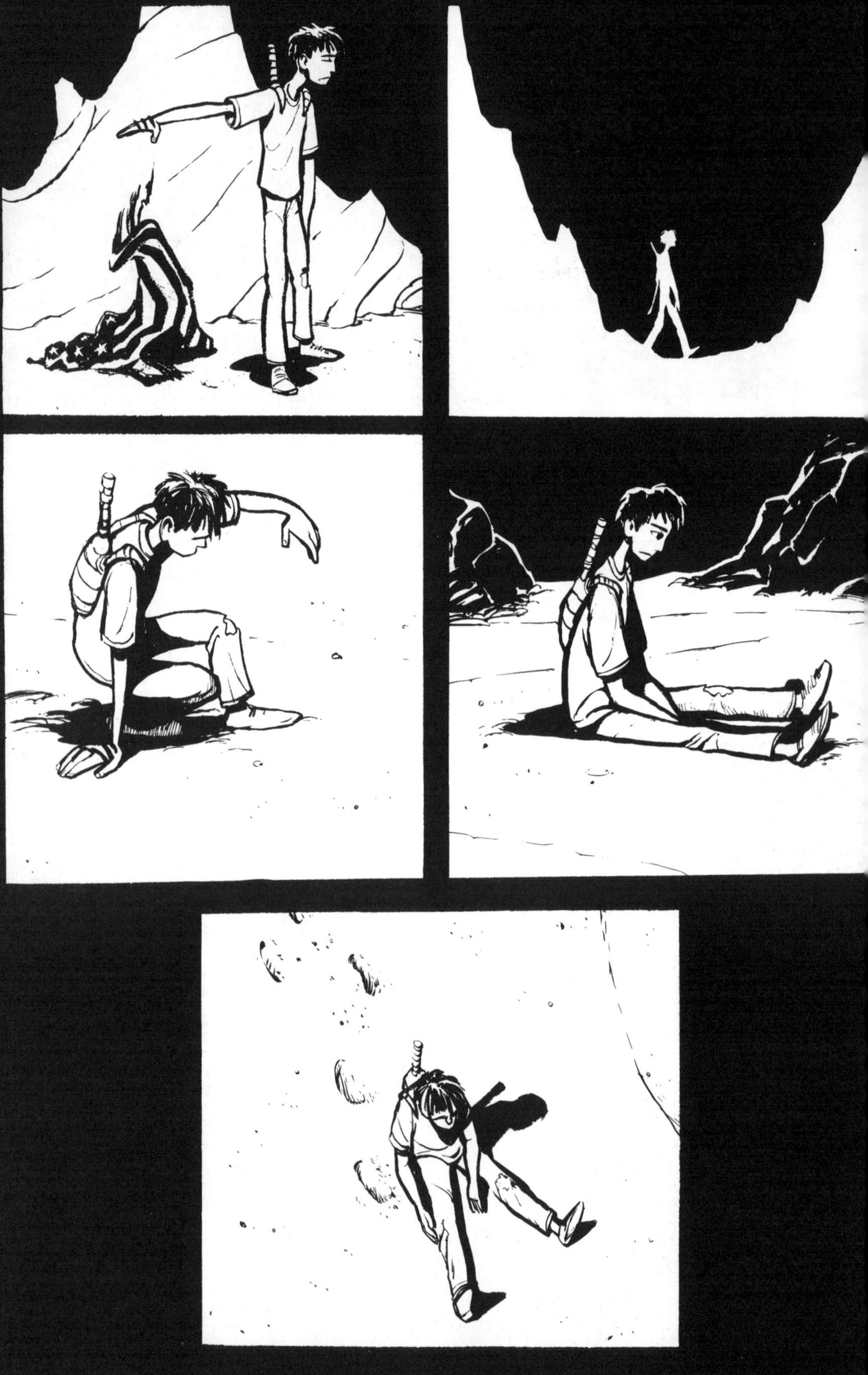

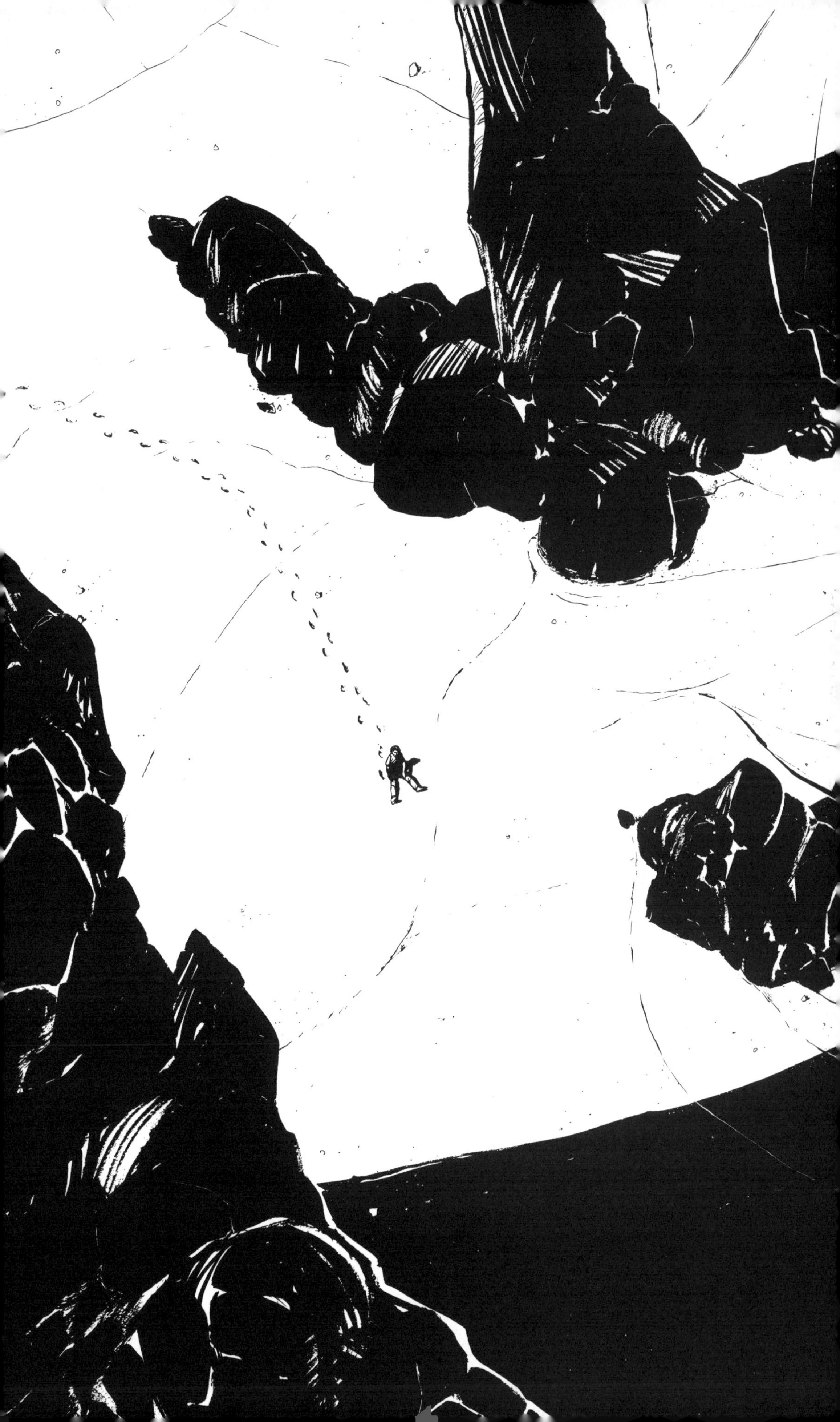

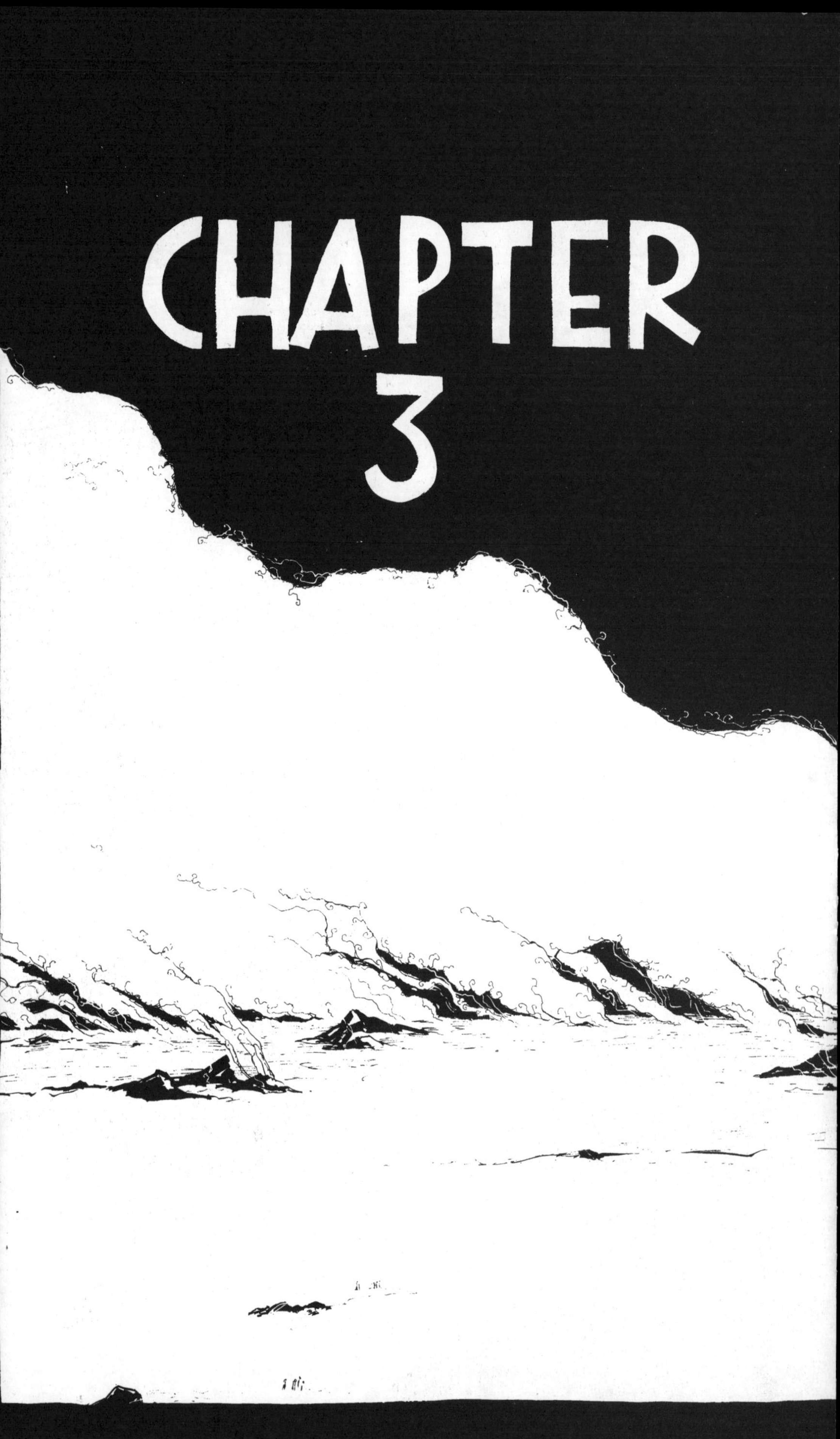
CHAPTER
3

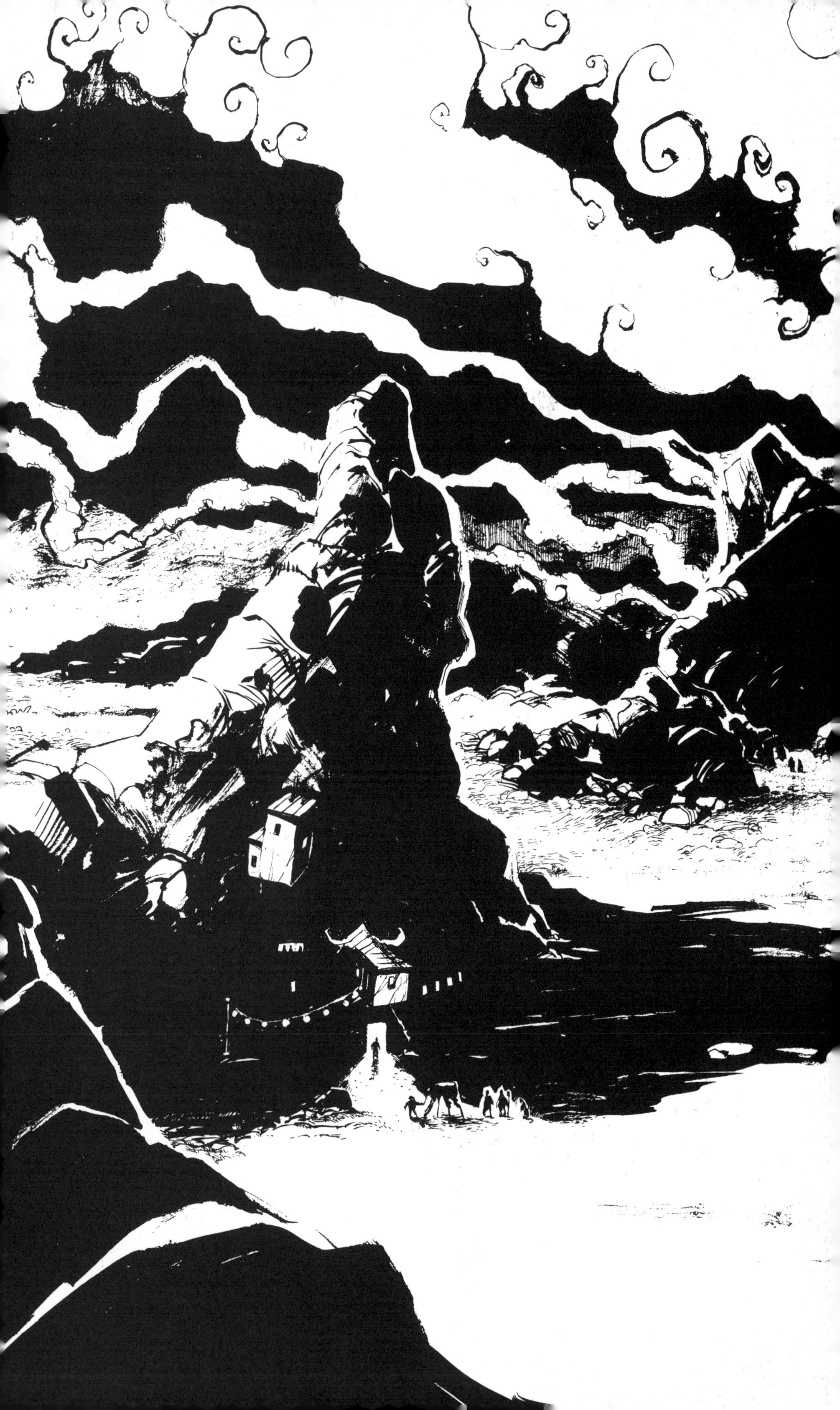

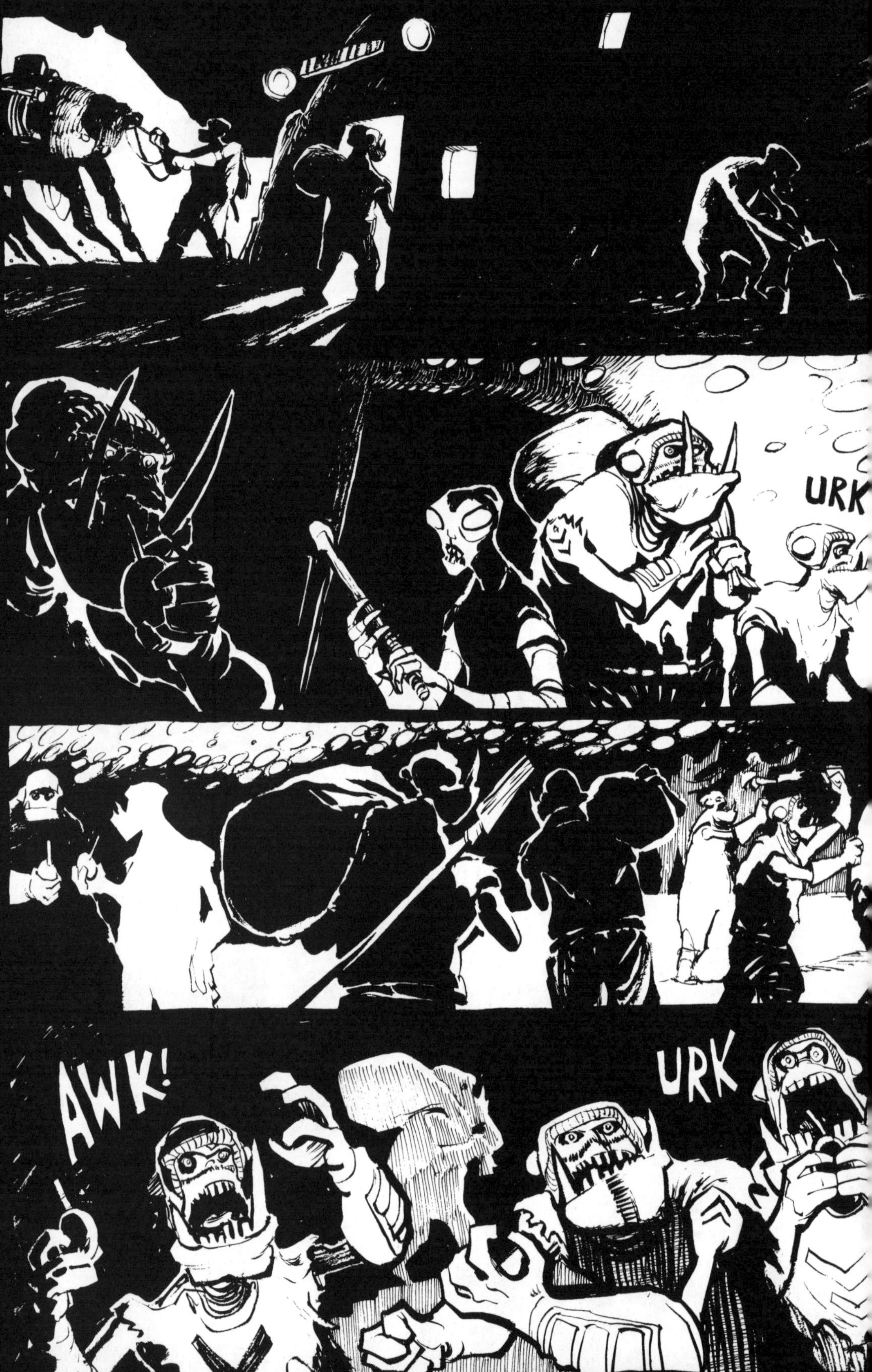
URK
AWK!
URK

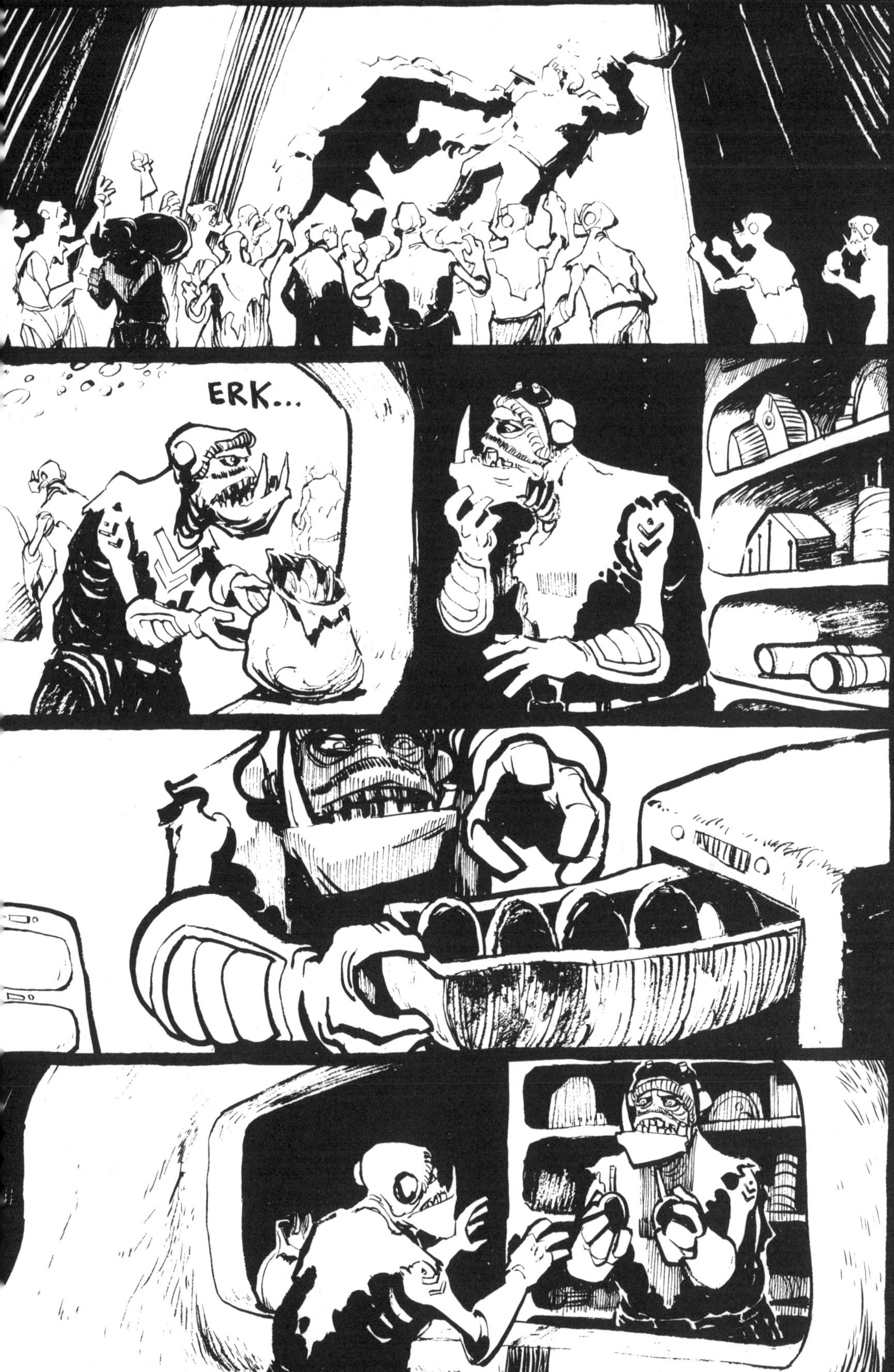
ERK...

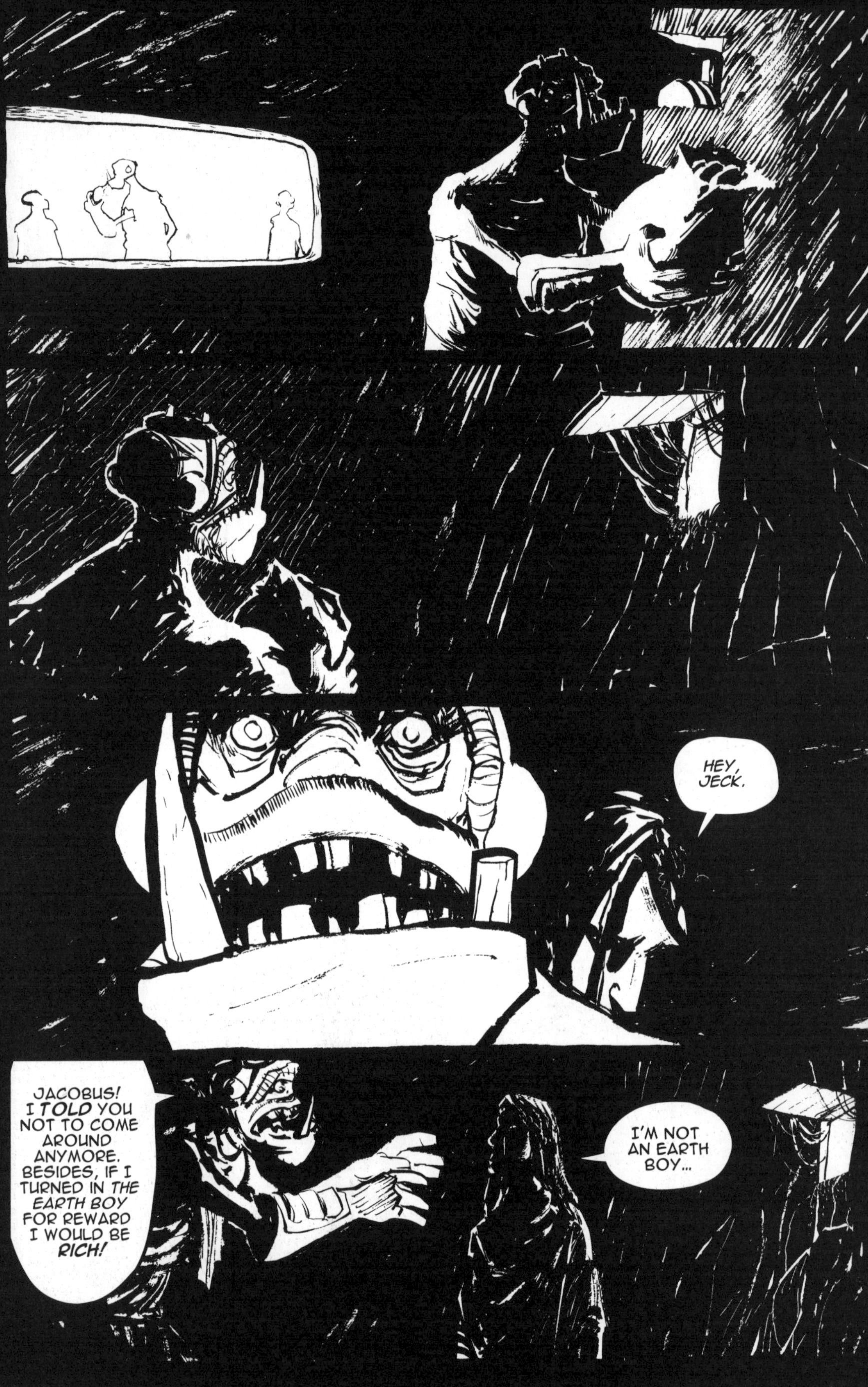
HEY, JECK.
JACOBUS! I *TOLD* YOU NOT TO COME AROUND ANYMORE. BESIDES, IF I TURNED IN *THE EARTH BOY* FOR REWARD I WOULD BE ***RICH!***
I'M NOT AN EARTH BOY...

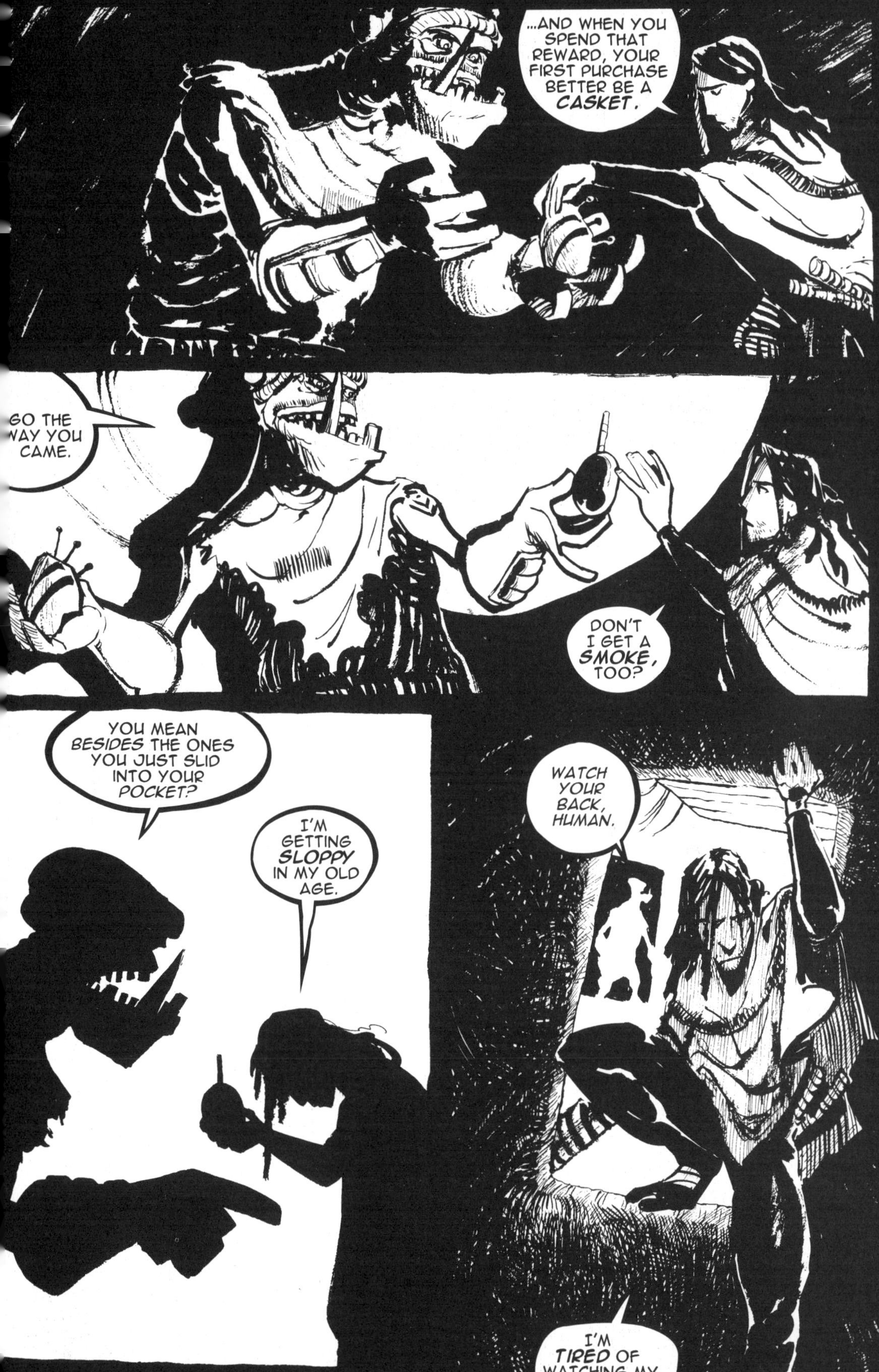
...AND WHEN YOU SPEND THAT REWARD, YOUR FIRST PURCHASE BETTER BE A CASKET.
GO THE WAY YOU CAME.
DON'T I GET A SMOKE, TOO?
YOU MEAN BESIDES THE ONES YOU JUST SLID INTO YOUR POCKET?
I'M GETTING SLOPPY IN MY OLD AGE.
WATCH YOUR BACK, HUMAN.
I'M TIRED OF WATCHING MY BACK.

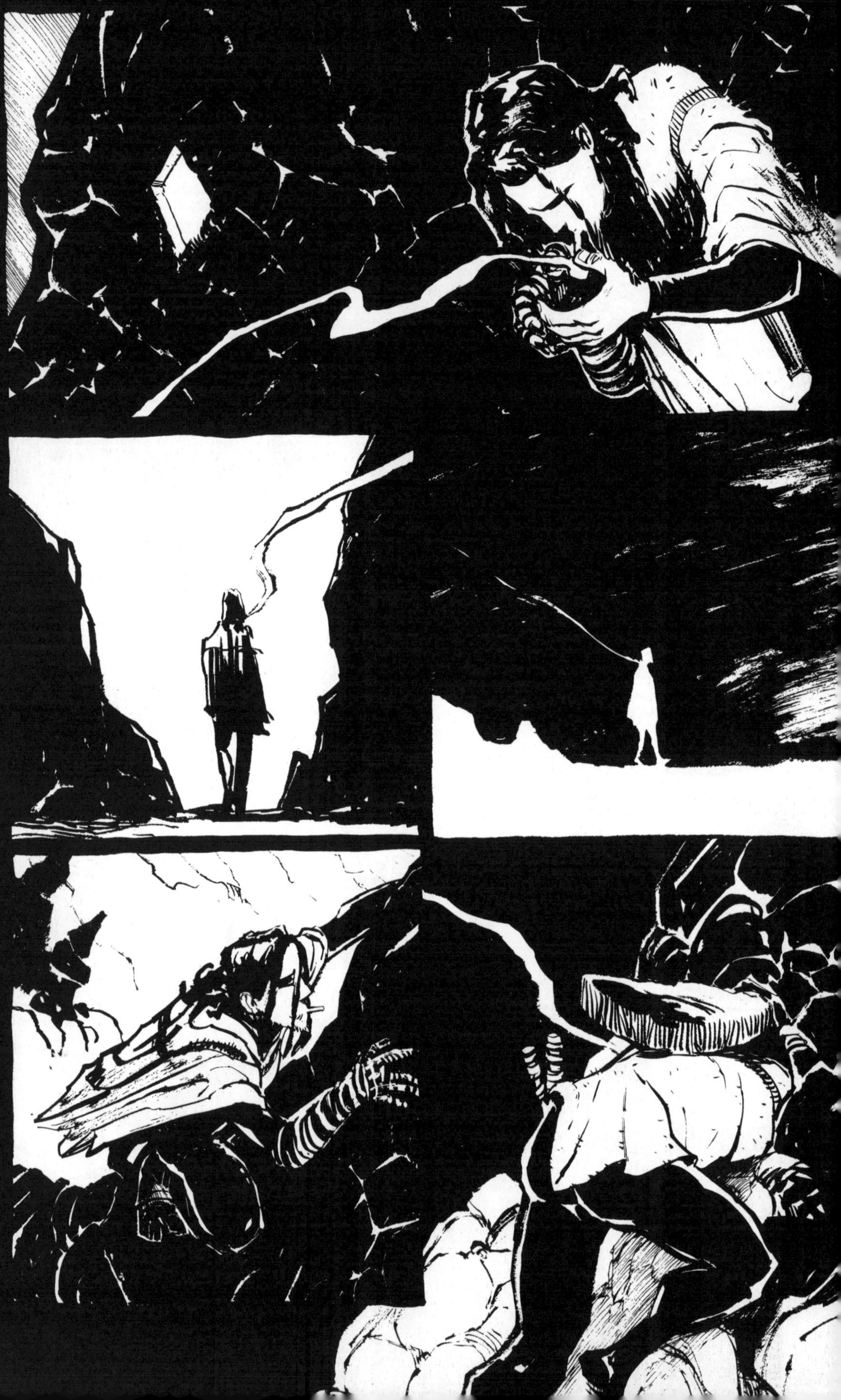

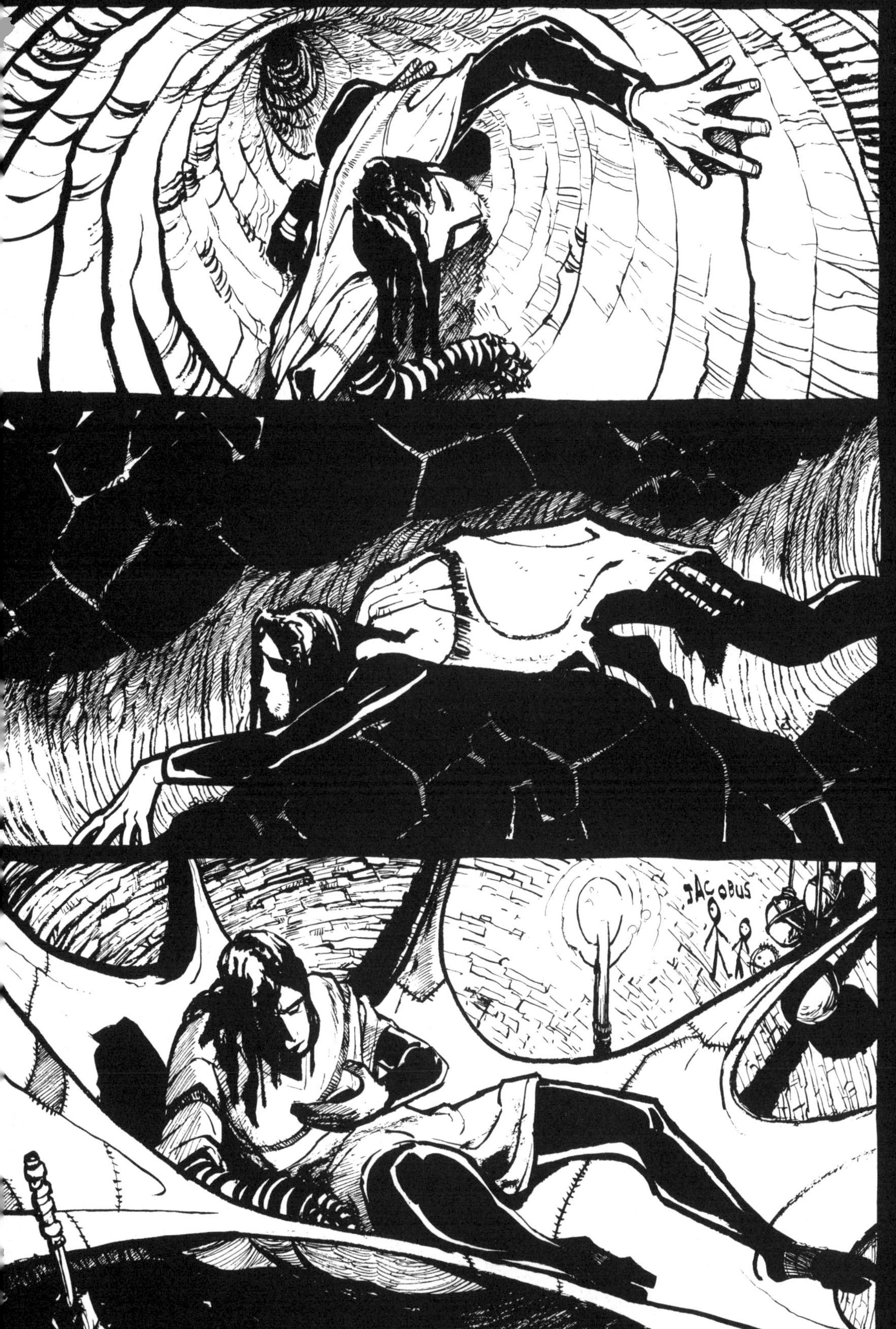
JACOBUS

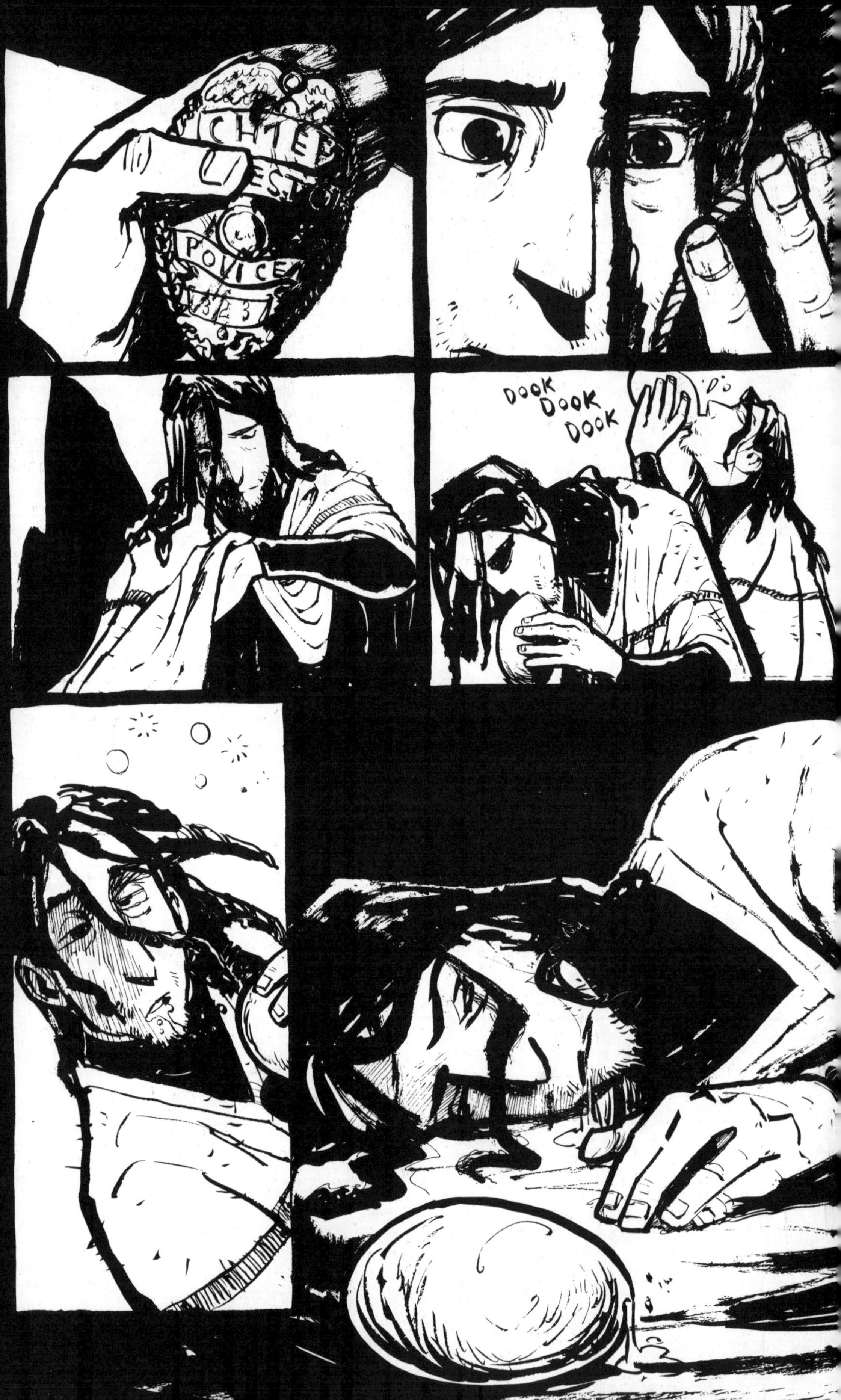
CHIEF
POLICE
DOOK
DOOK
DOOK

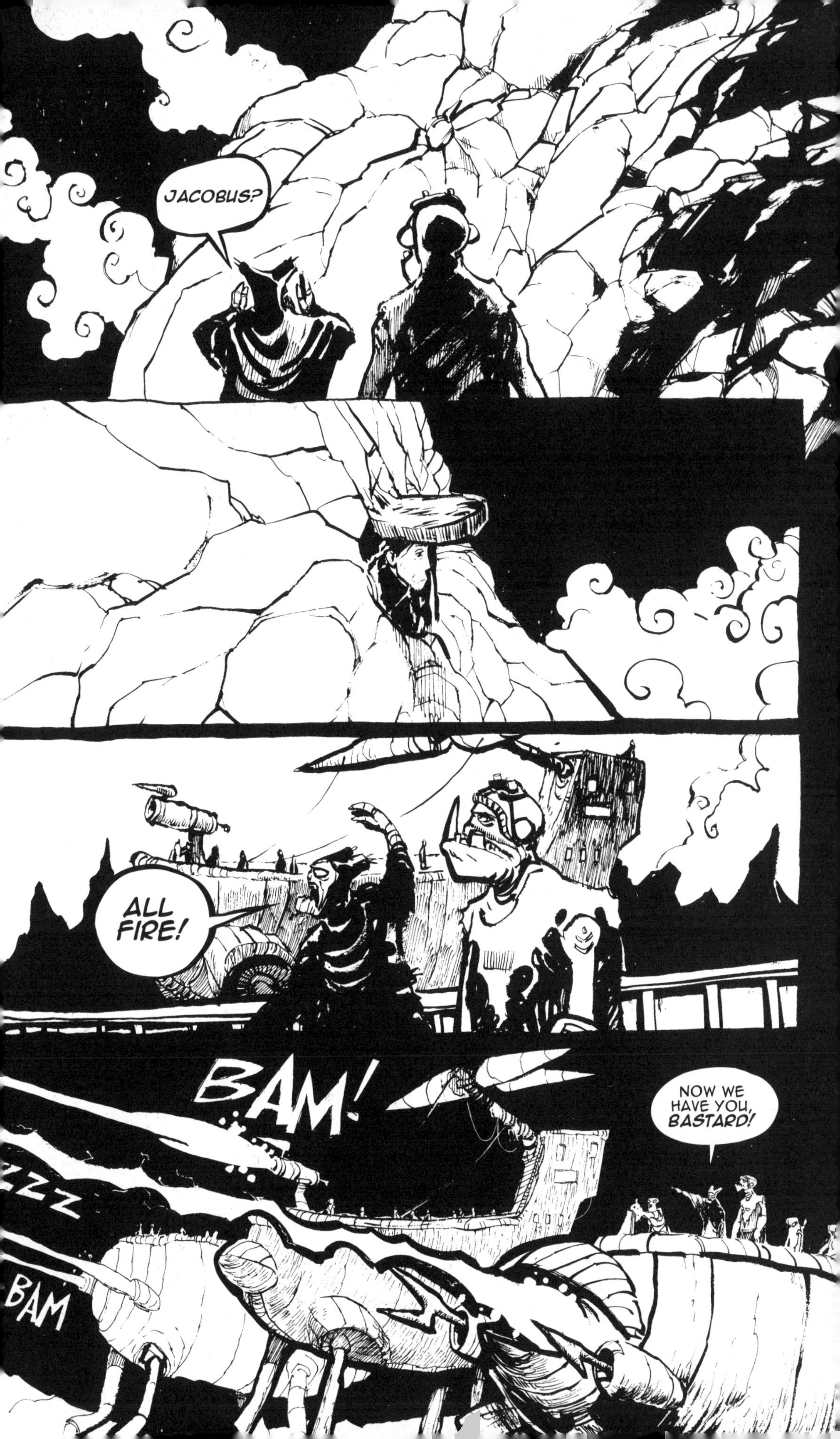
JACOBUS?
ALL FIRE!
BAM!
NOW WE HAVE YOU, BASTARD!
ZZZ
BAM

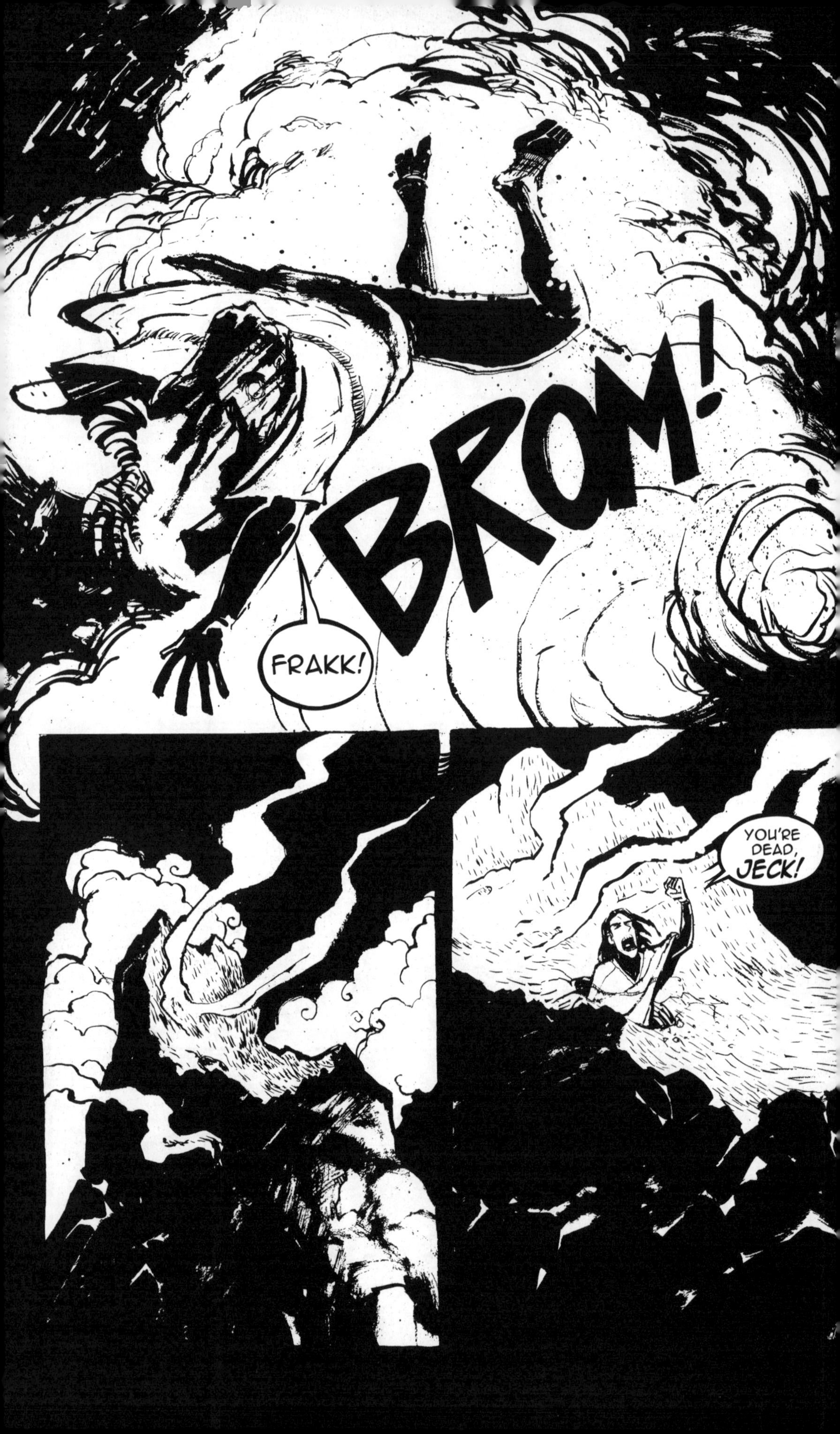
FRAKK!
BROM!
YOU'RE DEAD, JECK!

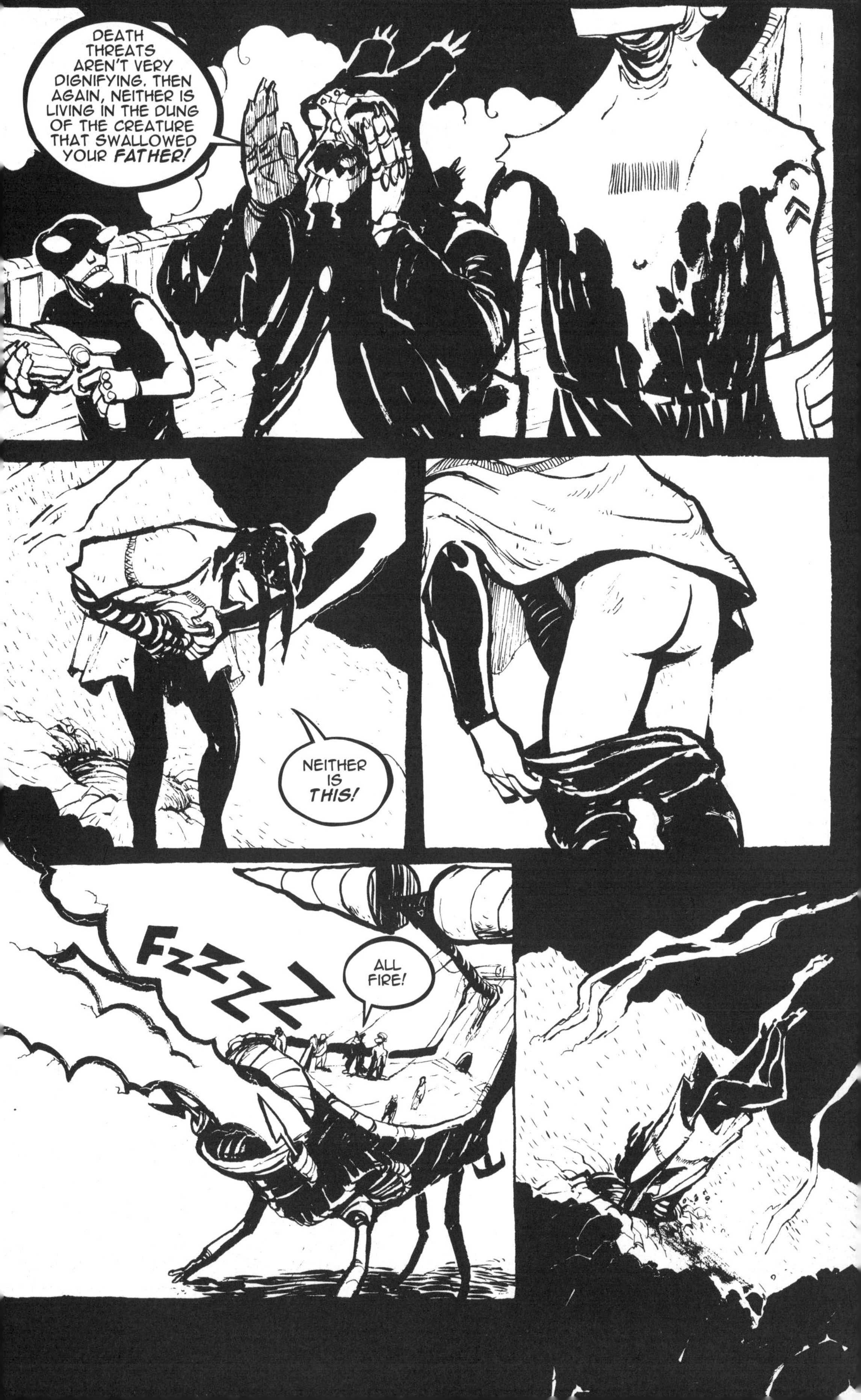
DEATH THREATS AREN'T VERY DIGNIFYING. THEN AGAIN, NEITHER IS LIVING IN THE DUNG OF THE CREATURE THAT SWALLOWED YOUR FATHER!
NEITHER IS THIS!
FzZZZZ
ALL FIRE!

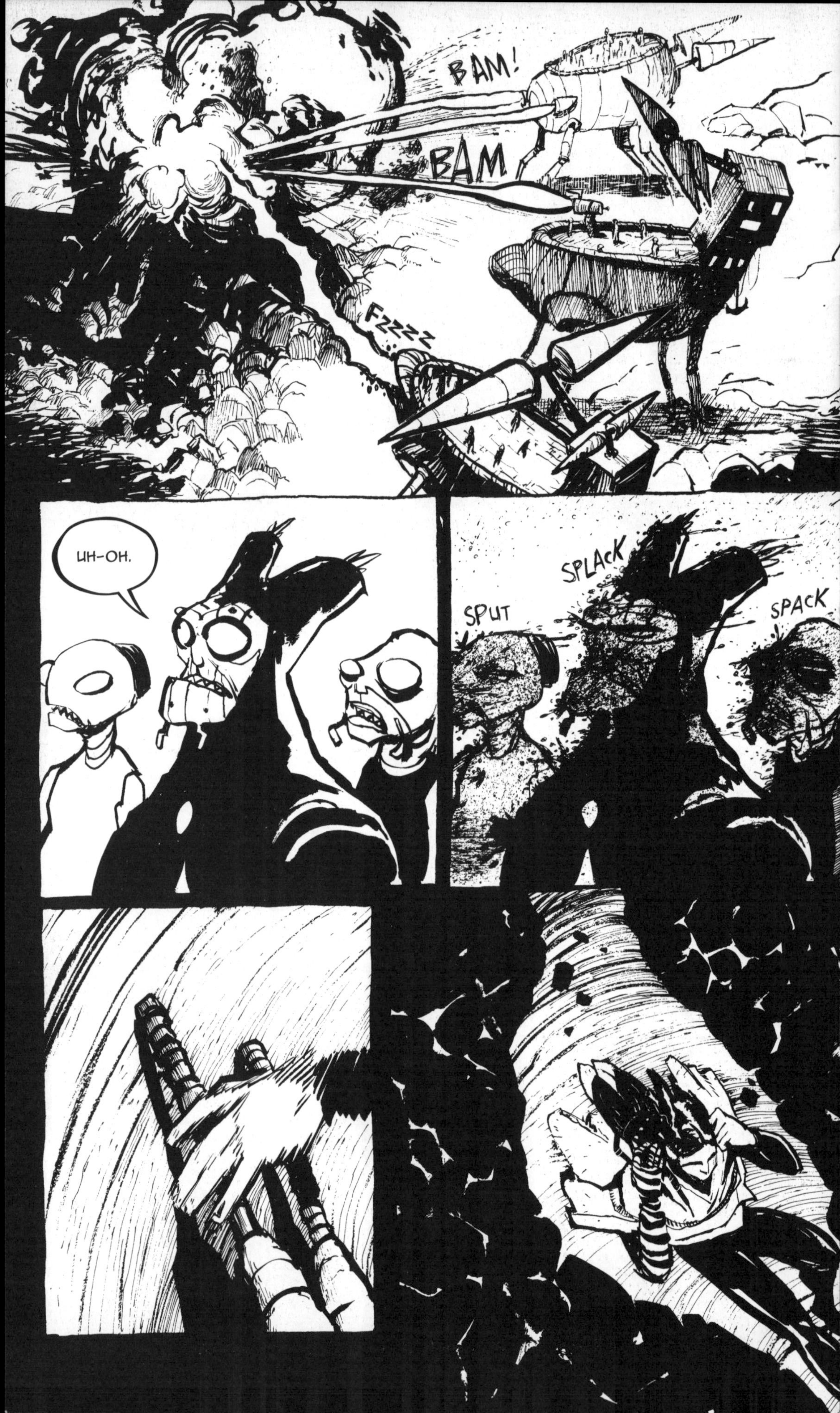
BAM!
BAM
Fzzzzz
UH-OH.
SPLACK
SPUT
SPACK

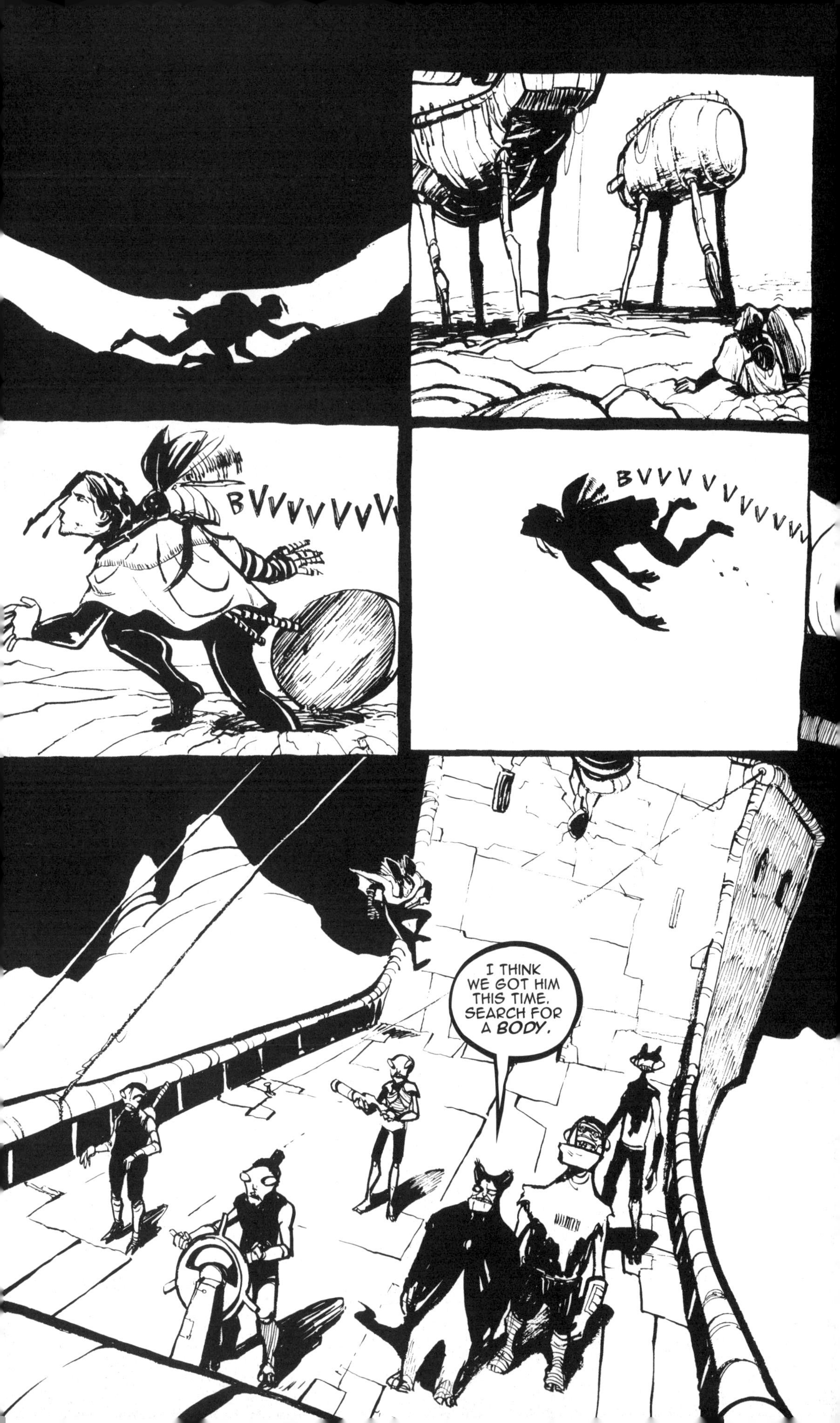
BVVVVVVVVV
BVVVVVVVVVVV
I THINK WE GOT HIM THIS TIME. SEARCH FOR A *BODY*.

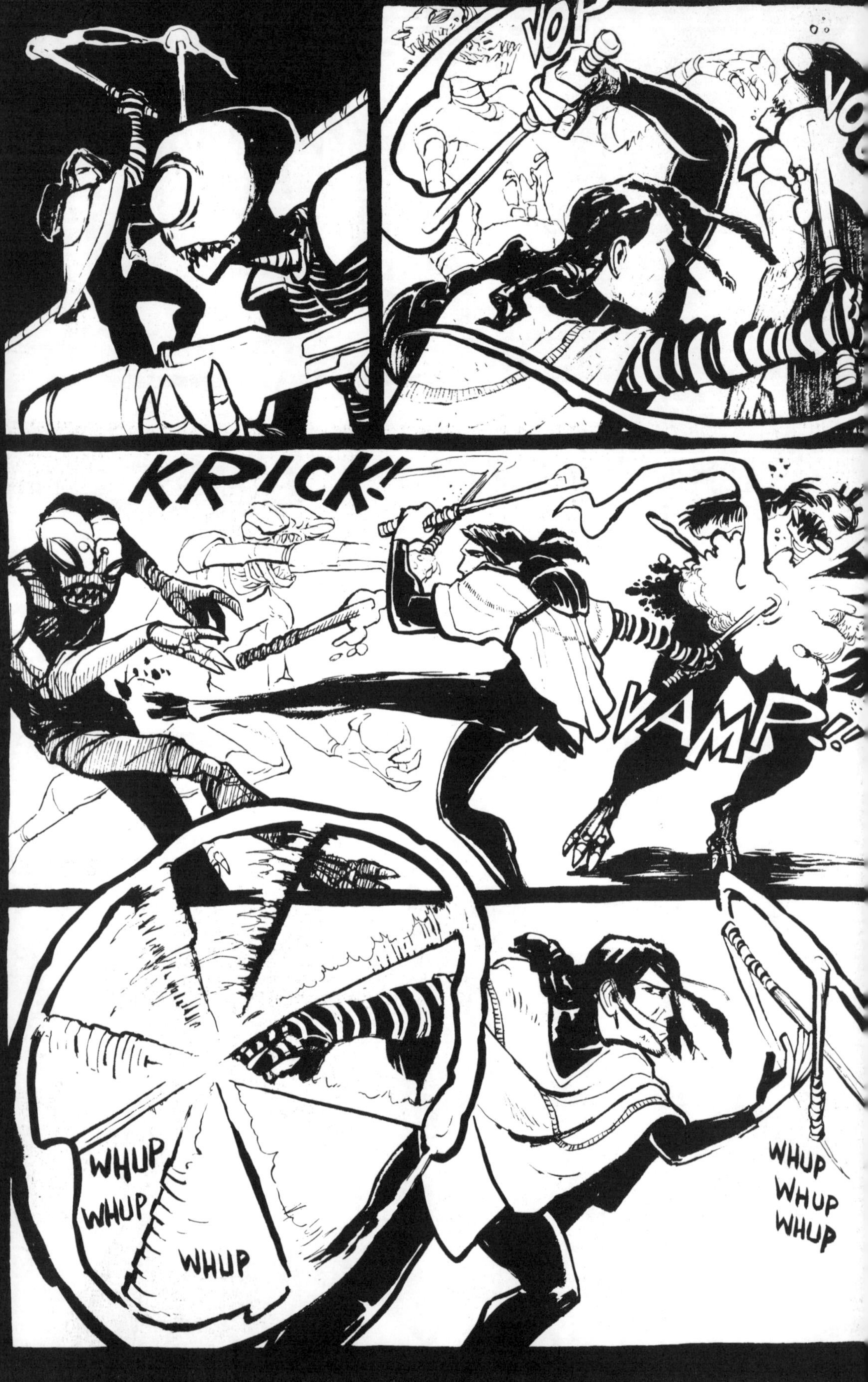
VOP
VOO
KRICK!
VAMP!!
WHUP
WHUP
WHUP
WHUP
WHUP
WHUP

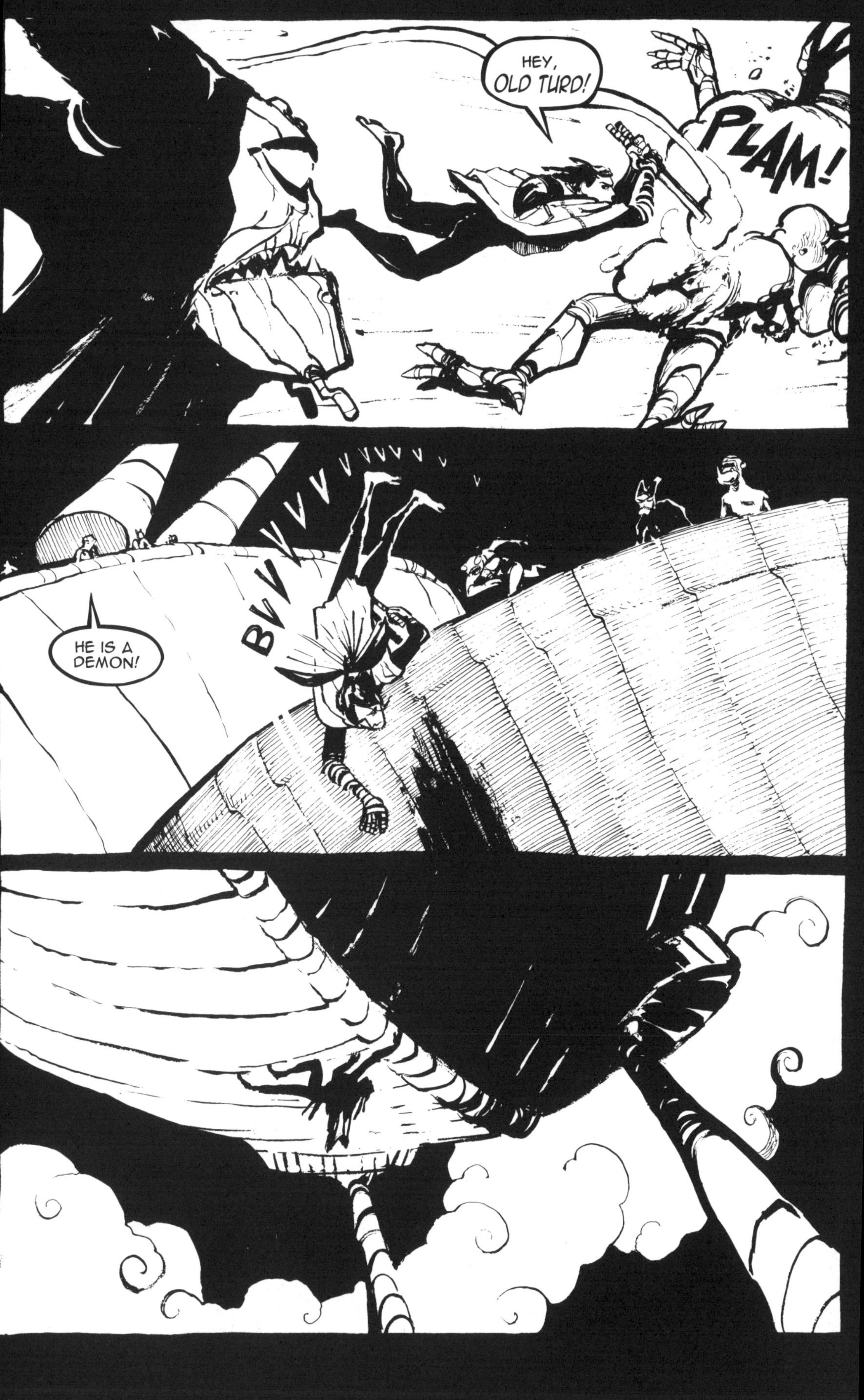
HEY, OLD TURD!
PLAM!
BVVVVVVVVVV
HE IS A DEMON!

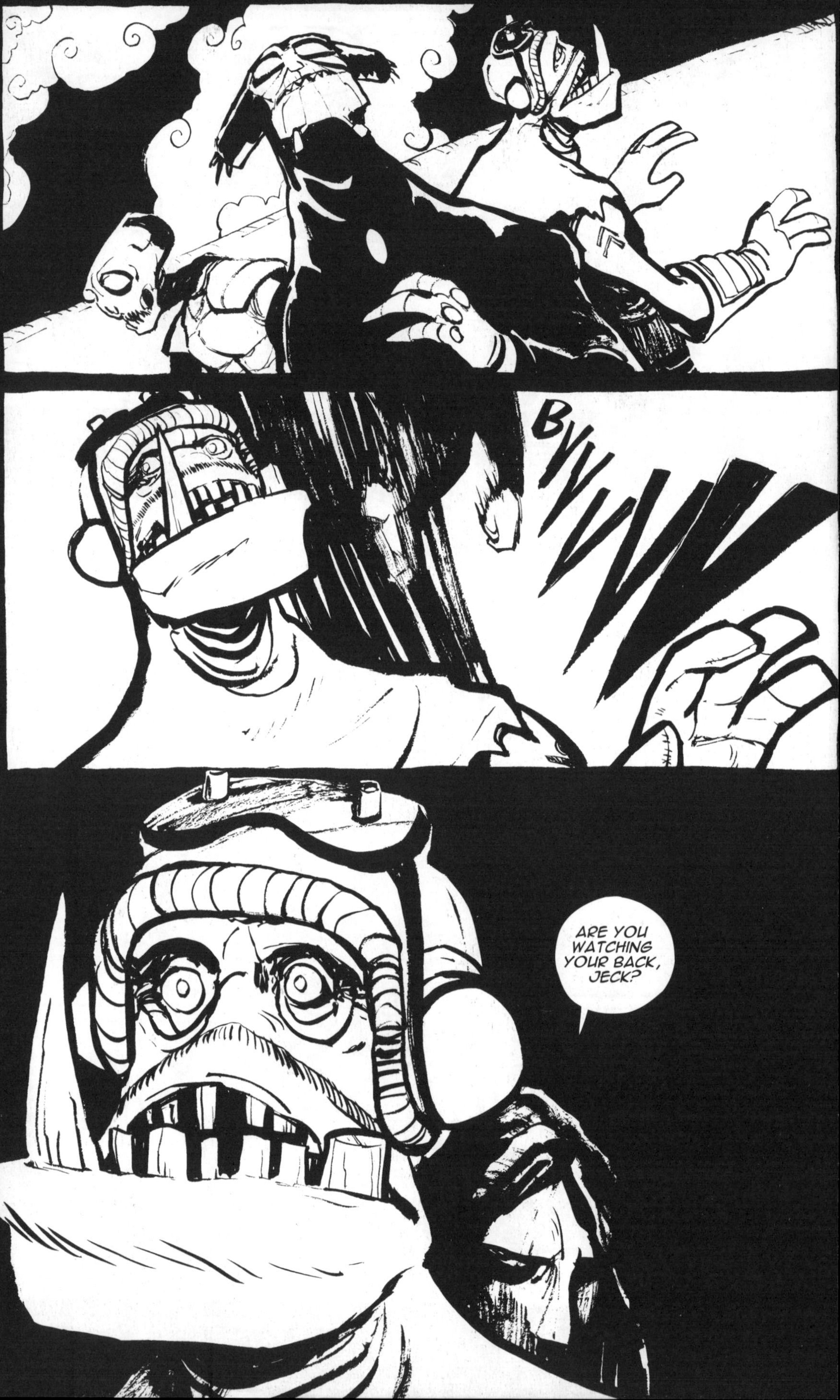
BVVVVV
ARE YOU WATCHING YOUR BACK, JECK?

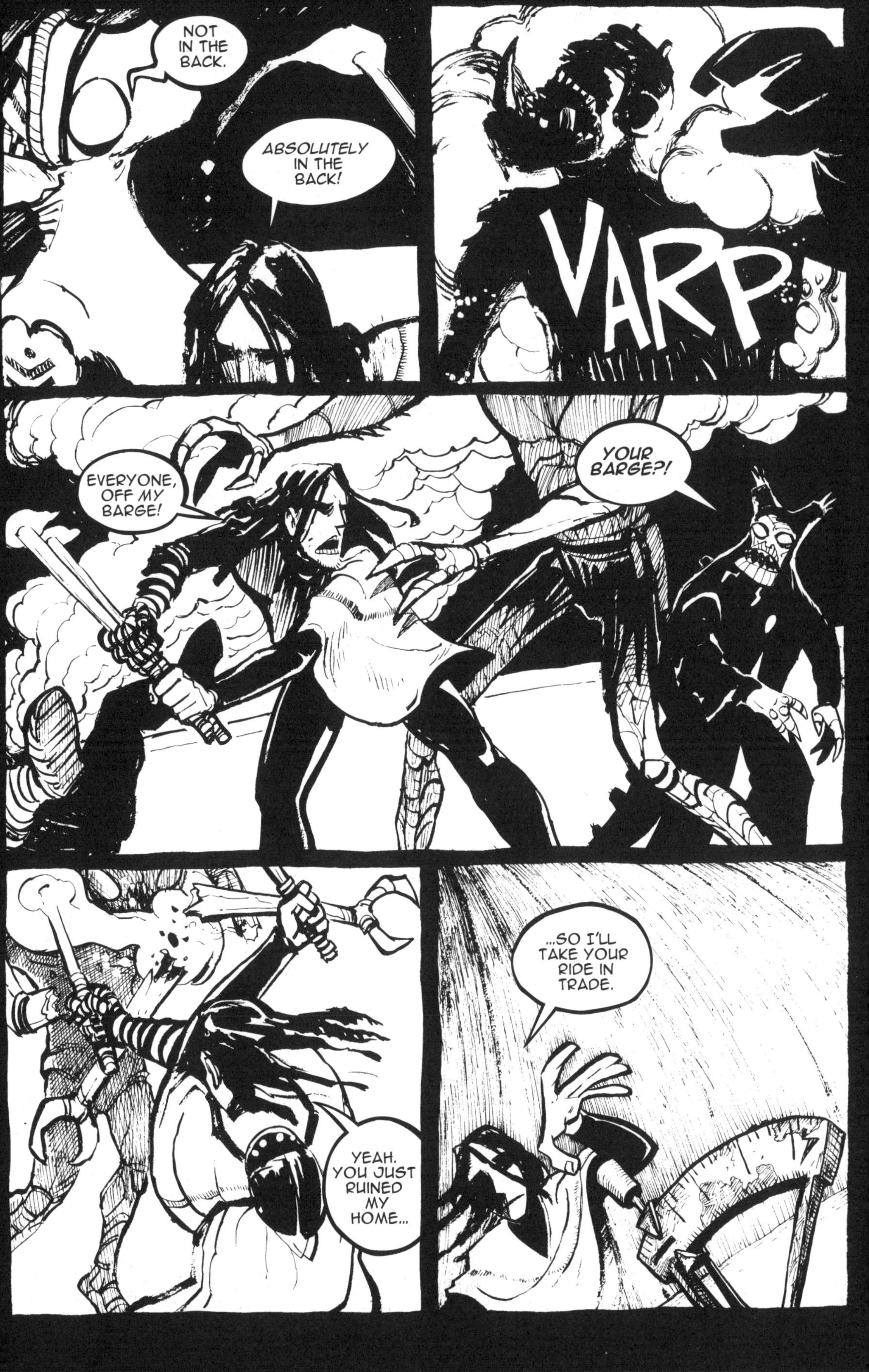
NOT IN THE BACK.
ABSOLUTELY IN THE BACK!
VARP
EVERYONE, OFF MY BARGE!
YOUR BARGE?!
YEAH. YOU JUST RUINED MY HOME...
...SO I'LL TAKE YOUR RIDE IN TRADE.

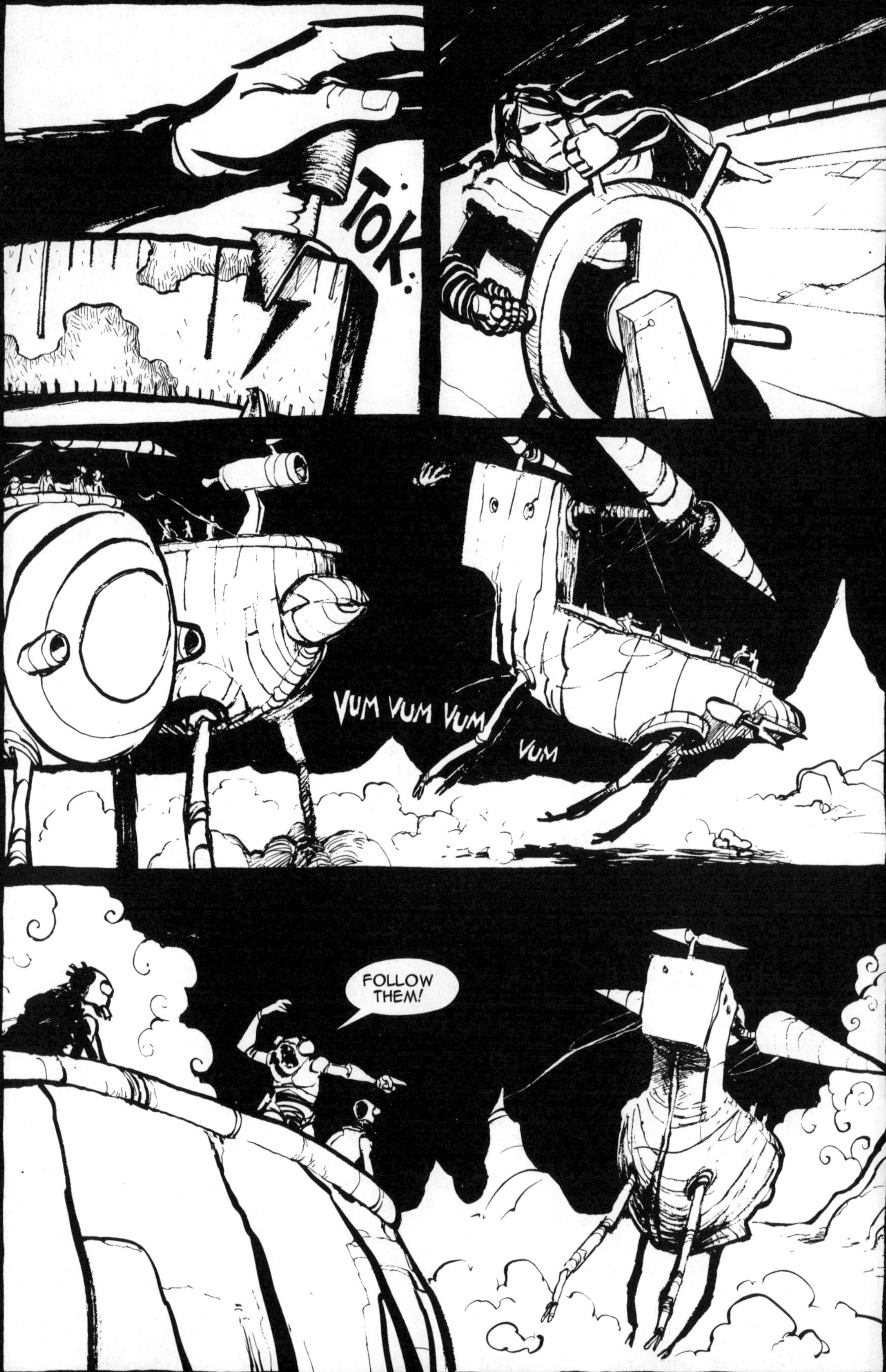
TOK!
VUM VUM VUM
VUM
FOLLOW THEM!

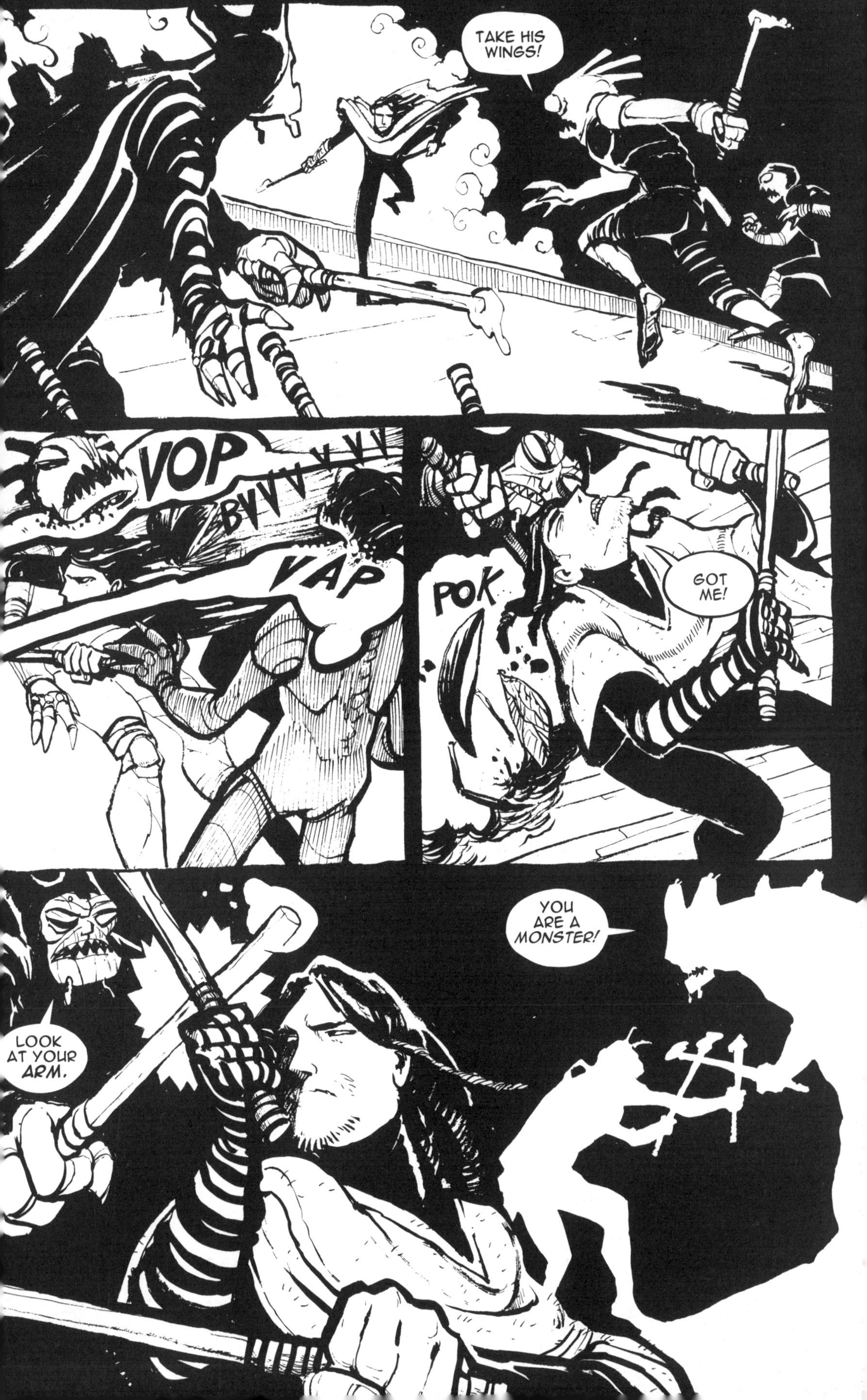
TAKE HIS WINGS!
VOP
BVVV
VAP
POK
GOT ME!
YOU ARE A MONSTER!
LOOK AT YOUR ARM.

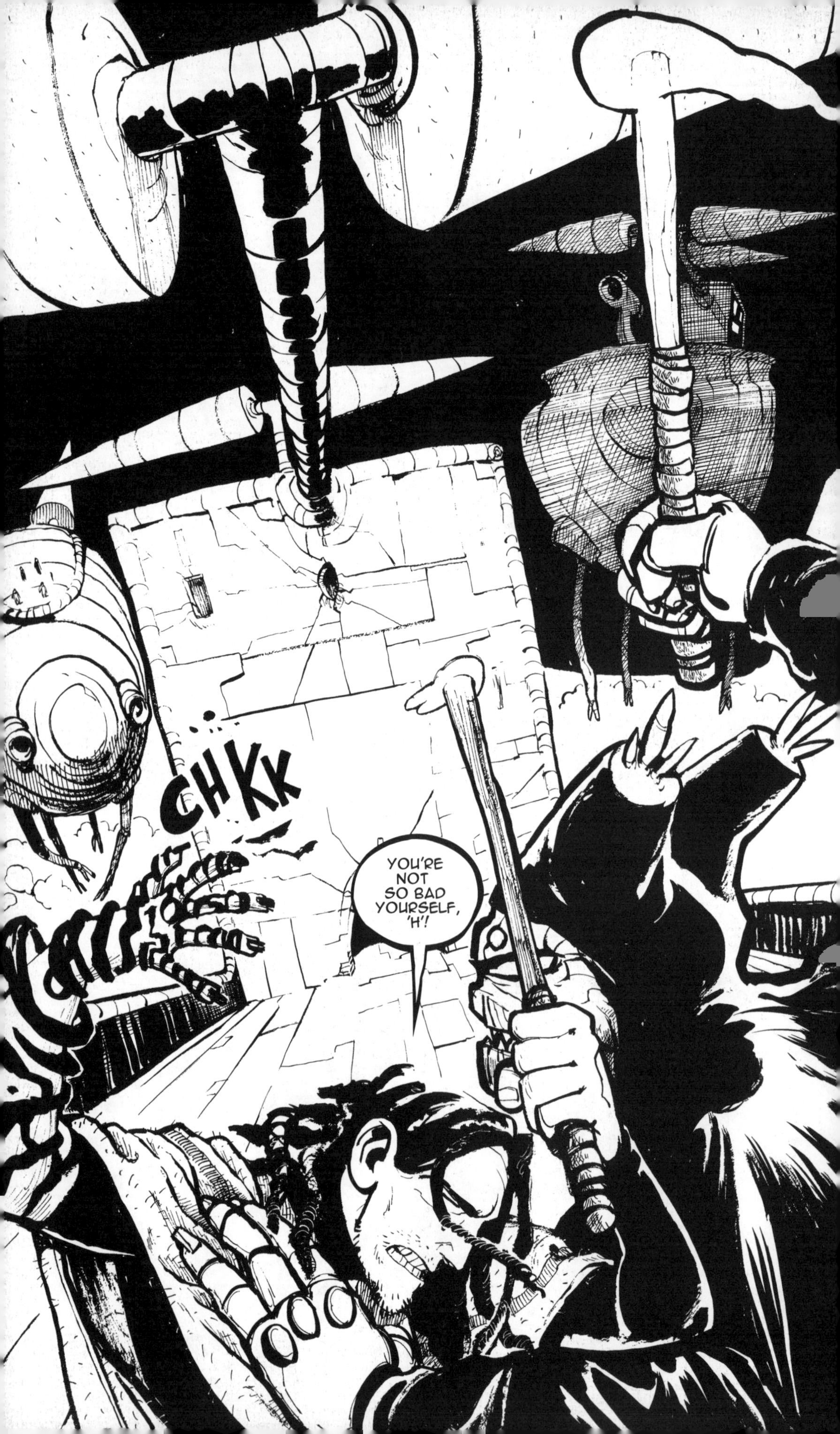
CHKK
YOU'RE NOT SO BAD YOURSELF, 'H'!

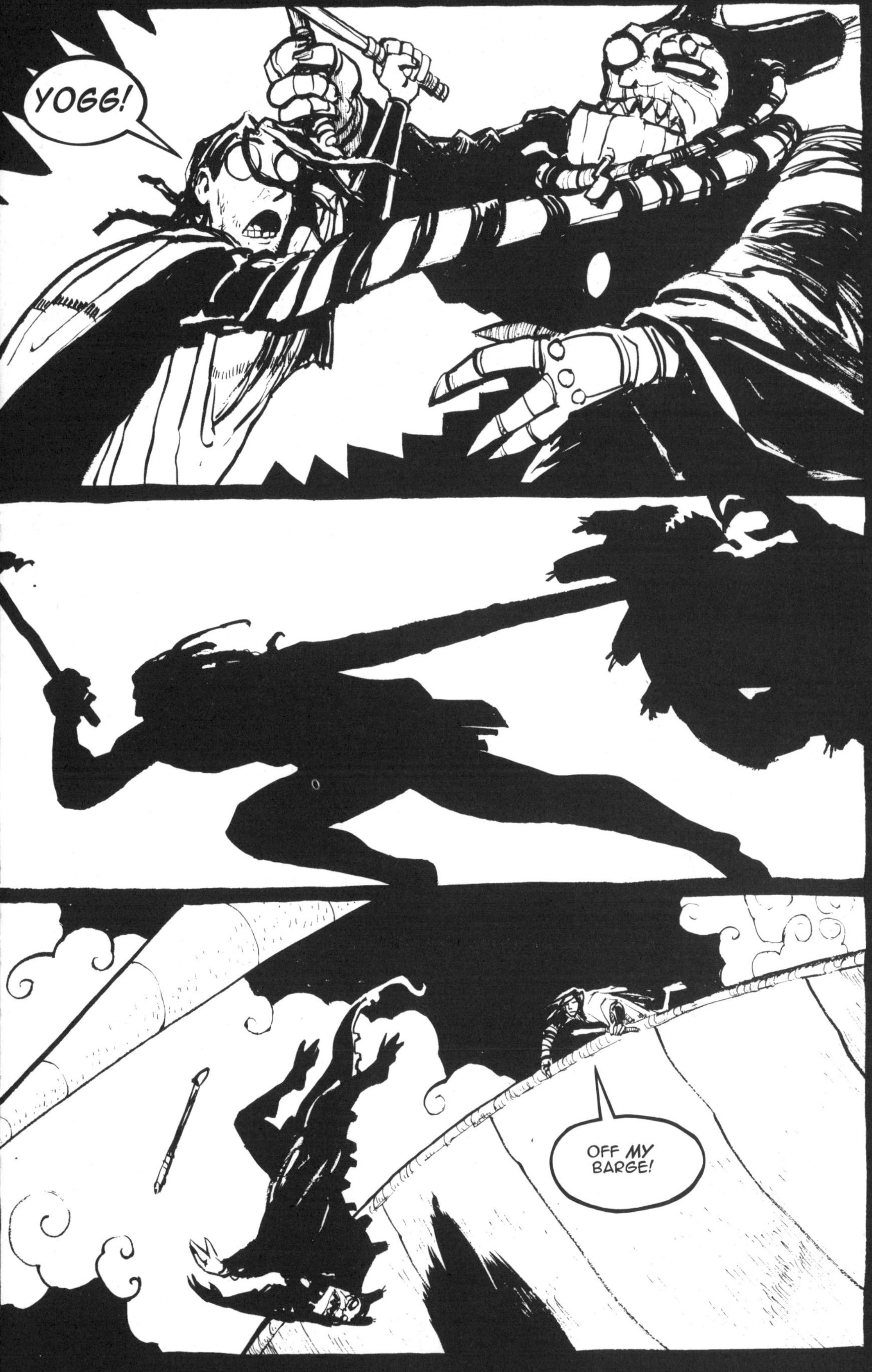
YOGG!
OFF MY BARGE!

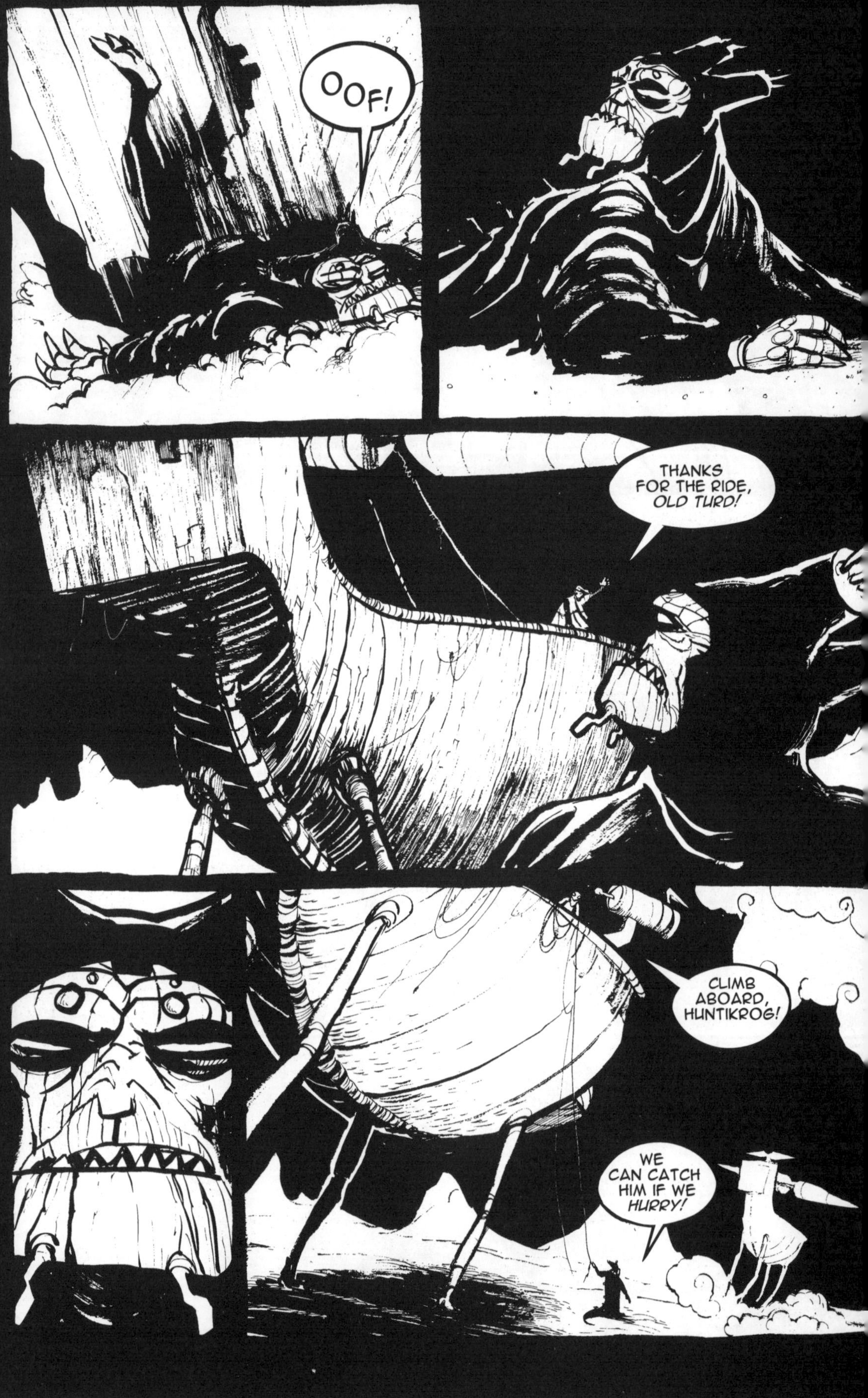
OOF!
THANKS FOR THE RIDE, OLD TURD!
CLIMB ABOARD, HUNTIKROG!
WE CAN CATCH HIM IF WE HURRY!

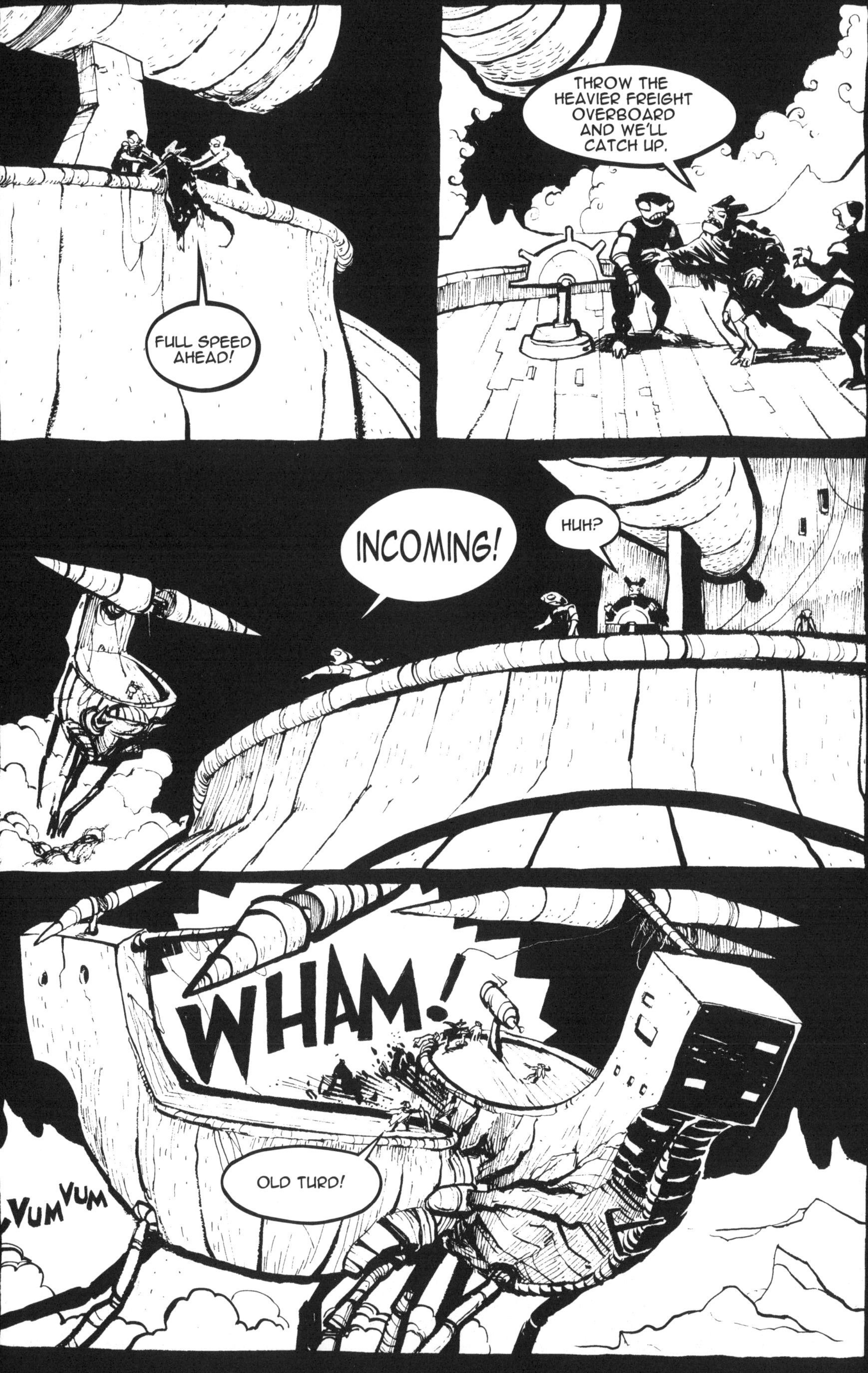
FULL SPEED AHEAD!
THROW THE HEAVIER FREIGHT OVERBOARD AND WE'LL CATCH UP.
INCOMING!
HUH?
WHAM!
OLD TURD!
VUM VUM

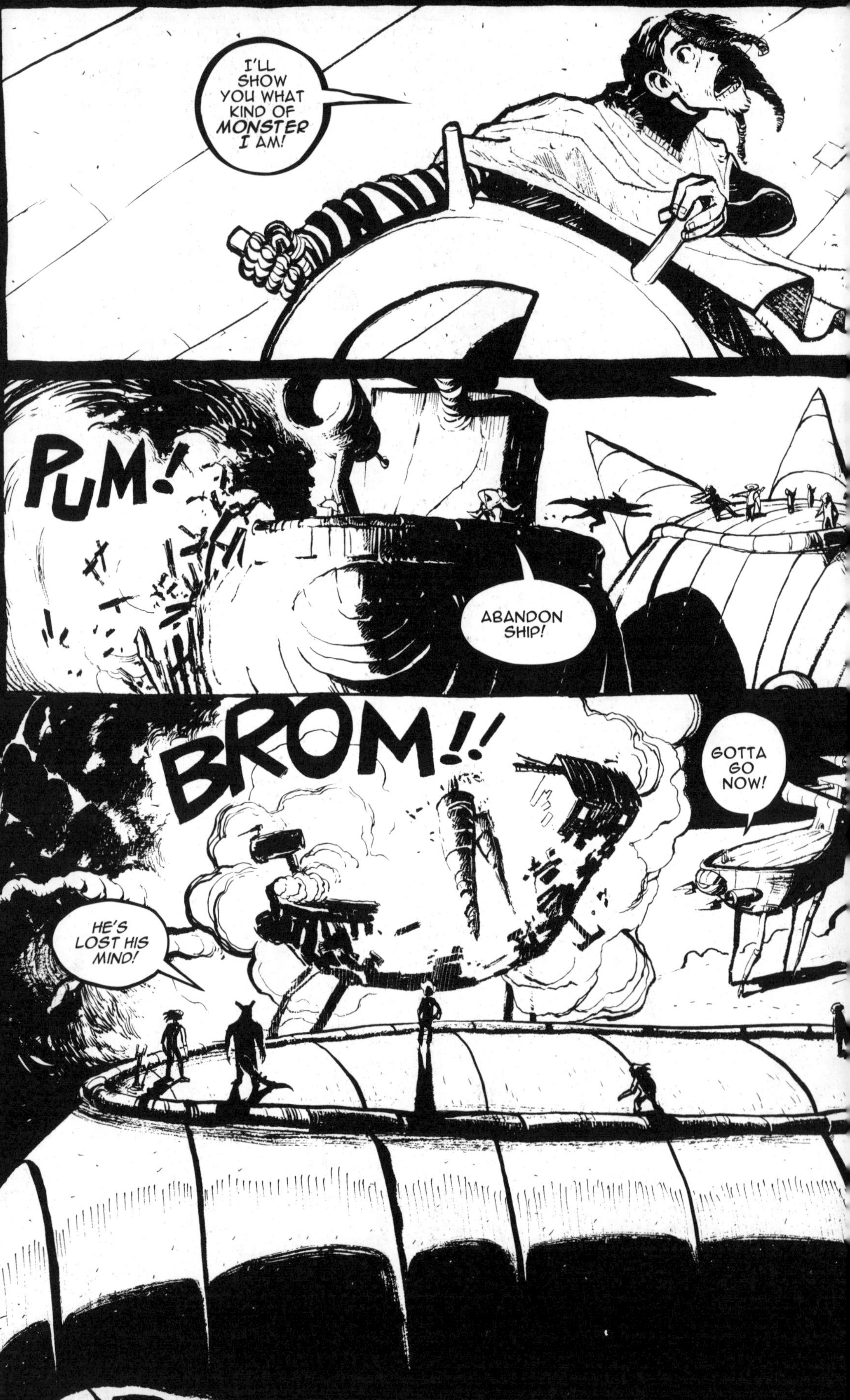
I'LL SHOW YOU WHAT KIND OF MONSTER I AM!
PUM!
ABANDON SHIP!
BROM!!
GOTTA GO NOW!
HE'S LOST HIS MIND!

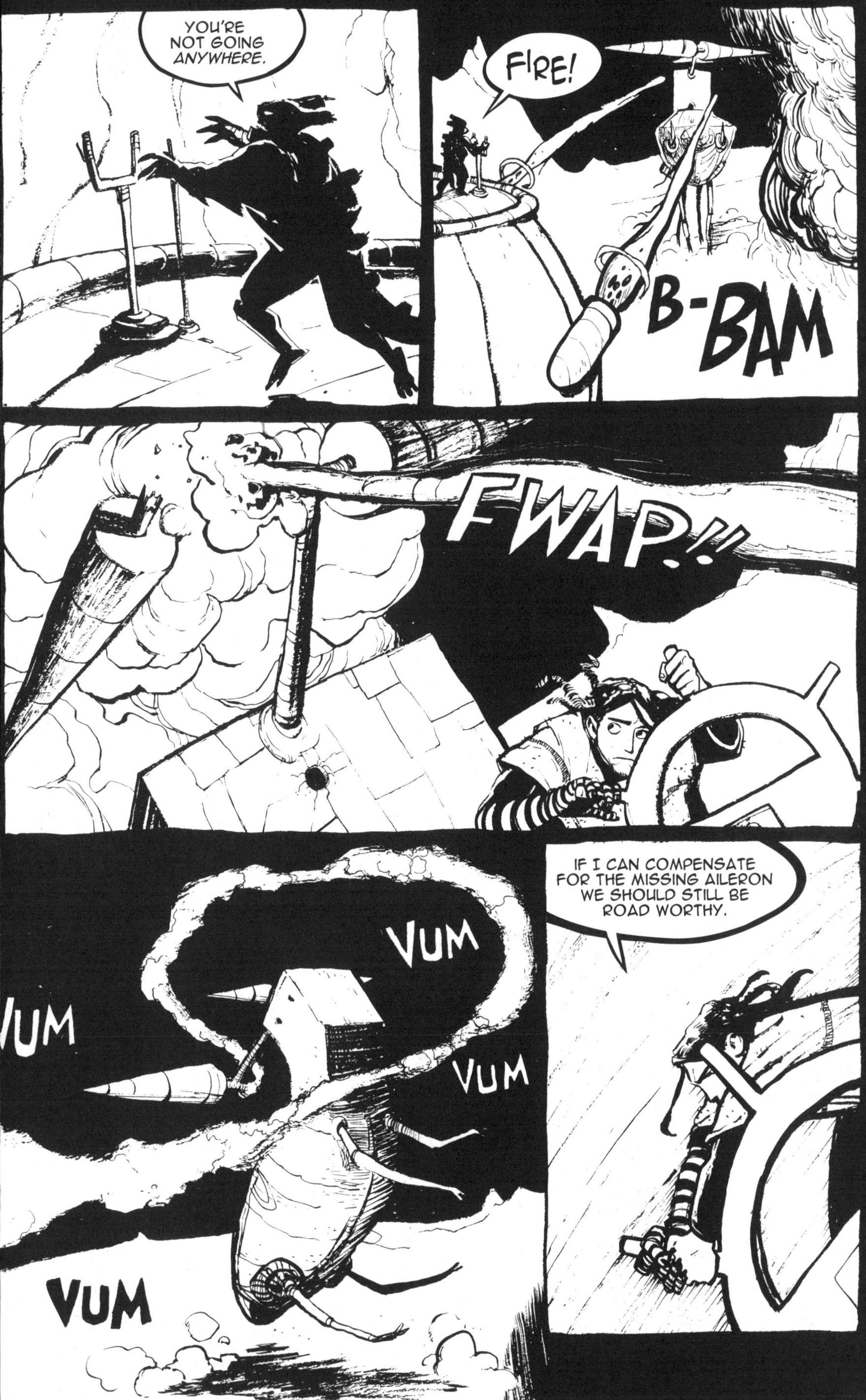
YOU'RE NOT GOING ANYWHERE.
FIRE!
B-BAM
FWAP!!
VUM
VUM
VUM
VUM
IF I CAN COMPENSATE FOR THE MISSING AILERON WE SHOULD STILL BE ROAD WORTHY.

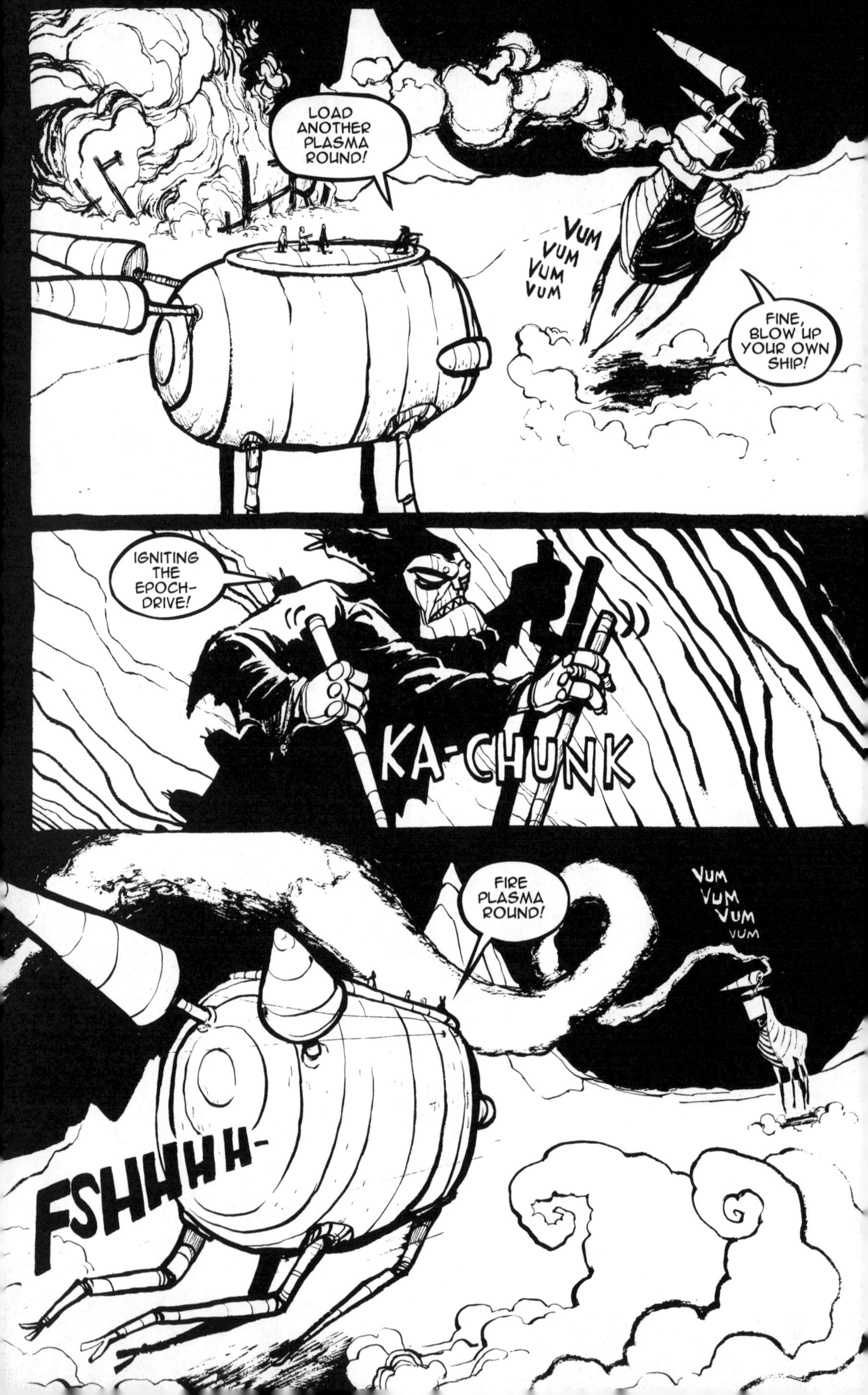
LOAD ANOTHER PLASMA ROUND!
VUM VUM VUM VUM
FINE, BLOW UP YOUR OWN SHIP!
IGNITING THE EPOCH-DRIVE!
KA-CHUNK
FIRE PLASMA ROUND!
VUM VUM VUM VUM
FSHHHH-

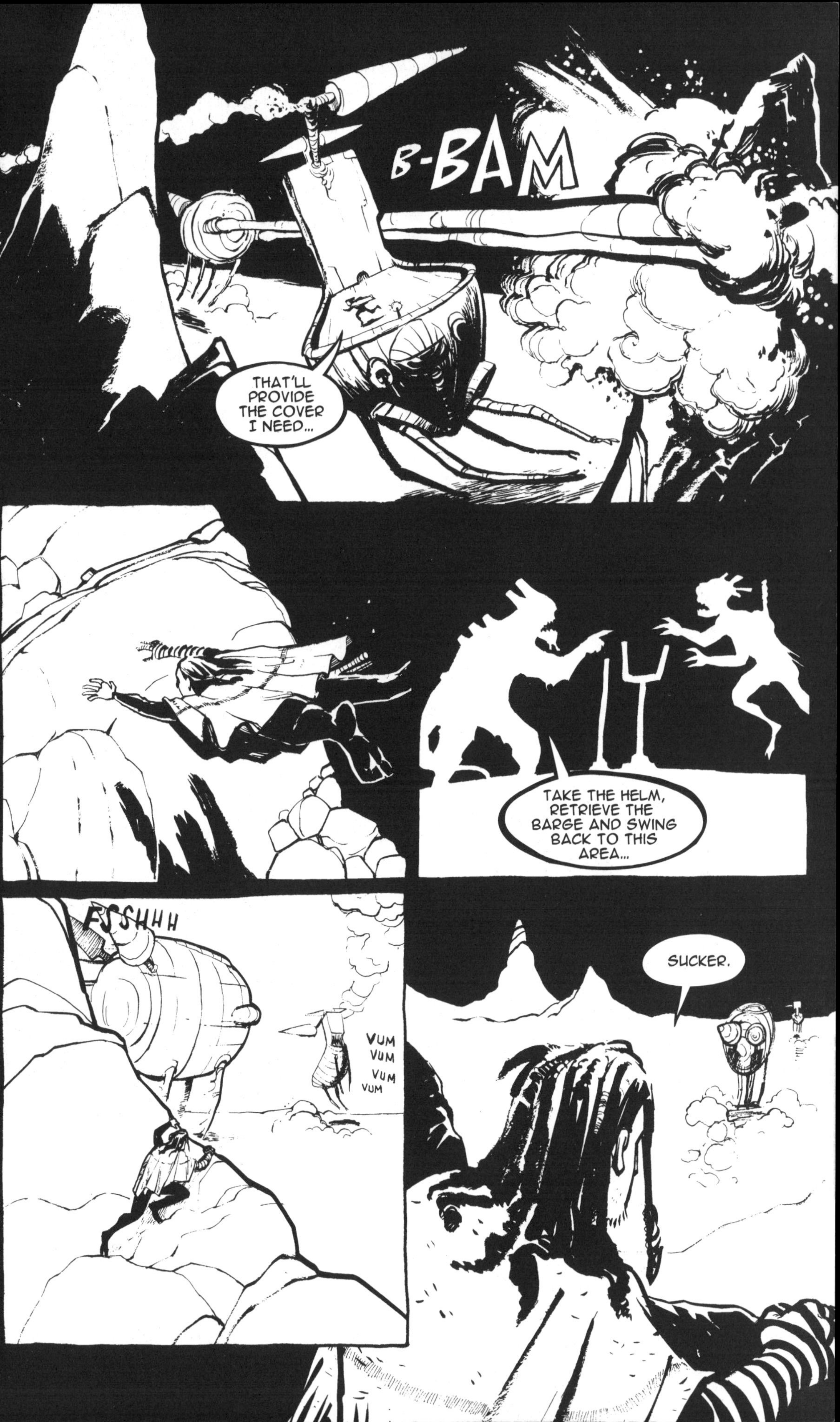
B-BAM
THAT'LL PROVIDE THE COVER I NEED...
TAKE THE HELM, RETRIEVE THE BARGE AND SWING BACK TO THIS AREA...
FSSHHH
VUM VUM VUM VUM
SUCKER.

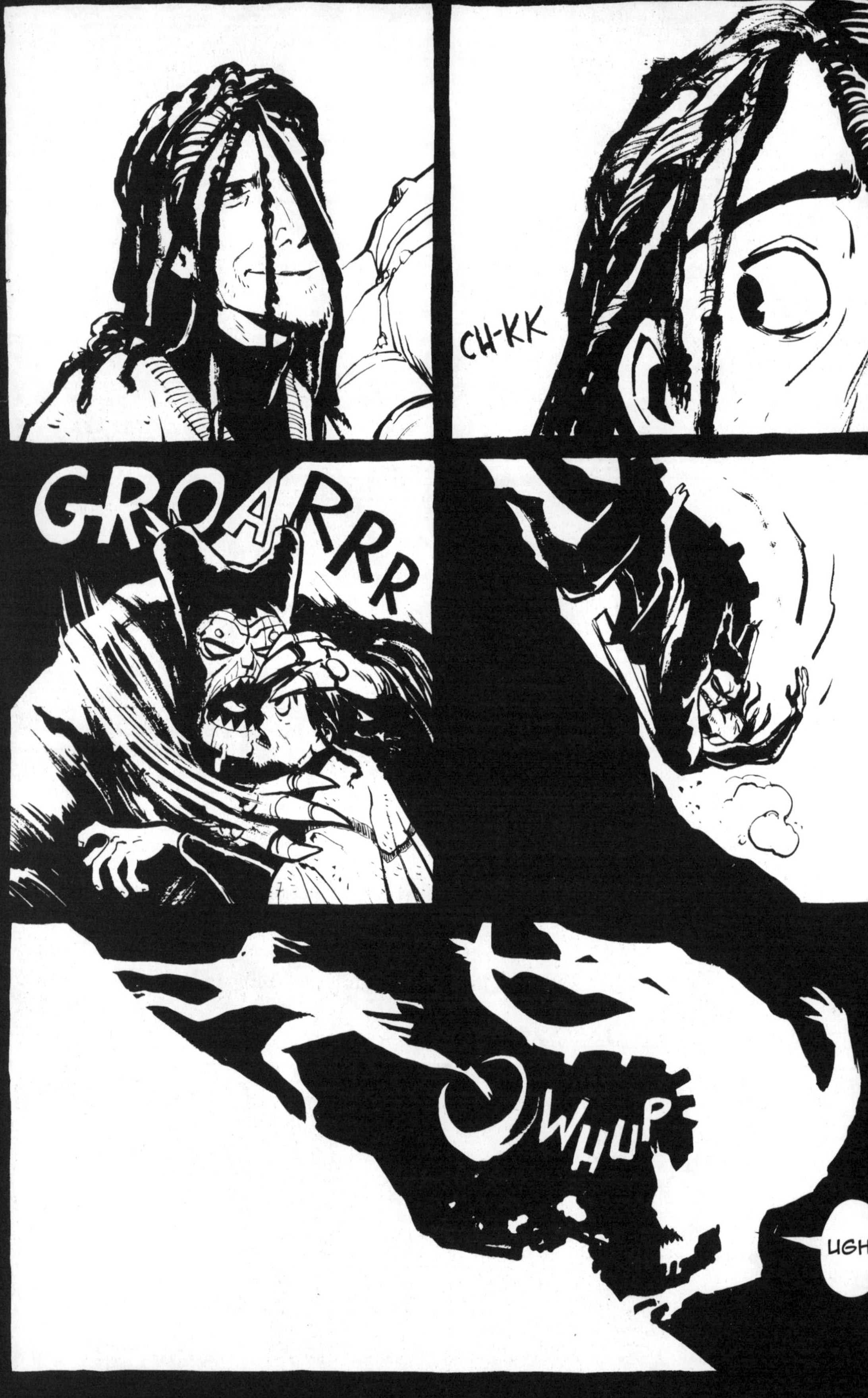
CH-KK
GROARRR
WHUP
UGH!

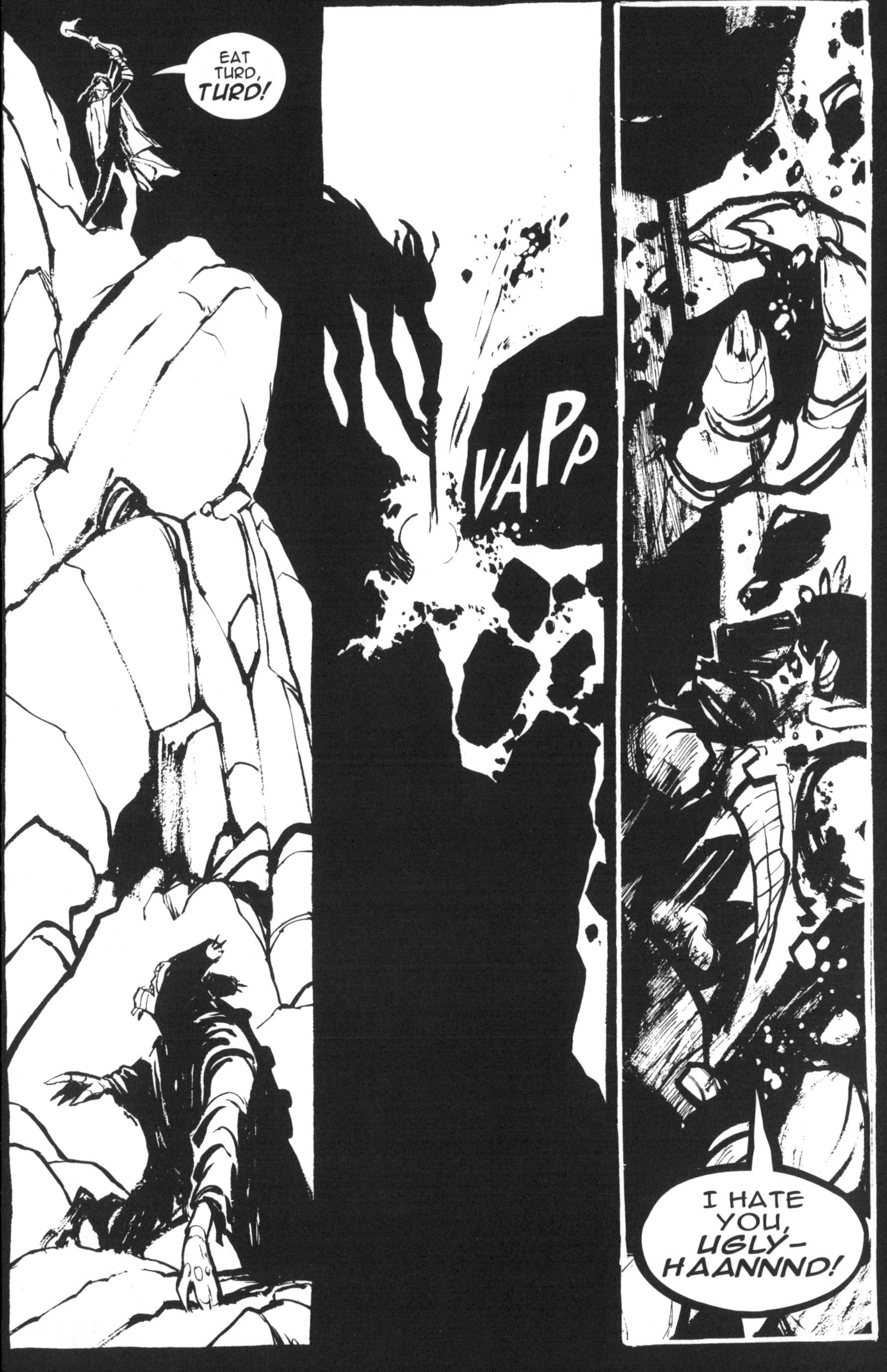
EAT TURD, TURD!
VAPP
I HATE YOU, UGLY-HAANNND!

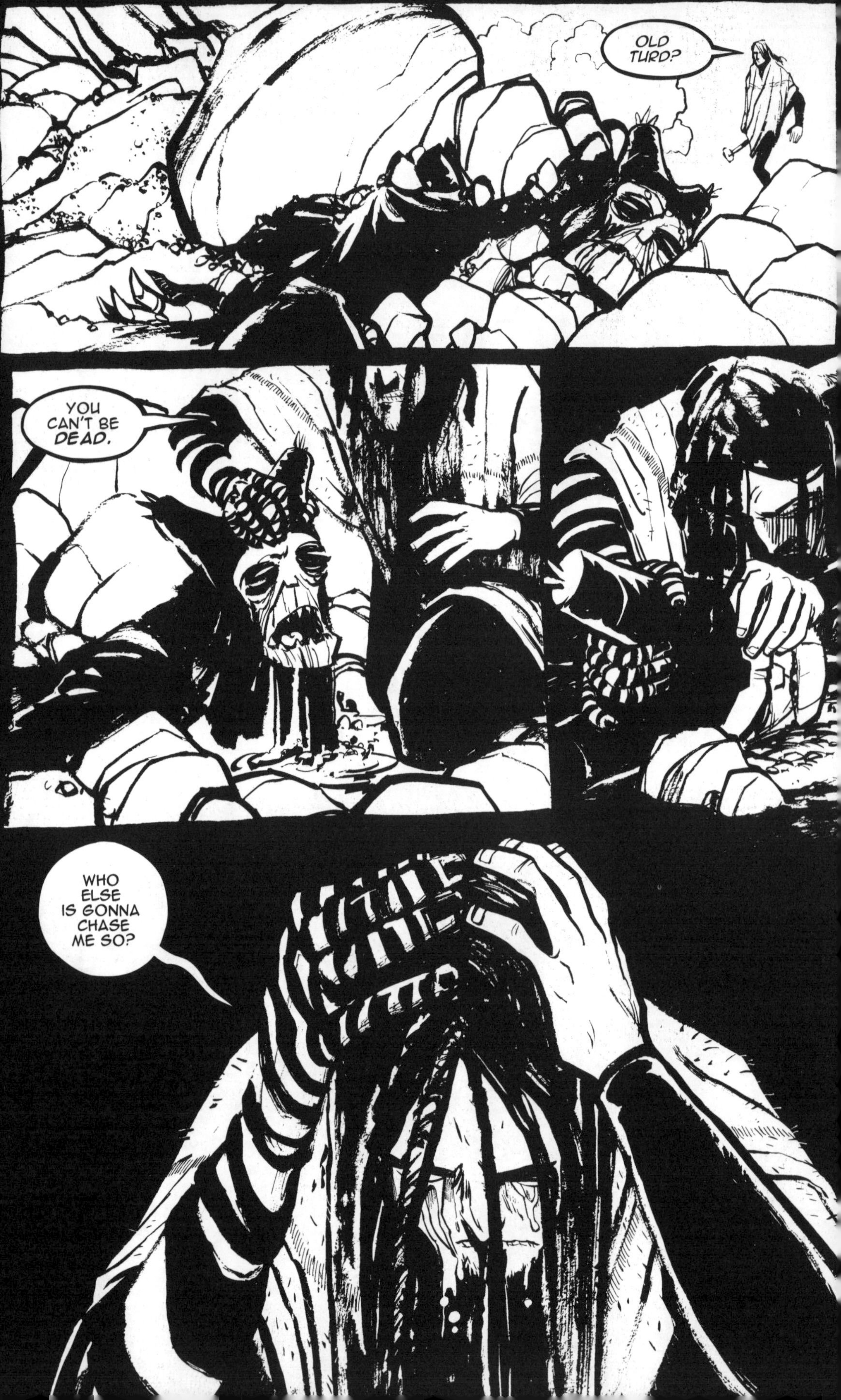
OLD TURD?
YOU CAN'T BE DEAD.
WHO ELSE IS GONNA CHASE ME SO?

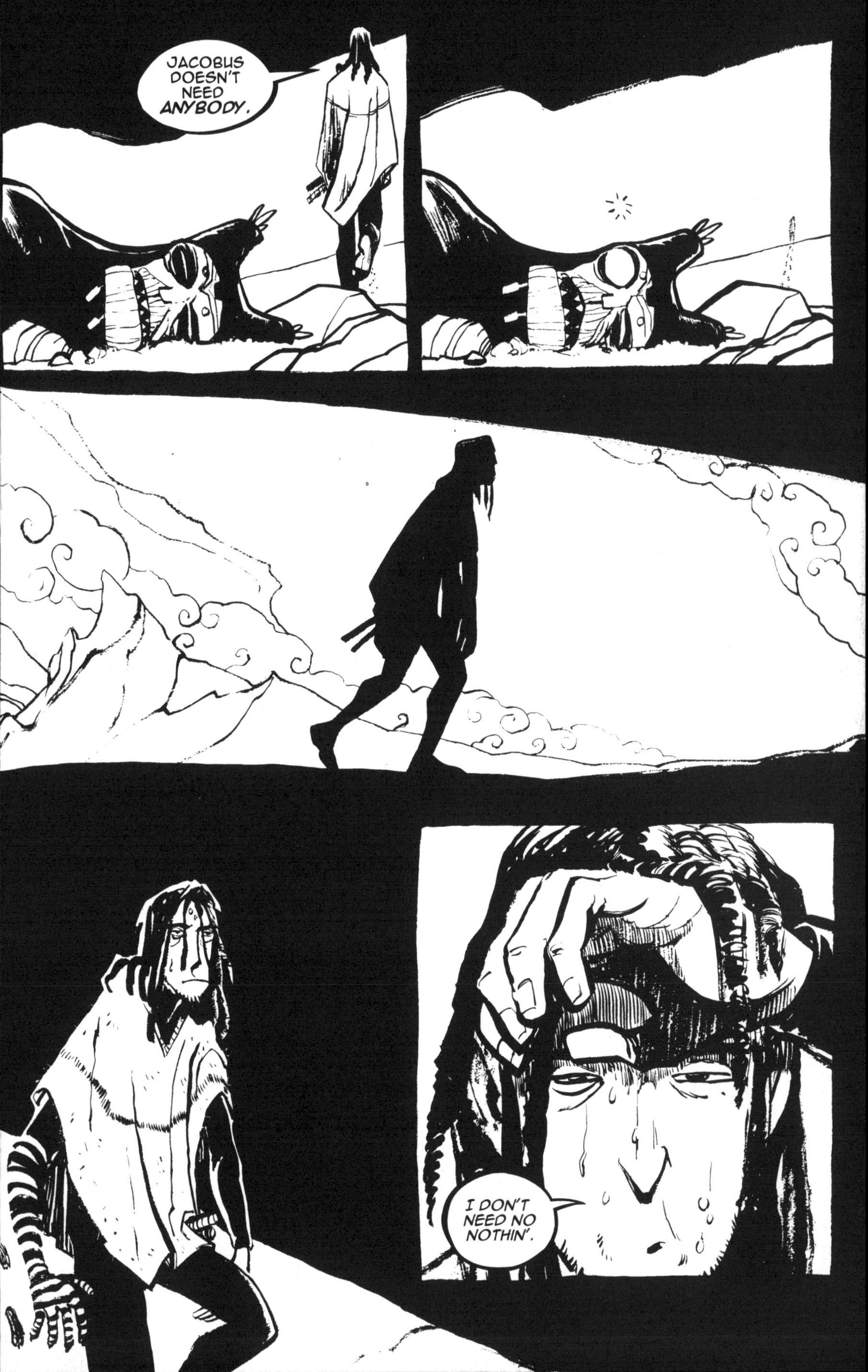
JACOBUS DOESN'T NEED ANYBODY.
I DON'T NEED NO NOTHIN'.

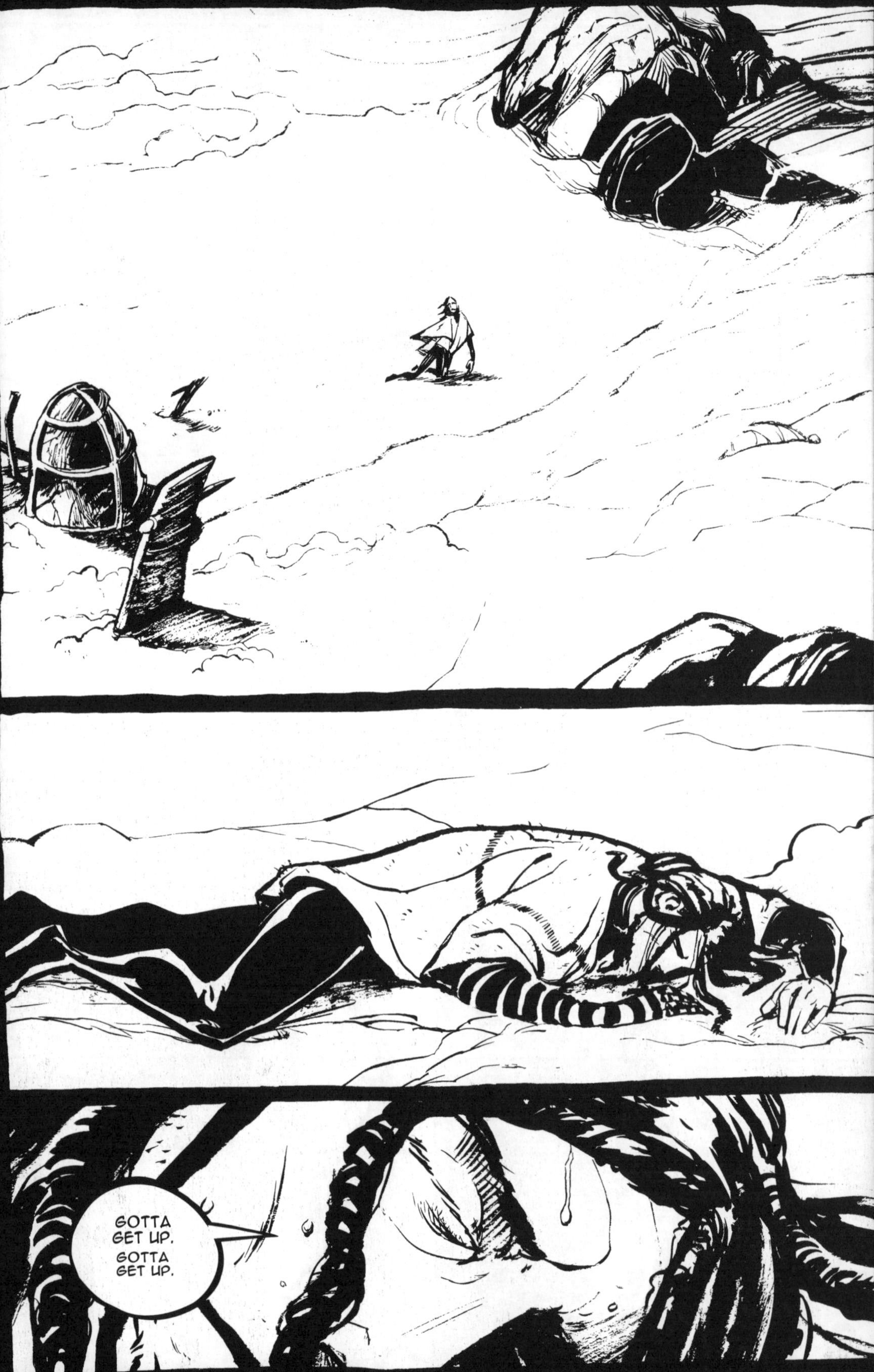
GOTTA GET UP. GOTTA GET UP.

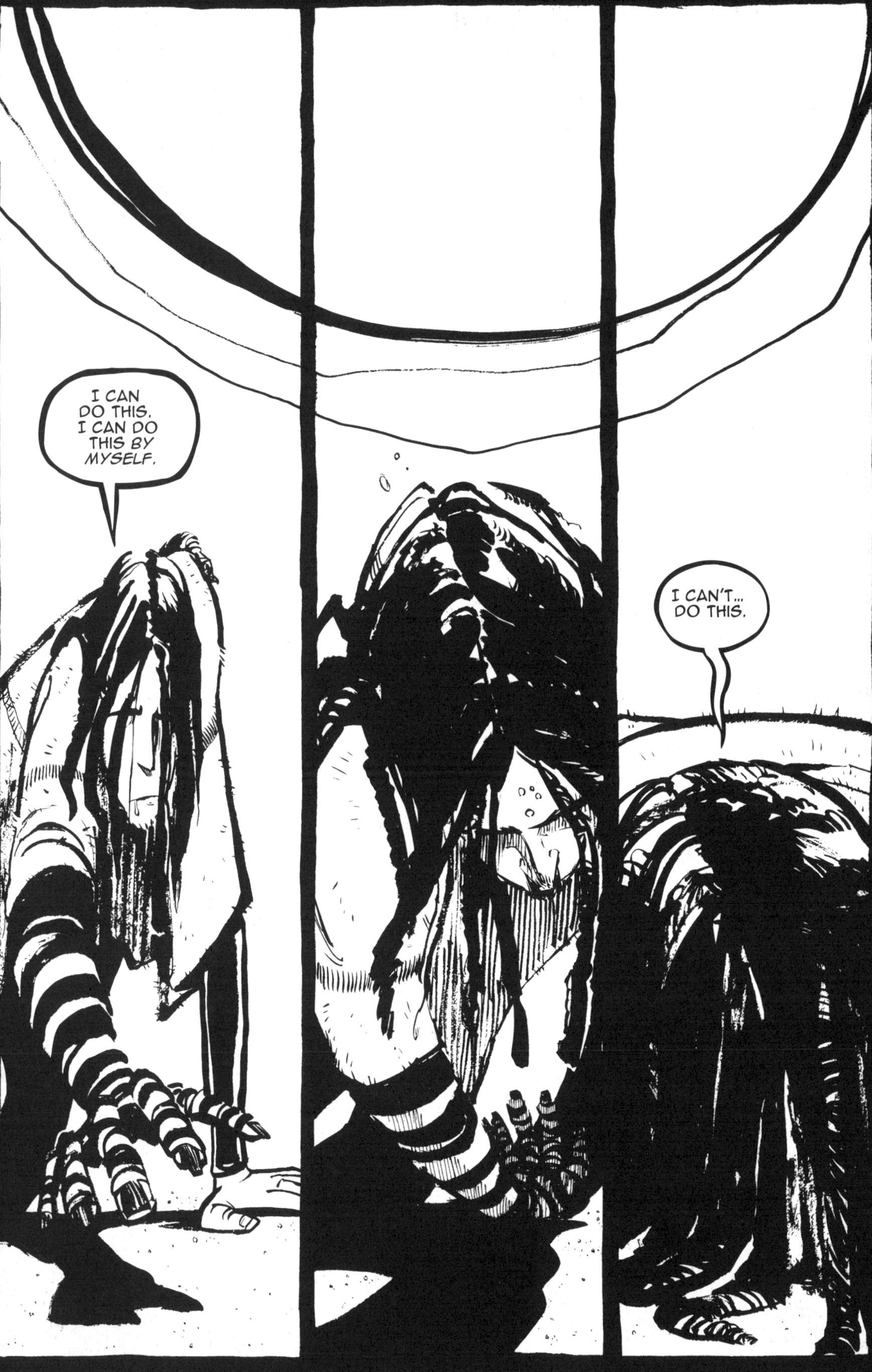
I CAN DO THIS. I CAN DO THIS BY *MYSELF*.
I CAN'T... DO THIS.

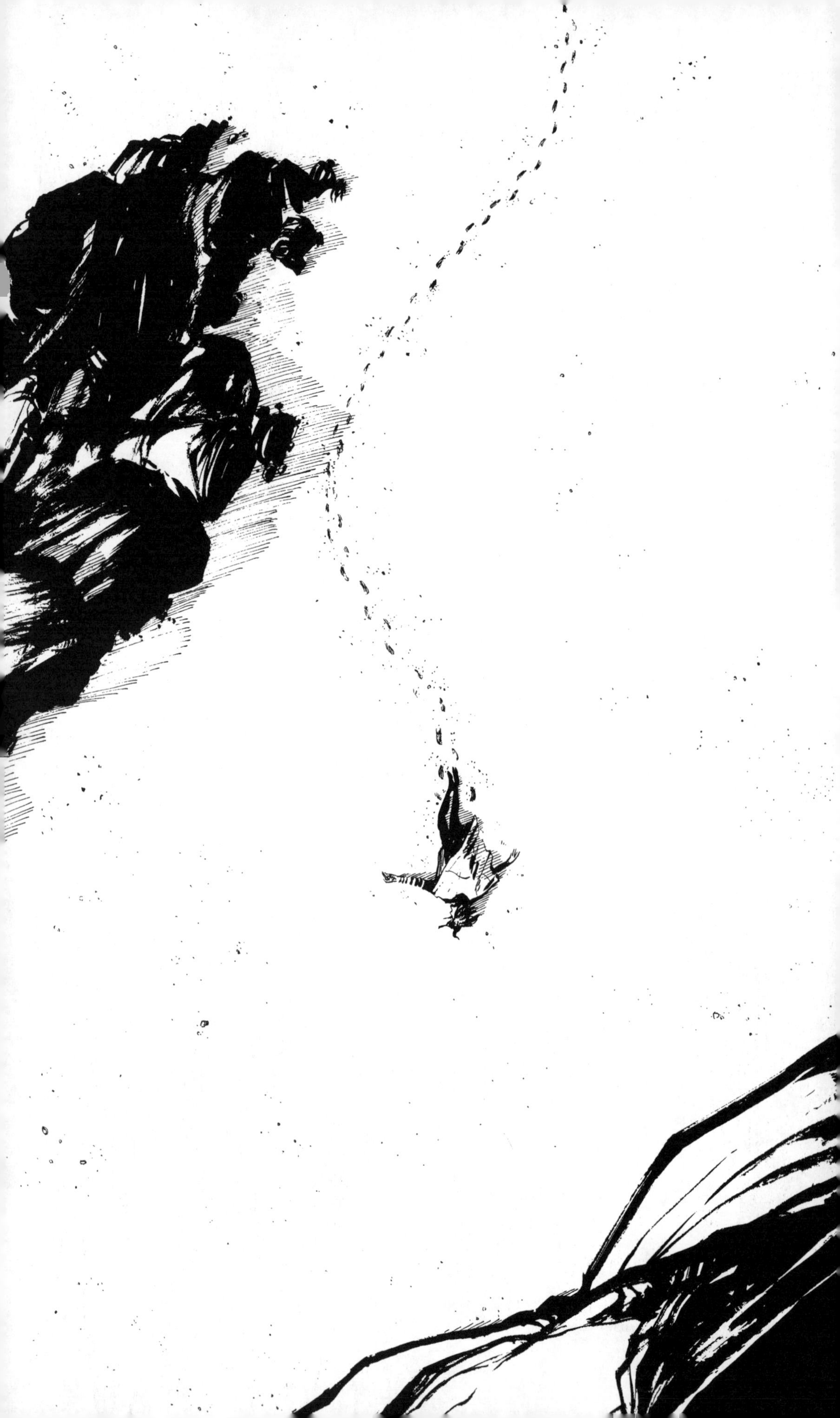

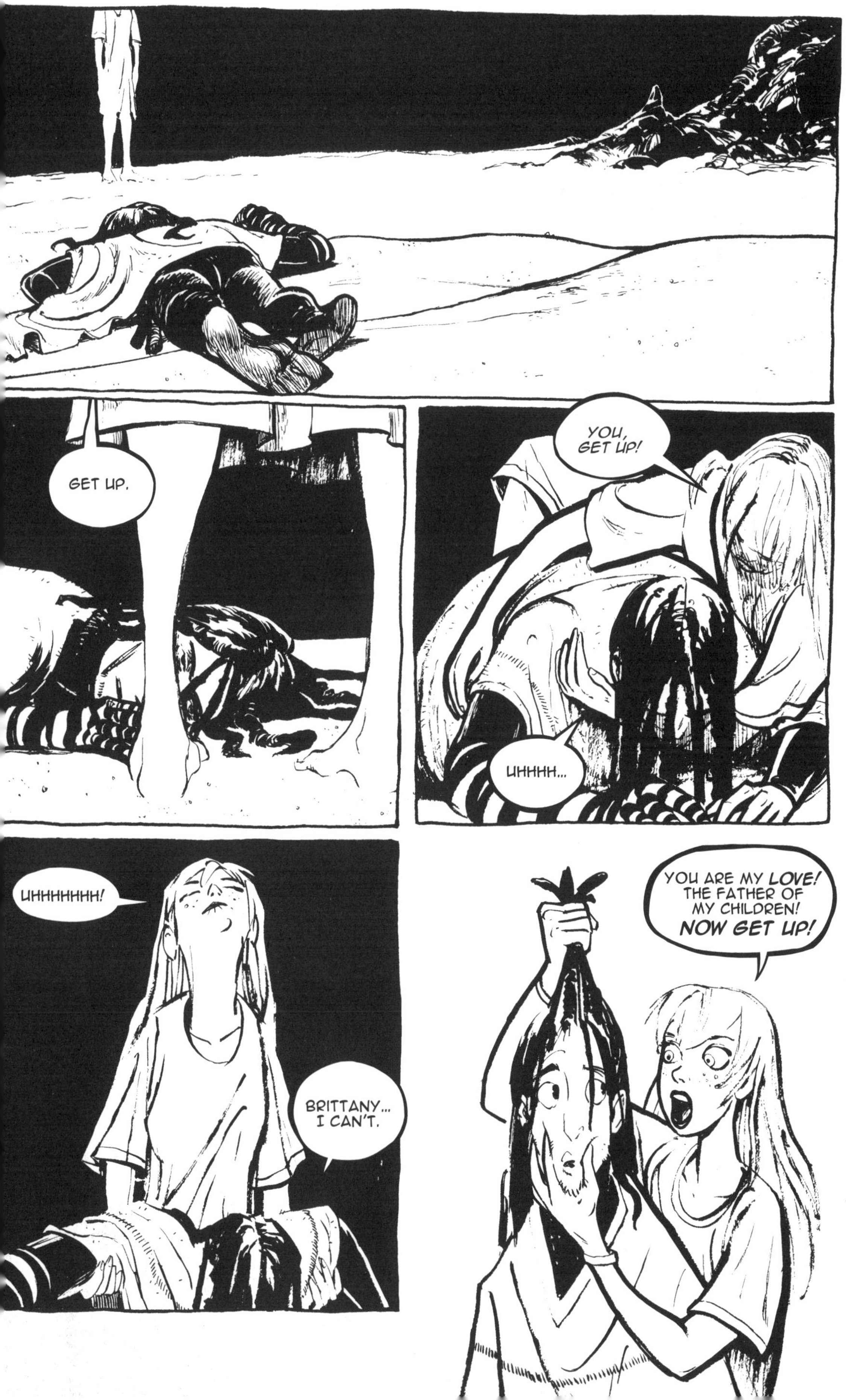
GET UP.
YOU, GET UP!
UHHHH...
UHHHHHHH!
BRITTANY... I CAN'T.
YOU ARE MY LOVE! THE FATHER OF MY CHILDREN! NOW GET UP!

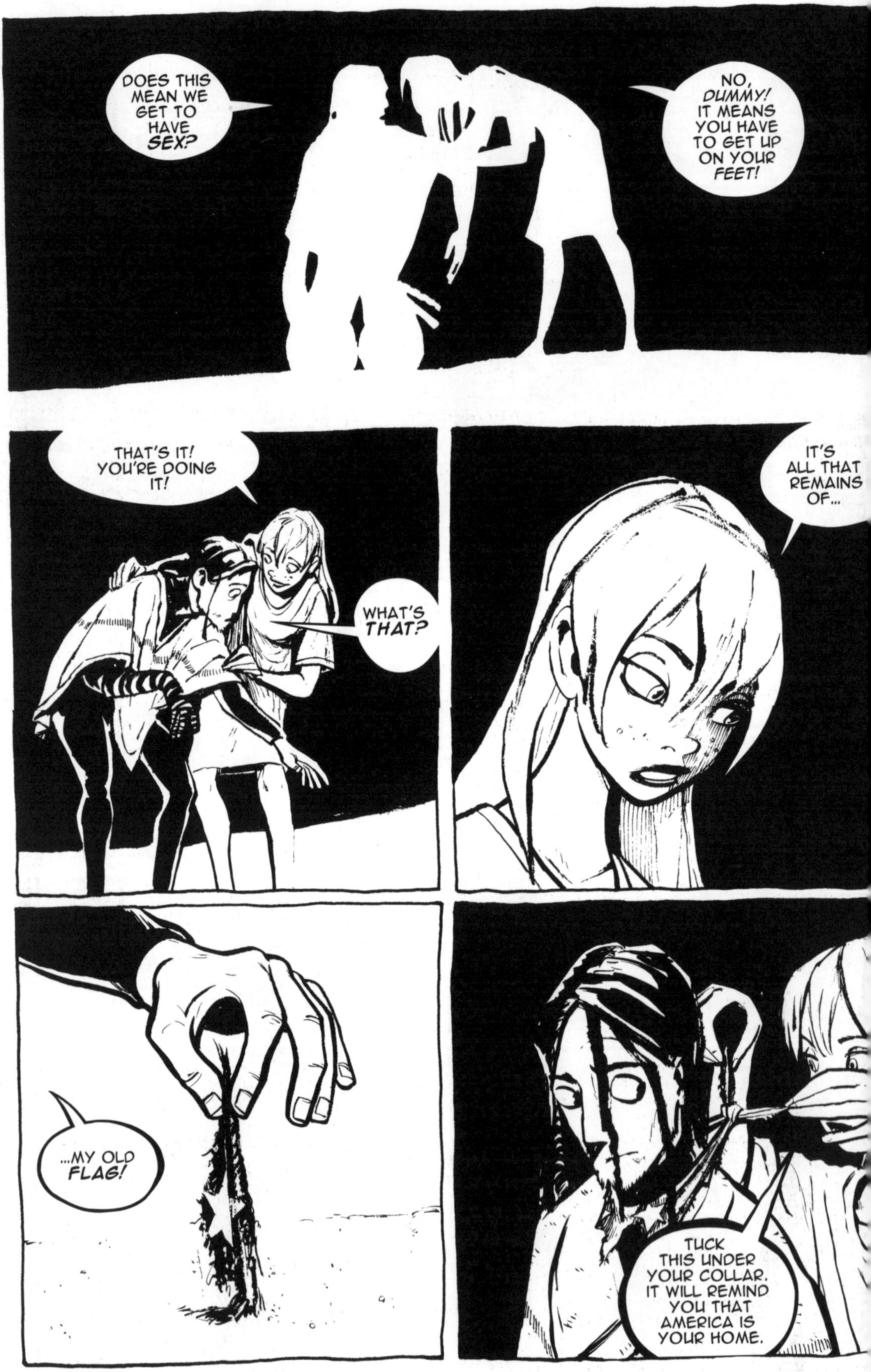
DOES THIS MEAN WE GET TO HAVE SEX?
NO, DUMMY! IT MEANS YOU HAVE TO GET UP ON YOUR FEET!
THAT'S IT! YOU'RE DOING IT!
WHAT'S THAT?
IT'S ALL THAT REMAINS OF...
...MY OLD FLAG!
TUCK THIS UNDER YOUR COLLAR. IT WILL REMIND YOU THAT AMERICA IS YOUR HOME.

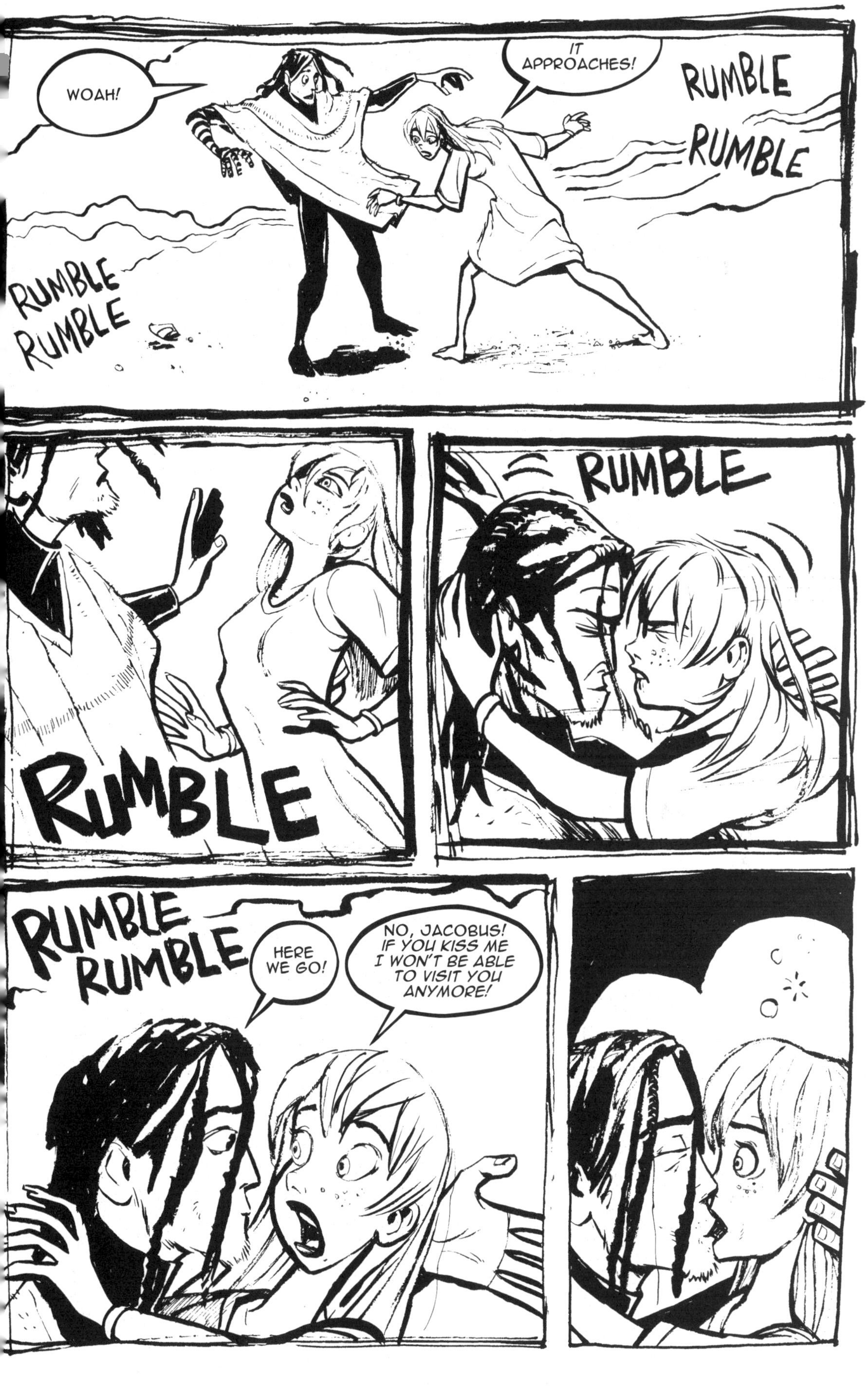
WOAH!
IT APPROACHES!
RUMBLE
RUMBLE
RUMBLE
RUMBLE
RUMBLE
RUMBLE
RUMBLE
RUMBLE
HERE WE GO!
NO, JACOBUS! IF YOU KISS ME I WON'T BE ABLE TO VISIT YOU ANYMORE!

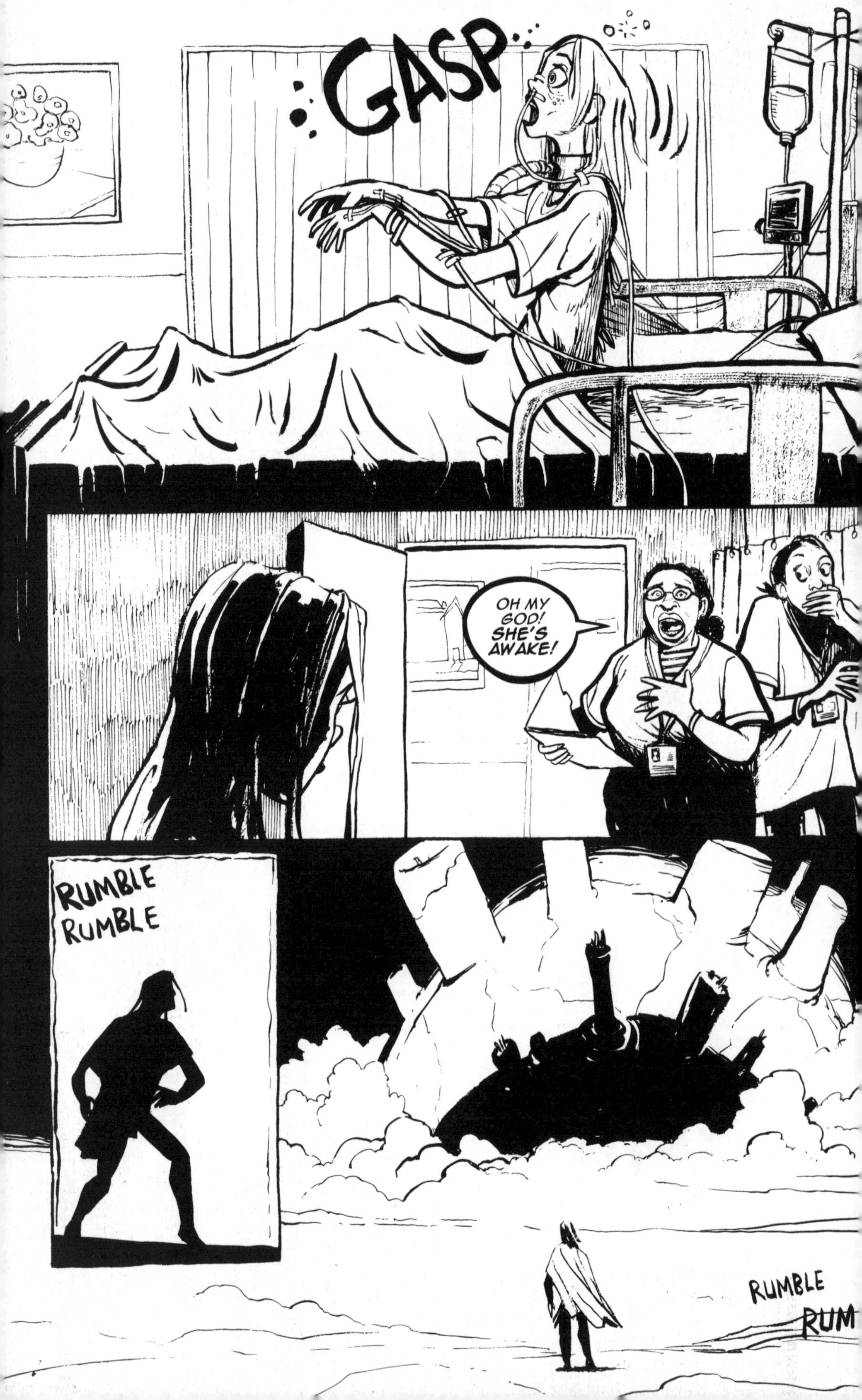
GASP
OH MY GOD! SHE'S AWAKE!
RUMBLE
RUMBLE
RUMBLE
RUM

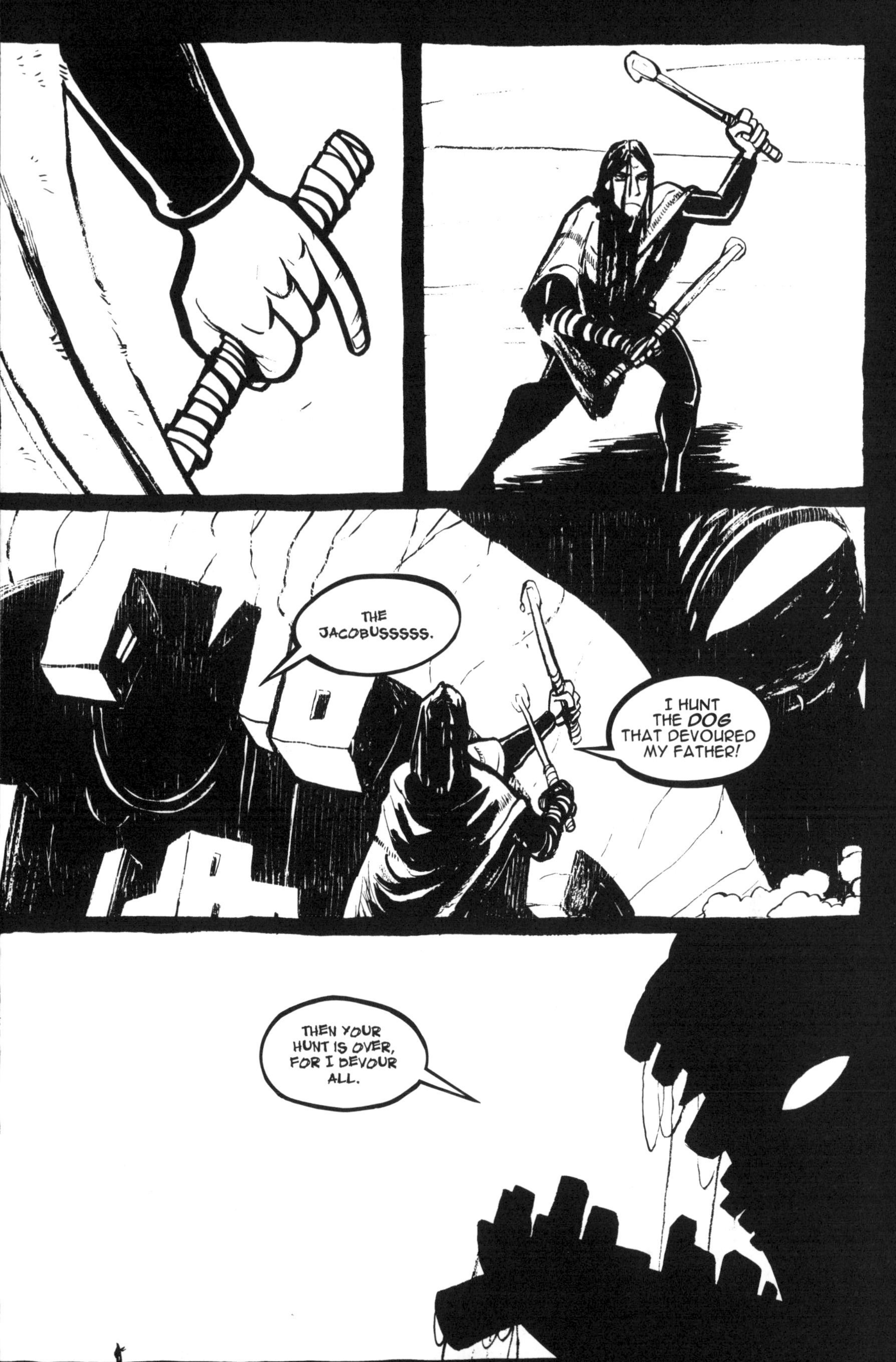
THE JACOBUSSSSS.
I HUNT THE *DOG* THAT DEVOURED MY FATHER!
THEN YOUR HUNT IS OVER, FOR I DEVOUR ALL.

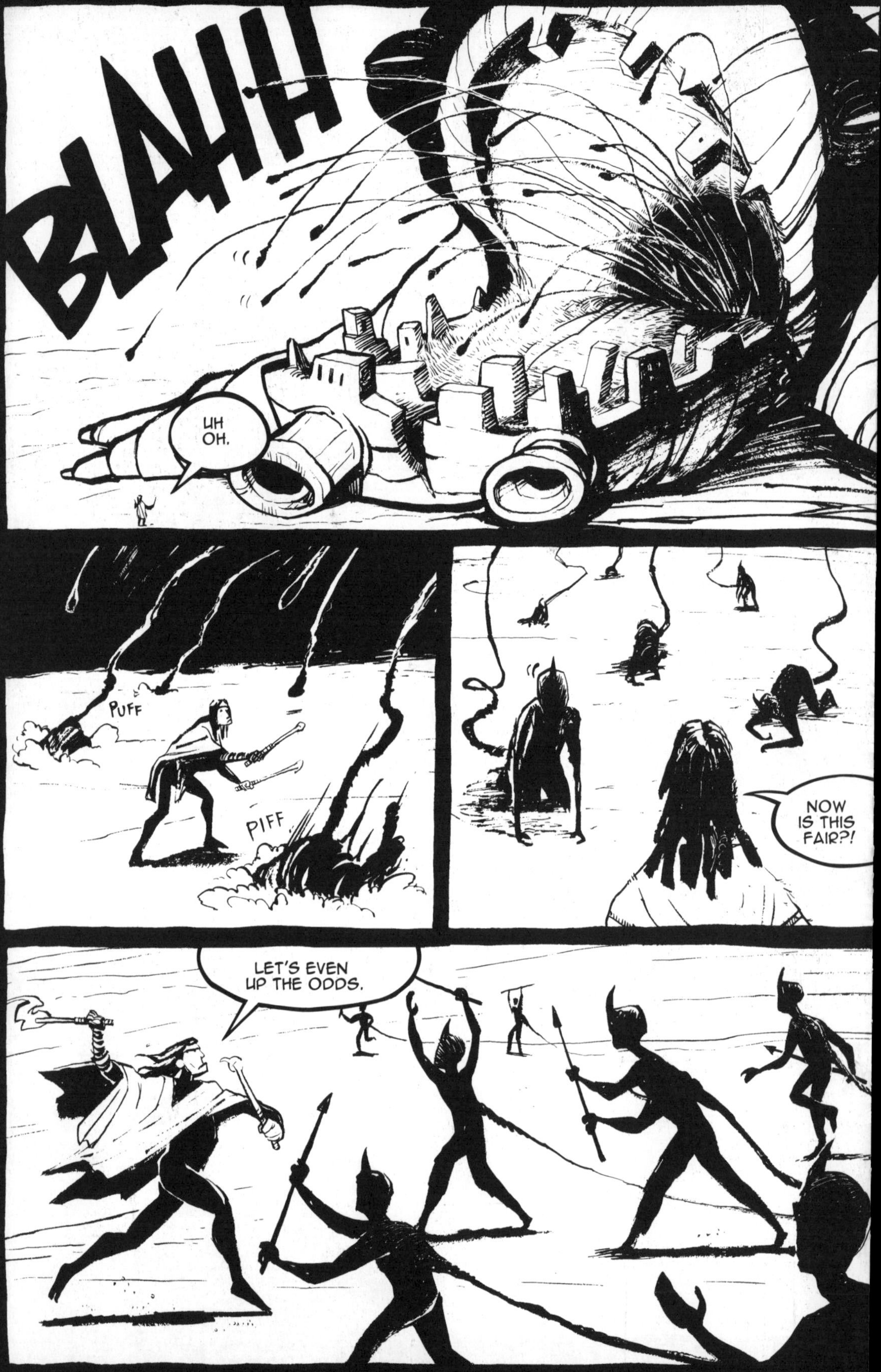
BLAHH
UH OH.
PUFF
PIFF
NOW IS THIS FAIR?!
LET'S EVEN UP THE ODDS.

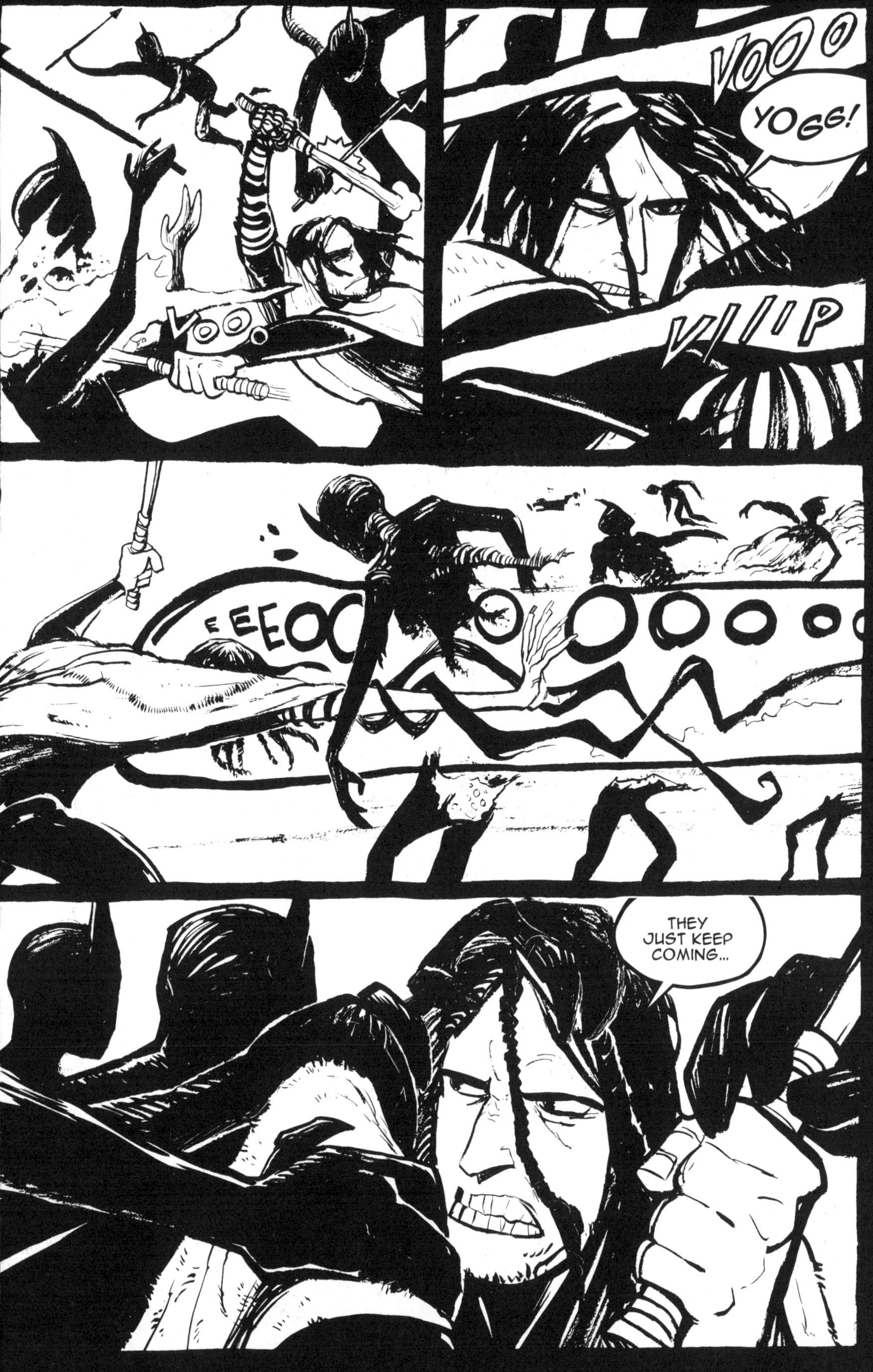
VOOO
VOOO
YOGG!
VIIIP
EEEOOOOOOOOO
THEY JUST KEEP COMING...

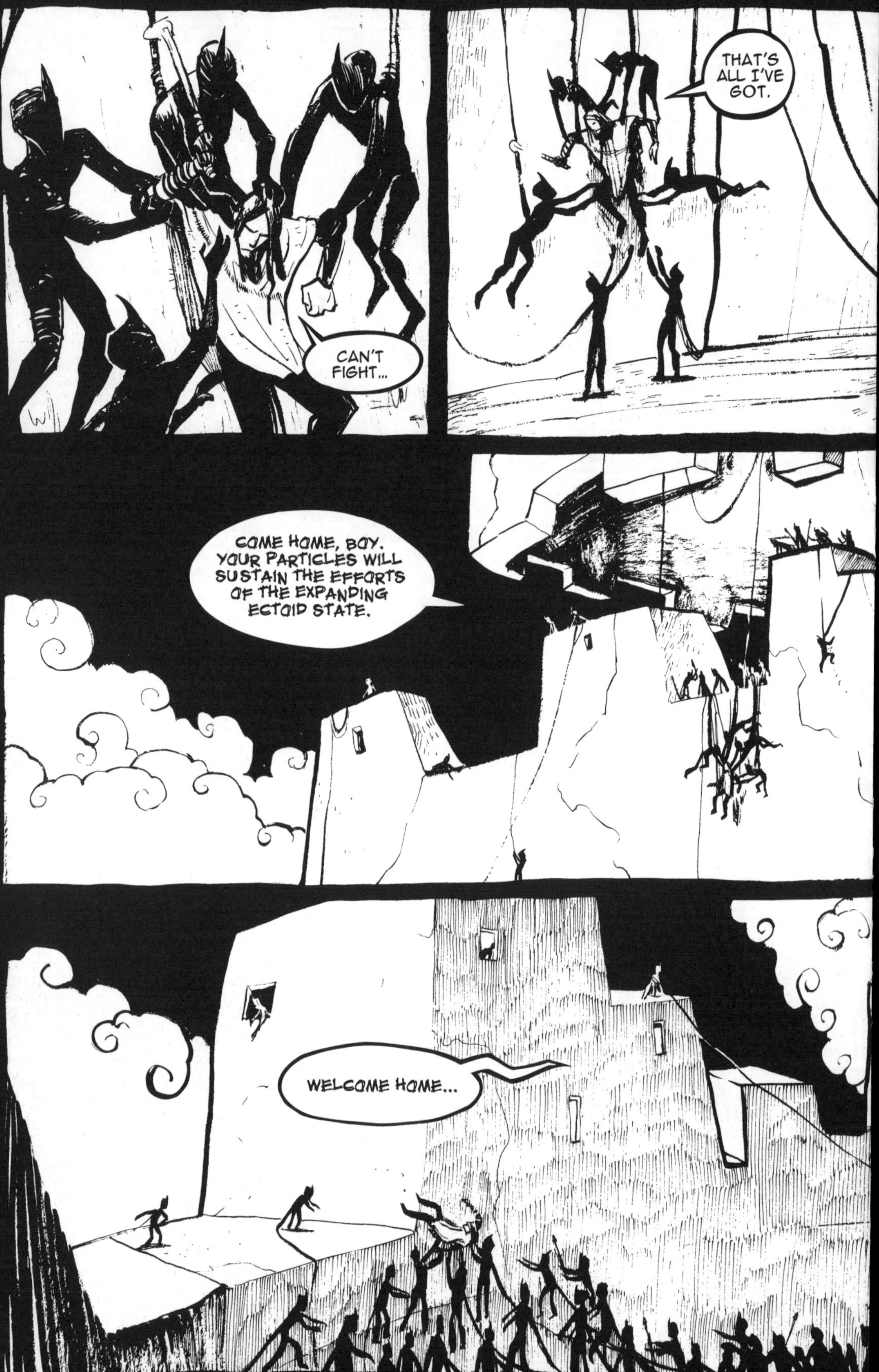

CAN'T FIGHT...
THAT'S ALL I'VE GOT.
COME HOME, BOY. YOUR PARTICLES WILL SUSTAIN THE EFFORTS OF THE EXPANDING ECTOID STATE.
WELCOME HOME...

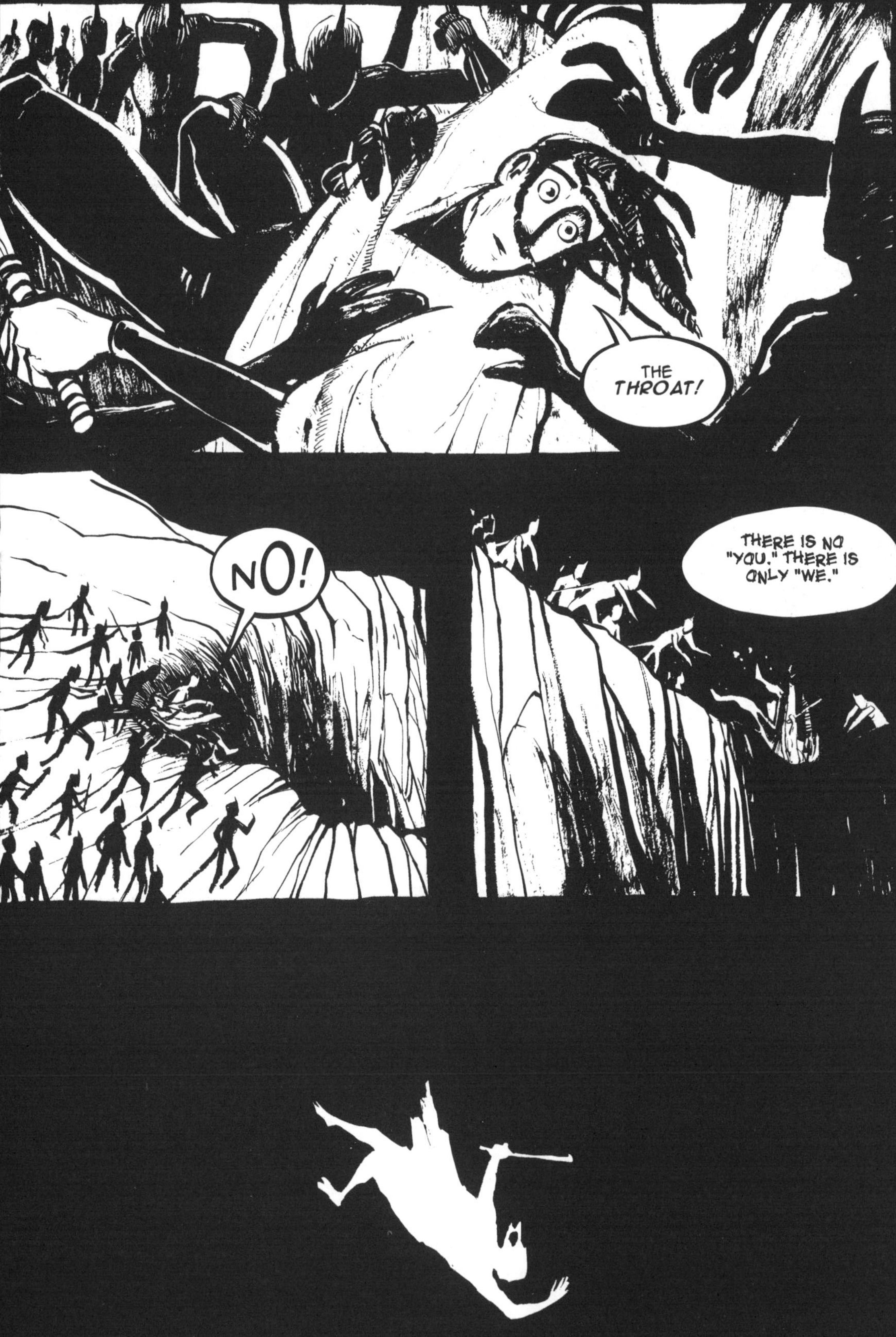
THE THROAT!
NO!
THERE IS NO "YOU." THERE IS ONLY "WE."

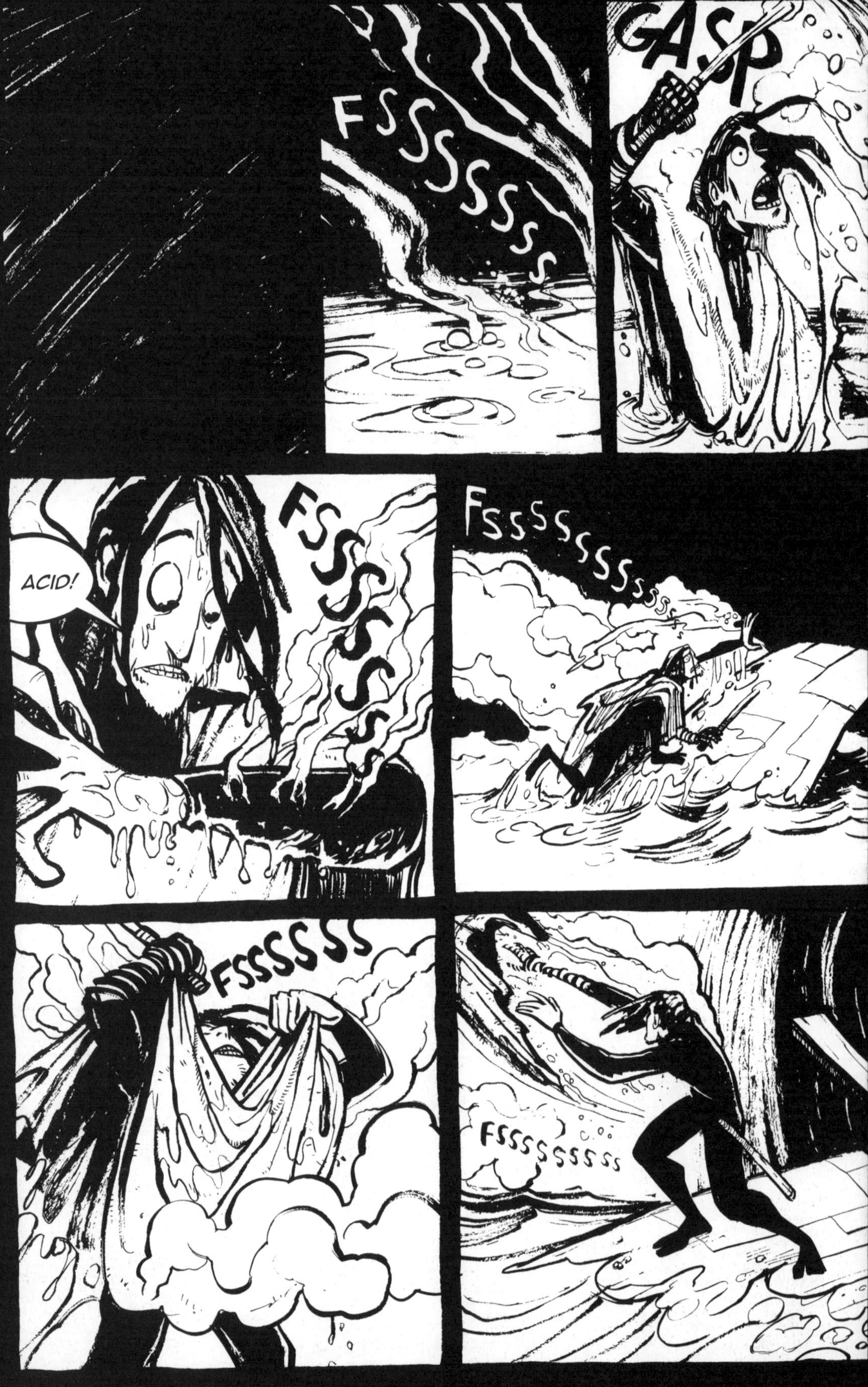
FSSSSSSSS
GASP
ACID!
FSSSSSSSS
FSSSSSSSSSSSS
FSSSSSS
FSSSSSSSSS

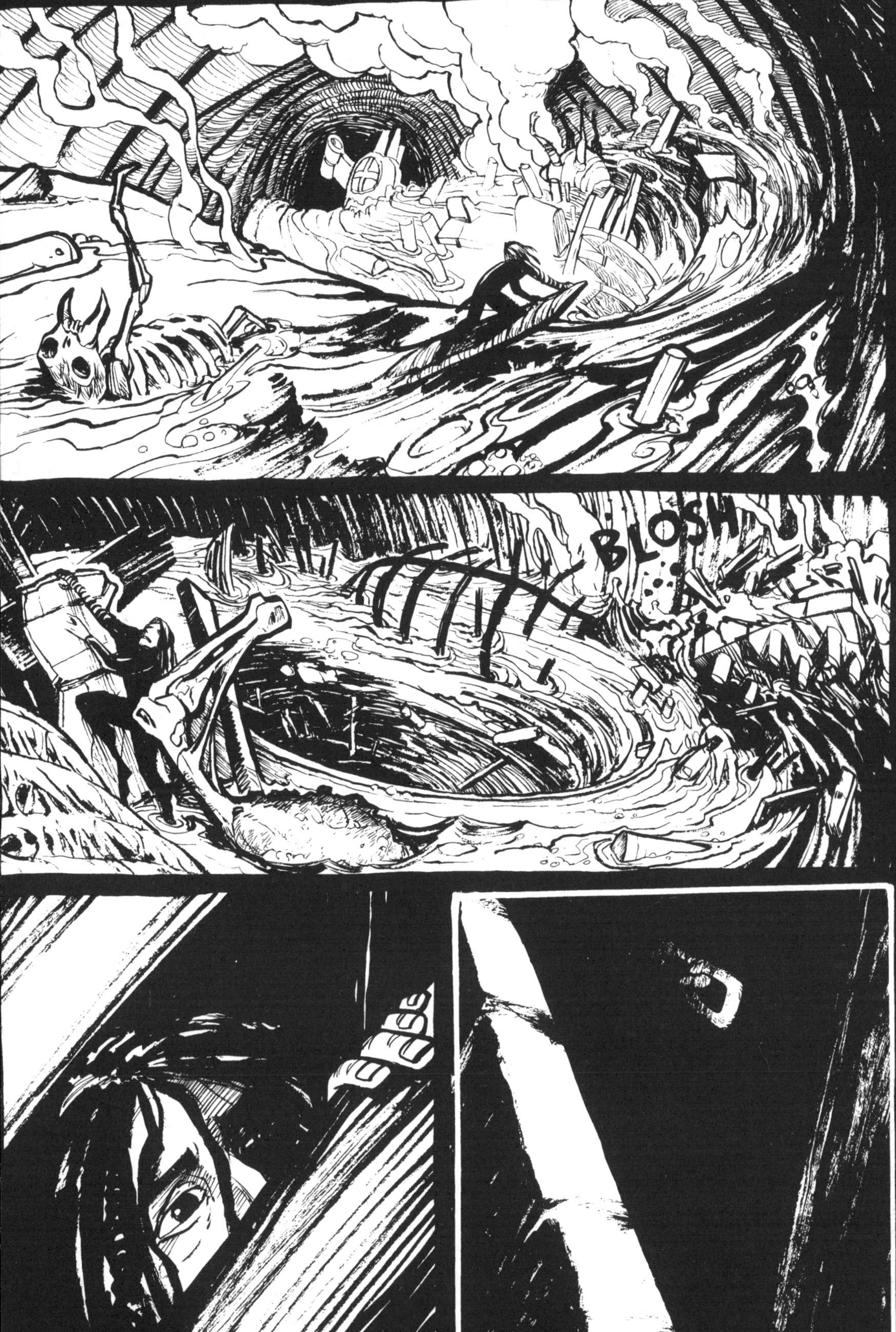
BLOSH

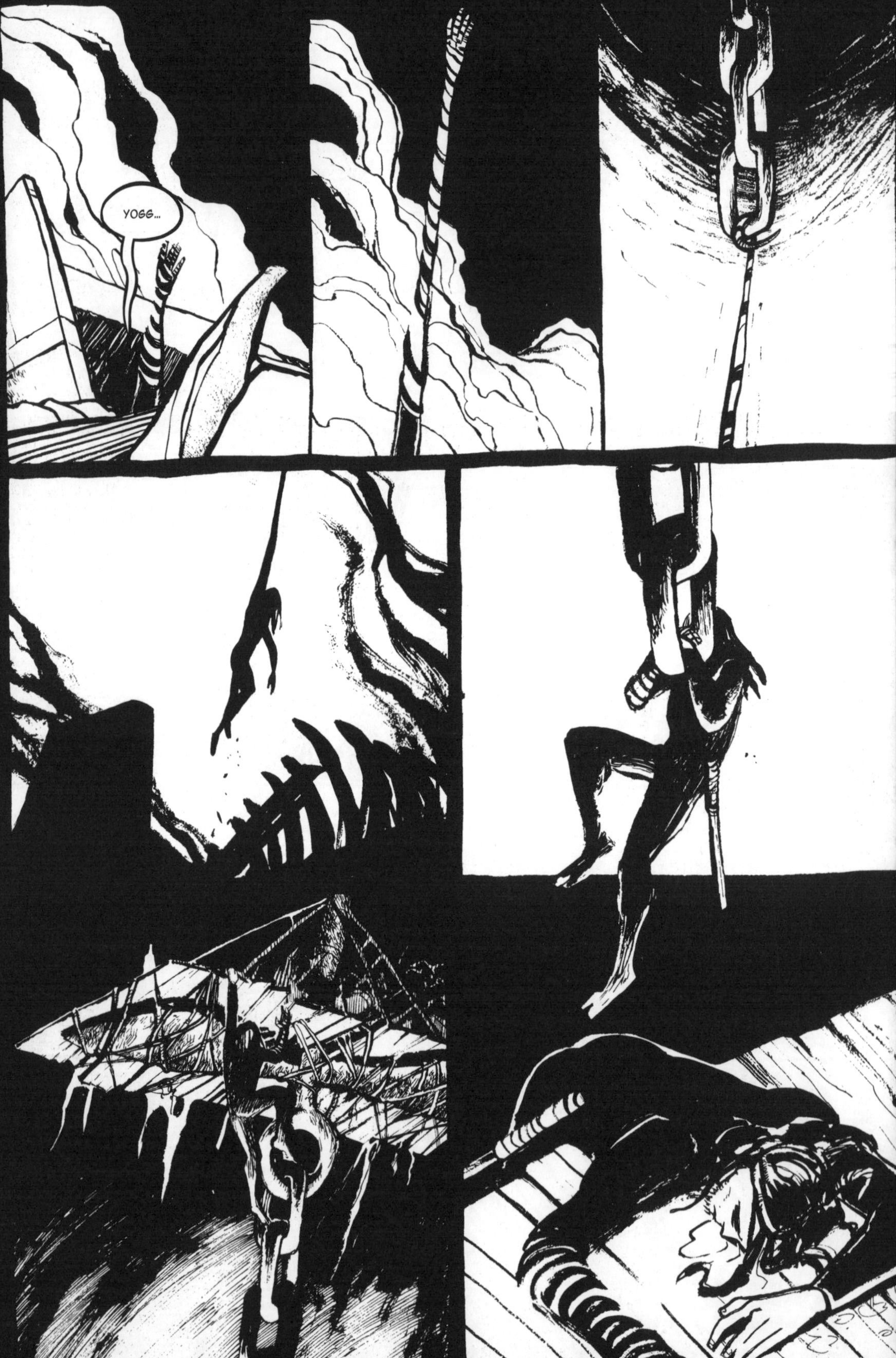
YOGG...

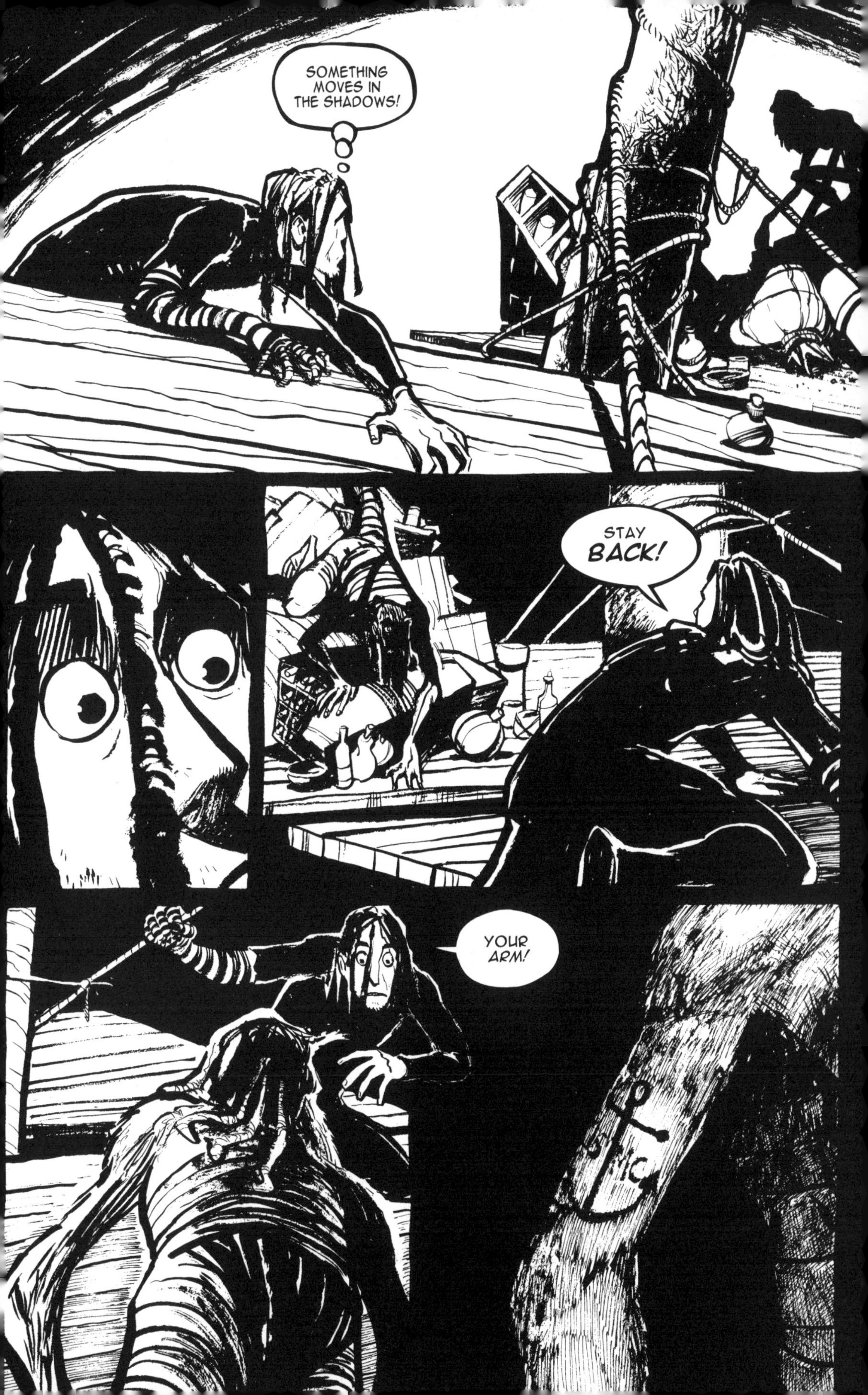
SOMETHING MOVES IN THE SHADOWS!
STAY BACK!
YOUR ARM!

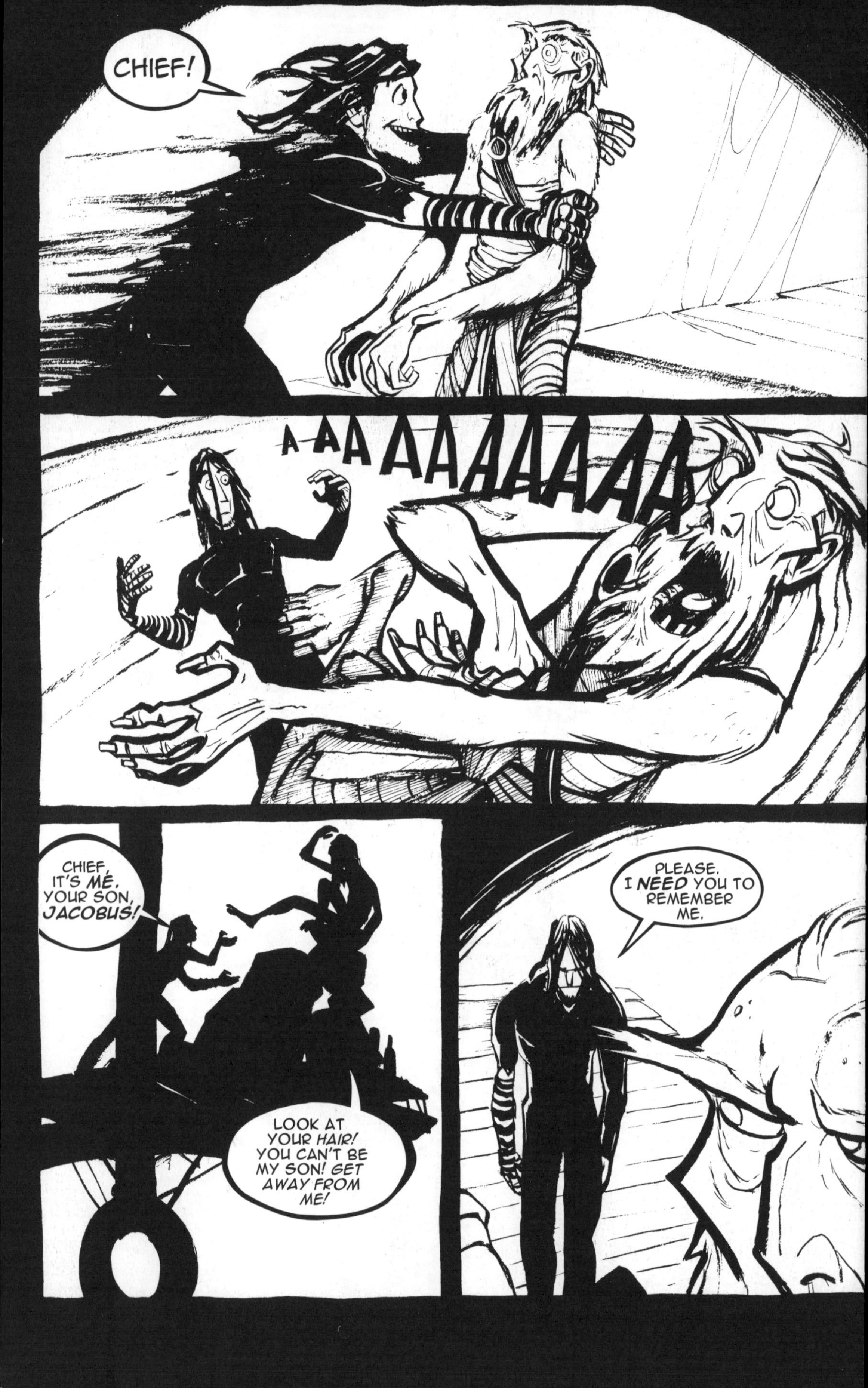
CHIEF!
AAAAAAAAAAA
CHIEF, IT'S ME. YOUR SON, JACOBUS!
LOOK AT YOUR HAIR! YOU CAN'T BE MY SON! GET AWAY FROM ME!
PLEASE. I NEED YOU TO REMEMBER ME.

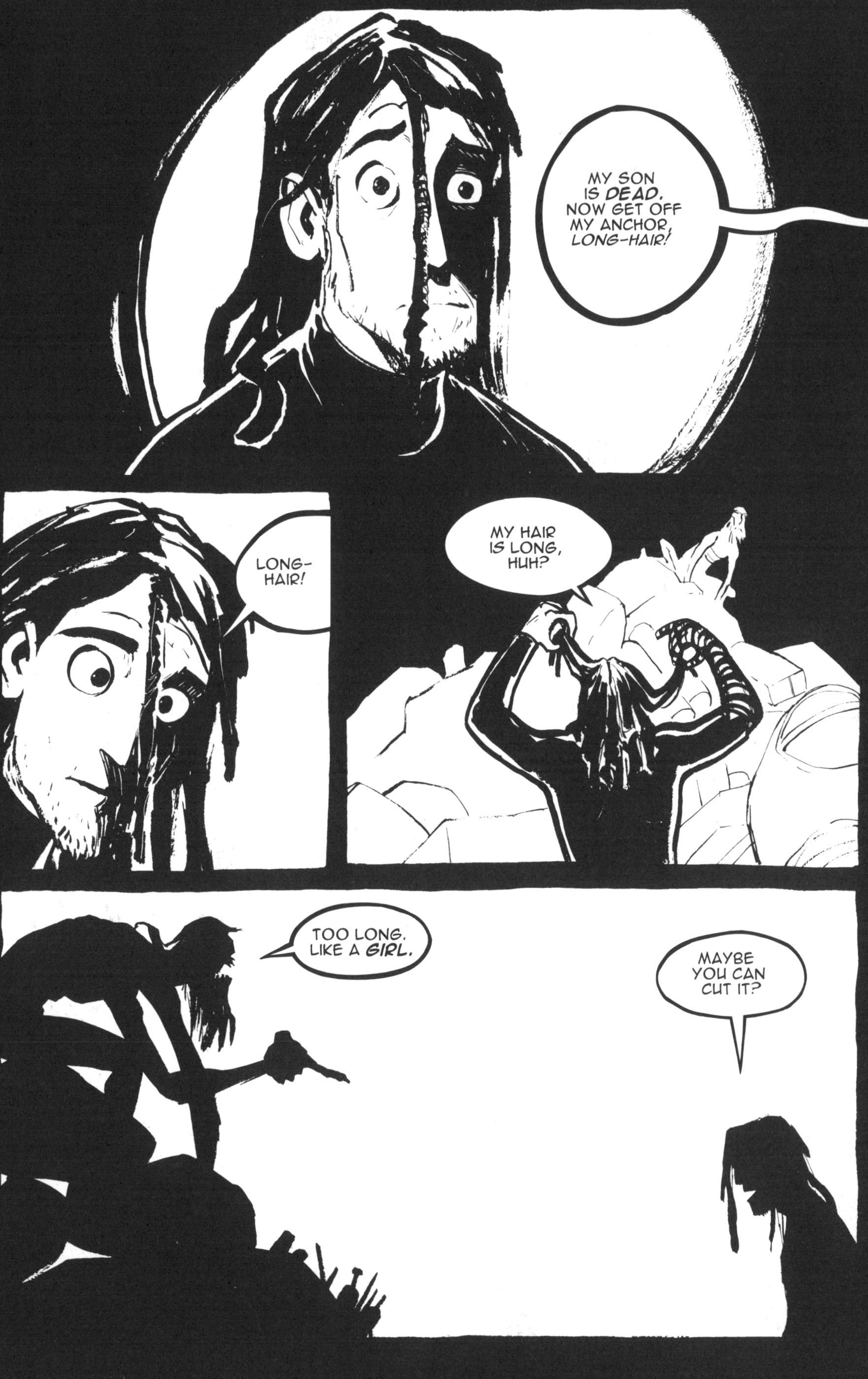
MY SON IS DEAD. NOW GET OFF MY ANCHOR, LONG-HAIR!
LONG-HAIR!
MY HAIR IS LONG, HUH?
TOO LONG. LIKE A GIRL.
MAYBE YOU CAN CUT IT?

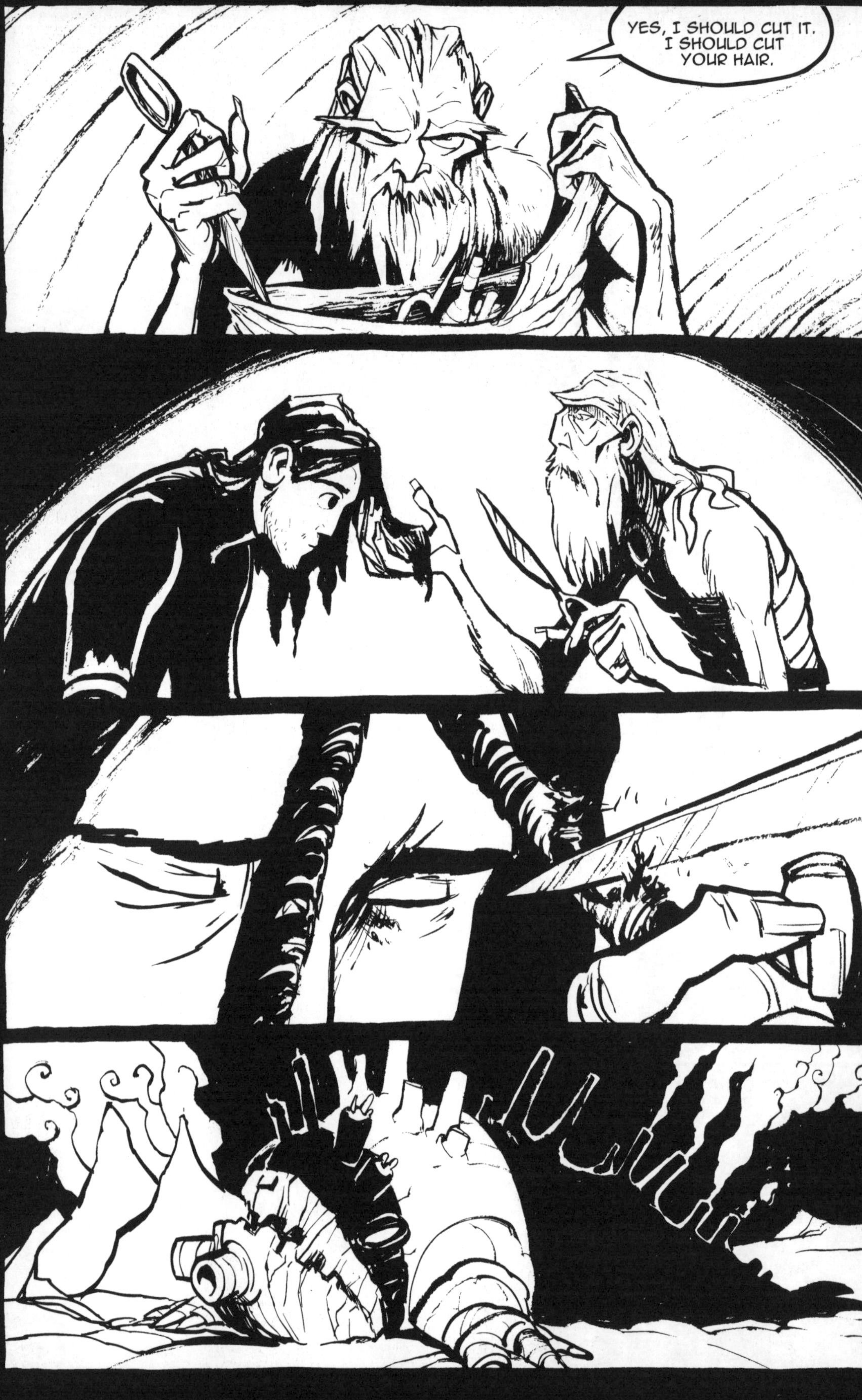
YES, I SHOULD CUT IT. I SHOULD CUT YOUR HAIR.

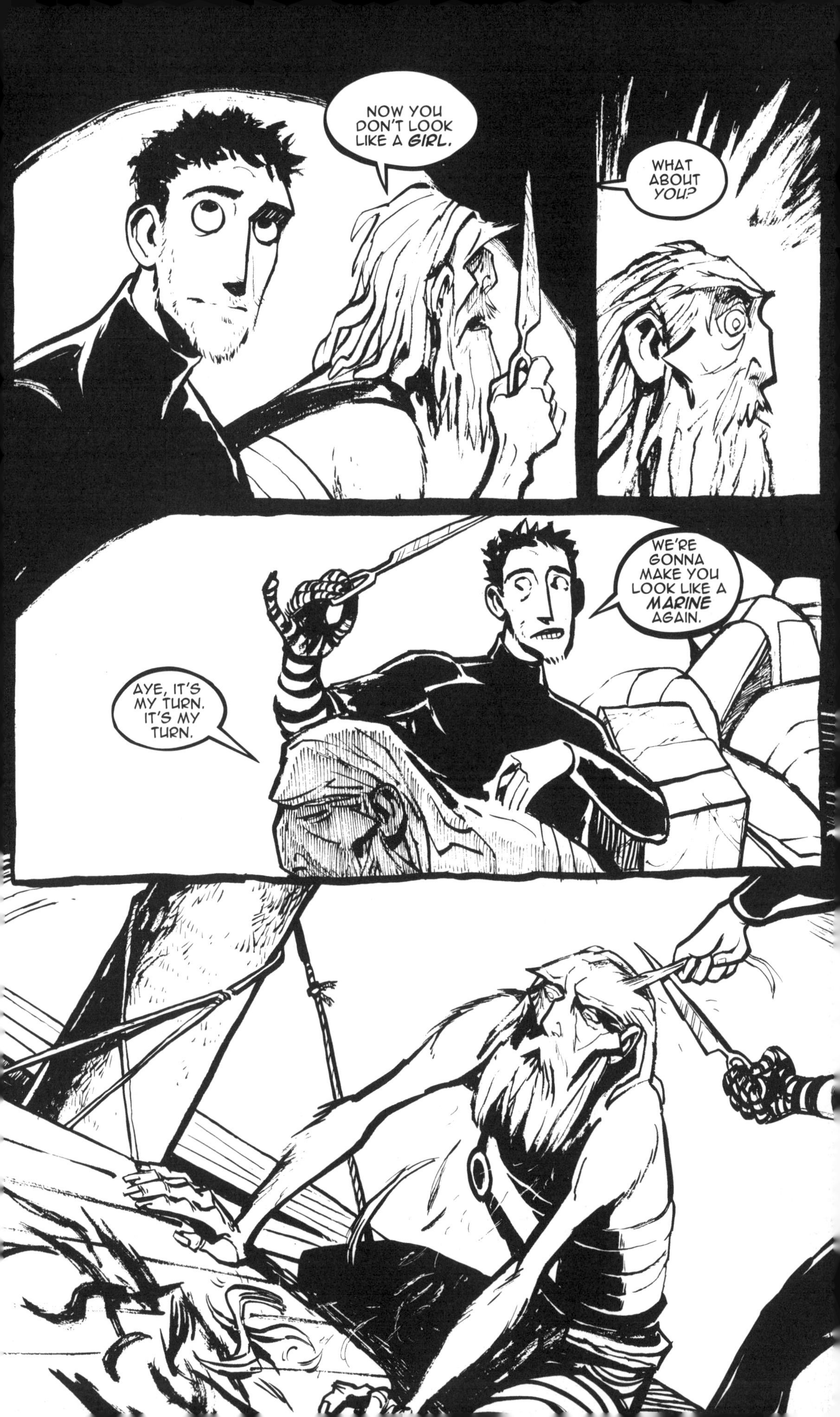
NOW YOU DON'T LOOK LIKE A GIRL.
WHAT ABOUT YOU?
WE'RE GONNA MAKE YOU LOOK LIKE A MARINE AGAIN.
AYE, IT'S MY TURN. IT'S MY TURN.

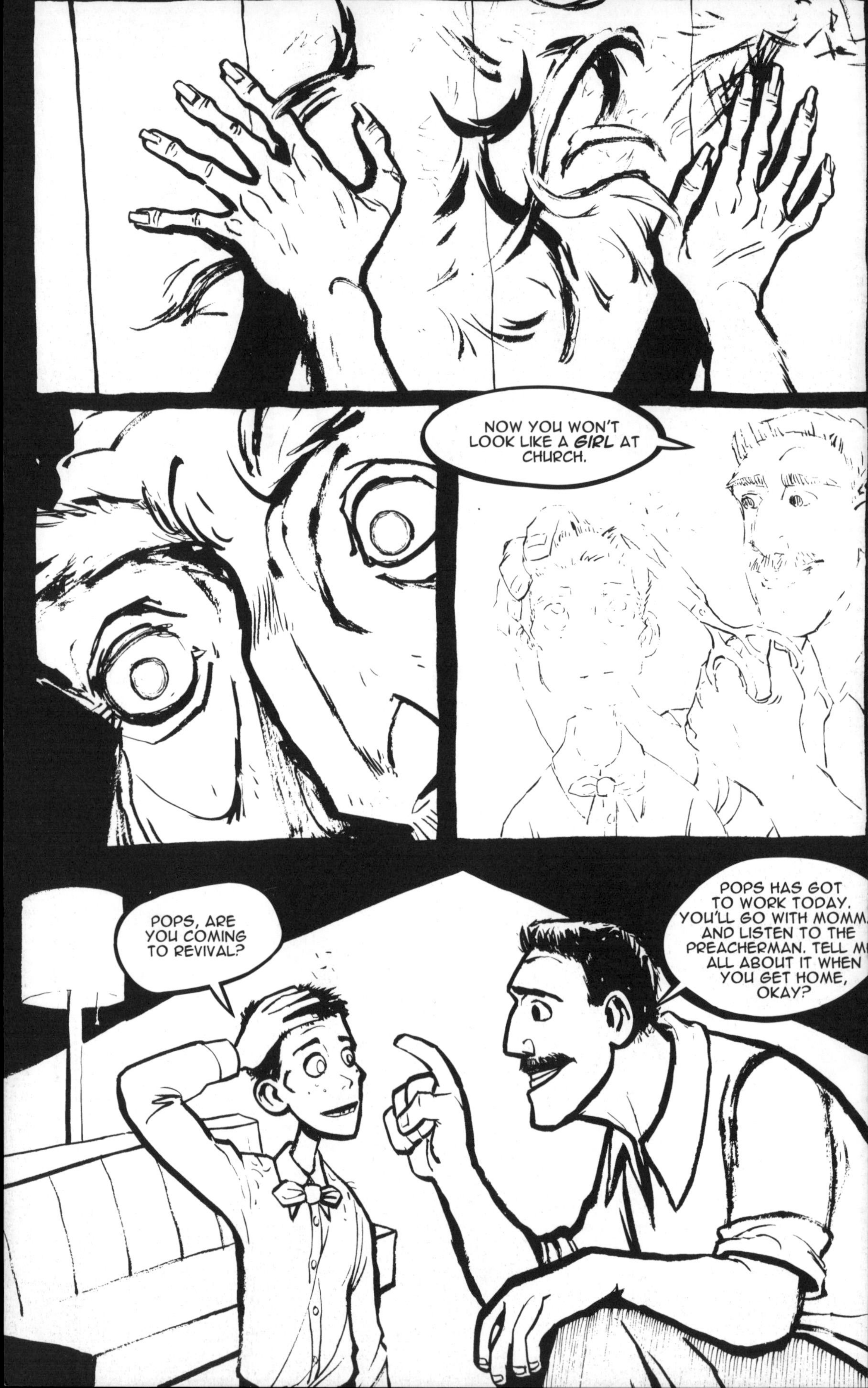
NOW YOU WON'T LOOK LIKE A *GIRL* AT CHURCH.
POPS, ARE YOU COMING TO REVIVAL?
POPS HAS GOT TO WORK TODAY. YOU'LL GO WITH MOMM[A] AND LISTEN TO THE PREACHERMAN. TELL M[E] ALL ABOUT IT WHEN YOU GET HOME, OKAY?

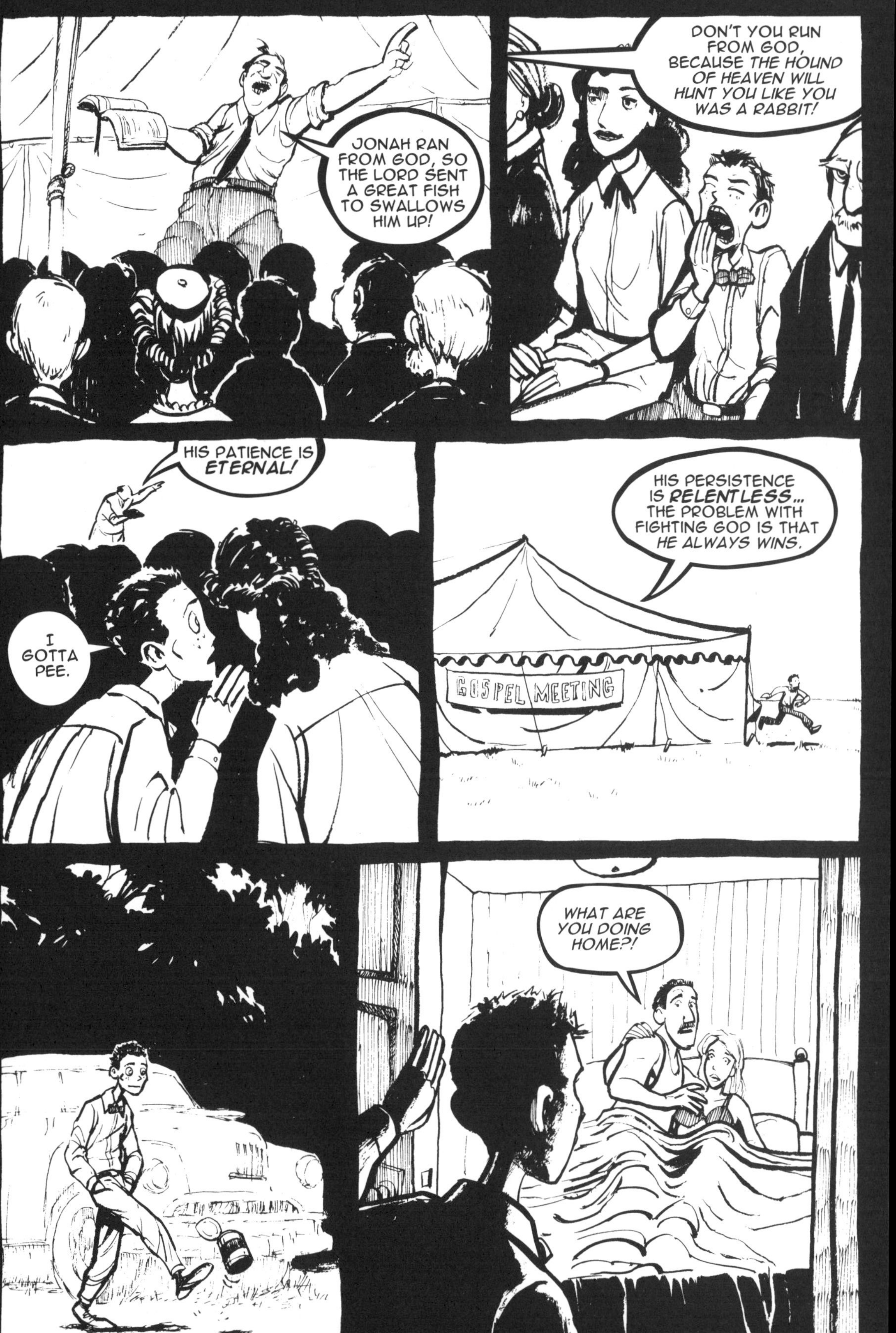
JONAH RAN FROM GOD, SO THE LORD SENT A GREAT FISH TO SWALLOWS HIM UP!
DON'T YOU RUN FROM GOD, BECAUSE THE HOUND OF HEAVEN WILL HUNT YOU LIKE YOU WAS A RABBIT!
HIS PATIENCE IS ETERNAL!
I GOTTA PEE.
HIS PERSISTENCE IS RELENTLESS... THE PROBLEM WITH FIGHTING GOD IS THAT HE ALWAYS WINS.
GOSPEL MEETING
WHAT ARE YOU DOING HOME?!

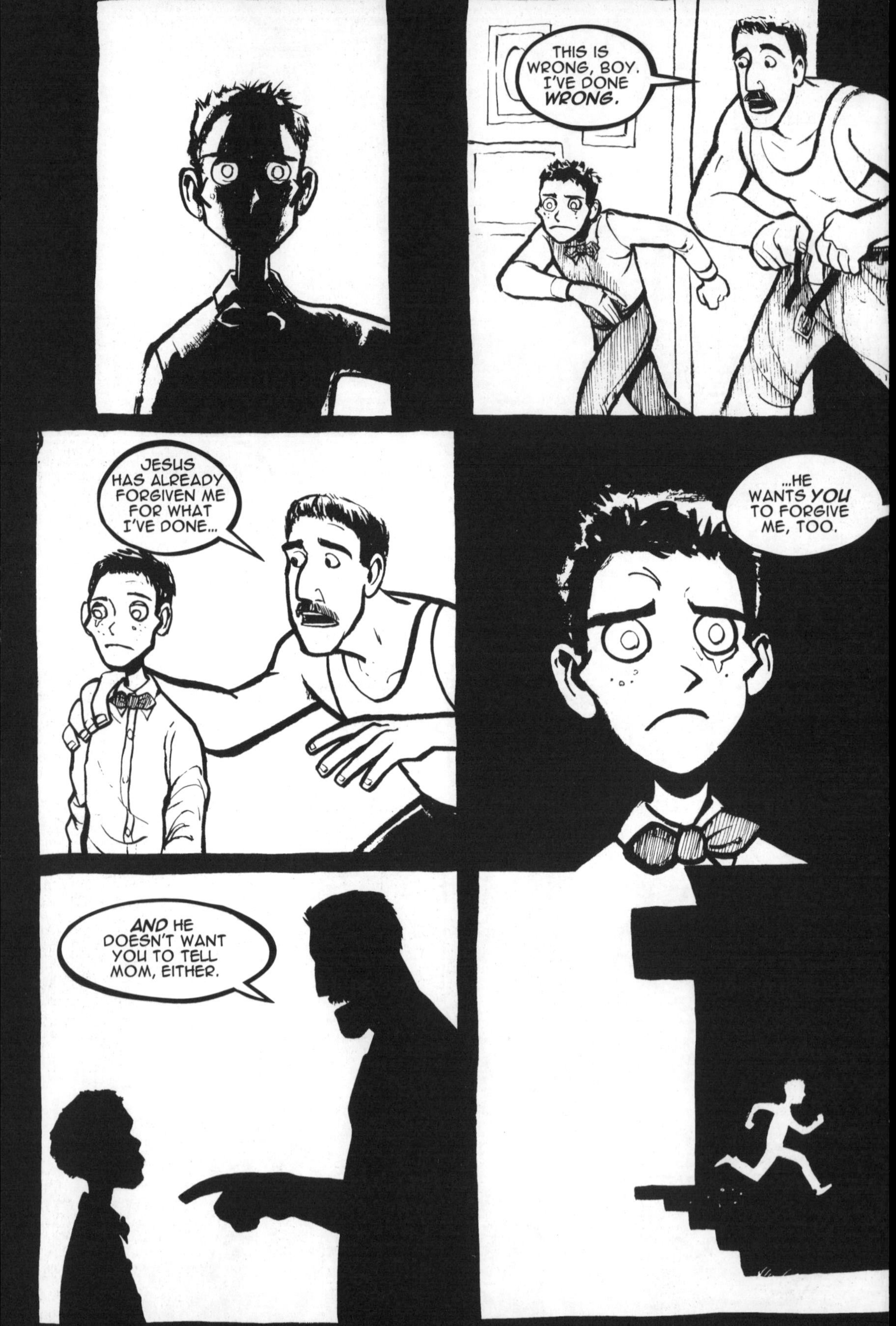
THIS IS WRONG, BOY. I'VE DONE *WRONG*.
JESUS HAS ALREADY FORGIVEN ME FOR WHAT I'VE DONE...
...HE WANTS *YOU* TO FORGIVE ME, TOO.
AND HE DOESN'T WANT YOU TO TELL MOM, EITHER.

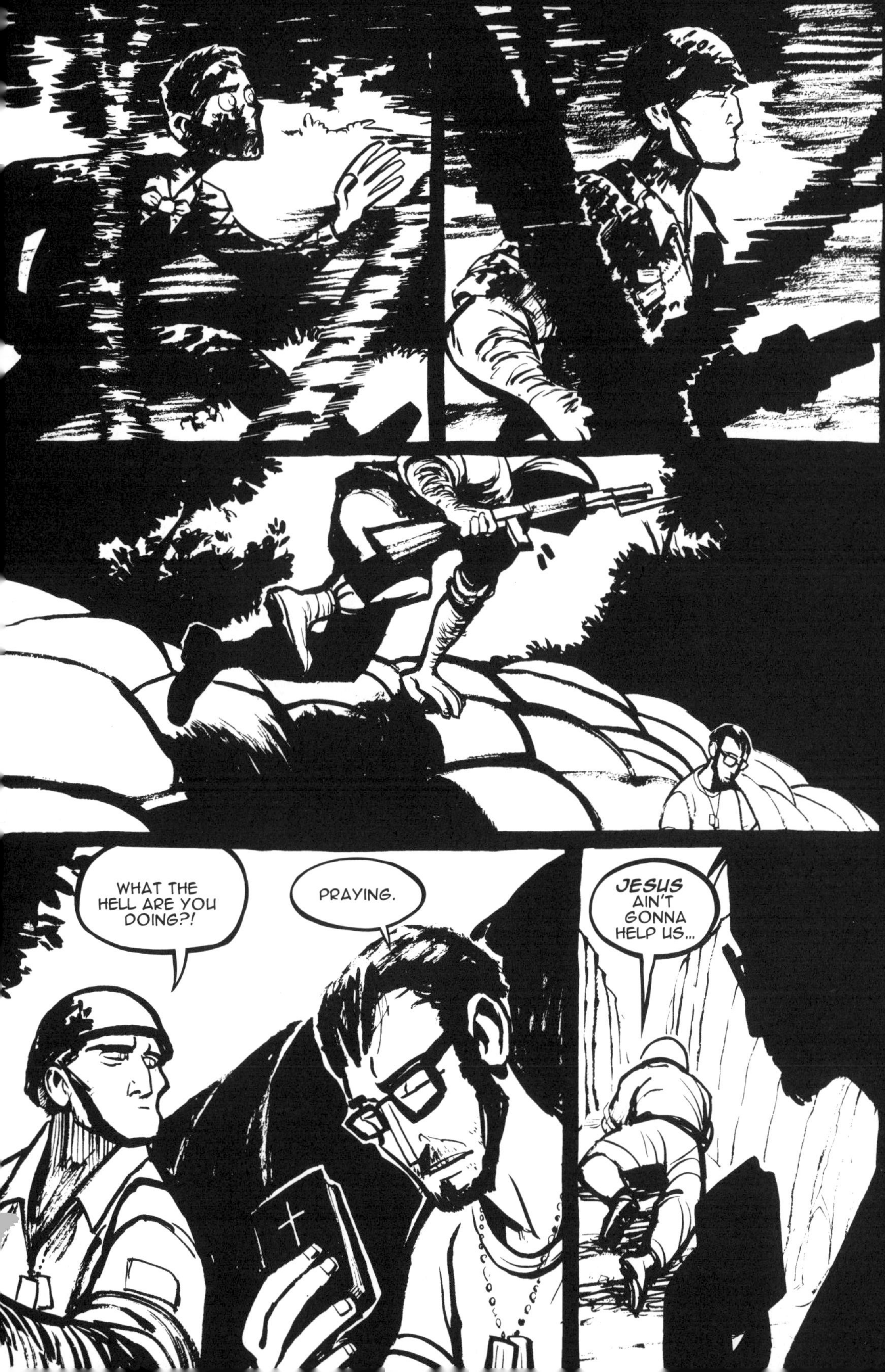
WHAT THE HELL ARE YOU DOING?!
PRAYING.
JESUS AIN'T GONNA HELP US...

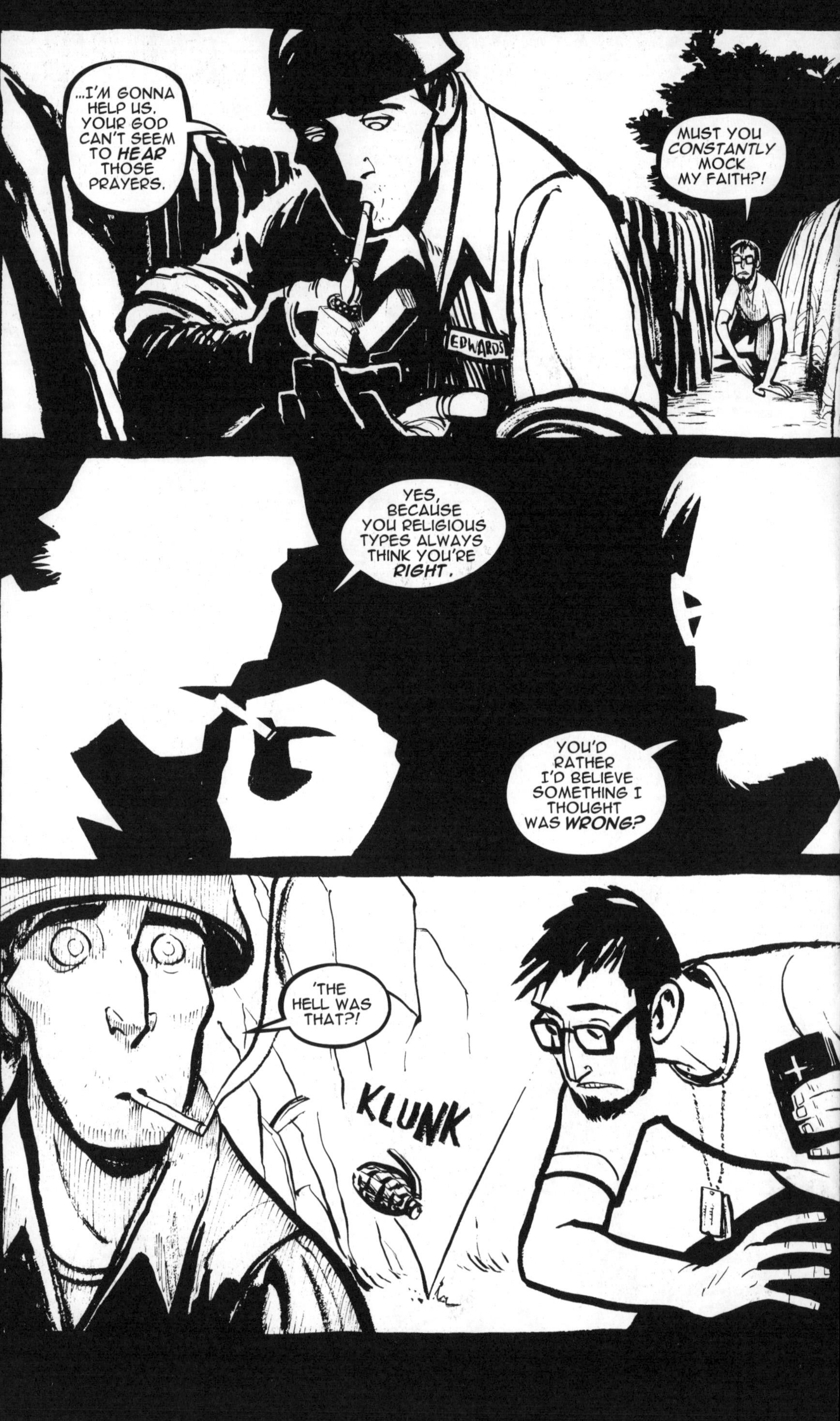
...I'M GONNA HELP US. YOUR GOD CAN'T SEEM TO HEAR THOSE PRAYERS.
MUST YOU CONSTANTLY MOCK MY FAITH?!
EDWARDS
YES, BECAUSE YOU RELIGIOUS TYPES ALWAYS THINK YOU'RE RIGHT.
YOU'D RATHER I'D BELIEVE SOMETHING I THOUGHT WAS WRONG?
'THE HELL WAS THAT?!
KLUNK

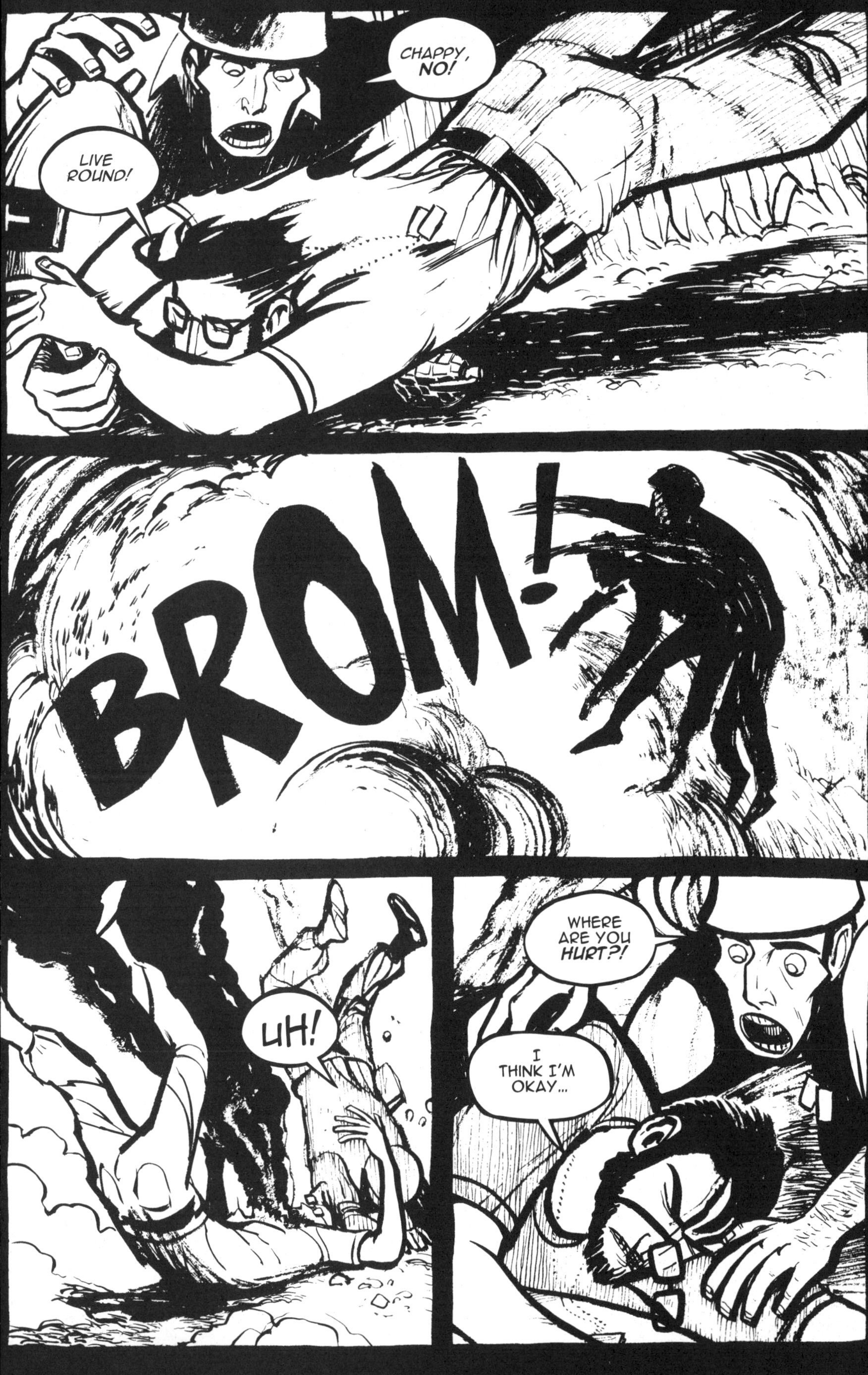
CHAPPY, NO!
LIVE ROUND!
BROM!
UH!
WHERE ARE YOU HURT?!
I THINK I'M OKAY...

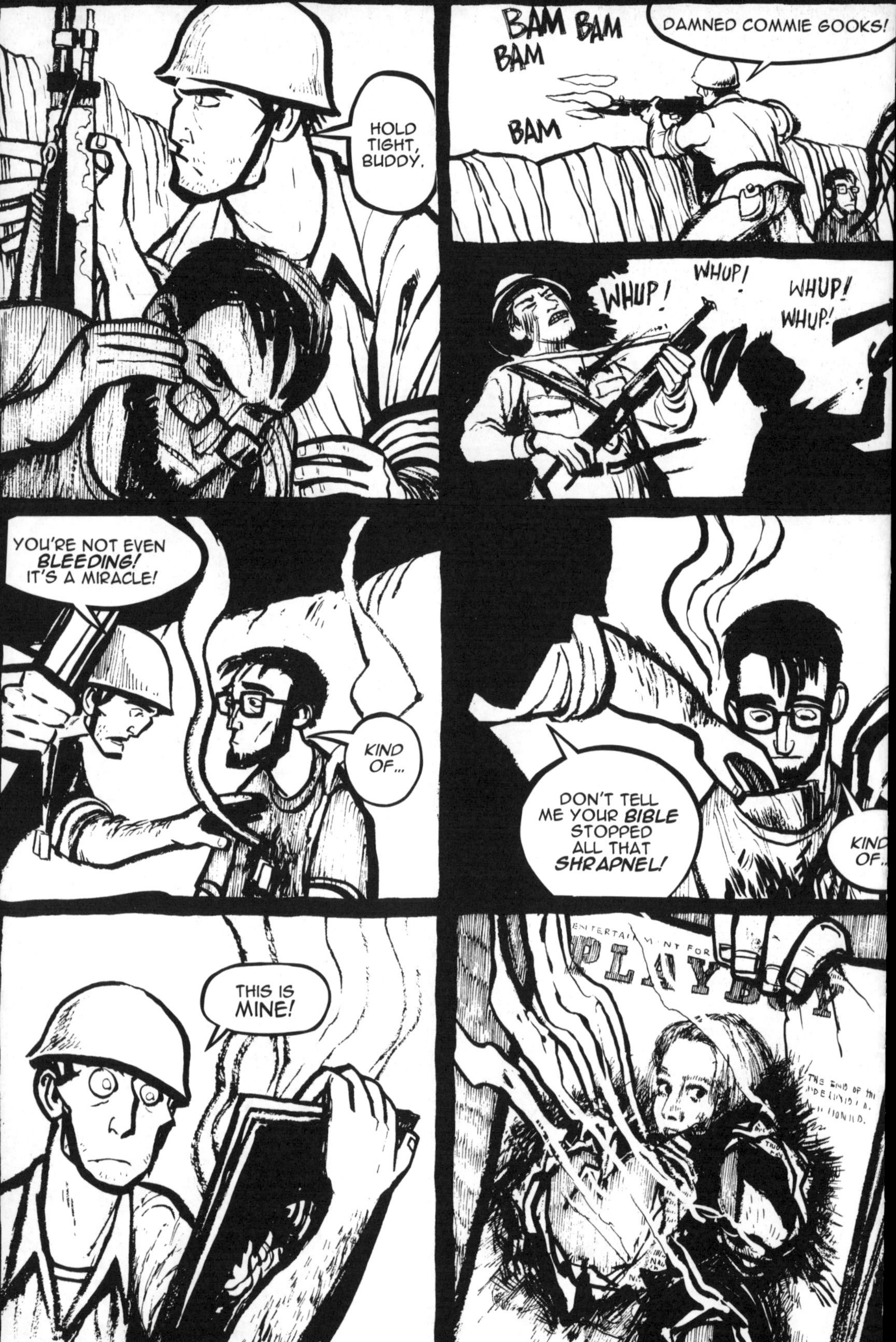
HOLD TIGHT, BUDDY.
BAM BAM BAM
BAM
DAMNED COMMIE GOOKS!
WHUP! WHUP! WHUP! WHUP!
YOU'RE NOT EVEN BLEEDING! IT'S A MIRACLE!
KIND OF...
DON'T TELL ME YOUR BIBLE STOPPED ALL THAT SHRAPNEL!
KIND OF...
THIS IS MINE!

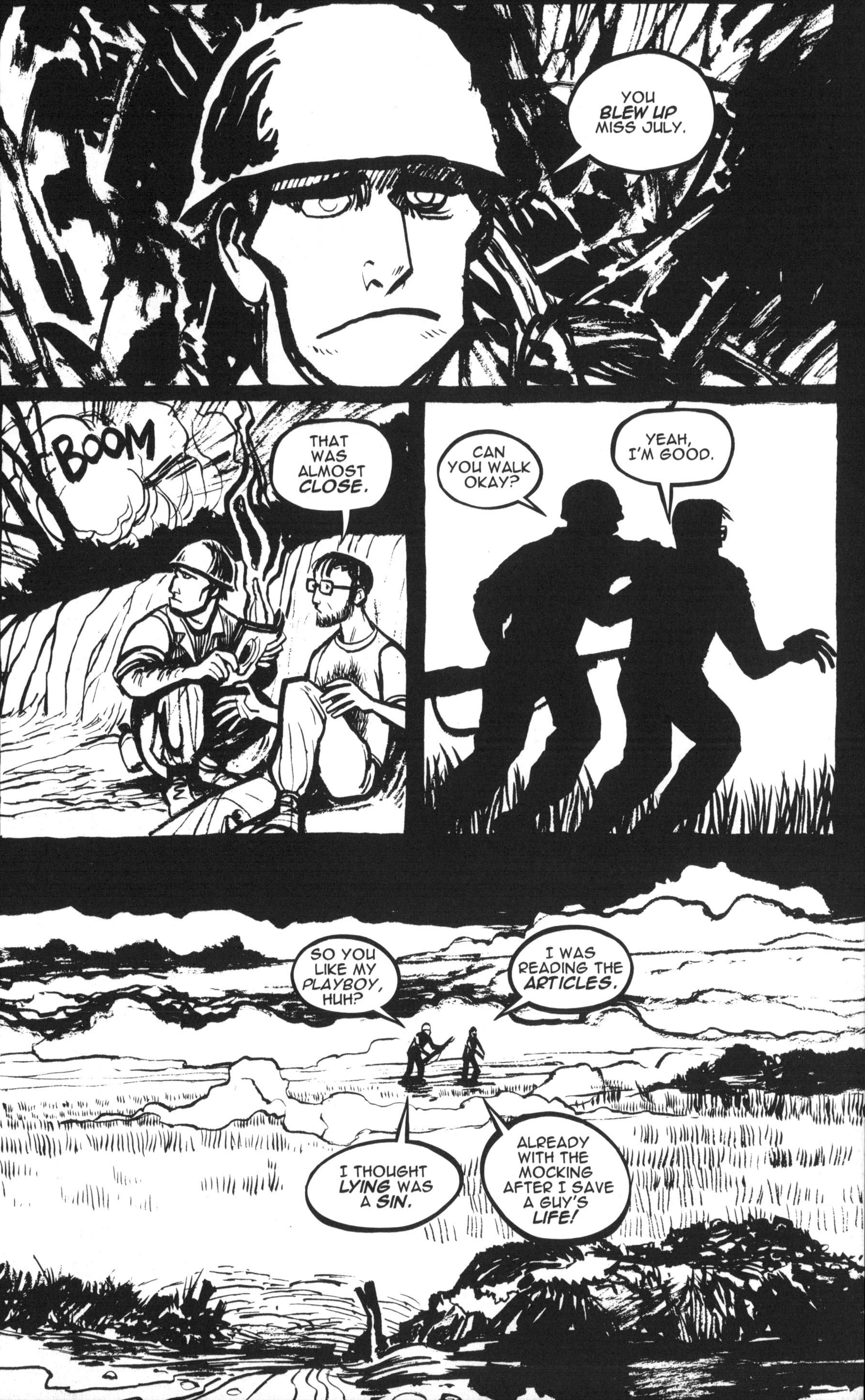
YOU BLEW UP MISS JULY.
BOOM
THAT WAS ALMOST CLOSE.
CAN YOU WALK OKAY?
YEAH, I'M GOOD.
SO YOU LIKE MY PLAYBOY, HUH?
I WAS READING THE ARTICLES.
I THOUGHT LYING WAS A SIN.
ALREADY WITH THE MOCKING AFTER I SAVE A GUY'S LIFE!

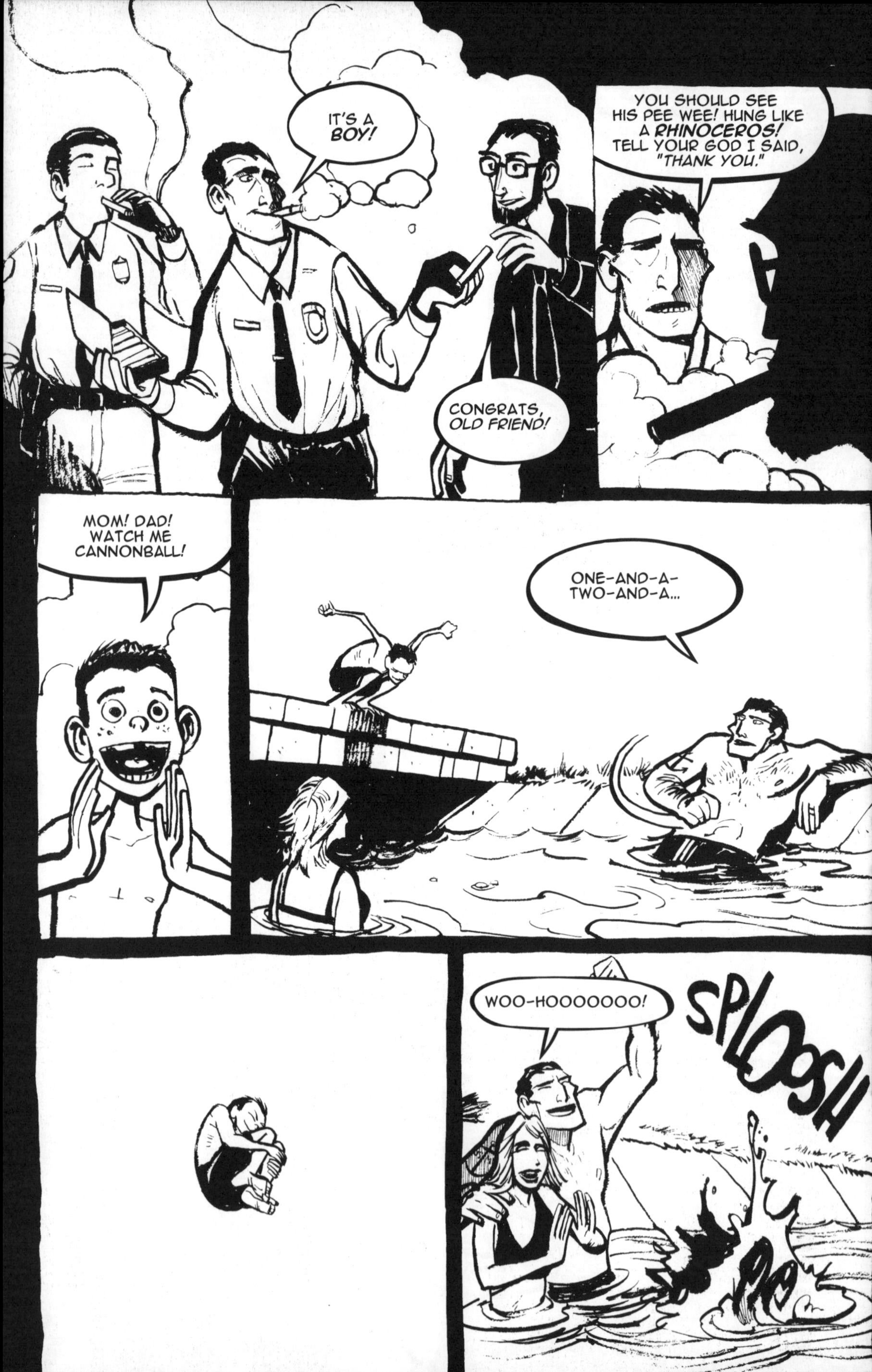
IT'S A BOY!
CONGRATS, OLD FRIEND!
YOU SHOULD SEE HIS PEE WEE! HUNG LIKE A RHINOCEROS! TELL YOUR GOD I SAID, "THANK YOU."
MOM! DAD! WATCH ME CANNONBALL!
ONE-AND-A-TWO-AND-A...
WOO-HOOOOOOO!
SPLOOSH

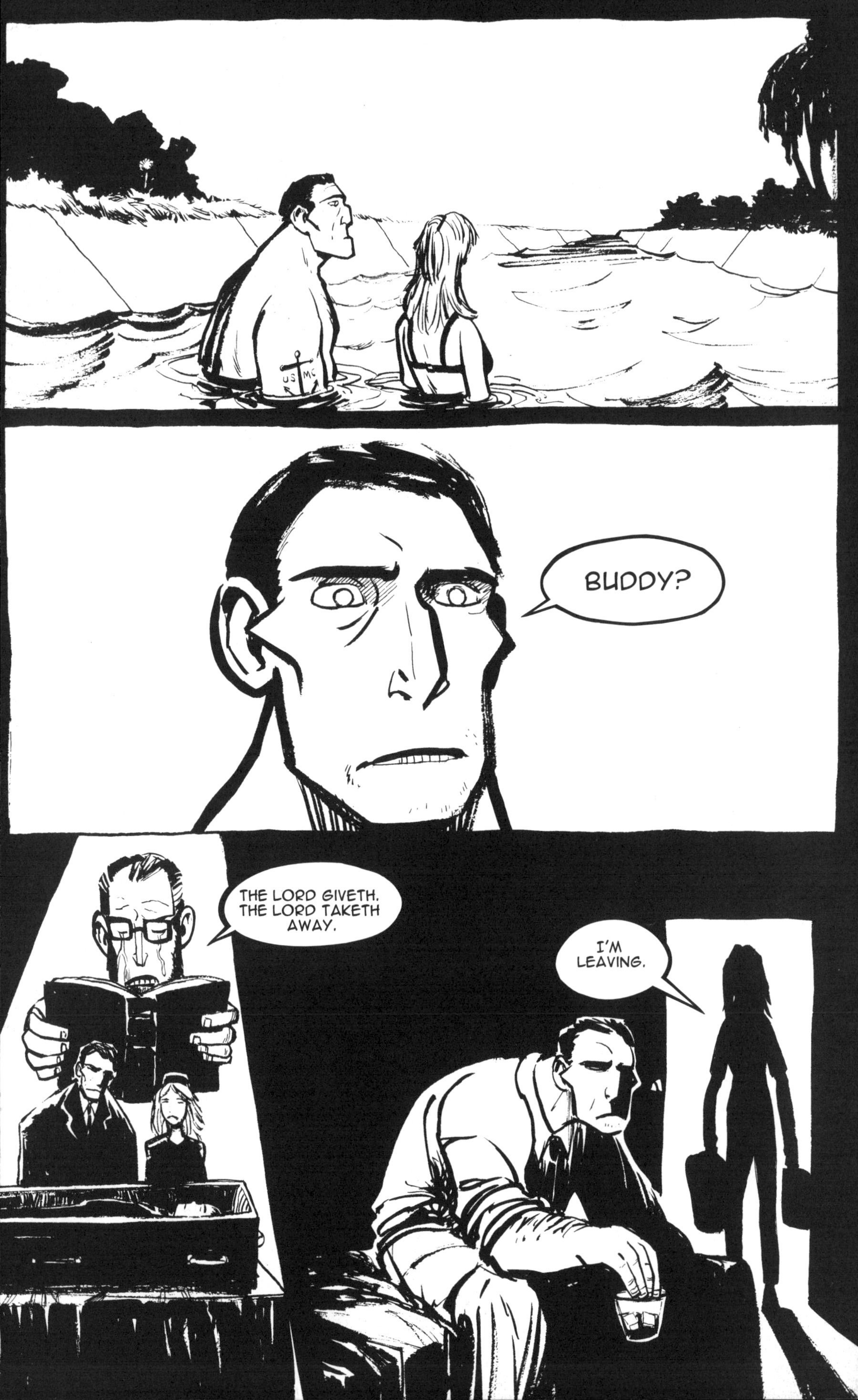

US MC
BUDDY?
THE LORD GIVETH. THE LORD TAKETH AWAY.
I'M LEAVING.

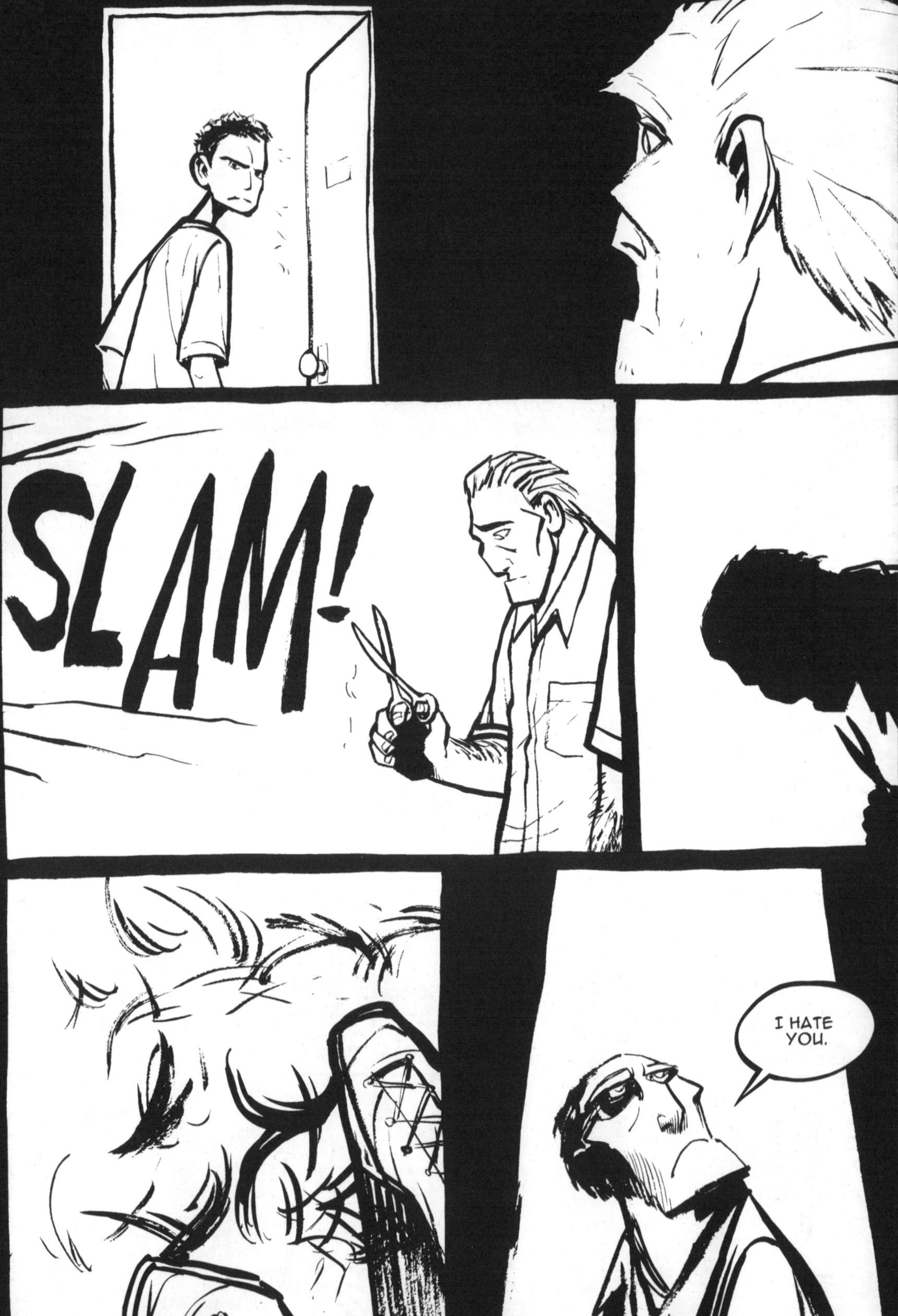
SLAM!
I HATE YOU.

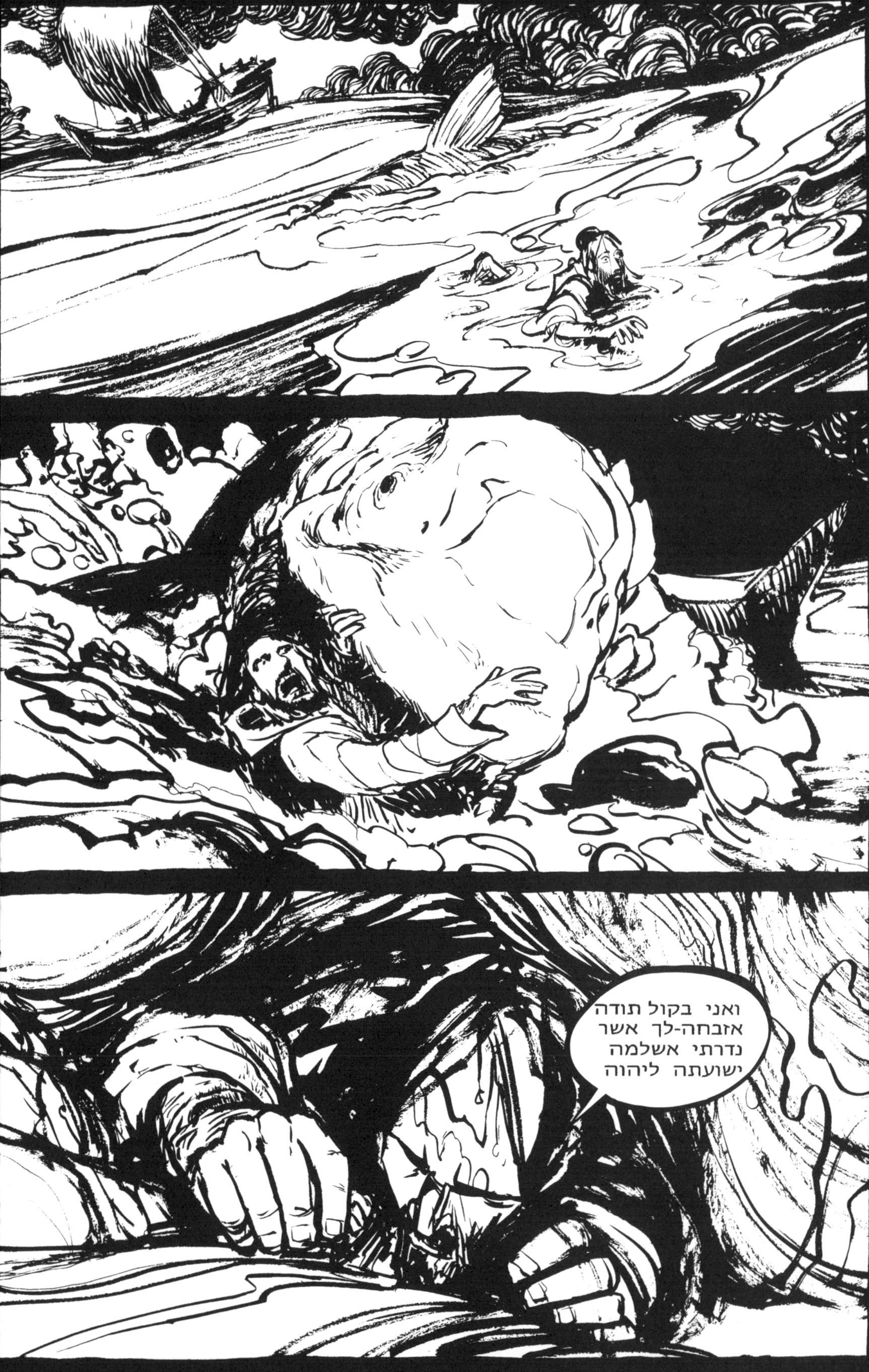
ואני בקול תודה
אזבחה-לך אשר
נדרתי אשלמה
ישועתה ליהוה

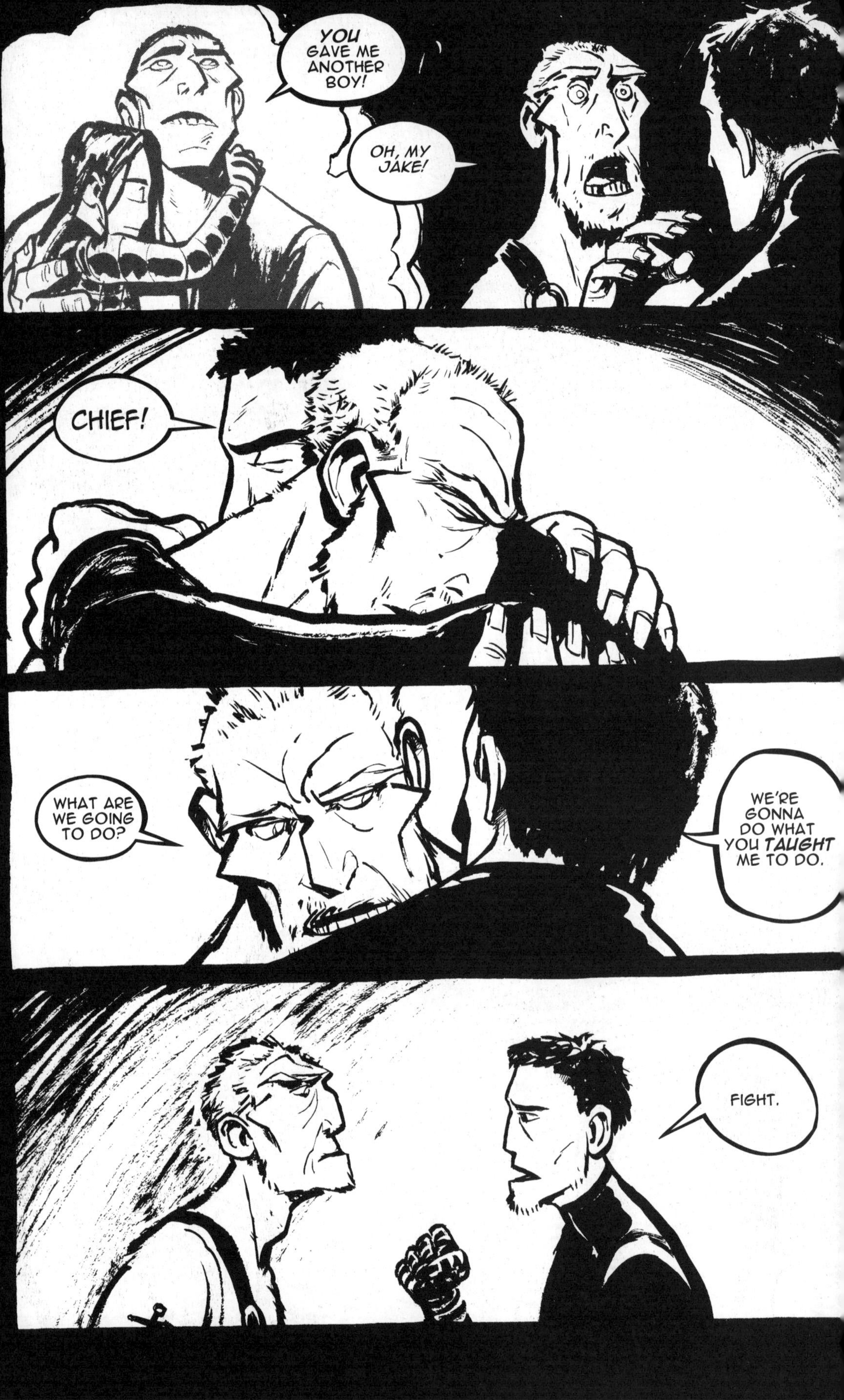
YOU GAVE ME ANOTHER BOY!
OH, MY JAKE!
CHIEF!
WHAT ARE WE GOING TO DO?
WE'RE GONNA DO WHAT YOU TAUGHT ME TO DO.
FIGHT.

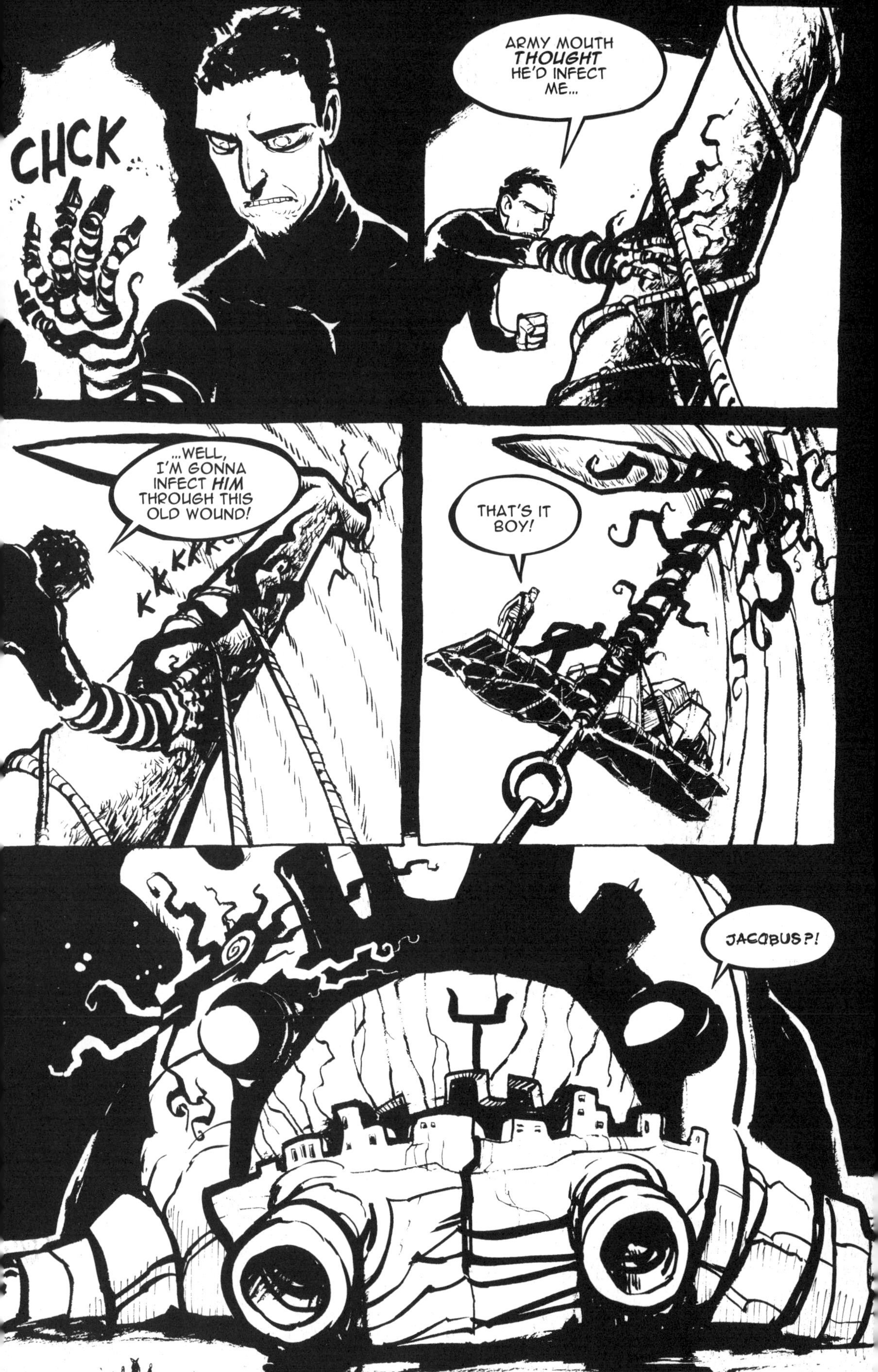
CHCK
ARMY MOUTH THOUGHT HE'D INFECT ME...
...WELL, I'M GONNA INFECT HIM THROUGH THIS OLD WOUND!
KKKKKK
THAT'S IT BOY!
JACOBUS?!

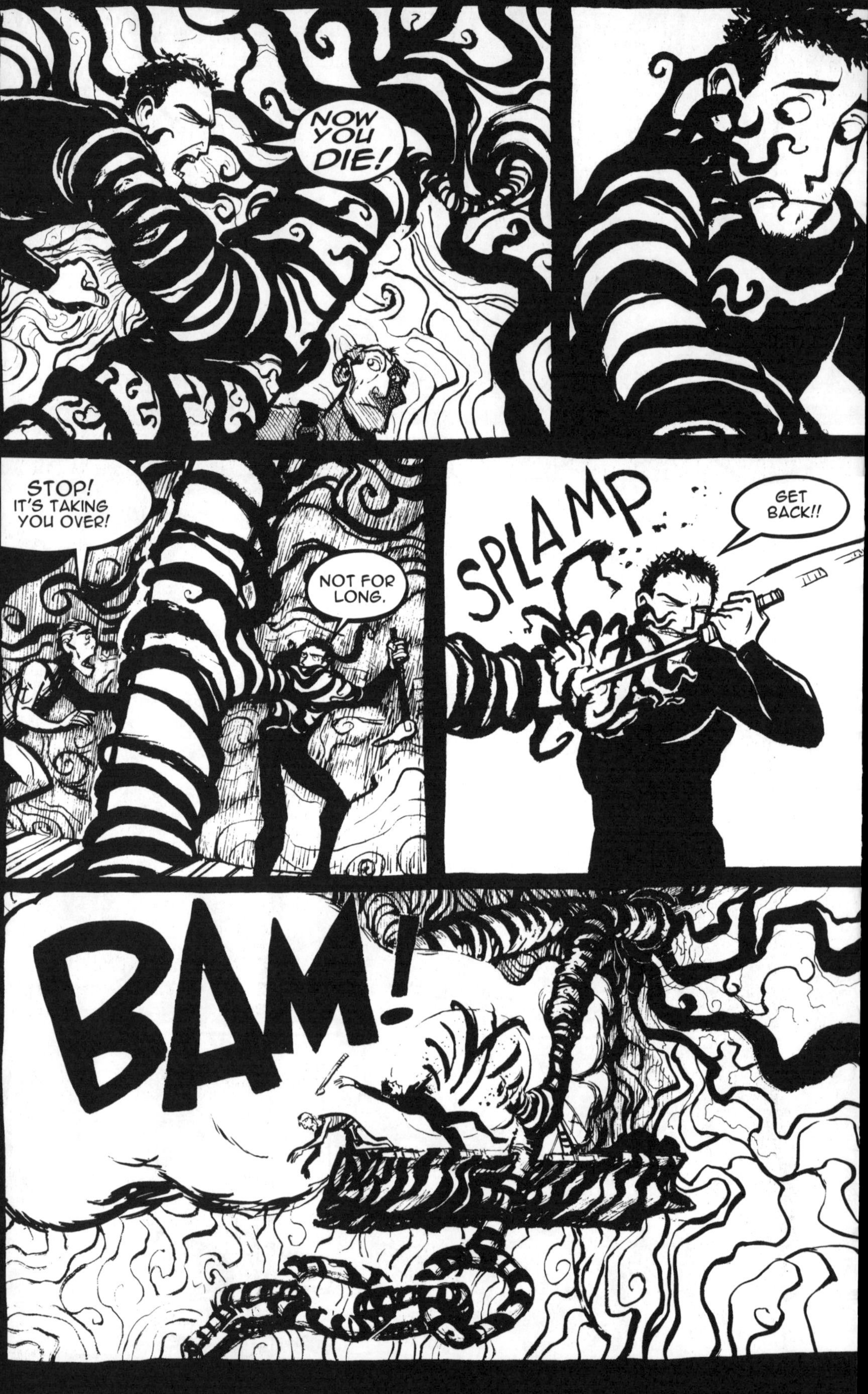
NOW YOU DIE!
STOP! IT'S TAKING YOU OVER!
NOT FOR LONG.
SPLAMP
GET BACK!!
BAM!

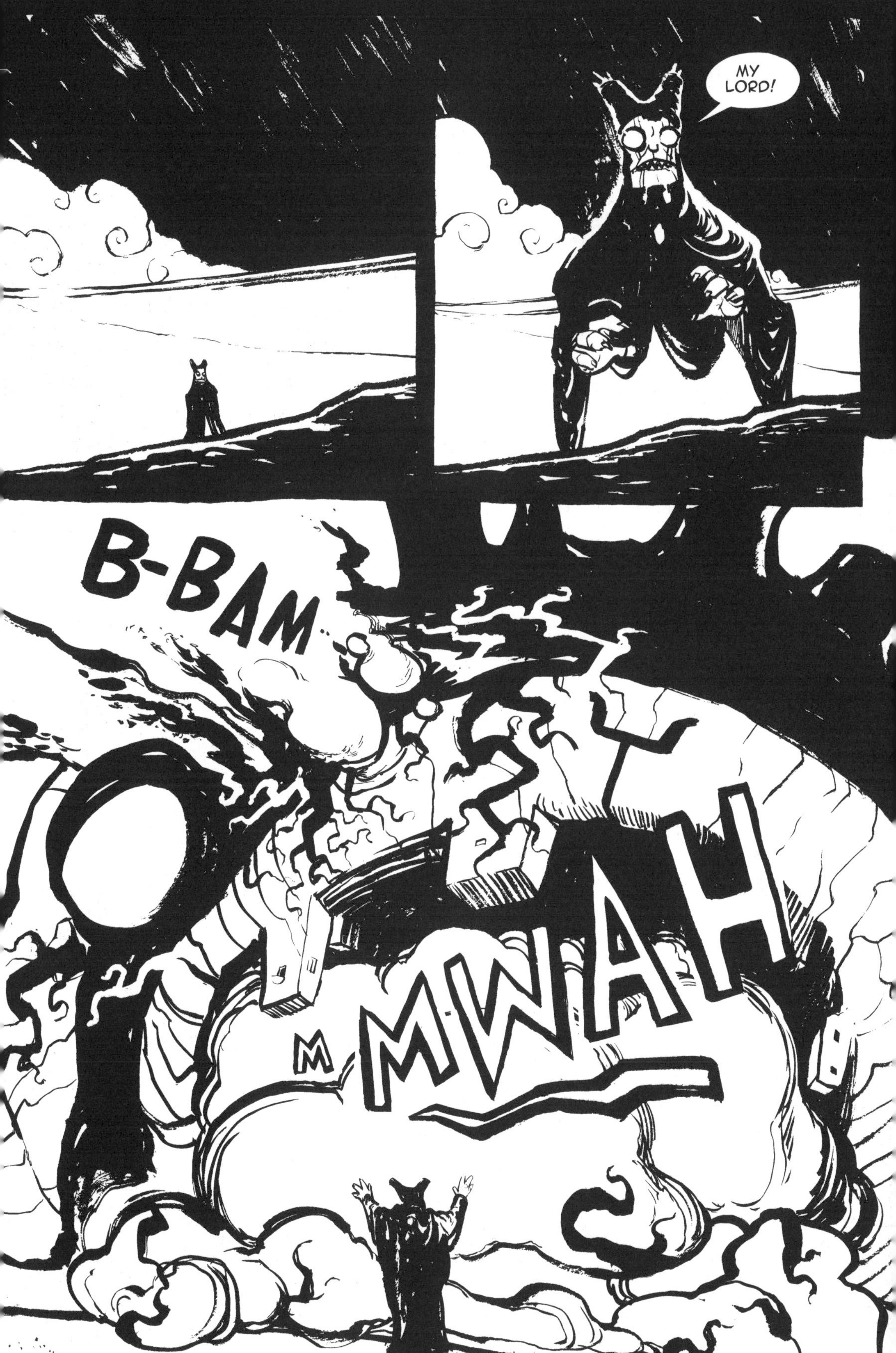
MY LORD!
B-BAM
MMWAH

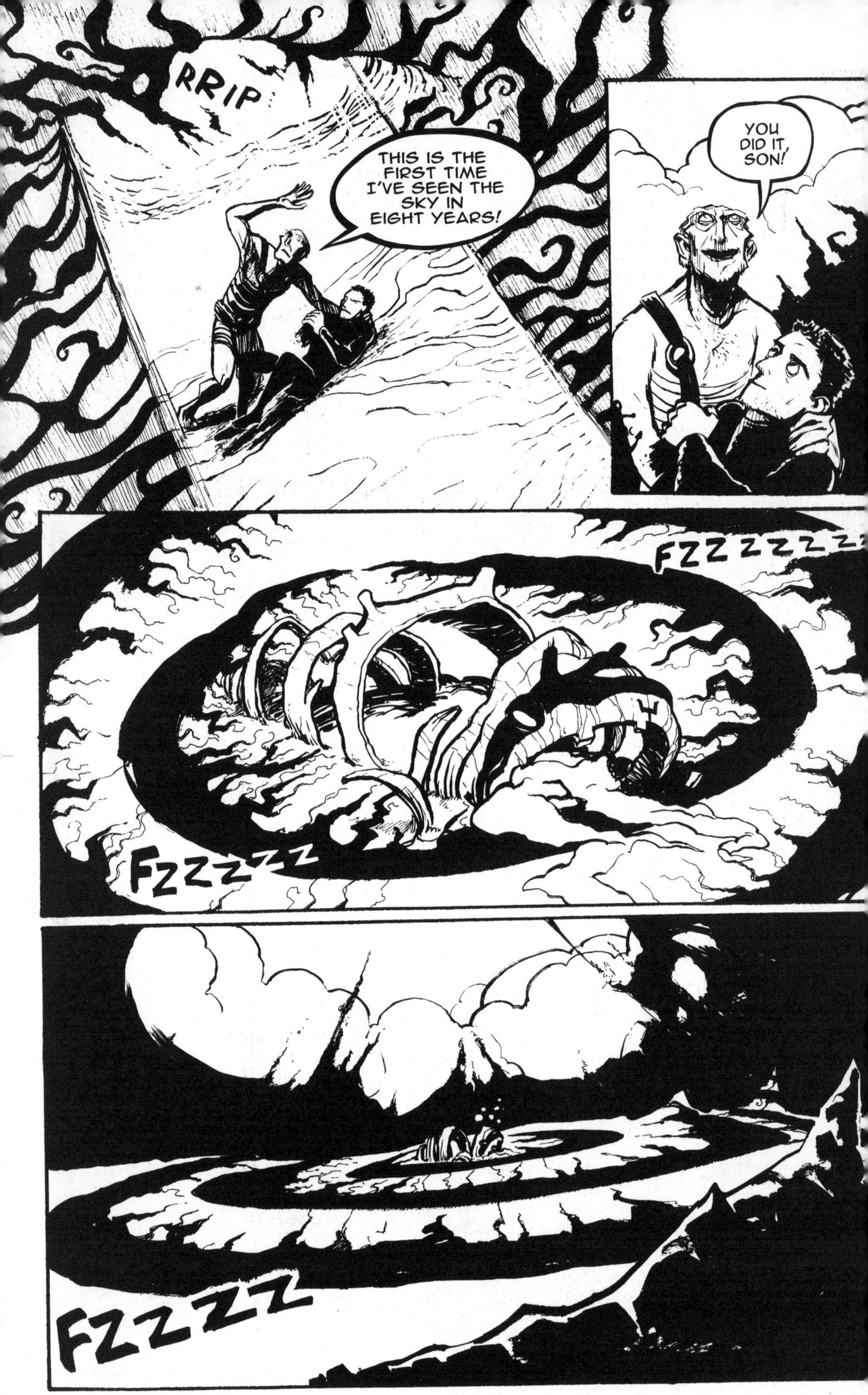
RRIP
THIS IS THE FIRST TIME I'VE SEEN THE SKY IN EIGHT YEARS!
YOU DID IT, SON!
FZZZZZZZ
FZZZZZ
FZZZZZ

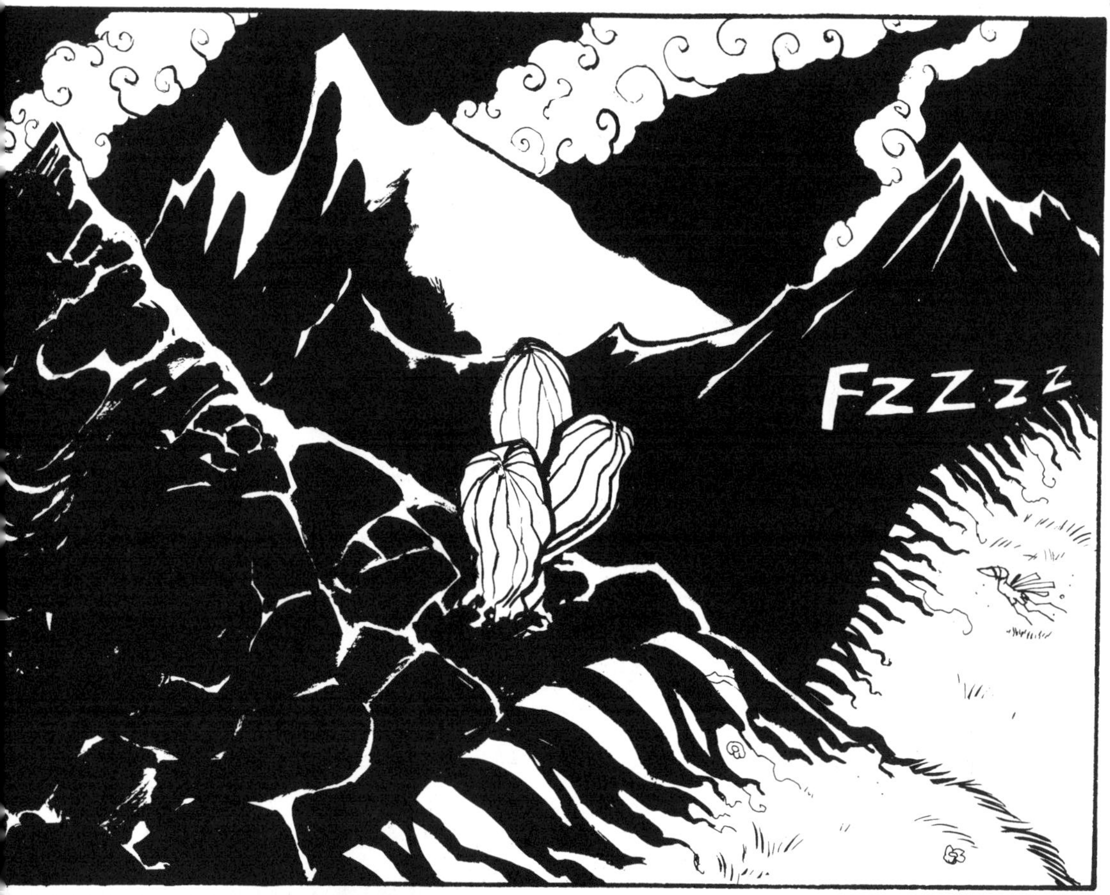
FzZzzz

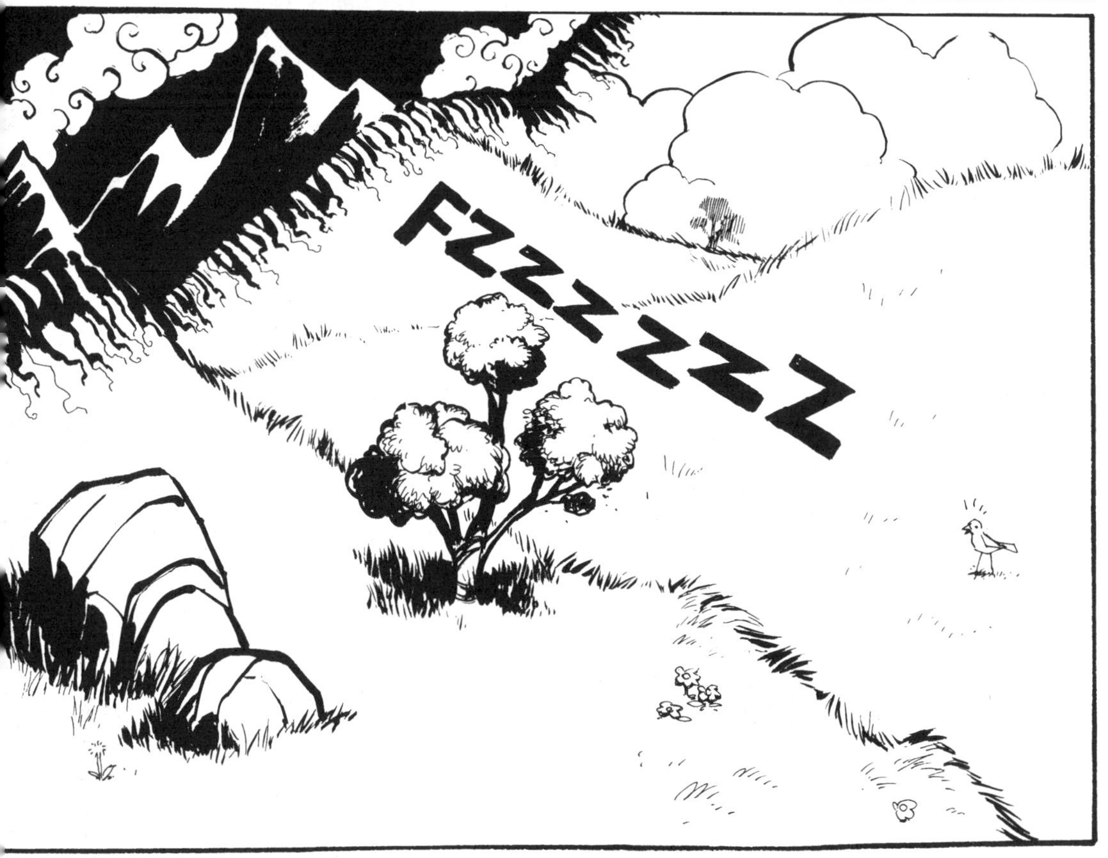
FZZZZZZ

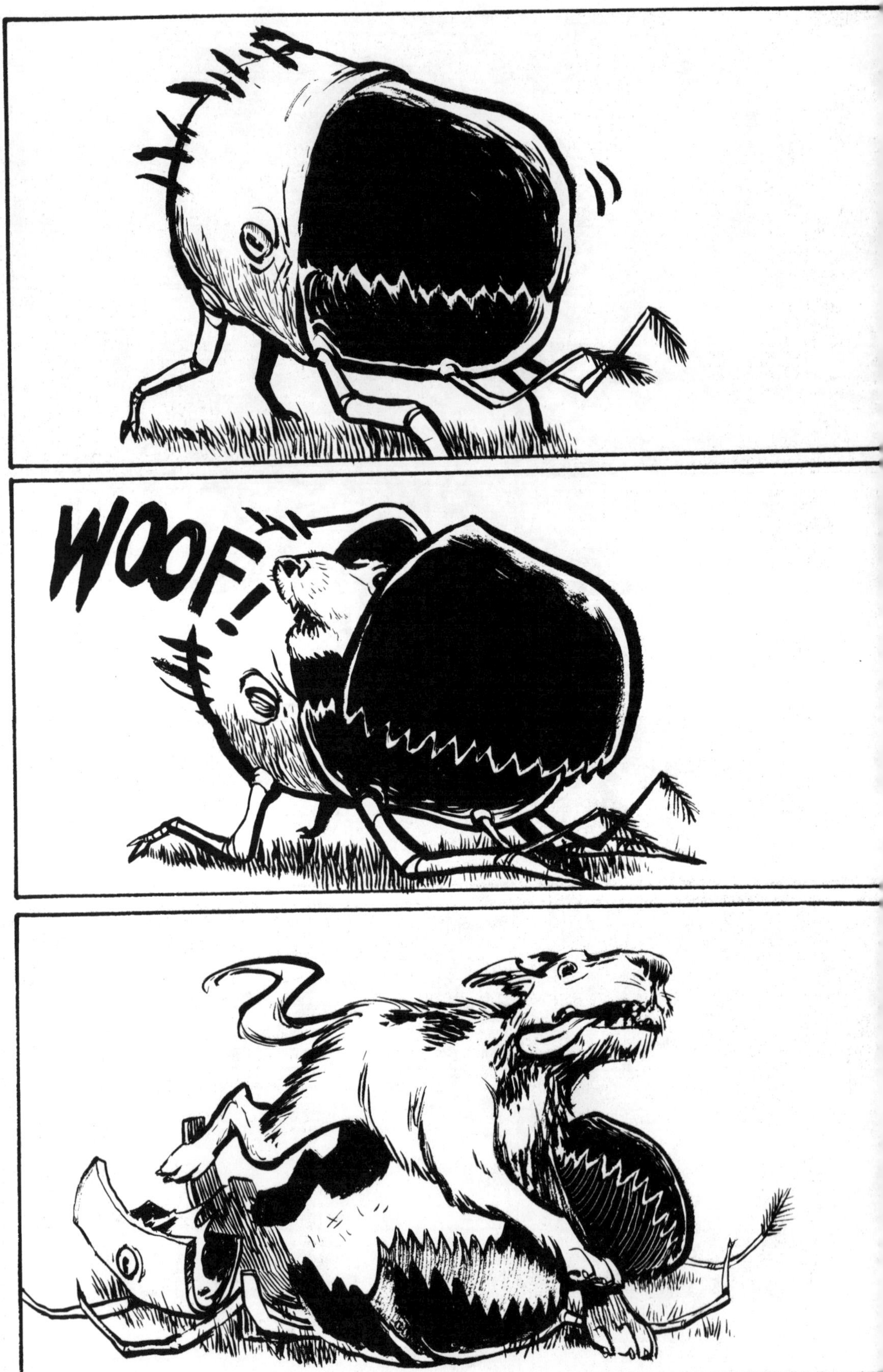
WOOF!

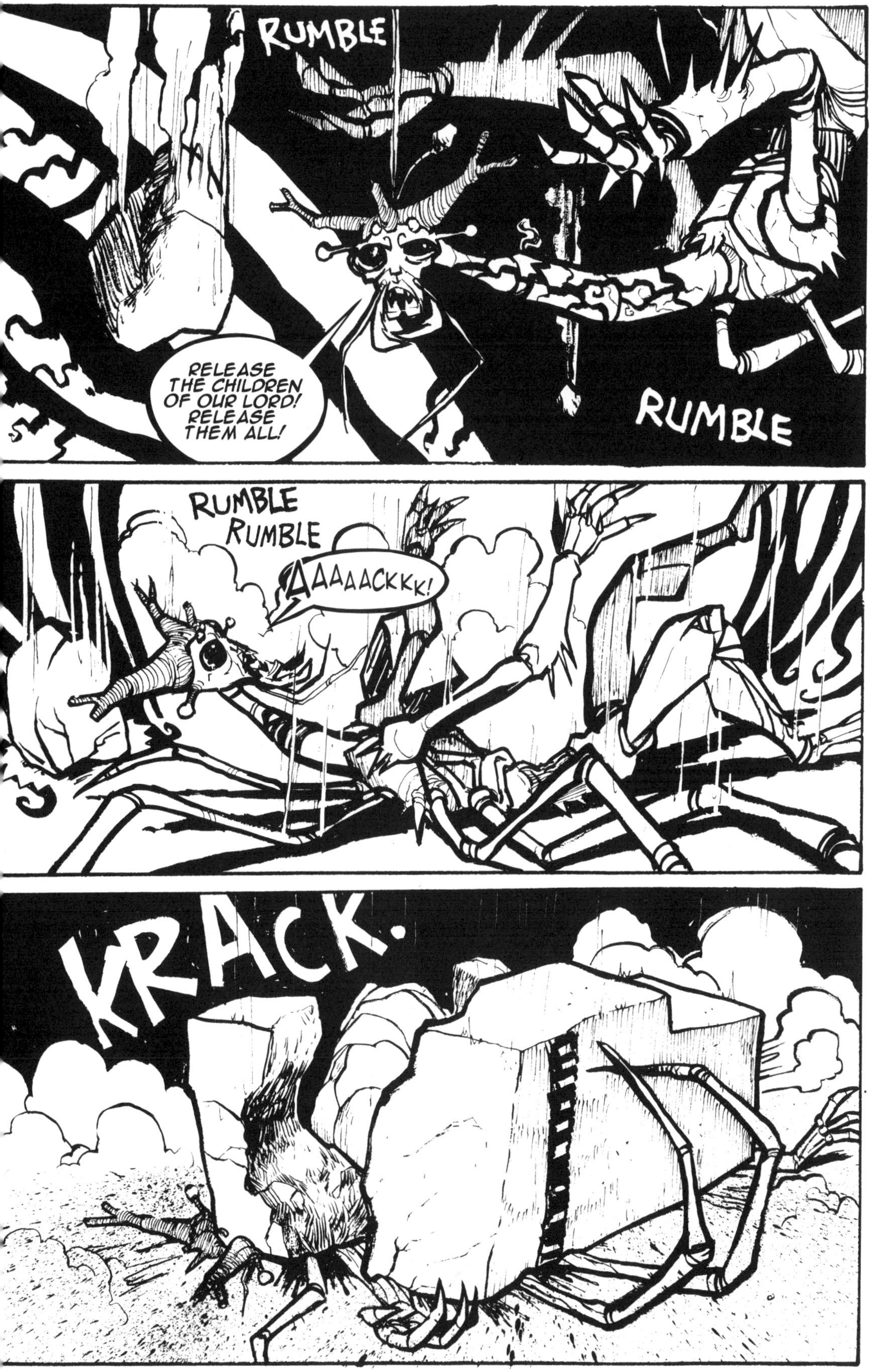
RUMBLE
RELEASE THE CHILDREN OF OUR LORD! RELEASE THEM ALL!
RUMBLE
RUMBLE RUMBLE
AAAAACKKK!
KRACK.

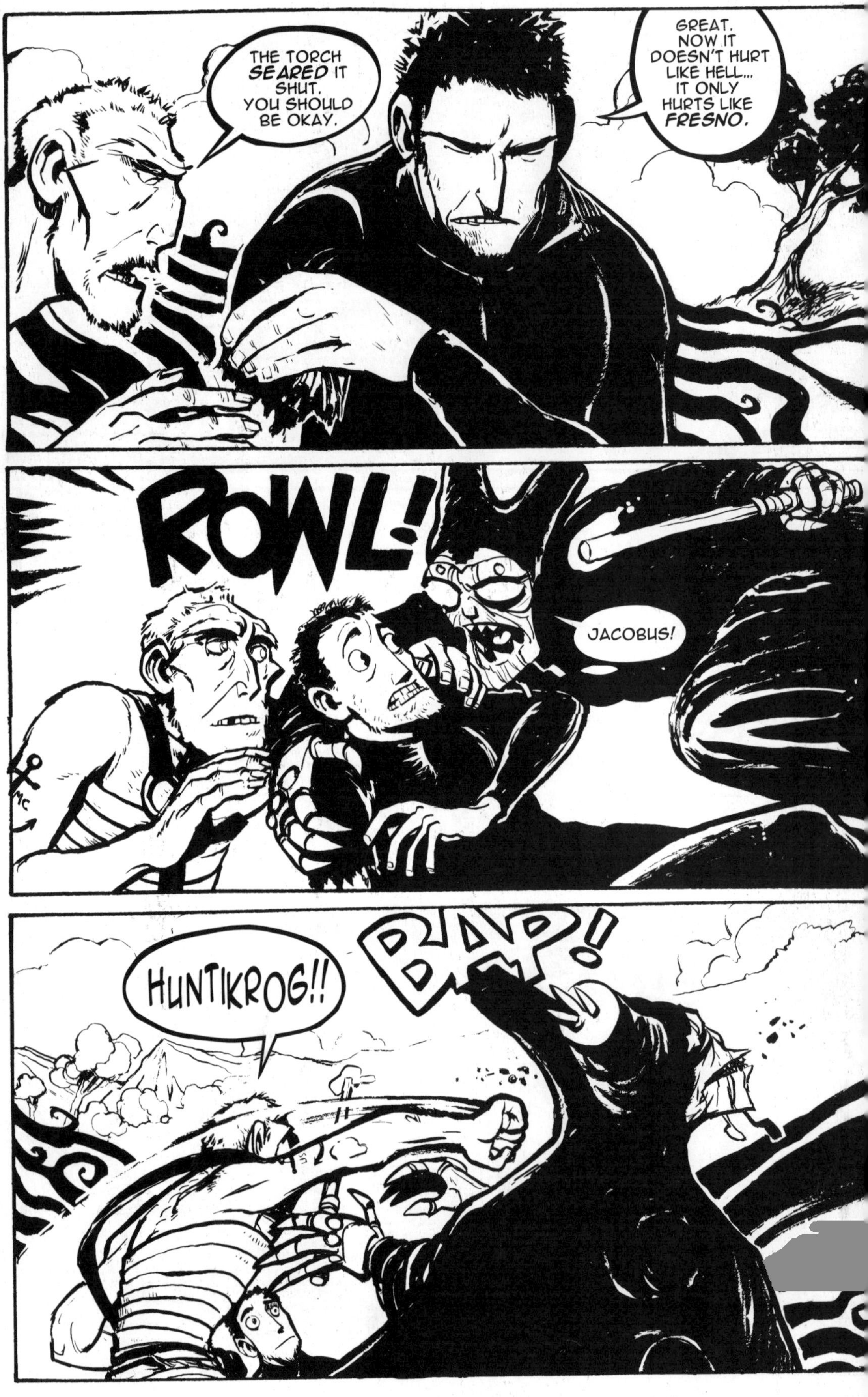
THE TORCH SEARED IT SHUT. YOU SHOULD BE OKAY.
GREAT. NOW IT DOESN'T HURT LIKE HELL... IT ONLY HURTS LIKE FRESNO.
ROWL!
JACOBUS!
HUNTIKROG!!
BAP!

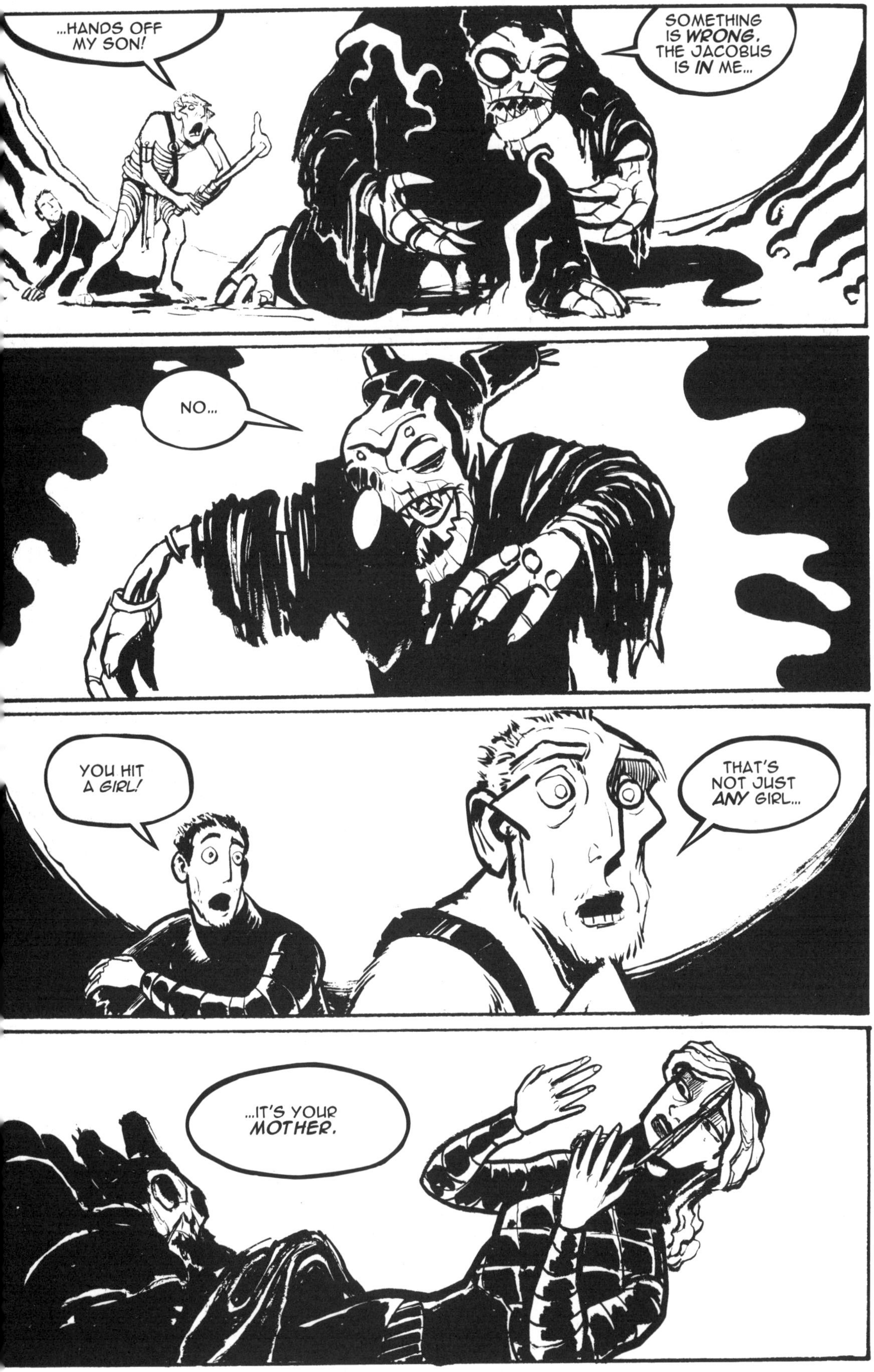
...HANDS OFF MY SON!
SOMETHING IS WRONG. THE JACOBUS IS IN ME...
NO...
YOU HIT A GIRL!
THAT'S NOT JUST ANY GIRL...
...IT'S YOUR MOTHER.

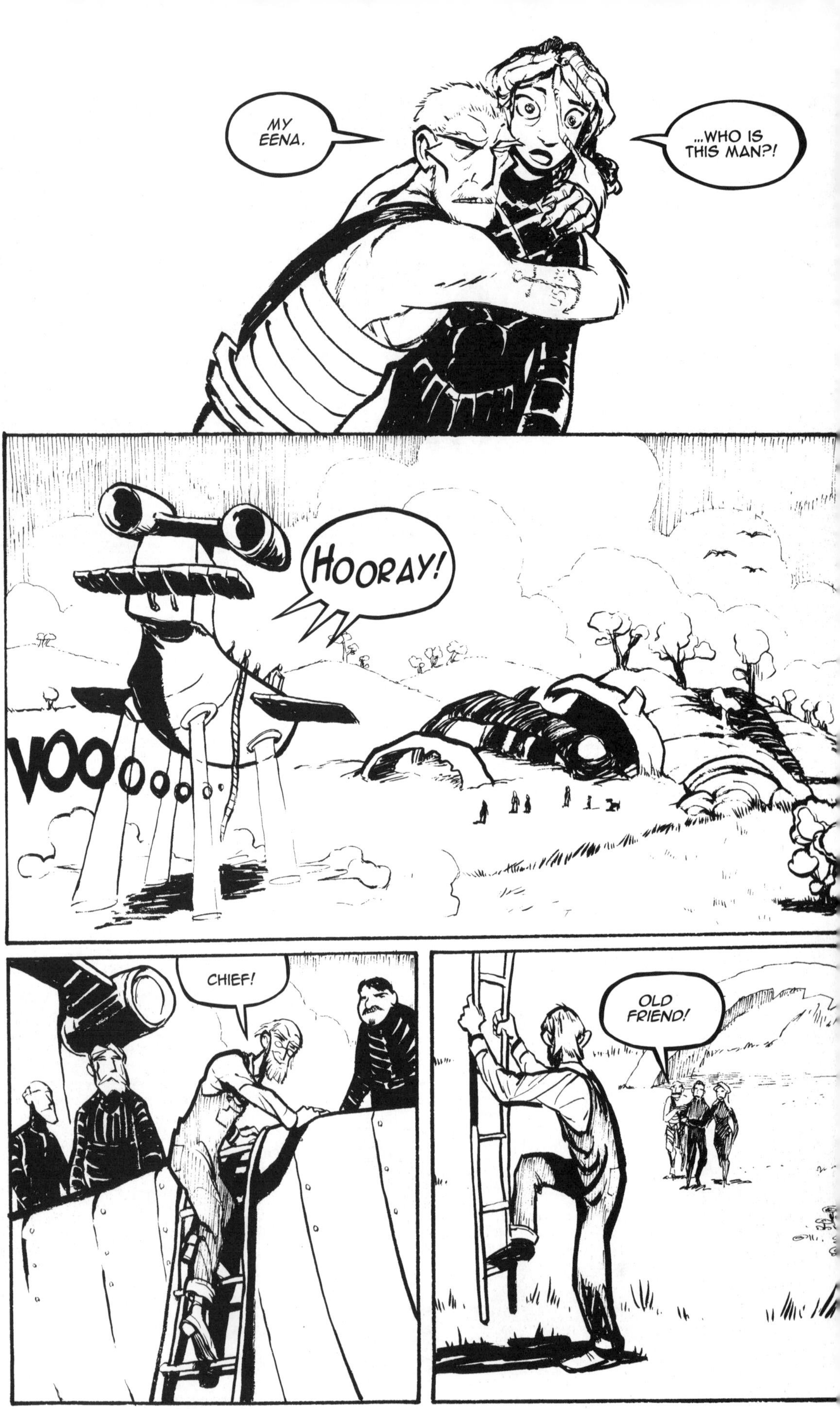
MY EENA.
...WHO IS THIS MAN?!
HOORAY!
VOOooooo
CHIEF!
OLD FRIEND!

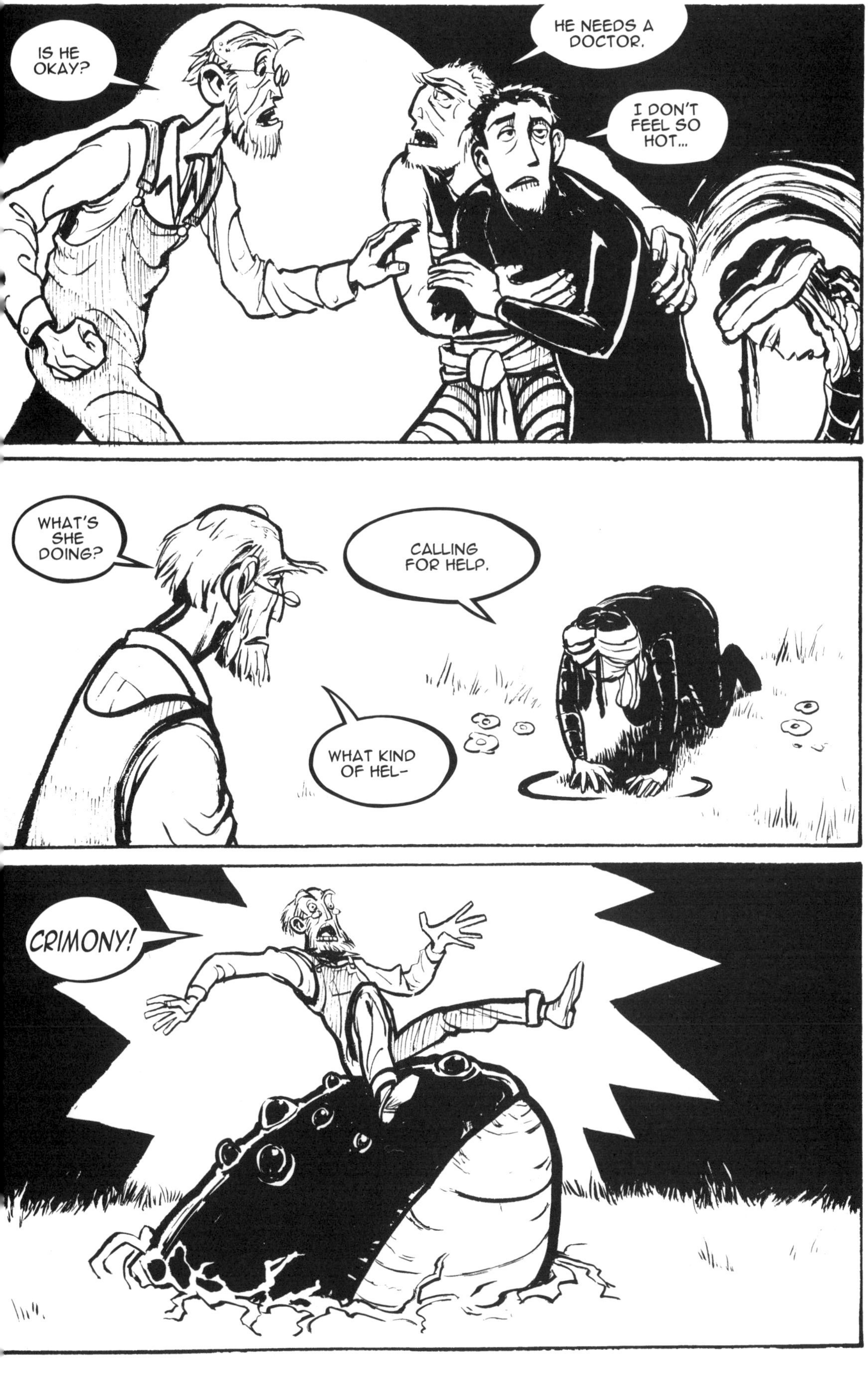
IS HE OKAY?
HE NEEDS A DOCTOR.
I DON'T FEEL SO HOT...
WHAT'S SHE DOING?
CALLING FOR HELP.
WHAT KIND OF HEL-
CRIMONY!

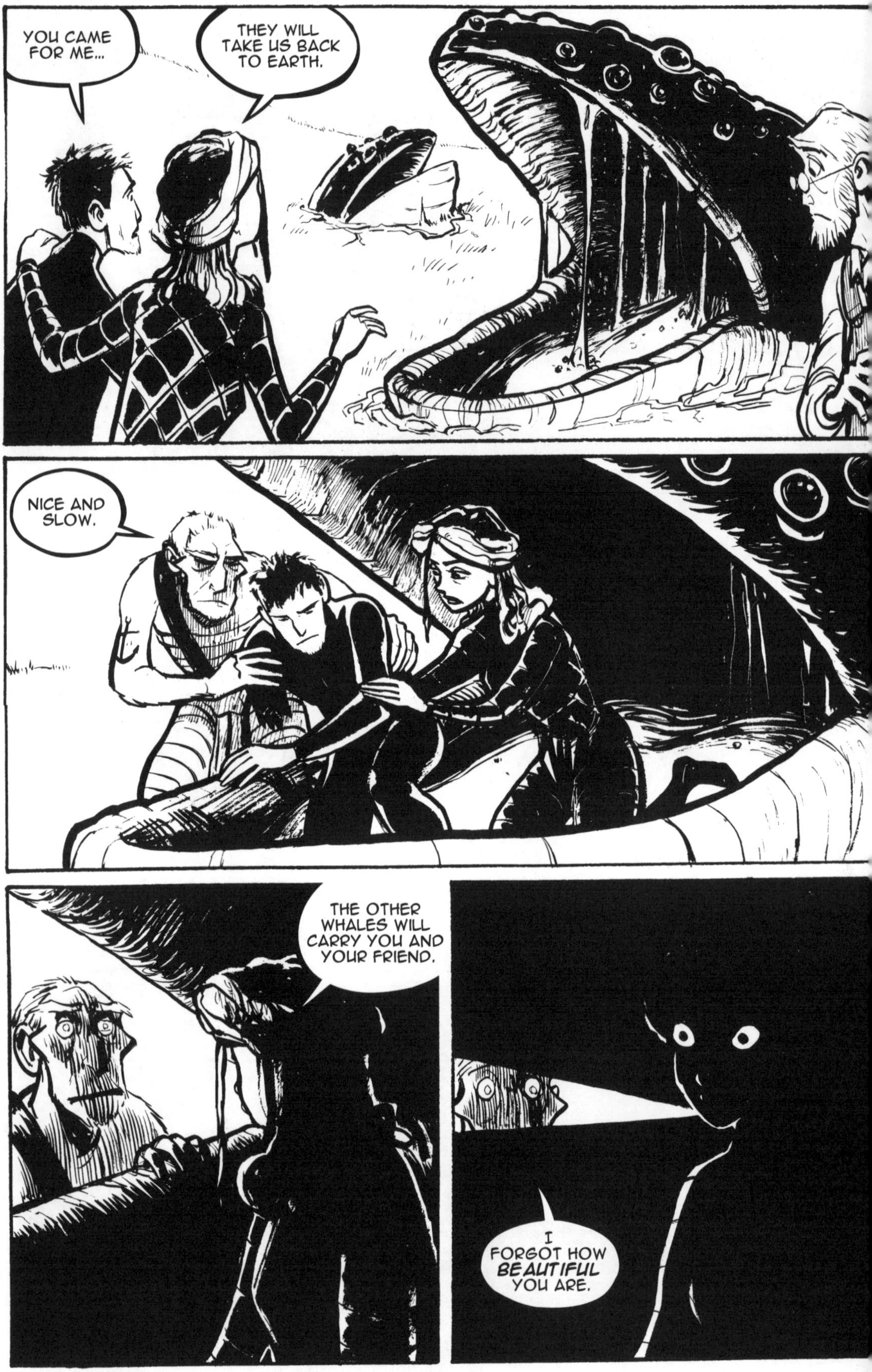
YOU CAME FOR ME...
THEY WILL TAKE US BACK TO EARTH.
NICE AND SLOW.
THE OTHER WHALES WILL CARRY YOU AND YOUR FRIEND.
I FORGOT HOW *BEAUTIFUL* YOU ARE.

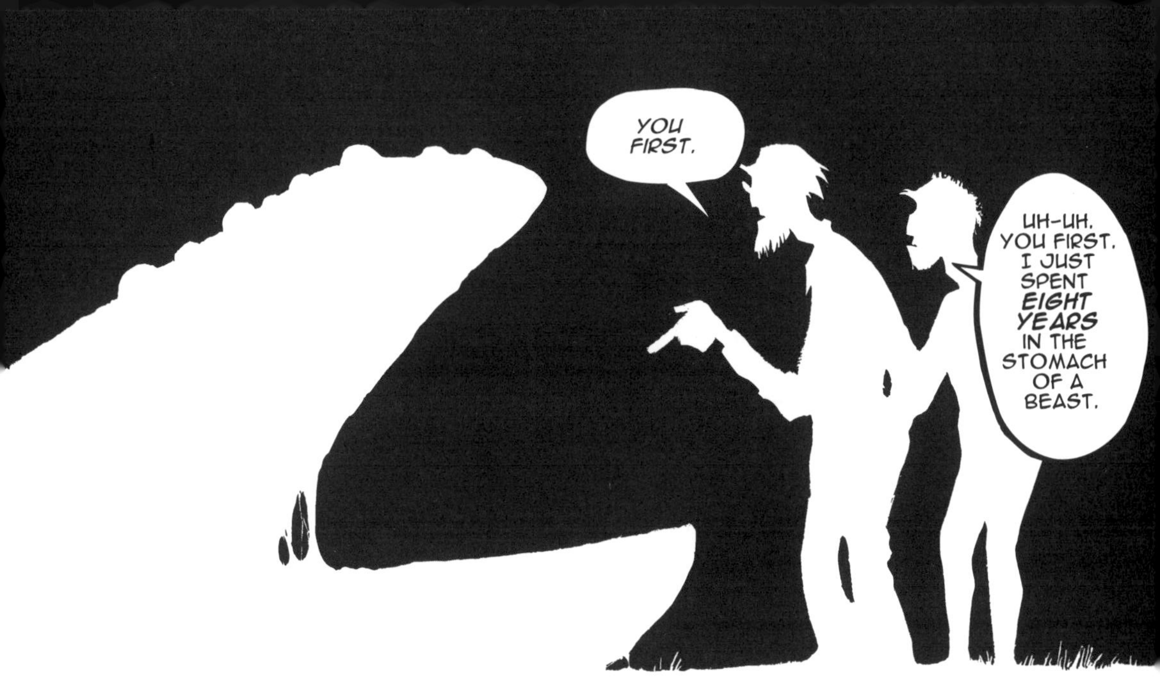
YOU FIRST.
UH-UH. YOU FIRST. I JUST SPENT EIGHT YEARS IN THE STOMACH OF A BEAST.

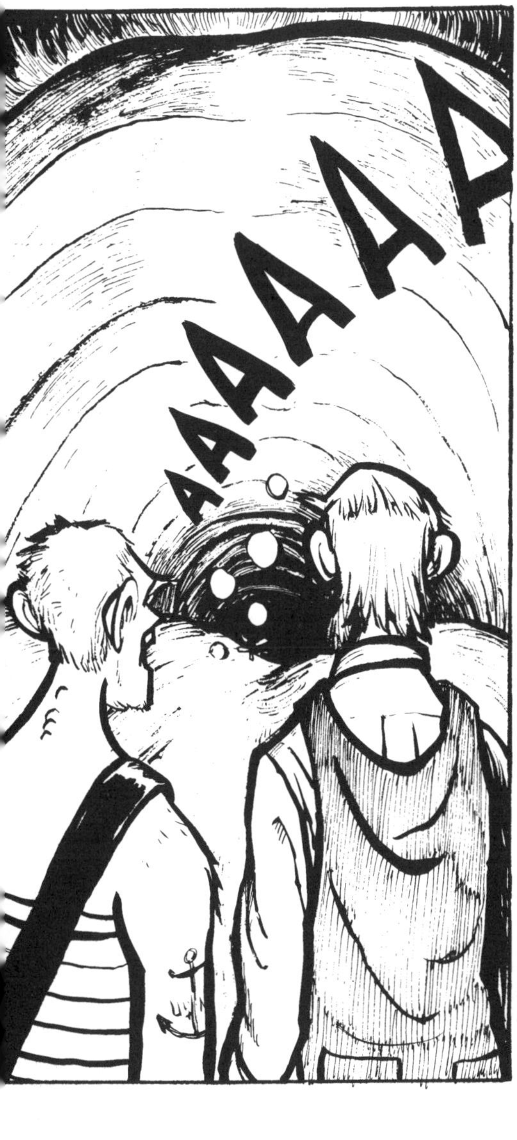
AAAAAAA

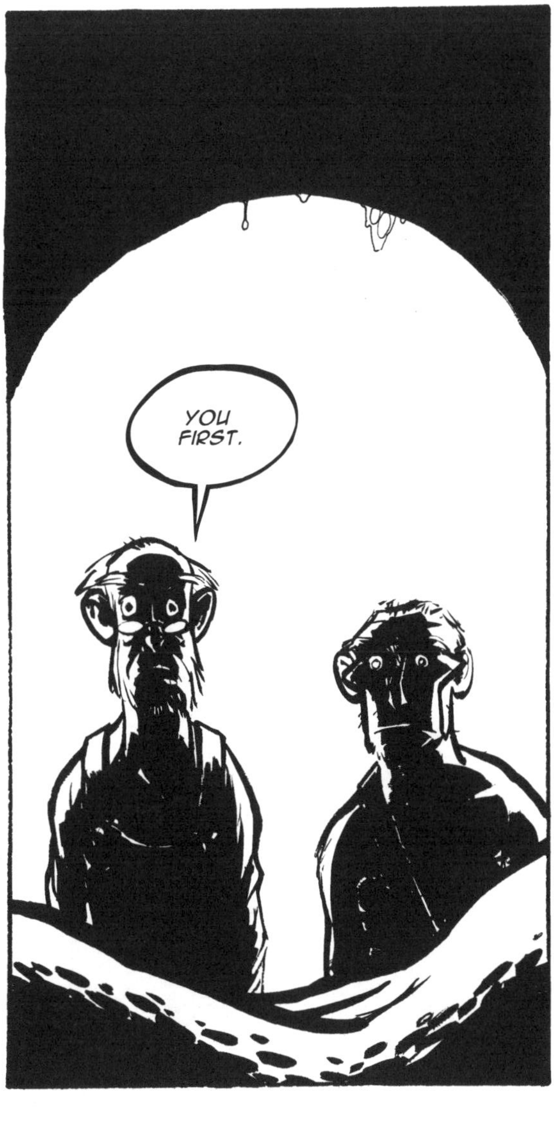
YOU FIRST.

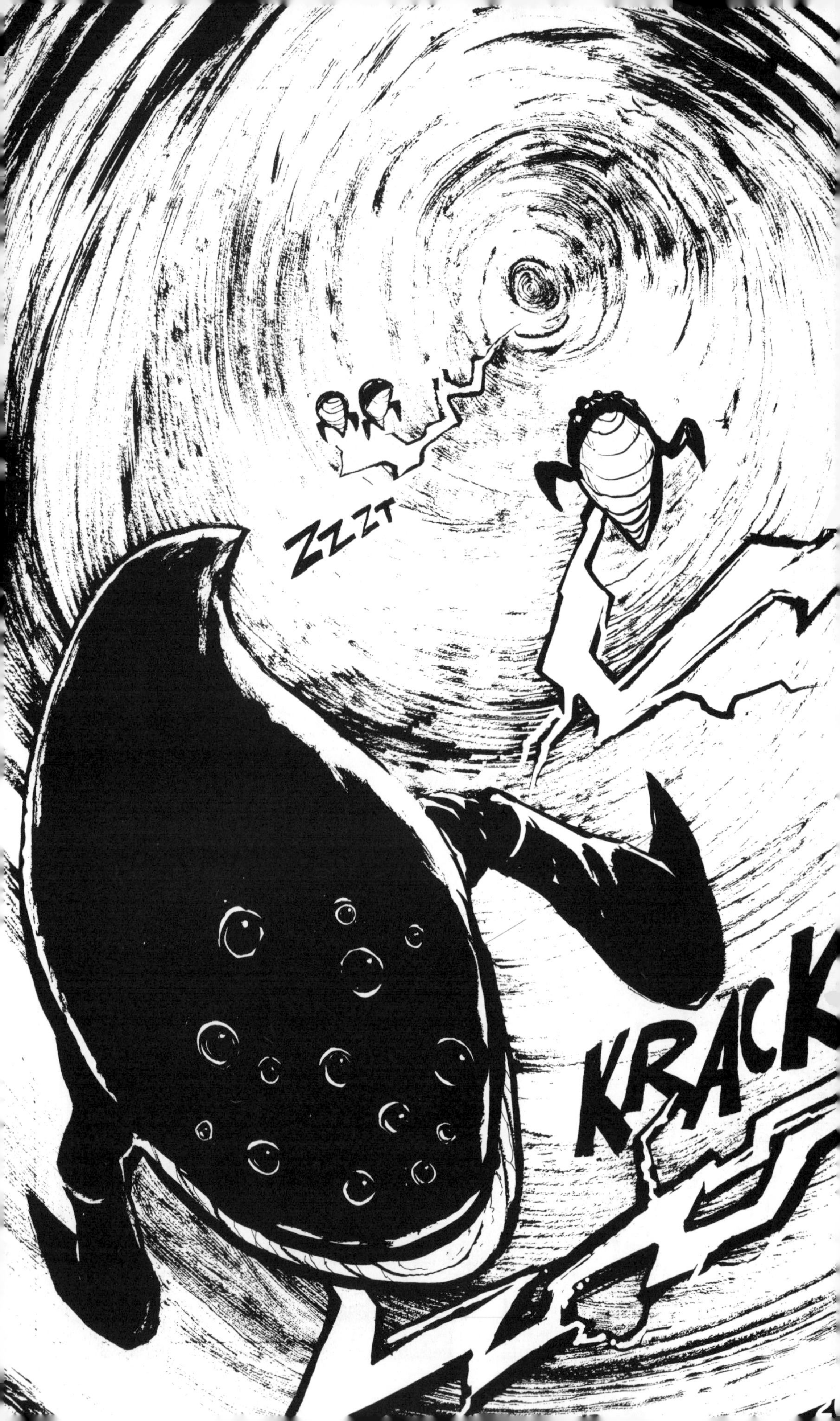
ZZZT
KRACK

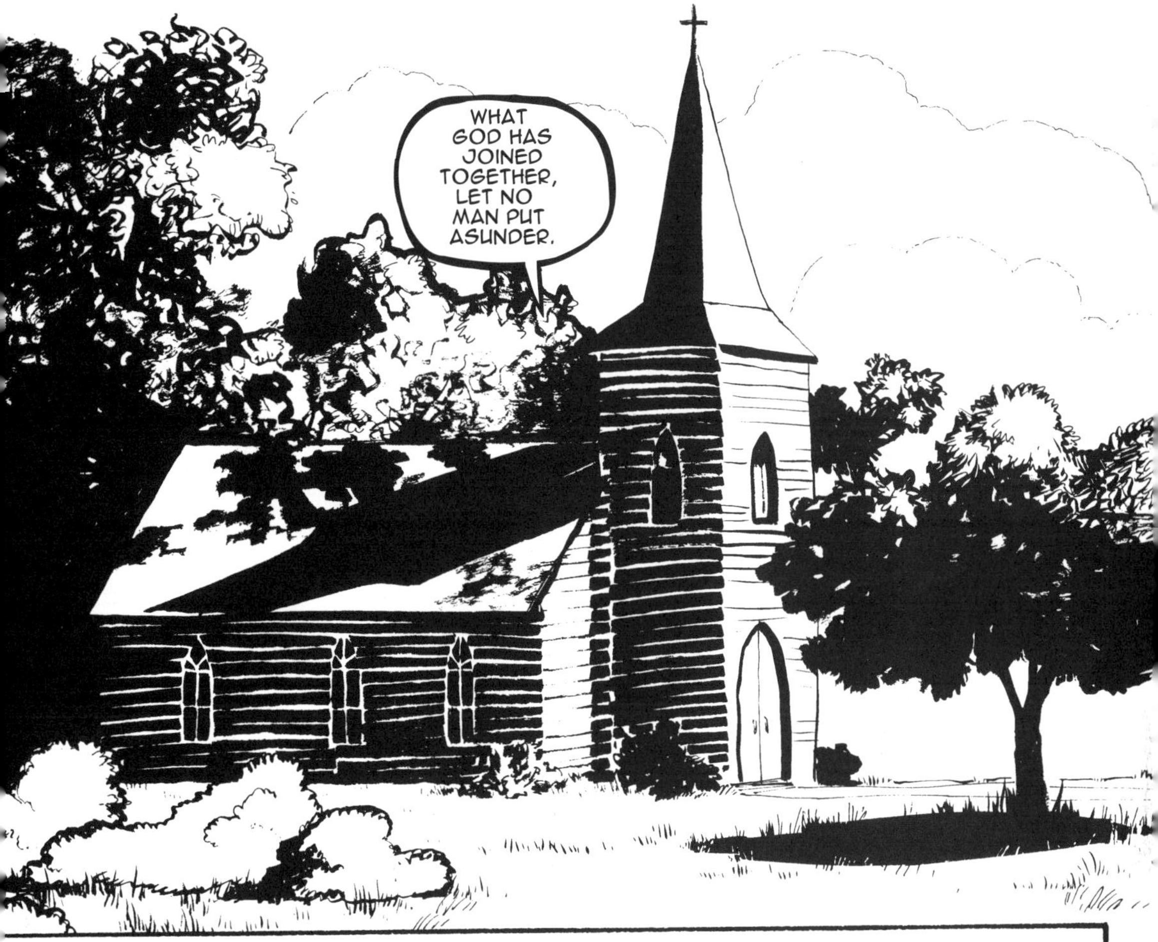
WHAT GOD HAS JOINED TOGETHER, LET NO MAN PUT ASUNDER.

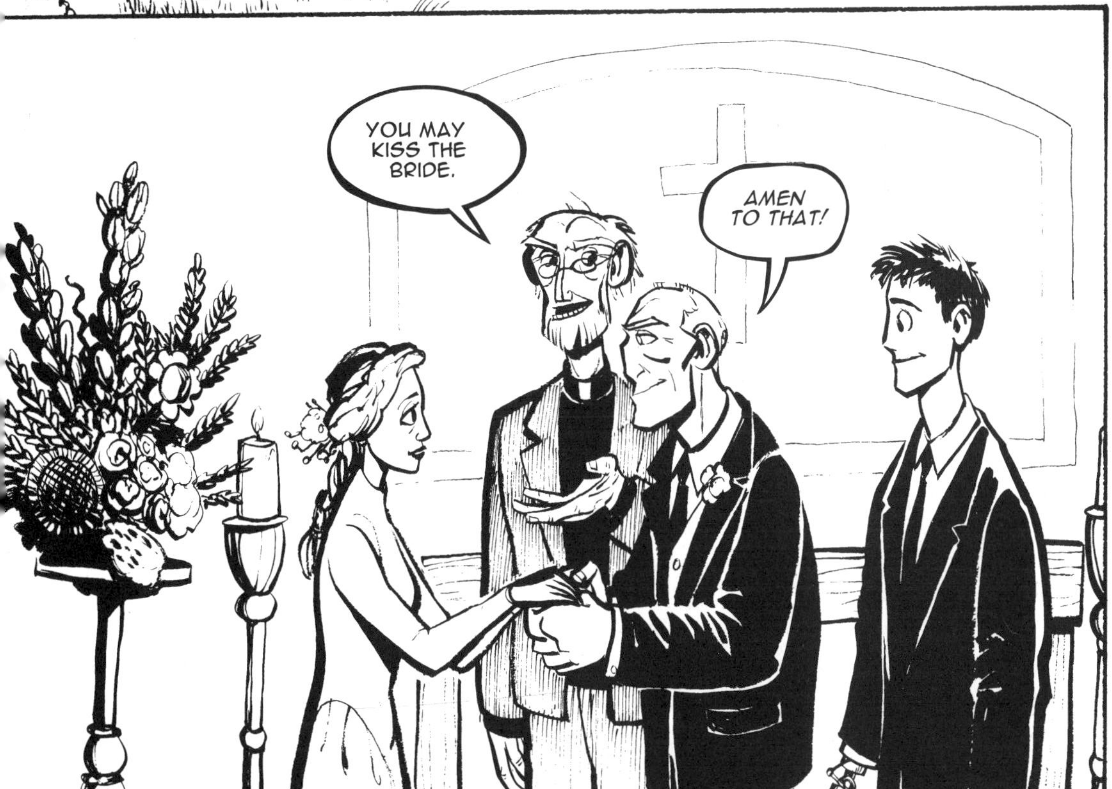
YOU MAY KISS THE BRIDE.
AMEN TO THAT!

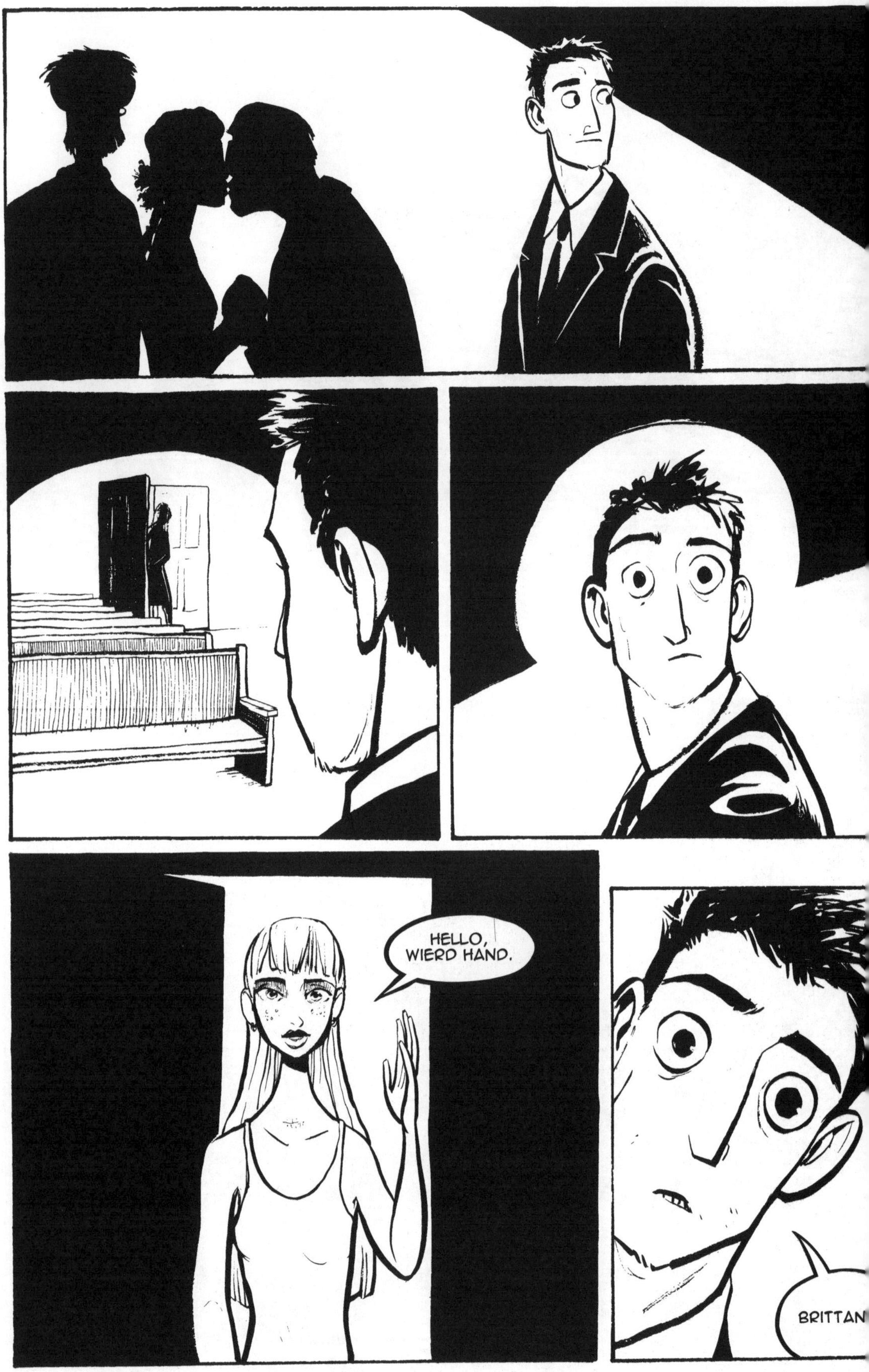
HELLO,
WIERD HAND.
BRITTAN

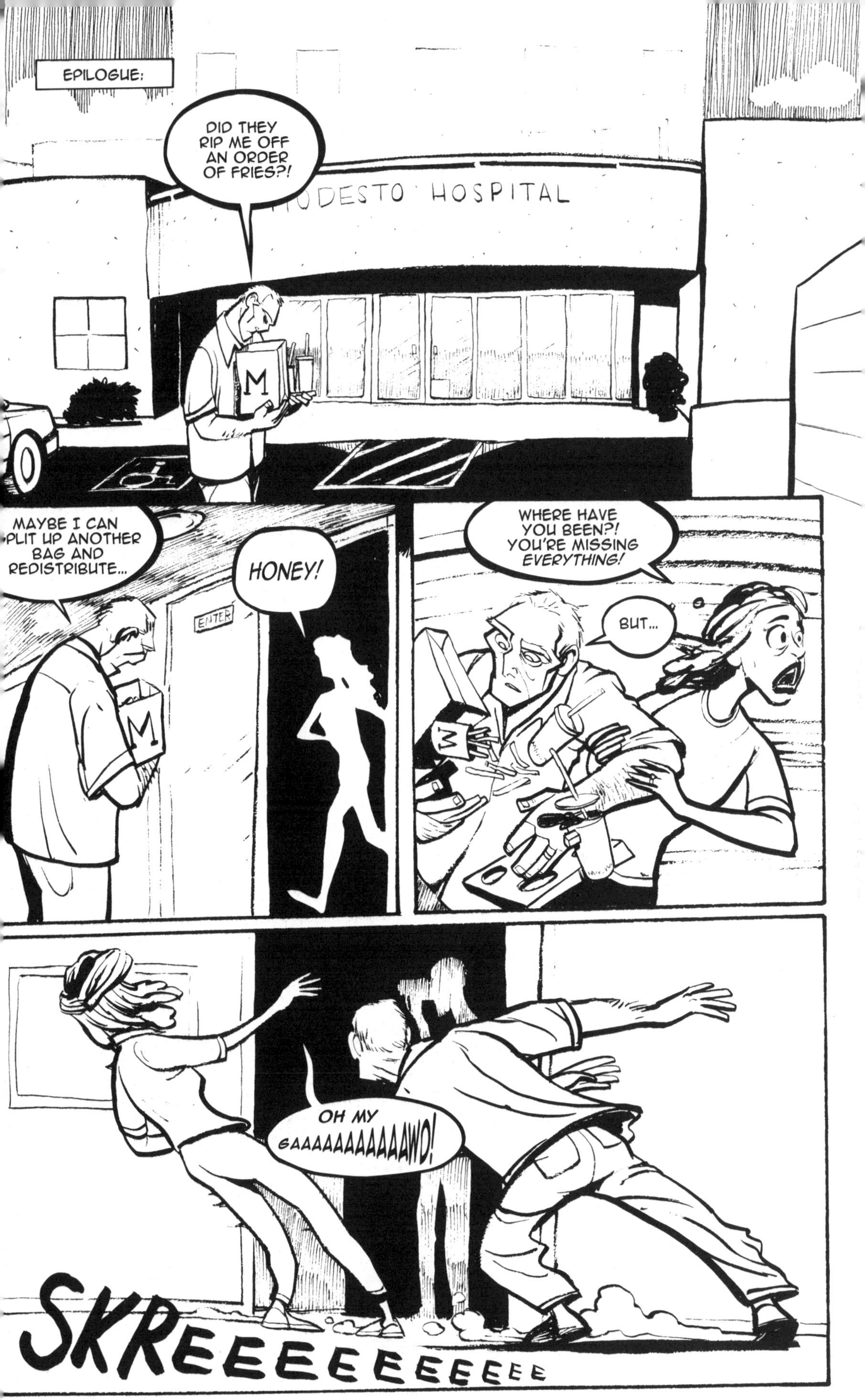
EPILOGUE:
DID THEY RIP ME OFF AN ORDER OF FRIES?!
MODESTO HOSPITAL
MAYBE I CAN PLIT UP ANOTHER BAG AND REDISTRIBUTE...
ENTER
HONEY!
WHERE HAVE YOU BEEN?! YOU'RE MISSING EVERYTHING!
BUT...
OH MY GAAAAAAAAAAAWD!
SKREEEEEEEEEEE

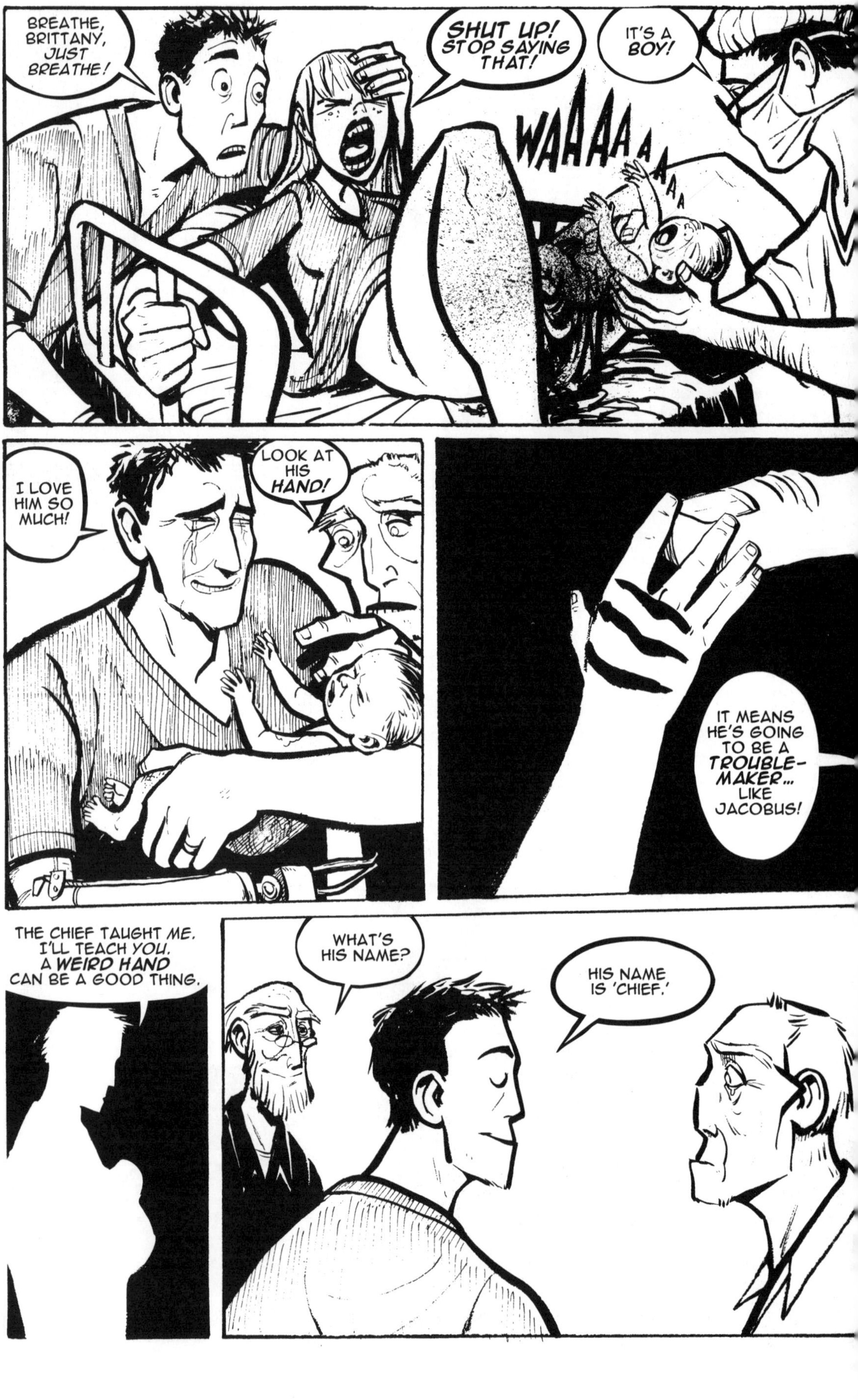
BREATHE, BRITTANY, JUST BREATHE!
SHUT UP! STOP SAYING THAT!
IT'S A BOY!
WAAAAAAAAA
I LOVE HIM SO MUCH!
LOOK AT HIS HAND!
IT MEANS HE'S GOING TO BE A TROUBLE-MAKER... LIKE JACOBUS!
THE CHIEF TAUGHT ME. I'LL TEACH YOU. A WEIRD HAND CAN BE A GOOD THING.
WHAT'S HIS NAME?
HIS NAME IS 'CHIEF.'

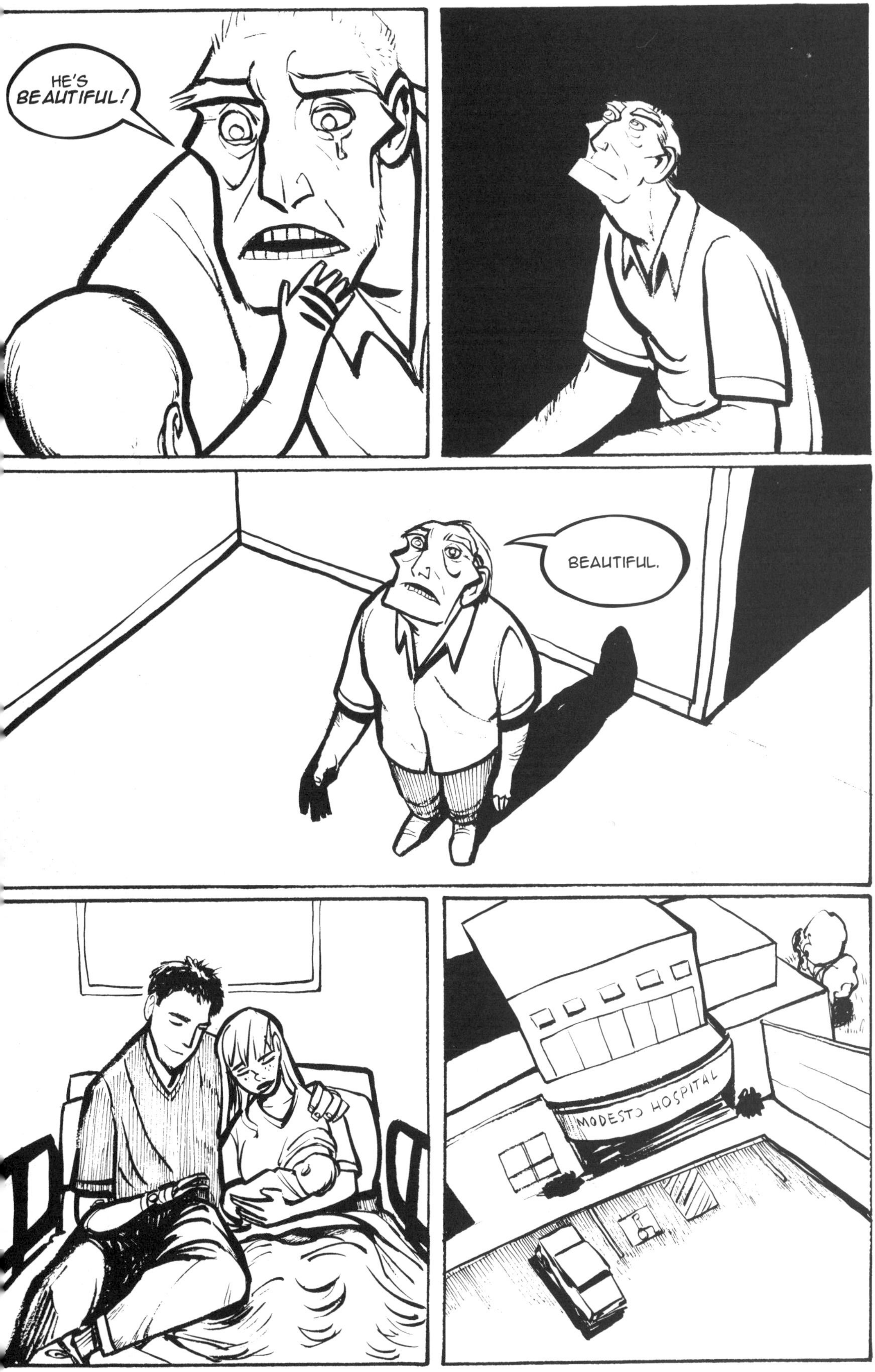
HE'S BEAUTIFUL!
BEAUTIFUL.
MODESTO HOSPITAL

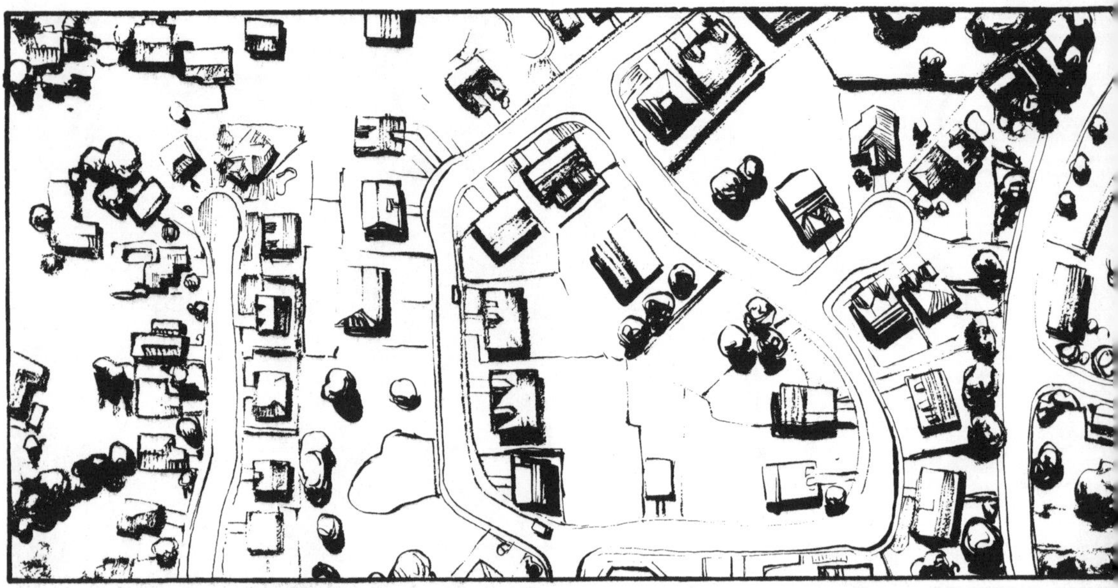
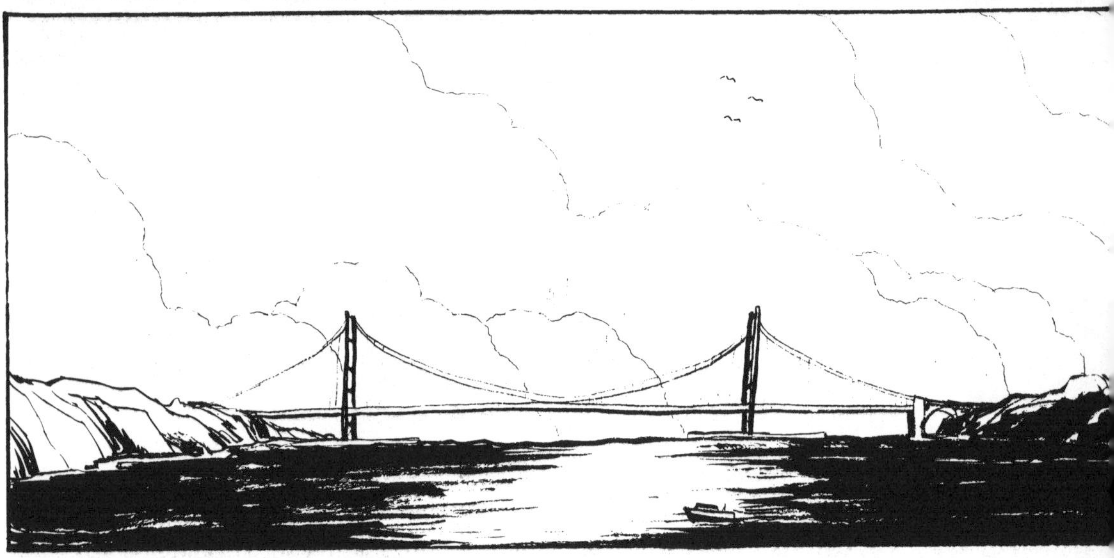
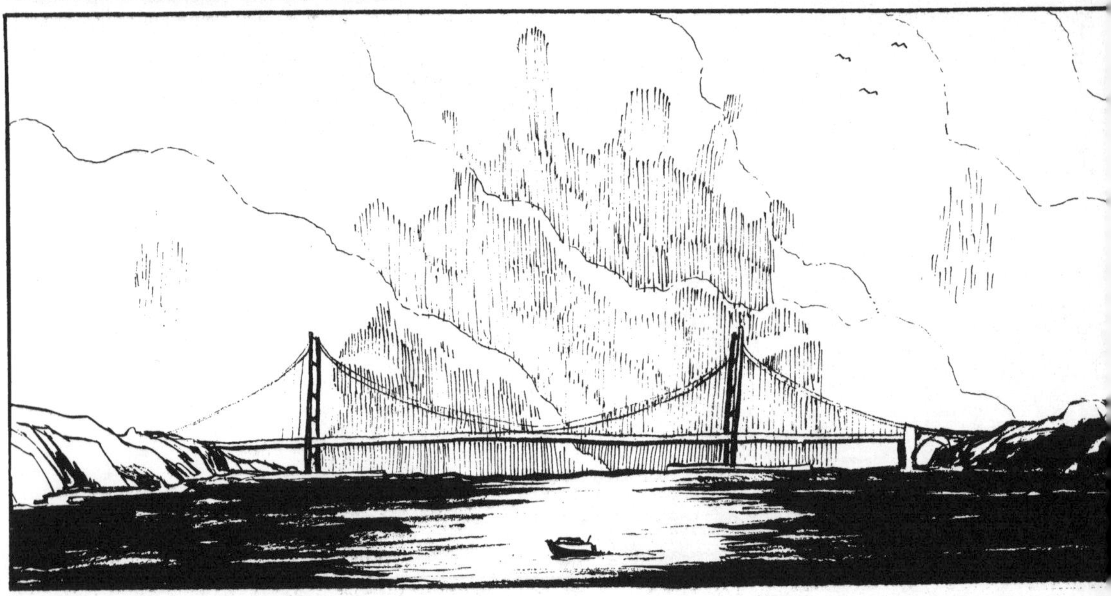

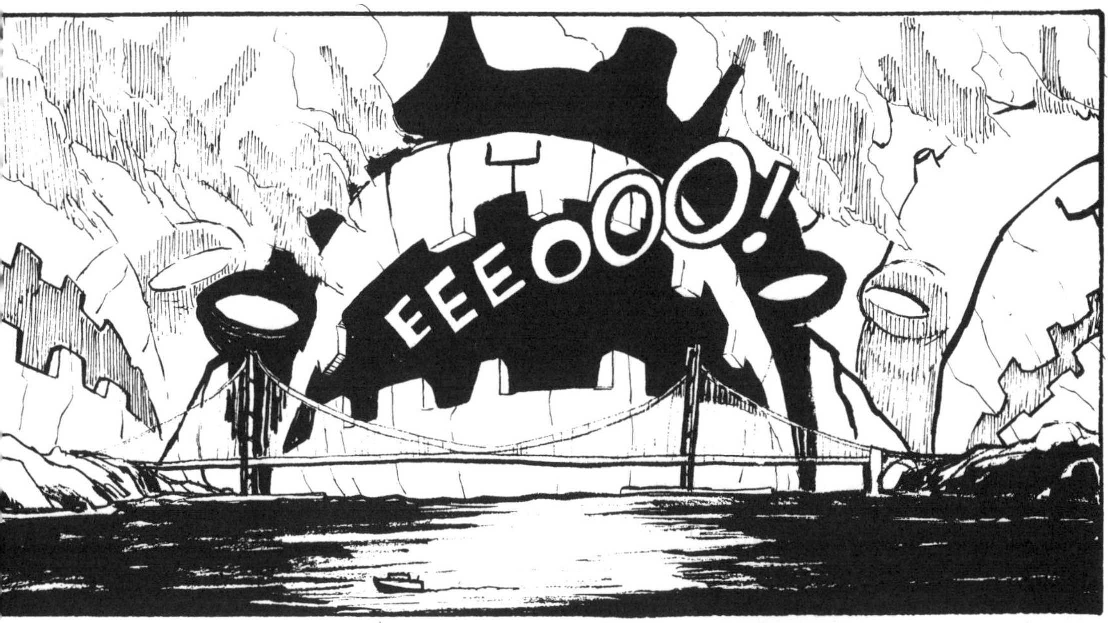
EEEOOO!

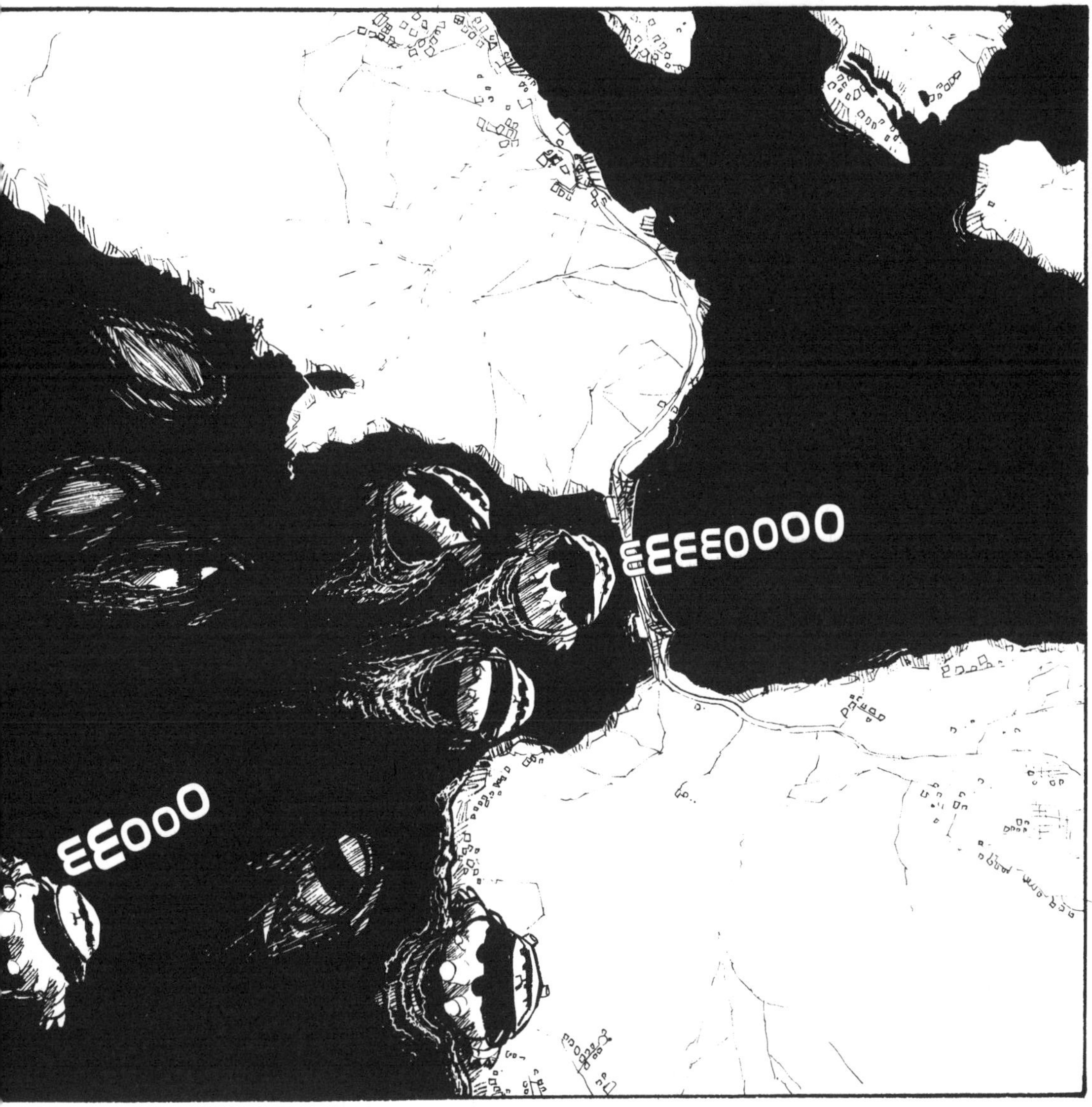
EEEOOOO
EEOOO

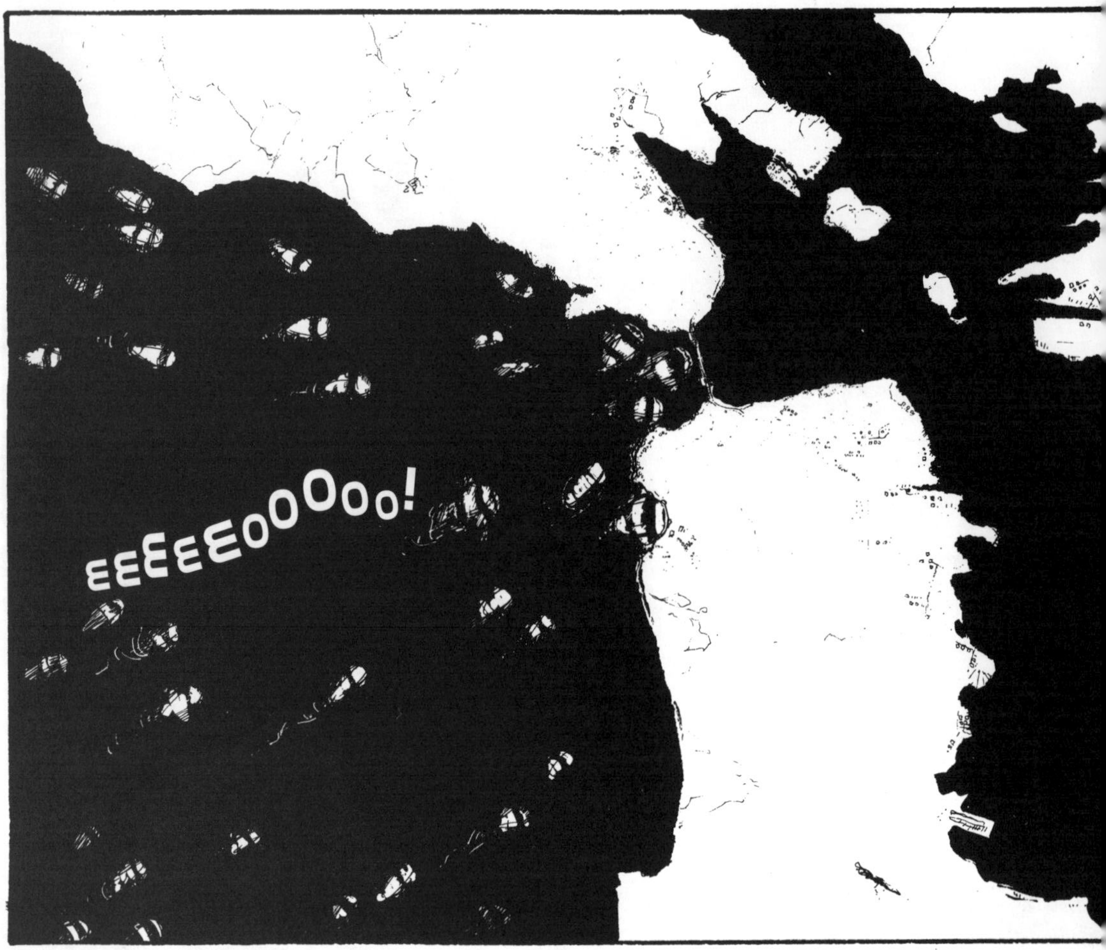

EEEEEEoOOOoo!

THE END

FOR MY FATHER, ED.

FOR MY SON, ED.